Correctional Counseling

Robert D. Hanser, Ph.D.
University of Louisiana at Monroe

Scott M. Mire, Ph.D.
University of Louisiana at Lafayette

With contributions by
Alton Braddock, M.A.
University of Louisiana at Monroe

Prentice Hall

Boston Columbus Indianapolis New York San Francisco Upper Saddle River
Amsterdam Cape Town Dubai London Madrid Milan Munich Paris Montréal Toronto
Delhi Mexico City São Paulo Sydney Hong Kong Seoul Singapore Taipei Tokyo

Editor in Chief: Vernon R. Anthony
Acquisitions Editor: Eric Krassow
Editorial Assistant: Lynda Cramer
Director of Marketing: David Gesell
Marketing Manager: Adam Kloza
Senior Marketing Coordinator: Alicia Wozniak
Project Manager: Renata Butera
Operations Specialist: Renata Butera
Creative Art Director: Jayne Conte
Cover Designer: Jayne Conte
Audiovisual Project Manager: Janet Portisch
Cover Image: Shutterstock, Inc.
Full-Service Project Management: Shiny Rajesh, Integra Software Services, Ltd.
Composition: Integra Software Services, Ltd.
Printer/Binder: Bind Rite Robbinsville
Cover Printer: Bind Rite Robbinsville
Text Font: Minion

Credits and acknowledgments borrowed from other sources and reproduced, with permission, in this textbook appear on appropriate page within text.

Library of Congress Cataloging-in-Publication Data

Cataloging-in-Publication Data for this title can be obtained from the Library of Congress.

18 2022

Prentice Hall
is an imprint of

www.pearsonhighered.com

ISBN 10: 0-13-512925-7
ISBN 13: 978-0-13-512925-8

CONTENTS

PREFACE

TEXT ORIENTATION AND THEME

First and foremost, students and instructors should understand that this text is written by authors who have had significant experience with the offender population and have also been involved with the treatment of offenders at many different levels. This means that this textbook has been written by practitioners in the field and, as a result, it has a strong practitioner orientation to the presentation and content of the text. It is from this perspective that the authors intend for the text to be used, enabling students to literally become proficient in providing basic correctional counseling services to the offender population, presuming they adequately practice the techniques provided, study the issues associated with different offender typologies, and obtain the necessary credentials to legally provide therapeutic services in their own jurisdiction. In other words, it is our belief that this text, in and of itself, contains all of the basic information that a student will need to perform this type of specialized counseling within a correctional agency.

The desire to provide a teaching-and-learning aid that will create correctional practitioners who are competent in offender treatment is perhaps the overarching goal of this text. While students will be provided with basic information regarding underlying theoretical perspectives among a variety of counseling approaches, it is important to emphasize that this text is not a theoretical overview of the counseling process nor is it a systemic presentation of treatment. Rather, this text addresses the micro-level details of the counseling and treatment process itself, explaining exactly how correctional counseling is done in the field. This is particularly what sets this text apart from others that have been produced in the past. In our estimation, this makes our text a superior product.

Intended Audience and Intended Use

This book is ideally written for the undergraduate or graduate criminal justice students. Most other criminal justice texts on correctional counseling or offender treatment provide a simple overview of the treatment process, leaving most criminal justice students uninformed in regard to how the specific process of treatment is implemented. We believe that this provides criminal justice students with an incomplete picture of the treatment process. Because correctional treatment courses are coming into vogue within the criminal justice discipline, we believe that students will increasingly need more than a mere introduction to the treatment process; they will need exposure to the tools of the trade when considering work in clinical services.

In addition, this text could easily be used by other disciplines such as counseling and social work for courses that are geared toward offender counseling and treatment. In fact, this text would be a perfect adjunct or primary text for many introductory counseling courses or courses that are technique-driven. The advantage of using this text in disciplines such as counseling and social work is twofold. First, the material on the counseling process itself should provide good reinforcement material for students since this text covers the basics of the counseling process all the way from intake to discharge. Second, this text provides students with information pertaining to specific offender typologies as well as treatment approaches for the offending population in general. To date, there is no counseling text widely disseminated in the market that provides detailed information regarding counseling treatment of this type of a variety of offenders. Thus, the inclusion of this text would enhance the budding counselor's expertise in regard to correctional counseling, providing often-lacking information and resources that are typically overlooked in most counseling programs.

Organization of the Text

This text is organized in a manner that presumes that the student will have had little or no true exposure to offender treatment. However, it is presumed that the student will have at least a basic understanding of basic issues in corrections within the criminal justice system. Therefore, this text is not organized to provide lengthy explanations related to the day-to-day operations of correctional facilities but instead begins with a definition and description of correctional counseling. From this point, the text includes a number of chapters that address the general counseling process involved in individual and group service delivery. Later chapters of the text address specific types of offenders and/or challenging issues within the correctional counseling field. The final chapter concludes with information on the evaluation of treatment programs, tying the evaluation process back to earlier chapters in the text.

Chapter 1 provides a basic introduction to criminal behavior, motivations for criminal behavior, and the means by which treatment should be approached with the offender population. The necessary ingredient of motivation for change and the means by which such motivation can occur are discussed. Likewise, the various characteristics of good counselors and effective counseling are discussed. Lastly, this chapter also covers material unique from most criminal justice–oriented texts but common to counseling texts, such as the importance of collaboration, clinical training, and the clinical supervision that one receives when beginning their career.

In **Chapter 2**, the importance of ethics as well as the boundaries and parameters related to ethical behavior are provided. Students are given clear guidance on the initial processes involved in the counseling relationship where informed consent, the limits to confidentiality, and other legal and ethical aspects of counseling must be addressed prior to actually conducting services with any client. Further, this chapter also provides extensive information regarding the counselor's ethical responsibility to provide culturally competent services for his or her clients. Ensuring that clinical services meet the needs of diverse groups is a critical component to the clinician's career development and also safeguards against the provision of substandard services to the general public.

Perhaps most unique aspects of this text would be found in **Chapter 3**. As noted in that chapter, assessment is often not understood by many correctional counselors but, ironically, is perhaps the most important aspect of correctional treatment because most counselors do not have in-depth training in regard to the use of assessment instruments or standardized scales. As pointed out in the chapter the use of various scales and instruments helps to provide assurance that the initial appraisal of the client's situation is based on factors more solid than the single perception of the client or the therapist. The chapter concludes with techniques that provide for collaborative treatment planning and action between the client and the counselor.

Chapter 4 provides an extensive presentation of the importance of the therapeutic relationship between client and counselor. This relationship is referred to as the therapeutic alliance and is a critical component within the therapeutic relationship. As students will learn, the existence of a strong affective bond between the counselor and offender is more important than any particular modality of intervention. This is because it is the positive therapeutic alliance, not the particular modality of treatment delivery, that assists in identifying the offender's true needs as well as uncover important information related to the offender's perceptions, coping mechanisms, and future goals.

Chapter 5 provides an overview of the more common therapeutic modalities in counseling, particularly, those modalities that are frequently used in the correctional setting. This chapter illustrates the theoretical underpinnings that serve as the foundation for techniques designed to alter cognitions and behaviors. Regardless of the modality is affective based or behavioral in orientation, the underpinnings to the counseling process are important for the counselor since they determine the approach and vantage point from which services will be provided.

Chapter 6 provides students with a fairly comprehensive presentation of family systems therapy. We have chosen to showcase this type of therapy because it is often used with juvenile offenders and with the addicted population. Further, many correctional counseling textbooks make mention of this type of therapy and some may provide a brief overview, but few (if any) provide a thorough examination of this commonly used counseling approach. Often, family issues lie at the base of many offender problems and family therapy offers an option of rectifying dysfunctional family influences. Additionally, family therapy offers a venue by which well-adjusted families can aid in the offender's treatment and/or recovery.

Chapter 7 presents the use of group counseling services with offender treatment programs. In most circumstances, the primary advantages of group counseling include cost and also the fact that much learning takes place in the form of peer interaction. Further, this type of approach allows offenders to confront one another and this can be particularly useful since offenders are likely to detect deceit and manipulation from amongst one another. This can greatly enhance the therapeutic benefits for offenders in treatment. Other issues related to resistance in therapy and the ability of counselors to work through observed resistance is also presented.

Chapter 8 provides an examination of substance abuse treatment processes. This chapter covers a very important topic that is relevant to the vast majority of the offender population. However, this chapter also provides detailed coverage of common co-occurring disorders. It is important for students and instructors to understand the various co-occurring disorders and issues that are involved with substance abuse. Additional topics covered in this chapter include the need for accurate and effective screening, assessment, and diagnosis as a fundamental component of the substance abuse treatment process. Lastly, this chapter provides information on self-help recovery programs. Due to their widespread use among the offender population, any discussion related to drug treatment would be incomplete without the inclusion of such information.

Chapter 9 addresses juvenile offenders and the various issues that confront them. Issues related to clinical disorders among juveniles, including depression, anxiety, and suicidal ideation, are examined as are a number of other issues related to mental health. Family issues, substance abuse, as well as teen sex and pregnancy are addressed. This chapter provides unique coverage related to teen sex, STDs and HIV, as well as birth control and teen parenting. Lastly correctional counselors are encouraged to be informed on different subcultural groups and their importance among juvenile offenders and prevalence within the juvenile justice system. Lastly, the issue of multicultural competence is addressed in this chapter since recent literature demonstrates that a disparate proportion of juvenile offenders are of minority status.

Chapter 10 provides information related to anger management and domestic abuse but makes a point to distinguish between these two areas of problematic behavior. Specifically, this chapter proposes that while anger management and domestic abuse interventions may have many similar techniques, the two problem behaviors should not be confused as being one and the same. This is an important point that is illustrated throughout the chapter. Indeed, domestic batterers require extensive intervention that goes beyond simple anger control. Issues of sexism, a sense of entitlement, views on relationships, and power and control must also be addressed.

Chapter 11 presents the female offender as one of several specialized offenders that correctional counselors should consider. Though female offenders are only a small portion of the institutional offender population, they consist of a fairly substantive proportion of offenders on community supervision. Further, the differences between male and female offenders goes beyond simple physical differences; women throughout society experience a different socialization process than do men, and this must be included as a component within any treatment program for female offenders. Throughout this chapter, social, psychological, and physiological aspects of female offenders are taken into account while discussing treatment processes.

Chapter 12 addresses one of the most heinous types of criminal offenders—the sex offender. Indeed, the sex-offending population is perhaps the most difficult and controversial group of offenders that correctional counselors will treat. These offenders tend to be very manipulative in treatment and can be very convincing. Because of this, correctional counselors must be careful in their assessments and appraisals of sex offenders, who on the surface often appear compliant but in most cases are resistant to treatment. This means that correctional counselors must become skilled at detecting and addressing denial with this population. A variety of techniques to break through this denial as well as the corresponding forms of treatment that are implemented with this population of offenders are discussed.

Chapter 13 addresses death and dying, terminal diseases, and the elderly offender population. Correctional counselors who deal with terminal illness and/or offenders who are advanced in age must be prepared to assist offenders in developing a coping strategy that provides them with dignity and respect when facing death.

The stages of grief and loss as identified by Kübler-Ross are presented and the student is shown how the correctional counselor can assist offenders in grief and/or facing loss process their emotional reactions to the grieving process and to the experience of loss or trauma. This chapter also addresses elderly offenders and the need for mental health services that tends to occur. Because elderly offenders will become increasingly more common in correctional facilities and community supervision programs throughout the nation, they are an important population to identify. Complications associated with elderly offenders and the differences between categories of elderly offenders are discussed, providing the student with a specific information for interventions with elderly offenders.

Chapter 14 provides the student with an introduction to evaluative research within treatment programs. It is our contention that correctional counselors need to understand this process since this is what allows programs to refine their efforts. Further, an understanding of the evaluator's role in the agency leads to understanding of the cyclic nature of the continual improvement process. The use of standardized scales, issues related to validity and reliability, as well as ethics in mental health research are all discussed in this chapter.

PEDAGOGICAL ASPECTS

Immediately noticeable among the pedagogical aids is the fact that this text has a discernable and consistent sense of organization in relation to the presentation of the material. This is evident at the very beginning of each chapter where the chapter objectives are listed, making the purpose and emphasis of the chapter clear to the student and instructor. These chapter objectives are further reinforced by section summaries that exist within each of the chapters. Dividing the chapters into sections provides a more organized and structured presentation of the information and, by utilizing the section summaries, the student is reminded of the main points to the content that they have previously read.

Further, these section summaries also include section learning checks. These learning checks are intended to simply support the information presented throughout the section of the chapter and reinforce those chapter learning objectives that are included in that section. It is in this manner that information in each chapter is broken down into manageable sections of content that, at the same time, is connected back to the overall purpose of the chapter. Taken together, the section summaries and the section learning checks provide a sense of order, consistency, and repetition that enhances content learning. These features are further reinforced by the end-of-chapter conclusion that is followed by end-of-chapter essay questions. The end-of-chapter essay questions are designed to specifically require the student to respond to inquiries related to the chapter learning outcomes, once again tying together the various concepts that are included throughout the chapter.

Throughout several chapters the use of case vignettes has been included to provide examples of how counseling techniques might be utilized. This is an approach that is frequently used in many counseling textbooks but is not often seen in texts within the criminal justice or corrections discipline. The use of these vignettes demonstrates our desire to provide both a strong counseling orientation as well as a criminal justice orientation to this text. The use of teaching-and-learning aids that are familiar to most persons involved in the counseling field will ensure that this text comports with that the needs and expectations of persons who seriously intend to work in the field of offender treatment.

In addition, this text includes a treatment planning exercise at the end of each chapter. We believe that this application-oriented exercise sets our text apart from other textbooks on this topic because it encourages students to actually use and/or apply the techniques that they have learned and the knowledge that they have accumulated while reading each successive chapter of our text. In many cases, students are required to use specific techniques that they have learned in chapters that cover counseling techniques and/or approaches, such as with Chapter 5 where students must pick a theoretical orientation and demonstrate how they would provide counseling services to a specific client scenario; Chapter 6, where students must identify specific family therapy concepts and techniques used in an exercise; or Chapter 3, where students are required to use a specific prediction instrument to assess a hypothetical client.

Other chapters may require the student to use basic counseling skills covered in Chapters 3 through 7 to specific types of offenders, such as with Chapter 9 where students must use basic person-centered (called "youth-centered" techniques in Chapter 9) techniques originally covered in Chapter 5 to a case involving a juvenile offender. Other chapters, such as Chapter 10, require the student to consider counseling dynamics first presented in Chapter 4 as they relate to a client who is a domestic batterer. Chapters such as these and several others included in this text accomplish two important requirements for effective correctional counseling: (1) the need to identify, learn, and apply specific techniques to specific client cases, and (2) the need to become familiar with the various characteristics common to diverse hard-core offender populations.

While most counseling textbooks and programs are effective at accomplishing the first requirement, they fail miserably in meeting the second requirement. Conversely, most criminal justice texts and programs that provide courses on correctional treatment/counseling provide adequate coverage related to security concerns and challenges with specific offender populations but they fail to provide the student with any true training or guidance that illustrates *exactly how* the counseling process should be conducted. Our text meets both of these requirements: the student learns how to use the more common skills and techniques of the counseling discipline and they are given very detailed information on how to provide interventions to specific and diverse offender populations such as young offenders, elderly offenders, female offenders, substance abusing offenders, offenders with HIV/AIDS, offenders with *DSM-IV-TR* diagnose, sex offender, domestic batterers, and offenders from different racial and/or cultural backgrounds.

Further, this text includes a very strong emphasis on assessment, classification, and evaluation. We think that this is a very important aspect of the correctional counseling process since, in every institution throughout the United States, classification processes are implemented and assessments for treatment and security purposes are typically either required or strongly encouraged by most agencies. Further, the use of evaluation processes (Chapter 14) is considered equally important since, in almost every case where federal funding is given, agencies are being required to provide evidence-based proof that their programs are making an identifiable and quantifiable difference with the client population that they serve. Further, the treatment planning exercise in Chapter 14 requires the student to integrate information from Chapter 8 (substance abuse issues) and Chapter 9 (juvenile offenders) with evaluation approaches learned by the student, demonstrating how evaluative processes might be used to examine a variety of aspects related to correctional counseling.

Regardless of the specific pedagogical aid that is considered, we believe that each one of these features further enhances the intention behind this text to show the student specifically how treatment is conducted with the offender population. To our knowledge, there are few, if any, textbooks on correctional counseling that provide a similar approach. Likewise, this text is much different from others that on many occasions are anthologies which bring together disparate articles from various authors in a quasi-structured fashion. Our text provides a comprehensive presentation of correctional counseling and does so in a consistent manner that provides a seamless overview of this area of intervention. In addition, our text is much more up-to-date, both in research and modalities that are emphasized. Because of this, it is our sincere belief that this text will prove to be a superior teaching-and-learning tool among instructors and students alike.

ACKNOWLEDGMENTS

We would like to thank the following reviewers of the manuscript for their helpful recommendations and for their kind comments: Nancy L. Hogan, Ferris State University; Elizabeth C. McMullan, Grambling State University; J. Michael Olivero, Central Washington University; and Irina R. Soderstrom, Eastern Kentucky University.

We do welcome your comments concerning the text. Please feel free to contact us at the appropriate e-mail address:

Robert Hanser: hanser@ulm.edu
Scott Mire: smm6281@louisiana.edu

1

The Role of the Correctional Counselor

CHAPTER OBJECTIVES

After reading this chapter, you will be able to:

1. Identify the functions and parameters of the counseling process.
2. Discuss the competing interests between security and counseling in the correctional counseling process.
3. Know common terms and concerns associated with custodial corrections.
4. Understand the role of the counselor as facilitator.
5. Identify the various personal characteristics associated with effective counselors.
6. Be aware of the impact that burnout can have on a counselor's professional performance.
7. Identify the various means of training and supervision associated with counseling.

PART ONE: A BRIEF INTRODUCTION TO COUNSELING AND CORRECTIONS

There are many myths concerning the concept of counseling. Although the image of the counseling field has changed dramatically over the past two or three decades, much of society still views counseling and therapy as a mystic process reserved for those who lack the ability to handle life issues effectively. While the concept of counseling is often misunderstood, the problem is exacerbated when attempting to introduce the idea of correctional counseling. Therefore, the primary goal of this chapter is to provide a working definition of correctional counseling that includes descriptions of how and when it is carried out. In order to understand the concept of correctional counseling, however, the two words that derive the concept must first be defined: "corrections" and "counseling." In addition, a concerted effort is made to identify the myriad of legal and ethical issues that pertain to counselors working with offenders.

It is very difficult to identify a single starting point for the counseling profession. In essence, there were various movements occurring simultaneously that later evolved into what we now describe as counseling. One of the earliest connections to the origins of counseling took place in Europe during the Middle Ages (Brown & Srebalus, 2003). The primary objective was assisting individuals with career choices. This type of counseling service is usually described by the concept of "guidance." In the late 1800s Wilhelm Wundt and G. Stanley Hall created two of the first known psychological laboratories aimed at studying and treating individuals with psychological and emotional problems (Brown & Srebalus, 2003). Around the same time (1890), Sigmund Freud began treating mental patients with his patented technique of psychoanalysis. As a result, the origins of counseling can be traced to two different but simultaneous movements: (1) guidance and (2) psychotherapy.

Guidance

Guidance has been used as a concept to describe the process of helping individuals identify and choose what they value most (Gladding, 1996). Guidance can occur in any instance where one individual, usually more experienced, helps another to identify choices that best reflect their interests and strengths. In the United States, Frank Parson is generally considered to be the founder of the guidance movement (Brown & Srebalus, 2003). Much of Parson's work, along with those of other pioneers, focused on vocational guidance usually provided in schools (Brown & Srebalus, 2003; Gladding, 1996). The primary objective was to help students identify occupations for which their particular skill sets would be best suited. In addition to vocational guidance, another area that received substantial focus was helping students identify specific areas of study that they were interested in and were also well suited for intellectually. It is important to note, however, the broad processes for which the concept guidance is used to describe. In essence, guidance occurs in any circumstance where one individual helps another make choices that are best suited for his or her intellectual, physical, psychological, and emotional skill set.

Psychotherapy

Psychotherapy is a concept generally used to describe a process that focuses on serious psychological and emotional disorders. Most often these disorders are characterized as being associated with intrapsychic, internal, and personal issues and conflicts (Gladding, 1996). "Psychotherapy" is the term often used by psychiatrists and psychologists to describe their work (Gladding, 1996), which generally focuses on past events and the development of insight or personal awareness. In addition, psychotherapy (or therapy) is also thought of as a process that usually consists of a long-term relationship between the therapist and client that focuses on reconstructive or transformational change in the client. Exploring and identifying subconscious reasoning and motivations for behavior and thoughts are also central components to some therapeutic modalities couched within the concept of psychotherapy.

Counseling

In the1940s, largely due to the work of Carl Rogers, counseling began to evolve into a profession that incorporated more than just guidance (Brown & Srebalus, 2003). Today, counseling is often thought of as a profession that encompasses both guidance and psychotherapy. Gladding (1996) describes counseling as a "relatively short-term, interpersonal, theory-based process of helping persons who are basically psychologically healthy resolve developmental and situational problems" (p. 8). If one carefully scrutinizes Gladding's definition, it is clear that the concept of counseling describes a broad profession aimed at helping individuals resolve issues ranging across personal, social, vocational, and educational matters.

Realistically, the only tangible distinction between counseling and therapy is one of duration. As mentioned above, therapy is the concept usually used to describe a professional relationship between a therapist and client that occurs over long periods of time, in some cases lasting several years. But this distinction is ambiguous because many of the same techniques are applied in both settings. In most circumstances counselors and therapists receive the same foundational focus in training. As a result, Egan (2007) uses the concept of formal and informal helpers to capture the true essence of the goal to be achieved regardless of whether the facilitator is identified as a counselor, psychiatrist, psychologist, social worker, or minister of religion. Ultimately, the goal is "to help people manage the distressing problems of life" (Egan, 2007, p. 3). Henceforth, the concept of **counseling**, as used in this text, is drawn largely from the work of Egan (2007) and will be used to describe the process of helping individuals to better manage distress by further development or refinement of their own resources.

What Is Corrections?

Corrections is a concept that describes one component of the criminal justice system that is responsible for offenders once they have been convicted of a crime. The term "corrections" can be thought of as an "umbrella" that generally encompasses a multitude of entities such as prisons, jails, detention facilities, probation, parole, community treatment programs, and others. In essence, any agency that is responsible for housing, monitoring, or providing services to a convict falls under the milieu of corrections. There is a rich history behind the concept of corrections that is beyond the scope of this text. However, some background information is warranted in order to understand the remaining portions of this chapter and text from the proper perspective.

There are two essential objectives of corrections: (1) the punishment of offenders and (2) the prevention of future crime (Clear & Dammer, 2003). **Punishment** is a concept that describes the process of causing an offender to suffer through the infliction of a penalty. As early philosophers have stated, one true way society can declare an act forbidden or wrong is by imposing a form of punishment on the individual responsible for its commission. In addition, through the imposition of suffering society is better able to forgive the offender for his actions. And, as mentioned by Clear and Dammer (2003), "When communities come together to punish deviant members, a sense of shared values and togetherness becomes a part of that community's identity" (p. 19).

The concept of **crime prevention** describes the process of preventing future illegal acts based upon the punishment received by the offender. The ideology behind this concept is that the punishment meted out should be appropriate to deter any future wrongdoing and begins with the incarceration of the offender. One way to prevent crime is by **incapacitating** the offender so that his or her movements and actions are restricted. This may be accomplished through incarceration or more modern techniques such as electronic monitoring and the prescription of certain medications. Another way to prevent crime is through the process of rehabilitation.

Rehabilitation is a concept that describes the process of restoring one's effectiveness in carrying out a "normal" life through training and exposure to different modalities and techniques of treatment. There are many strategies aimed at rehabilitating offenders. Naturally, as one might guess, this text will lean strongly in the direction of rehabilitation rather than punishment. However, this is not to say that punitive elements are not employed in corrections (or correctional counseling, for that matter) but it is the intent of this text to provide both the theory and the technique necessary for the reformation of offenders. Lastly, **restoration** is one of the oldest forms of correction and it describes the process of bringing the offender back to his or her original state in the community by their working with victims and community members to repair the damage caused by the criminal act. Both rehabilitative and restorative elements will be emphasized throughout this text and the strategies used toward these ends will be covered in the coming chapters. Much of the information provided will be directed at two broad components: (1) helping offenders identify and correct dysfunctional patterns of thinking and behaving, and (2) reintegrating the offender into the community in a manner that does not compromise the safety or security of the public at large.

What Is Correctional Counseling?

"Correctional counseling" is a broad term that has been defined in various ways depending on the context in which it is used. For example, Bennett (1978) defines correctional counseling as any "planned interaction between the correctional worker and a client or group of clients—probationers, prisoners, or parolees—with the aim of changing the pattern of the recipients' behavior toward conformity to social expectation" (p. 10). Kratcoski (1981) uses the term "correctional treatment" and defines it as "any planned and monitored program of activity that has the goal of rehabilitating or 'habilitating' the offender so that he or she will avoid criminal activity in the future" (p. 4). This definition was criticized by Walters (2001) for being too broad and not providing appropriate parameters for the true essence of correctional counseling. Schrink and Hamm (1990) also argue that the true goals of correctional counseling are actually much narrower in scope than suggested by most of the definitions found in the literature. According to Schrink and Hamm (1990), the counseling that does take place is most often aimed at addressing crises related to being in prison and has little to do with past or future situations or circumstances. More recently, Masters (2004) uses the concept of criminal justice counseling and describes it as a process of counseling offenders in various modes and settings. For example, counseling may take place in "prisons, probation agencies, parole agencies, diversion programs, group homes, halfway houses, prerelease facilities, and to some extent U.S. jails" (Masters, 2004, p. 2). In addition, Masters (2004) notes that "At the heart of criminal justice counseling philosophy is protection of society" (p. 3).

Therefore, the question still remains: What is correctional counseling? One of the most salient factors to consider when attempting to define a concept is to first identify the audience for whom it is intended. For our purposes, the targeted audience is both correctional counseling practitioners and students studying to become counselors in correctional settings. With these parameters in mind, we provide the following as the working definition of correctional counseling for the purposes of this text. **Correctional counseling** is a concept that describes the process of trained counselors helping offenders identify and incorporate better behavioral, psychological, and emotional responses to life events that serve to improve their quality of life and reduce or eliminate their involvement in criminal activity. Correctional counseling can occur in any setting where a counselor and offender(s) are able to gather in an attempt to carry out these goals. The essence of our definition is aimed at the process of a trained counselor screening, diagnosing, and assessing an offender in order to carry out a planned method of intervention aimed at correcting dysfunctional learning. The one component that makes our definition of correctional counseling different from most definitions provided in previous literature is the concept of training. Most previous works identify police officers, probation officers, parole officers, correctional officers, and so on as mechanisms through which correctional counseling takes place. For our purposes, however, we believe it is most appropriate to utilize the concept of correctional counseling when describing a process of helping offenders that is being carried out by trained counselors.

Defining Trained Counselor

The business of defining concepts can sometimes be difficult. This is particularly true when one considers that the field itself has gone through a process of definition formulation throughout the past two or three decades. Ideally, the definition should be broad enough to capture the full requisites of the concept, and yet sufficiently narrow to eliminate similar constructs that detract from its fundamental purpose. Our fear is in providing a definition for "trained counselor" that might eliminate certain professionals within the criminal justice system who may be able to deliver sound advice to offenders that does in fact stymie their participation in further criminal acts.

As a result, we provide the concept of trained counselor to describe professional counselors who have received theoretically based education and training regarding the fundamental principles of counseling. In addition, a trained counselor should have knowledge of a variety of theoretical approaches that inform the underlying mechanisms of dysfunctional learning and behavior. At a minimum this training would consist of a bachelor's degree in an appropriate discipline that is scientifically based. However, training with an advanced degree, masters, or doctorate, in an appropriate, scientifically based discipline is preferred. Noticeably, our concept of a trained counselor stops short of requiring full licensure as a licensed professional counselor. We do believe, however, that any counselor not licensed should be under the direction of a licensed supervisory counselor available for consulting and advice when necessary.

The primary reasoning driving the construction of these definitions is the need to accurately evaluate the concept of correctional counseling. Over the years there have been a variety of reports and recommendations that have generally portrayed the idea of counseling offenders in a negative light. The most notable of these reports was generated by Robert Martinson and colleagues in 1966. In essence, Martinson was hired by the State of New York to evaluate what worked in rehabilitating criminal offenders. The variables used to operationalize the concept of rehabilitation consisted of adjustment to prison life, vocational and educational achievement and success, changes in personality and attitude, general adjustment to society, and rates of recidivism. After reviewing the findings of 231 studies, Martinson ultimately concluded that rehabilitative efforts had no appreciable effects. Both at the time of Martinson's report, and still today, the primary variable used to measure the success of rehabilitation is the concept of recidivism.

Recidivism is a concept used to describe the process of an offender relapsing into criminal behavior. What followed, based on Martinson's report, was an immense emphasis on behalf of politicians and the media highlighting the shortcomings of rehabilitative efforts within the criminal justice system. The report served as an official document on which leaders and politicians could rely in order to advocate the concepts of stricter punishments and longer prison sentences. It also served as a tool to greatly reduce the amounts of funding allocated toward counseling and rehabilitative efforts. All of this was in spite of the fact that Martinson and colleagues cautioned politicians and the public that many of their findings should be considered in light of the enormous methodological complications of conducting such a study. These cautions, however, received very little attention from the media. The concept of "Nothing Works" was found, by the media, to be much more stimulating and capable of creating the frenzy, which drives interest, generates sales, and later culminates in money.

In essence, the concept of correctional counseling and its attendant components should be defined and described based on the same standards from which they will be evaluated. The foundation on which these standards should stand is the scientific method of inquiry. This is the only way to provide a fair evaluation of the strengths and weaknesses of correctional counseling that is able to produce reasonable coefficients related to reliability and validity. The scientific method of inquiry allows us to examine a given question and explore that question in an objective manner. Yet, once an answer is found, the scientific method of inquiry then provides counselors and counseling programs with answers related to outcomes. If a program is found to achieve its objectives, then all is well. However, few programs achieve every single objective that is necessary for true overall reform of the offender within the first point of implementation. Rather, the process of scientific inquiry can allow treatment providers to determine those areas of intervention that work well while also identifying those areas that will need improvement. From that point, treatment providers are able to refine their efforts in a constant cycle of continuous improvement.

This process of inquiry allows counselors and treatment agencies to constantly stay up-to-date with challenges facing their populations. Further, the process is one of constant hypothesis generation, producing fresh new ideas over time as interventions are examined and revised. As students will see in the following chapters, this process of hypothesis generation and inquiry will be relevant to the assessment and diagnosis components of the treatment process and will even be relevant to the process of developing the therapeutic alliance between offender client and correctional counselor. In addition, this process and the means by which it provides guidance to further program improvement will be demonstrated in Chapter 14, where evaluation processes are explored.

Lastly, we do not believe that recidivism rates should be the sole factor considered when attempting to judge the success of correctional counseling. In private settings, occasions of relapse and regression are common and expected. They may consist of clients returning to substance abuse or obsessive-compulsive behaviors that inflict harm on themselves as well as others. In these instances the goal is to stabilize clients quicker than what would have been possible prior to counseling. The same logic should apply to counseling offenders in correctional settings. It is not practical or realistic to assume that all offenders who undergo counseling will henceforth lead a crime-free life. A more logical approach, especially for hardened offenders who are likely to return to their original crime-ridden neighborhoods, would be to try to reduce the extent of their criminal activities as they continue to learn and process new methods of responding to life events. In the end, however, it is really up to the offender. If the offender is not willing to change, progress is not likely, and based on this fact that we believe a variety of circumstances, and not just recidivism rates, should be considered when attempting to gage the effectiveness of correctional counseling.

Concerns of Custodial Staff versus Concerns of Treatment Staff

One of the most problematic issues in the administration of counseling services in correctional settings is the fact that custodial staff and counseling personnel often have different goals. The primary goal of corrections facilities and their staff is security. There are two broad components of security that are especially relevant to correctional agencies: (1) security and safety for the inmate population as well as staff, and (2) security and safety of society through maintaining control and custody of offenders and preventing escape. For the management and staff of correctional facilities, security is paramount and will forego concerns or attempts at rehabilitating offenders through the provisions of counseling services.

Trained counselors, on the other hand, are primarily motivated by the idea of helping offenders identify and incorporate better responses to stressful life events. The heart of this process requires that trust be established between the counselor and offender at an appropriate depth whereby the offender feels safe to share intimate details pertaining to their dysfunctional learning and thoughts. The literature is replete with examples of how these differing goals significantly impact the outcomes of counseling services provided to offenders. For example, Masters (2004) clearly states that "American society still demands, first and foremost, protection of society over treatment efforts on the part of counselors in the criminal justice setting" (p. 3). Lester (1992) asks, "Is the primary goal of counselors who work in prisons one of correcting offenders for successful readjustment to the outside world, or is their primary role more concerned with offenders' adjustment to the institutional world of the prison" (p. 25), thereby enhancing security? Our answer is that even for counselors who are employed by correctional agencies, security concerns will override the philosophies and procedures known to be necessary for the creation of an environment conducive to successful intervention. This is evidenced by the assertion of Schrink and Hamm (1990), who state that counselors working in correctional settings "are not even expected to worry about inmates' post institutional behavior" (p. 137).

At this point, a couple of logical questions may arise: What are the motivations behind these differing goals? Why is that, from a realistic standpoint, the issue of security is and will continue to be paramount? Our assertion is that the primary reason for the concept of security being the paramount concern for any correctional facility is due to the issue of liability—both civil and criminal liability. **Liability**, within the context of corrections, is a concept that describes the process of being accountable or legally bound to ensure that one's basic rights are not violated. Even though they may be in a correctional setting, offenders still have basic rights of due process, including rights to safety and life. What happens when these rights are found to be violated and offenders are injured or killed due to negligence? Either correctional personnel lose their own freedom, or agencies may have injunctions imposed against them, or the agency or its staff may be required to pay monetary damages. There is no question that both of these results generate powerful motives aimed at their avoidance.

The student should understand that one of the best means of ensuring the safety of offenders while avoiding liability is through the maintenance of tight and strict security measures within the agency. In addition, agency personnel tend to be insulated from liability when they are sure to follow the written policies and procedures of the agency. Further highlighting the salience of this issue is the fact that most legal decisions governing the discipline of corrections uphold the concept of maintaining security and in most cases defer to prison officials to determine how to best achieve safe and secure environments. In essence, the concept of helping offenders learn better skills to cope with difficult life situations is, and will remain, secondary to the security of the facility.

As a result of this reality, trained counselors have a very realistic problem that somehow has to be addressed if they are to have any chance of helping offenders. In essence, the problem for trained counselors hired to provide a professional service is one of disclosure. Offenders must be informed that any information that they disclose found to be relevant to the issue of security or safety may be turned over to correctional officials. As a result, a game is often initiated between the counselor and offender. The offender participates in counseling because he knows it will be beneficial to do so when release factors are considered. No real attempt, however, is made on the offender's behalf to disclose necessary information because of the fear that it may later be disclosed and incriminating.

Therefore, our approach in this text is not to try and provide further information regarding how the competing goals hinder the results of counseling. Previous literature is more than sufficient to address that issue. Our goal is, however, to explore various methods that may be employed by correctional counselors that may serve to reduce some of the conflict between issues of security and counseling offenders in correctional settings. For now, it may be most salient for the correctional counselor to accept the reality of these competing goals and begin to understand that this will likely remain the case for many years to come.

Correctional Counseling: Facility Settings versus Community Settings

It is important to note that correctional counseling can take place in a variety of settings. Most of the information presented thus far is primarily geared toward counseling services being provided in a secured correctional institution. Examples of secured correctional institutions include federal and state prisons, local jails, juvenile detention facilities, as well as privately owned correctional institutions responsible for the security of offenders. In addition to these institutional settings, however, are the various locations and circumstances in which counseling may occur within the community. For example, offenders who are on probation or parole or under any sentencing guideline that allows them to remain in the community or have access to community services are most likely to receive counseling services. These services may be provided by trained counselors employed by local mental health centers, employment agencies staffed by trained guidance counselors, as well as private helping centers.

Currently, there is a strong movement in American Criminal Justice toward further implementing a concept called **community corrections**. Community corrections describe the process of attempting to help offenders learn to better manage life circumstances through education, counseling, job placement, and housing centers. In fact, it may be that some of the best opportunities for professional counselors to have significant impacts on the lives of offenders are in these various community corrections programs. One example of a program that would fall under the category of community corrections is jail diversion. **Jail diversion** is a concept that describes the process of diverting offenders, convicted of nonviolent offenses, away from a jail cell and into the care of community health providers. It is a comprehensive, federally funded program that incorporates further education, counseling services to be provided by a licensed professional, psychiatric services primarily geared toward prescribing necessary medications, as well as housing that serves to remove the offender from his or her typically crime-ridden neighborhoods, or dysfunctional family environments.

In the late 1980s, the first drug treatment court had emerged. During this time, the drug court principles and processes were integrated into the overall criminal justice response involving addicted criminal defendants (Watson, Hanrahan, Luchins, & Lurigio, 2001).

The **drug court** concept synthesizes therapeutic treatment and judicial processes to optimize outcomes with the drug-addicted offender population (Watson et al., 2001). This means that drug addiction is not just viewed as a problem solely within the domain of the criminal justice system, but it is also a problem that affects the health of society. Current evaluations of drug courts have found promising results in the reduction of drug use, criminal behavior, and costs (Schma & Rosenthal, 1999). But, as the number of drug courts increased, so did the influx of individuals with mental health problems. This was perhaps one of the earliest official recognition that substance abuse disorders were frequently connected with other co-occurring mental health disorders. As a result, many practitioners became concerned about the continued appearance of the mentally ill in the criminal court system and it was at this time that "the mental health court movement emerged out of recognition of inequities in the experiences of mentally ill offenders . . ." as well as ". . . the drug court movement" (Watson et al., 2001, p. 3).

In response, several jurisdictions in several states developed mental health tracks within the drug treatment courts themselves (Watson et al., 2001). Eventually, these became what are known today as drug courts. According to the Bureau of Justice Assistance (2004), the term **mental health court** is most often used to refer to a specialized docket for defendants with mental illnesses that provides:

1. the opportunity to participate in court-supervised treatment;
2. a court team composed of a judge, court personnel, and treatment providers;

3. continued status assessments with individualized sanctions and incentives; and
4. resolution of case upon successful completion of mandated treatment plan.

The development of mental health courts has been witnessed in a variety of states, including California, Hawaii, New York, and Oregon (among others). Some jurisdictions have separate drug courts and mental health courts but with the same judge presiding over both. Other jurisdictions have created mental health courts that are independent of the drug courts. Prior to this, most police agencies simply jailed the mentally ill whenever they were considered a community nuisance. The problem for police as well as traditional court systems was that there was typically no specific legal agency that could have legal jurisdiction over the offender and provide suitable services to address their specific needs. Once established, mental health courts provide both therapeutic and criminal justice strategies through techniques like the use of a computer link between the jail facility and a mental health provider so that mental health workers can check the names of defendants against their client roster. If a client's name appears on the list then the caseworker is able to visit the jail and intervene (McNutt, 1999). Strategies such as these (and many others) have been utilized to optimize services for those offenders who present with mental illness, whether or not their disorders co-occur with drug abuse. Nevertheless, it is in the manner just described that the genesis of the mental health court is linked to the development of the drug treatment court.

SECTION SUMMARY

It is important for the student to be able to distinguish between *guidance*, *counseling*, and *psychotherapy*. All of these terms have similarities, but they are not identical. In addition, it is important for the student to understand what is meant by corrections. Corrections and correctional programs can be both institutionally based and community based. Each type affects the type of counseling setting that is likely to be encountered. Likewise, the underlying tenets to corrections are important to understand since they impact the correctional counseling role and function. Thus, students have many factors to consider when using the term "correctional counseling," which is a composite of concepts and ideas.

Lastly, the concerns and motivations for correctional security staff are different from those of the counseling or treatment staff. Correctional counselors must learn to work within an environment that is not always supportive of their efforts, understanding that the practitioner culture can also exacerbate problems facing offenders. Lastly, the scientific method is presented as a friend to the correctional counselor. Indeed, as one will see throughout this text, this process of continued evaluation of treatment effectiveness is never-ending. It is this process of inquiry that provides a skilled clinician with a clear framework from which client problems can be analyzed, techniques tested, and continual improvements implemented as a means of aiding the therapeutic process.

I. LEARNING CHECK

1. When referring to the term "counselor," this text is predominantly referring to those persons who have educational and clinical training, not lay counselors.
   a. True
   b. False

2. ________________ describes the process of trained counselors helping offenders identify and incorporate better behavioral, psychological, and emotional responses to life events.
   a. Psychotherapy
   b. Psychology
   c. Counseling
   d. All of the above
   e. None of the above
3. Guidance has been used as a concept to describe the process of helping individuals identify and choose what they value most.
   a. True
   b. False
4. Even though they may be in a correctional setting, offenders still have basic rights of due process, including rights to safety and life.
   a. True
   b. False
5. The scientific method of conducting research is generally described by which of the following components:
   a. Designing a test of this hypothesis
   b. Interpreting the results of the analysis, and by the process of induction
   c. Confirming, modifying, or rejecting the theory
   d. All of the above
   e. Only a & c, but not b.

PART TWO: THE ROLE OF THE COUNSELOR

The Counselor as Facilitator

Many people think of counseling as a process that is similar to "advice giving." As such, it is often the case that clients may come to a counseling session expecting the counselor to have specific details and guidance as to how they should handle a situation that confronts them. This is unfortunate because this is precisely where feelings of disappointment can quickly surface, with the client feeling as if they are getting no help for whatever issue that is identified as problematic. However, it is not the intended role of the counselor to be an advisor. Rather, counseling presumes that clients have the capacity to solve their own problems and address challenges, if only they can be shown the way. This is where the counselor enters the picture.

Often, people may have the means to solve their problems but they may simply not know how to proceed and/or they may not know how to utilize their own unique talents or abilities. The counselor, as a helping professional, is tasked with assisting these individuals in finding their own resolution. In this regard, counselors build on the strengths of the client to help mobilize the client's own natural ability to cope with and overcome challenges that bring them into counseling. The counselor acts as a grand facilitator and empowers the clients to handle issues in their lives, thereby enhancing a client's ability to make necessary changes in their life.

Through the process of facilitation, counselors will often assist the client in identifying goals in treatment and in developing the means by which they can achieve those goals. Ultimately, it is the task of the client to actually achieve his or her own goals, but it is the counselor who serves as a sounding board and source of inspiration and encouragement. By building a relationship of trust, exhibiting empathy, and providing tools for effective coping, the counselor provides the client with additional assistance to implement self-change and/or life changes that may be necessary to resolve challenges and difficulties. Through a collaborative partnership between the counselor and the client, trust is established where the client is encouraged to make honest and genuine progress toward an agreed-upon goal. All the while, the counselor respects the autonomy of the client, avoiding any desire to fully dictate the course of action that a client may take.

It is worth noting that the traditional role of the counselor as facilitator may not always mesh well with the requirements that exist within the criminal justice system. The fact that offenders do have certain requirements placed upon them does put the counselor in some bit of an authoritative role. Thus, the process of facilitation may sometimes have to be counterbalanced against the need to maintain security requirements imposed by the correctional system. This is a common challenge to correctional counselors but is perhaps best navigated through maintaining honesty and congruence as to the limits of the counselor's influence within the correctional environment. Ensuring that clients know the counselor's limits at the start and refraining from being overly coercive in therapy can be effective approaches to maintaining a facilitative role rather than one that is too directive, domineering, and counter to the internal change that is desired from the offender population in treatment.

Personality and Background for Becoming a Counselor

While there is no one single personality type that is ideal for the counseling profession, there are some characteristics that may be particularly well suited for persons wishing to enter the field of counseling. Generally, personalities that are given to excessive emotionality are not likely to be suitable for the counseling profession. Yet, at the same time, persons in the counseling profession must be in tune with the emotional framework of others. This is particularly true if the counselor hopes to achieve the minimal of empathetic bonds with the client.

Further, counseling requires that the counselor have a stable frame of mind. Otherwise, they cannot be effective in aiding others who in many cases may prove to be quite unstable. Persons with fragile ego development, inability to withstand stress, or a lack of concern for others will not typically be well suited for the counseling profession. Rather, persons who enjoy communicating with others, have at least some degree of patience, and who respect people for their inherent value will most probably find the counseling field to be to their liking. Because the counseling process can be very taxing upon one's patience and mental stamina, it is important that would-be counselors take an honest inventory of their own personal framework and the background that has shaped them to determine if the counseling field is appropriate for their own combination of strengths and limitations. Failure to do this can result in future impairment of others who will later seek the assistance of the counselor. Thus, it is important that persons contemplating such a career do so with careful consideration.

Personal Qualities of an Effective Counselor

According to Gladding (2007), there are a number of positive personal qualities that are well-suited to the counseling profession. Gladding provides a list of 10 qualities that are presented below:

1. ***Curiosity and inquisitiveness:*** A natural interest in people
2. ***Ability to listen:*** The ability to find listening stimulating
3. ***Comfort with conversation:*** Enjoyment of verbal exchanges

4. ***Empathy and understanding:*** The ability to put oneself in another's place, even if that person is a different gender or from a different culture
5. ***Emotional insightfulness:*** Comfort dealing with a wide range of feelings, from anger to joy
6. ***Introspection:*** The ability to see or feel from within
7. ***Capacity for self-denial:*** The ability to set aside personal needs to listen and take care of other's needs first
8. ***Tolerance of intimacy:*** The ability to sustain emotional closeness
9. ***Comfort with power:*** The acceptance of power with a certain degree of detachment
10. ***Ability to laugh:*** The capability of seeing the bitter–sweet quality of life events and the humor in them.

Even though correctional counselors may work with offenders who are hardened and potentially resistant, all of the above qualities are nevertheless very useful. Indeed, it is especially important that the correctional counselor possess these qualities (at least to some degree) if they expect to model them for offenders. Regardless of the population that a counselor is working with, these qualities are essential to basic counseling process and serve to aid the facilitative nature of counseling.

Professional Aspects of Counseling (Levels of Helping)

According to Gladding (2007), there are three levels associated with the helping relationship: nonprofessional, paraprofessional, and professional. For counselors to practice at a certain level, they must acquire the requisite skills associated with that level of helping. The first level of helping is that which consists of **nonprofessional helpers** (Gladding, 2007). These persons may be friends, family, or even untrained volunteers who offer assistance. The second level of helping consists of **human service workers**. These persons have some bit of formal training in human behavior but they are not likely to be licensed. Further, these types of helpers tend to work in teams rather than individually. Gladding notes that these types of professionals tend to be mental health technicians, child-care workers, and probation and/or parole personnel. The final and highest trained level of helpers are the **professional helpers**. These are the persons who have formal educations in prevention and intervention programming and implementation. This group consists of licensed counselors, psychologists, social workers, and psychiatrists. These professionals have advanced and specialized degrees as well as practical and internships where they will demonstrate their ability to provide therapeutic services.

Credentialing of Counselors

Therapeutic personnel come in many forms, particularly when dealing with specialized populations. Further still, state laws often have different distinctions between types of therapeutic providers and the level of credential and/or license that they may hold. For, instance, a person may be certified, but this is not the same as licensure. **Certification** implies a certain level of oversight in that a minimum standard of competency exists, but it is **licensure** that provides the legal right to see clients and receive third-party billing. Third-party billing is when insurance companies, employment assistance programs, or state programs are billed to reimburse the therapist. Obviously, this is important for the therapeutic practitioner working in private practice or in a non-profit but private facility. In addition, not all mental health specialists can give assessment tests. Many of the assessment tests that will be discussed later need to be administered by a fully licensed psychologist with a Ph.D. whereas the other tests may be administered by people with no other qualification than the requisite training to successfully administer and score the test. However, in some states, counselors who have obtained the adequate psychometric training may also be qualified and permitted to administer standardized mental health tests on their own. Thus, the distinctions in credentials can be a bit blurred, but it is the possession of license that is paramount to the counseling professional.

SECTION SUMMARY

It is important for persons interested in correctional counseling to understand the true nature and role of the counseling process. Counseling is a collaborative process where the counselor and the client engage in a shared form of interaction and goal-setting. In other words, the counselor acts as a facilitator rather than the leader of the session. Further, there are some personality characteristics and personal qualities that make a person more ideally suited for counseling. In general, the counselor should be a person who enjoys working with people, is a good listener, has an appropriate sense of empathy, and is of stable mind and character. While there are many more characteristics that make an effective counselor, the basic requirement is that counselors should be able to convey a sense of genuine care for their clients.

Lastly, there are different types of helping that range from help from a layperson to that from a clinically trained professional. Each of these approaches to helping have their appropriate uses but, as the clinical demands of the client become more serious, the more formally trained clinician is likely to be needed. This also leads to distinctions in the person's officially recognized credentials. Knowing the difference between certification and licensure is important because it is licensure alone that qualifies a person to make many of the advanced clinical decisions during treatment and it is this credential that is required to charge reimbursements for formal billing. This means that insurance companies, employee assistance programs, and other such organizations recognize the superior and advanced training that is associated with licensure.

II. LEARNING CHECK

1. Professional helpers usually work independently in delivering services.
   a. True
   b. False
2. Human service workers usually work independently in delivering services.
   a. True
   b. False
3. Introspection is a good quality for counselors to possess.
   a. True
   b. False
4. Licensure is required to obtain third-party billing.
   a. True
   b. False
5. Counselors should be facilitators rather than problem solvers when conducting therapy.
   a. True
   b. False

PART THREE: DEVELOPMENT OF THE CORRECTIONAL COUNSELOR

Watching for Burnout

Burnout is a concept that describes the process of emotional exhaustion, and cynicism along with hardened and calloused attitudes toward helping others (Egan, 2007; Masters, 2004). Burnout is a formidable foe that usually manifests itself based on a myriad of circumstances. According to Brown and Srebalus (2003), burnout is an extremely serious health problem within the workforce and is second only to infectious diseases and pollution-related illnesses as a health hazard. In essence, over time counselors often become fatigued due to demands from their work, causing them to be less effective or, in extreme cases, inoperable.

It is important that counselors be aware of some of the symptoms that may present themselves in the case of burnout. Masters (2004) provides a list of symptoms that are identified in counselors who have begun to feel overwhelmed by the process of helping. The following selection is not meant to be all inclusive but is instead intended to serve as a reference point to help identify certain situations or behaviors that are indicative of burnout:

- Loss of objectivity toward an offender
- Belief that the offender will never change
- Belief that the criminal justice system does not work
- Feelings of futility due to not being able to find effective methods of intervention
- Manipulating offenders
- Becoming detached and noninvolved with the counseling process
- Not properly attending to the offender during counseling sessions
- Calling in sick
- Excessive consumption of alcohol or other drugs.

There are a variety of causes commonly associated with burnout. One of the most salient causes is stress. **Stress** is a concept that describes the process of feeling strained due to reaching one's limits of emotional or physical capacity. When one begins to experience stress, an abundance of physical and emotional energy is needed to combat the unpleasant feelings. Over time, this massive expenditure of energy fatigues the body and mind. Once fatigued, counselors are vulnerable to physical and emotional ailments as well as a general lack of productivity. Common factors that together produce stressors include being overworked; lack of or perceived lack of money; organizational characteristics; family problems; as well as inadequate feedback from supervisors (Brown & Srebalus, 2003).

It is critical that counselors first recognize symptoms and stressors early on and then take appropriate actions to effectively combat them. One of the most powerful methods of reducing stress is through social support. It is not uncommon for counselors to correlate periods of time where they were experiencing significant stress with times where they had become emotionally isolated from significant others, including spouses, family and friends, as well as their professional colleagues. Other methods of combating burnout include regular exercise, vacations when possible, as well as reconnecting with friends and loved ones. In addition, Brown and Srebalus (2003, p. 341) provide the following list of possible actions that may serve to stave off the powerful forces of burnout:

- Time and boundary management
- Detached concern for clients
- Work sharing and job rotation

- Supervision for professional development
- More effective peer/supervisor feedback
- See counseling as a job not a "calling"
- Cultivate nonwork friendships
- Realism about the power of counseling interventions
- Written professional development plan
- Join a social support/mutual aid group
- Treat spouse and children as different from clients
- Improve body image
- See health as holistic
- Preserve privacy better
- Cultivate hobbies or take vacations
- Reevaluate personal/professional ambitions.

Professional Collaboration

Professional collaboration among counselors is a process where counselors may ask for input and/or suggestions from other professionals regarding clients who are on their clinical caseload. This is an important process because this allows counselors to solicit the advice of counselors who may have invaluable firsthand experience with a certain clinical issue. In correctional counseling, this is also a useful means of exchange when a counselor is tasked with working with a particularly difficult population, such as sex offenders or domestic batterers. In such cases, it may prove useful to have the advice of a colleague.

Professional collaboration is also very useful for newly minted counselors who have received their degree or training in counseling but have not had much clinical experience. In such cases, the advice and guidance of a more seasoned therapist can provide effective mentoring for the junior counselor. However, the use of professional collaboration should not be thought of as being sought only out by junior counselors. Many counselors who have had years of experience may find it useful from time-to-time to consult with colleagues regarding a specific clinical case that proves challenging. This is a normal and routine process within the world of counseling and tends to improve overall service delivery and also helps the counselor seeking such collaboration to identify blind spots that might exist in his or her own clinical judgment. Having another professional examine the issues associated with a client can provide a wealth of ideas and perspectives that might otherwise be overlooked by a counselor who does not seek the benefit of collaboration.

It is important to note that during this period of collaboration, the counselor may discuss various aspects of the client's problems or challenges. The counselor may also discuss his or her own internal reactions to the client. However, even in the collaboration process, the identity of the client is kept anonymous. In other words, the client's confidentiality must be respected since collaboration is not an acceptable exception to the client's right to confidentiality. Counselors should not allow themselves to become lax in safeguarding the confidentiality and/or anonymity of the client, even while engaged in professional collaboration.

Supervision and Continued Training

The issue of supervision and continued training is very important for the professional counselor. The supervision process is often associated with faculty supervision of counselors who take a practicum and/or an internship when enrolled in a professional counseling degree program.

However, supervision tends to continue well beyond gaining the degree since most all states require graduates to obtain several thousand hours of clinical experience after the completion of their degree. These additional clinical hours are required so that the counselor, commonly referred to as an intern at this point in training, can obtain a license to practice independently without the use of a supervisor. In such cases, the site supervisor is likely to supervise these budding counselors. This early supervision is an important aspect of the development of the counselor, so it is important that the supervisor take an active interest in the counselor intern's development.

Lastly, it is important that counselors continue their training well beyond obtaining their degree and/or their initial training. In fact, most all licensing and certification boards require that counselors complete at least a minimum amount of training every year or two. While this changes in specific criteria from state to state, the requirement that extended training be completed seems to be universal. In many cases, counselors attend workshops or conferences where they will obtain Continuing Education Units (CEUs), which are awarded to the counselor who attends the training. The specific number of CEUs depends on the length of the workshop or training experience, but generally one CEU is the equivalent to one hour of training. It is very common for counselors to routinely attend these types of training events since there are so many issues with which they may have to contend. Further, attendance at these training functions also leads to further opportunities for collaboration and networking. This, in turn, provides further support for counselors who have challenging client caseloads.

SECTION SUMMARY

Effective professional collaboration, supervision, and training are critical to the development of a correctional counselor. These means of support for the counselor can also alleviate the stress and burnout that tends to occur when counselors become overworked and/or impacted by the nature of their work. Counselors must recognize their own symptoms of stress to ensure that they maintain the level of psychological fitness that is required to be effective in attending to their clients. Professional development activities can help the counselor to achieve higher levels of competence and, in the process, can also improve the counselor's sense of confidence. Professionally competent and adequately confident counselors are less likely to suffer from the ravages of stress and burnout. This then ensures that counselors are likely to deliver appropriate services to the public, the public welfare being the ultimate priority within the counseling profession.

III. LEARNING CHECK

1. One effective means of preventing stress is to cultivate friendship with those who are not associated with one's work environment.
   a. True
   b. False
2. One symptom that might indicate that a counselor is feeling overwhelmed by the demands of the helping role is if he or she begins to manipulate offenders who are under treatment.
   a. True
   b. False
3. During professional collaboration, the counselor may receive feedback from colleagues in regard to a challenging clinical case on their caseload.
   a. True
   b. False

4. When engaged in professional collaboration, the counselor may reveal the identity of the client; confidentiality is not a concern since the counselor is collaborating with other counselors.
   a. True
   b. False
5. The awarding of Continuing Education Units is a common practice when attending workshops or receiving routine training within the counseling profession.
   a. True
   b. False

CONCLUSION

The actions and behaviors of people are a manifestation of their experiences with caregivers, social groups, social and societal experiences, and interpretations of how they are viewed by others. In essence, criminal behavior should be viewed as a symptom of dysfunctional learning. Individuals who are mostly psychologically and emotionally healthy are less likely to engage in criminal behavior. This is because to engage in a criminal activity, such as drug use, for example, produces a result that is analogous to "gumming things up." The fruits of criminal activity are not capable of allowing someone to reach their fullest potential. Regardless of the circumstances, "most" criminals know, at some level of consciousness, that their actions are either harmful to themselves or someone else. Therefore, one way to phrase the goal of correctional counseling is to transform the offender's emotional landscape from barren to being able to feel (from an emotional standpoint) and capable of making decisions that contribute to, and reflect, growth and development.

In order for this transformation to take place, however, offenders must be willing to change and must have the capacity and courage to make hard decisions. This one fact alone probably removes at least a portion of offenders who are capable of being helped through counseling. If the offender is not willing or able to view the criminal lifestyle as destructive, then counseling techniques are not likely to have the intended result. It may be that the offenders not ready to change would benefit more from educational-type programs aimed at informing the offender of the likely consequences of continuing criminal behavior.

In addition, as will be highlighted throughout this text, is the fact that what works for one offender may not work for another. Correctional counselors must be flexible and able to adapt to the differing needs and learning styles of different offenders. Also, counselors must remain vigilant in their efforts to stay abreast of the laws governing the counseling relationship. Confidentiality is a critical factor and is related to the success of counseling. Counselors must be aware of the state laws in which they practice because as of yet there is no national legislation that clearly articulates what information can and cannot be disclosed. From an ethical standpoint counselors must be willing to inform offenders that at the current time there can be no guarantee to strict confidentiality.

Further, counselors should always present themselves in a professional manner, with the sole intention of attending to the needs of the offender in an effort to help. It is always unethical for a counselor to enter into sexual relationships or dual relationships with offenders. One of the best ways for a counselor to guard against burnout as well as engaging in the process of countertransference is to continuously and actively participate in further self-development programs. This may include participating in personal counseling sessions for the counselor, continued educational programs, as well as developing and maintaining social contacts and activities.

Finally, matters of ethics and appropriate counseling practice are shaped by the professional collaboration, clinical training, and supervision that one receives. Thus, it is important for counselors and, for the entire counseling profession, that they are well trained in clinical aspects of practice as well as the ethical aspects of practice. This training, supervision, and professional support can also serve as a buffer to stress and burnout. This is important because counselors suffering from professional fatigue and burnout can impair a client's attempt to change. Since the ultimate maxim for counselors is to do no harm to their clients, it stands to reason that all counselors should openly embrace the process of training, education, and professional collaboration as a means of ensuring that they deliver appropriate services to society. There is no other objective that is more important to the field of counseling in general, and the field of correctional counseling in particular.

Essay Questions

1. Define correctional counseling. Is correctional counseling different from other forms of counseling? Why or why not?
2. Describe and discuss two key legal and ethical considerations that must be attended to when providing counseling services within the correctional setting?
3. What is the most important legal issue that counselors must be aware of when providing services to an offender? Why is this issue so important and what are the possible repercussions if this legal parameter is violated?
4. Describe the difference between guidance and counseling? Are these two concepts mutually exclusive or can they overlap?
5. In your own words, describe the concept of stress. What are some of the physical and emotional consequences of stress? What is the likely result of prolonged stress that is not properly defused?

Treatment Planning Exercise

Though students have completed just one chapter at this point, it is important that they begin to connect the ethical and legal issues relevant to the treatment planning process. For this exercise, divide the class up into pairs of students and have them read the case vignette that follows. Once they have read the vignette regarding Jeff, have the students select at least five specific legal or ethical issues that are relevant to this case.

Note that issues related to confidentiality, *Turner* reasonableness test, *Tarasoff*, informed consent, and/or issues associated with potential HIV/AIDS could all be considered particularly suitable.

The Case of Jeff: Pedophile in Institution

Jeff is a 35-year-old male who is an inmate in your maximum security facility. Jeff has recently been transferred to your facility from another facility, largely for protective reasons. Jeff has come to you because he is very, very worried. Jeff is a pedophile and he has been in prison for nearly five years. His expected release date is coming up and he may very well get released due to prison overcrowding problems and his own exemplary behavior. He has been in treatment and, as you look through his case notes, you can tell that he has done very well.

But there were other inmates at his prior prison facility who did not want to see him get paroled. In fact, it is a powerful inmate gang, and Jeff had received "protection" from this gang in exchange for providing sexual favors to a select trio of inmate gang members. Jeff discloses that while humiliating, he had to do this to survive in the prison subculture, particularly since he was a labeled and known pedophile. The gang knew this, of course, and used this as leverage to ensure that Jeff was compliant. In fact, the gang never even had to use any physical force whatsoever to gain Jeff's compliance. Jeff notes that this now bothers him and he doubts his own sense of masculinity.

Jeff has performed well in treatment for sex offenders. But he has also been adversely affected by noxious sexual experiences inside the prison. You are the first person that he has disclosed this to. Further, he is beginning to wonder if he may have HIV/AIDS; he notes that he feels fatigued more frequently and that he gets ill more easily. However, he makes it very clear that he does not want to be tested until he is out of prison and he does not want his fears known to others in the prison.

As you listen to his plight, you begin to wonder if his issues with sexuality are actually now more unstable than they were in prison. Though his treatment notes seem convincing, this is common among pedophiles. But what was not known to the other therapist was how Jeff had engaged in undesired sexual activity while incarcerated. This activity has created a huge rift in Jeff's masculine identity. Will this affect his likelihood for relapse on the outside? Will Jeff be able to have a true adult–adult relationship on the outside? If not, will he be more enticed to have an adult–child relationship? Does Jeff need to resolve his concerns with consensual versus forced homosexual activity? You begin to wonder.

Now as you listen, you realize that if you make mention of this, then the classification system is not likely to release Jeff, and this condemns him to more of the same type of exploitation (gang members are in this prison, too; they just are of different gangs but will eventually learn of his past and follow suit with the prior gang). Oh, and if you do say something, will Jeff feel that honesty and counseling are simply an exercise in vulnerability and betrayal? Or do you not mention this information and by the same token allow someone to be released with a highly questionable prognosis.

You sit there listening to Jeff, who is on the verge of tears. You begin to wonder what you should do and what ethical and/or legal bounds you need to consider . . .

Bibliography

Bennett, L. A. (1978). Counseling in correctional environments. New York: Human Science Press.

Brown, D., & Srebalus, J. (2003). *Introduction to the counseling profession* (3rd ed.). Pearson Education, Inc: New York.

Bureau of Justice Assistance. (2004). *Mental health courts program.* Washington, DC: Office of Justice Programs, United States Department of Justice.

Clear, T. R., & Dammer, H. R. (2003). The offender in the community (2nd ed.). Thompson/Wadsworth: Toronto, Ontario Canada.

Egan, G. (2007). *The skilled helper: A problem management and opportunity development approach to helping* (8th ed.). Belmont, CA: Thompson Brooks/Cole.

Gladding, S. T. (1996). *Counseling: A comprehensive profession* (3rd ed.). Englewood Cliffs, New Jersey: Prentice Hall.

Gladding, S. T. (2007). *Counseling: A comprehensive profession* (5th ed.). Englewood Cliffs, New Jersey: Prentice Hall.

Kratcoski, P. C. (1981). *Correctional counseling and treatment.* Monterey, CA: Duxbury Press.

Lester, D. (1992). *Correctional counseling* (2nd ed.). Cincinnati, OH: Anderson Publishing.

Masters, R. (2004). *Counseling criminal justice offenders* (2nd ed.). Thousand Oaks, CA: Sage Publications.

McNutt, R. (1999). Court for mentally ill offenders advocated: Judicial officials at seminar told that treatment is lacking. The Cincinnati Enquirer. Available at: http://www.enquirer.com/editions/1999/11/10/loc_court_for_mentally.html.

Schma, H. P., & Rosenthal, W. (1999). Therapeutic jurisprudence and the drug court movement: Revolutionizing the criminal justice system's response to drug abuse and crime in America. *Notre Dame Law Review, 74*, 439–555.

Schrink, J., & Hamm, M. S. (1990). Misconceptions concerning correctional counseling. *Journal of Offender Counseling, Services & Rehabilitation, 14*(1), 1989.

Walters, G. D. (2001). Book review. *International Journal of Offender Therapy and Comparative Criminology, 45*, 129–131.

Watson, A., Hanrahan, P., Luchins, D., & Lurigio, A. (2001). Mental health courts and the complex issue of mentally ill offenders. *Psychiatric Services, 52*(4), 477–481.

Weed, L. L. (1964). Medical records, patient care and medical education. *Irish Journal of Medical Education, 6*, 271–282.

2

Legal, Ethical, and Cross-Cultural Issues

CHAPTER OBJECTIVES

After reading this chapter, you will be able to:

1. Know the basic legal rights of offenders who may be engaged in the correctional counseling process.
2. Know the key ethical and legal considerations when providing counseling services within the institution and within the community.
3. Be aware of the various legal issues associated with the delivery of counseling services.
4. Understand the SOAP process of maintaining case notes and the importance of documentation and records management in counseling.
5. Understand the dynamics associated with the counseling relationship that can lead to ethical violations.

PART ONE: LEGAL AND ETHICAL ISSUES

Rights of the Correctional Offender

One of the most important aspects of correctional counseling that practitioners and students need to be aware of involves the myriad of legal issues that must be considered. In addition, it is important to identify the sources of these rights so that a comprehensive understanding is possible. Before proceeding, however, a quick note should be made. It is likely that legal and ethical issues concerning correctional counseling are not usually the areas of interest to most persons wishing to learn about the correctional counseling process. However, this area of knowledge is fundamental for every counselor working in the criminal justice system for several reasons. First, offenders can be litigious by nature and it is wise for counselors to understand the legal parameters within their field to avoid pitfalls or manipulation by their offender clientele. Second, ethical practice is a key to developing genuine rapport between the counselor and the client. Third, a counselor is essentially incompetent if he or she is not familiar with his or her profession's strictures on conduct and practice.

Confidentiality

In relation to counseling, confidentiality is a concept that describes the process of keeping private or secret the information disclosed by a client to a counselor during a counseling session. The essence of confidentiality is very important to the success of counseling. This point was highlighted in the U.S. Supreme Court case of *Jaffee* v. *Redmond* (1996). In its opinion, the Court clearly articulated that an atmosphere of confidence and trust is necessary for a client to feel comfortable enough to disclose his or her emotions, memories, and fears. The Court further reasoned that because of the nature of the problems for which clients seek the assistance of counselors, embarrassment or disgrace may be endured if information is not properly contained and is likely to impede the confidential relationship necessary for effective treatment.

Beyond these, however, the issue of confidentiality becomes much less clear, especially within the domain of correctional counseling. Remember, correctional counseling describes the process of a trained counselor helping an offender identify and implement better methods of handling stressful life circumstances. Usually, confidentiality will be maintained unless the offender presents a danger to self or others. *What needs to be made exceptionally clear, however, is the fact that the client is a convicted offender under the care of the criminal justice system.* In these circumstances confidentiality will always yield to issues of security, safety, and order, as well as the concept of punishment in the event the offender discloses participation or knowledge of past, present, or future criminal behavior. This is the reality of correctional counseling.

As Masters (2004) states, "In a criminal justice setting, whether during probation, incarceration, or some form of aftercare such as parole, it is impossible to assure a client of complete confidentiality" (p. 170). This is why it is of paramount importance to practice informed consent in all circumstances, and the stipulations governing the informed consent need to be articulated clearly and accurately. The concept of **informed consent** describes the process of a trained counselor educating the offender on all legal and ethical parameters governing the counseling relationship. In other words, offenders must be told that it is possible that anything they discuss in counseling may be under certain circumstances disclosed to the courts. Masters (2004) captures the essence of this point well by stating "It is ethically indefensible to assure the client of confidentiality or have the client assume that privacy exists when it does not" (p. 171). Offenders have the right to know what kind of treatment they are receiving, the associated risks, as well as the benefits and alternatives.

Duty to Warn and the Case of Tarasoff

One of the leading court cases governing the concept of confidentiality as it applies to information concerning the safety of a third party is *Tarasoff* v. *Regents* (1976). In essence, the court ruled that mental health professionals have the duty and obligation to protect a third party (public) in cases where they reasonably believe a client might endanger the third party; and this duty overrides any obligation to confidentiality. Prosenjit Poddar was a graduate student at the University of California at Berkeley. He was also a voluntary outpatient at the University's student health center. During a counseling session Poddar told the psychologist that he intended to kill his former girlfriend, Tatiana Tarasoff, when she returned to campus from visiting her aunt in Brazil. In a counseling session he disclosed that he was upset and depressed due to the fact that Tatiana was involved in relationships with other men. Poddar stated that he was going to get a gun and shoot Tatiana. Based on this information the psychologist notified the campus police and informed them of what Poddar had stated. The campus police detained and questioned Poddar, who denied any intention of killing Tatiana. The campus police found Poddar to be rational and released him after he promised to stay away from Tatiana. Meanwhile, Poddar no longer sought counseling from the psychologist and no further action was taken. Two months later, when Tatiana returned, Poddar first stalked her and then stabbed her to death. Based on these circumstances the court stated, "When a therapist determines, or pursuant to the standards of his profession should determine, that his patient presents a serious danger of violence to another, he incurs an obligation to use reasonable care to protect the intended victim against such danger. The discharge of this duty may require the therapist to take one or more of various steps. Thus, it may call for him to warn the intended victim, to notify the police, or to take whatever steps are reasonably necessary under the circumstances" (*Tarasoff* v. *Regents*, 1976, p. 430).

Ethics in Correctional Counseling

Ethics is a concept that describes the process of focusing on principles and standards that are used to guide the relationships between people and, specifically for our purposes, the relationship between counselor and client (Gladding, 1996). The concept of ethics is often used in conjunction with describing whether certain behaviors are considered legal. For example, someone may state, "Such conduct, within the context of counseling would be considered illegal and unethical." Appreciate, however, that in such a statement two different disciplines have been called on; one being the study of ethics and the other dealing with law. It may be that one way of teasing out the intended meaning of "ethics" is to think of the term as describing a discipline aimed at studying and identifying the parameters of human behavior and values within particular contexts.

When counselors are faced with situations that are difficult to resolve, they are expected to handle these situations in ways that are professionally appropriate for the well-being of the client and the integrity of the counseling process.

For example, the American Counseling Association (ACA, 2005) publishes a code of ethics aimed at providing direction and guidelines for counselors to address certain circumstances and this code will be primarily relied upon in this section. Section A.1.a., titled **Primary Responsibility**, states, "The primary responsibility of counselors is to respect the dignity and to promote the welfare of clients" (ACA, 2005, p. 4). Although not specific in providing dictates of exact behavior, the above section does provide crucial guidance. In essence, when attempting to figure out what behavior is most appropriate, one question to ask oneself is, "Are my actions in accordance with the best interest of my client?"

Case Notes and Session Recording

One of the most important elements of the correctional counseling process, and which is directly addressed by ethical codes of conduct, is the accurate recording of notes pertaining to the activities of all counseling sessions. Recording and maintaining accurate records is no longer something counselors should do but instead something counselors must do. This is partly due to the litigious nature of current society and the accurate recording of notes is one way to guard against potential liability concerns. In addition, case notes are vital to the process of keeping counseling sessions focused on pertinent issues of concern to the offender(s). To keep counseling sessions on track case notes should reflect the offender's progress, or lack thereof, especially as it relates to the particular goals of an offender. Case notes provide one avenue for counselors to stay focused on particular issues as well as to verify compliance with legal issues. Regarding clients' records, the code of ethics, the ACA, in Section A.1.b. (2005) states, "Counselors maintain records necessary for rendering professional services to their clients and as required by laws, regulations, or agency or institution procedures. Counselors include sufficient and timely documentation in their client records to facilitate the delivery and continuity of needed services. Counselors take reasonable steps to ensure that documentation in records accurately reflects client progress and services provided. If errors are made in client records, counselors take steps to properly note the correction of such errors according to agency or institutional policies" (p. 4).

One of the most popular methods of capturing necessary information regarding the events that transpire during counseling sessions is described by the acronym SOAP. SOAP notes originally developed by Weed (1964) provide a method of collecting and documenting information that help counselors identify, prioritize, and track the needs of offenders so that they may be attended to in a timely and systematic fashion (Cameron & Turtle-Song, 2002). Each letter of the acronym represents a particular component of the data collection method:

Subjective (S)—is a concept that describes the process of interpreting observations based on one's own mind. This is where a counselor describes his or her impression of a particular offender. Particularly salient to this section is the description of an offender's expression of feelings, concerns, plans, or goals, as well as the attendant levels of intensity attached to them each (Cameron & Turtle-Song, 2002).

Objective (O)—is a concept that describes the process of a particular phenomenon that is observable. The objective portion may consist of an offender's appearance, certain behaviors, abilities, and so on. In this section counselor observations should be stated in precise and descriptive terms that are quantifiable. Labels, judgments, and opinions should be avoided.

Assessment (A)—is a concept that describes the process of a trained counselor providing an evaluation of an offender that incorporates the subjective and objective observations. It usually contains diagnostic terms such as *depression*, *anxiety*, *anti-social disorder*, *bi-polar disorder*, and *obsessive-compulsive disorder* (OCD), among others. The assessment component is the section mostly read by outside reviewers or auditors. It should be complete and based on factual evidence that is supported by information contained in the subjective and objective portions of the format (Cameron & Turtle-Song, 2002).

Plan/Prognosis (P)—is a concept that describes the particular actions that will be carried out as a result of the assessment. Information contained in the plan usually consists of such entries describing the particular interventions used, educational components used to assist comprehension, the offender's progress, direction that will be taken in the next session, and the date of the next section.

Accountability is a vital component of the counseling process that must be adhered to. The best way to ensure accountability is to accurately and ethically note all happenings of the counseling process and then record these notes in appropriate files. SOAP is one format, among many, that provides guidelines that serve to help counselors ensure they are recording necessary information. Tables 2.1 and 2.2 serve as a guide or reference point. They are not all inclusive, but instead serve as a tool in assisting counselors to make sure they are capturing the essence of what is required in documenting the status of a particular client. The tables contain selections borrowed from the work of Cameron and Turtle-Song (2002).

TABLE 2.1 Summary of definitions and examples

Section	Definitions	Examples
(S) Subjective	What the client tells you. What others tell you about the client. Basically, how the client experiences the world.	Client's feelings, concerns, plans, goals, and thoughts. Intensity of problems and impact on relationships. Client's orientation time, place, and person.
(O) Objective	Factual. What the counselor personally observes/witnesses. Quantifiable—what was seen, counted, smelled, heard, or measured.	The client's general appearance. Client's demonstrated strengths and weaknesses.
(A) Assessment	Summarized the counselor's clinical thinking. A synthesis of the analysis of the subjective and objective portion of the notes.	Include clinical diagnosis and impressions.
(P) Plan	Describes the parameters of treatment based on the assessment.	Includes interventions used, progress, and direction of future intervention.

Informed Consent

As discussed earlier, informed consent is a critical component of any respectable counseling process. It is important to note that there are ethical guidelines that inform the proper process and circumstances in which consent should be obtained from clients. In addition, informed consent is often obtained in separate circumstances that may fall under the umbrella of counseling. For example, within correctional counseling offenders will often be asked to provide consent to the initial assessment. In addition, it is common to have an evaluation component attached to many of

TABLE 2.2 Guidelines for note taking

Dos	Dont's
Be brief and concise. Keep quotes to a minimum. Use an active voice. Precise and descriptive terminology. Record immediately after each session. Use proper spelling, grammar, and punctuation. Document all contact or attempted contacts. Use only black ink if notes are handwritten. Sign off using legal signature and include your title.	Do not use names of other clients, family members, or other individuals named by the client. Avoid terms like *seems* or *appears*. Avoid common labels that can be interpreted in various ways. Only use terminology that you are trained to use. Do not leave blank spaces. Do not use margins or try to squeeze additional commentary between lines.

the correctional counseling programs, which also require informed consent. Evaluation studies are primarily aimed at measuring selected variables at different points in time to determine if there is any progress in the offender. It is important that clients know the nature of the data that will be collected and the uses of such data. In its ethical standards, the ACA (2005) directly addresses the issue of informed consent as it relates to assessment for the purposes of research as well as counseling relationship.

Prior to assessing a client, counselors should "explain the nature and purposes of assessment and the specific use of results in language the client (or other legally authorized person on behalf of the client) can understand, unless an explicit exception to this right has been agreed upon in advance. Regardless of whether scoring and interpretation are completed by counselors, by assistants, or by computer or other outside services, counselors take reasonable steps to ensure that appropriate explanations are given to the client" (ACA, 2005, p. 12).

In addition, clients need to be informed, in a manner in which they understand, the likely processes that will take place during counseling sessions. The ACA (2005) makes this clear in Section A.2.a., where it states, "Clients have the freedom to choose whether to enter into or remain in a counseling relationship and need adequate information about the counseling process and the counselor. Counselors have an obligation to review in writing and verbally with clients the rights and responsibilities of both the counselor and the client. Informed consent is an ongoing part of the counseling process, and counselors appropriately document discussions of informed consent throughout the counseling relationship" (p. 4).

Further, clients need to be given clear and distinct information in regard to the counselor who delivers therapeutic services. Beyond matters of confidentiality, clients have a right to know other parameters related to their counselor and their perspective before any counseling begins. Clients should be informed of the counselor's qualifications and credentials, the parameters related to those credentials, the nature of the counseling relationship, the counselor's areas of expertise, fees and services offered, the boundaries of privileged communication, the limits of confidentiality, client responsibilities, and any potential risks that may occur as a result of the counseling process. Each of these points of information are important because they educate the client on the process and they ensure that no feelings of betrayal emerge from the client as the counselor administers services and/or ensures compliance with the agreed-upon treatment plan. The information just noted is typically included on what is referred to as a *Disclosure Statement* in many states. In other states, the official term may be a *Declarations and Procedures Form* (see Box 2.1). Regardless of the specific name given to the hardcopy form that is used, the counselor should emphasize that it is his or her desire that clients know, upfront, all of the specific details about the counseling process that they are about to become involved in. This is important because this goes well beyond being informed of limitations of confidentiality; it tells the client exactly what he or she should expect in therapy. While the boundaries of confidentiality are indeed important, clients need to understand the mechanics behind the therapeutic process since this optimizes their ability to participate. In many cases, clients may see the process of completing the disclosure statement as a mere formality and some may even find it to be a trifling issue, but the counselor should make sure that this information is understood by the client prior to conducting counseling. If done correctly, the counselor can use this process as a rapport-building opportunity by emphasizing that it is important to him or her, as a professional, to ensure that the client is as fully informed as is possible. The counselor should emphasize that it is his or her desire to provide ethical counseling services when requiring that the client become fully familiar with the

BOX 2.1
Declarations and Procedures Form

DECLARATION OF PRACTICES AND PROCEDURES

John Smith
101 Main Street, Mayberry, USA 11001
(000) 000-000

Qualifications: I earned an MA degree from the University of ______________________ in 2010. I am a **Licensed Professional Counselor** (LPC #0000) with the LICENSED PROFESSIONAL COUNSELORS BOARD OF EXAMINERS, 8631 SUMMA AVENUE, BATON ROUGE, LOUISIANA 70809, TELEPHONE (225)765-2515. I am also a **Licensed Addiction Counselor** (LAC #0000) with the *Addictive Disorder Regulatory Authority of Louisiana*, Baton Rouge, Louisiana 70809. Telephone: (225)922-7700.

Counseling Relationship: I see counseling as a process in which you, the client, and I, the counselor, have come to understand and trust one another, work as a team to explore and define present problem situations, develop future goals for an improved life, and work in a systematic fashion toward realizing those goals.

Areas of Expertise: I have a specialty in addictions counseling and I am licensed to provide services that are related to the addicted population as well as general counseling services to a wide variety of populations.

Fee Scale: The fee for my services typically range from $50.00 to $75.00 per session. However, I do operate on a sliding scale for remuneration, depending on the individual client's particular financial circumstances and their state of need. Payment is due at the time of service and clients are seen by appointment only. Clients will be charged for appointments that are broken or canceled without 24-hour notice. Payment is not accepted from insurance companies.

Services Offered and Clients Served: I approach counseling from a cognitive-behavioral perspective in that patterns of thoughts and actions are explored in order to better understand the client's problems and to develop solutions. I work in a variety of formats, including individual counseling, couples counseling (related to addiction issues), and family counseling (as related to addiction and recovery). I also conduct group therapy. I see clients of all ages and backgrounds with the exception that I do not work individually with children under the age of six.

Code of Conduct: As a counselor, I am required by state law to adhere to the Code of Conduct for Licensed Professional Counselors that has been adopted by my licensing board. A Copy of this code is available upon request.

Privileged Communications: Materials revealed in counseling will remain strictly confidential except for:

- **a.** The client signs a written release of information indicating informed consent of such release.
- **b.** The client expresses intent to harm himself or herself or someone else.
- **c.** There is a reasonable suspicion of abuse or neglect against a minor child, elderly person (65 years of age or older), or a dependent adult.
- **d.** A court order is received directing the disclosure of information.

It is my policy to assert privileged communication on the behalf of the client and the right to consult with the client if at all possible, except during an emergency, before mandated disclosure. I will endeavor to

(*continued*)

apprise the client of all mandated disclosures as conceivable. In the event of marriage or family counseling, material obtained from an adult client individually may be shared with the client's spouse or other family members only with the client's permission. Any material obtained with a minor client may be shared with the client's parents or guardian.

Emergency Situation: If an emergency situation should arise, you may seek help through hospital emergency room facilities or by calling 911.

Client Responsibilities: You, the client, are a full partner in counseling. Your honesty and effort is essential to success. If you have suggestions or concerns about your counseling as we work together, I expect you to share these with me so that we can make the necessary adjustments. If it develops that you would be better served by another mental health provider, I will help you with the referral process. If you are currently receiving services from another mental health professional, I expect you to inform me of this and grant me permission to share information with this professional so that we may coordinate our treatment plan and any medication schedules that you are now under.

Physical Health: Physical health is an important factor in the emotional well-being of an individual. If you have not had a physical examination in the last year, it is recommended that you do so. Also, please provide me with a list of the medicines that you are now taking.

Potential Counseling Risk: The client should be aware that counseling poses potential risks. In the course of working together additional problems may surface of which the client was not initially aware. If this occurs the client should feel free to share these concerns with me.

I have read and understand the above information

Counselor Signature: ______________________ **Date**: ______________________

Client Signature: ______________________ **Date**: ______________________

I, signature of parent or guardian ______________________, give permission for **John Smith** to conduct counseling with my (relationship), ______________________ (name of minor) ______________________.

elements of the counseling relationship. See Box 2.1 for an example of a *Declarations and Procedures* document which includes all of the information just discussed.

Professional Boundary Setting

Critical to the survival of any counseling relationship is the fact that certain boundaries must be established and not breached. From a geographical standpoint a boundary is relatively clear. It is a line, often marked by a fence or other physical structure that clearly demarcates where one property begins and another ends. Boundaries between people, however, are often complex and not as clear. Emotions and feelings often add to the complexity making it difficult to decipher what actions are appropriate in certain situations. The concept of a power differential is what usually provides the foundation for the formation of a counseling relationship. The power differential exists because of the specialized knowledge and training the counselor possesses that is ultimately being sought by the client. It is precisely the result of this differential that certain boundaries must not be crossed. To do so would in essence change the foundation of the relationship which in most cases would prove harmful to the client. Especially, in light of the fact that the counseling relationship is one of the most powerful components of the counseling process capable of fostering meaningful transformation in the client.

Transference

Not all clients, especially those within correctional settings, will be open to the concept of counseling. They may be participating as a result of court order, or in an attempt to garner a lighter sentence or an earlier release. In fact, some clients may be difficult and troublesome for the trained counselor, who may at times feel abused. It is vital that counselors be able to respond to such feelings without inflicting punishment on the client. A particular phenomenon that is common in some counseling relationships is the concept of transference. **Transference** is a concept that involves a client projecting onto the counselor traits or characteristics of others in the client's life (Brown & Srebalus, 2003). For example, if a client sees the counselor as possessing traits similar to those of authority figures, the client may respond to or treat the counselor similar to the way he or she has treated other authority figures. This could result in the client becoming hostile or openly agitated with the counselor. Another possibility is that the client may withdraw and become silent if the counselor is perceived as a figure of authority. This response is especially likely for some clients who have experienced abuse at the hands of caregivers and were never allowed to express their feelings or emotion.

Countertransference

In the event that transference takes place in the counseling relationship, counselors must be vigilant and not allow themselves to further contribute to the phenomenon through the concept of countertransference. **Countertransference** is a condition where a counselor projects onto the client undeserved qualities or attributes. If a client reacts in a hostile fashion, the counselor may respond emotionally, portraying inappropriate intensity that does not foster growth or functional learning on the part of the client. In such a case the counselor has reacted in a manner described by the concept of countertransference. In essence, the counselor has reacted to the traits or characteristics of the client in the same way the counselor may treat others with similar attributes. As a result, counselors must be able to manage the process of transference in a manner that helps the client become more aware of his or her own emotion and feelings. For the counselor to become a participant, through the process of countertransference, in an unproductive exchange is damaging to the overall health of the counseling relationship.

Sexual Attraction

In correctional counseling sexual attraction does occur between counselors and offenders. The success of the counseling relationship depends, in large part, on the depth of the connection between the counselor and offender. Sufficient depth within the counseling relationship is needed to foster an environment conducive to offenders so that they share deep feelings and emotions. This requires trust that is established based on the counselor's genuine expressions of care, compassion, and empathy. As noted by Masters (2004), however, this can sometimes result in the counselor's professional warmth being misunderstood by offenders, resulting in attraction and crushes. Counselors also need to ensure that their motivations for entering into a counseling relationship are pure. In other words, counselors need to avoid trying to get their own needs met through the counseling relationship.

In essence, it is unethical for a trained counselor to engage in a sexual relationship with a client. It is not unethical for a counselor to find a client attractive; it is unethical, however, if the counselor acts on the attraction or serves to perpetuate a sexual relationship through inappropriate behavior. This is primarily because counseling relationships are not based on mutuality. In most cases clients are more vulnerable and perceive the counselor as someone with special knowledge. When sexual relations begin the true objectives of the counseling relationship are lost. In addition, the counselor will be held responsible. In most cases involving sexual relationships between counselors and offenders in criminal justice settings, the counselors will be terminated.

Dual Relationships

Dual relationship is a situation where a counselor and client enter into a relationship(s) that is beyond or distinguished from the counseling relationship. As mentioned above, sexual relationships certainly constitute dual relationships. In addition, nonsexual dual relationships should also be avoided. Nonsexual dual relationships include business transactions where the counselor and offender engage in some type of business venture while the counseling process is still under way. For example, during a counseling session the offender tells the counselor that he is a skilled carpenter. The counselor needs work done on the house and asks the offender if he would be willing to make some repairs. The offender agrees and the two decide that the work to be done would equate to approximately the same cost of three counseling sessions.

The problem with this kind of arrangement lies in the possibility of the services rendered not being satisfactory. In such a case where the repairs are not done properly or the counselor "slacks off" and does not properly attend to the client, the counseling relationship will likely suffer. As a result, counselors should refrain from doing business or accepting gratuities from clients. In addition, due to the same ethical reasons, Gladding (1996) suggests that counselors should not enter into a counseling relationship with close friends, family members, students, lovers, or employees.

SECTION SUMMARY

Legal issues in counseling can often be important since counselors are charged with protecting the rights of their clients. This is particularly true in regard to the client's confidentiality and other such concerns. However, the correctional environment opens up a number of additional concerns that are not usually found within the realm of the traditional counseling setting. It is important for the correctional counselor to understand basic legal principles common to the correctional setting so that counselors do not find themselves at cross purposes with the environment in which they work.

Correctional counselors have many responsibilities and obligations when providing therapeutic services. First, they have a responsibility to their client. As such, they must promote the dignity and the welfare of their client, even though that client is an offender. This can actually be much more difficult than many novice counselors may realize. Second, counselors must take careful and complete notes of the clinical experiences during each session. These notes are records that are often referred to as case notes. The use of the Subjective, Objective, Assessment, and Plan/Prognosis approach, otherwise known as "SOAP" is presented as an organized and widely recognized method of constructing case notes.

Lastly, it is important that the counselor safeguards his or her relationship with the client. To do this, it is important that the client is given informed consent and that this is obtained in writing—typically, a disclosure statement and/or a declarations of practices page. These documents simply inform the client of the counselor's credentials while also explaining the parameters associated with confidentiality. Though many offenders will already be aware of much of this information, still it is strongly advised that counselors complete the process of obtaining signed informed consent; this safeguards the client and the counselor. Other ethical considerations associated with the client–counselor relationship, such as transference and/or countertransference, dual relationships, stress, and burnout must be attended to by the counselor.

LEARNING CHECK

1. ______________________ describes the process of a trained counselor educating the offender on all legal and ethical parameters governing the counseling relationship.
   a. Notice of confidentiality
   b. Informed consent
   c. Dueces Tecum
   d. Waiver of confidentiality
   e. HIPAA
2. Transference is the process where the counselor identifies and/or projects expectations onto the client.
   a. True
   b. False
3. A(n) ______________________ is a situation where a counselor and client enter into a relationship(s) that is beyond or distinguished from the counseling relationship.
   a. excess relationship
   b. dual relationship
   c. ineffective relationship
   d. none of the above
4. Countertransference is a concept that describes the process of a counselor projecting onto the client undeserved qualities or attributes.
   a. True
   b. False
5. When using SOAP with one's case notes, we are referring to the process of keeping them clean of incriminating or derogatory information.
   a. True
   b. False

PART TWO: CULTURAL COMPETENCE AS PART OF ETHICAL SERVICE DELIVERY

Defining Cultural Competence

Cultural competence describes the process of effectively attending to the needs of individuals through proper consideration of the salient components of their particular culture. One definition that is congruent with our assertion that cultural competence is a theoretical construct is provided by the Department of Health and Human Services (DHHS, 2003) in its report titled

Developing Cultural Competence in Disaster Mental Health Programs. "Cultural competence is a set of values, behaviors, attitudes, and practices within a system, organization, program, or among individuals that enables people to work effectively across cultures. It refers to the ability to honor and respect the beliefs, language, interpersonal styles, and behaviors of individuals and families receiving services, as well as staff who are providing such services. Cultural competence is a dynamic, ongoing, developmental process that requires a long-term commitment and is achieved over time" (DHHS, 2003, p. 12). This definition was chosen because its essence implies a philosophy that is meant to incorporate all necessary components of providing quality mental health services to all individuals including minorities.

Much of the information that follows relies heavily on a 2001 report produced by DHHS titled *Mental Health: Culture, Race and Ethnicity—A supplement to Mental Health: A Report of the Surgeon General.* This supplemental report was created in an attempt to directly address the issue of cultural competence as it applies to mental health services through better understanding the nature and extent of mental health disparities, providing evidence of the need for mental health services, and providing possible avenues of action aimed at eliminating mental health disparities. Four groups will be directly addressed: African Americans, Hispanics, American Indians and Alaska Natives, and Asians and Pacific Islanders.

Why Cultural Competence Is Important

Currently, there is sufficient evidence that shows the rate of mental illness among minority populations is similar to the rate encountered across the population of the United States. Roughly 21% of U.S. population suffers from or has suffered from some type of mental illness. **Mental Illness** refers to mental disorders, which are considered health conditions characterized by alterations in thinking, mood, or behavior associated with distress and/or impaired functioning (DHHS, 2001). The overall rate of approximately 21% of minority populations suffering from mental illness is important to note, primarily because minority populations do not have proportionate access to mental health services. In essence, minority populations contain the same percentages of individuals suffering from mental illness as non-minority populations; however, services are not equitably distributed between the groups. This results in many individuals in minority populations going untreated for mental illness and also suggests that unmet mental health needs are disproportionately higher for minority populations in relation to Caucasian Americans.

One important reason for studying cultural competence is to acquire a better understanding of different cultures and the corresponding barriers to mental health services that may exist due to cultural differences and/or misunderstandings. Some of the most common barriers to treatment must first be illuminated in order to have a chance at removing or minimizing them while also improving the quality of services that are provided to minority clients once they reach treatment providers. Some of the more common barriers include cost of mental health services, societal stigma attached to mental illness, need for help, no clear organization of service providers, clinicians' ignorance concerning cultural issues and bias, and inability to speak the client's native language (DHHS, 2001). In essence, counselors who provide services to minorities must understand salient cultural issues and their impact on cognition and behavior, especially in light of the fact that minority populations are increasing. In addition, counselors who are unable to adequately appreciate cultural issues must have the courage to admit it and properly refer clients to another provider better equipped to effectively provide competent service.

Culture of the Client

Prior to examining the impact of the culture on offender mental health issues it is important to note that there is significant diversity within cultural groups. In fact, as mentioned by DHHS (2001) there is more diversity within groups than between groups. This is an important point and is meant to highlight the fact that none of the information provided should be used to stereotype any particular group or culture. The counselor should accumulate as much knowledge on a given racial and/or ethnic group yet at the same time, he or she should follow the client's lead in distinguishing the degree of racial and/or cultural affiliation that exists. In other words, let the client lead the way in determining what is culturally relevant and what is not.

Once baseline cultural underpinnings are established in the therapeutic process, the counselor should integrate the resulting knowledge with his or her own presentation of mental illness as a concept. Indeed, the manner in which the counselor presents "mental illness" (indeed, the very use of the term itself) can be critical to getting minority clients to consider therapeutic possibilities. One of the most problematic issues underlying an individual's perception of "mental illness," is the pervasive stigma that still exists in regard to that term. **Stigma** is the feeling of shame or disgrace due to a circumstance or because of some imperfection. According to Lin and Cheung (1999), Asian patients will often report somatic symptoms such as fatigue or dizziness while omitting emotional symptoms such as fear, shame, or sadness. In essence, it is important that counselors be aware of cultural beliefs in order to decipher symptoms that are likely being presented in ways acceptable to a particular culture. In the foregoing example, it is likely that somatic symptoms of distress are more culturally acceptable and carry less stigmatization than emotional symptoms, which may be interpreted as personal weakness.

Indeed, some social groups may emphasize a need to be "tough" or strong in the face of adversity. Though this may not necessarily be the best approach in coping, it may actually be the most adaptive response available to these groups under the circumstances that they find themselves in. Simply put, there may be no other alternative for the person and the social group but to simply make do with their circumstances. When an entire group is traumatized, it may be difficult to provide extended support as all persons are equally taxed emotionally. Thus, the need for individual members to be "strong" and "adaptive" may be a matter of survival for other members of the group as well as the individual in question since other members may be well beyond their stress threshold and incapable of providing extended empathy. Further, when few resources exist, a sense of helplessness may exist among other family members and friends who might desire to help the individual afflicted by coping challenges but find themselves unable to do so. In such a case, the emphasis on "bucking up" may be the most suitable option that the family member has. In such cases, it is likely that individuals having difficulties will be viewed as lacking self discipline, mental toughness/weakness, perseverance, and other such characteristics commonly reinforced by these groups. Such individuals who display vulnerability to trauma and depressive-related disorders will then tend to be viewed as "weak," "thrown off," or inadequate in functioning. This is unfortunate in light of the fact that once biological changes have occurred the only viable solutions are in-depth interventions coupled with, in some cases, medication. Amidst this reality, the social or cultural group undermines the ability of the therapist to effectively administer proper services because of the stigma of shame and embarrassment that is attached to seeking mental health assistance.

Another factor that counselors should thoroughly explore is the offender's family environment. Indeed, it is widely known that "many features of family life have a bearing on mental health and mental illness" (DHHS, 2001, p. 27), both genetically and due to social learning mechanisms that are passed down from generation to generation. Supportive families characterized by healthy relationships among members can provide protection against the development of symptoms of mental illness. Conversely, where familial relationships have broken down and are instead sources of stress symptoms of mental illness can be activated or exacerbated. For all cultural groups, it tends to be true that marital discord, overcrowding or occupancy with inadequate space, as well as general abuse and neglect all tend to exacerbate mental illness (DHHS, 2001). Thus, counselors should attempt to explore family-of-origin dimensions to determine sources of support and to determine sources of familial stressors that may contribute to mental illness.

One useful tool that could be implemented is family-of-origin genogram. The **genogram** is similar to a family tree illustration, but the client and the counselor construct the illustration in a collaborative fashion, with the client providing input while the counselor details and fills out the illustration with information pertaining to family relationships, interactions, history, and issues. The use of the genogram allows the client to compare relationships, to reexamine family-of-origin issues, and to essentially discuss the future of the family system. If used during the beginning phases of the counselor–client relationship, this can be a very effective means of establishing a rapport. Further, because genograms include both immediate and extended family members, it may be especially useful in preventing relapse among minority men who desire to repair the bonds in their families (Suzuki et al., 1996).

One barrier to the receipt of mental health services is that of inherent mistrust that minority groups may have of social service agencies and mental health practitioners (particularly practitioners of another racial or ethnic group). **Mistrust** involves being suspicious or having little confidence in a service or product. Regarding counseling environments mistrust among minorities is widespread (Harper & McFadden, 2003; Sue & Sue, 1990). One study conducted by Sussman, Robins, and Earls (1987) reported that almost half of African Americans expressed fear of mental health treatment as opposed to just 20% of whites. In a 2000 research report, specifically examining cultural issues and minority perceptions of mental health treatment, Senturia, Sullivan, Cixke, and Shiu-Thornton (2000) identified several factors that limit the ability of African American women to seek intervention services. These factors included racism, lack of economic resources, lack of availability of services, perception that such services were for Caucasian women, and hesitancy to involve persons other than their family or local community because of fear of ostracism or being viewed as disloyal to their race. Subjects also indicated fear that stereotypes about race would be reinforced by the system at large (Senturia et al., 2000). This again demonstrates that stereotyping has lead to serious impairments in developing therapeutic connections with the minority community. In fact, from this research it is known that, the impairment exists before the counselor even has a chance to meet with the client. Because of this, counselors must be aware of this, approach this issue with concern, and they must be willing to meet the client where they are at that point and time.

Because of the inherent mistrust that may exist, the priority issue that must be taken into consideration by all correctional counselors providing cross-cultural therapeutic services is the stigma often attached to the helping professions. In fact, this stigma has been reported to be the most formidable obstacle to better acceptance and progress within the area of mental illness and mental health (DHHS, 1999). Corrigan and Penn (1998) accurately note that there are still widespread beliefs and attitudes, pertaining to mental illness, that foster negative attitudes, fear, and general discrimination and avoidance of people suffering from mental illness. All of these issues are commonly encountered within the offender population and naturally will impact the prognosis of the offender on the correctional counselor's caseload.

Culture of the Counselor

To begin, it is important to understand that there are two broad and comprehensive cultures that tend to influence most trained counselors. When considering this, it should be kept in mind that culture is a concept that describes the process of groups sharing a set of beliefs, norms, and values. Going from this point, counselors need to understand that they are impacted by the counseling culture itself. Indeed, the first broad component of culture that influences a trained counselor is directly related to their training. In the United States, most educational programs offering training in counseling consist of theories and concepts rooted in Western medicine (Harper & McFadden, 2003). In essence, Western medicine focuses on the human body in attempting to understand and uncover causal factors related to disease. As pointed out by Porter (1997), the ideologies of Western medicine are different from many previous healing systems that focused on the relationship and balance between human beings and nature. Many people of varying cultures still view the harmonious relationship between themselves and nature as paramount to their overall mental health (Harper & McFadden, 2003; Sue & Sue, 1999). A counselor's dismissal or lack of attendance to these important cultural views is likely to result in the client terminating the relationship and not receiving proper care for their mental health problems (Harper & McFadden, 2003; Pederson, 2003; Sue & Sue, 1999).

Two additional concepts that have particularly significant impact on the mental health of minorities are racism and discrimination. **Racism** and **discrimination** refers to treating individuals or groups adversely based primarily on certain characteristics such as skin color and/or facial features. For our purposes there are two categories of racism and discrimination that are of particular interest. The first deals with racism and discrimination on behalf of the counselor working with a minority offender. The second category of racism and discrimination that must be understood is the consequences or effects of a minority populations' sustained exposure to racist and discriminative views from the society in which they live.

Racist and discriminative views of a counselor have the potential to destroy any possibility of establishing a meaningful and helpful relationship with an offender. Underlying racism and discrimination is the concept of judgmentalism. The primary component of judgmentalism, and what makes this phenomenon so destructive, is the concept of superiority (Elliot & Elliot, 2006). In essence, racism and discrimination stem from feelings of judgmentalism, which is based on an individual's perception of being superior to another based on race, physical characteristics, or societal status. If an offender perceives the counselor as judgmental, the offender's likely reaction will be to shut down emotionally thereby limiting any potential growth as a result of the counseling relationship. As is mentioned in various places throughout this text, one of the best ways to guard against judgmentalism is to work toward becoming more open to differing views and methods.

The second component of racism and discrimination that counselors must understand is that many incidents that minority offenders endure as a result of discriminatory perceptions are empirically real incidents. The consequences of racism and discrimination will often manifest themselves through mental disorders such as depression and anxiety. Sadly, because these offenders may present with these disorders, there may be a tendency to ignore or disbelieve any contentions they may hold regarding discriminatory actions and/or the effects of institutional racism within the justice system. Minorities in the United States are seldom able to fully distance themselves from the overt or covert implications of racism and discrimination. The cumulative effect is often increased stress which is likely to lead to elevated levels of both anxiety and depression. Counselors should be aware of this phenomenon and be able to work with clients in an attempt to reduce the effects of racism and discrimination. It is unacceptable for non-minority counselors to simply dismiss the effects of racism and discrimination on minority offenders due to erroneous beliefs that racism and discrimination no longer exist.

SECTION SUMMARY

Before getting into the different minority groups, it is important to understand that the population of the United States is very heterogeneous. This is the point most often implied through the use of the concept *melting pot.* The United States described as a melting pot is usually an attempt to portray the vast differences among the many different groups occupying the territory. Minority population refers those groups of people smaller in number, and often thought to be different from the larger group of which it is a part. In addition, minority groups usually possess less political power than the majority. As a result, minority groups will often face discriminative practices not commonly experienced by members of a majority. As a result, it is not uncommon to have minority offenders who present symptoms that are in some ways related to their discriminative experiences.

One way of effectively working with minority offenders is by counselors being culturally competent. Cultural competence is the idea of understanding how a multitude of different factors influence one's reasoning and decision-making processes. This general description applies to both counselors and offenders. In order for counselors to successfully work with minority offenders they must intimately understand their own feelings and biases. Without this understanding it is doubtful that a counselor will be able to enact meaningful change within the population of minority offenders on a consistent basis.

LEARNING CHECK

1. Culture is not related to mental illness.
   a. True
   b. False
2. Cultural competence is usually important in the counseling process but not always.
   a. True
   b. False
3. Which of the following often result from racism and discrimination?
   a. Depression
   b. Anxiety
   c. Suspiciousness
   d. All of the above
4. The counselor's culture is important to understand when attempting to provide culturally competent counseling.
   a. True
   b. False
5. It is uncommon for minority offenders to mistrust mental health providers
   a. True
   b. False

PART THREE: SPECIFIC RACIAL AND CULTURAL GROUPS

African Americans

One of the most important components that has to be taken into consideration when providing effective mental health services to minority offenders is the historical context of their race. As of 2001, there were approximately 34 million African Americans, roughly 12% of the population, living in the United States (U.S. Census Bureau, 2001). Most, if not all, African Americans currently residing in the United States can trace their ancestry to the slave trade from Africa. It is estimated that millions of Africans, over a period spanning two centuries, were kidnapped or purchased to be brought to the United States in order to perform manual labor. These African slaves were considered personal property of their owners. According to Thernstrom and Thernstrom (1997), even after the Fourteenth Amendment extended citizenship to African Americans many continued to live in poverty as they still remained dependent and were mostly being kept uneducated.

Currently, many African Americans still live in poor neighborhoods largely segregated and clearly delineated from other non-minority settlements. Among these neighborhoods there are few resources and high rates of unemployment, homelessness, crime, and substance abuse (Jones & Hanser, 2005; Wilson, 1987). It is important that counselors understand that due to these circumstances many African Americans experience prolonged perceptions of personal vulnerability. These perceptions of vulnerability and attendant psychological and emotional consequences that originate at the community level will often overpower individual control (Shusta, Levine, Harris, & Wong, 2005; Sue & Sue, 1999). In essence, it is important that counselors truly appreciate the environments and conditions of many African Americans and embrace these factors as part of the counseling process and not limit their roles within the offenders' decision-making process.

Although poverty rates are decreasing many African Americans are still relatively poor. African Americans are much more likely than whites to live in severe poverty with a rate of more than three times that of whites (Joiner, 2006). Currently, there is sufficient evidence indicating that poverty is one of the most frequent correlates in relation to criminal behavior (Joiner, 2006; Shusta et al., 2005). In order to be effective, counselors need to be aware of the effects of poverty and how these effects manifest themselves into cognition and behavior. The historical adversity experienced by African Americans through slavery and exclusion from educational as well as social and economic resources is largely responsible for many of the socioeconomic disparities they face today. Socioeconomic status is linked to mental health. In essence, poor mental health is more common among the impoverished than those who are more affluent (DHHS, 2001). Poor mental health will often translate into criminal behavior especially among those who are homeless or have substance abuse problems.

IMPORTANT CONSIDERATIONS WHEN COUNSELING AFRICAN AMERICANS There is extensive literature that compares therapeutic outcomes between African Americans and Caucasian Americans. Amidst this research, numerous studies have sought to determine whether common counseling techniques are equally effective for both Caucasian Americans and African Americans (Jones & Hanser, 2007; Sue & Sue, 1999; McGoldrick, Giordano, Pearce, & Giordano, 1996). One of the most salient components that must be understood by correctional counselors is that the cultural history of minorities is often different from whites. To add to this enigma is the fact that most, if not all, counseling modalities were created by white, Judeo-Christians to address psychological and emotional problems experienced by mostly non-minority clients. In essence, many of the counseling modalities are not equipped to specifically address some of the most salient issues affecting minorities. For example, most counseling modalities stress the importance of introspection and assuming responsibility for one's decisions. The problem with this when attempting to work with minority offenders is that oftentimes minorities have a clear understanding of their identity as a historically oppressed population (Brown & Srebalus, 2003). In essence, they are able to identify social issues that are independent of themselves as the underlying mechanism of much of their struggle (Brown & Srebalus, 2003), thereby creating a real conflict between counseling theory and group identity among minority populations.

This lack of congruence between counseling theory and characteristics specific to cultural history is surely part of the reason why only about half of African Americans, as compared to whites, seek out and receive counseling services. In addition, African Americans are much more likely than whites to prematurely terminate counseling and generally express greater dissatisfaction with the entire helping process (Sue & Sue, 1999). In essence, many of the counselors responsible for providing services to African American populations, as well as other minority populations, are ill equipped to provide culturally effective services largely because they do not fully understand the cultural history and identity of minority populations.

Latino Americans (Hispanic Persons)

"Hispanic" is a term generally used to describe people of Spanish origin living in the United States (Gladding, 1996). Before discussing the central components related to Hispanic Americans' mental health issues it is first necessary to distinguish the different groups commonly classified as Hispanic. Currently, the U.S. Census Bureau recognizes four different groups as Hispanic: **Mexicans, Puerto Ricans, Cubans, and Central Americans**. As described below, Hispanic Americans are very heterogeneous in most circumstances including those that led to or contributed to their migration and, are rapidly expanding. The U.S. Census Bureau projections indicate that by 2050 the number of Hispanics will be roughly 97 million, or one fourth of the U.S. population.

MEXICANS There are several important factors (both historical and therapeutic in nature) to consider when counseling Mexicans or Mexican Americans. First, it is useful to remember that after the Mexican war large territories of Mexico became part of the United States. This included land from Texas to California in which many Mexican citizens chose to stay, thereby becoming Americans citizens. In addition to the Mexican war, and as noted by DHHS (2001), there are a myriad of both push and pull factors that heavily influence the flow of Mexicans into the United States. Poor economic conditions in Mexico contribute to the push factor and the need for laborers in the United States influence the pull factor. It is important to note that much of the reasoning behind the origins of migration among all of the Hispanic groups is closely tied to economic factors. In essence, the overwhelming majority of Hispanics who choose to migrate to the United States do so in hopes of providing better circumstances for themselves and their family. The one factor, however, largely responsible for the overwhelming majority of Hispanic Americans being Mexican is the fact that the two countries border each other. Logistically, it is usually easier for Mexicans to come to the United States simply because they do not have as far to travel and especially because migrant travel is often by land, much of which is often covered on foot.

It is important for correctional counselors to understand that many of their clients may come from families that are illegally in the United States. The cultural variables associated with this type of extralegal existence must be taken into account. Likewise, the levels of acculturation and assimilation may vary from one Mexican client to another. In a similar vein, the ability to speak the English language can be a barrier unless the correctional counselor speaks Spanish sufficiently well to conduct therapy sessions. Therapy with this and other Hispanic groups can be greatly impaired due to linguistic challenges, and, in some dire cases, the use of an interpreter may be necessary.

PUERTO RICANS One of the characteristics that distinguishes Puerto Ricans is that as of 1917, by way of the Jones Act, Puerto Ricans are considered American citizens. Hence, they can enter and exit the mainland of the United States at their will. After World War II many Puerto Ricans began migrating to the mainland in order to find work. Rising populations on the island of Puerto Rico contributed to the high unemployment and made it difficult to find meaningful employment. As the work force began to age many Puerto Ricans who had come to the United States began to return home creating a circular pattern that commenced in the early to mid-1980s (DHHS, 2001).

CUBANS The most significant migration of Cuban immigrants began in 1959 after Fidel Castro toppled the Batista government and assumed control of the country. Many of the initial Cuban immigrants were well-educated professionals who have become well established in America. Other immigrants who were not as well established in Cuba also attempted the trip and are commonly referred to as Balseros. Balsero means less than secure and often makeshift watercrafts that were used by many Cuban immigrants because of their poor economic situations. Finally, many of the Cubans who have come to the United States have received full rights to citizenship due to their declared status as political refugees.

CENTRAL AMERICANS Central Americans are generally considered those immigrants whose country of origin is El Salvador, Guatemala, or Nicaragua. Central Americans are considered to be the newest Hispanic subgroup in the United States as their distinction is relatively recent. Many of the Central Americans migrated to the United States because of political turmoil and massive atrocities carried out by rivaling political factions in their homeland. A large number of Central Americans arrived in the United States during the 1980s. As with all of the subgroups, however, it is important to understand that migration is a constant process with ebbs and flows. There have been historical and political events over the past decades that have contributed to spikes or shifts in the flow of immigrants but below these peaks lie the relatively stable fact that large numbers of individuals travel toward and often into the United States each year.

IMPORTANT CONSIDERATIONS WHEN COUNSELING LATINO AMERICANS One key reason for at least briefly describing the characteristics of each group's circumstances causing their migration is because we are able to glean valuable insight into their experiences and possible mental health needs. In addition, how these groups have been received once in the United States is also important. For example, Puerto Ricans, regardless of whether born in the United States or Puerto Rico are considered U.S. citizens. This is important to note because citizenship allows access to government programs and sponsored services aimed at providing needed support. Similarly, many Cuban immigrants have achieved citizenship due to their declared status of political refugees.

Mexican and Central American immigrants, however, are much less likely to be granted citizenship. Many of the Central American immigrants were fleeing war-struck countries mired in political turmoil. Despite these circumstances Central American immigrants are not considered political refugees. Therefore, many Hispanics migrating to the United States arrive without proper documentation. Central Americans, in addition to being undocumented, are also likely to suffer symptoms of post traumatic stress disorder (PTSD) as a result of their experiencing trauma and terror prior to their departure. Also, immigrants who are undocumented live in constant fear of deportation. This reality makes it difficult to find and sustain meaningful employment let alone advance in one's career. In addition, due to their illegal status immigrants rarely establish permanent homes as they fear the risk of loosing their property if deported. Therefore, adjustment to migration can often be difficult especially for Mexicans and Central Americans. Current trends indicate, however, that migration is difficult for all groups of Hispanics largely because many of the immigrants are unskilled laborers. They work long, hard hours for relatively little pay.

Mexican Americans are by far the most populous subgroup of Hispanics living in the United States. Research has shown that the Mexican Americans living in the United States are further divided into two groups: those born in Mexico and those born in the United States. Another research has found that Mexican Americans born in the United States reported higher rates of depression and phobias as compared to those immigrants born in Mexico (Burnam, Hough, Karino, Escobar, & Telles, 1987). This is an important component related to the Mexican American population that counselors need to understand especially since this finding is far from being considered intuitively obvious. In other words, most people would likely believe that Mexicans born in Mexico and then later coming to the United States would suffer greater degrees of mental illness due to the harsh conditions. In fact, according to Vega et al. (1998) those Mexican immigrants living in the United States for at least 13 years suffered higher rates of mental disorders than those living there for less than 13 years. This consistent pattern of findings among independent investigations begs the question, why? Why is it that Mexican immigrants who have been in the United States the longest suffer from mental illness at greater rates? Some have pointed to the process of acculturation but it is not clear what aspects of acculturation are related to higher rates of disorders.

Native Americans: American Indians and Alaskan Natives

American Indians and Alaskan natives occupied North America long before Europeans made their way over to this continent and Russians arrived in what is now Alaska. The plight of American Indians and Alaskan natives is legendary and they have had to overcome and survive ever since European settlers first landed in America and began their push westward. First, American Indians were greatly affected by the various diseases spread through their initial contacts with early European settlers. As they lacked immunity against such new diseases, the population of American Indians plummeted. One common theme in treating this group is the need to address what is called **historical trauma**, which underscores the generations of suffering and traumatic experiences that have been attributed to this group of people.

Currently, American Indians and Alaskan natives are considered to be the most impoverished ethnic minority group in the United States (DHHS, 2001). Oppression, discrimination, and removal from native lands are directly related to their lack of educational achievements, lack of economic opportunities, and high rates of mental illness and disorder. In a study conducted by Robin, Chester, Rasmussen, Jaranson, and Goldman (1997) more than 70% of American Indians met the guidelines for a lifetime diagnosis of alcohol disorders. Alcohol problems and mental disorders often occur together as evidenced in the fact that of the 70% of American Indians suffering from alcohol disorders many were also found to be suffering from psychiatric disorders. Because of this, substance abuse treatment is one of the most common forms of therapy required for offenders from this cultural group.

In general, studies have found that American Indians and Alaskan natives experience greater psychological distress than the overall population. Almost 13% of American Indians and Alaskan natives report experiencing psychological distress as compared to 9% of the general population (DHHS, 2001). Evidence in support of the above postulations is gleaned from the prevalence of suicide, which is often an important indicator of need. The suicide rate among American Indians and Alaskan natives is estimated to be 1.5 times the national rate. Rates are particularly high among Native American males between the ages of 15 and 24.

Asian Americans and Pacific Islanders

Asian Americans and Pacific Islanders are extremely diverse groups. Lee (1998) reports as many as 43 different ethnic groups are classified as Asian Americans and Pacific Islanders. Asian immigrants now account for approximately 4% of the U.S. population and are rapidly increasing. By 2020 the Asian American and Pacific Islander population is expected to reach 20 million accounting for approximately 6% of the U.S. population. Further, a very substantial portion of Asian Americans are born outside of the United States, collectively comprising more than 25% of all the foreign-born citizens in the *United States* (Bennett, 1978; Shusta et al., 2005). Indeed, throughout the United States, over 60% of all Chinese Americans, 70% of all Asian Indian Americans, and a full 90% of all Vietnamese Americans are not born in the United States.

Though this population consists of disparate national origins, there are some characteristics that are common to most all Asian American ethnic groups in the United States. Understanding of these characteristics can benefit the correctional counselor to provide services to an Asian American caseload. Shusta et al. (2005) note that each of these characteristics given below can hinder the ability of correctional counselors to develop an effective rapport with Asian Americans:

1. Generational status in the United States (first, second, third generation)
2. Degree of acculturation and assimilation
3. Comfort with and competence in English
4. Religious beliefs and cultural value orientation
5. Family cultural dynamics.

Some are more relevant than others to specific groups but almost all of these issues are relevant at one point or another when considering Asian Indian Americans, Chinese Americans, Vietnamese Americans (the three largest Asian groups in the United States), as well as Pacific Islanders.

As was noted earlier, proficiency in the English language is a particular hindrance that can cause serious misunderstandings between police officers and Asian American citizens. This issue is somewhat tied to the generational status of an individual Asian American because large percentages of the population of those groups that have immigrated most recently do not speak English. This is particularly true among the Southeast Asian groups. Indeed, nearly 38% of all Vietnamese Americans do not speak English (Shusta et al., 2005). In addition, it is estimated that an approximate 23% of Chinese Americans also do not speak English (Shusta et al., 2005). On the other hand, this is not typically an issue for Asian Indians because of the fact that almost all speak English as a result of prior subjugation during the reign of the British Empire (Almeida, 1996).

Further, Asian families tend to be close-knit and this still tends to be true even though divorce is becoming more prevalent (attributed to Westernized values regarding the role of Asian American women) and Asian American youth are becoming more independent in mindset. However, there are specific dynamics unique to Asian families that may be important to consider. For instance, the father of the house typically acts as the spokesperson for the household, but he may consult with grandparents who may live with him, his spouse, and other key persons in the home. With this in mind, correctional counselors should remember that any family-oriented issues will be seen as a "private manner" and as Shusta et al. (2005) note, ". . . self-control and keeping things within the family are key values for Asian Americans" (pp. 145–146). Thus, it should not be surprising that the use of genograms and other instruments designed to gain insight into family dynamics are likely to produce limited results. This is especially true if the correctional counselor is not of the same cultural group as the Asian offender. Thus, Asian offenders who have problems with domestic abuse are likely to present unique challenges that will require patience and savvy on the part of the correctional counselor.

SECTION SUMMARY

It is important to understand some of the distinguishing characteristics of each racial group mentioned above. As indicated, each group is comprised of different subgroups and all share considerable diversity. The essence of this portion of the chapter is to highlight some of the critical factors central to each group. For example, when working with African American offenders it is important that counselors be aware of how their ancestry is linked to slave trade. In addition and also related to their origins as slaves, it is important that counselors understand the impact of poverty and the often violent surroundings that many African American offenders often find themselves associated.

Hispanic Americans consist of Mexicans, Cubans, Puerto Ricans, and Central Americans. Each of these groups shares a Hispanic origin but has endured different circumstances surrounding their arrival and presence in America. American Indians and Alaskan Natives are the most impoverished minority group. They have suffered extreme oppression throughout their history that must be considered when attempting to diagnose and treat current symptoms. Similarly, Asian Americans and Pacific Islanders have also suffered from oppression. It is also important to note that some of their oppressive experiences have been at the hands of the criminal justice system. In essence, the histories of these minority groups are a vital part to comprehensively understand how to treat them.

LEARNING CHECK

1. Most violent encounters are perpetrated by strangers as opposed to someone the victim knows well.
   a. True
   b. False
2. An African American's origin to the slave trade is not an important factor within the context of current symptoms.
   a. True
   b. False
3. Generalizations are acceptable when dealing with minority groups and will often serve to save the counselor time so that real work can begin immediately.
   a. True
   b. False
4. One of the most significant factors associated with American Indians is the high rate of alcoholism and depression.
   a. True
   b. False

5. It is not really important that counselors understand the histories of minority offenders but instead focus should be on the ability to identify current problems and how these problems are manifested in daily circumstances and interactions.
   a. True
   b. False

CONCLUSION

Correctional counselors bear a responsibility to their client. This means that correctional counselors must promote the dignity and the welfare of their client, regardless of the fact that they have engaged in criminal behavior. This can be challenging for the counselor, particularly when the offender has committed a crime that is particularly heinous and/or contrasts with the inherent beliefs of the counselor. While ensuring that they are balanced and nonjudgmental in approach, correctional counselors must be sure to take careful and complete notes of their clinical sessions with the offender client. The use of the SOAP is presented to students as the preferred means by which such records should be organized and written.

In addition, it is important that correctional counselors maintain professional boundaries in their relationship with their client. As part of this process, counselors should ensure that the client is given informed consent and that this is obtained in writing, typically in a disclosure statement and/or a declaration of practices page. This process simply informs the client of the counselor's credentials while also informing the offender of the parameters of confidentiality. Given the client's criminal background, this can be a very sensitive and important aspect of the initial counseling process. Therefore, it is still strongly advised that counselors complete the process of obtaining signed informed consent; this safeguards the client and the counselor. Other ethical considerations associated with the client–counselor relationship, such as transference and/or countertransference, dual relationships, stress, and burnout, must also be considered by the counselor.

In order to effectively provide mental health services to all offenders, correctional counselors must be culturally competent. Especially among minority offenders, counselors must understand the impact of their cultural experiences and how these experiences influence cognitions and behavior. Correctional counselors must do more than be simply sensitive to cultural issues; they must be able to competently address cultural differences and they must be able to incorporate these differences into their treatment approach. Importantly, correctional counselors must understand the implications of stigma often attached to mental health services and needing help "from the outside," as well as historical events that heavily impact current behavior. Given the prevalence of minorities within the offender population, it is clear that any person working in correctional treatment will be inept if they fail to make at least a cursory attempt to familiarize themselves with the various cultural issues associated with offenders from various minority groups.

Essay Questions

1. How would you define cultural competence? In your own words, describe why it is so important that counselors understand the essence of cultural competence, especially within the offender population.
2. Explain and describe two of the most common barriers to treatment.
3. Define the concept of stigma. What are some of the origins of stigma especially as it relates to counseling?
4. What is the difference between covert and overt racism? Provide two examples of each. Is one type of racism more destructive than the other? Why or why not?
5. What is meant by the concept of a melting pot? How is this related to the significance of counselors being culturally competent in their ability to effectively provide services?

Treatment Planning Exercise

In this exercise, the student must consider the case of Ming and provide a discussion of how they might approach the problems that face Ming's family. Consider all of the issues relevant to acculturation and assimilation, paying particular attention to the dynamics between the younger and the older generation of the Chung family. List and discuss at least eight cultural considerations that you would employ and place them each in the order of priority, noting those that you would address early and those that might remain on the periphery of your clinical concerns.

The Case of Chung Ming

Chung Ming is a teenager, 14 years old, and he is ethnic Chinese. His parents immigrated from China when Ming was roughly 9 years old. Ming's parents have not yet mastered the English language and in some cases, he has had to translate for his family. Lately, Ming has been skipping school and he has been hanging out with a group of other Asian (mostly Chinese) youth that have established a small gang.

Ming's parents are humiliated by his behavior and do not act as if they are really ready to conduct counseling. They express that they are very troubled by Ming's behavior and even that he brings dishonor on his family. Ming, on the other hand, is much more Westernized than his parents and he notes that many of his friends have forsaken much of their Chinese views for those more consistent with mainstream American society.

Ming seems indifferent as you watch him while his parents talk, noting that Ming stays out late, drinks at age 14, and he has even stolen small items from various stores in the neighborhood. You can tell by observing that Ming's father has difficulty with English and is a bit withdrawn. The mother is also withdrawn and does not offer anything to the conversation throughout most of the session.

Ming is on juvenile probation and he seems to meet the requirements of his supervision. The mere fact that he is on probation is problematic with his parents and is also a source of shame for all members of the family.

After the session, you are fairly sure that Ming is still engaged in illegal activities with his prior gang. You make it a point to ultimately contact his probation/parole officer during the next week.

Given the dynamics of this traditionally Chinese family, Ming's advanced acculturation in Western culture, and the lack of concern that Ming has, you realize that there are many more factors at play than Ming's simple misbehavior. You consider the cultural dynamics and begin to develop a plan.

Bibliography

Almeida, R. (1996). Asian Indian families. In M. McGoldrick, J. Giordano, & J. K. Pearce (Eds.), *Ethnicity and family therapy* (pp. 394–423). New York: Guilford.

American Counseling Association (2005). *ACA code of ethics.* Alexandria, VA: Author

Bennett, L. A. (1978). *Counseling in correctional environments.* New York: Human Science Press.

Brown, D., & Srebalus, J. (2003). *Introduction to the counseling profession* (3rd ed.). Pearson Education, Inc: New York.

Burnam, M., Hough, R., Escobar, J., Karno, M., Timbers, D. M., & Telles, C. A. (1987). Six-month prevalence of specific psychiatric disorders among Mexican American and Non-Hispanic Whites in Los Angeles. *Archives of General Psychiatry, 44*, 687–694.

Cameron, S., & Turtle-Song, I. (2002). Learning to write case notes using the SOAP format. *Journal of Counseling & Development, 80*, 286–292.

Corrigan, P. W., & Penn, D. L. (1998). Lessons from social psychology on discrediting psychiatric stigma. *American Psychologist, 54*, 765–776.

Elliot, J., & Elliot, K. (2006). *Disarming the inner critic.* Lafayette, LA: Anthetics Press.

Gladding, S. T. (1996). *Counseling: A comprehensive profession* (3rd ed.). Englewood Cliffs, NJ: Prentice Hall.

Harper, F. D., & McFadden, J. (2003). *Culture and counseling: New approaches.* New York: Allyn & Bacon.

Huang, K. (1991). Chinese Americans. In N. Mokuau (Ed.), *Handbook of social services for Asian and Pacific Islanders* (pp. 79–96). Westport, CT: Greenwood Press.

Jencks, C. (1994). *The homeless.* Cambridge, MA: Harvard University Press.

Joiner, T. (2006). *Why people die by suicide?* Cambridge, MA: Harvard University Press.

Lee, S. M. (1998). Asian Americans: Diverse and growing. *Population Bulletin, 53*(2). Washington, DC: Population Reference Bureau.

Lin, M. K., & Cheung, F. (1999). Mental health issues for Asian Americans. *Psychiatric Services, 50*(6), 774–780.

Masters, R. (2004). *Counseling criminal justice offenders* (2nd ed.). Thousand Oaks, CA: Sage Publications.

McGoldrick, M., Giordano, J., Pearce, J. K., & Giordano, J. (1996). *Ethnicity and family therapy* (2nd ed.). New York: Guilford Press.

Porter, R. (1997). *The greatest benefit to mankind: A medical history of humanity.* New York: Norton.

Robin, R. W., Chester, B., Rasmussen, J. K., Jaranson, J. M., & Goldman, D. (1997). Prevalence, characteristics, and impact of childhood sexual abuse in a Southwestern American Indian tribe. *Child Abuse and Neglect, 21*, 769–787.

Senturia, K., Sullivan, M., Cixke, S., & Shiu-Thornton, S. (2000). *Cultural Issues Affecting Domestic Violence Service and Utilization in Ethnic and Hard to Reach Populations*, Project number 98-WT-VX-0025.

Shusta, M., Levine, D. R., Harris, P. R., & Wong, H. Z. (2005). *Multicultural law enforcement: Strategies for peacekeeping in a diverse society* (3rd ed.). Upper Saddle River, NJ: Prentice Hall.

Sommers-Flanagan, R., Elliot, D., & Sommers-Flannagan, J. (1998). Exploring the edges: Boundaries and breaks. *Ethics & Behavior, 8*(1), 37–48.

Substance Abuse and Mental Health Services Administration. (2001). Cultural competence standards in managed care mental health services: Four underserved/underrepresented racial/ethnic groups. Rockville, MD. (SMA00-3457).

Sue, D. W., & Sue, D. (1990). *Counseling the culturally different: Theory and practice.* New York: John Wiley & Sons.

Sussman, L. K., Robins, L. N., & Earls, F. (1987). Treatment seeking for depression by black and white Americans. *Social Science and Medicine, 24*, 187–196.

Suzuki, L. A., Meller, P. J., & Ponterotto, J. G. (Eds.). (1996). *Handbook of multicultural assessment: Clinical, psychological, and educational applications.* San Francisco: Jossey-Bass.

Tarasoff v. *Regents of the University of California*, 17 C. 3d 425, 131 (Calif. Rptr. 14, 551 P2.d 334 1976).

Thernstrom, S., & Thernstrom, A. (1997). *America in black and white.* New York: Simon & Schuster.

U.S. Census Bureau. (2001). The black population in the United States: March 2000 (update) (Report No. PPL-146).

U.S. Department of Health and Human Services. (1999). Mental Health: A report to the Surgeon General. Rockville, MD: Author.

U.S. Department of Health and Human Services. (2001). Mental health: Culture, race, and ethnicity—A supplement to mental health: A report of the Surgeon General. Rockville, MD: U.S. Department of Health and Human Services, Substance Abuse and Mental Health Services Administration, Center for Mental Health Services.

U.S. Department of Health and Human Services. (2003). Developing cultural competence in disaster mental health programs: Guiding principles and recommendations. DHHS Pub. No. SMA 3828. Rockville, MD: Center for Mental Health Services, Substance Abuse and Mental Health Services Administration.

Vega, W. A., Kolody, B., Aguilar-Gaxiola, S., Alderate, E., Catalano, R., & Carveo-Anduaga, J. (1998). Lifetime prevalence of DSM-III-R psychiatric disorders among urban and rural Mexican Americans in California. *Archives of General Psychiatry, 55*, 771–778.

Weed, L. L. (1964). Medical records, patient care and medical education. *Irish Journal of Medical Education, 6*, 271–282.

Wilson, W. J. (1987). *The truly disadvantaged: The inner city, the underclass, and public policy.* Chicago: University of Chicago Press.

3

Data Gathering, Assessment, Diagnosis, Classification, and Treatment Planning

CHAPTER OBJECTIVES

After reading this chapter, you will be able to:

1. Understand the importance of assessment in developing effective treatment plans for correctional clients.
2. Know about the different types of assessment (subjective and objective) and assessment instruments presented in this chapter.
3. Know and fully understand the stages of the supervision and treatment planning process namely data gathering, assessment, diagnostic, recidivism prediction, classification, and case management.
4. Know false positives, false negatives, true positives, and true negatives.
5. Understand the difference between static and dynamic risk factors.
6. Be familiar with the Level of Supervision Inventory—Revised and understand the strengths associated with that instrument.
7. Understand why the MMPI-2 Criminal Justice and Correctional Report is important to correctional treatment.

PART ONE: DATA GATHERING AND ASSESSMENT STAGES

Assessment processes and procedures are primary to any effective intervention or treatment plan. Assessment processes lay a foundation upon which all subsequent interventions will follow and it is because of this that correctional counselors must understand the point and purpose to the process. What is sad is that in many cases this is an area of the treatment process that is often least understood by therapists in the field. Further, many therapists may initially use the assessment information that is obtained but over time will lose sight of this information and will instead rely only upon the information obtained from their own sessions with the client. This is unfortunate because it undoubtedly has a negative impact on the continuity of the treatment program and it may lead to a scattered treatment approach that meanders from issue to issue with little focus or clarity on actual objectives.

It is important that the correctional counselor understand that assessment is not a means to an end but that it is instead a continuous process. In reality, the assessment of a client never actually ends. Rather, once the initial screening and assessment takes place, the client should be continually reassessed to ensure that treatment goals are being adequately and appropriately met. The integration of assessment processes throughout the entire treatment process ensures continual feedback loops in the process and augments the eventual evaluation of the treatment process once the client has been processed out of treatment. Maintaining a continual assessment scheme helps to reinforce accountability for both the client and the therapist since neither is allowed to wander aimlessly in the therapeutic process. Rather, each participant has a clear and shared role, both being complicit in the therapeutic relationship and both indicating understanding and agreement as to the parameters of that relationship. The assessment information is, quite naturally, drawn within that relationship with both participants having mutual obligation to address issues that are obtained from the assessment data. In crude terms, it keeps everyone honest.

In basic terms, **assessment** is the process that is used by clinicians to determine the characteristics, needs, and prognosis of a given client. This information is simply mandatory if the therapist is expected to have the ability to assist the client. With this in mind, it is clear that this process requires that the counselor obtain a large amount of information pertaining to the client. Some of this information will be obtained by other staff during intake (unless the counselor actually conducts the initial intake), while other information may be obtained from official reports, such as arrest records, hospital information, and so forth. Because of this, it is necessary to view the data-gathering process as the first component to effective assessment.

Data Gathering

The first and most basic component of assessment is data gathering. Indeed, without data there is nothing to assess. With most correctional clients, there will typically exist a great deal of data that is readily available to the counselor. This is particularly true with adult offenders and will also tend to be true with juvenile offenders. Various forms of records such as arrest information, drug tests, hospital records, and information from probation/parole agencies can provide good background information for the therapist. In fact, it would behoove any counselor to peruse such documents before any initial session with their clients, just to ensure that they are familiar with the client. Such knowledge of the client can also be very helpful in building a rapport with the client. This is a definite benefit during the treatment and intervention phases that follow the assessment and intake process.

DOCUMENT REVIEW For correctional treatment personnel, a large amount of information related to the criminality of the client, their previous incarceration, probation periods, terms of parole, and so forth are required. This information allows treatment personnel to assess the need for client structure and their likely receptivity to the therapeutic process. While the clinician will not rely solely on written records, of course, the use of such information can provide one with a clear snapshot of the client's current level of functioning and a degree of familiarity that could not otherwise be achieved.

HOME VISITATION The correctional counseling setting may or may not entail home visitation. This naturally depends on the nature and function of the mental health worker. For example, it is quite common for social workers and/or community supervision personnel to visit the home of a person on their caseload. This provides an inside view of the client's lifestyle, circumstances, and surroundings. However, few counselors who work in a purely counseling setting will visit the home of a client, even in the case of offenders who are on community supervision. However, in some cases it may be that the counselor does indeed visit the client's home on some form of official visit, particularly when family interventions are involved. One example where this may occur would be with adolescent offenders, where the therapist pays a home visit to talk with parents and/or conduct some form of family session within the family's own area of comfort.

The counselor should be aware that some of the behaviors observed may be contrived and/or modified due to acts of **impression management**. Impression management is simply when clients act in a way that provides the most positive impression or when they present their best image possible to influence the therapist's own observations and deductions. Chaotic lifestyles or those that are laden with conflict can serve as triggers for relapse—the stress of such conditions contributing to a client's potential for relapse and recidivism. This is especially true for substance abusers and it is therefore important that the counselor observe others in the household as well as the client. Such observations provide insight as to the influences impacting the client.

COLLATERAL CONTACTS The term "collateral contacts" is borrowed from Enos and Southern (1996, p. 67). It aptly describes those persons who are tangent to the client and who are typically most knowledgeable of the client—his or her temperament, lifestyle, and day-to-day behavior. Collateral contacts are those contacts with people who may live with the client (relating to home visits just discussed in the preceding section), work with the client (both supervisors and other work associates), or those that have other connections with the client (such as close friends or extended family members). In all cases, these contacts can prove to be very good sources of client information that might otherwise not be discovered. Further, Enos and Southern note that "since it is very common for offenders to be deceptive and dishonest, it is important to check client self-report data against information provided by persons who know and have regular contact with the offender" (1996, p. 67). This does aid the therapeutic process because it ensures that goal setting and other aspects of the therapeutic session are not impaired by false client input and it also serves as a deterrent for offender dishonesty when disclosing to therapists.

It should be pointed out that this may, in some respects, actually serve to close off genuine rapport with some offenders. Knowledge that they will be "checked on" may build resentment and may also lead to less disclosure from the client. While in most counseling relationships this would be discouraged, it should perhaps be seen as a necessary and an expected element of the correctional counseling process when dealing with highly manipulative clients. Offenders with diagnoses of antisocial personality disorder, borderline personality disorder, substance abuse disorders, and other such manipulative clinical diagnoses will present unique challenges to the therapist that will warrant the use of techniques and approaches not typically considered consistent with most counseling relationships. While this may sound counterintuitive, the need for leverage in the relationship cannot be overemphasized when dealing with manipulative offenders.

Naturally, not all offenders will be manipulative. Some will genuinely desire to do well and will work to make progress in their treatment regimen. In these cases, relationships with collateral contacts should still be fostered, but for different reasons. In these cases, the collateral contacts can (and should) be used as a support network for the client. These contacts can provide helpful input and can also be used as external support that continues well beyond the confines of the therapy sessions that may occur in a counselor's office or even during potential home visits.

Collateral contacts, home visitation, interviewing, and document review are all means of obtaining and compiling information that pertains to a particular offender on a counselor's caseload (Enos & Southern, 1996). When taken together, these various methods of collecting client information serve to connect and integrate the professional judgments and perceptions of a variety of workers in the process of service delivery. This information, if completed correctly, can be quite extensive. Such information, when attended to by the therapist, can improve the overall ability of treatment providers in providing sessions that are both data driven but also client driven. The more the therapist knows about his or her client, the better he or she is able to understand client problems and challenges from the perspective of that client. This is important because this is a necessary precursor to empathy building within a relationship and, if done correctly, can help the client to feel understood. When therapists have a full docket of information, multiple types of personal observations, and the benefit of accurate and appropriate assessment tools, they are likely to improve the prognosis of the client, simply by being knowledgeable of their client.

Assessment Stage

SUBJECTIVE ASSESSMENT It is difficult to accurately assess correctional offenders during treatment planning because their needs tend to be complicated and because they have a variety of criminal justice issues that constrain many therapeutic modalities. When considering assessment, it is much easier to assess offenders for security purposes than it is for therapeutic purposes. These offenders tend to be an extremely heterogeneous group with diverse concerns. This means that a "one-size-fits-all" approach is destined to fail with these specialized populations. Given the wide range of needs and security considerations involved with these offenders, proper assessment is absolutely critical. Many of these offenders have a wide range of mental health and physical health considerations that require some form of diagnosis, and if this diagnosis is not correct, the consequences could mean harm to someone in society. Thus, the wisest investment for any correctional system desiring to perfect its ability to ensure public safety will be in the arena of assessment. More money and resources in assessment means that the subsequent stages (diagnostic, recidivism prediction, and classification) in the equation will also operate better, resulting in increased public safety as the ultimate answer.

One method of assessment, the **subjective assessment process**, consists of interviews and observations that are less structured than are objective forms of assessment and are used in determining the security and treatment needs of the offender. Typically, only clinical professionals will conduct these forms of assessment because they are considered qualified to use their sense of judgment and experience in determining the offender's possible dangerousness, treatment needs, and their likelihood of responding to treatment (Hanser, 2006, 2009). This process, though an important augmentation to objective forms of assessment, should not be the primary form of assessment but should serve as a component of a "two-pronged" assessment process (Hanser, 2009, p. 85). In some cases, clinicians may provide assessments but they may not have seen the offender face to face. Rather, they may look through an offender's client file of information (such as the Pre-sentence Investigation file) to make their determination. This should never be allowed. Instead, each offender with special needs should be seen, in person, by the practitioner who provides this subjective assessment.

There are some drawbacks to this process, just as there are with any form of assessment. For one, the process is subjective, which means that the determination is based upon the impressions of an individual. Thus, these assessments are likely to vary from one professional to another. Second, these assessments can be lengthy in nature as they tend to rely on open-ended questions

Closed Question	Open-Ended Question
Do you feel you have a problem with alcohol?	What problems has your alcohol use caused for you?
Is it important to you to complete supervision successfully?	How important is it for you to complete supervision successfully?
Anything else?	What else?

FIGURE 3.1 Closed versus Open-Ended Questions *Source:* Walters, S. T., Clark, M. D., Gingerich, R., & Meltzer, M. L. (2007). *A guide for probation and parole: Motivating offenders to change*. Washington, DC: National Institute of Corrections.

rather than closed questions. Basically, open-ended questions elicit full responses from the offender and require that the offender provide more than simply "yes" or "no" responses. In interviews that have numerous open-ended questions, offenders are encouraged to talk at length and this, understandably, takes some bit of time to complete the process. Closed questions, on the other hand, simply require that the offender provide a simple "yes" or "no" response to a direct, focused, and limited inquiry. Figure 3.1 provides a comparison between both types of questions, showing how both can ask about similar topics but yet be structured in a fashion that modulates the amount of information that the offender is likely to provide.

As one can see, there are various approaches to the interview process and this may require that facilities have staff who are well trained in interviewing processes. Thus, any interview is only as good as the personnel who administer it. This then means that subjective forms of assessment that uses extensive open-question formats can be very costly because only highly educated and/or well-trained staff will be able to utilize this form of assessment.

To limit personal bias and/or quirks of the individual interview, it is recommended that the structured interview processes be utilized. A **subjective structured interview** is a process whereby an interviewer asks the client a set of preconstructed and open-ended questions so that the interview seems informal in nature (as if a conversation), yet, because of the structure and construction of the questions, certain bits of desired data are gathered from the client throughout the process of the conversation. These forms of interviews can guide clinicians who conduct intakes and they can be effective rapport builders when conducted by a skilled interviewer. In addition, the structure of these interviews allow for consistency of information that is kept among different staff in the agency; this means that agencies can ensure that similar criteria are considered despite the nuances and/or individual tendencies of the individual interviewer (Hanser, 2006, 2009). Indeed, correctional counselors who conduct structured interviews can even utilize methods that provide a type of quantification to the offender's response.

One example of how interviews can be quantified would be the use of scaling in the interview. **Scaling** is a process where the offender is asked to choose a number along a preset continuum that describes their agreement or disagreement, willingness or unwillingness, and/or motivation or lack of motivation when presented with a particular question. In such circumstances, the offender may be asked to indicate his or her willingness to engage in the group counseling process by choosing a number from 1 to 10, with a "1" indicating low motivation and "10" indicating high motivation. This process not only provides more of a range of responses than does a simple "yes" or "no"

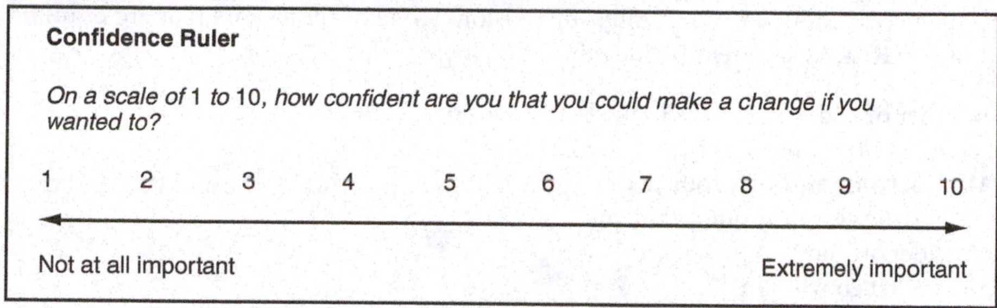

FIGURE 3.2 Scaling Question Related to Client Confidence *Source:* Walters, S. T., Clark, M. D., Gingerich, R., & Meltzer, M. L. (2007). *A guide for probation and parole: Motivating offenders to change.* Washington, DC: National Institute of Corrections.

response but also focuses the interview into a specific range of response that is selected by the offender. An example of a scaled question related to offender confidence and motivation is provided in Figure 3.2.

Since this scale provides a specific number that is attached to the offender's response, this technique of questioning is ideal for standardized interviews that are designed to collect the same type of information from all respondents. Not only is the same type of answer collected, but the manner or response is provided some degree of uniformity and comparability. With such interviews, offenders are asked the same questions in the same order, and the answers are recorded identically (Drummond, 1996).

OBJECTIVE ASSESSMENT As noted earlier in this chapter, when making determinations about security levels (especially when community supervision is involved) it is strongly recommended that determinations be based solely on objective assessment instruments. However, there are a variety of specific assessment instruments that are employed by correctional agencies throughout the United States. These types of objective assessments can range from behavioral checklists that staff complete after observing a client's behavior to the traditional paper-and-pencil test that is usually completed by the offender (Hanser, 2009; Van Voorhis, Braswell, & Lester, 2000). Most of the later types of assessments require manual scoring by the counselor. Some tests are also given on computer and require that the offender complete the assessment at a specific location, unless the instrument is put on a portable laptop. In most cases, these versions of assessment instruments are computer scored, saving time and effort of assessment personnel. With the use of a portable laptop and a computer-loaded assessment program, the evaluator can eliminate the need to keep track of hardcopy files to track offender results.

Perhaps, one of the best types of risk assessment systems is the **Wisconsin Risk Assessment System.** Indeed, this structured assessment has become the standard tool used by many probation and parole systems. Supervision personnel who use this instrument must score probationers on the predictors contained on the list, and from that point the offender is classified into either "high-," "medium-," or "low-risk" categories of supervision (Van Voorhis et al., 2000). The items that are included on this list are all statistical predictors of likely failure while on probation. These predictors are all based on previous probation histories among probationers and are based on the premise that the best predictor of future aggregate probationer behavior is the typical prior behavior of offenders who have had similar scores as the offender currently being assessed. Over time, offenders have been tracked so that follow-up data could be collected. The follow-up data from this instrument has allowed researchers to determine those factors that are associated with failure and success while on community supervision. Some of the factors that are examined via the **Wisconsin Risk Assessment** include the following:

1. Number of address changes in the last 12 months
2. Percentage of time employed in the 12 months
3. Alcohol consumption problems
4. Other drug consumption problems
5. Offender attitude
6. Age at first conviction
7. Number of prior periods of probation/parole supervision
8. Number of prior probation/parole revocations
9. Number of prior felony convictions
10. Type of convictions or prior adjudications.

It is important to understand that not all risk factors are the same and not all of them have the same priority. Indeed, some risk factors are fairly permanent or at least they occur due to no fault or cause of the offender. On the other hand, other risk factors, such as criminal activity, are solely due to the behavior of the offender or his or her reactions to one's environment. Different risk factors may carry more "weight" in determining the likelihood that the offender is likely to benefit from treatment and, correspondingly, refrain from recidivism. Thus, some risk factors are more attuned to security issues and the need to maintain custody and control of the offender, whereas others are more applicable to treatment planning.

Static risk factors are characteristics that are permanent and/or unchanging, being inherent to the offender's psychological framework. Any number of factors may qualify as static risk factors that have a permanent bearing on the offender's ability to change. Consider the age at first conviction, the gender, the sex, disabilities, and mental impairments; each of these have a serious impact on offenders and the existence of each of these are permanent (Hanser, 2009; Van Voorhis et al., 2000). Identifying these types of characteristics is usually most effective for determining security classifications. These characteristics are often the best basis for security determinations. Opposite of the static risk factor is the dynamic risk factor. **Dynamic risk factors** are those characteristics that can and do change over time. Likewise, dynamic risk factors are those characteristics that are at least influenced, if not controlled by the offender. Examples of dynamic risk factors would be employment, motivation, drug use, and family relations, to name a few (Hanser, 2009; Van Voorhis et al., 2000). These characteristics do not do much to aid security but they are very good factors to consider when determining the needs of the offender and/or conducting the treatment planning process. Their fluid and changing nature is what makes them amenable to treatment and, since the offender does have some degree of influence over these characteristics, their efforts to improve can directly impact these factors (Hanser, 2006, 2009). Figure 3.3 gives an example of an instrument that utilizes both static and dynamic risk factors to determine an offender's risk of recidivism. These factors are specifically noted in the bottom section of this instrument.

While security issues are important, most persons in the counseling field will be assigned to duties that are related to treatment of the offender. This means that most persons in the counseling field will not necessarily be required to provide assessments for security status. Even if they are, they will most likely use those processes that are mandated by their agencies and will be given appropriate training in the use of those procedures. For counselors, the assessment process will utilize instruments that require client input and thus tend to have some bit of a subjective element. Though these instruments are standardized, they do require that the counselor

Juvenile Sex Offender Assessment Protocol-II
Scoring Form

Scoring Code: 0 = Stable; 1 = Moderate; 2 = Severe

1. Sexual Drive/Preoccupation Scale			
1. Prior Legally Charged Sex Offenses	0	1	2
2. Number of Sexual Abuse Victims	0	1	2
3. Male Child Victim	0	1	2
4. Duration of Sex Offense History	0	1	2
5. Degree of Planning in Sexual Offense(s)	0	1	2
6. Sexualized Aggression	0	1	2
7. Sexual Drive and Preoccupation	0	1	2
8. Sexual Victimization History	0	1	2
Sexual Drive/Preoccupation Scale Total			
2. Impulsive/Antisocial Behavior Scale			
9. Caregiver Consistency	0	1	2
10. Pervasive Anger	0	1	2
11. School Behavior Problems	0	1	2
12. History of Conduct Disorder	0	1	2
13. Juvenile Antisocial Behavior	0	1	2
14. Ever Charged or Arrested before Age 16	0	1	2
15. Multiple Types of Offenses	0	1	2
16. History of Physical Assault and/or Exposure to Family Violence	0	1	2
Impulsive/Antisocial Behavior Scale Total			
3. Intervention Scale			
17. Accepting Responsibility for Offense(s)	0	1	2
18. Internal Motivation for Change	0	1	2
19. Understands Risk Factors	0	1	2

FIGURE 3.3 A Sample Instrument Using Static and Dynamic Risk Factors *Source:* **Note that this assessment form was adapted from the U.S. Government publication as referenced as follows:** Prentky, R., & Righthand, S. (2003). *Juvenile sex offender assessment protocol-II (J-SOAP-II) manual*. Washington, DC: Office of Juvenile Delinquency and Prevention. Retrieved from: http://nicic.org/Library/019361.

20. Empathy	0	1	2
21. Remorse and Guilt	0	1	2
22. Cognitive Distortions	0	1	2
23. Quality of Peer Relationships	0	1	2

Intervention Scale Total

4. Community Stability/Adjustment Scale

24. Management of Sexual Urges and Desire	0	1	2
25. Management of Anger	0	1	2
26. Stability of Current Living Situation	0	1	2
27. Stability in School	0	1	2
28. Evidence of Positive Support Systems	0	1	2

Community Stability/Adjustment Scale Total

Juvenile Sex Offender Assessment Protocol-II

Summary Form

Static/Historical Scales

1. Sexual Drive/Preoccupation Scale Score:
   (Add Items 1–8 [range: 0–16]) ________/16 = ________

2. Impulsive-Antisocial Behavior Scale Score:
   (Add Items 9–16 [range: 0–16]) ________/16 = ________

Dynamic Scales

3. Intervention Scale Score:
   (Add Items 17–23 [range 0–14]) ________/14 = ________

4. Community Stability Scale Score:
   (Add Items 24–28 [range: 0–10]) ________/10 = ________

Static Score

(Add items 1–16) ________/32 = ________

Dynamic Score

(Add items 17–28) ________/24 = ________

Total J-SOAP Score

(Add items 1–28) ________/56 = ________

FIGURE 3.3 Continued

ask the client for his or her own answer to a series of questions. These are often referred to as "objective" assessments because they go beyond a mere interview and/or checklist procedure. However, these instruments do tend to be psychometrically normed and validated for use with a given group of clientele and these instruments serve as a tool for guiding the therapeutic process. When a test is **normed**, this means that it has been used with a sample that is reflective of a population that we wish to assess. Thus, if we wish to assess substance abuse in our clients, we would need to pick an assessment tool that had been normed on substance abusers to ensure that the instrument is appropriate for our purposes. In addition, when we use the term **validated**, this simply means that an instrument has been tested (usually statistically) to ensure that it actually measures what we intend for it to measure. On some occasions, a question on an assessment or instrument may seem clear to the person creating the question but it may be interpreted in a different manner by the person completing the assessment instrument. In such a case, the response would then not be valid since it is not based on the actual, intended interpretation of the question. Validated instruments guard against these types of problems. Later, in Chapter 14, we provide a much more detailed discussion on standardized and validated instruments since these instruments are often used by program evaluators for agencies that provide mental health services.

SECTION SUMMARY

The assessment and classification of offenders is critical to ensure that services delivered are suitable and appropriate. The data collection process comes before any processes such as assessment or classification of the offender can take place. During this process, a number of methods might be used—from the review of documents in the offender's file to the use of personal interviews with the offender, and even including home visits with the offender and/or their family. Gaining information from collateral contacts likewise provides additional external information that can serve as cross-validation of the data collection process.

Beyond the data collection/gathering stage, the assessment stage consists of two broad categories of assessment. These are the subjective and the objective forms of assessment. Subjective assessments typically consist of interviews and observations. In many cases, the use of structured interviews may be used. A subjective, structured interview is a process whereby an interviewer will ask a respondent a set of prearranged and open-ended questions so that the interview will address certain bits of desired data that are gathered from the respondent. Objective assessments include standardized instruments, often having psychometric characteristics, and can range from behavioral checklists that staff complete to paper-and-pencil test completed by the offender. Among the best-known and most widely used objective instruments is the Wisconsin Risk Assessment system. Two types of factors are typically examined by objective instruments: static risk factors and dynamic risk factors. Static risk factors are characteristics that are inherent to the offender and are usually permanent in nature. These characteristics often form the best basis for security determinations. Opposite of the static risk factor is the dynamic risk factor. Dynamic risk factors are those characteristics that can change and are more or less influenced or controlled by the offender, such as employment, motivation, drug use, and family relations.

LEARNING CHECK

1. Objective forms of assessment are best for treatment planning purposes.
   a. True
   b. False

2. ______________________ are those characteristics that can change and are more or less influenced or controlled by the offender, such as employment, motivation, drug use, and family relations.
   a. Dynamic risk factors
   b. Static risk factors
   c. Random risk factors
   d. Baseline typology risk factors
   e. None of the above
3. The objective assessment used for security purposes should always be based upon the response of supervision staff and should never incorporate self-report data from the offender.
   a. True
   b. False
4. The "halo error" is the tendency to be influenced by your first impression of an individual or by an exceptional trait. This influence can lead to bias in perception.
   a. True
   b. False
5. When a test is normed, this means that it has been used with a sample that is reflective of a population that we wish to assess.
   a. True
   b. False

PART TWO: DIAGNOSTIC STAGE AND CLASSIFICATION STAGE

Diagnostic Stage

PSYCHOSOCIAL HISTORY Psychosocial history is a common component within most client records that are kept by a mental health facility. In most cases, this history will at least document details related to the client's lifestyle that was current at the time of intake. The documentation of psychosocial history, usually conducted at intake, may be updated throughout an offender's tenure of participation in therapeutic services. This is often the case due to reclassifications, mental health updates, and presentence investigations that are conducted prior to a client's sentencing. The psychosocial history is a primary means of collecting various personal information related to an offender's past, typically presenting this information in a manner that is relevant to the client offender's presenting problems, ability to cope with these problems, and other issues related to day-to-day functioning.

Enos and Southern (1996) provide a good presentation of the utility of psychosocial histories, noting that such records are excellent means of gaining information on the lifespan development of a client. From this history, recurring problems and patterns of behavior may be recognized that would have shaped the individual, being inherent to their own personality development and sense of self. The modes of behavior may have drawbacks and advantages, leading to aptitudes and opportunities for the individual. Indeed, through an examination of the past behavior in a psychosocial history, an attentive clinician may be able to find trends that give clues as to specific diagnoses applicable to the client but that were never officially detected by authorities or mental health providers. Consider an adult client who reports to a counselor and provides an account of his youth that indicate a troubled childhood. From this history, the therapist might find that the characteristics of the client, garnered from the psychosocial history, match with known features of conduct disorder, demonstrating a consistency of behavior that provides a clinical explanation for the persisting problem that may continue into adulthood (Enos & Southern, 1996).

The psychosocial history will contain an extensive amount of information that ranges from birth and early childhood to teenage years and beyond. Early childhood circumstances such as medical conditions; accidents; family interactions; physical, social, and cognitive development; academic performance; and so forth will all be included in this history (Enos & Southern, 1996). When considering the correctional treatment process, juvenile and adult offending history will naturally be included and will typically be a focus of court-mandated treatment programs. However, it should be noted that the therapist is best served using the psychosocial history as a means of obtaining familiarity with the client as a multidimensional person rather than a unidimensional offender. While community supervision officers and other official agents may wish to focus on offending history, the role of the counselor is one where a therapeutic alliance is sought between the therapist and the client. Excessive attention to the simple act of offending tends to impair the development of an effective therapeutic alliance and also creates an atmosphere where the client will certainly feel judged by the therapist. This must be avoided or it is extremely unlikely that the therapist will gain positive therapeutic movement from the client. Instead, distance and resistance are likely to develop since the client will not trust the intentions of the therapist as being benevolent.

The key reason for noting that the psychosocial history is of therapeutic value lies with the observation that some treatment providers may simply use this history during the initial periods of a client's treatment but will later fail to continue the incorporation of this information throughout the remainder of the therapeutic process. This is especially true when therapists have large caseloads or are employed in grass-root organizations where constraints on treatment services may call for less detailed approaches to service delivery. This less than flattering point is not intended to be a criticism of such facilities but instead demonstrates how routinely the psychosocial history may be considered a tool of value restricted to early treatment programming. Yet, if such agencies were to incorporate psychosocial stories throughout the span of their treatment programming, a coherent theme will emerge and money can be saved since there is no need for additional products, forms of disjointed interventions, and/or other specialists or treatment providers. Indeed, this technique, when woven into a program, simply extends the initial intake and assessment period throughout the treatment process, making maximum use of the data that are gathered while also making maximum use of the group therapy process.

PSYCHOLOGICAL EVALUATION In many respects, psychological evaluation is similar to the previously discussed psychiatric examination. However, psychological evaluation tends to have a greater emphasis on testing. The measurement of intelligence, academic and vocational abilities, personality, psychopathology, and other attributes tend to be those areas that psychologists focus on in the correctional treatment. One name for this field of specialization is **psychometrics**, which deals with psychological measurements. It should be noted that psychological evaluations are not always used in correctional systems. This is because psychological measurement tends to be less focused on the use of diagnoses and is instead more focused on describing various traits related to human functioning (Enos & Southern, 1996).

Psychological tests tend to fall within three broad categories: objective, projective, and performance tests. **Objective tests** measure a dimension or characteristic in a relatively direct manner that compares the individual's scores with those of the norms of the sample from which the instrument was created. **Projective tests** use indirect measures of characteristics related to human adjustment through the use of client responses to various unstructured tasks. In these cases, "verbal, written, and even graphic responses to projective test protocols reveal underlying psychodynamics and psychic contents relevant to the study of personality, as well as perceptual processes" (Enos & Southern, 1996, p. 77). **Performance tests** are similar to projective tests since both tend to ask the client to perform a given set of tasks. Performance tests differ from projective tests in that they score the client with respect to accuracy, time required to complete the task, and level of difficulty involved in the task (Enos & Southern, 1996).

Objective tests are most often administered in pencil-and-paper format with the client providing answers in a test booklet. Lengthy objective tests such as the Minnesota Multiphasic Personality Inventory (MMPI), which will be discussed later in this chapter, may have a number of subscales that are designed to measure domains of functioning. These scales often use the aid of grading templates that are placed over the response booklet and help facilitate grading of the subscales and determining offender profiles. In many cases, computerized scoring systems may also be available, though they are of course more costly. If computerized scoring systems are used, all responses must either be keyed into the computer system or (depending on the particular test) the response sheet can be scanned into the computer.

Projective tests are purchased from commercial manufacturers such as Western Psychological Services or Psychological Assessment Resources, Inc. These suppliers provide the tests and additional supporting materials to those that have sufficient training and experience in the use of psychological testing instruments. This is a very important point to note because many counselors (i.e., licensed professional counselors) may not have sufficient credentials to administer projective psychological tests. This often includes social workers and other correctional treatment workers who do not have official degrees in psychology (particularly a Ph.D. in a clinical track) or those who have not opted to take the additional statistics courses and courses on intelligence, individual, and pathological testing. Thus, many correctional counselors are simply not qualified to administer these tests unless they have obtained additional credentials to do so. Thus, it is most often psychologists who interpret the client's test, using their training and discretion to unravel the client's response to ambiguous tasks designed to open the unconscious thought processes. These tests are considered "projective" in nature because they project (or speculate) the likely thoughts that a person has during a specific testing point, looking for typologies, similarities, and patterns that prior research has identified. Naturally, this takes extensive skill and understanding that goes well beyond that contained in a two-year graduate program for counselors and other such mental health service providers.

Lastly, performance tests compare what a person is able to do in completing a given task with normed standards that exist when others are required to complete the same task. Usually, these standards will be based on increments by physiological age, mental age, or academic levels of achievement. The main distinction between performance testing and objective and projective testing is the fact that clients are required to literally perform some type of actual task. Some examples might include testing persons with the creation of block formations, solving a puzzle, completing a maze, or even tasks that require hand–eye coordination. The key is to test more than simple intellect and/or psychological factors; it is used to test the degree of integration that the client has when using both mind and body to complete a challenge in the physical universe.

THE MULTIAXIAL SYSTEM OF THE DSM-IV-TR Mental health assessments are designed to answer questions related to how and why people think, feel, and behave as they do (Carbonnell & Perkins, 2000). There is a wide variety of issues and challenges that may "push" and "pull" on one's coping such as day-to-day stress, traumatic stress, intensely emotional circumstances, and challenges with problem solving, which may all become the focus of scrutiny among those who deal with such a person. When such challenges rise to a level that impairs his or her day-to-day functioning, the involvement of mental health professionals may be necessitated and, in some cases, the need for an appropriate diagnosis may arise. Mental health assessment tools are designed to judge for suitable criteria related to a diagnosis and this process is intended to ensure that the correct diagnosis is applied.

Before going further, it is important that we take a moment to explain why the use of diagnosis is important to correctional counseling. We would also like to address the fact that many persons, even in the mental health field, may not be supporters of the use of diagnoses. First, in order to correct something, we believe that one must be able to define exactly what it is that needs to be corrected. A failure to do this will simply result in a scattered and unorganized approach toward treatment planning and this will, in turn, result in a scattered approach to therapy with the client; this must be avoided at all costs. Later, in Chapter 14, we demonstrate the value of evidence-based practices in treatment, and, it is our contention that without a clear definition of the problematic behavior (defined as a specific disorder with specific criteria) there will not be clarity in determining if the intervention has worked to rectify the problem that has manifested itself in treatment. Further, if there is no clear definition at the beginning stage of treatment, it is difficult to obtain a baseline that we can compare with upon the conclusion of treatment. Without the clear ability to compare mental health problems at intake with those upon release, we are severely limited in our ability to determine if our treatment "worked" to correct the behavioral problems that were initially presented. If we cannot demonstrate that our program "works" then we are not evidence based and are therefore reduced to speculation. Thus, the use of assessment tools and diagnoses helps us (at the front end) to evaluate our effectiveness as treatment providers once clients have completed the treatment regimen (the back end) and are considered "cured" of their mental health affliction.

Further, we are aware that some practitioners are concerned with the labeling of persons who have received mental health services. We are receptive to this concern but believe that it is not near as problematic as was the case in years past. Given the number of public commercials regarding medications for depression and anxiety, the general acceptance of counseling as a service that many people utilize, the fact that there is less mystique attached to most mental health professions, and given that HIPAA laws and other recent legal innovations have emerged to protect the personal privacy and confidentiality of the client, we believe that the risks and consequences associated with diagnoses are minimal, if they exist at all. This is particularly true when one considers that offenders tend to have a stigma attached that has less to do with their mental health diagnosis and more to do with the fact that they have been processed through the criminal justice system. Thus, we believe that, for the most part, correctional clients are not negatively impacted by diagnoses, particularly when this is counterbalanced with the benefits that will be derived if the true problem is identified and if it is given the correct intervention. Thus, we are supportive of the use of clinical diagnoses because they provide focus to the treatment process and ensure that the baseline start of the evaluation process is appropriately established.

Further, the selected forms of mental health assessment that we have discussed tend to identify psychopathology because it is the offender population who disproportionately possesses those diagnostic factors related to psychopathology. Research has demonstrated that there is an inflated representation of mental illness among offenders in prison and on community supervision (Ashford, Sales, & Reid, 2002; Bartol, 2002). Researchers consistently estimate that about 30 to perhaps 35% of all offenders in maximum security institutions may have antisocial personality disorder (Ashford et al., 2002). In addition, conduct disorder, oppositional defiant disorder, and attention-deficit hyperactivity disorder tend to be strongly correlated with juvenile offending (Hanser, 2006). Various mood and substance abuse disorders are found among those offenders with communicable diseases. It is well known that in most state systems, the majority of inmate offenders have some form of substance abuse problem (Bureau of Justice Statistics, 1999). Further, approximately 73% of federal and 83% of state prison inmates noted that they had abused substances within the 12-month period prior to incarceration. Fully 70 to 80% of all prisoners are thought to have some form of substance abuse problem (Belenko, 1998; Reentry Media Outreach, 2005). Because substance abuse disorders are considered diagnosable disorders, mental health again becomes central to the assessment and diagnosis of the offending population. Further, offenders subjected to substance abuse disorders also have cooccurring disorders (discussed in more depth in Chapter 8), which again makes diagnosis a necessary function of correctional treatment planning.

The information that follows regarding the diagnosis of disorders and the organization of those diagnoses comes from the ***DSM-IV-TR***, which is the common terminology among practitioners for ***Diagnostic and Statistical Manual of Mental Disorders***, *Fourth Edition, Text Revision*. This text is considered the clinical "bible" among mental health professionals and diagnosticians. The *DSM-IV-TR* allows mental health practitioners to label, or diagnose, an individual (in this case an offender) so that they can be better categorized for further treatment interventions (Hanser, 2006, 2009). This is a necessary process when attempting to match the right client with the correct treatment modality. Further, as will be seen in many subsequent chapters, some offenders will qualify for two or more diagnoses, making them dual or comorbid in their diagnosis. In spite of the complexity, the *DSM-IV-TR* diagnostic categories provide important information when developing treatment plans for the offender.

It is important to understand that the use of the *DSM-IV-TR* criteria is all based upon the judgments of the practicing clinician. Thus, there is some degree of subjectivity involved with the development of a diagnosis that can only be balanced if the clinician is adequately qualified and trained to work with the offender population. Presuming the clinician is appropriately trained and experienced, the diagnostic process can be very effective and it can greatly improve approaches to treatment. On the other hand, if the process of diagnosis is faulty, it can have detrimental outcomes for the client and for the evaluation of agency services. As one might guess, the diagnostic process is closely tied to the effectiveness of the clinician to engage in structured interviews and observations, all necessary in the formulation of a diagnosis. This also brings us to another point: under no circumstances should a correctional counselor or other professional ever apply a diagnosis to clients whom he or she has not personally and physically seen. Even with this said, the amount of contact must be sufficient for the clinician to reasonably derive professional judgments related to the diagnosis of a given individual. Thus, clinicians are required to conduct routine interviews and they need to be skilled at this process. Ideally speaking, the same clinician who conducts the initial structured interview should also be the one who applies any diagnoses from the *DSM-IV-TR*.

The organization of disorders in the *DSM-IV-TR* is based on what is referred to as a multiaxial system. This system of assessment involves an examination of the offender along several different "axes." Each axis refers to a different area of content information that can assist a clinician to plan treatment for an offender and it can also aid in the prediction of the treatment outcome with that offender (American Psychiatric Association, 2000). There are five axes included in the *DSM-IV* multiaxial classification as shown below:

Axis I	Clinical Disorders Other Conditions that May Be a Focus of Clinical Attention
Axis II	Personality Disorders Mental Retardation
Axis III	General Medical Conditions
Axis IV	Psychosocial and Environmental Problems
Axis V	Global Assessment of Functioning

The use of this multiaxial system facilitates comprehensive and systematic evaluation while paying attention to the various mental disorders and general medical conditions, psychosocial and environmental problems, and the offender's overall levels of functioning. This approach examines a variety of areas related to the offender's functioning, providing a multidimensional view of the person who includes mental health functioning but does not overlook other factors that might impact such a functioning. We provide a brief overview of the various "axes" and their corresponding disorders so that students will understand the overall organization of mental disorders in the *DSM-IV-TR*. While we do not provide a step-by-step discussion of individual disorders, it is important to understand that these disorders will be included in the content of the chapters that follow. It is at this time that more depth and detail will be given to relevant disorders. However, we think that it is useful for the student to become familiar with the organization behind these disorders. If nothing else, this provides additional clinical context for students when they read later chapters of this text. It is the purpose of this chapter to simply acquaint the student with the *DSM-IV-TR* and to demonstrate how this clinical guide is organized. The main point of presenting this information is to give the student a clear and specific idea of how disorders are organized.

Axis I consists clinical disorders or conditions that may be the focus of clinical attention (American Psychiatric Association, 2000). The disorders included in this category are as follows:

1. Disorders diagnosed in infancy, childhood, or adolescence (excluding mental retardation)
2. Delirium, dementia, amnestic, and other cognitive disorders
3. Mental disorders due to a general medical condition
4. Substance-related disorders
5. Schizophrenia and other psychotic disorders
6. Mood disorders
7. Anxiety disorders
8. Somatoform disorders
9. Factitious disorders
10. Dissociative disorders
11. Sexual and gender identity disorders
12. Eating disorders
13. Sleep disorders
14. Impulse-control disorders not otherwise classified
15. Adjustment disorders.

The **Axis II** category includes both personality disorders and mental retardation. This axis is also sometimes used to note maladaptive personality characteristics. In some cases, clinicians may refer to content in this axis when describing defense mechanisms that a client may use to cover symptoms of his or her disorder (American Psychiatric Association, 2000). These disorders were deliberately placed on a separate axis to ensure that symptoms from personality disorders do not get confused with symptoms related to disorders in Axis I. This ensures organization and accuracy of the clinical diagnosis, which, as was discussed earlier, is a key issue in using diagnoses. An incorrect diagnosis can do harm and this organization scheme helps to safeguard the process. The disorders included in this category are as follows:

1. Paranoid personality disorder
2. Schizoid personality disorder
3. Schizotypal personality disorder

4. Antisocial personality disorder
5. Borderline personality disorder
6. Histrionic personality disorder
7. Narcissistic personality disorder
8. Avoidant personality disorder
9. Dependent personality disorder
10. Obsessive-compulsive personality disorder
11. Mental retardation

The **Axis III** category includes general medical conditions that may be relevant to the understanding and treatment of a client's mental disorder (American Psychiatric Association, 2000). It is important to keep in mind that Axis III considerations are common among those offenders possessing communicable diseases and among geriatric offenders (Hanser, 2006, 2009). A partial list of general medical conditions that are included in this axis are noted below:

1. Infectious and parasitic diseases
2. Diseases of the nervous system and sensory organs
3. Immunity disorders
4. Diseases of skin, musculoskeletal, and connective tissue
5. Diseases of the digestive, circulatory, and respiratory systems

The **Axis IV** category of disorders presents psychosocial problems that are tertiary to the actual disorder but have the capability of negatively impacting the disorder. Most of these problems have to do with the social environment of the offender, such as with educational, occupational, housing, and economic challenges and are therefore not necessarily clinical in nature. However, when one is attempting to reform offenders, all of these areas of concern are critical and have an overall global effect on the offender's prognosis. In short, these issues can quite easily aggravate the treatment process and can impair the prognosis of mental disorders possessed by an offender. According the American Psychiatric Association (2000), a psychosocial or environmental problem may be a negative life event (financial problems, loss of employment), an environmental difficulty or deficiency (such as being in prison), familial or other interpersonal stress (such as divorce), inadequate social support (no family or reliable friends), or other problems that relate to the overall context in which the offender's problems have developed. The list that follows illustrates some of the key problem areas that are included within the Axis IV category:

1. Problems with primary support groups
2. Problems related to the social environment
3. Educational problems
4. Occupational problems
5. Housing problems
6. Economic problems
7. Problems with access to health care services
8. Problems related to interaction with the legal system/crime.

Axis V is the last category in the *DSM-IV* multiaxial classification system. This axis deals with the overall functioning of the individual and is often referred to as the "GAF scale" which is simply an abbreviation for the Global Assessment of Functioning Scale. The GAF scale is an easy-to-use clinical tool that provides an "at a glance" indicator of the client's overall sense of functioning. This scale does not provide in-depth clinical details but instead provides a general guide as to where the client's functioning ranks when scaled on a continuum that has very high functioning at one end and very low functioning at the other. The GAF scale summarizes the client symptoms and sense of functioning to provide one single measure that provides an approximation of the client's functioning. This number is assigned by the clinician and is based on the overall details of the offender's mental health, social, occupational, and educational functioning. The GAF scale criteria are listed on Table 3.1.

Though simple in design, the GAF scale is an effective tool for providing a general sense of how an offender is functioning on a day-to-day basis. This scale is sometimes utilized as a supplemental screening device by correctional counselors when conducting structured interviews. This scale can be used by paraprofessionals in an informal sense and, even if such professionals may not make diagnostic decisions, it is still good for such staff to understand the criteria related to a given numerical rating from the GAF scale. Thus, it behoove agency administrators to train all treatment staff on the use of this scale, if nothing else, to ensure that they will understand what

TABLE 3.1 Global Assessment of Functioning (GAF) Scale

Score	Narrative Level of Functioning
100–91	Individual exhibits superior functioning; never seems disturbed by life's problems; free of psychological symptoms; is popular among others who respect the individual for their many positive characteristics.
90–81	Only minimal signs of disorder (mild anxiety before a stressor); good functioning in all domains; tends to be involved in a wide range of activities; is socially connected; only common day-to-day problems.
80–71	Few if any symptoms; any emergent symptoms or transient in nature and seem balanced in relation to the psychosocial stressor concerned; only slight social, occupational, or educational impairment.
70–61	The existence of mild symptoms such as depression or sleeplessness; some minor difficulties with social, occupational, or educational functioning; is involved in at least a few meaningful interpersonal relationships.
60–51	Symptoms are in the moderate range; moderate difficulty in social, occupational, or educational functioning; has few friends.
50–41	Serious symptoms such as thoughts of suicide, obsessions, or criminal behavior; serious impairment in social, occupational, or educational functioning.
40–31	An impaired and distorted sense of reality; weak or poor communication skills; major impairment in social, occupational, or educational functioning; poor family relations.
30–21	Delusions and hallucinations affect the behavior of individual; serious communication deficits; poor judgment and/or function in social, occupational, or educational settings.
20–11	Some degree of suicidal ideation or desire to hurt others; fails to maintain minimal hygiene standards; profound communication deficits.
10–1	Serious suicidal ideation with genuine intent to cease living; unwillingness to take care of oneself.
0	Information is not adequate to appraise.

Source: The table was adapted from the American Psychiatric Association. (2000). *Diagnostic and statistical manual of mental disorders*. Arlington, VA: American Psychiatric Association.

the rating is when they see it entered by advanced clinical personnel who have made note in the client's records. Further, GAF scale accounts for both static and dynamic risk factors and hence makes it useful to clinicians for treatment planning purposes as well as security staff who are responsible for the safety and security of the offender.

SECTION SUMMARY

The diagnostic stage is critical to the counseling process since it provides a sense of direction for the overall treatment process. Though counselors will not typically diagnose offenders on their own (most being unqualified to do so), they will often have to work with offenders who do have any number of diagnoses. These diagnoses often will be derived from psychiatric evaluations and other sources that require psychiatrists or psychologists. Thus, it is important that correctional counselors are at least marginally familiar with the common content of such psychiatric reports. Counselors should also be familiar with different types of tests, these consisting of objective, projective, and performance-based tests.

Lastly, correctional counselors must develop a sense of appreciation for the *DSM-V-TR* since a variety of diagnoses are encountered among the offender population. Correctional counselors should be familiar with all axes of the *DSM-IV-TR*, particularly Axis I and II as these deal with the various disorders that offenders will tend to have. In addition, GAF scale is presented as a useful tool to assess an offender's ability to function in a prosocial manner. This scale is both easy to understand and easy to utilize. Use of the GAF scale provides counselors with a simple but effective numerical indicator of a client's state of functioning and does so in a manner that allows the result to be easily used by other counselors or treatment specialists.

LEARNING CHECK

1. The GAF scale has a range from 1 to 100, with a score of 1 indicating that the offender is free of dysfunction, for the most part.
   a. True
   b. False
2. Antisocial personality disorder is an ____________________ disorder.
   a. Axis I
   b. Axis II
   c. Axis III
   d. Axis IV
   e. none of the above
3. According to Enos and Southern (1996), true psychiatric examinations are fairly common in correctional case management.
   a. True
   b. False
4. Mood disorders are ____________________ disorders.
   a. Axis I
   b. Axis II
   c. Axis III
   d. Axis IV
   e. none of the above

5. Problems related to the social environment fall along which *DSM-IV-TR* Axis?
   a. Axis I
   b. Axis II
   c. Axis III
   d. Axis IV
   e. None of the above

PART THREE: RECIDIVISM PREDICTION AND CLASSIFICATION STAGES, TREATMENT PLANNING, AND REFERRAL

Recidivism Prediction Stage

The recidivism prediction stage incorporates information derived during assessment and diagnosis (Hanser, 2006, 2009). It is at this stage where correctional counselors attempt to determine the risks involved with providing security level assignments to the offender, whether in the institution or under community supervision. With this in mind, we recommend one of the more commonly accepted clinical inventories that has been used to determine offender suitability; this is the **Level of Supervision Inventory—Revised (LSI-R)**. This instrument has been adopted by many correctional agencies because of its effective recidivism-prediction characteristics (Hanser, 2009; Van Voorhis et al., 2000). The LSI-R, as designed by Don Andrews and James Bonta, can be administered by correctional counselors. The initial process of utilizing the LSI-R consists of a semistructured interview, but this instrument has additional utility because it allows for the continued reassessment of an offender's risk score. The use of risk reassessment scores can be useful both from a security-setting and a program evaluation standpoint. In other words, as the assessment of the offender is completed throughout several iterations, the determination will continue to be accurate to the offender's situation at that current point in time. This ensures that the assessment does not become outdated over weeks, months, or years of supervision. Further, the use of multiple measures provides numerous points from which to determine outcomes and, as will be seen later in Chapter 14, provides a more robust evaluation of the program's overall effectiveness.

The LSI-R inventory is a quantitative survey of attributes that consider the offender and his or her situation relevant to the level of supervision and treatment decisions (Andrews & Bonta, 2003). Further, the LSI-R was intended for use with offenders who are aged 16 and older, making it usable for clinicians dealing with older teens as well as adults. This instrument includes 54 items that are based largely on legal requirements and also factors relevant to security risk levels and treatment success (Andrews & Bonta, 2003; Hanser, 2006, 2009). However, the LSI-R is not intended to replace the professional judgment of the correctional worker. Rather, the use of objective risk-needs assessments should be to augment professional judgment, add to the fairness of offender assessment, and alert correctional counselors to the need for effective offender risk-needs assessment (Andrews & Bonta, 2003). Research with the LSI-R shows that scores on the instrument have predicted a variety of outcomes important to offender security and supervision (Hanser, 2009). Among probation samples, the LSI-R has predicted violent recidivism and other forms of violations to supervision with a great deal of accuracy (Andrews & Bonta, 2003; Hanser, 2009). Among incarcerated offenders, the LSI-R has predicted such varied outcomes as success in correctional halfway houses and institutional misconduct (Andrews & Bonta, 2003).

When going beyond the use of specific instruments and inventories, students should understand the underlying presumptions behind risk prediction. These assumptions help to ensure that agency decision makers understand the broader implications for their agency when making release decisions. Among these considerations are those related to **False Negatives** and **False Positives**. The chronic occurrence of these two mistakes in risk prediction can lead to tragic consequences for society and/or costly expenditures for correctional agencies. When decision makers are making release decisions for offenders, they will ultimately have to decide if the offender be allowed within the community or if the offender must remain behind bars. There are some implications in making these decisions that may not be readily apparent to the casual observer, and these implications, as well as the official professional terms associated with these implications, should be understood by the student.

First, when correctional decision makers predict that an offender is not likely to reoffend (making them a good risk for community supervision) this is called a prediction in the negative. If later, the offender is released into the community and he or she does not commit any future offense, then this is referred to as a true negative. This is because the prediction turns out to be true. Therefore, the **True Negative** implies that the offender will not recidivate and the prediction turns out to be true (Hanser, 2006, 2009). On the other hand, if correctional personnel predict that an offender is not likely to offend, and when upon release to the community that offender does commit some form of crime, this is referred to as a false negative. This is because the agency made the prediction in the negative (meaning that the agency thought the offender would not reoffend) yet it turned out that their prediction was "false" or incorrect. Thus, the **False Negative** implies that the offender was predicted not to recidivate but, in reality, he or she does, making the prediction false (Hanser, 2006, 2009).

On the other hand, if an offender is predicted to reoffend this is referred to as a prediction in the positive. If then, the offender is predicted to reoffend yet he or she is allowed on community supervision because of either the effectiveness of his or her legal representation or some other odd course of events, and later he or she does in fact commit an offense, it is called a **True Positive**. Simply put, the true positive predicts that the offender will reoffend and this prediction later turns out to be true. However, if another offender is likewise predicted to be likely to commit a crime but later the offender somehow is released onto community supervision and is found to never reoffend, this would be a **False Positive**. The prediction was in the positive, indicating risk of reoffending, yet it was false and thus not accurate (Hanser, 2006, 2009).

As one might guess, it is the **True Positive** and **True Negative** that agencies hope to obtain as often as possible. These are perfect predictions of offender behavior. However, life not being perfect, the **False Positive** and **False Negative** predictions will be inevitable at some point (Hanser, 2006, 2009). Because of this, there are a couple of key points that should be mentioned related to false positives and false negatives. First, false positives can be viewed as a "safe-bet" for persons making release decisions, because if the offender remains behind bars, he or she simply cannot commit any further crimes in society. Because of this, it may seem prudent from the decision maker's perspective to simply incarcerate as many offenders as possible (the more the better) as a means of ensuring public safety (Hanser, 2009). However, this would be very costly and would result in excessive expenditures on inmates who are neither dangerous nor likely to repeat their criminal behavior. In addition, this will also tend to ruin even the best prognosis for treatment since prisons are not environments that are highly conducive to treatment programs, particularly among offenders whose status does not, in reality, warrant custodial supervision.

Though the focus of recidivism prediction is largely centered on security rather than treatment, Hanser (2006) has noted repetitively that the two are not mutually exclusive of one another, especially when dealing with complicated offender caseloads. Further, there is an abundance of research that clearly demonstrates that prisonization can and does serve as a training ground for offenders who are kept in a long-term confinement with one another (Hanser, 2009). This can essentially "create" recidivism as those who would normally refrain from further criminality are placed in an environment where they can learn to commit crimes more effectively and network with large offender groups represented in the prison (i.e., gang members, organized crime members, and just random malcontents), thereby becoming more socialized into the underground and often unseen world of the mainstream criminal; this simply increases their incentive to reoffend in the future. Thus, overpredicting recidivism is not a good long-term strategy as it will result in further overcrowding of prisons; creating ever more costs to taxpayers (Hanser, 2009). Rather, this strategy is one that is certain to lead state governments toward bankruptcy.

On the other hand, false negatives result in dangers to public safety and also damage the public perception of treatment programs that are aimed at offender reintegration within the community. Naturally, the ultimate goal of correctional counseling is to have the offender "fixed" so that they can be returned to society as effective members who provide a constructive contribution so that they can lead meaningful lives. Public sentiments will not realize this possibility if constant false negatives occur within a given recidivism-prediction scheme. This can be very damaging to a treatment program inside a correctional facility since this will further exacerbate the schism that tends to exist between custodial and treatment personnel. This is also damaging to treatment programs in the community since the public will be reluctant to work with such programs.

Because of the fear of committing a false negative, some correctional counselors may decide to deliberately make more false positives. No criminal justice professional wants to see people in the community get hurt, and the use of false positives helps to safeguard against this possibility. Since no agency wants its credibility at risk due to incorrect predictions, supervisors tend to become so risk aversive that treatment processes are completely stifled. As noted previously, this further fuels the cycle of recidivism since offenders are not afforded an adequate opportunity to break free of the criminal crowd. Further, this detracts from the ability of treatment specialists to address issues and challenges that might be characterized as Axis IV problems since occupational and social improvements cannot be realistically pursued inside the prison.

Classification Stage

As noted at the beginning of this chapter, this stage is largely tied to the recidivism prediction stage. Thus, once the general risk level of the inmate or offender on community supervision is known, the job of the correctional agency, whether institutional or community based, is to correctly "match-up" the offender's treatment plan with the level of security determined by the LSI-R and other risk prediction tests and procedures. One of the best instruments for this process is the MMPI-2, which is perhaps the most widely used objective test instrument in corrections. The **MMPI-2** is an objective personality adjustment inventory that can be administered to a large number of offenders simultaneously, making it a very practical tool within the institutional setting. The MMPI-2 consists of 567 true/false questions that require the offender to be able to read at the sixth-grade level. Further, the MMPI-2 has been updated and renormed to ensure that the instrument's standardized features remain current. Further, this instrument is available on tape for blind, illiterate, semiliterate, or disabled individuals. This instrument is intended to be a clinical tool, meaning that the MMPI-2 is not a security-oriented instrument. It is best suited for detecting mental health disorders among abnormal populations.

The MMPI-2 consists of a number of "subscales" within its construction. These subscales consist of a series of questions that are embedded within the remainder of the 567 total questions, being undetectable by the test taker. These questions are all designed to measure specific points of interest to provide a multifaceted profile of the offender's personality. In addition, the MMPI-2 is robust from deceit and the tendency for manipulative offender to "fake good" with their responses. This is because the MMPI-2 contains three specific subscales that are included to specifically detect untrue or manipulative responses. These subscales are the lie (L), infrequency (I), and the correction (K) scales.

The lie or "L" scale consists of 15 questions (out of 567 total questions) such as "I never get angry." This scale indicates whether the client is consciously or unconsciously presenting as a perfectionist. The "I" scale contains 64 questions but does not measure a trait. Rather, this subscale determines if the client has serious psychological disturbances. Indeed, items on this subscale are answered in a deviant direction by fewer than 10% of all test takers—meaning that a high score indicates that the offender has indicated as having serious psychological difficulties. Lastly, the "K" or correction scale measures client defensiveness when taking the test. The "K" subscale has 30 items that cover a wide range of content areas. Low scores indicate a deliberate attempt on the part of the offender to appear bad. However, some offenders may have a poor self-image and may, as a result, endorse responses that indicate pathological problems (this is common among addicts, some pedophiles, or offenders who feel remorse). Beyond this, the MMPI-2 is an effective instrument in determining underlying pathology within the offender. Table 3.2 provides the additional subscales that examine separate area of mental health.

Further, the MMPI-2 Criminal Justice and Correctional Report is based on decades of research and evaluation where it has been designed to fit the data produced from the MMPI-2 to agency classification schemes (Megargee, 2004). Therefore, the **MMPI-2 Criminal Justice and**

TABLE 3.2 Clinical Scales of the Minnesota Multiphasic Personality Inventory-2

Scale	Item Total	Item Content
Hypochondriasis	32	Undue concern with physical health
Depression	57	Depression, denial of happiness and personal worth, lack of interest, withdrawal
Hysteria	60	Specific somatic complaints, discomfort in social situations
Psychopathic Deviate	56	Activity/Passivity, identification with culturally conventional masculine and feminine choices
Paranoia	40	Delusions of persecution, suspiciousness, moral self-righteousness
Psychasthenia	48	General dissatisfaction with life, indecisiveness, self-doubt, obsessional aspects
Schizophrenia	78	Feeling of being different, feelings of isolation, bizarre thought processes, tendency to withdraw, sexual identity concerns
Hypomania	46	Elevated energy level, flight of ideas, elevated mood, increased motor activity, expansiveness
Social Introversion/Extroversion	69	Introversion/extroversion, social insecurity

Source: Adapted from Drummond, R. J. (1996). *Appraisal procedures for counselors and helping professionals* (3rd ed.). Englewood Cliffs, NJ: Prentice-Hall, Inc.

Correctional Report (MMPI-2 CJCR) is well suited to ensure consistency between the offender's treatment plan and his or her level of security. This means that this instrument can be triangulated with results from the LSI-R to improve overall security determinations. Further, this report is designed to identify those offenders who may suffer from thought disorders, serious depression, and substance abuse. This instrument further distinguishes those who are likely to exhibit hostility and/or behave in a predatory fashion, as well as those who will likely be bullied or victimized while in an institution. This comprehensive report even includes predictor items related to self-injury and suicide, making it a useful instrument for many of the issues discussed in Chapter 13. The **MMPI-2 Criminal Justice and Correctional Report** also consists of nine behavioral dimensions. These behavioral dimensions are normed off of substantial offender populations rather than the general outside population. This ensures that the results are correctly suited for the offender population. A list of these nine behavioral dimensions of the MMPI-2 follows below:

- Apparent need for further mental health assessment or programming
- Apparent leadership ability; dominance
- Indications of conflicts with or resentment of authorities
- Likelihood of positive or favorable response to academic programming
- Indications of socially deviant behavior or attitudes
- Apparent need for social participation; extroversion
- Likelihood of mature, responsible behavior; positive response to supervision
- Likelihood of positive favorable response to vocational programming
- Likelihood of hostile or antagonistic peer relations.

In addition, the MMPI-2 Criminal Justice and Correctional Report also provides nine possible areas relevant to the offender's functioning. This provides correctional counselors with indicators of potential clinical challenges that may affect the offender. These nine identified problem areas are as follows:

- Difficulties with alcohol or other substance abuse
- Manipulation or exploitation of others
- Thought disorders
- Overcontrolled hostility
- Family conflict or alienation from family
- Depressive affect or mood disorder
- Awkward or difficult interpersonal relationships
- Anger control problems
- Tendency to get sick/ill frequently.

When combined, the MMPI-2 and the MMPI-2 Criminal Justice and Correctional Report (MMPI-2 CJCR) provide a fully comprehensive classification system that takes both mental health and security concerns into consideration. The use of the LSI-R, in tandem with the MMPI-2 and the MMPI-2 CJCR, adds further accuracy in predicting recidivism among offenders. In fact, when considering recidivism, it is usually best to have one instrument that is specifically designed for this purpose and, as noted earlier, the LSI-R is the best tool that we can recommend. It is important to understand that these instruments are lengthy; afterall, they are quite comprehensive. However, these instruments also work and achieve superior results. This simply demonstrates that there is a price for quality; the development of a high quality assessment and classification system will therefore entail costs, both in financial capital and in human resources.

Because of the effectiveness of each of the tools presented (all have been shown to have better-than-average validity and reliability) and because of the manner in which each precisely fulfills the intended functions of the *assessment, diagnostic, recidivism prediction*, and *classification* stages, these instruments are presented as a "Cadillac program" of providing for all four stages of offender treatment. Indeed, the MMPI-2 serves to aid during both the "classification" and the "diagnostic" stage, and the MMPI-2 CJCR serves to aid during the "recidivism prediction" and "classification" stage. Thus, each instrument also provides a dual-purposed overlap in functions ensuring that each stage and each instrument optimally complements one another.

Treatment Planning: Moving from Assessment to Action

First, it should be understood that treatment planning is not a one-time occurrence in the process of providing treatment services to the client. Rather, it is a continual process that is refined over time as new challenges emerge and as the client has successes and failures throughout the process. It is very important that counselors understand this and remain flexible throughout the process. While on the one hand it is important to be flexible as the counseling relationship unfolds, it is likewise important to get as clear and accurate an assessment at the beginning stages of treatment as is possible. If counselors find themselves shifting modalities constantly or if they find that a new unrelated issue occurs every week so as to make the initial treatment plan ineffective, then it is likely that they either did not get a good assessment of the client's initial condition or circumstances or, less frequently but sometimes occurring, the client may be manipulating them.

It is important that the client get a clear picture of the underlying issues relevant to his or her overall recovery in treatment. This may not always be what the client overtly states to the counselor. As noted, the client may be manipulative and may desire to throw the therapist off course throughout the treatment process. Because of this, it is important that correctional counselors have the appropriate skills to conduct interviews (particularly at intake) and to use those interviews as constructive mechanisms not only to gain information but also to motivate clients toward positive change. Indeed, the entire rationale behind data gathering, assessment, and classification is to aid in the treatment planning process as well as the therapeutic service delivery that follows.

One promising, evidence-based practice for motivating offenders and fostering positive behavioral changes is motivational interviewing. The use of motivational interviewing was first developed in the addiction treatment field but now has been applied with positive results in a number of correctional settings (Walters, Clark, Gingerich, & Meltzer, 2007). This approach has a good track record in studies with schizophrenic, depressed, and antisocial clients, as well as others who have relatively low cognitive functioning (Hettema, Steele, & Miller, 2005; Rubak, Sandboek, Lauritzen, & Christensen, 2005; Walters et al., 2007). Recent findings from large alcohol and drug treatment studies suggest that motivational techniques may work particularly well with offenders who are angry and/or frustrated or more resistant to change (Project MATCH Research Group, 1997, 1998; Walters et al., 2007). Because of this, we contend that motivational techniques should be the primary method of interaction used by correctional counselors who must take the offender from the initial assessment stage to the treatment planning stage. These techniques work well with persons who have clinical disorders (including antisocial personality disorder) and with offenders who are resistant (a common occurrence). Thus, this approach is ideal for the correctional counseling approach.

The principle behind motivational techniques is that by listening to an offender and following up on the positive aspects of his or her speech and thinking, correctional counselors can help increase the offender's motivation to make positive changes in one's own life that will reduce his or her likelihood of reoffending. These techniques are also congruent with the rapport-building and person-centered techniques that will be discussed in Chapter 4. Because of this, we believe motivational interviewing and motivational techniques are the ideal link between the assessment/classification/diagnosis junctures and the actual process of getting clients to commit to goals that are set in the treatment plan.

Further, motivational interviewing techniques are evidence based in practice. In Chapter 14, we discuss the importance of the evaluation process in treatment programs and, as students will learn, the demonstration of evidence-based practices will be again highlighted. There is a national push toward these types of practices, particularly among federal agencies that fund many public treatment programs. This push toward evidence-based practices is partially in response to research suggesting that effective correctional treatment programs share similar characteristics that tend to be effective in reducing recidivism. One finding is that brief interactions can significantly influence offender outcomes. This is true whether the person conducting an interview or initial intake is a paraprofessional or full-fledged mental health provider. Thus, motivational techniques provide the specific means by which correctional counselors can take assessment and classification determinations and gain offender motivation and compliance, creating a collaborative method whereby the counselor and the client create a treatment plan that will result in genuine behavior change.

Treatment planning helps connect assessment, planning, and supervision. The use of motivational techniques in interviewing and consultation can help to integrate the assessment results with the treatment planning process. Quite naturally, the use of assessment outcomes with the treatment planning process is highly desired, and motivational techniques can help to cement the two functions throughout the offender–counselor relationship. With this in mind, we would like to highlight four basic steps to treatment planning as presented by Walters et al. (2007), with the use of motivational techniques being included in the process:

- Consult the assessment results for information on risk, needs, and responsivity.
- Ask the offender what problem(s) he or she thinks are most closely related to his or her crime.
- Factor in any relevant court- or board-ordered conditions.
- Given the information from all three areas, use motivational techniques to help resolve ambivalence and motivate positive behavior.

Walters et al. (2007) note that although motivation techniques suggest some tangible strategies, this approach is better thought of as a style of interaction that follows these basic principles:

Express Empathy. Empathy is about building good rapport and a positive working environment. It is an attempt to understand the offender's mindset, even though the agent may not agree with the offender's point of view. Empathy also involves an effort to draw out concerns and reasons for change from the offender, instead of relying on the agent's (or court's/board's) agenda as the sole persuasion strategy.

Work with Resistance. It is normal to have mixed feelings when thinking about change. Hence, the agent does not argue with the offender. Arguing or debating with clients will seldom be effective. Rather, correctional counselors must work with resistance by finding other ways to respond when the offender challenges the need for change. Later chapters of this text will provide specific techniques for working with resistance in the offender population.

Identify and Process Discrepancies. Discrepancy is the feeling that one's current behavior is out of line with one's goals or values. Rather than telling the offender why he or she should change, the agent asks questions and makes statements to help the offender identify his or her own reasons for change.

Support self-efficacy. A client is more likely to follow through with behavior he or she believes to have freely chosen and believes that he or she can accomplish. Therefore, the agent remains optimistic, reminds the offender of personal strengths and past successes, and affirms all efforts toward change.

Though clients will of course deviate from the initial plan and present new and varied issues, correctional counselors can use motivational techniques to help keep them on track with the structure of the plan—a plan that should be grounded in the subjective and objective assessment, classification, and diagnostic processes described in previous sections of this chapter. While it is important that the counselor stay with the client, they must not lose sight of the originally agreed upon treatment planning issues. On the other hand, this is difficult because a degree of flexibility is desirable when working through the stages of a treatment plan, as was noted earlier. If the counselor adheres to the initially prescribed plan and works the process faithfully, it may still be that the client shows no improvement. In such a case, it is likely that the treatment plan was good but the assessment was poor. No matter how good a treatment plan is and no matter what forms of motivation are provided, if the assessment is faulty then the plan will simply be a poor fit with the client. Stubbornly sticking to that plan with a hope that it will work will not produce effective results. Thus, identification of the key underlying issues through a sound assessment is still critical, with or without the use of motivational techniques.

A counselor must also identify the needs of a client in an effective and realistic manner. Much as with Maslow's hierarchy of needs pyramid, it is important that clients' basic needs are met before they can be expected to effectively dwell on any metaneeds such as belonging or actualization. Thus, basic needs must be attended to for most all correctional clients. It is important to keep in mind that when we talk about correctional clients, we are typically referring to clients who have a lack of material resources, few job skills, a social stigma of being an offender, likely housing problems, medical issues, and so forth. Any attempt to deliver services amidst this chaotic set of events will probably have dismal results. This is an important element to remember with correctional clients. Among those being released from incarceration, there may be issues with trauma (incarceration is traumatic though the client may not address this issue without some guidance from the counselor), depression, and/or other comorbid problems. Further, special needs related to physical disabilities and such need to be considered when the counselor seeks to determine the best approach in proceeding with a given client.

In addition to the needs of the client, the strengths and resources that the client has must also be considered. In many cases, clients will not necessarily be aware of their own strengths and/or understand the resources that they have. Sometimes this may be because of esteem issues (not recognizing their own strengths due to a negative self-image) and at other times it may be because they simply have not realized their given strength or resources. This can be an area of insight as you, the correctional counselor, train the client to look for the good within them in order to find those bright spots that exist for that person. Further, integrating their strengths and resources in the treatment process will give some tools to you and the client as you brainstorm possibilities. Lastly, it is important that when setting up the treatment plan or process, it should be structured so that the client is able to realistically achieve at least minor forms of therapeutic success. This can be motivating and it also conditions the client to harness his or her strength in a manner that leads to positive therapeutic outcomes. Once the strengths and resources have been determined, the goal setting can begin.

Setting goals is one of the most important aspects to the counseling process for several reasons. First, this is a point and time where the client should collaborate and provide input on the goals and the likelihood of his or her success. It is because of this that counselors should assist clients in achieving short-term goals that ultimately lead to long-term goals. Clients can easily become discouraged and this can increase their likelihood of recidivism and/or relapse. It is best to have subgoals within broader overarching goals that are able to be obtained, on bit at a time, in a clear, step-by-step, reasonable fashion. This helps to build confidence in clients and also allows the collaborative relationship to generate more "successes" than failures. To be sure, correctional clients will have setbacks and will experience failures, but if given the appropriate guidance, an adequate level of motivation, and a clear direction for success, many can and do benefit on a long-term basis from treatment. Second, by setting clear goals the overall success of the treatment plan is easier to record and to measure. This aids greatly when one wishes to later evaluate the effectiveness of their intervention program.

Naturally, the counselor will want to ensure that the client has clear objectives that are written. It is best if the counselor is able to have the client write out the objectives themselves as this has a positive therapeutic effect because of the reinforcing properties that are involved. In fact, in some programs, clients may be required to either write or read the objectives several times throughout a given day or week. These objectives should of course be prioritized, but, just as importantly, the client should clearly understand why a given order of prioritization has been assigned to goals and objectives. This is also important because it teaches and reinforces a valuable skill that many correctional clients tend to lack—long-term and sequential planning. In addition, a list of steps to be undertaken for each objective should be made. While this may seem mundane and perhaps a bit overly detailed, this is important for clients who may not have had optimal socialization and/or educational training. Planning and organizing are critical skills to life success and they should be emphasized when clients are in treatment. Lastly, it is important that deadlines be set within the treatment regimen. While a degree of discretion must be maintained if clients cannot meet all deadlines, a general emphasis on doing the required activities or tasks within the allocated timeframe helps to encourage client accountability and also generates the need for being self-motivated to ensure that the goals and objectives are achieved.

In an ideal case, the correctional client fulfills all of his or her goals and objectives. In the real world, this seldom happens, at least initially. However, this does not mean that overall these clients are not successful with their programs and that many do not recidivate in the future. Regardless, once the client has met the criteria for program completion, they should be discharged. Naturally, the counselor will need to, among other things, write a summary of the discharge elements as a means of recording the final outcome of the client while in the treatment program. In addition, the counselor will need to have additional referrals available in case the client has other issues or circumstances that he or she may wish to address. These may be corollary to the issues that the correctional client addressed with his or her counselor and the client may not be under any obligation to address such issues (often, court-mandated treatment can be very specific, overlooking key areas of needed treatment). However, some clients may wish to do so anyway. In such cases, it is important that agencies and/or private counselors have an integrated system of services and resources available to aid the client in their post-treatment functions and routines. If the counselor is successful in arranging this, then it is likely that a continuum of care can be achieved for the correctional client, providing a seamless transition from the role of a criminal justice number to be processed to that of a full-fledged, pro-social member of society.

SECTION SUMMARY

This section provides the student with an overview of the **Level of Supervision Inventory—Revised (LSI-R)**. This inventory has been found to be highly predictive of recidivism among a variety of correctional offender clients and is frequently used in the field of corrections. Further, students are introduced to the concept of true positives, true negatives, false positives, and false negatives. All of these general aspects of assessment accuracy are important for students to understand. Likewise, the **MMPI-2 Criminal Justice and Correctional Report (MMPI-2 CJCR)** is presented as an instrument that is highly complementary to the LSI-R. Indeed, the MMPI-2 CJCR is ideally suited to match the offender's treatment plan with his or her level of security while also serving as an additional backup scale when making security decisions from the LSI-R. This makes these two tools ideal for any program that seeks to address both security and clinical issues in as accurate a manner as possible, all the while aiding the ultimate treatment planning process through effective assessment and identification of areas needing further clinical exploration.

Lastly, it is important for assessment and classification processes to be useful and applicable to the treatment planning process. The ability to take the client from the assessment process to a point of therapeutic action is a skill that requires therapists to shift from an emphasis on mere identification of the problems to one where the offender is encouraged to make behavioral changes to remedy those problems. While effective diagnosis will allow for definition in determining problems facing offenders and while this will also provide specific and concrete planning tools, the treatment plan will only work if the offender makes the choice to incorporate those treatment goals and activities that are identified as necessary. The use of motivational techniques during the intake process and during early junctures in treatment can greatly aid correctional counselors who must facilitate the process where the client moves from the identification of treatment issues to a process of action in modifying their life-course circumstances.

LEARNING CHECK

1. In this case, the offender is predicted to reoffend but he or she is allowed on community supervision due to the effectiveness of his or her legal representation or some other odd course of events, but then he or she later does in fact commit an offense.
   a. False Positive
   b. True Positive
   c. True Negative
   d. False Negative
2. The ____________________________ implies that the offender is predicted not to reoffend but the prediction turns out to be false.
   a. False Positive
   b. True Positive

c. True Negative
d. False Negative

3. The MMPI-2 and the MMPI-2 CJCR both go beyond mere recidivism prediction but instead include mental health and security classification determinations.
a. True
b. False

4. Which of the following is among the nine behavioral dimensions of the MMPI-2?
a. Indications of socially deviant behavior or attitudes
b. Apparent need for social participation; extroversion
c. Likelihood of mature, responsible behavior; positive response to supervision
d. Likelihood of positive favorable response to vocational programming
e. All of the above

5. ________________________ are what agencies hope to obtain as often as possible. These are perfect predictions of offender behavior.
a. False Positive
b. True Positive
c. True Negative
d. False Negative

CONCLUSION

Assessment processes are among those that are least understood by many correctional treatment specialists but, ironically, are perhaps the most important aspects of correctional treatment. Often this is because the processes associated with assessment are more structured, linear, and systematic than is a typical counseling relationship. Further, the assessment process tends to focus on details, from data gathering to assessment testing, all the way through classification and treatment planning, it is clear that a sense of detail and structure is inherent to the process. This process, while utilizing both subjective and objective forms of assessment, tends to distill the efforts of the clinician to a refined determination that can often seem constraining to many counselors.

However, assessment provides clarity in purpose when proceeding with the counseling relationship. The ability to set realistic and structured treatment plans that are tailored to achieve some basic therapeutic goal is enhanced by the assessment process. The use of various scales and instruments help to provide some sort of assurance that the initial appraisal of the client's situation is based on factors more solid than the single perception of the client or the therapist. This alone implies a degree of implicit collaboration between the client and the counselor. Further, when clients provide information during assessment, they are in fact contributing to their own treatment planning and wise therapists will be sure to articulate this to the client. Further still, the keen therapist will utilize the assessment process throughout the components of the treatment planning process and will continually reassess or evaluate the progress of the client in terms of the initial assessment. Such comparisons, over time, ensure that progress remains pointed in the correct direction and also provides a therapeutic map from which the therapist and the client may proceed.

In the end, it should be found that most successful clients will be those who had a successful assessment. The ability to plan treatment strategies will be based from the information that is obtained from this process. The process of moving from the assessment and treatment planning phases to action stages where clients provide collaborative input on the process can be enhanced by using techniques of motivational interviewing. Such techniques provide for collaborative treatment planning and action between the client and the counselor. When clients are collaboratively involved in goal setting that incorporates the assessment information, success is increased due to the fact that more relevant issues will be addressed with the client's motivation being woven into the process due to the collaborative nature of the agreed-upon goals. With each passing juncture in treatment, it may prove therapeutic for the client to take a reflective glance to the point and time of assessment as a means of determining how far they have come. For the therapist, such reflection provides moments where therapeutic delivery can be enhanced, providing evidence-based insight to the client that positive change can be obtained, both in peripheral and in measurable terms.

Essay Questions

1. In your own words, how would you define the concept of assessment? Why is it important to properly assess offenders prior to the implementation of a treatment plan?
2. In general, what type of information is produced by the MMPI? Why is this information useful and how is the information best used?
3. Describe the difference between false positives and false negatives as well as the difference between true positives and true negatives. What is the likely consequence of counselors not properly identifying the presence of each of these concepts?
4. Describe and discuss static and dynamic risk factors. What is the difference between these types of factors? From a counselor's standpoint, is one more important than the other? Why or why not?
5. What is the difference between objective and subjective forms of assessment? Provide an example for each.

Treatment Planning Exercise

For the case below, students must identify the clinical issues that confront Rick. Specific diagnoses should be identified and the *DSM-IV-TR* clinical Axis to which each disorder belongs should also be identified. Further, students should attempt to guess the overall level of functioning for this youthful offender using the criteria from the GAF Scale. Students should provide a specific number that they believe corresponds with the identified level of functioning.

For this assignment, students should refer to Figure 3.3. This figure provides a copy of the **Juvenile Sex Offenders Assessment Protocol-II** (JSOAP-II), use this instrument to assess Rick as a juvenile sex offender. Specifically, students should identify the static and dynamic risk factors on the JSOAP-II that they believe apply to Rick. Using this scale students should identify and generate what they believe would be the static score, the dynamic score, and the total JSOAP score for Rick. In doing so, students should also explain why they have chosen to give the scores that they settle upon.

It is important that students not focus on the specific number that they award but instead focus on their justification for their award as related to the JSOAP-II and Rick's clinical description.

The Case of Rick

Rick is a 16-year-old male who has had numerous encounters with law enforcement. Currently, Rick is on juvenile probation and attends an alternative school. Among other things, Rick was diagnosed with attention-deficit hyperactivity disorder in his early childhood. Rick's parents have brought Rick in for counseling to your office because even they do not believe that his probation supervision is sufficiently restrictive.

Rick has routinely been in trouble at school and in the community. He surrounds himself with a number of younger youth who look up to his acts of violence and intimidation. Rick also experiences periods of very serious anger and is given to outbursts when he is frustrated. He has been known to hit other kids when he is angry and he has even made threats at teachers during his periods of intense fury.

Rick is also very good at lying. He lies constantly about his whereabouts and is difficult to locate. He is fond of going from house to house and friend to friend. He also stays out late despite his parent's attempts to keep him from doing so. He breaks the city ordinance curfew for juveniles. In fact, two nights ago Rick was reportedly out in a neighborhood at 2:00 a.m. with some other youth, drinking beer and beating mailboxes with an aluminum bat. One of the girls who was with the group told him that he was immature and he should stop. Rick called her a number of inappropriate names and then threw a brick at the girl, luckily he missed.

At age 11, Rick was diagnosed with conduct disorder in addition to his diagnosis of ADHD. He exhibited acts of cruelty toward pets and other animals and seemed indifferent to the pain they suffered. In fact, he indicated a bizarre and morbid fascination with their death. The violence committed by Rick continued to progress and, by the age of 13, Rick had coerced one of his 9-year-old female cousins into sexual intercourse. In fact, he had done this on three different occasions, and, were it not for another family member accidentally walking in on the third circumstance of victimization, it is unknown how many times he would have done that. This was reported to the authorities and Rick was charged with this offense in juvenile court.

Bibliography

American Psychiatric Association. (2000). *Diagnostic and statistical manual of mental disorders*. Arlington, VA: American Psychiatric Association.

Andrews, D., & Bonta, J. (2003). *Level of supervision inventory—revised (LSI-R)*. Retrieved from: http://www.mhs.com/LSI.htm.

Ashford, J. B., Sales, B. D., & Reid, W. H. (2002). *Treating adult and juvenile offenders with special needs*. Washington, DC: American Psychological Association.

Bartol, C. R. (2002). *Criminal behavior: A psychological approach* (5th ed.). Upper Saddle River, NJ: Prentice Hall.

Belenko, S. (1998). *Behind bars: Substance abuse and America's prison population*. New York: National Center on Addiction and Substance Abuse at Columbia University.

Bureau of Justice Statistics. (1999). *Drug use and crime*. Washington, DC: U.S. Department of Justice, Office of Justice Programs.

Carbonnell, J. L., & Perkins, R. (2000). *Diagnosis and assessment of criminal offenders*. In P. Van Voorhis, M. Braswell, & D. Lester (Eds.), *Correctional Counseling & Rehabilitation* (4th ed.). Cincinnati, OH: Anderson Publishing Company.

Drummond, R. J. (1996). *Appraisal procedures for counselors and helping professionals* (3rd ed.). Englewood Cliffs, NJ: Prentice-Hall, Inc.

Enos, R., & Southern, S. (1996). *Correctional case management*. Cincinnati, OH: Anderson Publishing.

Hanser, R. D. (2006). *Special needs offenders in the community*. Upper Saddle River, NJ: Prentice Hall.

Hanser, R. D. (2009). *Community corrections*. Belmont, CA: Sage Publications.

Hettema, J., Steele, J., and Miller, W. R. (2005). Motivational interviewing. *Annual Review of Clinical Psychology, 1*(1), 91–111.

Project MATCH Research Group. (1997). Matching alcoholism treatments to client heterogeneity: Project MATCH posttreatment drinking outcomes. *Journal of Studies on Alcohol, 58*, 7–29.

Reentry Media Outreach. (2005). *Health challenges of reentry: Briefing paper*. Indianapolis, IN: Reentry Media Outreach. Retrieved from: http://www.reentrymediaoutreach.org/pdfs/health_bp.pdf.

Rubak, S., Sandboek, A., Lauritzen, T., & Christensen, B. (2005). Motivational interviewing: A systematic review and meta-analysis. *British Journal of General Practice, 55*(513), 305–312.

Van Voorhis, P., Braswell, M., & Lester, D. (2000). *Correctional counseling and rehabilitation* (4th ed.). Cincinnati, OH: Anderson Publishing Company.

Walters, S. T., Clark, M. D., Gingerich, R., & Meltzer, M. L. (2007). *A guide for probation and parole: Motivating offenders to change*. Washington, DC: National Institute of Corrections.

4

Basic Rapport Building, Goal Setting, and Implementation

CHAPTER OBJECTIVES

After reading this chapter, you will be able to:

1. Understand the importance of the therapeutic alliance.
2. Know the different skills necessary for the formation of a positive therapeutic alliance (practical and interpersonal).
3. Understand the need for problem identification.
4. Identify various types of coping techniques.
5. Be familiar with the process of goal setting and implementation as well as the termination of the counseling relationship.

PART ONE: THE THERAPEUTIC ALLIANCE

According to various researches, the **therapeutic alliance** is one of the most powerful constructs, within a counseling relationship, able to produce positive changes in behavior and cognition. It is important to understand that the therapeutic alliance is largely an intellectual concept that describes both practical and interpersonal skills. And, one of the problems with intellectual concepts is that they can often be difficult to define. In fact, a working definition of a therapeutic alliance for one counselor may be wholly different from the definition provided by another counselor. This is because the therapeutic alliance is as much subjective as objective, or as much art as science.

Generally, the therapeutic alliance is a concept that describes the process of counselors and offenders collaboratively identifying goals and tasks to be accomplished within the counseling relationship. The most important component of this relationship, however, is the degree to which counselors and offenders are able to establish an interpersonal bond through which much of the healing and corrective action takes place. Bordin (1979) describes the therapeutic alliance as the vehicle through which psychotherapies are effective. In essence, it is not so much the counseling modality that is important, but rather the degree to which counselors and offenders are able to establish an affective bond that produces the necessary trust that fosters an environment in which an offender is willing to psychologically and emotionally expose himself or herself in order to heal.

Offenders are more likely to respond positively to counseling when counselors are able to consistently portray themselves as nurturing and understanding allies. A number of studies have found that the therapeutic alliance is directly related to such outcomes as whether or not a person will continue counseling (CSAT, 2005). Petry and Bickel (1999) found that among clients with moderate to severe psychiatric problems, less than 25% of those reporting weak therapeutic alliances completed treatment. Obviously, this is an important point, largely because it is unlikely that offenders will undergo substantive change without structured and professionally delivered services aimed at reconfiguring cognitive and behavioral responses to certain stimuli likely to produce criminal behavior. Green (2004) provides additional support by stating he believes that "treatments (counseling) succeed mainly on the therapist's ability to develop and maintain an emotionally positive therapeutic alliance with all members of the system in treatment" (p. 2).

How then do we define therapeutic alliance—a concept deemed so critical to the counseling process? One way of defining a therapeutic alliance is to again borrow from Green's (2004) language and say that it is a positive emotional connection between a counselor and an offender. But, what is a positive emotional connection? This is where the task of defining a social science concept becomes challenging. For our purposes, we believe the following definition of a therapeutic alliance best captures the essence of how it contributes to the process of an offender enriching his or her emotional landscape leading to the reformation of cognitions and behavior that are in better alignment with societal norms.

Put in less scientific way, the therapeutic alliance is simply a genuine interest in a fellow human being and a respect for the person being in a potentially therapeutic setting. It is the first and critical step in the counseling process in which a bond is established between the counselor and offender that serves to enhance the likelihood of producing lasting, positive change.

Creating a Therapeutic Alliance

Creating a therapeutic alliance with an offender requires both practical skills as well as interpersonal skills. Practical skills include such concepts as probing, proper use of questions, accurately paraphrasing what an offender has articulated, and providing appropriate feedback. These skills are thought to be the most teachable to new counselors. There are specific protocols and procedures that can be employed for each. Interpersonal skills such as empathy and genuineness are much more difficult to teach. A counselor's ability to express empathy and genuineness in a therapeutic setting has more to do with personal qualities as well as their views of the specific offender. And, although more difficult to teach, it is the interpersonal skills that have been consistently found to be responsible for more of the variance in the establishment of a positive therapeutic alliance (Summers & Barber, 2003).

Practical Skills

Probing is a concept that describes the process of attempting to ascertain the essence of an offender's emotional and psychological problems through the use of guided questions. The **use of questions** is an important component of probing, and as mentioned by Gladding (1996) usually begins with *who, what, where, or how.* In addition, Masters (2004) notes that probing questions

Therapeutic Alliance—An intellectual concept that describes the process of a real, authentic, and sincere connection between a counselor and an offender based on the attributes of professionalism, openness, honesty, and decency that provide the foundation for effectively identifying and working through psychological and emotional-based dysfunction.

should not be used to trick an offender or as an attempt to avoid an offender's questions. In order for meaningful information to be obtained through the employment of probing, the technique must be accompanied by empathic genuineness. An example:

OFFENDER: My life is very stressful!

COUNSELOR: What is it about your life that you find most stressful?

Here the offender is making a broad statement in which the primary goal is to communicate that his or her current life circumstance is difficult to manage and troublesome. It is likely that there are a variety of events and circumstances that are contributing to the global assessment of his or her life being stressful. At this point, the possible stressors are legion and precisely why a good probing question may consist of guiding the offender to explore what he or she considers to be the most salient of the stressors. "Explore," however, is the key word. In many circumstances the offender will not immediately identify the most pressing of the stressors. In fact, the most significant stressor may be the circumstance that triggers the most shame, which is where much of the upcoming work will take place, but also an area the offender is likely to try and avoid. Therefore, even though the counselor's response is an attempt to uncover the most pointed stressor it is probable that the offender will provide a broad snapshot of his or her current life circumstance inadvertently providing the counselor with rich and useful information that will guide future questions.

This technique also allows the counselor to begin intellectually organizing the direction of the session through the extrapolation and exploration of what the offender deems most critical. In addition, this type of question may also serve to inform the offender of the counselor's awareness that it is not uncommon, or surprising, that individuals often experience many different stressors at single points in time, reducing the negative psychological effects of feeling as if he or she is the only one in such dire circumstances.

As noted by Gladding (1996), most probing questions should not begin with the word *why*? Initiating a question with the word "why" can sometimes be interpreted as a subtle form of judgmentalism (e.g., "Why would you do such a thing?"). In addition, a probing question that begins with why will often be interpreted by the offender as a sign of disapproval which is likely to lead to defensive behaviors. Defensive behavior will undermine the counseling process via its damage to the creation of a therapeutic alliance.

Egan (1990) provides several good suggestions regarding the appropriate use of probing questions that were later adopted by Masters (2004) and specifically worded to address offenders. They include the following:

1. Do not assault offenders with a lot of questions.
2. Ask questions that serve a purpose.
3. Ask open-ended questions that get offenders to talk about specific experiences, behaviors, and feelings.
4. Keep the questions focused on the offender (Masters, 2004, p. 42).

In essence, each question should serve a purpose by attempting to identify problems that are stymieing the offender's ability to live and function in a healthy manner. Below are additional questions that may serve as a guide:

- What are some of the issues you think should be addressed in order to solve the problem?
- What type of plan do you think would be most successful in reaching your goal?
- How can others help you?
- In your past interactions, who is responsible for causing you the most amount of pain?

Often these types of questions will be helpful because they not only serve a purpose but they also "allow the offender to take responsibility for the change process, and lead to the expression of the offender's feelings, experiences, and behaviors" (Masters, 2004, p. 42).

Once a counselor has successfully initiated a probing question that elicits a response from an offender it is critical that the counselor fully understand the intended meaning of the response. Successful interpretation of the offender's intended meaning is often accomplished through the employment of the remaining practical skills, vital to the formulation of a positive therapeutic alliance. These skills include **paraphrasing**, **reflective listening**, **summarizing**, and **feedback.** Each of these concepts describes the process of a counselor verbally responding to an offender in a method that demonstrates one of several positions:

1. The counselor fully understands the offender's intended message
2. The counselor understands some of the offender's intended message
3. The counselor completely "missed" the offender's intended message.

Often these skills can occur simultaneously. For example, a counselor may first paraphrase an offender's statement in order to summarize the key points and through the process of feedback provide guidance or suggestions meant to inform the offender, as well as solicit additional statements meant to explore deeper psychological and emotional issues.

Reflective listening is a skill in which a counselor demonstrates that he or she has accurately heard and understood an offender's communication by restating its meaning. That is, you provide a guess about what the offender intended to convey and express this in a responsive statement, not a question. "Reflective listening is a way of checking rather than assuming that you *know* what is meant" (Miller & Rollnick, 1991, p. 75).

Reflective listening strengthens the therapeutic relationship between the counselor and the offender and encourages further exploration of problems and feelings. This form of communication is particularly appropriate in early stages of counseling. Reflective listening helps the offender by providing a synthesis of content and process. It reduces the likelihood of resistance, encourages the offender to keep talking, communicates respect, cements the therapeutic alliance, clarifies exactly what the client means, and reinforces motivation (Miller, Leckman, Delaney, & Tinkcom, 1992).

This process has a tremendous amount of flexibility, and you can use reflective listening to reinforce your offender's positive ideas (Miller et al., 1992). The following dialogue gives some examples of counselor's responses that illustrate effective reflective listening. Essentially, true reflective listening requires continuous alert tracking of the offender's verbal and nonverbal responses and their possible meanings, formulation of reflections at the appropriate level of complexity, and ongoing adjustment of hypotheses.

COUNSELOR: What else concerns you about your drinking?

OFFENDER: Well, I'm not sure I'm concerned about it, but I do wonder sometimes if I'm drinking too much.

COUNSELOR: Too much for . . . ?

OFFENDER: For my own good, I guess. I mean it's not like it's really serious, but sometimes when I wake up in the morning I feel really awful, and I can't think straight most of the morning.

COUNSELOR: It messes up your thinking, your concentration.

OFFENDER: Yes, and sometimes I have trouble remembering things.

COUNSELOR: And you wonder if that might be because you're drinking too much?

OFFENDER: Well, I know it is sometimes.

COUNSELOR: You're pretty sure about that. But maybe there's more . . .

OFFENDER: Yeah, even when I'm not drinking, sometimes I mix things up, and I wonder about that.

COUNSELOR: Wonder if . . . ?

OFFENDER: If alcohol's pickling my brain, I guess.

COUNSELOR: You think that can happen to people, maybe to you.

OFFENDER: Well, can't it? I've heard that alcohol kills brain cells.

COUNSELOR: Um-hmm. I can see why that would worry you.

OFFENDER: But I don't think I'm an alcoholic or anything.

COUNSELOR: You don't think you're that bad off, but you do wonder if maybe you're overdoing it and damaging yourself in the process.

OFFENDER: Yeah.

COUNSELOR: Kind of a scary thought. What else worries you?

Most counselors find it useful to periodically summarize what has occurred in a counseling session. Summarizing consists of distilling the essence of what an offender has expressed and communicating it back. "Summaries reinforce what has been said, show that you have been listening carefully, and prepare the client to move on" (Miller & Rollnick, 1991, p. 78). Summarizing also serves strategic purposes. In presenting a summary, a counselor can select what information should be included and what can be minimized or left out. Correction of a summary by the offender should be invited, and this often leads to further comments and discussion. Summarizing helps offenders consider their own responses and contemplate their own experience. It also gives the counselor and offender an opportunity to notice what might have been overlooked as well as incorrectly stated.

Throughout the literature it is clear that feedback is a necessary component to successful counseling and usually works best when it is personal and individualized to the specific offender. When providing feedback, however, the counselor must take every precaution to ensure it is provided in a respectful manner. A confrontational or judgmental approach is likely to leave the offender unreceptive (CSAT, 1999).

Not all offenders respond in the same way to feedback. One person may be alarmed to find that he or she drinks much more in a given week than comparable peers but be unconcerned about potential health risks. Another may be concerned about potential health risks at this level of drinking. Still another may not be impressed by such aspects of substance use as the amount of money spent on substances, possible impotence, or the level of impairment especially with regard to driving ability caused by even low blood alcohol concentrations. Personalized feedback can be applied to other lifestyle issues as well and can be used throughout the counseling process. Feedback about improvements is especially valuable as a method of reinforcing progress.

Masters (2004) draws on the work of Corey (2000) and provides the following suggestions meant to help correctional counselors provide effective feedback to offenders:

1. Global feedback should be avoided in favor of specific feedback.
2. Feedback should be cogent and clear-cut.
3. Positive feedback zeroing in on the offender's strength is more helpful than negative feedback.

4. Timing is important in giving feedback. Immediate feedback is more valuable than waiting until later.
5. Delivering feedback in a nonjudgmental way is important to minimize defensiveness on the part of the offender.
6. Corrective feedback has greater probability of being accepted if it emphasizes observable behaviors.
7. Feedback may be easier to take if the counselor indicates to the offender how he or she has been affected by the offender's behavior (Masters, 2004, p. 43).

Interpersonal Skills

As mentioned above, creating and maintaining a positive therapeutic alliance requires both practical and interpersonal skills. The practical skills mentioned are much more amenable to direct instruction or training. For example, within the context of a counseling class, a student may be taught how and when to provide feedback, or how to use probing questions and then paraphrase. And, students may even be provided with handouts that can be taken into actual counseling sessions and used as guides. Interpersonal skills such as genuineness and empathy, however, are much more difficult to teach. This is because the ability to display genuineness and empathy, so vital to the establishment of a positive therapeutic alliance, has much more to do with the counselor's own internal congruence. In other words, how comfortable is a counselor with his or her own feelings? How aware is the counselor of his or her own negative emotionality as well as the origins of such negative emotion? In this context **congruence** is a concept that describes "a state of wholeness and integration" within the counselor (Witty, 2007, p. 37). The first necessary step to provide genuine and empathic counseling services to offenders is the counselor's own deep exploration into the midst of his or her own dysfunction.

According to Ormont (1999), empathy is the ability to "experience another person's feeling or attitude while still holding on to our own attitude and outlook" (p. 145); it is the foundation counselors should operate from when relating to and interacting with offenders. The ability of a counselor to express empathy enables clients to begin to recognize and own their feelings, an essential step toward managing them and learning to empathize with the feelings of others. What often gets many offenders into trouble is their lack of ability to empathize with other human beings. Due to their own abuse and neglect, often experienced at the hands of their caregivers, many offenders have become "numb" to the harmful effects of their actions. Unfortunately, for many offenders, their first experience with genuineness and empathy will be as a result of their interaction with a correctional counselor.

Furthermore, genuine and empathic relating must be used consistently over time in order to keep a positive therapeutic alliance intact. This caveat is even more critical for offenders with co-occurring disorders, because they usually have lower motivation to address either their mental or substance abuse problems. In addition, they may have greater difficulty understanding and relating to other people and need even more understanding and support to make a major lifestyle change such as adopting a healthier lifestyle and abstinence from substance abuse and criminality in general. Support and empathy from the correctional counselor can help create and maintain the therapeutic alliance, increase offender motivation, assist with medication adherence, model behavior that can help the offender build more productive relationships, and support the offender as he or she makes a major life transition.

One of the biggest proponents of employing an empathic style of relating within the counseling process is Carl Rogers. In fact, Rogers (1957) person-centered style of therapy is predicated on the idea that change is possible if the right climate of facilitative conditions is present. Rogers

(1957) also believed that some persons and environments undermine and inhibit growth instead of fostering growth. A positive therapeutic alliance is the first step in fostering growth.

When trying to create the foundation on which a positive therapeutic alliance can be cultivated, a very important concept must be discussed. This concept is called judgmentalism. Judgmentalism has been discussed in various places throughout this book due to its profound ability to disrupt relationships. **Judgmentalism** is a concept that describes the process of displaying condemning or critical reactions to the thoughts, statements, or actions of another. Appreciate that judgmentalism can be displayed through both verbal and nonverbal means of communication. A counselor's rolling of the eyes may display a judgmental reaction to an offender's statement. Additionally, a counselor's question, "Why would you commit such a ridiculous act?" can significantly "zing" an offender and substantially harm or destroy a positive therapeutic alliance.

Threats to the Therapeutic Alliance

One of the greatest threats to the successful formation of a positive therapeutic alliance is attempting to work with offenders who are either reluctant or resistant to treatment. The reluctance and/or resistance may manifest itself in various ways. Some offenders will play "mind" games with the counselor; some offenders may just simply respond with lethargy or a lack of interest; some offenders may inappropriately disclose important information just as the session is ending, knowing there is not enough time to address the disclosure. These actions are usually an attempt to avoid the difficult process of exploring deep psychological pain and trauma necessary for healing. Before delving into the psychodynamics of resistance and reluctance, however, it is important to note the difference between the two and appreciate that both reluctant and resistant offenders challenge the counselor's ability to foster a positive therapeutic alliance.

A **reluctant offender** is the offender who has been referred to counseling by a third party. And, this is often the case in correctional counseling. Usually, counseling will be initiated as a result of a judge's mandate stipulating that the offender attend counseling in lieu of being incarcerated, or as part of his or her incarceration. The main issue with reluctant clients is the fact that they often do not believe that they need counseling and view it as a process to be tolerated until adjudication is complete (Gladding, 1996).

A **resistant offender** is the person who seeks out the counseling process and willingly attends but is unwilling to change. In essence, the resistant offender has not yet committed to the necessary work change demands. Often times, the resistant offender will initiate counseling to stave off painful internal recognitions that change is necessary but is not yet able to engage the often grueling process. Sack (1988) mentions "that one of the most common forms of resistance is the simple statement 'I don't know' " (p. 180). Such responses often make it very difficult for counselors to proceed primarily because of the offender's unwillingness to explore feeling and emotion as opposed to "surfacy" thoughts (Gladding, 1996).

Gladding (1996) cites several different authors who provide suggestions on how to deal with reluctant and resistant offenders. Elliot and Elliot (2006) suggest that one way to deal with reluctance is by asking the offender, "What did you feel when you found out you had to come to counseling?" Here the counselor's most important function is to make sure the response provided by the offender is one grounded in feeling or emotion as opposed to just a thought. An example of an offender answering the question with a thought as opposed to a feeling may be, "Oh nothing really—just something I have to tolerate to get out of this trouble." Not much a counselor can do with this type of a response. The offender must be guided into exploring his or her emotion. A feeling- or emotion-based response would consist of an answer that may contain such concepts as anger, fear, or sadness. For example, an offender may say, "Well I felt scared when I was told I had to attend counseling." In this case the counselor has just gained rich and meaningful information. And, the counselor's response should be, "Can you tell me more about that?" This question when accompanied with genuineness and empathy may open the door to the beginnings of a positive therapeutic alliance. It may be that the offender felt scared because he or she knew it would be necessary to explore painful and traumatic events, which up to this point the offender did not have the strength to confront.

Additional threats to the therapeutic alliance may come in the form of various defense mechanisms commonly enacted by offenders. Common defenses displayed by offenders include denial, projection, rationalization, displacement, reaction formation, regression, and sublimation. Before exploring each of these mechanisms it is important to understand that, similar to both reluctance and resistance, these defense mechanisms must be confronted by the counselor because they "involve denials or distortions of reality" (Schultz & Shultz, 2005, p. 58). The only way the counselor will get to the offender's emotion is by first removing the armor constructed of these defense mechanisms. The offender's employment of these mechanisms must be confronted; however, the confrontation must take place in the spirit of empathy and understanding. Trying and appreciating that defense mechanisms are primarily a response aimed at reducing anxiety will help counselors to proceed with this difficult task. The counseling process may be very scary to many offenders, and the idea of disclosing personal and painful information is likely to produce disturbing levels of anxiety. Therefore, the counselor must be vigilant in remaining cognizant of the fact that these behaviors are normal and should not be taken personally. The following description of each defense mechanism is borrowed in large part from the work of Schultz and Schultz (2005).

Denial—is a concept that describes the process of repressing troubling thoughts usually related to some threat(s) or traumatic event(s). It is the offender's way of avoiding anxiety likely to be experienced in the event his or her true feelings are exposed. For example, some offenders may adamantly deny their feelings of fear in the presence of certain stimuli because of their belief that the expression of fear shows weakness that can be exploited by others.

Projection—is a concept that describes the process of attributing disturbing thoughts or impulses onto another in an attempt to alleviate their threatening nature. An offender accused of rape may deny his need to control in favor of a less threatening thought such as, "She wanted to have sex; I could tell by the way she was dressed."

Rationalization—is a concept that describes the process of an offender reframing one's behavior so that it becomes less threatening and more acceptable. The offender who beats his wife may rationalize his actions by saying, "She knows better than to look at another man—what else am I suppose to do?"

Displacement—is a concept that describes the process of shifting one's impulses from an unavailable object to one that is available. For example, an offender may feel helpless in his ability to stand up to his condescending boss who routinely treats him with a lack of respect. In stead of confronting his boss, however, the offender redirects his anger toward his family in a misguided attempt to reduce his tension and stress.

Reaction formation—is a concept that describes the process of an offender actively displaying a feeling or impulse that is opposite of what is truly being felt or experienced. For example, an offender who feels threatened by his impulse toward violence against women may repress these feelings and attempt to replace them with more acceptable behaviors like actively advocating for stiffer sanctions against men who batter their wives.

Regression—is a concept that describes the process of an offender cognitively retreating to a time in life where there was less anxiety and frustration. An example of regression may be where the offender simply wants the counselor to tell him what to do as opposed to exploring the pain of past events.

Sublimation—is a concept that describes the process of altering one's impulses. It is important to note that sublimation is a form of displacement. It is a compromise. An example of sublimation could be where an offender diverts uncomfortable sexual energy into some type of artistically creative endeavor. The essence of sublimation is that it is an attempt to alleviate anxiety caused by socially unacceptable impulses by engaging in activities that are socially acceptable and maybe even admirable.

Each of these defense mechanisms poses a serious threat to a positive therapeutic alliance, as well as to the offender's ability to experience meaningful change. These mechanisms work to reduce the offender's level of anxiety but are not capable of producing real satisfaction or happiness. These defenses, at best, are only able to disguise human flaws; they are not able to resolve them. The truth about oneself is always present. And, because of their inability to resolve deep-seated psychological and emotional issues the prolonged use of these defense mechanisms will often lead to a massive buildup of tension. Unfortunately, when this tension is finally discharged, usually in the presence of multiple stressors, it is often by way of a violent criminal act. The best way for a counselor to begin the process of reducing an offender's reliance on these defense mechanisms is by first identifying when they are being used and then responding with empathic and understanding guidance in an attempt to build trust through which the offender is more likely to explore the revelation of true feeling and emotion.

SECTION SUMMARY

Creating a therapeutic alliance is the first and most important step in the counseling process. Through the alliance the offender must feel safe to share and explore feelings and emotion. In order to develop effective alliances, counselors must be internally congruent and able to traverse a variety of threatening feelings and emotion. The process of sharing negative emotion is not natural for most people. Offenders will often exert significant effort in the attempt to disguise their true feelings. Counselors must remain cognizant of the fact that many of the defensive behaviors enacted by offenders are attempts to stave off powerful pangs of anxiety. An effective counselor will recognize this fact and not take the resistance personally. If taken personally, the alliance will be all but impossible to establish and the possibility of the offender experiencing a genuine corrective transformation is greatly diminished.

LEARNING CHECK

1. The interpersonal skills needed to create a therapeutic alliance are difficult to be taught to new counselors.
   a. True
   b. False
2. Defense mechanisms are primarily employed to reduce feelings of anxiety.
   a. True
   b. False
3. The therapeutic alliance should be created later in the counseling process.
   a. True
   b. False

4. Reflective listening is not an important component within the therapeutic alliance.
   a. True
   b. False
5. Summarizing is meant to dictate to the client what he or she needs to do in order to change his or her behavior.
   a. True
   b. False

PART TWO: PROBLEM IDENTIFICATION

In identifying and defining the problem that an offender may report, it is important for the correctional counselor to gain an understanding of the circumstances that occurred prior to the problematic event or behavior. This is particularly true if the event or problem behavior is repetitive. One example would be the typical reference to *people*, *places*, and *things*, often heard among recovering addicts who discuss the factors that lead to relapse. In this example, certain places, certain people, or certain things are present that tend to lead these individuals to relapse.

Identification of the precipitating event is very important because the counselor must identify the offender's perception of the situation. If the cognitions associated with the event are not identified properly, there will be no therapeutic interactive communication. Changing offender perceptions of these events is essential if increased functioning is desired (Kanel, 2003). It is clear that this is true for persons contending with some form of trauma or for those persons going through substance-abuse relapse. Indeed, these types of problems are well known as having triggered events that aid in the onset of lowered functioning or disruptive behavior. However, the process of addressing cognitions that result in personal distress may not be so easy with other disorders or problems, such as depression or symptoms associated with various personality disorders. The process of recognizing the precipitating event, addressing the offender's perception of that event, identifying subjective distress, and impacting the overall functioning of the offender is best presented by an illustration from Kanel's (2003) text. This process and the means by which offenders are aided in improving their overall functioning is illustrated in Exhibit 4.1, which provides a good schematic of the process that we are referring to.

EXHIBIT 4.1

Perception of Precipitating Event and Its Impact on Functioning

Process Leading to Lowered Functioning

Precipitating Event	=	Perception of Event	=	Subjective Level of Stress Increased	=	Overall Functioning Is Impaired

Process Leading to Increased Functioning

Client Perception of Precipitating Event Is Chanced & Coping Mechanisms Are Learned	=	Subjective Level of Stress Is Reduced	=	Overall Functioning Improves

Source: Kanel, K. (2003). *A guide to crisis intervention* (2nd ed.). Pacific Grove, CA: Brooks/Cole.

In some cases it may be difficult to get the offender to realize his or her own personal distress. Clients in both the offender community and in other populations may simply be oblivious to their impaired functioning because they black out painful memories and cultivate alternate perceptions. Also, there may be cultural norms at play where offenders are less likely to disclose information related to problem-evoking events due to feelings of shame or weakness. Further, readers should always keep in mind that this text is aimed at the offender population. In many offender groups, it is considered a personal weakness to discuss events that cause lowered functioning. Discussion of anxiety-producing events is not likely to be valued activities among the criminal subculture.

Consider, for example, a bona fide gang member who is incarcerated. These offenders have likely been involved in numerous crimes and altercations, and have probably had exposure to a number of trauma-inducing incidents. In a group counseling context, these offenders will typically only address their feelings related to these experiences on a topical level due to strong disapproval among the gang culture. Further, if the counselor is not trained in gang lore and behavior, but is otherwise able to relate to that offender population, the entire process of addressing the gang member's perception of the event will likely be fruitless. The effects of gang culture upon the individual member's thinking are strong and all-consuming; the gang is that person's family and it is through the gang family that the offender has his or her esteem needs met. The gang is that offender's world and the correctional counselor must be able to operate from that world's perspective in order to both reach the offender and to encourage him or her to change some of his or her perceptions regarding events that result in low functioning and/or criminal behaviors.

If such an offender client were in distress, he or she might never admit it and/or might genuinely not recognize the experience as distress. Indeed, if he or she were a substance abuser he or she may be masking that distress with alcohol (a common technique, albeit a dysfunctional technique) because this is acceptable within the gang culture. They may moderate the effects of anxiety with various forms of marijuana since this drug is known to most frequently produce feelings of elation and happiness. Each of these forms of coping would be condoned in most criminal groups but yet would keep the offender from addressing his or her own personal trauma, distress, or impaired functioning.

One other point to be noted in our discussion regarding the recognition of distress is that the dysfunctional forms of coping may not always be so clear and obvious as the examples just given. One primary example is the use of anger and/or violence. Often, male offenders going through states of depression and/or anxiety will resort to violent activity to mask these feelings as well. This may sound counterintuitive to the reader, and it should. Over time, many offenders have learned, either through early socialization in dysfunctional family systems, their peer groups, or through criminal subcultures, that being violent gets respect. Likewise, acting, threatening, and/or bluffing can get the same benefits. Over time, these persons may be conditioned to address their negative affects through the heightened and adrenaline-charged feelings associated with violent activities. Further, the use of such violence (or threat of violence) keeps other criminals at bay and allows their trauma, lowered esteem, and sense of anxiety to remain undiscovered among their other dangerous peers.

This can create a very difficult psychological conundrum for the correctional counselor because such negative forms of coping have been learned and reinforced over years and the reward mechanisms are so powerful. Indeed, some of these reward mechanisms might be physiological (i.e., increased serotonin levels when winning physical altercations) resulting in a physical high for that offender. Other rewards might be social in nature, such as obtaining respect from peers as reinforcement of this activity thereby meeting esteem needs of belonging and acceptance. Yet again, some rewards might achieve basic needs for security, as their violent acts work to deter other potentially violent offenders from instigating conflict due to their desire to avoid potential injury. It is clear then that these mechanisms can lead to a reliance on violence as a means to solve problems, and, as the offender becomes more and more accustomed to this, he or she will lose sight of one's own fears, sense of fragile esteem, and/or source of anxiety, burying that and/or deliberately not addressing such issues.

In the criminal subculture (and this is especially true in many larger prison systems) it is not considered "manly" to expose such feelings of vulnerability. Thus, strong external mechanisms will often undermine the counselor's ability to address affect that is associated with the precipitating event. Given that many offenders are recycled in and out of the jail or prison and that many will return to the same communities (gang members will in many cases come from the same area and recycle together, in and out of the jail system and back-and-forth within the same neighborhood), an exportation of these prison values occurs and is thus transmitted to persons acting on the streets. In such cases, it may well be that these values are further cultivated among street offenders who may not have yet experienced long-term incarceration. This then creates a set of values that are also taught in the neighborhood and are then imported back into the prison. In addition to this, many of these members (particularly hard-core teens and youth) may have dysfunctional family systems that further contribute to this environment, and it is very easy to see why these offenders may have absolutely no incentive in recognizing their own distress and why they simply may not be willing to address their own perceptual sets that have emerged in reaction to this combination of psychological and sociological influences.

Blind Spots

Issues such as these may then result in corresponding blind spots among many of the offender population. For purposes of this text, **blind spots** refer to misperceptions that persons have regarding social realities either due to a lack of exposure, a lack of knowledge, or due to faulty perceptions that the person has developed. Blind spots are not deliberate forms of resistance but may, over time, emerge due to a series conditioning experiences that limit the perceptual view that a person may have of the world or of themselves. Egan (1994) perhaps sums up our intent in bringing up blind spots in offender therapy by stating that:

> The focus here is on the discrepancies, distortions, evasions, games, tricks, excuse making, and smoke screens that keep clients mired in their problem situations. All of us have ways of defending ourselves from ourselves, others, and the world. But our defenses are two-edged swords. Daydreaming may help me to cope with the dreariness of my everyday life, but it may also keep me from doing something to better myself. Blaming others for my misfortunes helps me save face, but it disrupts interpersonal relationships and prevents me from developing a healthy sense of self-responsibility. The purpose of helping clients challenge themselves is not to strip clients of their defenses, which in some cases could be dangerous, but to help them overcome blind spots and develop new perspectives (p. 165).

This description, as presented by Egan (1994), is precisely what we mean when we refer to blind spots in the counseling context. Further, Egan notes that "if clients are comfortable with their delusions and profit by them, they will obviously try to keep them. If they are rewarded for playing games, inside the counseling sessions or outside, they will continue a game approach to life" (1994, p. 169).

It is important that the correctional counselor handle blindspot issues delicately or they will inadvertently damage the therapeutic alliance by building resistance and distrust in the offender. One means by which the counselor can aid the offender in challenging blind spots is through the use of a variety of techniques such as the empty chair exercise. The **empty chair technique**/exercise occurs when the counselor instructs the client to engage in a dialogue with an imaginary person who is sitting in an empty chair arranged across from them. The client is instructed to ask that "person" a series of questions and then the client must provide responses to those questions from the viewpoint of the "person," who would be sitting in that chair. Correctional counselors can have any number of imaginary persons assigned to the empty chair, such as a famous icon valued by the offender (this can be effective with teens), or perhaps a valued or respected family member, or a member of the community (i.e., a priest or a pastor from the community that the offender knew while growing up). In such cases, the counselor provides a series of questions that are relevant to the offender's own personal circumstance; the offender asks these questions of the chair and provides answers from the perspective of the imaginary person in the chair.

Further still, counselors can have their clients engage in such a dialogue but pretend as if they are themselves sitting on the chair, are talking to themselves, and are observing the dialogue from a third person point of view. This can be very effective in building introspection in the client and also tends to avoid defensiveness between the client and the therapist. This restructuring of the conversation allows the offender to both ask the questions (even though the questions are provided by the counselor) and to respond. This can deflect potential resentment and hostility and allows the offender to engage in the process on his or her own terms. This technique can be particularly useful for clients who grapple for control in their interactions. The counselor can (and should) provide simple affective reflections (reflection of feeling) while the client engages in this dialogue. Naturally, the correctional counselor should maintain the use of common attending behaviors that one would normally expect while the client engages in this exercise. The main point, however, is that counselors must let offenders complete the exercise on their own, with the counselor providing gentle (not coercive) support as they engage in the dialogue.

Leverage Points

Lastly, this and other exercises similar to this help offenders to identify and work on problems, issues, and concerns that can change their lives. This generates what Egan (1994) refers to as leverage points. **Leverage points** are those points in a therapeutic alliance between the counselor and the client that are optimal for client change and that have the most probable impact on the offender's overall future functioning. Offenders and counselors should identify those areas that are most ripe for positive gain and, in a collaborative manner, should prioritize these areas of clinical potential. If a given area of attention is important to the offender's overall functioning and if the client is willing to work on that area, then the counselor is well advised to allow the offender to work on that specifically chosen area of focus. There is a very constructive reason for this.

First, the counselor must develop a positive therapeutic alliance and maintain that alliance with the offender. Allowing the offender to have choice in the issue of focus provides a sense of autonomy and empowerment for that offender. This also aids in maintaining motivation of the offender, thereby translating to a better likelihood that the offender will be able to successfully accomplish any goals set in regard to the chosen issue. If the offender is successful in achieving the first set of objectives (agreed upon by the client and the counselor) then this also builds confidence in the offender and provides a commonly shared success between the offender and the counselor. Such an experience also increases the rapport between the client and the counselor. Second, the counselor can then progress on to another area of focus—being careful to allow the offender to have the maximum input allowable under circumstances.

The third point that should be noted about leverage points is that the counselor must focus on the "sideline" issues. It may well be that the offender has an identified area of focus that is assigned due to their offending history. Some examples might be substance abuse, domestic abuse, or sex offending, where the offender is mandated to treatment for a specific criminal behavior. While it is important that this area of focus be addressed (indeed, it is mandated), it may work well if the counselor allow for other "sideline" issues to be the area of focus over time. These other areas are not so challenging and allow the advantages to the counseling relationship that were just discussed in the preceding paragraph. However, this may be difficult in programs that are highly structured and do not allow for flexibility in the administration of the treatment regimen. In such cases, changes in the curricular approach to client intervention may be warranted in a treatment agency to accommodate the use of therapist latitude in service delivery.

Lastly, the use of the *Axis V Global Assessment of Functioning* Scale, as provided in the *DSM-IV-TR*, is critical when prioritizing leverage points. While the client may be allowed to select lower priority issues for intervention, as a means of developing rapport and ensuring client commitment to therapy, the counselor should continue to track his or her level of functioning according to the GAF scale. The point is that counselors may have to compromise with the client as to the specific issues that are addressed. In other words, even in the correctional setting, the counselor may find it necessary to "meet the offender where they are at" rather than insisting that the offender conform to the parameters developed through assessment scales. Conversely, this is not meant to undermine the utility of these scales; if they are valid and reliable then they are just that—valid and reliable.

Coping

As has been discussed earlier, offenders may have a multitude of methods by which they justify, rationalize, or excuse their problematic behaviors. Further, they may simply develop cognitive processes that allow them to overlook details or shift perceptions that define an event or problem in a manner that is divergent from their police report or other similar definition assigned by the criminal justice system. This is understandable and should be expected because these are common defense mechanisms that aid a person in coping with challenges to one's sense of self.

While these mechanisms should not be allowed to excuse the behavior, it should again be noted that counselors may have to meet offenders "where they are" psychologically if they do not want the therapeutic message to be entirely shut out from the offender's frame of reference. Rather than judging or challenging these past means of coping, the correctional counselor should encourage the offender to discuss incidents and the means by which they coped with past incidents. When doing so, the therapist is advised to use his or her active listening skills, reflecting affect and cognitive content of the offender's message. In addition, the therapist can use probing questions to express interest and to gain understanding of the client's perspective, particularly in regard to the external family, peer, or cultural factors that may impact the client's perception of these events.

Factors affecting the offender's ability to cope may result in their relapse when the client is a substance abuser. Stressors and circumstances that negatively impact the offender often result in decreased coping with subsequent challenges and are what often result in the offender's return to drugs and/or alcohol. The return to illicit drugs is, in its own right, a return to criminal behavior, and substance abuse relapse provides the impetus behind further offending. Thus recidivism rates become related to the coping ability of many offenders. Given that so many offenders present with substance abuse issues, the claim that coping correlates with recidivism likelihood is not at all unreasonable.

Lastly, any number of internal and external issues might affect an offender's ability to cope. Internally, the offender may have cognitive deficits or even health problems that limit his or her ability to handle stress. Indeed, consider the fact that the offender population tends to have physiological symptoms that are more advanced than their chronological age (Hanser, 2007). The ravages of the offender lifestyle, unhealthy choices, and the debilitating effects of incarceration lead to a more rapid physiological breakdown and this takes a toll on the offender's overall functioning and ability to cope with daily challenges. External factors may also affect this, such as with institutional racism and discrimination (remember again that a large proportion of offenders in the United States are minorities) that may have created social structure stressors that the offender is unable to overcome. Other external stressors, particularly those related to basic needs (i.e., food, shelter, clothing, and safety) may exist that further deplete the offender's resource coping ability and exacerbate his or her likelihood of relapse and/or recidivism.

For this reason, the correctional counselor should aid the offender in obtaining support systems that maximize coping. If family and friends are available and if they are functional, then the offender should be encouraged to reach out for their assistance. Family involvement and the use of family systems therapy might be an effective modality in such cases. (See Chapter 7 for more on family systems approaches.) Other support systems might be community groups, religious groups, and/or self-help groups. The main point is that the offender develops connections with others, particularly other persons who are not also offenders, so that the offender is not left on his or her own. Regardless of how well intentioned the counselor may be, they cannot be present at every moment and the offender should have multiple sources of human support, when necessary. Lastly, the counselor will need to aid the offender by teaching alternative coping skills. Many of these forms of coping and the specific techniques used go beyond the scope of this current chapter and will therefore be discussed in subsequent chapters. Nevertheless, clients should be given the interpersonal and interactional skills to cope with challenges, thereby providing a multifaceted approach to client welfare.

SECTION SUMMARY

Once a positive therapeutic alliance has been established, offenders must begin the difficult work of accurately identifying events proceeding problem behaviors. Perceptions of these events are critical. Often, it is the immediate perception of some event that strongly influences resulting behavior. Therefore, events and then perceptions must be carefully investigated and reparations must begin in order to reframe the offender's cognitive processes that foster safer and healthier responses and actions. Once cognitions are properly reframed the concept of coping becomes very important in order to maintain progress and continued positive behavior. Among the coping mechanisms covered in this section, the idea of creating a robust repertoire of coping skills is critical. Offenders need to have as many options as possible to alleviate the powerful negative emotions created by certain events and the perceptions that coincide with these events.

LEARNING CHECK

1. It is not important to identify the event preceding the problem behavior.
   a. True
   b. False
2. Perceptions of certain events are very important to identify in order to reframe an offender's cognitive processes.
   a. True
   b. False
3. External factors have more of an impact on coping than internal factors.
   a. True
   b. False
4. Offenders should rely on only one method of coping.
   a. True
   b. False
5. Family and friends should never be relied upon in order to assist with coping.
   a. True
   b. False

PART THREE: GOAL SETTING AND IMPLEMENTATION

A goal refers to a desired result, purpose, or objective. Within counseling, the process of setting goals is often described as the second phase (Egan, 2007), the first phase consisting of the formation of a positive therapeutic alliance. Once the alliance is formed, however, the proper identification of goals becomes paramount and is a very powerful component of the counseling relationship. Goals will often provide offenders with a clearer sense of direction. And, according to Egan (2007), "People with a sense of direction tend to experience the following:

- have a sense of purpose
- live lives that are going somewhere
- have self-enhancing patterns of behavior in place
- focus on results, outcomes, and accomplishments
- avoid mistaking random actions for accomplishments
- have a defined rather than an aimless lifestyle" (p. 251).

Counselor/Offender Collaboration

It is important that both the counselor and offender be active participants in the process of identifying and setting goals. In essence, the counselor and offender should collaborate on the direction and focus of counseling based on the offender's needs. This collaboration will often serve as a process through which offenders are more likely to assume ownership of their role in the counseling relationship and enhance motivation to succeed. The offender's experience as being considered an equal in identifying goals may also serve to strengthen the therapeutic alliance. An important product of a strong therapeutic alliance, within the context of goal setting, is the greater likelihood the offender will feel comfortable enough to fully disclose threatening and personal information that need attention within the counseling relationship. Masters (2004) asserts that counselors are often in a better position to guide the process of goal setting because they are functioning from a more objective standpoint and not "blinded by the offender's problems" (p. 51). Although an accurate statement, counselors should not assume the role of dictating to offenders what their needs are and subsequent goals aimed at addressing those needs. The spirit of collaboration should be carefully cultivated and rigorously safeguarded.

Clearly Defining Goals

Through the process of collaboration, counselors and offenders should work to clearly define goals. The goals need to be operationalized in a manner in which what is expected of the offender is clear. Green (2004) states that "successful therapy requires establishing relatively clear collaborative goals with clients (a focus) and using interventions that are relevant to those therapeutic goals throughout" (p. 3). In essence, three important steps in the counseling relationship should now be clearly discernable:

1. The establishment of a positive therapeutic alliance
2. The establishment of clear goals
3. Establishing interventions specific to the goals.

Once the goals have been collaboratively established, and possible interventions discussed, it is important to get client's commitment toward working to fulfill the goals. This process is often described as **the contract**, whereby counselors and offenders agree to work toward identified goals, in collaboration, through the counseling relationship. The contract is generally a verbal and nonformal agreement that displays the commitment of both the counselor and offender in doing everything possible to achieve the established goals. An example of entering into a contract with an offender may include the following:

COUNSELOR: You have indicated that you are feeling depressed. Would you like me to help you with this?

OFFENDER: Yes, being depressed is negatively impacting my relationship with my family. I want help!

Now that goals have been established and the contract is in place it is critical that counselors remain focused on the task at hand. This takes diligence and careful concentration on the part of the counselor to remain focused on directing the counseling relationship in a manner specific to the desired outcomes. Green (2004) provides a good example in which he highlights the criticalness of this point. He states, "in consultations for 'stuck' cases, I frequently have found that a clear sense of direction was never established at the outset of a treatment; or, once having been established, the therapy conversations meandered or avoided dealing with the main presenting problems" (p. 3). The true task of both counselor and offender is to spend as much working time as possible dealing with the offender's feelings and emotion as they relate to various life circumstances that have historically disrupted the offender's ability to function in a healthy manner.

Perception Clarification Techniques and Insight Development

Often in the counseling dialogue between the offender and the counselor, there may come times where both persons may need to clarify a range of perceptions. Often, these techniques are used to add focus to the session and to give definition to a problem. This is important because it allows both the client and the counselor to gauge concepts that would otherwise be vague and perhaps unwieldy. Likewise, the counselor who uses perception clarification techniques is engaged in an informal and personal "check" as to whether both persons are on the same page, so to speak. This is, in actuality, nothing less than an informal assessment and should be viewed as such; the counselor is ensuring that the session is on track and also is checking that he or she perceives the client's message in a manner that the client intends. If these techniques should determine otherwise, then the counselor will know that he or she must take stock of the imagined progress and determine where miscommunications may be taking place.

The first clarification technique that will be discussed is called scaling. **Scaling** requires that the client provide the counselor with a rating, between 1 and 10, that explains the severity, importance, or degree to which an issue or concept exists, as perceived by that client. In other words, scaling provides a measure. An example, provided below, shows the use of scaling. Please note that the use of the actual scaling technique itself is placed in italics. The example is as follows:

OFFENDER: I am looking forward to getting out of prison soon, but I am just not sure if I will be able to make it once I am out.

COUNSELOR: So, on the one hand, you are looking forward to more freedom but, on the other hand, you feel uneasy about the outcome once you are finally released.

OFFENDER: Yeah, kind of strange, huh? I go years behind bars looking forward to this day. Then, once it is near, I start to get all choked up.

COUNSELOR: It is a new experience, the process of reentry, that is. Under the circumstance, exercising a sense of concern or caution is healthy. But, just so I can get a better notion of your level of concern, *let me ask you to give me a number from 1 to 10 that would express your amount of concern about release, with 10 being the highest and 1 being the lowest.*

OFFENDER: Well, I would say about a 5. Somewhere in the middle would probably describe it best.

COUNSELOR: That sounds about average. Why don't we just explore that a bit to weight things out and see what might help facilitate your experience in the free world?

From the example above, it is hoped that students can see that the counselor is actually using several techniques in a simultaneous fashion. First, the counselor is reflecting the client's comments, addressing both affect (feelings of anxiety about release) and content (the client has become institutionalized, being adapted to prison life and is therefore nervous about life on the outside). In addition, while the correctional counselor does reflect the affect of the client, the counselor avoids powerful feeling words like *anxiety*, *fearful*, or *worried* because hardened offenders might not be willing to engage in strong affective display or dialogue (keep in mind the subculture of the prison, as has been discussed). Rather, the reflection uses a subdued feeling word—*uneasy*—to describe the emotions related to the client's upcoming release.

With respect to the scaling technique, the correctional counselor asks the client to provide a numerical value for the client's concern. Notice that the counselor gently shifted the feeling word from "uneasy" to "concern," a little more directive and a bit more related to the client's feelings, but still not overladen with emotional content. In addition, when the client provides a numerical value to his or her level of concern, the counselor reflects with a comment that describes that number as "average," perhaps an apt description when the number 5 is produced from a range of numbers between 1 and 10. As can be seen, the counselor then uses this as an opportunity for further exploration in the session, with goal of facilitating the client's transition from the prison to outside society.

Another clarification technique is known as the *Lazarus Technique* (Egan, 1994; Lazarus, 1976). Egan used this term to describe a technique that Arnold Lazarus employed in his film on multimodal approaches to therapy. In this film, Lazarus used a focusing technique where the client was asked to use just one word to describe her problem (Egan, 1994). After contemplating her situation she then provided a word. Then Lazarus asked the client to put the word in a sentence that would describe that problem in a bit more detail. Lazarus then asked the client to provide a set of phrases and or summary of the problem that emerged from the sentence that was provided. Thus, the **Lazarus technique** clarifies a client's issue of focus and challenges the client to provide definition to his or her issue, and, after providing such definition, the client is then given a prompt to further explore that issue in detail. Using the prior session between the correctional counselor and the inmate client that is nearing release from prison, consider the following example:

COUNSELOR: After talking about this for a while, I am wondering if you could provide one word that might best define what you hope for upon release?

OFFENDER: Yeah, I would like to have stability. . . . "Stability" is the word that I would choose.

COUNSELOR: All right, you would like to have stability. Now put that in a sentence. Describe what you would like to achieve in a short sentence.

OFFENDER: I want to have a stable income and be free of any legal hassles.

COUNSELOR: Okay, now provide a brief explanation of how that might occur. What would need to happen?

At this point the client explained that he would need to keep his job and stay away from problem areas where he might be prone to resort to old habits. This technique is an effective method of bringing a session into focus. Indeed, Egan (1994) notes that this method of clarification can be used at any stage in the helping process. This is an important point that some counselors may overlook. This technique can even be a good summarization technique—one that brings the session to a close (as when the hour-long session is coming to its end) in a constructive manner. Further, the use of this technique requires that the offender—not the counselor—provides the summary and therefore conducts a "rehash" of the session, ensuring that the client considers the happenings throughout the session. Using our previous examples, consider this use of the Lazarus technique as a means of closing the session.

COUNSELOR: We have been talking for a while now and I believe that we have covered a lot of ground. Because we have discussed so much in a short period of time, I would like you to pick another word. But this time, pick a word that describes how you feel as we come to the end of the session.

OFFENDER: I feel optimistic.

COUNSELOR: Go ahead and put that in a sentence that describes why you picked that word.

OFFENDER: I feel optimistic about my release because I realize I have a lot to look forward to.

COUNSELOR: Okay, good, so "bring it on home" at this point and explain exactly what you mean by that, as related to this session.

OFFENDER: I feel optimistic because, after talking things out, I realize how many good things there are to look forward to. I also realize that much of the outcome is within my own power of choice. If I choose to keep my nose clean, the odds are stacked in my favor that I will get the stability that I am wanting. That makes me much more optimistic than I was just an hour ago.

COUNSELOR: That's good. As we close this session, I would like you to take some time throughout the week and think about what you have just said. You can talk to others about it, if you want, but it is not necessary. Simply consider the points you just stated while making plans for life in the free world. Think of the specific means by which you might pursue those plans and bring those ideas with you next week so that we can touch on those a bit. This might help you with your transition . . .

As one can see, the use of this technique not only helped to place focus on the session, but it also gave the client some introspective direction throughout the week until the next session. This is empowering for the offender, gives him or her focus throughout the next week, and ties sessions together so that he or she does not become disjointed. The Lazarus technique is a very powerful technique that is quite versatile. However, counselors should not rely on a technique repetitively or the session will become artificial and mechanical in nature. Much of the art of counseling is just that, an art, where counselors must exercise effective judgment in selecting tools and techniques by which they work their craft.

Incidentally, the counselor could have even chosen to use the scaling technique at the end of the session. Just prior to the second use of the Lazarus technique, before the session was about to draw to a close, the dialogue might have gone as follows:

COUNSELOR: We have been talking for a while now and it seems as if we have covered a lot of ground. I am not completely sure about that, so I thought that I would ask you to once again give me a number from 1 to 10 that would express your amount of concern about release, with 10 being the highest and 1 being the lowest.

OFFENDER: I would say somewhere between a 2 and a 3. Let's say my level of concern would be about a 2.5 on a 10-point scale.

COUNSELOR: Well, that does seem to be a step in the right direction. With that in mind, I would like you to go ahead and pick another word for this session. But this time, pick a word that describes how you feel about the session as we draw to a close.

OFFENDER: I feel optimistic.

COUNSELOR: Okay, put that in a sentence that describes why you picked that word.

OFFENDER: I feel optimistic about my release because I realize I have a lot to look forward to.

COUNSELOR: Good, so "bring it on home" at this point and explain exactly what you mean by that, as related to this session.

OFFENDER: I feel optimistic because, after talking things out, I realize how many good things there are to look forward to. I also realize that much of the outcome is within my own power of choice. If I choose to keep my nose clean, the odds are stacked in my favor that I will get the stability that I am wanting. That makes me much more optimistic than I was just an hour ago. . . .

The session would then conclude just as the prior example demonstrated. This last example shows how different techniques can be effective in channeling and focusing a counseling session. They can be used at different points and in a different order, depending on the specific circumstances of the session and the counselor's own professional judgment. It is important to once again note that techniques should not be used too much or they make the session sterile. Rather, they add in facilitating the session and providing additional means by which the counselor can better guide the client through a process of self-discovery. The main ingredient of an effective counselor–offender relationship is the therapeutic alliance whereby mutual respect, empathy, congruence, genuineness, and unconditional positive regard are communicated to the offender. The use of technique should not become a crutch for the correctional counselor, lest the underlying theory and purpose behind an intervention get lost in the process itself, a process that is about people rather than theoretical applications or techniques of implementation.

Termination of the Counseling Relationship

The goal of any good counselor is to get his or her client into a position where counseling is no longer necessary. That is the most laudable and ethical goal of a good correctional counselor. With that in mind, it is the responsibility of the correctional counselor to indicate that termination of the offender–counselor relationship looms in the future when it is clear that the offender has met their agreed-upon goals or when it is clear that the offender is not benefiting from the therapeutic relationship. In most cases with correctional counseling, offenders will be mandated to treatment, regardless of whether they are in a prison or a community corrections environment. However, there will come a time when offenders will finish their program requirements and/or the required number of therapeutic sessions, and correctional counselors should be prepared to process the offender through this last segment of the counseling relationship.

While conducting therapy with the offender, the counselor will have undoubtedly made contact with various custodial personnel, such as the offender's probation and/or parole officer. This is important because the correctional counselor will typically share information regarding the offender's progress with these individuals. Keep in mind that the offender will be aware of this, and in all cases, correctional counselors obtain *release of information* that demonstrates the offender's knowledge of and consent to this sharing of information. A **release of information** is simply a formal and signed agreement where the client consents to the counselor's sharing of information with another person and/or persons at another agency. The specifics of this arrangement are not necessary to discuss at this time, but the parameters of such a release must be clear, specific, and with the client's signed consent. However, such releases are routine in the field of counseling and should not be seen as a hurdle to any process of treatment provision. The use of releases of information is so commonplace that agencies typically have numerous black forms prepared so that counselors can quickly fill in the relevant information and expedite the process of ethical information sharing. Obtaining offender compliance in the correctional setting is usually not problematic because the treatment aspect of an offender's sentence is usually part of his or her overall sentencing requirement. Whether this seems right or wrong, such coercive elements do exist as a means of maintaining offender compliance, both from a security standpoint and a therapeutic one.

Throughout the counseling relationship, the correctional counselor will have likely provided several notes, observations, and recommendations regarding the offender to prison or community supervision officials. These are the same officials (a parole board or some such body if such is warranted, a warden or his or her designee in a prison, a judge or the chief probation officer in a community supervision environment) that will make decisions regarding the ultimate discharge of the offender from the justice system. The correctional counselor's input, through an official recommendation based on clinical observation and expertise of the counselor, will be used to make subsequent decisions regarding the offender. Because of this, it is important that correctional counselors take this role seriously; the fate of both the offender and the public hang in the balance when making critical decisions regarding custody-level changes and/or full release.

Once it is clear that the offender will make suitable progress to soon exit the program, the correctional counselor should make arrangements for the last session to be one for closure of the relationship. If possible, the offender should know this in advance to aid them in processing the eventual end of the relationship. Many programs may even go so far as to have ceremonies or celebrations for the offender, providing certificates of completion and such. This is definitely a kind and worthy gesture that can hold substantial meaning for the offender. However, this should not suffice for the official termination session between the offender and the counselor. Indeed, such a process does not actually address the termination of the relationship, in and of itself. It is important that, regardless of any celebrations or graduation ceremonies, the counselor ensures that an actual session is held that addresses the offender's progress throughout the program and that addresses the offender's feelings regarding the termination. While many clients may address this topically, it is nonetheless important. It tells the offender that the counselor cares and that the client was not simply "another number," but was and is a human being who has completed a major milestone. If the offender was in a group counseling setting, it allows the group to say goodbye and lets the client know that they will be missed. Yet at the same time, such a session puts a sense of official closure on the relationship, thereby maintaining effective professional boundaries between the counselor and the offender.

Further, the counselor does not want to leave the client feeling abandoned. Though the therapeutic relationship between the offender and counselor will end, the counselor should provide at least three referral clinicians who are trustworthy and accessible, in case the offender should need such services. This is important, though in many cases where the offender works within an agency that processes offenders on a routine basis, a pre-established list of such referrals may readily exist. This ensures that sufficient follow-up resources are available once the offender is out of therapy. Lastly, when and where agency policy deems appropriate, counselors may wish to provide a brief follow-up phone call after a suitable period of time has elapsed (such as three or six month intervals). This can aid offenders in their relapse prevention and also aids in the informal evaluation process. This particular aspect of the termination cycle is followed in many private practices but may not be common practice in state- or country-run agencies. In all cases, correctional counselors will need to know and understand agency policy regarding this aspect of post-termination.

The primary task of the counselor during termination, aside from common record keeping concerns, is to ensure that the offender has a continuum of care that continues beyond the individual offender and counselor. The offender should not be exited without having sufficient knowledge of potential treatment providers in the community. Though the official counseling mandate may have ended in such cases, the requirement that counselors put offender welfare as their first and foremost concern does not. This is the obligation of an ethical correctional counselor and is also the final message that an offender will receive—the message that regardless of mandates or other displays of formality, the correctional counselor's empathetic positive regard remains as a bastion of hope amidst a vast array of persons affected by a myriad of personal and social challenges. However, the correctional counselor provides aid and assistance to face these challenges, with a goal of providing a better future for the offender and society alike.

SECTION SUMMARY

Goals must be clearly defined as early as possible in the counseling process. The clear identification of goals allows counseling sessions to be focused and guided by factors most salient to the offender. It is very important that goal setting and subsequent methods of implementation be agreed upon by the offender and counselor. Collaboration within this process is extremely important. Counselors must refrain from overtly or covertly inserting their own biases in this process and forcing upon the offender what they think would be the best. A lack of collaboration will significantly damage the therapeutic alliance. Finally, termination must occur within a continuum. Termination of the counseling process may be best viewed as the beginning of the next phase of care. And, it is critical that the offender understand that the counseling process may be reinstituted if the need arises.

LEARNING CHECK

1. Offenders can sometimes benefit from feelings of abandonment within the counseling process.
   a. True
   b. False
2. The Lazarus technique is an effective method of clarifying an offender's feelings.
   a. True
   b. False
3. If a therapeutic alliance has been successfully created, a release of information is never required.
   a. True
   b. False
4. When used properly, scaling can be an effective method of clarification.
   a. True
   b. False
5. A contract is a mechanism through which offenders and counselors are able to work together toward identified goals.
   a. True
   b. False

CONCLUSION

A positive therapeutic alliance is a critical component within the therapeutic relationship. Regardless of treatment modality, there must be a strong affective bond between the counselor and offender that produces an environment in which the offender feels safe in disclosing deep, personal, and often shameful information. The therapeutic alliance is built primarily on the counselor's ability to display genuineness and empathy when responding to the myriad of statements and actions displayed by the offender. The positive therapeutic alliance is also the vehicle in which counselors will be able to effectively identify the offender's true needs as well as uncover important information related to the offender's perceptions, coping mechanisms, and future goals.

It is important to understand that the therapeutic alliance is a concept that requires continuous attendance throughout the counseling relationship. It is not something that is established in the beginning phase of counseling and then forgotten about. It must be revisited throughout the process especially in the presence of negative emotion. Counselors must remain aware of the destructive nature of even subtle forms of judgmentalism. Offenders in counseling are not usually emotionally capable of properly processing the idea of being judged without feeling rejected. Even the slightest form of judgmentalism is likely to emotionally "turn off" the offender rupturing the alliance. In the event a counselor senses the offender emotionally shutting down it is critical the counselor immediately stop and tend to the cause(s). In such an event, the therapeutic alliance may have been damaged and will need to be reestablished.

To sum up the essence of this chapter, Green (2004) provides three important points regarding a positive therapeutic alliance:

1. Give sufficient emotional support and validation to the offender
2. Successfully manage negative emotion within the offender
3. The counselor must regulate his or her own negative emotion in response to the offender.

Finally, Green (2004) states that "the very best therapists tend to be those who can easily establish and maintain positive therapeutic alliances with the widest range of clients, both in terms of clients' cultural diversity and in terms of managing negative emotionality" (p. 2). In essence, the counselor's ability to effectively provide lasting and quality services to an offender is in large part directly related to his or her own internal congruence.

Essay Questions

1. Discuss the importance of a therapeutic alliance?
2. Identify and discuss two factors that threaten the establishment of a strong therapeutic alliance.
3. Discuss two coping techniques that you feel are most effective. What makes these techniques, in your opinion, so effective?
4. Discuss the idea of problem identification. Why is this so critical to the counseling process?

Bibliography

Bordin, E. S. (1979). The generalizability of the psychoanalytic concept of the working alliance. *Psychotherapy: Theory, Research and Practice, 16*(3), 252–260.

Center for Substance Abuse Treatment. (1999). *Enhancing motivation for change in substance abuse treatment.* Treatment Improvement Protocol (TIP) Series 35. DHHS Publication No. (SMA) 99-3354. Rockville, MD: Substance Abuse and Mental Health Services Administration.

Center for Substance Abuse Treatment. (2005). *Substance abuse treatment for persons with co-occurring disorders.* Treatment Improvement Protocol (TIP) Series 42. DHHS Publication No. (SMA) 05-3922. Rockville, MD: Substance Abuse and Mental Health Services Administration.

Corey, G. (2000). *Theory and practice of group counseling* (5th ed.). Belmont, CA: Wadsworth.

Doyle, R. E. (1992). *Essential skills and strategies in the helping process.* Pacific Grove, CA: Brooks/Cole.

Egan, G. (1990). *The skilled helper: A systematic approach to effective helping* (4th ed.). Pacific Grove, CA: Brooks/Cole.

Egan, G. (1994). *The skilled helper: A problem-management approach to helping* (5th ed.). Pacific Grove, CA: Brooks/Cole.

Egan, G. (2007). *The skilled helper* (8th ed.). Belmont, CA: Thompson Brooks/Cole.

Elliot, J., & Elliot, K. (2006). *Disarming the inner critic.* Lafayette, LA: Anthetics Press.

Gladding, S. T. (1996). *Counseling: A comprehensive profession* (3rd ed.). Englewood Cliffs, NJ: Prentice Hall.

Gordon, T. (1970). *Parent effectiveness training: The no-lose program for raising responsible children.* New York: Wyden.

Green, R. J. (2004). Therapeutic alliance, focus, and formulation: Thinking beyond the traditional therapy orientations. *Pscychotherapy.net* (Electronic Journal). Retrieved date: www.psychotherapy.net/articles/articlesframe.html.

Hanser, R. D. (2007). *Special needs offenders in the community.* Englewood Cliffs, NJ: Prentice Hall.

Kanel, K. (2003). *A guide to crisis intervention* (2nd ed.). Pacific Grove, CA: Brooks/Cole.

Lazarus, A. A. (1976). *Multimodal behavior therapy.* New York: Springer.

Masters, R. (2004). *Counseling criminal justice offenders* (2nd ed.). Thousand Oaks, CA: Sage Publications.

Miller, W. R., Leckman, A. L., Delaney, H. D., & Tinkcom, M. (1992). Long-term follow-up of behavioral self-control training. *Journal of Studies on Alcohol, 53*(3), 249–261.

Miller, W. R., & Rollnick, S. (1991). *Motivational interviewing: Preparing people to change addictive behavior.* New York: Guilford Press.

Ormont L. R. (1999). Establishing transient identification in the group setting. *Modern Psychoanalysis. 24*(2), 143–156.

Petry, N. M., & Bickel, W. K. (1999). Therapeutic alliance and psychiatric severity as predictors of completion of treatment for opioid dependence. *Psychiatric Services 50*(2), 219–227.

Ritchie, M. H. (1986). Counseling the involuntary client. *Journal of Counseling and Development, 64,* 516–518.

Rogers, C. R. (1957). The necessary and sufficient conditions of therapeutic personality change. *Journal of Consulting Psychology, 21,* 95–103.

Sack, R. T. (1988). Counseling responses when clients say 'I don't know.' *Journal of Mental Health Counseling, 10,* 179–187.

Schultz, D. P., & Schultz, S. E. (2005). *Theories of personality* (8th ed.). Belmont, CA: Thompson/Wadsworth.

Summers, R. F., & Barber, J. P. (2003). Therapeutic alliance as a measurable skill. *Academic Psychiatry, 27*(3), 160–165.

Witty, M. (2007). Client-centered therapy. In N. Kazantzis and L. L'Abate (Eds.), *Handbook of homework assignments in psychotherapy research, practice, and prevention* (pp. 35–50). US: Springer.

5

Common Theoretical Counseling Perspectives

CHAPTER OBJECTIVES

After reading this chapter, you will be able to:

1. Discuss behavioral approaches to counseling.
2. Identify common techniques used in behavioral therapy.
3. Discuss cognitive approaches to counseling.
4. Identify basic techniques used in cognitive therapy.
5. Discuss reality therapy.
6. Identify common techniques used in reality therapy.
7. Discuss Gestalt therapy.
8. Identify common techniques used in Gestalt therapy.

INTRODUCTION

A variety of counseling perspectives have been created since the birth of psychology and the helping professions. Counseling perspective is a particular approach to counseling based on specific assumptions regarding determinants of cognition and behavior. Most counseling perspectives also include specific techniques of intervention directly related to the perspective's assumptions concerning human behavior.

An important prelude to what follows is that each perspective contains unique contributions to help people identify and overcome psychological and emotional issues causing distress. The various causes of distress are broad and diverse. As a result we encourage students to maintain an open mind while critically reviewing each perspective. The extreme diversity within the offender population cannot be overemphasized. In addition, our society is becoming more diverse as different cultures are increasingly forced to interact due to spatial limitations as well as the process of globalism. Based on these facts we suggest the following intellectual framework as a foundation for readers of this chapter:

1. There is no right or wrong counseling perspective.
2. Each perspective contains parameters that may be useful under certain conditions with certain offenders.

3. Counselors should be flexible in their approach to help and should be able to draw techniques and reasoning from various perspectives.
4. In order to effectively help others counselors, themselves must have a good understanding of their own strengths and weaknesses.
5. As you examine each counseling perspective reflect on the following question: "How can this information help me to better understand my own intellectual perceptions and behavior?"

In this chapter we present four counseling perspectives: (1) Behavioral Therapy, (2) Cognitive Therapy (including Cognitive Behavior Therapy), (3) Reality Therapy, and (4) Gestalt Therapy. Obviously, there are additional therapeutic approaches found throughout the literature. Some of these approaches are very specific aimed at particular types of dysfunction and prescribe specific types of treatment. The reason for our selections is that each perspective is used extensively within the offender population. We make no claim that one perspective is superior to the other. In fact, we urge the opposite and once again invite students to explore this information from a point of neutrality accompanied by personal introspection. Finally, we would like to point out that we rely heavily on the work of Corey (2005) in creating the foundation for much of the information contained in this chapter.

PART ONE: BEHAVIORAL APPROACHES

One of the most significant proponents of behavioral theory was B. F. Skinner (1904–1990). Skinner spent much of his career researching various behavioral techniques all of which are aimed at increasing one's personal choices through the creations of new conditions of learning. Behavior therapy is heavily grounded in objectivity with the basic assumption that behavior can be learned. For example, behavior theorists posit that addiction is a learned behavior and because it is learned new behaviors can also be learned in order to replace the dysfunctional qualities of addiction.

Corey (2005) provides 10 key factors related to behavior therapy that provides a robust foundation from which one is able to intellectually frame the basic underpinnings of behavior therapy. In addition to Corey (2005), several other authors including Kazdin (2001), Miltenberger (2004), as well as Speigler and Gueveremont (2003) have made significant contributions to the following factors.

1. As mentioned above, behavior therapy is primarily rooted in objectivity. **As such, the scientific method of conducting research and experiments is central to behavior therapy.** Corey (2005) notes, "the distinguishing characteristic of behavioral practitioners is their systematic adherence to precision and to empirical evaluation" (p. 232). The problem is clearly stated, the intervention is clearly identified, outcomes are empirically tested, and the entire process undergoes continual revision.
2. The primary interest of behavior therapy is the specific nature of the offender's current problem. Past events may be useful at times but are not considered primary. For example, an offender suffering from substance abuse would be examined and treated based on the positive and negative reinforcers associated with the substance abuse. Ultimately, the goal is to find alternative behaviors that maximize positive consequences based on freedom to choose responses other than the use of substances. **Behavior therapists are most interested in current behaviors associated with distress and the environmental stimulants that contribute to and maintain the behavior.** Once the distressing behavior is identified

the behavior therapist will then begin exploring various measurable techniques aimed at altering the environmental stimuli correlated with the problem behavior.

3. **Behavior therapy requires specific actions from the offender aimed at altering and enhancing his or her possible responses to certain stimuli.** Behavior therapy is not talk therapy. Action and learning is paramount.
4. **Behavioral therapy relies heavily on educating a client in regards to new behaviors.** Therapists take an active role in pointing out alternative behaviors that may produce more desired results. For example, an offender who routinely turns to marijuana when faced with anxiety-provoking decisions may be taught to exercise instead.
5. **The focus of behavior therapy is on assessing behavior through which problems can be identified.** Once identified, specific and measurable interventions are introduced and results are evaluated.
6. **Self-control is central to behavior therapy.** In order for behavior therapy to be effective clients must be able to identify problem behavior and then consciously choose to carry out learned behavior more capable of reducing distress and negative consequences.
7. There is no universal behavioral treatment protocol appropriate for all individuals. **Instead, interventions and teaching are specific to the individual and the problem behavior.** This is an important characteristic of behavior therapy. We must remain cognizant of the fact that human beings are extremely diverse and complex.
8. As mentioned above, behavior therapy relies heavily on the participation of the client. In essence, a partnership must be forged between the counselor and client where both are active participants in the path to change. **The counseling process is open and clients are generally informed about the decisions and process of treatment.**
9. **The focus is on developing interventions aimed at reducing problem behavior that can be practically applied in all areas of one's life.** "Practicality" is the key word in this characteristic. Theoretical postulations that are unable to be measured in daily life are not generally part of the main focus.
10. Counselors must be culturally competent in order to provide treatment protocols best suited for a particular client and the client's problem behavior.

Classical Conditioning

Classical conditioning refers to a process of learning based on the idea of pairing. Ivan Pavlov, a Russian physiologist, is a central figure in classical conditioning based on his work with dogs. Through various experiments, Pavlov found that when food was presented to dogs they salivated. Pavlov considered both the presentation of food and the process of salivating to be unconditioned responses. Through additional experiments he found that a conditioned response could be generated through the pairing of an unconditioned stimulus with a conditioned stimulus. Specifically, Pavlov learned that after several repetitions of pairing food with a buzzer the dogs began to salivate in response to the buzzer even in the absence of food. And, maybe even more significant in the context of criminal offending is the fact that Pavlov also found that if the conditioned stimulus (buzzer) is repeatedly presented without the pairing of food the salivation response is reduced and over time is extinguished. Classical conditioning provides the foundation of one form of learned behavior.

As noted by Gladding (1996) a variety of human emotions are often experienced as a result of classical conditioning via paired associations. Phobias are also often linked to paired associations. For example, a person may learn that he or she cannot trust others due to repeated exposure of disappointment by not being adequately attended to by caregivers. In fact, it could be argued that antisocial behavior, commonly used to describe criminal offending, is in part a result of classical conditioning. In essence, a person learns through paired associations that it is dangerous to overly rely on or openly present oneself to others.

Operant Conditioning

Whereas classical conditioning refers to what takes place prior to learning, operant conditioning describes learning in which behavior is influenced by the consequences that follow them (Corey, 2005). Generally, operant conditioning describes a process of learning that is heavily influenced by rewards and punishments. If a person is rewarded for a particular action it is more likely that the action will be repeated. When an action is followed by a punishment it is less likely to be repeated. Therefore people often learn to discriminate between actions that result in reward and those that result in punishment (Gladding, 1996). To once again contrast classical and operant conditioning, it could be said that classical conditioning is the conditioning of involuntary responses whereas operant conditioning is the conditioning of voluntary responses. People will often repeat behaviors that produce some type of desired attention, feeling, or emotional gain. Within the offender population one's toughness is often viewed in high esteem. Therefore one may learn that the ability to intimidate or physically overtake others results in the elevation of status among peers. This is a very powerful motivator for someone who has nothing else to rely on for feelings of worth and acceptance, especially when this is due to inadequate early child care. The same is true in relation to money and the ability to obtain material possessions. The bedrock of operant conditioning as noted by Skinner (1953) is that individual behavior is primarily driven by one's environment.

Operationalizing Behavior Therapy with Criminal Offenders

According to behavior theorists behavior that is learned can be unlearned. Therefore the goal is to help offenders identify problem/criminal behavior and replace it with socially acceptable law-abiding behavior. In order for behavior therapy to be effective there must be significant collaboration between the counselor and offender. Offenders take an active role in deciding which behaviors to address and also the formulation of specific goals. "Goals must be clear, concrete, understood, and agreed on . . . This process of determining therapeutic goals entails a negotiation between client and counselor that results in a contract that guides the course of therapy" (Corey, 2005, p. 234). The importance of collaboration in the therapeutic process cannot be overstated. In fact, Corey (2005) notes the work of Cormier and Nurius (2003) who provide five guiding principles illuminating the importance of collaboration:

1. The counselor provides a rationale for goals, explaining the role of goals in therapy, the purpose of goals, and the client's participation in the goal-setting process.
2. The client identifies desired outcomes by specifying the positive changes he or she wants from counseling. Focus is on what the client wants to do rather than on what the client does not want to do.
3. The client is the person seeking help, and only he or she can make a change. The counselor helps the client accept the responsibility for change rather than trying to get someone else to change.

4. The cost–benefit effect of all identified goals is explored, and counselor and client discuss the possible advantages and disadvantages of these goals.
5. The client and counselor then decide to continue pursuing the selected goals, to reconsider the client's initial goals, or to seek the services of another practitioner (p. 234).

One of the most important tasks of a behavior therapist is to conduct a functional analysis of the problem behavior. Here, it is important to remember that all behavior serves some purpose. The goal is to identify environmental factors, parameters of the actions, and the results that accompany the problem behavior. For example, some offenders may use aggression to mask fear and anxiety. The aggression may consist of physically assaulting others to stave off appearances of being afraid. In certain cultures, this behavior is both acceptable and admired. Socially, however, it is disruptive and a criminal offense accompanied by sanctions. In this case, obviously the role of the counselor is to help the offender identify and define the problem of aggression; identify its destructive and dangerous nature; identify alternative responses to fear and anxiety that replace aggression; and evaluate the success of the alternative responses. The basic premise being dysfunctional behavior is learned and then integrated based on inappropriate reinforcement (Figure 5.1).

Common Techniques of Behavior Therapy

Systematic desensitization refers to the process of reducing anxiety primarily based on physical and mental relaxation. Systematic desensitization was developed by Joseph Wolpe (1958) and is a technique based on the principles of classical conditioning (Corey, 2005). Generally, a client will describe a particular situation that results in anxiety and then rank certain elements of the situation hierarchically ranging from little or no concern to extreme concern. The real task of the therapist is to help clients substitute feelings of anxiety with the competing response of relaxation. This is done by teaching the client to relax as successive elements of the anxiety-provoking circumstances are introduced beginning with those that are of little to no concern. Over time clients become desensitized and are then freer to make choices from an enhanced range of options. Masters (2004) notes systematic desensitization is often used with phobias, neurotic anxieties, interpersonal difficulties, as well as some forms of sexual problems. For specific steps in relaxation training see Wolpe (1990).

Implosive therapy first introduced in the 1960s by Thomas Stampfl (Gladding, 1996) is a concept that describes the process of guiding clients through imaginary details of a situation that may have catastrophic consequences. The offender is asked to imagine in detail circumstances that create extreme anxiety and then verbalize them. The anxiety is extinguished over

> A functional analysis probes the situations surrounding the client's problem behavior. Specifically, it examines the relationships among stimuli that trigger the behavior and the consequences that follow. This type of analysis provides important clues regarding the meaning of the behavior to the client, as well as possible motivators and barriers to change. In behavioral therapy, this is the first step in providing the client with tools to manage or avoid situations that trigger dysfunctional behavior. Functional analysis yields a roadmap of a client's interpersonal, intrapersonal, and environmental catalysts and reactions to problem behavior, thereby identifying likely precursors.

FIGURE 5.1 Functional Analysis *Source:* SAMHSA TIP 34.

time due to the repeated exposure in the counseling setting absent of the feared results. Gladding (1996) notes this technique should not be used by beginning counselors. Implosive therapy can produce extreme anxiety and even trauma if not properly delivered. One of the delineating factors between implosive therapy and systematic desensitization is that implosive therapy techniques of relaxation are not introduced prior to the presentation of the anxiety-provoking circumstance.

Assertive training is a process of teaching clients that they have the right to choose their own method of expression and do not have to continue with those responses that do not produce desired results. The major underpinning of assertive training is that a person should have the freedom to make choices without having to endure anxiety or emotional pain. Once a particular objective has been identified (speaking in front of groups, expressing true feelings, saying no to deviant peers), counselors will generally explore a client's current behavior in regards to the objective. Feedback from the counselor is an important part of assertive training. Especially once the desired behavior has been identified it is important that counselors are able to help clients engineer clever ways of implementing and maintaining healthier and more productive responses.

Coaching is a process of showing clients how to carry out or perform certain actions more conducive to healthy living. Sometimes referred to as modeling, coaching assumes that clients do not have to necessarily experience each aspect of a distressing circumstance in order to learn more effective behaviors. They can instead be taught by simply observing or watching others (Masters, 2004). Counselors are often in a powerful position to provide coaching. Corey (2005) notes, "Because clients often view the therapist as worthy of emulation, clients pattern attitudes, values, beliefs, and behavior after the therapist. It is essential that therapists be aware of the crucial role they play in the therapeutic process" (p. 235).

Behavioral homework is the process of practicing a desired behavior usually after it has been appropriately modeled for the offender by the counselor (Gladding, 1996). Typically, the offender will receive feedback as the desired behavior is shaped. Homework is designed to help the offender practice the behavior in a more natural setting outside the counselor's office. It is important that clients actively participate in this technique so that accurate reporting can be made on the outcomes of new behavior or responses. Accurate reporting is necessary so that further progress can be made in subsequent sessions usually in the form of modifications aimed at enhancing success and ultimately generalization of the more effective behavior.

Finally, specific measurement is an important component of behavior therapy. One of the hallmarks of behavior therapy is the ability to quantitatively measure the progress of clients. Success is largely gauged by the frequency in which an offender is able to substitute problem behavior with that which is more likely to produce desirable results. This is precisely why behavior therapists are interested in identifying the specific problem behavior, how the behavior is carried out, the circumstances in which the behavior occurs, and the general results that accompanies the behavior. These factors are critical in order to determine how best to treat a client. In the end the success of behavior therapy is contingent on the numerical observations of employed corrective behaviors taking the place of former behaviors unable to elicit desirable outcomes. Through the process of quantifying results counselors are able to hone in on circumstances in which the corrective behaviors were not employed. In these occasions the specific circumstances are further explored in order to modify or develop new corrective behaviors that may prove useful. In behavior therapy the scientific model is closely followed in an attempt to broaden one's repertoire of responses to aversive circumstances that are more likely to lead to healthier lifestyles and greater freedom to make choices.

SECTION SUMMARY

Behavior therapy is predicated on the assumption that behavior is learned and can therefore be unlearned. Classical and operant conditioning are the staples of behavior therapy and both describe types of learning. Classical conditioning refers to what takes place prior to learning and focuses largely on pairing. Operant conditioning focuses on learning that takes place based on the consequences that follow behavior. The types of reinforcements a person receives will determine whether the behavior is continued or extinguished. Behavioral interventions are individually tailored to the specific needs of a client. The relationship between client and counselor is one of collaboration and participation. Both must be active in the process of changing behavior.

LEARNING CHECK

1. Objectivity is not a major concern of behavior therapy.
   a. True
   b. False
2. Classical conditioning describes learning in which behaviors are influenced by the reinforcements that follow them.
   a. True
   b. False
3. A very important aspect of behavior therapy is the functional assessment of behavior.
   a. True
   b. False
4. Behavior therapy places strong emphasis on self-control.
   a. True
   b. False
5. The primary goal of behavior therapy is to increase personal choice and create new conditions for learning.
   a. True
   b. False

CASE VIGNETTE

Example of Behavioral Therapy Used with an Offender Convicted of Domestic Violence

Gus has recently been convicted of domestic violence. He has been sentenced to probation for one year and also ordered to receive counseling for his aggressive and violent outbursts. The incident that led to Gus's arrest happened one afternoon as he and his wife were watching television. Gus reports his wife began verbally assaulting him due to his lack of participation in carrying out household chores. Gus stated he had been drinking and when his wife failed to stop criticizing him he became violent and began to push and strike her. Gus stated that only after he initiates violence does his wife stop nagging him. Gus goes on to state that after the violent episodes he and his wife spend hours and even days not communicating. Gus claims to feel remorse for his violent actions and also extreme loneliness due to the lack of intimacy and connection following the violence. Gus also claims that he is concerned about his children growing up in an atmosphere of violence as he did. Gus states that while growing up he witnessed his father routinely batter his mother until finally his mother filed for divorce. Shortly after the divorce Gus's father committed suicide. Gus states he must learn how to change his behavior before he, too, loses his family and permanently damages his children.

The functional analysis of Gus's behavior is carefully reviewed:

COUNSELOR: When do you become violent?

GUS: Usually, after I have been drinking and just want to relax.

COUNSELOR: What typically triggers your violent outbursts?

GUS: Usually, when my wife begins nagging me about something that needs to be done around the house. I try to tell her that I do not feel like doing it at the time but she continues to nag saying that I never feel like doing anything.

COUNSELOR: How do you usually carry out the violence?

GUS: I just finally have enough and get up and grab her by the shirt or hair. By this point I can't take anymore. Once I have grabbed her I shake her and yell that I am tired of her constant nagging. Sometimes I punch her in the stomach or back. I never hit her in the face.

COUNSELOR: What does your violence accomplish?

GUS: Well, it gets her to shut up. I can finally sit and relax and watch TV without hearing her criticize me.

COUNSELOR: What else happens after your violent outbursts?

GUS: Well, to be honest, I hate it. I hate being violent with my wife. I really love her and she is wonderful to my kids. And, after the violence is over she is so scared and hurt by what I have done. She does not talk to me or even look at me. I know how much it hurts her and disappoints her. I am a people person and have to live in the same house with my wife and kids and not communicating with them is terrible. And, after the last time she took my kids and went to her mom's place for three days. She would not let me see or even talk to them. I can't take this anymore.

COUNSELOR: Ok, it seems as though the specific behaviors we need to work on consist of violent outbursts directed at your wife. Is this correct?

GUS: Yes.

COUNSELOR: How often do you use violence to keep your wife from nagging you?

GUS: Well, it depends on the nagging. Sometimes she says a few things and then stops. Other times, she just keeps going and says that she is not going to stop until I get up and do something. So when she says this I always get violent because my anger becomes too much.

COUNSELOR: So, when your wife continues to nag you use violence about 100% of the time?

GUS: Yes.

COUNSELOR: To what percentage would you like to reduce your violent outbursts?

GUS: 0%

COUNSELOR: What is your main motivation for wanting to eliminate your violent behaviors?

GUS: I want to save my marriage; I want to be closer to my wife and family; and I can't bear to think of my wife leaving me. I want my family to stay together.

COUNSELOR: I want to begin by suggesting alternative responses to violence. First, how would you feel about getting up and walking out of the room? This would create distance between you and your wife and allow you to implement a very important skill-breathing techniques aimed at helping you relax. When you feel yourself beginning to get angry, I want you to leave the room and begin concentrating on your breathing. I want you to concentrate, specifically, on slowing your breathing and focusing on the consequences of using violence.

GUS: I can try that. It will be difficult, but I think I can do it. See, where I grew up when the man said he had enough the woman knew to be quiet. The woman didn't keep talking because she knew what was going to happen.

COUNSELOR: I understand, however, if you continue to rely on this learned behavior what will happen?

GUS: I will end up in prison and I will lose my family. I get it. I am ready and willing to change my behavior. It is not worth it.

COUNSELOR: Ok, I want you to describe a typical circumstance that is likely to lead to violence? Do this slowly and I am going to help you work through it without resorting to violence. I am going to help desensitize you so that you have a fuller range of options to respond that does not include violence. In fact, I would like to get a working contract with you. The contract states that under no circumstances are you to engage in violence with your wife. How do you feel about this? Are you able to engage in this contract?

GUS: Yes, I can do it. I must do it. Usually, after I get home from work I like to sit around for a while and drink a few beers. I try to relax and unwind and let go of the stress. My wife stays home with the kids and if she wants me to do something she tells me to do it. This is where I usually begin to get upset. She could at least ask me instead of telling me.

COUNSELOR: Do you ever resort to violence when you are not drinking?

GUS: No, the only times I have been violent with my wife are after I have been drinking. I am able to relax after a few beers but I also get very angry and very quickly.

COUNSELOR: If you were not drinking, do you think you would get as angry with your wife based on her telling you to do something as opposed to asking?

GUS: Probably not.

COUNSELOR: How hard would it be for you to not drink alcohol?

GUS: Not that hard. As I get older, it is becoming harder to go to sleep after I have been drinking and it also makes me feel terrible in the mornings. I really need to stop drinking altogether. I am glad you brought this up because this is what I needed, to finally make the decision to stop. It is not helping me at all.

COUNSELOR: I want you to imagine coming home from work and sitting down to watch TV. Let's even assume that you are having a couple of beers. Your wife starts nagging at you to cut the grass. You tell her you do not feel like it and she continues. You feel yourself becoming angry. These are the steps I want you to follow:

1. Get up and create distance between you and your wife.
2. Begin to focus on your breathing. If you allow yourself to become enraged violence will be much more likely.

3. Think of the negative consequences of becoming violent. You will go to jail, and eventually lose your family.
4. In a calm voice, tell your wife that you need a little space to collect your thoughts. It is important to assert your rights in this instance because a violent outburst is at stake. Tell your wife that you would be happy to discuss household activities with her but you would like for her to please talk to you in a respectful manner.
5. If you feel as though violence is inevitable you will leave your house until you are able to return without engaging in violence.

GUS: I can do this. I feel better with the thought of having more options. I really felt stuck. I felt as though I had no options.

In this example, Gus must be lead from the point of no options other than violence to the point of having various options including leaving the house. Gus must understand that at no time is violence acceptable. In essence, Gus must begin to consider other options that are capable of producing the desired result. Gus would be given homework consisting of monitoring the interactions between him and his wife and the circumstances which produced the anger. Gus would be responsible for carrying out the objectives identified and evaluating their success. Based on the outcomes future sessions would be geared toward better enabling Gus to respond without violence.

PART TWO: COGNITIVE APPROACHES

Where behavior therapy is primarily concerned with behavior, cognitive therapy is primarily concerned with cognitions. Cognition is a concept that describes the process through which knowledge is acquired. The basic assumption of cognitive theory is that behavior is largely predicated on one's thoughts, beliefs, and perceptions and that it is through faulty perceptions that much of dysfunctional behavior is predicated. Cognitive theory attempts to identify and correct faulty thinking patterns responsible for behaviors that are distressing, destructive, and criminal. Ultimately, faulty cognitions must be replaced with those that contain balance and flexibility that foster healthier behavior patterns and responses to certain stimuli.

Cognitive therapy was developed by Aron T. Beck and resulted from his extensive work on depression (Corey, 2005). Psychoeducation plays a strong role in cognitive therapy as clients are taught how to identify internal cues and messages that are probably contributing to their distress. This process is often referred to as cognitive restructuring. Cognitive restructuring refers to a set of techniques that help people examine and reframe certain thoughts or beliefs that contribute to negative feelings or dysfunctional behavior (Beck, 1995). In essence, people's reactions to situations are determined by their thoughts and beliefs in those situations in particular, and about the world and themselves in general (Beck, 1995). Cognitive restructuring is a strategy aimed at enhancing one's awareness of one's own thoughts and especially perceptions and then challenging those that generate strong negative feeling or emotion.

Cognitive therapy builds on behavior therapy and attempts to account for the mental processes associated with behavior. In fact, although we keep the two separated in order to clearly depict the basics of each style, the combination of cognitive and behavior therapy techniques has led to one of the most robust therapeutic modalities known as cognitive behavioral therapy.

Cognitive behavioral therapy has been researched extensively and is among the evidence-based modalities shown to be effective with a wide range of people including offenders.

As noted by Corey (2005), Beck was primarily interested in automatic thoughts. Automatic thoughts are described as the often immediate intellectual reaction to some event or stimulus that culminates in an emotion-based response. Beck hypothesized that people suffering from emotional difficulties, especially depression, were highly prone to shift reality toward self-deprecation even in the absence of objectivity (Beck, 1967). "Cognitive distortion" is a term used to describe erroneous conclusions based on errors in reasoning. Cognitive restructuring, mentioned above, is the therapeutic response to cognitive distortion under many circumstances due to the assumption that healthy behavior is unlikely if one is experiencing perceptions and thoughts not properly aligned with reality. Table 5.1 contains a list of many of the most common cognitive errors.

TABLE 5.1 Common Cognitive Errors

1. *Filtering*—taking negative details and magnifying them, while filtering out all positive aspects of a situation
2. *Polarized thinking*—thinking of things as black or white, good or bad, perfect or failures, with no middle ground
3. *Overgeneralization*—jumping to a general conclusion based on a single incident or piece of evidence; expecting something bad to happen over and over again if one bad thing occurs
4. *Mind reading*—thinking that you know, without any external proof, what people are feeling and why they act the way they do; believing yourself able to discern how people are feeling about you
5. *Catastrophizing*—expecting disaster; hearing about a problem and then automatically considering the possible negative consequences (e.g., "What if tragedy strikes?" "What if it happens to me?")
6. *Personalization*—thinking that everything people do or say is some kind of reaction to you; comparing yourself to others, trying to determine who's smarter or better looking
7. *Control fallacies*—feeling externally controlled as helpless or a victim of fate or feeling internally controlled, responsible for the pain and happiness of everyone around
8. *Fallacy of fairness*—feeling resentful because you think you know what is fair, even though other people do not agree
9. *Blaming*—holding other people responsible for your pain or blaming yourself for every problem
10. *Shoulds*—having a list of ironclad rules about how you and other people "should" act; becoming angry at people who break the rules and feeling guilty if you violate the rules
11. *Emotional reasoning*—believing that what you feel must be true, automatically (e.g., if you feel stupid and boring, then you must be stupid and boring)
12. *Fallacy of change*—expecting that other people will change to suit you if you pressure them enough; having to change people because your hopes for happiness seem to depend on them
13. *Global labeling*—generalizing one or two qualities into a negative global judgment
14. *Being right*—proving that your opinions and actions are correct on a continual basis; thinking that being wrong is unthinkable; going to any lengths to prove that you are correct
15. *Heaven's reward fallacy*—expecting all sacrifice and self-denial to pay off, as if there were someone keeping score, and feeling disappointed and even bitter when the reward does not come

Source: Beck, 1976. Adapted from TIP 34.

The Effects of Depression and the Cognitive Triad

As mentioned, much of Beck's work focuses on depression and the debilitating consequences of this disorder. According to Beck (1987) what triggers depression is the coexistence of three main components he calls the cognitive triad. The triad consists of (1) a negative view of oneself, (2) negative interpretations of experiences, and (3) a negative view of future outcomes. When one generally views oneself from a negative standpoint, it is very difficult to experience the actions and words of others from a balanced or accurate perspective. In essence, the starting point for any interaction is always negative. Negative views of oneself, especially when objective evidence does not support such a view, is usually the result of not being properly attended to in earlier formative years. And, this is the case for many offenders. The unfortunate reality is that many offenders, especially those engaged in persistent criminality, have experienced significant neglect and trauma. Common cognitions include, "I am not good enough; I must be wrong; No one will take me serious; if people really knew who I am they would not want to be around me." Especially, when something goes "wrong," or not as planned, the immediate reaction is that it is based on their failures. The list of examples is legion. The important element is that the negative view is central to one's mental landscape even in the absence of evidence.

The result of having a negative view of oneself manifests into negative interpretations of experiences. Regardless of the encounter, the default perception is lined with negativism. Beck (1987) referred to this tendency as selective abstraction. Generally, one will focus on negative aspects of an encounter and ignore anything positive. For example, "You have done a good job, overall. Your work ethic is good and you are always on time. Also, the quality of your work is exceptional and beyond that routinely performed by your colleagues. The only negative comment, worthy of mention, is that you are not always clear in your communication. If you could improve this aspect of your performance it would greatly enhance your overall contribution." A generally balanced and psychologically healthy individual is likely to interpret the above example as a positive review. Individuals with negative views of themselves, however, will focus solely on the suggestion to communicate clearer and construe this element as being an example of their failure. They will selectively abstract the one piece of information that is not positive and view their performance as a complete failure.

The third component of the triad relates to one's negative views of future experiences. A depressed person simply does not see the "light at the end of the tunnel." Most if not all of their conscious thoughts are centered around past, perceived failures, and the likelihood that nothing will change. Everything is grist for the mill. Even past attempts to change their faulty perceptions or behavior will be used to foster their negative perceptions. Thoughts such as, "I am going to begin working on aspects of my life that I can improve" are often met with judgmental retorts such as, "Yeah right, I said that a million times before and still haven't done anything."

Corey (2005) provides several examples of generally depressed people that do a good job of illuminating the core framework from which they operate. Depressed people often set goals that are impossible to attain, not only for them but for anyone. They are often very rigid and lack flexibility. If some event or circumstance does not go as planned they see it as a complete failure. Their worth is judged almost solely on external sources. In other words, what is most important is the view of others and anything short of perfection is not tolerable. Depressed people often hold rigid expectations of others as well. And, in the event that one is not able to meet certain expectations there is a profound feeling of disappointment. Failure is almost always anticipated. One way to guard against failure, for the depressed person, is to make exhaustive efforts to control all variables related to one's life or experience. This, too, however, is a futile attempt. The reality is that one is never able to control all circumstances. Trust is a very scary thought for someone suffering from depression. In essence, they have been "let down" so many times in the past that the only response they know is to not believe in anyone in a misguided attempt to stave off sadness, disappointment, and pain. Finally, depressed people often exaggerate the extent of their responsibilities and external demands. They feel overwhelmed which is accompanied by the expectation that they will not be able to get it done on time.

Beck Depression Inventory

Clearly, depression is among the most robust antecedents of psychological and emotional distress. As a result Beck (1967) created an instrument to objectively measure depression in an attempt to pinpoint the severity of a client's depression as well as possible origins. The Beck Depression Inventory (BDI) consists of 21 variables that depict common symptoms and basic beliefs of depressed people. The depth of one's depression is generally considered to be reflective of the scores provided for each of the variables. The variables measured in the BDI consist of the following:

1. Sadness
2. Pessimism
3. Sense of failure
4. Dissatisfaction
5. Guilt
6. Sense of punishment
7. Self-dislike
8. Self-accusations
9. Suicidal ideation
10. Crying spells
11. Irritability
12. Social withdrawal
13. Indecision
14. Distorted body image
15. Work inhibition
16. Sleep disturbance
17. Fatigue
18. Loss of appetite
19. Weight loss
20. Somatic issues
21. Loss of libido

Based on information gleaned through the BDI, cognitive therapists are able to focus specifically on problem areas and attempt to understand the origins of the symptoms. In essence, the BDI serves as a tool to provide clarity and direction for treating clients suffering from depression. As noted by Corey (2005) the goal is to persuade clients to buy into the idea that enacting some type of change is more likely to alleviate powerful pangs of distress rather than continuing with past behaviors.

Cognitive Behavioral Therapy

Cognitive behavioral therapy (CBT) is a therapeutic modality that combines various aspects of several different therapeutic approaches including behavioral, cognitive, rational, emotive, and others. The hallmark of CBT is the assumption that distress is a result of improper or faulty cognitive framing that provides the foundation for self-defeating thoughts that lead to maladaptive behaviors. Over the last couple of decades CBT has been the focus of extensive research aimed at validating its theoretical foundation and therapeutic techniques. Much of the research reports favorable outcomes within a variety of settings as CBT is often considered among the most diverse therapeutic modalities available to practitioners.

CBT is the logical extension to behavioral and cognitive therapy. It combines the basic components of behavior and cognitive therapy in an attempt to better attend to a fuller range of psychological and emotional stressors that significantly influence behavior. Mahoney and Lyddon (1988) argue that many of the most exciting and advanced therapeutic techniques developed since the 1970s have been within the theoretical construct of CBT.

Ultimately, a person's behavior is driven and guided by a combination of external and internal events. External events driving behavior are well accounted for with the theoretical foundation of behavior therapy. Classical and operant conditioning, when combined, account for behavior that occurs prior and subsequent to learning usually in the form of a reward or punishment. Internal events are more complex and "sneaky" in the manner in which they drive behavior. Internal event refers to internal dialogues that take place within a person's cognitive structure as a result of some stimuli. For example, "*You should put in for that award.*" "*Oh no, Gosh, if they really knew how screwed up I am. Well, you are doing a great job with the offenders. Yes, but these offenders are really doing all of the work. I am just lucky I have them on my caseload. Really, there is nothing that I have done that makes a difference.*" The internal message within this hypothetical is one of not being good enough and low self-esteem among others. The result of this basic cognitive structure is likely to limit one's ability to reach his or her fullest potential which results in stress that accumulates and demands some type of release.

The type of release is what is critical and we would argue that the type of release is related to the level of one's dysfunction and distress. For example, one would be hard pressed to find a human being who is so well adjusted that he or she does not experience anxiety or depression. We are all flawed; however, the extent is what is critical. Criminal offenders, especially those whose criminality has persisted over time, are likely to have the most negative and destructive internal dialogues. The result of these negative dialogues is often criminality, a behavioral act considered wrong by society as well as our legal system. The essence on which the following information is constructed is that most people who engage in persistent criminal behavior over prolonged periods of time and have experienced various correctional responses from incarceration to probation are likely to possess the most negative and destructive internal dialogues that must be restructured if criminal behavior can realistically be expected to be reduced or eliminated. Bartol and Bartol (2008) provide direct support for our basic thesis by stating, "CBT has become the preferred treatment approach for dealing with certain groups of offenders, including sex offender, violent offenders, and a variety of persistent property offenders" (p. 621).

Cognitive Restructuring

"Cognitive restructuring is a process through which offenders are taught to identify, evaluate, and change self-defeating, or irrational thoughts that negatively influence their behavior" (Gladding, 1996, p. 274). Irrational thoughts often occur in the form of "shoulds," "oughts," or "musts." Many offenders have developed a powerful cognitive structure that demands they appear tough, strong, smart, and powerful. These demands have been learned via social processes throughout one's life usually from caretakers and those in his or her immediate environment that seem to garner the most respect. What makes these cognitive schemas so powerful is they are backed by emotional punishments if disobeyed. For example, an offender who has learned that it is important to be tough may feel extreme shame in the face of showing weakness or "backing down."

The experienced shame is very powerful because it is directly related to a prototype the offender views as more powerful than him. The offender who has internalized and accepted the cognitive structure of having to be tough at all times may have heard this from his father. He may have heard his father refer to others perceived as weak in a derogatory fashion. Furthermore, the offender may have even received instruction from his father that he better not find out his son is weak and that no son of his will ever be "seen" as weak. This type of dialogue and learning is extremely powerful due to the authority of the source. This experience manifests itself into the creation of powerful prototypes (authoritative sources) that continuously provide cognitive messages even when they are not physically present. If the offender does not obey the "must" to be tough he has in essence let down his father. For some offenders the emotional pain resulting from such a circumstance may be sufficient to warrant extreme violence. Within the offender population the concept of respect is so powerful that it is likely a factor within the context of most murders.

How does CBT attempt to restructure these dysfunctional cognitions? Meichenbaum (1977) provides a well accepted three-phase process. Phase one is self-observation where the offender begins the process of learning how to identify faulty cognitions and dysfunctional behavior. This can be a very challenging phase for correctional counselors because the task is to disassemble the structure of the dysfunctional, internal message that was crafted and sealed by an important source of authority within the offender's life. The real task of phase one is to get the offender to realize that many of the cognitive structures and internal dialogues governing his life are faulty and will never lead to an existence described as psychologically and emotionally healthy. Phase two is the process of re-creating internal dialogues that are more adaptive and less likely to lead offenders into conflict. They may begin to recreate the dialogue pertaining to respect. It may be that the new dialogue says that if someone disrespects me it does not mean that I have to engage in violence to "save face." This is not the only option I have. In phase three new skills are taught and learned. This is where offenders are taught specific behavioral responses to aversive stimuli that in the past have led to problems. For example, instead of violence the offender may be taught to immediately remove himself from the situation.

SECTION SUMMARY

CBT is a robust therapeutic modality that has received favorable results among many empirical tests. Cognitive and cognitive behavior therapy both focus on the importance of cognition and internal dialogues. Within the offender population a large percentage operate from a skewed cognitive structure heavily influenced by various associations with authoritative sources. The hallmark of CBT is that offenders learn to identify self-defeating messages and behaviors, begin the process of altering faulty messages, and then adapt new behaviors that are more likely to lead to positive results.

LEARNING CHECK

1. Overgeneralization is when someone holds extreme beliefs based on many past incidents.
   a. True
   b. False

2. Cognitive therapy attempts to alleviate distress by teaching offenders new behavior.
   a. True
   b. False

3. According to Beck, people with emotional distress often tilt objective reality toward self-deprecation.
   a. True
   b. False

4. The cognitive triad describes a pattern that triggers depression.
   a. True
   b. False

5. The first phase of Michenbaum's approach is to immediately begin a new internal dialogue.
   a. True
   b. False

CASE VIGNETTE

An Example of CBT with an Offender

John a 23-year-old male residing in an urban area on the west coast has been arrested numerous times for a variety of charges. His most recent charge involves domestic violence as a result of him assaulting his girlfriend after she failed to return home within 30 minutes of completing her shift at work. Sally, John's girlfriend, works for a fast-food restaurant approximately 15 minutes from her apartment (depending on traffic). On the afternoon of John's arrest, Sally was 45 minutes late which infuriated John. When Sally did return home John demanded to know exactly why Sally was late. Sally seemed confused and unsure as to how to answer John because she was late due to her stopping off to pick up John a surprise gift. Sally did not want to ruin the surprise so she hesitated when pressed about her whereabouts. To John, the fact that Sally did not have a definitive and immediate answer proved that she had something to hide. John became convinced that Sally was hiding something from him and was likely cheating on him. In fact, John had been suspicious of one of Sally's co-workers for some time. This was the final bit of evidence he needed. At this point, in John's mind, Sally was being unfaithful and this was not acceptable. John was raised in an environment where men were dominant and made all important decisions. In addition, the men in John's life were free to come and go as they pleased but the females were not allowed the same freedom. In fact, the females were expected to be home and tend to domestic duties. In John's upbringing he was taught that a female who was not obedient needed to be put in her place. John was arrested for twice striking Sally in the back of her head.

COUNSELOR: Can you tell about the day of the incident for which you were arrested?

JOHN: Yes, my girlfriend was late. She did not have any explanation for why she was late. I know that she was probably with another guy. I am a man, and she is not going to disrespect me that way. I will not tolerate it. She is going to understand that I am incharge.

COUNSELOR: Do you have any evidence that your girlfriend was with another man?

JOHN: No, but what would you think if your wife was 45 minutes late?

COUNSELOR: Well, I would probably begin by asking her if she is ok?

JOHN: Asking her if she is ok, man, where I come from a woman is not late and if she is she better have a good reason and she better not start hesitating when questioned. At this point the counselor has identified several important cognitive structures from which John is operating that are faulty. In this case the counselor will probably have to spend a significant amount of time, maybe several sessions, establishing a strong therapeutic alliance with John. For some counselors John's cognitive framework may be very troubling. This must be worked through in order to avoid any hint of judgmentalism. In order to form a strong therapeutic alliance, John will have to grow to trust the counselor and feel that the counselor has valuable information. This will be the foundation on which the counselor is able to slowly begin to teach John how to begin the process of cognitive restructuring. First, the counselor will need to train John to be attentive to his basic internal dialogues. Second, John will need to develop new internal dialogues that are more functional and reflective of objective reality. Finally, John will need to identify behaviors that are first, not illegal and second more conducive to establish meaningful connections with significant others.

COUNSELOR: John, as you were standing in the yard, furious, and waiting for Sally, what was going through your mind?

JOHN: Well, I kept thinking about how my dad used to say that no woman should be allowed to disrespect her man. He used to say that it was not tolerable for a woman to be late and if she was she was probably up to no good. I also started thinking, what is wrong with me? What is it that some other guy has that I don't?

COUNSELOR: Where is your dad?

JOHN: He is in jail. He has been married three times and his last wife just left him. He began drinking one night and when he came in the house she was hanging up the phone. She was said she was talking to her mother but he did not believe her. He roughed her up and the neighbors heard what was going on and called the police. He is probably going to spend some time in prison for this charge because this is like the fifth time he has been arrested for domestic violence.

COUNSELOR: How long have you been in jail?

JOHN: I have been locked up for three weeks because I do not have the money to make bail. And, I hate it in here. I hate to admit it but I am scared. I see people getting beaten up all the time.

COUNSELOR: Ok, John, are you ready to begin working on bettering your life and ultimately identifying healthier responses to certain aversive stimuli?

JOHN: Yes, but how do I do it?

COUNSELOR: First, you have to begin closely monitoring your internal messages regarding such issues as respect and self-worth. Can you envision a scenario where Sally may be late from work but yet have a very valid reason? Can you envision a time where Sally may not immediately come home from work simply because she wanted to go shopping for a while? Can you begin to envision a time where you do not relate such incidents to your self-worth or to the concept of respect?

JOHN: Yes, I think so, but it will be hard.

COUNSELOR: I understand it will be difficult. It is hard to let go of deep, entrenched thought processes that are laced with "shoulds," "oughts," and "musts." However, it will be necessary to change the basic messages you send and receive to yourself regarding the appropriate behavior of Sally or any other woman with whom you may engage in a relationship.

JOHN: So, what types of thoughts should I have? How do I not immediately get angry because I feel disrespected?

COUNSELOR: You can begin by first recognizing that it is never acceptable to strike another person. Regardless of the circumstance, it is never legal to assault another person because you feel disrespected. Your father has engaged in this type of behavior and look where he is at. You have tried it and look where you are at.

JOHN: Yes, you are right. I do not want to spend my life in jail. I also do not want to go through several divorces. I want to marry someone I love and I want to remain with them.

COUNSELOR: What if you tried something different when you begin to feel angry? For example, what if you said to yourself, ok, I am feeling angry because Sally has not yet returned home. But, I am not going to overreact. I am going to wait to hear from Sally. It is possible that there is a valid reason for her not being home yet.

JOHN: Yes, I think I can do this because, really, Sally has never done anything to hurt me. I hate that I scared her so bad and got so angry with her. All I can think about is telling her how sorry I am. And, you know, I really want to be different. I remember my dad telling my mom he was sorry but then he would hit her again the next time he got mad. I want to change so that we can be happy.

COUNSELOR: Ok, so far we have accomplished two important tasks: (1) You have learned that you must be aware of and monitor your internal dialogues. Such messages like a woman's place is in the home and a woman should never be late are not healthy messages from which to make decisions or base your actions; (2) you have learned that it is ok for Sally to be late. It does not mean that she does not respect you. It may be because she is not ready to come home and that is ok. Or, it may be that she has somewhere to go prior to coming home. Regardless of the circumstance, it does not mean that you are being disrespected.

At this point, the counselor may check with John to ensure that the therapeutic alliance is still strong. It may also be beneficial to probe John as to whether he is truly able to internalize these suggestions and new cognitive structures. If so, the counselor is ready to proceed to the final phase which is helping John identify new behaviors. If not, the counselor may need to spend more time with John talking about his concerns as there may be additional information that will need to be explored prior to John being ready to proceed.

JOHN: So what type of suggestions do you have that can help me change my behavior?

COUNSELOR: First, remember that it is never acceptable to assault another person. So that is the first step, to commit to the fact that violence is not an option. And, when you feel yourself beginning to feel threatened that you remember that you will at least talk to Sally before concluding that she is doing something hurtful.

JOHN: Ok, I get it. I know that I can not hit Sally. And, I have committed to never doing this again. Like I said before, I do not want to spend my life in jail. I am better than that. And, I don't have to believe everything I learned from my dad. Look where he is at. And, even when he is not in jail he is not happy because he is constantly worried about making sure he is the "man" of the house.

COUNSELOR: Yes, and you may try this also: When you feel yourself getting worked up and anxious tell Sally how you are feeling. Begin the conversation by first acknowledging that you are feeling angry or fearful. Let Sally begin to help you work through this. Instead of immediately attacking Sally for something she probably did not do, tell her that you are angry and that you are going to do all that you can to remain calm but that you may need some help. Tell Sally that you are working very hard to not buy into the old cognitive structures that demand you not be disrespected. If necessary, you may also take a little time to gather your thoughts before talking with Sally. In fact, you may create distance between you and Sally until you feel ready to talk in a nonthreatening manner.

JOHN: It will not be easy but at least now I have a new way of thinking about things. In the past I was not open or familiar with any alternatives other than feeling disrespected and feeling as though I must do something about it or I was not a real man. I realize that this is crazy and will only lead to trouble.

PART THREE: REALITY THERAPY

Reality therapy was created by William Glasser, born in 1925 in Cleveland, Ohio. Glasser's initial training was in chemical engineering where he received a degree from Case Institute of Technology. He then decided to attend graduate school and in so doing began studying clinical psychology. After completing his master's degree, Glasser then chose to attend medical school graduating in 1953 from Western Reserve University. Glasser specialized in psychiatry and was board certified in 1961. By 1962 Glasser had created the structure for what he called reality therapy (Corey, 2056; Gladding, 1996).

The foundation of Glasser's reality therapy is predicated on a few central postulates. First, Glasser and Zunin (1979) delineated old and new brain needs. Formerly, humans were mostly guided by physical needs to survive. Paramount concerns included those related to food and drink. In modern times, however, most humans do not experience these same concerns. Therefore, with basic (old brain) needs mostly met humans began grappling with the powerful pangs and often elusive new brain needs. According to Gladding (1996) new brain needs consist of the following four psychological needs:

1. Belonging—the need for friends, family, and love
2. Power—the need for self-esteem, recognition, and competition
3. Freedom—the need to make choices and decisions
4. Fun—the need for play, laughter, learning, and recreation (p. 279).

How do we best satisfy each of these new brain needs? According to reality therapy new brain needs are best satisfied through healthy relationships with others. Therefore, the second major postulate is the realization that modern humans need to establish nurturing, loving, and lasting relationships with others. Without satisfying relationships through which people are able to connect in meaningful and fulfilling ways modern human needs can not be met.

When humans are not able to establish meaningful connections with others most will begin to engage in maladaptive behaviors that are misguided attempts to fulfill basic needs. For reality therapists this is the crux of most dysfunctions. People are either not meaningfully connected to others or the connection is unsatisfying. And, it is from this basic framework that Glasser largely rejects the medical model related to mental illness (Glasser, 2003) and adamantly denounces the use of medication to treat emotional and psychological symptoms related to a lack of satisfying human connections (Corey, 2005).

The third major postulate of reality therapy is that people make choices in relation to how they respond to various stimuli. This is an important component of reality therapy. In essence, behavior is purposeful and based on conscious thoughts that direct us in ways we feel are most likely to get our needs met. Total behavior is a concept used by reality therapists that describe four interrelated components of all behaviors:

1. Doing—the outward, overt, physical act of taking some form of action
2. Thinking—the thought process of driving the specific physical actions we choose to carry out
3. Feeling—the feelings associated with our thoughts and actions that can be either positive or negative
4. Physiology—the physiological reactions related to what we do, think, and feel. Similar to feelings, physiological reactions can be positive or negative. An example could include the energized feeling one gets as a result of exercise (Corey, 2006; Gladding, 1996).

Fundamental to reality therapy is its emphasis on personal responsibility. Especially, with offender populations this concept is critical. Many offenders avoid taking responsibility for their actions and instead adopt the role of victim. Choice therapy, however, operates from the assumption that people do have choices and it is based on these choices that one will achieve our most basic desire—closeness with another.

In order to accentuate this concept, Glasser published *Positive addiction* (1976) and also the *Identity society* (1972). The essence of both of these works is fundamentally related to the idea of choice as well as the need for identity. We all have a basic psychological need to establish an identity that is unique and meaningful. Glasser (1972) made these points clear in what he called the success identity. Central to developing a success identity is being accepted for who you are, including faults and imperfections, by others. When one feels accepted by others there is usually a transfusion of feelings of love and worth, both of which are central components to a success identity. The antithesis is a failure identity usually developed in the absence of love and acceptance. Common characteristics of a failure identity include a basic sense of insecurity where one's conclusions based on some stimuli are often erroneous. In addition, people suffering from a failure identity usually lack confidence to try new things and tend to give up easily. In essence they see life as a string of failures and come to accept this as normal. Common verbiage coinciding with a failure identity may include, "Why try, I never succeed. I guess my family was right, I am useless."

The Function and Role of the Therapist

Reality therapists work to create success identities and help offenders gain psychological strength. The first and most important goal is to establish a strong therapeutic alliance. This is important to understand when one considers that most offenders are offenders because they never felt truly accepted by their caregivers. Most offenders have developed a failure identity as a result of being abused and/or neglected. The reality therapists' first task is to therefore accept the offender via nonjudgmental caring and empathy. This is the foundation that will eventually allow the therapist to gently confront the offender when necessary or to focus on reality and also what is rational. Without building a strong therapeutic alliance, subsequent techniques will be rejected primarily due to the lack of feeling perceived by the offender in relation to the therapist and the therapeutic process. According to Gladding (1996) therapists may even choose to disclose personal information as a gesture to help establish understanding and acceptance as well as an attempt to express to the offender the therapist's belief and faith in his or her ability to change. In essence, counselors get involved with the offender and work to establish a meaningful relationship.

Once a strong relationship between offender and therapist has been forged various action-oriented techniques may be deployed. Gladding (1996) notes that reality therapists routinely use techniques such as teaching, humor, confrontation, role-playing, feedback, plans, and contracts within the therapeutic process. The most important task beyond the therapeutic alliance is identifying behavior that is dysfunctional. Reality therapists work to help offenders face the reality of their behaviors and that their behavior is their responsibility. This recognition often requires confrontation in order to help an offender identify and accept responsibility for his or her actions. It is critical to note, however, that this process is delicate and as is always the case the counselor must be well grounded because the counselor must reject the offender's dysfunctional behavior without rejecting the offender as a person. Well-placed and cleverly guided humor may serve as an excellent tool in this process. Positive, nonjudgmental humor can be significantly lighten the emotional burden offenders carry into the counseling process as a result of the very natural fear of exposing oneself.

Once the problem behavior(s) have been identified reality therapists begin to work with offenders by helping them identify new behaviors more capable of producing desired results. This is often done through teaching and role-playing. Wubbolding (1991, 1998), a significant contributor to reality therapy, established the WDEP system which can be used as an excellent guide for reality therapists. Each of the letters within the acronym signifies one of the major components of reality therapy: W = wants, D = doing, E = evaluate, and P = plan. It is critical to find out what clients want. For example, what kind of person do you want to be? And, what are you doing to be the person you want to be? Counselors also help offenders evaluate their actions. For example, when you steal as opposed to buying what you want, what has happened? And, each time you are arrested, how does this affect your chances of obtaining meaningful employment? The remaining step is planning for future behaviors that are more likely to produce positive results. This is among the most difficult aspects of the reality therapy process. While in the presence of a sanitized environment, the counselor's office, most plans seem good and are readily agreed upon by the offender. In the real world of the offender, however, and in the presence of peers who are also likely to be involved in criminal activity, the fragility of most plans quickly resonates.

Plans must be concrete, executable, and realistic in relation to many of the variables most offenders must contend with. For example, it would not be realistic and even counterproductive to construct a plan with an offender that calls for him or her to no longer associate with anyone involved in criminal activity. It may be that his or her parents or brothers and sisters also engage in criminal acts. Obviously, this point would not be valid in the case of serious or violent crimes. What is critical is that the plan be one that is attainable and specific to the offender so that he or she is able to take ownership of the plan and make a sincere commitment to carry it out. In some cases the plan may be written out with each component clearly articulated simulating a formal contract. Once the contract has been agreed upon, reality therapists make clear that no excuses will be accepted for a lack of execution. Although this is a critical step that we strongly support, a word of caution is necessary. Counselors should only execute a contract followed up with strong expectations highlighted by no excuses when they are confident in their alliance with the offenders. Many offenders endure harsh verbal and physical abuse at the hands of authoritative figures. Without a strong alliance some offenders may aversely react to messages or language implying authority.

Finally, the reality therapist must be fully committed to the offender. As noted by Glasser (1965, 1980), counselors should not give up on clients even when they fail to follow through on agreements. In fact, we would argue that it would be the rare case where an offender would follow through with all agreements without any deviation. Most offenders will fail or relapse at various points in counseling. Counselors must understand this natural process and not take it personally. It may be that the mot significant gains are made after a breach of contract when the offender realized that the counselor is still there, still committed to his success, and is not going to abandon him. Most individuals whose criminal offending persists into adulthood have experienced chronic abandonment by those who were supposed to love them. A counselor's genuine care that clearly articulates that he or she will not abandon the offender may be sufficient to begin the process of restructuring the cycle of failure prevalent in the offender population.

SECTION SUMMARY

Reality therapy is a popular therapeutic modality with the offender population. Its primary focus is on the present and what the offender is doing now. The therapeutic alliance is critical and offenders must feel accepted, respected, and understood. It will be the alliance that will allow the reality therapist to confront dysfunctional behavior as well as the natural hesitancy to take ownership of behavior. Once the alliance has been established the focus turns to dysfunctional behavior that is inhibiting the formation of a meaningful success identity. Nonjudgmental guidance is paramount as the counselor begins to formulate a plan, in conjunction with the offender, aimed at identifying alternative responses and behavior to negative stimuli. Plans must be specific and concrete but also flexible. Plans should be drafted in the form of a contract in order to stimulate ownership as well as to ensure comprehension especially as it relates to realism and attainability. Finally, reality therapists need to be engaged with offenders. Counselors must be empathic and tenacious in their attempt to help offenders and always cognizant of the importance of reassuring offenders that they believe in their ability to change and that they will not be abandoned.

LEARNING CHECK

1. The successful creation of a therapeutic alliance is not that important as reality therapy techniques are designed to focus on analyzing subconscious processes.
   a. True
   b. False
2. Autonomy and accepting responsibility for behavior are primary components of reality therapy.
   a. True
   b. False
3. In reality therapy counselors should never confront offenders as this may damage the therapeutic alliance.
   a. True
   b. False
4. Reality therapists are more interested in present behaviors than they are in the past.
   a. True
   b. False
5. In reality therapy the counselor should always refrain from using humor.
   a. True
   b. False

CASE VIGNETTE

Using Reality Therapy with an Offender Arrested for Theft

John is a 24-year-old white male who has been arrested several times for theft. He began stealing things early in his life and the process continued up until his most recent arrest for attempting to steal a flat screen television set from the local Home Depot. John's parents divorced when he was 10 years old. His father was an alcoholic who frequently abused his mother both verbally and physically. His mother worked several different jobs and was rarely available to tend to anything more than John's most basic needs. John has been sentenced to probation and one of the requirements is that John attends weekly counseling sessions. The following dialogue generally captures the main components of John's exposure to reality therapy. A very important caveat, however, must be clearly expressed. The following dialogue is based on the assumption that John trusts and believes the counselor. In other words, a therapeutic alliance has been established.

JOHN: A lot of times it's just easier to take something. I don't have a regular job and things are expensive.

COUNSELOR: I understand; however, is stealing something getting you what you want?

JOHN: Well, not really because I am always worried about getting arrested and the judge told me that if I go back to court I am going to be sent to prison.

COUNSELOR: So, what do you want to do?

JOHN: I don't know, I am scared. I never went to college so I can't get a good job.

COUNSELOR: It is ok to be scared, however, to get what you are really needing you must change your behavior.

JOHN: That's easy for you to say.

COUNSELOR: It's also easy for you to continue to steal and not change your behavior.

JOHN: Well, if it is so easy, tell me what to do.

COUNSELOR: Tell me something, how would you describe the life you would like to be living?

JOHN: Well, I really would like to be a certified auto mechanic. I like working on engines and they make good money.

COUNSELOR: Then go do it.

JOHN: I can't, I don't know how to work on ALL engines.

COUNSELOR: How can you not do it? What is the alternative?

Once John was able to articulate a style of life that would be more fulfilling the process then progressed to formulating a plan capable of getting John what he wanted. This dialogue is primarily aimed at depicting the process of confronting an offender. Offenders involved with the criminal justice system will not usually give up behavioral adaptations easily. If they were open to alternatives they probably would not be in the criminal justice system. Once the offenders accept the fact that they will not get what they want unless they change their behavior they are usually ready to work with the counselor in constructing a plan. Some offenders, however, will not make this transition from openly acknowledging their current behavior is not able to get their needs met to actually constructing and taking ownership of a plan to change. If this occurs it is critical that counselors remain nonjudgmental and supportive. Some offenders may need more time. A counselor who takes this personal will likely do grave harm to the alliance. Finally, once the plan has been established and agreed upon the counselor will remain committed to the client, constantly providing reassurance.

PART FOUR: GESTALT THERAPY

Gestalt therapy is among the most popular therapeutic modalities in current practice. Gestalt is a concept that describes the process of becoming whole. The thrust of Gestalt therapy is aimed at helping individuals experience enhanced perceptions of wholeness. The focus is primarily on awareness and what a person is feeling and experiencing now as opposed to the past. Frederick Solomon Perls is regarded as being most responsible for popularizing Gestalt therapy (Gladding, 1996). Perls, born in 1893 to a middle class family in Germany, immigrated to the United States in 1946 where he established the Gestalt institutes providing training in Gestalt therapy through lectures and workshops. Throughout Perl's professional life he was fortunate to meet and work with some of the most significant contributors to the field of psychology including Sigmund Freud, Wilhelm Reich, and Karen Horney (Corey, 2006). It may be, however, that Perls's most significant association was with Kurt Goldstein. According to Gladding (1996) it was from Goldstien that Perls came to view people as whole or complete beings as opposed to being composed of separate parts. As noted by Perls (1969) individuals are more than simply the sum of their parts.

Basics of Gestalt Therapy

Gestalt therapy is a modality most focused on the concept of "now." Perhaps Perls (1970) articulates this best in a formula he developed stating, "Now = experience = awareness = reality" (p. 14). Perls believed that many people suffering distress were engaged in excessive intellectualization of life events that inhibited the flow of natural emotion. For example, intellectually, a person may reason that they "should" or "should not" react in a certain way to some stimuli. The result of this "intellectualizing" is the stymied flow of true emotion resulting in their suppression and over time will lead to distress. In essence, overintellectualization inhibits the natural self's expression and fractures the gestalt. This is precisely the reason that in Gestalt therapy, "why" questions are avoided. "Why" questions have a tendency to initiate intellectualization as opposed to what and how questions that focus more on the present (Gladding, 1996).

Another significant aspect of Gestalt therapy is working with unfinished business. In this context, unfinished business is past figures or experiences that manifest such feelings as anger, rage, guilt, fear, and abandonment. Unfinished business is significant and must be dealt with in order to restore the gestalt. Unfinished business from the past that results in powerful negative emotions in the present is generally the result of someone experiencing negative stimuli at a time or place where one did not feel he or she was in possession of significant power to respond authentically. As a result of these experiences emotions were again suppressed and in the present often provide the foundation from which one feels fractured. For example, someone who has experienced significant abandonment by primary caregivers while growing up may experience severe anxiety in certain circumstances that may be expressed in rage as one attempts to regain control. An adult suffering from the effects from such unfinished business is likely to engage in behavior that significantly reduces the individual's ability to reach his or her fullest potential.

Working with unfinished business can be difficult and extremely demanding. For most people, the thought of revisiting past events that were extremely painful and traumatic fosters fear and anxiety. These precise moments can be very beneficial to the counselor as the offenders are likely to respond in similar fashions as they would in real-world interactions. The offender who becomes defensive or hostile while attempting to work through unfinished business is likely to do the same in other settings. And, it will usually be these behaviors presented as troublesome and causing distress. For example, offenders may initially report that they often feel defensive or anxious when engaged with others and would like to work on this because it is limiting their ability to feel whole. What they may not realize initially is that these behaviors are a result of unfinished business regarding prototypes. Herein lies the essence of working with unfinished business and why it is paramount. The offender must be guided through the process of experiencing the real, unfettered emotion of harmful past experiences. Only by experiencing these suppressed emotions in the present will one be freer to choose his or her responses in the now.

It may be that offenders will be most open to working with unfinished business when they perceive themselves to be stuck or at an impasse. In other words, they do not know what else to do and their traditional responses of control, anger, violence, fear, and intimidation have failed them. At this point counselors may provide the most assistance by simply being there with the offender and providing an opportunity, free of judgmentalism, for the offender to experience and feel his or her frustrations fully. The goal is to become aware of their feelings and "accept whatever is, rather than wishing they were different" (Corey, 2006, p. 197).

The Value of Contact and Resistance to Contact

Contact in Gestalt therapy describes the process of interacting with the environment, especially with other people, in order to learn and grow as individuals (Corey, 2006). Human beings need contact in order to be whole. Positive contact allows us to experience sensations in the present that foster energy through the process of expression (Zinker, 1978). It is through contact with others that we get a sense of being "good enough" and that our authentic self is worthy. Through such positive interactions we are better able to experience gestalt and are free from having to pretend or appearing to be something we are not.

Unfortunately, contact with others is not always positive. In fact, some contacts can be extremely damaging and can greatly affect one's sense of self-worth. The most damaging contact is likely to result from being rejected by primary caregivers. This is usually the source of unfinished business most likely to be encountered within the counseling process. When one experiences negative contact whether from caregivers or others the result is usually in the form of painful emotion. In essence, we feel rejected and as a result of these painful experiences begin to construct defenses to reduce the likelihood of experiencing similar circumstances in future contacts. Often these defenses, or resistances to contact, are constructed early in life and become firmly ingrained as one proceeds through life. The power of these defenses is firmly rooted in our attempt to avoid painful feelings that detract from our self-concept and leave us feeling inadequate. The paradox lies in the fact that the defenses we use to protect our self are precisely what keep us from being whole.

E. Polster and Polster (1973), who have written prolifically in regards to Gestalt therapy, provide five primary defenses that must be challenged. **Introjection** describes the process of freely accepting information from others without any critique of one's own thoughts or ideas. In spite of any evidence, we internalize whatever we receive from our environment. If someone says "we are not good enough, or will never achieve what others have," we accept this without restructuring it into a realistic framework. **Projection** is commonly used as a defense and is the opposite of introjection. We project onto others the traits or characteristics that are not congruous with the person we would like to be. This defense allows us to blame others for the characteristics we refuse to face in ourselves. Subconsciously we decide that it is easier to blame others than face the painful reality that we are not perfect. **Retroflection** is the process of doing to ourselves what we would like to do to someone else. We may injure our self in an attempt to reduce strong feelings of pain or anger instead of directing our actions toward others whom we likely view as being too powerful. In some cases, prolonged drug abuse can be seen as an example of retroflection. Instead of confronting those who have harmed us we direct our pain inward through the use of foreign substances that eventually destroy our bodies. **Deflection** describes the process of diverting meaningful contact that is perceived to be threatening. People who do not have a basic sense of well-being often experience extreme difficulty with accepting praise or compliments; beneath the surface there is the rebuttal of, "Yeah, but . . . ," "If they only knew . . . " This defense greatly reduces one's ability to experience meaningful emotion. **Confluence** is a defense that describes the process of staying safe by not expressing one's feelings or opinions. People may engage in criminality with others because they are afraid to say no. They want to be liked and accepted and so they feel that the only way to accomplish this is through compliance.

These types of resistance to contact share a fundamental foundation. The attempt, albeit misguided, is to control one's environment in order to reduce his or her chances of being hurt. As noted above, however, when one or more of these defenses are employed the ability to experience wholeness is impossible.

The Function and Role of the Therapist

The first and most important role of the therapist is to create the foundation from which a strong therapeutic alliance can be built. This is a critical aspect of any therapeutic modality but is especially so with therapies that employ confrontation, such as Gestalt therapy. The atmosphere must be one that encourages offenders to freely and fully explore areas of their life that are creating or contributing to distress. Especially when working with offenders, counselors must be honest and involved. Counselors need to be energetic and exciting (Polster & Polster, 1973) and work to keep offenders focused in the now (Perls, 1969).

The Importance of Verbal and Nonverbal Communication

For Gestalt counselors one of the most important tasks is to guide offenders into the "now." The focus is on rationality and assisting offenders in taking ownership of thoughts and behaviors. To do this, counselors pay careful attention to verbal and nonverbal communication. Corey (2006) discusses several important clues that provide rich insight into an offender's internal dialogue that often needs to be modified. The central theme to the following clues is they are aimed at reducing the offender's sense of responsibility for actions. Often offenders will use "it" talk as opposed to "I" talk. "It" talk functions to depersonalize circumstances relegating them to the "general" instead of the "present." An offender may say, "it is very difficult to stay out of fights." The alert counselor may suggest the offender restate this in the form of "I have difficulty staying out of fights." "You" talk is similar to "it" talk. This type of verbal communication functions to keep the offender sheltered by globalizing circumstances. The implied question associated with "you" talk is "Wouldn't you?" "Would you not do the same thing?" The counselor's task is to get the offender to substitute "you" with "I." **Questions** also keep the offender sheltered and mysterious. Often offenders will respond with numerous questions instead of direct statements. Questions function to keep the offender from directly facing reality.

Language that denies power is very important to identify. As long as an offender is allowed to use language that detracts from his or her personal power he or she will not realize the essence of Gestalt therapy—wholeness. Qualifiers such as "maybe, perhaps, sort of, I guess, possibly and I suppose" (Corey, 2006, p. 201) need to be transformed into direct statements. Similarly, offenders will often use "I can't" instead of the accurate and direct statement of "I won't." Finally, **listening for language that uncovers a story** can provide a wealth of information regarding an offender's true mental and emotional landscape. This can be challenging because most offenders will not be accustomed in using direct statements that expose them. Indirect language should be viewed by the counselor as a defense mechanism that is ultimately used to protect oneself from being rejected or harshly judged. During the process of communicating, offenders will often glaze over salient information regarding their life and who they are. In order to be effective, counselors must be alert to these subtleties in language and strategically and gently guide the offender back into the part of the offender's life story that is most frightening or exposing in order to experience real and meaningful interaction. Real progress and healing will take place in sessions where the counselor is able to create an environment where an offender is able to explore real emotions and not be critically judged but instead accepted as a human being.

Common Gestalt Techniques

"Some of the most innovative counseling techniques ever developed are found in Gestalt Therapy" (Gladding, 1996, p. 227). The one precursor, however, essential to the application of Gestalt techniques is the authenticity of the counselor. As noted by Corey (2006), to mechanically apply therapeutic techniques does little to provide the foundation on which offenders are able to transform inauthentic living to that which is filled with feeling and the ability to express oneself wholly. Also, it is important to differentiate between two different concepts, exercises, and experiments, commonly used in Gestalt therapy. Exercises are ready-made techniques (Corey, 2006; Gladding, 1996) applied to certain circumstances in order to provoke a response from an offender or further exploration of feeling. Experiments are spontaneous and grow out of specific interactions taking place within the counseling relationship. For example, an offender filled with anger and rarely able to experience joy or playfulness may be asked to do something silly. He may be asked to lie on his back on the floor and flail his arms and legs. To the offender this may seem bizarre and completely void of any practical reasoning. The point, however, is to demonstrate that it is ok to be silly—it can be fun and invigorating even if control is set aside only for a short time. Experiments are vital to Gestalt therapy and provide the path for exploring stimuli responsible for much of the offender's distress.

Among the most poignant of Gestalt techniques is **confrontation**. It is critical that counselors be able to point out incongruencies in what offenders are doing and saying. The ability to effectively confront offenders requires counselors to be authentic and also brave enough to endure negative reactions as offenders struggle to maintain the "props" that have supported their egos and justified their actions. It is important to note that confrontation in contemporary Gestalt therapy is not meant to be harsh or delivered in the form of attacks. Modern Gestalt therapy has far advanced many of the techniques exhibited by its founder, Fritz Perls. As noted by Yontef (1993) it appears as though Perls, in many cases, was more interested in meeting his own needs than those of his clients. Confrontation is the attempt to gently transform an offender into a more real person by showing him or her acceptance for who he or she really is and that denying one's responsibility is not capable of providing wholeness.

Another technique common to Gestalt therapy is **dialoguing with polarities**. The polarities are commonly depicted as the "top dog" and "under dog." The top dog is the part of our personality that is associated with governing our thoughts and actions. It is perfectionistic and overly demanding. The top dog is where "shoulds" originate. The underdog takes the opposite stance and usually relies on the perception of being powerless and is very capable of creating clever excuses for not acting or changing one's behavior. Without intervention these two sides become embroiled in a bitter battle that deflates one's energy and sense of wholeness. One of the most effective techniques in dealing with polarities is the **empty chair**. The offender is guided through a process where the use of an empty chair is used as a prop to illuminate the internal struggle caused by conflicting messages. The essence of the empty chair technique is to enhance awareness and reduce fragmentation. The offender is guided through the process of placing each polarity into the empty chair and then verbalizing its demands. Ultimately, the offender is able to internalize how each polarity is bombarding the authentic self with messages that are impossible to carry out, or place extreme demands on the authentic self that if carried out will greatly detract from one's quality of life.

Role-playing is a technique used to help offenders identify and adapt more functional responses to aversive stimuli. This can be a very beneficial exercise for offenders who feel "trapped" or "locked in" to certain responses that they feel must be carried out under certain circumstances. For example, the offender who feels he must respond with violence to any circumstances where there is the perception of being disrespected may begin to explore various alternatives by playing out different roles within the safety of the counseling process.

Staying with feelings is the process through which counselors help offenders remain in the present with feelings that are frightening or shameful. Most human beings have a very difficult time remaining in the present with feelings that threaten our cognitive equilibrium. Humans are well served by arranging feelings and emotions in ways that reduce anxiety. The problem with this, however, is that it is impossible to reach the origins of dysfunction by attempting to alter or rearrange feelings on the surface. The consequence of not staying with feelings and investigating the origins is that the same defensive techniques will continue to be employed when presented with threatening stimuli. The counselor's task is to encourage the offender to stay with feelings for as long as possible. The longer the offender is able to remain in the present with feelings the better the chances of uncovering the origins of the feelings which can then be processed and evaluated.

Making the rounds is a Gestalt technique commonly employed in group settings. This can be a very powerful technique as offenders are encouraged and guided through the process of "checking out" their feelings with the members of the group. Corey (2005) provides a good example of how he has used this technique with clients having difficulty trusting others. Offenders are also likely to find it very difficult to trust most human beings because they would have often experienced rejection and neglect during their formative years. For those offenders having a difficult time taking the risk associated with sharing their feelings, making the rounds may prove very beneficial. An offender may be encouraged to address each member of the group and begin the dialogue with "What makes it hard for me to trust you is . . ." (Corey, 2005, p. 211). The goal is to help offenders begin the process of taking risks and understanding that not everyone will judge them with the harshness they have experienced in the past.

Exaggeration is often used in Gestalt therapy to heighten awareness surrounding various messages the offender may be sending. Exaggeration is usually used in conjunction with behavior but can be adapted to cognitive processes as well. An example could include a counselor guiding an offender through the "worst case scenario" of some real or imagined stimuli. The ultimate goal is to reduce fear in relation to a circumstance or encounter the offender perceives as distressing.

CASE VIGNETTE

An Example of Gestalt Therapy Used with an Offender Suffering from Substance Abuse

Sandra is a 38-year-old African-American woman who has abused a number of substances, including cocaine, heroine, alcohol, and marijuana over the past 15 years. She left high school and was a prostitute for five years. Later she found a job as a sales clerk at a home furnishings store. Sandra had two children in her early 20s, a daughter who is now 15, and a son, aged 18. Because of her substance abuse problems, they live with other relatives who agreed to raise them. Sandra has been in treatment repeatedly and has remained substance-free for the last five years, with several minor relapses. She has been married for two years to Steve, a carpenter; he is substance-free and supports her attempts to stay away from substances.

Last month she became symptomatic with AIDS. She has been HIV-positive for five years but had not developed any illnesses related to the disease. Sandra has practiced safe sex with her husband who knew of her HIV status. Recently, after learning from the physician at her clinic about her HIV symptoms, she began to "shoot up," which led her back into treatment. Out of fear, she came to the treatment center and asked to see a counselor at the clinic one day after work. She is worried about her marriage and that her husband will be devastated by this news. She is afraid she is no longer strong enough to stay away from drugs since discovering the onset of AIDS. She is also concerned about her children and her job. Uncertain of how she will keep on living, she is also terrified of dying.

Response to the case study

The Gestalt therapist begins with Sandra's current experience of the world, starting with awareness and attention. The therapist may simply help her become aware of basic sights, sounds, somatic reactions, feelings, and thoughts as well as what her attention drifts to. The immediate contact between therapist and client is a component of the "now" where these sensations are explored directly. The therapist might notice and ask about her style of eye contact, or her fidgeting body, or stream of thoughts (e.g., "What is it like to make eye contact now? What is the sensation in your body at this moment?").

Sandra may also identify certain issues such as substance abuse, relationship difficulties, and the threat of death from AIDS that seem to dominate her life. The therapist might invite her to name and explore the sensation that the thought of death, for example, brings; perhaps this involves a sense of a void, or feeling cold and dark, or a feeling of engulfment. She then may be asked to become these sensations—for example, the therapist may ask her to be "the void" and encourage her to speak as if she were that void. This may then open possibilities for a dialog with the void through acting out the opposite polarity: separateness and choice. This might involve using an empty chair technique in which the client would literally move into the chair of the "void," speak as if she were that, and then move into an opposite chair and respond in a dialog. A therapist could also explore her introjection through questions such as, "How is this void different or the same as from the feeling of alcohol or in relationships with your children or husband?" She might also use this same technique to dialog with family members, or certain aspects of herself.

Sandra seems to have a great deal of "unfinished business" that involves unexpressed feelings (e.g., anger, longing, hurt). Experimentation with these sensations may begin to free her to express and meet these feelings more directly. All of this work encourages Sandra's experimentation with new ways of relating both during and outside of the session in order to move into the "here and now" and work toward the resolution of "unfinished business."

Source: Barry, K. L. (1999). *Brief interventions and brief therapies for substance abuse.* DHHS Publication No. (SMA) 99-3353. Substance Abuse and Mental Health Services Administration. Rockville, MD.

SECTION SUMMARY

Gestalt therapy is primarily aimed at helping offenders modify dysfunctional behavior through enhanced awareness of feeling and emotion. The essence of Gestalt therapy is wholeness. In other words, as long as one is fragmented and not functioning from a unified perspective there will be distress. Gestalt therapy is direct and firmly predicated on a strong alliance between the counselor and offender. Reality or "realness" is also a big part of Gestalt therapy. The work of the counselor is to help offenders identify troublesome behavior and begin to develop new ways of getting their needs met. Confrontation is the mainstay of Gestalt techniques. However, it is delivered gently and with empathy.

LEARNING CHECK

1. Modern Gestalt therapy is still practiced in the same manner in which it was introduced by Fritz Perls.
   a. True
   b. False
2. Wholeness is important to Gestalt therapy but not as important as intellectualization.
   a. True
   b. False
3. The empty chair is a common technique used in Gestalt therapy.
   a. True
   b. False
4. In Gestalt therapy, counselors rarely confront offenders due to the fact that this may damage the therapeutic alliance.
   a. True
   b. False
5. In most cases the "top dog" will be correct and should be obeyed, especially in light of the fact that most "shoulds" have been ingrained through the interactions with care givers.
   a. True
   b. False

CONCLUSION

In this chapter various therapeutic modalities have been explored. Each modality consists of specific theoretical underpinnings that provide the foundation for techniques aimed at altering cognitions and behaviors. For example, some modalities believe it essential that past experiences be fully explored while others pay no attention to past experiences and concentrate solely on present feelings and actions. In the end, most modern therapeutic modalities have more in common than not. First, the therapeutic alliance is central to all. Without a strong alliance little progress should be expected. The counselor should lead this process and foster the alliance through respect and nonjudgmental modeling aimed at creating a comfortable and safe environment. Second, once the alliance has been established each modality begins the process of attempting to change behavior.

Behavior therapy is concerned with altering dysfunctional behavior via the process of classical or operant conditioning. Reward and punishment are central to behavior therapy with little concern for underlying psychological issues that may be contributing to distress. Cognitive therapy and cognitive behavior therapy are most concerned with altering behavior via the alteration of cognition. Over the past several decades, cognitive modalities have received an abundance of support as being very effective in producing meaningful change. Reality and Gestalt therapy are both concerned with the "now" and strive to create wholeness through mending fractured parts of the self. They are also heavily focused on rationality and pay careful attention to what is realistic for an individual offender.

Finally, we would like to aggressively assert that these modalities are a small sampling of a very rich field containing many more techniques all aimed at helping people realize more of their natural self. Over the last couple of decades there have been strong movements to integrate several different theories in order to capture more of the variance associated with distress. We encourage students to carefully explore the basic foundations of each therapeutic modality. Often the one that will fit best will be the one that is most aligned with an individual's own preferred methods of learning. Effective counseling is really about the counselor and not the specific modality. The modalities provide direction, insight, and techniques all of which are very beneficial. The true worth of their application, however, will be decided by the quality of the counselor which is usually most correlated with the depth of one's own self-exploration and understanding.

Essay Questions

1. Explain why behavior therapy may be very successful in some circumstances. Also, identify several circumstances in which behavior therapy may not be successful. Why?
2. Discuss the basic tenets of cognitive therapy. Why, in your opinion, was much of Beck's work concerned with depression?
3. Explain the basic premise of reality therapy. Discuss two of the techniques you think would be most effective with offenders.
4. Explain the basic premise of Gestalt therapy. Discuss the importance of the *Impasse*.
5. Explain, using your own words, why the therapeutic alliance is so important in confronting offenders.

Treatment Planning Exercise

During this exercise, the student should consider the case of Mike. Mike has Narcissistic personality disorder, which makes him very difficult to treat. Students should choose two theoretical approaches from behavioral, cognitive, reality, and/or Gestalt theoretical perspectives. The student should explain how they would provide counseling with Mike using their first chosen theoretical perspective and then they should do the same again with their second theoretical perspective. Once the students have done this, they should then compare and contrast both approaches noting how each would address Mike's issues while also noting some limitations to any of the theoretical perspectives that were chosen.

The Case of Mike

Mike is a 20-year-old male who has just recently been released from jail. Mike is technically on probation for car theft, though he has been involved in crime to a much greater extent. Mike has been identified as a cocaine user and has been suspected, though not convicted, for dealing cocaine. Mike has been tested for drugs by his probation department and was found positive for cocaine. The county has mandated that Mike receive drug counseling but the drug counselor has referred Mike to your office because the drug counselor suspects that Mike has issues beyond simple drug addiction. In fact, the drug counselor's notes suggest that Mike has Narcissistic personality disorder.

Mike seems to have little regard for the feelings of others. Coupled with this is his complete sensitivity to the comments of others. In fact, his prior fiancé has broken off her relationship with him due to what she calls his "constant need for admiration and attention. He is completely self-centered." After talking with Mike, you quickly find that he has no close friends. As he talks about people who have been close to him, he discounts them for one imperfection or another. These imperfections are all considered severe enough to warrant dismissing the person entirely. Mike makes a point of noting how many have betrayed their loyalty to him or have otherwise failed to give him the credit that he deserves.

When asked about getting caught in the auto theft, he remarks that "well my dumb partner got me out of a hot situation by driving me out in a stolen get-a-way car." (Word on the street has it that Mike was involved in a sour drug deal and was unlikely to have made it out alive if not for his partner.) Mike adds, "you know, I plan everything out perfectly, but you just cannot rely on anybody . . . if you want it done right, do it yourself."

Mike recently has been involved with another woman (unknown to his prior fiancé) who has become pregnant. When she told Mike he said "tough, you can go get an abortion or something, it isn't like we were in love or something." Then he laughed at her and told her to go find some other guy who would shack up with her.

Incidentally, Mike is a very attractive man and he likes to point that out on occasion. "Yeah, I was going to be a male model in L. A., but my agent did not know what he was doing . . . could never get things settled out right . . . so I had to fire him." Mike is very popular with women and has had a constant string of failed relationships due to what he calls "their inability to keep things exciting."

As Mike puts it "hey, I am too smart for this stuff. These people around me, they don't deserve the good life cause they're a bunch of dummies. But me, well I know how to run things and get over on people. And I am not about to let these dummies get in my way. I got it all figured out . . . see?"

Bibliography

Bartol, C. R., & Bartol, A. M. (2008). *Criminal behavior: A psychosocial approach* (8th ed.). Upper Saddle River, NJ: Pearson/Prentice Hall.

Beck, A. T. (1967). *Depression: Clinical, experimental, and theoretical aspects.* New York: Harper & Row.

Beck, A. T. (1976). *Cognitive therapy and emotional disorders.* New York: International University Press.

Beck, A. T. (1987). Cognitive therapy. In J. K. Zeig. (Ed.), *The evolution of psychotherapy* (pp. 149–178). New York: Brunner/Mazel.

Beck, A. T. (1995). *Cognitive therapy: Basics and beyond.* New York: Guilford Press.

Corey, G. (2005). *Theory and practice of counseling and psychotherapy* (7th ed.). Belmont, CA: Brooks/Cole.

Cormier, S., & Nurius, P. S. (2003). *Interviewing and change strategies for helpers: Fundamental skills and cognitive behavioral interventions* (5th ed.). Pacific Grove, CA: Brooks/Cole.

Gladding, S. T. (1996). *Counseling: A comprehensive profession* (3rd ed.). Englewood Cliffs, NJ: Prentice Hall.

Glasser, W. (1965). Reality therapy. *New York State Journal for Counseling and Development, 7*(1), 5–13.

Glasser, W. (1972). *The identity society.* New York: Harper & Row.

Glasser, W. (1976). *Positive addiction.* New York: Harper & Row.

Glasser, W. (1980). Reality therapy: An explanation of the steps of reality therapy. In W. Glasser (Ed.), *What are you doing? How people are helped through reality therapy.* New York: Harper & Row.

Glasser, W. (2003). *Warning: Psychiatry can be hazardous to your mental health.* New York: Harper Collins.

Glasser, W., & Zunin, L. M. (1979). Reality therapy. In R. Corsini (Ed.), *Current psychotherapies* (2nd ed., pp. 302–339). Itasca, IL: Peacock.

Kazdin, A. E. (2001). *Behavior modification in applied settings* (6th ed.). Pacific Grove, CA: Brooks/Cole.

Mahoney, M. J., & Lyddon, W. (1988). Recent developments in cognitive approaches to counseling and psychotherapy. *Counseling Psychology, 16,* 190–234.

Meichenbaum, D. (1977). *Cognitive behavior modification: An integrative approach.* New York: Plenum.

Miltenberger, R. G. (2004). *Behavior modification. Principles and procedures* (3rd ed.). Pacific Grove, CA: Brooks/Cole.

Perls, F. (1969). *In and out of the garbage pail.* Moab, UT: Real People Press.

Perls, F. (1970). Four lectures. In J. Fagan & I. L. Shepherd (Eds.), *Gestalt therapy now* (pp. 14–38). Palo Alto, CA: Science and Behavior Books.

Polster, E., & Polster, M. (1973). *Gestalt therapy integrated: Contours of theory and practice.* New York: Brunner /Mazel.

Spiegler, M. D., & Gueveremont, D. C. (2003). *Contemporary behavior therapy* (4th ed.). Pacific Grove, CA: Brooks/Cole.

Wolpe, J. (1958). *Psychotherapy by reciprocal inhibition building.* Stanford, CA: Stanford University Press.

Wolpe, J. (1990). *The practice of behavior therapy* (4th ed.). Elmsford, NY: Pergamon Press.

Wubbolding, R. E. (1988). *Using reality therapy.* New York: Harper/Collins.

Wubbolding, R. E. (1991). *Understanding reality therapy.* New York: Harper/Collins.

Yontef, G. M. (1993). *Awareness, dialogue and process: Essays on Gestalt therapy.* Highland, NY: Gestalt Journal Press.

Zinker, J. (1978). *Creative process in Gestalt therapy.* New York: Random House.

6

Family Systems Therapy and Counseling

CHAPTER OBJECTIVES

After reading this chapter, you will be able to:

1. Know the basic principles of family systems therapy, including circular causality, cybernetics, homeostasis, and feedback loops.
2. Understand how correctional counselors can use family therapy and/or family counseling with the offender population.
3. Be aware of various techniques of family systems therapy that correctional counselors can utilize.
4. Be aware of cross-cultural considerations with family therapy.
5. Know the tenets to structural family therapy.
6. Know the theoretical aspects and techniques associated with Bowenian family systems therapy.
7. Know the theoretical aspects and techniques associated with behavioral family systems therapy.

PART ONE: FAMILY SYSTEMS IN GENERAL

Introduction

Family systems therapy is perhaps one of the most unique forms of therapy that will be presented in this text. This is simply due to the fact that family therapy is based on a "systemic" approach that is different from other approaches that focus on the individual. While group counseling techniques tend to naturally focus on more than one person, the focus is not on interactions in the outside environment but is instead focused on the interactions among members within the group setting. Family systems therapy, on the other hand, focuses on the interactions of members in the session both inside and outside the therapeutic setting. Further, these members will have typically known each other for a number of years, will have some sort of shared history, and will usually be linked by a number of other extended family and friends that are mutually known. These dynamics provide therapeutic strengths and challenges for the correctional counselor because, on the one hand, the counselor can utilize family support to aid the offender in reforming, yet on the other hand, there is much more complexity to tracking the interactions, communication, and history of multiple members who share mutual knowledge—mutual knowledge that is unknown to the counselor until it is brought up in therapy.

With the aforementioned in mind, it can probably be surmised that this type of therapy is somewhat difficult to deliver, requiring a great deal of skill and experience for those wishing to implement it into their repertoire of therapeutic options. In fact, a person wishing to conduct marriage and family therapy (as opposed to a single or brief set of family counseling sessions) must have separate, formal, and extensive training to qualify him or her to deliver such services. Further, this typically results in an entirely different set of qualifications so that the counselor can effectively be referred to as a licensed marriage and family therapist (LMFT). The **licensed marriage and family therapist** is a therapist who has completed additional coursework beyond that required of the traditional graduate-level counseling education. Additional clinical hours providing services to families are also required, and additional testing, supervision, and record keeping often coincide with these advanced clinical hours. Only such therapists who complete these and other requirements set by the counselor's state ethics board may call themselves LMFT.

Nevertheless, it is often the case that many non-LMFT counselors may engage in what is commonly referred to as family counseling. **Family counseling** consists of therapeutic sessions that include the client's family members in the treatment plan. The use of these family members is typically short term and is not typically considered therapy for the entire family as much as it is considered therapy for the individual client, with the aid of other family members being solicited for additional individual client support. However, as we will see later in this chapter, some caution may need to be exercised for three reasons when using family systems approaches. First, the client's welfare must be considered as paramount and, with that in mind, the counselor must be assured that the family system delivering support to the client is not itself a major causal factor in the client's offending. Often, offenders are themselves enmeshed in dysfunctional family systems that may have generations of criminogenic patterns of behavior. Such families are not likely to be good candidates for therapeutic support since they are themselves in need of pro-social change. These families would require long-term family therapy and this would typically not occur unless the treatment program could gain their willingness to attend and this would then require the services of an LMFT. Second, the client who acts out in a family is often synonymous with what family therapists refer to as the identified patient. The **identified patient** is often referred to as the "symptom bearer" of the family; this individual is most likely to be the individual first sent for treatment and it is their disruptive behavior that serves as the social glue for the family, giving the family an issue to rally around. This is especially the case with adolescent members of the family, and correctional counselors who work with juvenile offenders need to keep this possibility in mind whenever they deal with delinquent youth who are referred by their own family. Third, counselors will need to ensure that they understand their bounds of competence if they are not licensed family therapists, because a failure to do such can result in a violation of state law and/or their code of ethics.

As the student may now understand, the focus of family systems therapy is on the family and the individual's dysfunctional behavior that stems from family interactions. Specific theoretical orientations and techniques exist within these approaches that can serve the correctional counselor in effectively addressing families in need of treatment. Further, this mode of treatment has been found to be very effective with the substance-abusing population (SAMHSA, 2005). Family therapy (particularly functional family therapy) has also been found to be particularly successful with the juvenile population (SAMHSA, 2005). Given that the majority of offenders in the correctional population have had some kind of substance-abuse issue and given that a large portion of the correctional system consists of young males, family systems therapy should be considered an important modality within the field of correctional counseling.

In general, all family therapy approaches are built on the tenets of general systems theory. General systems theory holds the family as an entity that is maintained by the interactions of its members. This theory also contends that the best way to understand the individual is through the study of the context of his or her interactions. In addition, the family can be viewed as either an open or a closed system. An open family system continuously receives input from and discharges output to the environment. Closed family systems tend to be isolated and are considered stagnant. These systems are typically considered stagnant and it is within these systems that family secrets may exist (such as with childhood sexual abuse and/or other forms of aberrant behavior within the family system). As will be discussed in Chapter 14, these types of systems (as well as chaotic and/or conflicted systems) are common among those that encounter types of sexual abuse and/or family violence. Lastly, systems theory holds that families engage in behaviors and modes of communication that ensure homeostasis of the system. **Homeostasis** is a tendency of families to behave in a manner that maintains the systemic equilibrium or the status quo of the system. In essence, the pursuit of homeostasis is what keeps dysfunctional families in their zone of comfort and serves to defy the attempts of therapists to influence such systems toward more adaptive form of functioning. The student should understand that while family members may act in a manner that supports homeostasis, they are not necessarily consciously cognizant of the fact that their behavior achieves such a balance. Rather, they tend to instinctively react in this manner regardless of their level of deliberation or forethought. This does not mean that members do not deliberately attempt to maintain their family's status quo but rather simply implies that members engage in such behaviors both deliberately and subconsciously.

Communication and the Family System

A primary area of focus for most family therapists is the communication processes within the family system. Much of this approach in family therapy is derived from the influence of cybernetics. When applied to the family communication process, cybernetics effectively incorporates that notion of feedback loops through which the family system processes information that it needs to maintain a steady and stable state of functioning. These feedback loops can be either negative or positive. **Negative feedback** loops reduce deviation from the norms and expectations of the family system and therefore increase equilibrium and stability within the system. **Positive feedback** loops serve to increase behavioral deviation and therefore disrupt that system. However, it should be understood that the results of a positive feedback system can initiate change that is healthy. Consider, for example, a family that is in equilibrium but the sense of stability in that system is maintained through abusive dynamics and/or uneven power structures between the primary adult couple. A break up in that sense of equilibrium may be effective in creating a more healthy family system.

One other common notion of family systems therapy is that of circular causality. This is one of the hallmark distinctions between family therapy and other individual-based forms of therapy. Indeed, where other forms of therapy tend to describe pathology and/or life-course problems in a linear cause-and-effect fashion, family system's notion of **circular causality** regards a symptomatic behavior as an actual part of the ongoing circular feedback loop. This is very important because family systems therapy will often address symptoms, in and of themselves. Most other forms of therapy tend to emphasize the need for addressing causal factors that are latent precursors to the symptomatic behaviors. However, family therapists will address symptoms and/or causal factors equally and independently since it is presumed that each ultimately "circles" back to being a causal factor of the other. This also is important when addressing issues between married couples and/or other family members because the emphasis often shifts any source of blame from one person or another and instead creates a schema where cause and effect are essentially the same. In essence, circular causality could be likened to a "cause-equals-effect-and-effect-equals-cause" perspective. This type of perspective is typically maintained in most types of therapy and in relation to most issues, except for those situations where abuse is encountered. In such situations, abuse is never considered appropriate behavior, though some cultural situations may modify the particular definition of what may or may not entail abusive behavior.

In the previous comment, it should be noted that family therapy is often effective in addressing parenting issues within dysfunctional families. The correctional counselor may have offenders on their caseload who are court mandated for abusive behavior (on one extreme) or they may even have offenders who are processed due to negligence in parenting (the other extreme). In both cases, family therapy may be an appropriate intervention. Further, inappropriate types of parenting are often intertwined with adolescent misbehavior and acting out among juveniles. This again makes it likely that such interventions can be productive for the family system and the correctional counselor.

Family therapists who focus on communication tend to operate from the perspective that all behavior is communicative, and thus people are always communicating, even when they seem not to be engaged in any overt or goal-directed behavior. Further, family rules are thought to set the structure of family communications. These rules are not necessarily officially stated but are mostly understood by family members. Covert rules between couples (i.e., she handles the domestic issues and he handles the bills) establish each partner's role in the family and provide a sense of homeostasis, regardless of whether this homeostasis is the most healthy means of operating. Dysfunctional communication patterns that family therapists might look for would include: (1) blaming and criticizing; (2) the use of incomplete statements (i.e., stating "I am angry" but not explaining why); (3) overgeneralizing (you *never* listen to me); and (4) mindreading or acting as if the partner should know what is on the client's mind. All of these patterns of interaction lead to breakdowns in communication. Family therapists seek to help "family members gain awareness of patterns of relationships that are not working well and create new ways of interacting to relieve their distress" (Corey, 1996, p. 467).

When addressing dysfunctional interactions, family therapists tend to use both direct and indirect techniques of intervention. Direct techniques include the following: (1) pointing out to family members problematic interactions as they occur; (2) teaching effective forms of communication (such as using "I" statements rather than "you" statements); and (3) interpreting interactional patterns, including nonverbal intentions that are wittingly or unwittingly communicated. Before proceeding to indirect techniques, it should be clarified that "I" statements are those where the client accepts ownership for his or her own feelings (i.e., "I feel that you should not do that") as opposed to statements that attribute blame to the other person (i.e., "you know that you should not do that"). Though seemingly minor, these differences in communication styles make all the difference in the outcome of communication interactions, and many clients and/or family systems are truly not aware of how damaging such negative communication patterns can be.

Indirect techniques of communicative intervention might include the use of what are called **double binds**, which are interventions where the client is required to do something contradictory to his or her desired behavior. For example, the therapist might have instructed a male client who dislikes his mother-in-law to give her a present each time he has an argument with her. The idea is based on the notion provided by the well-known Jay Haley, who said "if one makes it more difficult for a person to have a symptom than to give it up, the person will give up the symptom" (Haley, 1984, p. 5). The use of **paradoxical interventions** may also be used, though these must be carefully chosen and are reserved for the skilled therapist. An example might be when a counselor, hearing that a couple cannot get along pleasantly, instructs the couple to argue for two hours every day as required homework during the following week. Naturally, this is built on the premise that we all become bored with those things that become a task. Overall, the intervention can have good outcomes, but the counselor must again be careful in the use of this intervention and must be assured that the couple are not domestically violent.

Multigenerational Transmission of Dysfunction

Murray Bowen was the leading theorist and founder of family therapy processes during their formative years. Goldenberg and Goldenberg (1996) note that his theory "represents the intellectual scaffolding upon which much of mainstream family therapy has been erected," followed by the point that Bowen conceptualized "the family as an emotional unit, a network of interlocking relationships, best understood when analyzed within a multigenerational or historical framework" (p. 165). It is this multigenerational aspect of family systems theory that is of particular interest since this is often a dynamic that is relevant to the offender population. Indeed, many career offenders may belong to families that have a criminogenic history that spans generations. In fact, a criminal subculture may be part of the family culture. This can be evidenced by multiple generations of the same family that are processed through the criminal justice system and seen by many criminal justice practitioners within the correctional setting.

Bowen (1978) proposed that the **multigenerational transmission process** accounts for severe dysfunction within families, this dysfunction being the result of the operation of the family's emotional system over several generations. The nature of this familial emotional system is rooted in another concept attributed to Bowen's work—differentiation of self. **Differentiation of self** occurs in an individual when the person is able to distinguish between the intellectual process and the feeling process that he or she is experiencing. According to Bowen, persons who are mostly mentally healthy are able to achieve a balance between logic and emotion, achieving rationality but not at the expense of losing their capacity for spontaneous emotional expression. This is not to assume that Bowenian family systems theory holds that emotions should necessarily be suppressed as much as it implies that individuals should not allow their life decisions to be driven by emotion. Papero (1990) summarizes the notion of differentiation best by stating:

> To the degree that one can thoughtfully guide personal behavior in accordance with well-defined principles in spite of intense anxiety in the family, he or she displays a level or degree of differentiation. (p. 48)

The opposite extreme of differentiation is fusion. **Fusion** is when an individual has his or her logical decision making fused with his or her emotional framework, the two are thus inseparable. The more fused these two characteristics are, the worse that a given individual will function. Lastly, Bowen also introduced a related concept known as the **undifferentiated family ego mass**, which conveys the notion of a family that is emotionally "stuck together" in an unhealthy and counterproductive sense. For Bowen, maturity and self-actualization require that the individual become free of unresolved attachments to his or her family of origin. It is from this point that we again return to our original concept of multigenerational transmission of dysfunction. Families that have members who have their cognitive and emotional aspects fused are not sufficiently differentiated from the family system, and that are stuck together in maladaptive forms of closeness are those most likely to transmit their dysfunction from one generation to another. These types of dynamics are frequently seen within the offender population. This is particularly true in abusive families and those that have routine familial drug abuse. In such cases, it is obvious that these families are more detrimental to the offender's reform than anything and this would mean that the entire family would be in need of therapeutic services.

However, these types of families seldom make a collective and willing choice to mutually engage in treatment. In such cases, Bowen contends that therapists should focus the majority of their clinical attention on the *highest* functioning member that is present rather than the lowest. On the face of it, this seems to be opposite of what one might expect. But Bowen contends that lavishing clinical attention on the least functioning individual is more likely to lead to little or no outcome, particularly due to the negative influences of the rest of the family members. In fact, these persons will be the most susceptible to negative influences from the dysfunctional family. Rather, the highest functioning member is the most likely to weather the storm, so to speak, when the dysfunctional family is in conflict and/or crisis, and they are the most likely to have some sort of leadership impact on other family members. Further, Bowen observes that as that person becomes highest functioning member, there is an inherent tendency in other members to follow suit, thus increasing the overall functioning of the entire system.

The specific applications for correctional counseling may be difficult to see. But in cases where correctional counselors have juvenile clientele, it is important for counselors to identify those families that have these dynamics. In such cases, the correctional counselor would want to identify the higher functioning (more differentiated) family members who can balance the emotional content of the family with reasonable decision making. Such individuals are likely to function more adaptively during times of crisis and will likely have more positive influence over those that are less able to cope without emotional turmoil ensuing. Further, the correctional counselor should keep in mind the possibility that it is sometimes the troubled teen who has been selected as the *identified patient*, not because they were initially the worst off, but simply because they may not "fit" within the family system. In low functioning families, the counselor may find that ironically, the "troubled" teen does not fit within the family system because he or she is, in fact, the highest functioning member. Their behavior may simply be a skillful manner of keeping the family together and centered on one common issue—the identified patient.

However, the counselor must be careful with this progression in thought since such a client may actually suffer negative drawbacks from additional focus being provided to him or her. This may confirm in the family's consciousness that this person is indeed the source of the family's problems. This can have a negative effect on the family's progress and on the individual client. Further, in some cases, the identified patient may have genuine psychological difficulties such as a mood or personality disorder, perhaps coupled with substance abuse. The correctional counselor would not want to dismiss the aspect in treatment considerations (obviously) but most family therapists are interestingly opposed to the use of clinical diagnoses. We do not subscribe to that view and consider clinical diagnoses useful and necessary in the correctional setting. Nevertheless, these disorders may have underlying causal factors that are family secrets. Consider, for example, an adolescent female being treated for acting out, substance abuse, and potential histrionic personality disorder. It may be that later, the counselor finds a history of childhood sexual abuse. In such a case, the client may actually be the highest functioning client (when left to her own devices) within the family system but is simply manifesting clinical reactions to the sexual abuse.

As can be seen, correctional counselors must consider the approach and implementation of family interventions in a careful manner. Further, in the example just provided, the idea of circular causality might lead some therapists to the erroneous notion that the symptom and the abuse have circular causality. But keep in mind that, as was stated earlier in this chapter, there is no justification for victimization. Aggressive and exploitative behavior patterns are what correctional counselors are specifically tasked with addressing. However, the adolescent client's symptoms of personality disorder and substance abuse do play a circular role of causation in being singled out as the identified patient and also serve to increase the negative attention given to that client. It is in such a case that the correctional counselor would want to safeguard the client from any psychological harm that may be occurring within the family to ensure that the client is able to heal. Addressing the symptoms, in such a case, would be important to reduce conflict that aggravates the client's prognosis. However, the underlying trauma associated with sexual abuse would have to be addressed and would, in all likelihood, result in long-term therapy as the client addressed this victimization while learning healthy means of coping.

Role of the Therapist and Common Techniques

Family therapists tend to be a bit more directive than are therapists who operate from other perspectives. It should be pointed out that there are a number of theoretical perspectives within the family therapy literature, more than can possibly be discussed in this one chapter. Indeed, there are textbooks that entirely address nothing but family therapy approaches. The purpose of this chapter is simply to give the student an understanding of the more common tenets found in the mainstream field of family therapy and to explain how correctional counselors might utilize such approaches with their own correctional caseload. Aside from this, it is hoped that the student learns a few specific techniques when conducting counseling sessions; some of these techniques have already been presented and others will follow. Regardless of the theoretical perspective and regardless of the specific technique, family therapy is known for being a more directive form of therapeutic assistance, with the therapist acting as a coach or a teaching in many respects.

The key to family therapy is getting clients to understand relationship effects and unhealthy patterns of interaction. Family therapists often give direct instruction and guidance to clients and their families. The therapy tends to be focused on the present point and time but does seek to have the client understand challenges in his or her own family of origin as a means of resolving issues in current relationships. As a means of doing this, family therapists have several techniques available that they will employ. These techniques are varied but they all tend to achieve one of three purposes: (1) to build rapport, (2) develop awareness within family members regarding their own family-of-origin issues, or (3) teach clients about healthy relationships.

The first technique is one that is borrowed from a leading forerunner in family therapy, Salvador Minuchin. This technique is **joining**, which is the process of building and maintaining a therapeutic alliance. This is a critical first step in family therapy and resounds earlier discussions in Chapter 4, with all the methods of building rapport (i.e., attending behaviors, reflecting affect, genuineness, paraphrasing, and exhibiting empathy) being relevant to the process of joining. Basically, one could simply incorporate all the aspects of Chapter 4 into the joining process in family therapy. However, the counselor joins the family for the strict purpose of modifying the means by which it communicates and functions but the counselor does not solve the family's problem. Rather, this is left to the family and requires that members develop their own means by which issues are resolved. While the counselor will aid in modeling effective communication, enlightening members about family dynamics, and guiding the process of interaction, it is the family that itself resolves disputes and/or problems that emerge. Corey

(1996) notes that "in order for the therapist to become a part of the family system, it is critical that he or she establish rapport by being sensitive to each of the members" (p. 396). This is particularly important because family members will be sensitive to any biases that may emerge. Naturally, this can impair the therapist's ability to build alliances with the group as a whole, so it is important that the correctional counselor keep this in mind, even when one of the members is the perpetrator of a crime against another family member. Obviously, the process of rapport building is much more challenging in the family setting than in the individual counseling setting because the therapist has to maintain a rapport with many different personalities that are enmeshed by common histories and experiences.

The next technique of interest is the genogram. To a certain extent, the genogram can be likened to a method of assessment, as this tool provides the therapist with a baseline understanding of where the family is at in terms of relationships, important family events, and issues that have occurred in the family (Corey, 1996; McGoldrick, Gerson, & Shellenberger, 1999). Further, since the genogram is developed in a collaborative fashion (the counselor draws the genogram, asks questions of the client, and fills in details using a variety of symbols and other aids), a sense of rapport is often developed once the genogram is complete. Essentially, a **genogram** is a:

> A pictorial chart of the people involved in a three generational relationship system, marking marriages, divorces, births, geographical location, deaths, and illness. This is typically explained to the client during an initial session and developed as sessions progress, is used for discussion points, and is especially helpful when client and therapist reach a point of being "stuck" in the therapeutic process. Genograms can be used to help identify root causes of behaviors, loyalties, and issues of shame within a family. (SAMHSA, 2005, p. 42)

The use of the genogram is fairly commonplace in family therapy and can serve as an excellent therapeutic tool. In fact, this tool can be used in a number of instances, even if the counselor does not intend to conduct family therapy or counseling. For families that have dysfunction that has been transmitted between generations, this can be a particularly useful tool.

Another technique often used by structural family therapists is the use of family mapping. This technique was developed by Salvador Minuchin, the founder of structural family therapy, a type of family therapy that focuses on the structural organization of the family itself, examining subsystems within the family system, such as the parental subsystem (the mother and father figures), the child or sibling subsystem (consisting of one or more children), and the extended subsystem (such as grandparents). Each subsystem has a specified set of roles and expectations within the broader family system, with healthy boundaries that exist between each subsystem, allowing for multiple subsystem relationships to emerge at different levels and in different contexts. The process of **family mapping** helps to illustrate the familial norms and expectations between persons and between subsystems. Family mapping utilizes a method for mapping the structure of the family by illustrating boundaries that are overly rigid (i.e., a parent who believes children should be seen but not heard), diffuse (enmeshment, such as with an overprotective parent), or clear and functional (boundaries allow subsystems to operate appropriately but are permeable so as to allow communication throughout the family). The use of family mapping highlights the functioning of the family and its communication patterns, providing insight and awareness for improvement in family functioning.

Another related concept, also developed by Minuchin, is the use of boundary setting. Boundaries are "the emotional barriers that protect and enhance the integrity of individuals, subsystems, and families" (Corey, 1996, p. 393). The demarcation of boundaries serves to maintain the amount of contact between family members. Healthy boundaries are necessary if families are to function adaptively within the home and especially in broader society. Family therapists often aid parents and other family members in **setting boundaries**, which simply consists of ensuring that appropriate relationships are maintained both in terms of closeness and distance, as is necessary for the effective day-to-day functioning of the family. Corey (1996) provides a clear illustration of the importance of subsystems and their corresponding boundaries as follows:

> When family members of another subsystem take over or intrude on one in which they do not belong, the result is usually some form of structural difficulty. For example, the sex life of the adults in the family belongs to the spousal subsystem; when children are allowed to witness, comment on, or investigate their parent's sexual activity, they are inappropriately involved in the spousal subsystem. This extreme example may be easier to understand than noting that parents ought to allow their children to form their own relationships. This second example, however, is just as important; working out brother and sister relationships is a task for the sibling subsystem, not the parental subsystem. Parents have their own activities and functions to address. (p. 393)

Another important technique used by many family therapists is reframe. **Reframing** is when the counselor provides an interpretation of family life events or circumstances that are different from those that are considered by the family itself. The use of reframes allow the counselor and the family to observe an issue from multiple angles, thereby providing additional means of addressing the problem that is at hand. Corey (1996) adds further clarity by noting that "through reframing it becomes possible to grasp the underlying family structure that is contributing to an individual's problem. In this way, one member does not bear the full burden of blame for a problem or the total responsibility for solving it" (p. 397). Thus, the effective use of reframes allows the counselor and the family to define the problem through a number of means, providing more options for correcting the problem while also deferring the responsibility for the problem among the family as whole. Such an approach provides significant leverage for the counselor and can greatly empower the family.

Benefits with Multicultural Counseling

Family therapy has been noted to have particularly useful applications among various ethnic and/or racial groups. Indeed, family systems therapy in a multicultural framework has significant appeal for those groups that place value on the inclusion of extended family members. Corey (1996) notes that families have their own cultures among members and yet the family system is intertwined to the larger culture from which the members belong. Corey adds that culture and ethnicity are so interrelated with family that it is difficult to know whether issues are particular to the family system itself or to the broader culture that the members share. From the information presented in Chapter 2, it is clear that there is extensive research on cultural competence and family therapy. However, there is very little research that has examined specific effects of culture and ethnicity on the actual clinical processes of the therapy itself (Santisteban, Muir-Malcolm, Mitrani, & Szapocznik, 2002, p. 331). More extensive research is needed on the interplay between "ethnicity, family functioning, and family intervention" (Santisteban et al., 2002).

It is important that counselors move beyond ethnic labels and consider a host of factors—values, beliefs, and behaviors—that are associated with ethnic identity (SAMHSA, 2005). In addition to the major life experiences that must be factored into treating families in a correctional counseling context is the complex challenge of determining how acculturation and ethnic identity influence the treatment process. Other influential elements that may need to be considered are the effects of immigration on family life and the circumstances that motivated emigration (migration due to war or famine is a far more stressful process than voluntary migration to pursue upward mobility), and the sociopolitical status of the ethnically distinct family, in particular how the host culture judges people of the family's ethnicity (SAMHSA, 2005; Santisteban et al., 2002).

Also, just as noted in Chapter 3, it is important to be aware of the various cultural factors associated with different client populations, but we must be careful when developing generalizations about barriers to treatment for racially and ethnically diverse men and women since characteristics are not identical among members within these groups. Still, some common cultural barriers to treatment, particularly among African-Americans and Hispanics/Latino-Americans, have been examined (SAMHSA, 2005). These include misperceptions in recognizing problematic behavior and/or the severity of that behavior (as with substance-abuse issues, for example, where there may be a cultural belief that one's alcohol use is not a problem, or not a severe one, and that those affected can handle the problem on their own), costs associated with seeking treatment, as well as doubt about the efficacy of treatment (SAMHSA, 2005). Further, some issues such as with parenting and the use of discipline may be much different from mainstream society but well accepted within the client's own cultural group. Other barriers to treatment for these groups include inherent mistrust of the therapeutic process and/or agencies that deliver such services (see Chapter 3).

Though Chapter 3 does cover a wide range of cultural issues relevant to counseling in great detail, we think that it is important to again provide some points relevant to specific groups that are likely to be encountered in the correctional context. Though the relevance for specific correctional systems will vary depending on the area of the nation, it is expected that the four groups discussed in the following subsections will provide an effective integration of some of the material from Chapter 3 within a family therapy (as opposed to individual therapy) context. This is not duplicate material but instead expands on the points associated with cultural issues in both contexts of therapy, demonstrating the interlocking nature of the individual and their culture as well as their family system and the cultural factors that have shaped that system. Further, the next subsection brings to light some additional considerations that were perhaps unwieldy for Chapter 3 but are better included in this section of the text. It should be noted that the material in the next few subsections has been adapted from the SAMHSA government document titled Substance Abuse Treatment and Family Therapy. This document lends itself well for a correctional counseling context due to the fact that points are easily extrapolated to a plethora of problems that offenders encounter (beyond substance abuse) and due to the fact that the overwhelming majority of offenders do have substance abuse issue. This government document is considered public domain and parts have been reproduced or copied with such automatic permission. With this noted, we now turn our attention to the cultural groups that follow.

AFRICAN-AMERICANS As with all individuals, African-American clients are sensitive to whether they are being treated with respect. Cultural information should be considered hypotheses rather than knowledge. Techniques shown to be effective with African-Americans will be rendered ineffective if the therapist assumes an attitude that is alienating to clients. People of African ancestry are widely divergent. Therapies effective for African-Americans may be inappropriate for immigrants from the Caribbean or Africa. The personal connection between family and therapist is the single most important element in working with African-American families. Without rapport, treatment techniques are worthless and the family will likely terminate therapy early (Wright, 2001).

African-American families also are sensitive to a patronizing approach that Boyd-Franklin (1989) refers to as missionary racism. Therapists should be sensitive to the ways in which this message may be conveyed. Clinicians must be aware of any biases or attitudes regarding their African-American clients. To address this issue effectively, therapists may need assistance from supervisors or colleagues or training in cross-cultural situations (Wright, 2001).

Santisteban et al. (1997) found that single-family therapy improved family relationships and reduced behavioral problems in African-American youngsters.

African-Americans also function very successfully in multiple family therapy. For many African-American Christians, the Bible is a longstanding source of truth and solace that helps them make sense of life (Reid, 2000). Because of the church's centrality to their lives, a Bible-related recovery program has been found to be effective for African-American Christian families (Reid, 2000).

LATINO-AMERICANS Perhaps the most widely acknowledged common thread among Hispanics/Latinos is the importance placed on family unity, the family's well-being, and the use of family as a support network. *Familialism* or *familismo* are terms that refer to a core construct among Hispanic and other ethnic-minority cultures. It has three components: (1) perceived obligations toward helping family members, (2) reliance on support from family members, and (3) the use of family members as behavioral and attitudinal referents (Marín & Marín, 1991). Generally, the typical nuclear family is embedded in an extended family with flexible and open boundaries. Hispanics/Latinos place a strong emphasis on extended family and clustering (Kaufman & Borders, 1988), and there tend to be fluid boundaries between family members such as cousins, aunts, uncles, and grandparents. "The family is usually an extended system that encompasses not only those related by blood and marriage, but also *compadres* (godparents) and *hijos de crianza* (adopted children, whose adoption is not necessarily legal)" (Garcia-Preto, 1996, p. 151).

Extended family members perform parental duties and functions, providing the children with the adult attention that is hard to come by in a large family (Falicov, 1998). Relationships between siblings and cousins are strong and it is not uncommon to have few peer friendships outside the sibling subgroup. Godparents are practically an additional set of parents, acting as guardians or sponsors of the godchildren and maintaining a strong relationship with the natural parents (Falicov, 1998).

Therapists who plan to work with Latino families who have migrated from Mexico should be familiar with spiritual healers, the *curandero* or *curandera* (i.e., folk healer). These healers can help resolve intrapsychic and interpersonal problems. *Curanderismo*, or the art of folk healing, is a particular treatment modality used primarily in Latino or Southwestern rural communities, although it is also prevalent in metropolitan areas with a large Latino population. *Curanderos* earn their trust from the community; the community validates their "practice." This modality contains a mix of psychological, spiritual, and personal belief factors. Since the *curanderos* are considered to be holy, they invoke God's and the saints' blessings on people seeking their aid.

ASIAN-AMERICANS Because extensive discussion was given to Asian-Americans in Chapter 2, this subsection will be a bit briefer than might otherwise occur. Correctional counselors should understand that due to the fact that Asian cultures are so intensively family centered, the responsibility of maintaining filial obligations is perhaps the dominant concern in the life of most

Asians (McGoldrick, Giordano, & Pearce, 1996). Given the central importance of family in Asian cultures, it is critical to assess the family's part when treating Asian-Americans with substance-use disorders. The psychological influence of the family, particularly the older members, is considerable even when key members are missing as a result of loss, nonmigration, or emotional estrangement (Chang, 2000). Family therapy with Asian-Americans is least likely to include older generations. The primary reason for this absence according to younger family members is that they hope to spare their elders any discomfort.

Working delicately and tactfully with elders is of foremost importance. When treating unresolved issues among older generations, therapists must demonstrate respect, reveal genuine empathy, and, above all, avoid embarrassing older family members. Often family members will try to shield older family members from shame. Family therapists must be cognizant not to rush into exploration of sensitive areas. One method is to initially join with the family at a broad experiential level—sharing their salient traumatic incident—without prying for embarrassing or threatening details (Chang, 2000).

Opinions vary on whether family therapy is an appropriate vehicle to counsel Asian-Americans with substance-use disorders. Paniagua (1998) states that family therapy is effective because the family is more important than the individual in Asian families and the act of withholding information from family members is unfamiliar to many Asians. May Lai (2001) urges therapists to work with the client's family, but to use individual counseling rather than family therapy. Debates on the efficacy of involving Asian families often revolve around the presumed skill level of the therapist, not the fundamental importance of the client's relationship to his or her family. Clearly, counseling Asian-American families requires skill, delicacy, and knowledge of cultural factors.

NATIVE AMERICANS Many tribes do not make any distinction between the nuclear family and grandparents, uncles, aunts, and cousins (Brucker & Perry, 1998). Many tribes characterize great uncles, great aunts, and grandparents (Brucker & Perry, 1998). Sometimes the family includes medicine people and nonrelated people (Brucker & Perry, 1998).

Within Indian culture, families work together to address problems. Family therapy's emphasis on systems and relationships is in particular cultural harmony with American Indians (Sutton & Broken Nose, 1996). Sutton and Broken Nose (1996) emphasize the preferred use of culturally appropriate, nondirective approaches involving "storytelling, metaphor, and paradoxical interventions" (p. 33). Networking and ritual approaches are preferable to strategic or brief interventions (Sutton & Broken Nose, 1996).

In certain cases a family member must go into inpatient treatment for substance abuse before family therapy can make any real impact. It is always possible, however, to continue to work with the family in preparation for the return of the family member to the home, with the goal of modifying family relations that may have contributed to the maintenance of the problem.

The historical trauma experienced by American Indians combined with the usual considerations of codependency and enabling, for example, make family therapy for substance-abuse treatment a challenging endeavor (Duran & Duran, 1996).

The model also must be congruent with the culture of the people that it intends to serve. For example, some parents from Asian cultures may be perplexed by the assumption that children have a "voice" in the family (e.g., children who take on adultlike responsibilities by interpreting for parents, but do not hold adultlike responsibilities in the family). The model selected must accommodate differences in family structure, hierarchies, and beliefs about what is appropriate and expected behavior.

Additional Guidelines for Cross-Cultural Family Therapy

McGoldrick et al. (1996) provide perhaps the single best text related to racial and ethnic issues associated with family therapy. Students who are particularly interested in cross-cultural counseling and/or family therapy are strongly recommended to refer to their text. However, there are eight specific recommendations that McGoldrick et al. (1996) provide for the would-be cross-cultural family therapist that are quite insightful, with five of them being highly relevant to correctional counselors. We include these five selected guidelines below since they tend to hold value for correctional counselors using family therapy perspectives, regardless of the specific cultural group being considered. These guidelines are as follows:

1. ***Assess the importance of ethnicity to clients and their families.*** Not all clients identify with their ethnicity or religious background identically and it is important for the counselor to determine the client's own perceptions before making any generalizations or drawing inferences.
2. ***Validate and strengthen the client's ethnic identity.*** McGoldrick et al. (1996) note that "under great stress an individual's identity can easily become diffuse. It is important that the therapist foster the client's connection to his or her cultural heritage" (p. 23). This is a particularly important point since such diffusion is undoubtedly likely to be relevant both to family dynamics (separation from others) and to cultural aspects of the client. See Exhibit 6.1 as an example of where a client (Darius) is diffused from his family, a family

EXHIBIT 6.1

Structural/Strategic Family Therapy in the Criminal Justice System

Darius, a 21-year-old male from the San Juan pueblo in New Mexico, was referred to a clinic for court-mandated substance-abuse counseling. He had just received his third violation for driving under the influence (DUI). Darius had been on probation since age 13 for various charges, including burglary and domestic violence, and he had a long history of alcohol and drug abuse. He had been on his own for eight years and had no family involvement in his life. Darius had participated in several residential treatment programs, but he had been unable to maintain abstinence on his own. When Darius entered outpatient treatment, he was extremely angry at "the system" and refused initially to cooperate with the therapist or his treatment plan. The therapist was pleasantly surprised that he did show up for his weekly sessions. The following interventions seemed to help Darius:

- The counselor suggested that one treatment goal might be for Darius to finally get off probation. At the time, he still had 18 months of probation remaining.
- The counselor helped Darius see the relationship of alcohol and drugs to his involvement with the criminal justice system.
- The counselor constructed a genogram depicting three generations of Darius' family of origin. This portrayal illustrated a great deal of family disintegration linked to poverty, substance abuse, and his parents' and grandparents' boarding school experience.
- The counselor initiated couples therapy to help Darius stabilize a significant relationship.
- After conferring with the probation officer, the counselor decided that Darius would benefit from a six-month trial of Antabuse treatment.
- The probation officer required that Darius find regular employment.

(*continued*)

During the course of treatment, Darius was able to stop drinking and reevaluate his belief system against the backdrop of his family and the larger judicial system in which he had been so chronically involved. He came to be able to express anger more appropriately and to recognize and process his many losses from family dysfunction. Although many of his family members continued to abuse alcohol, Darius reconnected with an uncle who was in recovery and who had taken a strong interest in Darius' future. Eventually, Darius formed a plan to complete his GED and to begin a course of study at the local community college. The counselor helped Darius to examine how the behaviors and responsibilities he took on in his family shaped his substance use.

Source: Substance Abuse and Mental Health Services Administration (SAMHSA). (2005). *Substance abuse treatment and family therapy*. Rockville, MD: Center for Substance Abuse Treatment.

that apparently has had drug and alcohol problems that have been transmitted between multiple generations.

3. ***Be aware of and use the client's support systems.*** "Often support systems—extended family and friends; fraternal, social, and religious groups—are strained or unavailable. Learn to strengthen the client's connections to family and community resources" (McGoldrick et al., 1996, p. 23). This is also relevant to the client case presented in Exhibit 6.1.
4. ***Do not feel as if you must know everything about other racial and/or ethnic groups.*** This is obviously an impossible task for anyone and counselors should not feel obligated to be an "expert" on all cultural groups. Counselors should be aware of their limitations, be honest about these limits (with the clients as well as with themselves), but should be "openheartedly curious" about the client's cultural background (McGoldrick et al., 1996, p. 23). This creates learning potential, expresses genuine care and concern, and can be a very good rapport builder within the therapeutic relationship. Such an approach is likely to maximize the therapeutic alliance that should be formed.
5. ***Avoid dichotomous thinking (yes or no, black or white) and consciously allow for three or more possibilities or outcomes for any issue discussed.*** Avoid categorizing issues into this-or-that categories. This also includes consideration of racial/ethnic categories. For instance, if you are exploring African-American and Caucasian-American differences, consider how a Latino-American might perceive the situation (McGoldrick et al., 1996). As another example, issues related to male and female relations among the African-American population might emerge, amidst this, consider how an African-American lesbian might perceive the discussion (McGoldrick et al., 1996). All of these points demonstrate that polar extremes in perception are detrimental to cross-cultural forms of intervention.

SECTION SUMMARY

Family systems therapy is an orientation that is much different from the training given to the typical counselor. In fact, only family therapists are qualified to actually practice family therapy. Nonetheless, counselors find it useful to integrate many of the techniques and/or approaches that are common to family therapy. These approaches have been found to be particularly effective with the juvenile and/or drug-abusing population.

Family therapy is much more directive than other forms of therapy. In most respects, the counselor will act as a family coach (when conducting therapy with the entire family) or will be directive in explaining how individuals may need to address interactions within their own family system (this is especially true if the family is more dysfunctional than the offender). There are numerous techniques that family therapists may employ, each of these are designed to address the interactive nature of families as a means of resolving conflict between members and issues that aggravate stress within the family system. The need to maintain equilibrium within families is presented as a primary reason for much of the behavior, whether functional or dysfunctional, in most family systems. Lastly, family therapy has been shown to be effective with diverse racial and/or ethnic groups. This provides another practical consideration for correctional counselors whose caseloads are drawn from a diverse offender population.

LEARNING CHECK

1. ______________________ occurs in an individual when the person is able to distinguish between the intellectual process and the feeling process that he or she is experiencing.
   a. Differentiation of self
   b. Differentiation of emotions and cognitions
   c. Cognitive override
   d. None of the above
   e. All of the above
2. ______________________ is a tendency of families to behave in a manner that maintains the systemic equilibrium or the status quo of the system.
   a. Family balance
   b. Collateral emotional exchange
   c. Order maintenance
   d. Equilibrium maintenance
   e. Homeostasis
3. A genogram is a pictorial chart of the people involved in a three generational relationship system, marking marriages, divorces, births, geographical location, deaths, and illness.
   a. True
   b. False
4. The **identified patient** is often referred to as the "symptom bearer" of the family.
   a. True
   b. False
5. Family systems therapy is a well-suited approach for diverse racial, ethnic, and cultural groups.
   a. True
   b. False

PART TWO: BOWENIAN SYSTEMS

Bowenian Family Systems

According to Bowenian family systems, all family dysfunctions (including, of course, criminal behaviors) come from ineffective management of the anxiety in a family system. More specifically, pathological behavior (i.e., sex offending, compulsive behaviors, substance abuse) is viewed as a means for both individuals and the family as a group to manage anxiety. Take for example a chronic drug addict within a family system, drug abuser is thought to do so in part as a means of reducing anxiety temporarily, and this also allows the entire family to focus on the individual who uses drugs as the problem, which then also allows all member to deflect attention from other sources of anxiety (SAMHSA, 2005).

A major source of anxiety can be a family's reactivity, or the intensity with which the family reacts emotionally to relationship issues instead of carefully thinking them through. Ideally, family members are able to strike a balance between emotional reactivity and reason and are aware of which is which. As noted earlier, this is referred to as differentiation and this is the hallmark of Bowenian family therapy. Family members who are adequately autonomous are neither fused with nor detached from others in the family. Bowen family systems therapy is also based on the premise that a change on the part of just one family member will affect the family system (Goldenberg & Goldenberg, 1996; SAMHSA, 2005). To reduce the family's reactivity, for example, counselors coach the most motivated family members in ways to curb their reactivity and behave differently in their relationships. Such changes can decrease or even eliminate the problem that brought the family into treatment.

The Bowenian approach to behavior change often works through one person, and its scope is highly systemic. For instance, Bowen attempts to reduce anxiety throughout the family by encouraging people to become more differentiated, more autonomous, and less enmeshed in the family emotional system. As noted earlier, Bowenian therapy seeks to focus on higher functioning members as a means of motivating the family system as a whole. However, this process requires that the therapist consider several interlocking elements that work hand in hand to enable dysfunctional processes. The correctional counselor must understand these processes since these are the social factors that will most likely offset any gains made during therapy once the client returns home. This is particularly true for juvenile offenders.

One of the primary points to attend to is the development and maintenance of emotional triangles. **Emotional triangles** are when a two-person system such as the husband and wife experience conflict or instability and a third person is drawn into the relationship as a means of increasing the sense of stability. This third person is essentially "in the middle of the relationship" and may act as referee or confidant to each person in some cases. In other cases, the person may instead be brought into the relationship as a problem person that the couple can focus on, thereby resolving their own instability by focusing on the third person introduced. However, even the three-person relationship may not always be sufficient to contain tension that is experienced, and this results in distress that is spread to others. Further, as more people become involved, the family system may become a series of interlocking triangles (Goldenberg & Goldenberg, 1996). This can even heighten the initial problems and sources of tension that the original triangle relationships sought to resolve.

Another aspect of family relationships that Bowenian family therapists tend to focus upon is called emotional cut-off. **Emotional cut-off** refers to the dysfunctional methods by which members use to distance themselves from their family. Often, relationships will be severed but they may simply be deliberately allowed to digress on their own. These members may try to place geographical distance between themselves and other members, they may use psychological barriers (i.e., ceasing to talk with family members), or they may engage in methods of self-deception, convincing themselves that no problem exists since no contact is maintained (Goldenberg & Goldenberg, 1996). However, the latent dysfunction, trauma, and anxiety reveal in many cases when the person is required to talk about their family history or worse yet when they must make intermittent contact with their family members. In such cases, persons that are emotionally cut-off have great difficulty with these activities.

Bowenian family therapists will nearly always seek to engage in processes of de-triangulation where family members are educated on the process and the ineffective means that these processes have on the communication process. Further, these therapists also tend to require that clients address emotion cut-offs that exist, though this is of course counterbalanced with a dose of common sense. For example, a Bowenian family therapist would not be likely to require the victim in a domestically abusive case or a victim of child molestation to repair the cut-off that would likely exist between the victim and the perpetrator. However, Bowenian therapists might have the victim develop awareness and explore their cut-offs with other family members that occurred after the victimization was discovered in the criminal justice system (i.e., extended family that are sympathetic to the perpetrator or at least forgiving of the perpetrator). Such occurrence happens routinely within dysfunctional and criminogenic families. Thus Bowenian therapy will tend to address both emotional triangles and emotional cut-off (two opposite relational reactions) as a means of helping the client to become more differentiated. Incidentally, there are some occasions where Bowenian objectives of addressing emotional cut-off between a victim and perpetrator might occur, even with domestic abuse cases and/or cases of sexual assault. This is particularly true in cases where restorative justice approaches are used to process offenders. **Restorative justice** being a term for interventions that focus on restoring the health of the community, repairing the harm done, meeting victim's needs, and emphasizing that the offender can and must contribute to those repairs. Restorative justice considers the victims, communities, and offenders (in that order) as participants in the justice process. In such cases, the victims willingly choose to engage in the restoration process and it would be likely that techniques of de-triangulation (encouraging direct communication of emotions) and the removal of cut-off (requiring that communication be undefensive, calm, and sincere) would be highly useful (Exhibit 6.2).

EXHIBIT 6.2

Use of Bowen Family Systems Therapy with Immigrant Populations

Although no demonstrated outcomes substantiate Bowenian therapy to address criminal offending, counselors have often used it to treat clients with criminogenic behavioral patterns (such as with substance-use disorders) who have immigrated to the United States. It is believed that this therapeutic approach is a good match for such clients because it emphasizes the intergenerational transmission of anxiety and the effects of trauma that are passed down through generations.

The perspective that the "past is the present" provides a mechanism to understand the lowered self-esteem of a person who has lost everything of importance: language, homeland, culture, possessions, and often, a sense of cultural identity. For many the circumstances of migration are traumatic. Such losses are not only carried from the past, but continue to occur in the present as family members are subject to the indirect consequences of migration, such as unemployment or underemployment, marginal or overcrowded housing, untreated health problems, and poverty. In this situation, criminal behavior may be a viable alternative to compensate for the lack of opportunities that exist, alcohol and drugs can provide an expedient way to blot out pain and hopelessness, and youth may engage in delinquent acts as a symptom of the challenges of acculturation (essentially being caught between two worlds, that of their parental culture and the broader American culture). Healing cannot begin until both the counselor and the client understand the significance of the loss of past cultural identification in light of the problematic behaviors that resulted in the immigrant offender's contact with the criminal justice system.

Source: SAMHSA. (2005). *Substance abuse treatment and family therapy*. Rockville, MD: Center for Substance Abuse Treatment. This insert is a modified version of the material adapted from the source document.

Characteristics of the Dysfunctional Family

When identifying the dysfunctional family, there are numerous characteristics that most all persons, professional and layperson alike, will understand to be counterproductive. For instance, most everyone intuitively understands that drug addiction, abusive parenting, or failing to pay one's bills would be considered dysfunctional. Though specific definitions of drug addiction, child abuse, or financial irresponsibility might have some variance from family to family, the general concept is not lost on most rational persons. For the most part, these are commonly accepted characteristics of dysfunction. However, Bowenian family therapists also look for other aspects of family functioning to determine whether its members are well adjusted and part of a healthy system or one that breeds anxiety and tension.

As stated earlier, dysfunctional families will tend to have members that are poorly differentiated; triangulation among relationships; and high levels of tension, conflict, and anxiety. These are common indicators that Bowenian therapists will seek to identify. In addition, Bowenian family therapists will examine sibling birth order positions among children in the family as well as the past histories of the parents. While **sibling birth order** dynamics go beyond the scope of this chapter to explain in detail, researchers have noted a variety of sibling personality profiles (i.e., the older brother, younger sister, older sister, younger brother, only child, middle child, twins, and so forth) that work together and against one another in a variety of dynamics, some being more harmonious than others (Corey 1996). This likewise affects marriages between adults, depending on their birth order position as children in their own families of origin. Bowenians will examine birth order characteristics to unravel problematic combinations (i.e., two firstborns are married) that provide guidance as to underlying sources of tension not overtly obvious.

Another aspect of dysfunctional families that has not been discussed is that of the societal-emotional process. According to Bowenian family systems, **societal-emotional process** refers to emotional factors in society that affect the emotional functioning of the family. This particular aspect is not well worked within the theoretical construct but makes intuitive sense, particularly for families that exist in underprivileged communities. As noted before, much of the prison population is drawn from offenders that come from backgrounds of poverty, low education, and diminished opportunities. Given these factors, it is easy to see how community factors (and those of the broader society) can create stress and strain for the family. Indeed, this is not much different from the notions of the criminological theorists, Messner and Rosenfeld, whose theory of institutional anomie contends that an emphasis on economic factors has placed strain on families throughout America, devaluing informal institutions and activities within the family and perpetuating a drive for increased activity in those areas that generate income in a competitive capitalistic market. While the tenets of this theory go well beyond the intent of this chapter, it is clear that other theorists contend that family dysfunction is as much a product of broader sociological pushes and pulls (that focus on the pursuit of economic stability). These same contentions would dovetail well with the Bowenian notion of societal-emotional process.

SECTION SUMMARY

This section familiarizes the student with Bowenian systems family therapy processes. Bowenian family therapy laid the groundwork for many other types of family therapy that followed. Bowenian family therapy is known for its emphasis on differentiation and for other key concepts such as emotional cut-off, emotional triangles, and other means of classifying family dysfunction and dynamics. This type of therapy is versatile and has provided a number of techniques that have been adopted by therapists practicing both family and individual therapy.

This type of therapy examines other issues such as sibling birth order, consisting of a variety of sibling personality profiles (i.e., the older brother, younger sister, older sister, younger brother, only child, middle child, twins, and so forth) that work together and against one another in a variety of dynamics, some being more harmonious than others. Other concepts, such as societal-emotional process refers to emotional factors in society that affect the emotional functioning of the family. Thus, at its base, Bowenian processes implement the basic feedback loop process between families and their broader social environment that affects them.

LEARNING CHECK

1. Societal-emotional process refers to emotional factors in society that affect the emotional functioning of the family.
   a. True
   b. False
2. ______________________ refers to the dysfunctional methods by which members use to distance themselves from their family.
   a. Emotional distance
   b. Geographical denial
   c. Ineffectual denial
   d. Relational emotions
   e. Emotional cut-off
3. Bowenian family therapists will nearly always seek to engage in processes of de-triangulation where family members are educated on the process and the ineffective means that these processes have on the communication process.
   a. True
   b. False
4. Emotional triangles are when a two-person system such as the husband and wife experience conflict or instability and a third person is drawn into the relationship as a means of increasing the sense of stability.
   a. True
   b. False
5. In Bowenian systems therapy, most of the clinical focus is given to the higher functioning client, not the one that is the least functioning.
   a. True
   b. False

PART THREE: BEHAVIORAL FAMILY THERAPY

Behavioral Family Therapy

Though we refer to this subsection as behavior family therapy, some elements of this type of therapy may occasionally include cognitive elements. The majority of this section will indeed focus on behavioral interventions, but when and where appropriate, aspects of cognitive behavioral therapy may be included. Behavioral therapy and cognitive behavioral therapy tend to be the modalities of choice in many criminal justice programs because they are clear, easy to measure, and straightforward in application. This often suits correctional systems that seek evidence-based outcomes with their treatment programs. Behavioral family therapy includes three subcomponents: behavioral marital therapy, behavioral parent training, and functional family therapy.

Behavioral marital therapy is based on the notion that "the behavior of both partners in a marital relationship is shaped, strengthened, weakened, and modified by environmental events, especially those events involving the other spouse" (Holtzworth-Munroe & Jacobson, 1991, p. 97). In general, the techniques of behavioral marital therapy are intended to (1) increase the couple's recognition, initiation, and acknowledgment of pleasing interactions; (2) decreasing the couple's aversive interactions; (3) training the partners in the use of effective problem-solving communication skills; and (4) teaching them to use contingency contracting in order to negotiate the resolution of persistent problems.

Behavioral parent training seeks to change parental responses to undesired behaviors from a child so as to ultimately produce a change (and expected improvement) in the child's behavior. This type of therapy is particularly important for the offender population since many of those processed through the criminal justice system will not have the necessary parental skills to raise their children in a pro-social manner. Further, such therapy is particularly useful for female offenders because over 70% of all female offenders are the primary caretakers of their children. Thus, this form of therapy is useful for correctional counselors as it provides specific tools for offenders who are parents, helping them to shape the behavior of their children in a manner that hopefully will not translate to future criminality in the next generation.

Tenets of Operant Conditioning

The most commonly used mechanisms that underlie behavioral family therapy are those associated with operant conditioning, as created by B. F. Skinner (1953). The primary notion is that most behavior is controlled and maintained by the consequences that occur. Essentially, this type of behavior modification relies of four primary and well-known principles: positive reinforcement, negative reinforcement, positive punishment, and negative punishment. A brief overview of each of these concepts will be provided, but before doing so, it should be noted that all four mechanisms are designed to aid in the *shaping* of desired behavior. **Shaping** is when behaviors are taught by reinforcing successive approximations of a desired behavior until the behavior is fully learned by the client. All aspects of behavioral family therapy center around this primary objective as a means of altering family functioning and the performance of individual members.

Reinforcement essentially refers to the use of consequences that immediately follow a behavior and are contingent upon that behavior in order to increase the likelihood of the behavior occurring again. In most all treatment regimens, positive reinforcement is used. **Positive reinforcement** occurs when a benefit or privilege desired by the client would be *presented after* the client engages in a behavior that is consistent with the treatment plan as a means of *increasing* the likelihood that the client will repeat the desired behavior. On the other hand, negative reinforcement, while seeking to increase the likelihood of the repetition of a behavior, does so by removing an unpleasant or aversive stimulus or event immediately after the desired behavior is completed. **Negative reinforcement** occurs when an event or stimulus that is unpleasant to the client is *removed after* the client engages in behavior that is consistent with the treatment plan as a means of *increasing* the likelihood that the client will repeat the desired behavior.

While most therapists do tend to emphasize the use of reinforcement rather than punishment, behavior psychology and/or behavioral therapy do also integrate the use of punishments as well. Essentially, the use of punishment is intended to decrease a behavior, but it should be made clear that punishment has been found to be much less effective than is reinforcement of desired behavior. In fact, it is generally held that if one does not reinforce a behavior, it will eventually become extinct. Therefore, **extinction** is when a behavior ceases due to a lack of reinforcement.

The use of extinction is generally preferred to the use of punishment, but nonetheless the use of punishment is widespread throughout society and is a definite reality in the criminal justice system. As such, it would be foolhardy to fail to include this in the current discussion on operant conditioning principles common to behavioral family systems. Positive punishment results from any stimulus that, when applied after an undesired behavior, it reduces the likelihood of that behavior being repeated. Thus, **positive punishment** occurs when an event or stimulus that is aversive to the client is *presented after* the client engages in a behavior that is not consistent with the treatment regimen as a means of *decreasing* the likelihood that the client will repeat the undesired behavior. On the other hand, **negative punishment** occurs when an event or stimulus that is desired by the client is removed after the client engages in a behavior that is not consistent with the treatment regimen as a means of decreasing the likelihood that the client will repeat the undesired behavior.

These principles of operant condition, reinforcement (both positive and negative), extinction, and punishment (both positive and negative) lie at the heart of behavioral family systems and are the main structure upon which this therapy is built. Though perhaps simplistic in its approach, it is a preferred modality in many criminal justice systems because of its straightforward approach and because it lends outcomes that are easily measured. It is with these mechanisms in mind that we now turn our discussion to the characteristics of a functional family and system as well as those of a dysfunctional family system, applying these mechanisms to both versions of family functioning.

Behavioral Assessment in Behavior Family Therapy

Behavioral therapy, like much of the field of psychology (as opposed to counseling), is grounded in scientific precision and empiricism. Behaviorists seek to operationalize a problem and employ quantitative methods of measuring behavioral change. In essence, behavioral family therapy is, in and of itself, evidence based. As discussed in Chapters 1 and 14, behaviorists will continually revise their hypotheses through an examination of their intervention's success and/or failure and they will conduct further observations to validate their results. At all times behaviorists use a quantifiable method of observations that allows for the testing of hypotheses (i.e., the intervention will reduce client anxiety during the next two-week period) so that the treatment regimen is refined as therapy progresses.

Behaviorist tend to place important emphasis on the assessment process, which "might include an objective recording of discrete acts exchanged by family members, along with the behaviors of others that serve as antecedent stimuli, as well as the interactional consequences of the problematic behavior" (Goldenberg & Goldenberg, 1996). Put in other terms, "assessment focuses on what the behavior or problem is and on the events that might influence that behavior. Further, assessment begins by clarifying the goals of the intervention and it is the assessment that is central to identifying the extent and nature of the problem before the intervention begins" (Kazdin, 2001, p. 7). A thorough behavioral assessment lends itself to effective post-treatment evaluation, an issue that is important to behaviorists who seek to measure and quantify the effects of the therapeutic process.

With behavioral interventions, "assessment of family functioning tends to occur at two different levels: (1) a problem analysis that seeks to pinpoint the specific behavioral deficits that underlie the problem areas, which, if modified, would lead to problem resolution; and (2) a functional analysis directed at uncovering the interrelationships between those behavioral deficits and the interpersonal environment in which they are functionally relevant" (Goldenberg & Goldenberg, 1996, pp. 254–255). Both the problem analysis and the functional analysis are peculiar to behavioral therapies but are instrumental in laying the groundwork for these types of interventions. It is the functional analysis that is most important for students to understand because it is the cornerstone to behavioral therapy. Functional analysis reflects a means of understanding behavior and using causal events to create effective interventions (Kazdin, 2001).

The key elements of a functional analysis are the assessment, development, and evaluation of hypotheses regarding circumstances that control behavior and the intervention. As one can tell, the process involved with functional analyses (particularly in regard to the generation of hypotheses) has many similarities to points that were made in Chapter 1. Kazdin (2001) notes that assessment is designed to "identify the relations of antecedents and consequences to the behavior of interest and hence the purposes or functions of the behavior. This assessment is likely to suggest patterns of when the undesired behavior is performed" (p. 104). For instance, the behavior may occur more at certain locations (i.e., school or home), or during certain times of the day or night (late and/or when there is a lack of sleep), or when certain persons are in the vicinity. The functional analysis of behavior then identifies these factors as a means of determining the antecedents to problematic behaviors. From this point, these antecedents are targeted with the idea that should one change the antecedent, changes in the problematic behavior will soon follow.

During the process of identifying these antecedents, hypotheses are generated as to factors that may be maintaining or controlling the behavior. Kazdin notes that "if at all possible, the hypotheses are tested directly by assessing the target behavior as various conditions are changed" (2001, p. 104). The primary means by which information is gathered to conduct the functional analysis is through the use of interviews of individuals who have contact with the client or clients that are the focus of the analysis. The interview focuses on the context in which the behavior appears to identify factors that can be systematically identified for modification. In the context of family therapy, there may be multiple family members who are involved in providing information, particularly if the focus is on a single offender (such as a substance-abusing offender whose family is consulted to aid in treatment). When the entire family is the focus of the therapy, multiple members might be interviewed in relation to the actions of the other members, resulting in multiple perspectives being individually shared by multiple family members and giving the correctional counselor a unique perspective when examining family behavioral dynamics. It is from the point of assessment that the behavioral therapist then identifies dysfunctional areas of family behavior that are in need of modification (Exhibit 6.3).

EXHIBIT 6.3

The 10 Underlying Assumptions of Behavioral Therapy

1. All behavior, normal and abnormal, is acquired and maintained in identical ways (just as with any of the basic leaning principles).
2. Behavior disorders represent learned maladaptive patterns that need not presume some inferred underlying cause or unseen motive.
3. Maladaptive behavior, such as symptoms, is itself the disorder, rather than a manifestation of a more basic underlying disorder or disease process.
4. It is not essential to discover the exact situation or set of circumstances in which the disorder was learned; these circumstances are usually irretrievable anyway. Rather, the focus should be on assessing the current determinants that support and maintain the undesired behavior.
5. Maladaptive behavior, having been learned, can be extinguished (i.e., unlearned) and replaced by new learned behavior patterns.

6. Treatment involves the application of the experimental findings of scientific psychology, with an emphasis on developing a methodology that is precisely specified, objectively evaluated, and easily replicated.
7. Assessment is an ongoing part of treatment, as the effectiveness of treatment is continuously evaluated and specific intervention techniques are individually tailored to specific problems.
8. Behavioral therapy concentrates on the "here and now" problems, rather than uncovering or attempting to reconstruct the past.
9. Treatment outcomes are evaluated in terms of measurable change.
10. Research on specific therapeutic techniques is continuously carried out by behavioral therapists.

Source: Adapted from Goldenberg, I., & Goldenberg, H. (1996). *Family therapy: An overview* (4th ed., p. 254). New York: Brooks/Cole.

SECTION SUMMARY

Behavioral family therapy contends that the behavior of persons in a family relationship is shaped, strengthened, weakened, and modified by environmental events, especially those events involving other family members. Behavioral family therapy utilizes many concepts that are familiar to psychologists and students of psychology, such as operant conditioning, social learning/modeling, and the use of functional analyses of behavior. It is important that the student understand the basic points and concepts to behavioral psychology and/or therapy since family therapy systems designed around this modality stay true to the ideas presented by those who established the behavioral school.

Behavioral family therapy and cognitive behavioral interventions are the preferred methods of intervention in many criminal justice treatment programs. Likewise, this is a good basic form of intervention that is easy to understand, measure, and evaluate. This also has strong appeal within the criminal justice system. As has been emphasized throughout this text, the use of effective assessment is considered extremely important in this type of intervention, but behavioral psychology uses a unique approach called the functional analysis of behavior. This form of assessment also aids in the treatment planning process and lends itself well to the implementation of the various mechanisms of reinforcement and punishment that are akin to operant conditioning.

LEARNING CHECK

1. ________________________ occurs when an event or stimulus that is desired by the client is removed after the client engages in a behavior that is not consistent with the treatment regimen as a means of *decreasing* the likelihood that the client will repeat the undesired behavior.
   a. Positive reinforcement
   b. Negative reinforcement
   c. Positive punishment
   d. Negative punishment
2. ________________________ occurs when an event or stimulus that is unpleasant to the client is *removed after* the client engages in behavior that is consistent with the treatment plan as a means of *increasing* the likelihood that the client will repeat the desired behavior.
   a. Positive reinforcement
   b. Negative reinforcement

c. Positive punishment
d. Negative punishment

3. **Social learning** occurs when one person observes another engage in operant learning conditions and when the observing person then, in turn, repeats the behaviors that were reinforced for the person that had been observed.
a. True
b. False

4. ________________________ occurs when a benefit or privilege desired by the client is *presented after* the client engages in a behavior that is consistent with the treatment plan as a means of *increasing* the likelihood that the client will repeat the desired behavior.
a. Positive reinforcement
b. Negative reinforcement
c. Positive punishment
d. Negative punishment

5. ________________________ occurs when an event or stimulus that is aversive to the client is *presented after* the client engages in a behavior that is not consistent with the treatment regimen as a means of *decreasing* the likelihood that the client will repeat the undesired behavior.
a. Positive reinforcement
b. Negative reinforcement
c. Positive punishment
d. Negative punishment

Effective Family Functioning and Dysfunctional Family Functioning

As just noted, for behaviorists, the notions of operant conditioning stand at the heart of determining whether a family is functional or dysfunctional. When examining family systems, one of the key determinants of a high-functioning family is whether maladaptive behavior is reinforced. Obviously, in a functional family, such behaviors would not be reinforced. Though there may be some question as to specific definitions of adaptive behavior (considering family variability, the effects of culture, and etc.), it is nonetheless the case that effective families will not reinforce behaviors that are generally considered inappropriate in the broader mainstream society and that the same family system will reinforce those that are considered desirable. Further, high-functioning families do not often have a need for the use of punishment, the presumption being that a satisfactory set of reinforcers and reinforcement schedules will typically elicit the desired behavior in lieu of behavior that is not desired.

Further, in most all functional families, social learning will take place that further reinforces the impact of operant conditioning. **Social learning** occurs when one person observes another engage in operant learning conditions and when the observing person then, in turn, repeats the behaviors that were reinforced for the person that had been observed. In other words, the person learns vicariously as a product of another person's learning experiences. For example, if an older sibling is given praise for completing chores around the house, it is likely that the younger children will observe this and also do their chores, in the hopes of also getting praise. In addition, parents that are effective will also engage in modeling. **Modeling** is when desired behavior is deliberately produced by one person knowing that it is being observed by another. Thus, children will tend to repeat the behavior that is modeled by their parents, this being a product of social learning. If the parents then reward the child, then the social learning is further reinforced with operant conditioning and social learning mechanisms working hand in hand in an interlocking fashion. This further strengthens the learning processes that take place.

It is important that functional families ensure that the benefits of pro-social behavior outweigh the costs of engaging in that behavior. Otherwise, there is little likelihood of motivating family members into engaging in a desired behavior. In addition, it is important that a sense or reciprocity is maintained among families members, this resulting in the mutual reinforcement of desired behaviors between family members and this also serving to further add to the social learning that takes place as family members observe reciprocal behaviors that reinforce each other. In terms of behavioral family systems, all of these elements are part and parcel of any well-functioning family. Naturally, behavioral therapists must attend to these when they attempt to motivate families toward change and they will attempt to instill such methods of interaction, the ultimate goal being that the family members reinforce one another, one step at a time, into functional and healthy means of operating.

Naturally, dysfunctional families will tend to lack many of these qualities. In such families, there are often haphazard approaches to reinforcement, with inconsistent rewards and punishment. Indeed, consistency is the key to effective forms of behavioral shaping. This is not to say that desired behaviors must be rewarded every time that they occur (in fact, there is substantial research that demonstrates that ratio forms of reinforcement are much more effective), but it does mean that the same types of behaviors should be reinforced and that the same types of behaviors should be punished. Effectively attending to this requires effort on the part of the parents who may see themselves as too busy or too tired to maintain such a state of vigilant parenting. However, this is specifically where the problems with dysfunction can emerge. In short, maintaining a functional family takes work and effort; parents who guide their families will need to be prepared to provide such effort. In criminogenic families it can be very challenging to gain the motivation necessary to achieve effective outcomes. Further, the parents (whether they are offenders or otherwise) will need to model pro-social and adaptive behaviors since social learning will occur within the environment as family members observe one another.

Lastly, communication within many dysfunctional families will often tend to be impaired and will usually be laden with conflicted intent, sarcasm, and/or inappropriate content. This obviously will impact the likely reaction that other family members will have to such means of message delivery. Because behavioral family therapy is so focused on the measurable outcomes and content of the behavior itself, a word of advice should be given. Families in counseling should all be given instruction in appropriate forms of communication. The delivery of the content is just as important (in many cases) as is the content itself, at least if one expects to have his or her content heard. The correctional counselor will do well to attend to the processes involved in a family's communication patterns and will be best off if they have family members model effective communication patterns (the use of "I" statements, use of active listening effective reflection) during therapeutic sessions and at home. This is important because many challenged families cannot implement higher functioning forms of operation due to the crippling effects of inappropriate or ineffective communication. Indeed, in many of these families, verbal abuse may be present and this along will impair the effectiveness of any treatment plan that can be implemented. Thus, correctional counselors are encouraged to make this a part of their intervention plan when using behavioral family system perspectives.

CONCLUSION

Family systems therapy offers a set of treatment options that are very different from those used in individual counseling. While it is not necessary that correctional counselors be actual family therapists, it is useful if they are aware of the basic dynamics associated with family therapy and family counseling. Often, family issues lie at the base of many offender problems, and family therapy offers an option of rectifying dysfunctional family influences. Additionally, family therapy offers a venue by which well-adjusted families can aid in the offender's treatment and/or recovery. It is with substance abuse and juvenile offenders that family therapy has been used extensively. Among both populations, this type of intervention has proven to be quite successful.

There are many types of family therapy, just as with individual therapy. Each type reflects a different orientation but all consider the interaction process to be important in determining dysfunction. Further, all methods of family intervention examine issues associated with the homeostasis of the family system as well as other aspects of family functioning. Whether the family issues are those rooted in the past or those that occur in the present, there are a number of interventions that can aid correctional counselors in addressing this element of an offender's clinical circumstances. Because of this and because this type of therapy tends to work well with diverse populations, it is a method of clinical practice that should not be ignored. Rather, it is a method that should be specifically utilized whenever practical for the agency that delivers therapeutic services. Given the trauma that tends to plague the backgrounds of many offenders, this type of intervention perhaps holds a greater degree of utility than is associated with many other types of interventions.

Essay Questions

1. Describe the basic principles of family systems therapy. In your description, be sure to define the concepts of circular causality, cybernetics, homeostasis, and feedback loops.
2. Describe two techniques of family systems therapy that correctional counselors can utilize. Also, can you think of situations in which these techniques may not be useful?
3. Describe the essence of structural family therapy. Provide an example of when this type of therapy may be particularly useful and why.
4. What is Bowenian family systems therapy? What are the central tenets of this system of therapy? How is this system different from other family system therapies?
5. Why is it important to identify and use an offender's support system within the counseling process? Describe some of the advantages of doing so. Are there times where this may not be a good idea? Why or why not?

Treatment Planning Exercise

The case scenario for this chapter was selected for several reasons that are beneficial to showcasing family systems interventions and are also likely to enhance student learning. This case provides the student with a scenario where they can read and observe how a family therapist would address problems presented by a client family. Further, this case scenario includes a family of minority status (Latino-American) and thus also illustrates the utility of family therapy with diverse cultural groups. As noted in this chapter, the ability to apply family therapy to diverse racial, ethnic, and/or cultural groups is one of the strong suites of this mode of intervention. For this exercise, the student will not be responsible for applying aspects of the chapter to the scenario; rather this assignment works in a backward fashion. In this case, the student must read the scenario and identify concepts, terms, and/or techniques from the chapter(s) identified and must then explain how that identified concept, term, or technique was used by the therapist. This is intended to integrate the material even further through diversified learning processes, allowing students to analyze the scenario from the perspective of their readings. Lastly, note that students will need to identify components from this chapter as well as Chapter 3 on cultural competence. This further integrates the material provided throughout this text. For this assignment, the student must do the following:

1. Students should list five concepts, terms, or techniques from Chapter 6 that were mentioned or utilized by the therapist in this scenario. For each, be sure to provide a specific explanation of how your example was used, the area from the chapter to which this example corresponds, and explain whether you believe that the therapist used the concept, term, or technique in an effective manner.
2. Identify at least three issues, concepts, or other considerations from Chapter 3 that were relevant to this case scenario. Also explain why you chose those three in particular and explain whether the therapist considered those issues, concepts, or considerations in an effective manner.

The Case of the Hernandez Family

Initial Presentation: The Hernandez family was referred to the clinic by the public defender at the time of Isabelita's third arrest, this time for drug possession. Isabelita was 15 years old, and she lived with her mother, a single parent, and a 12-year-old brother. Because the mother only spoke Spanish, the case was assigned to a Hispanic BSFT counselor who called home and heard screaming and fighting in the background. The counselor spoke with the mother, who sounded overwhelmed. When the counselor explained that he was calling to set up a family session, Ms. Hernandez angrily told the counselor that she could never get Isabelita to attend.

The counselor asked Ms. Hernandez for permission to come to her home when she and Isabelita were both likely to be home. Because Ms. Hernandez worked as a domestic during the day, the appointment was set for 7 o'clock the next evening. When the counselor arrived at the home, he found the mother alone with her 12-year-old son. Ms. Hernandez explained that Isabelita often stayed out with her friends, and she could not predict what time Isabelita would be home. The 12-year-old son was quick to confirm his mother's story and added that Isabelita was always upsetting his mother and that he wished she would just go away.

Establishing the Therapeutic System: The counselor began to join with Ms. Hernandez by listening to the story of her hardships in this country and with Isabelita. Ms. Hernandez said how overwhelmed she felt by Isabelita's behavior and that she did not know what she could do. In fact, she said, "It is all in God's hands now," as if there was nothing else she could possibly do. It appeared from the story that Ms. Hernandez did not have well-established rules or consequences for Isabelita's behavior. It also appeared that most of the communication that occurred between daughter and mother was angry, blaming, and fighting. Ms. Hernandez felt that they could argue for hours about the same thing and then have the same argument all over again the next day. It was about 8:15 p.m., when Isabelita arrived. It was obvious to the counselor that her gait was unsteady and her speech was slurred.

(continued)

Her eyes were red. She barged into the home and went straight to the kitchen. When Ms. Hernandez said to Isabelita, "Come here, there is someone here who has come to see you about your arrest," Isabelita answered, "F—k them, I am hungry." Ms. Hernandez went to the kitchen to serve Isabelita her dinner, screaming at her "Your food is already cold. You are late again. We had dinner two hours ago." The screaming between mother and daughter continued for another 10 minutes before the counselor came to the kitchen to attempt to introduce himself to Isabelita, as a way of extending the joining process. In this first encounter, the counselor listened and joined.

Diagnosis: While the counselor listened and joined, he also observed the interaction between mother and daughter. Armed with these observations, the counselor understood the family's interactions along the following diagnostic dimensions.

Organization: There is a problem with this family's hierarchy and leadership. The identified patient is in a powerful position, while the mother is powerless and feels overwhelmed. The mother has no control over the identified patient's behavior. There is no sibling subsystem. The 12-year-old son triangulates between the mother and the identified patient.

Resonance: The family is very enmeshed. The quality of the enmeshment between the mother and the identified patient is conflictive and hostile.

Developmental Stage: All three members of this family appear to be functioning below what would be appropriate for their ages and roles. The identified patient's demands on her mother are those of a younger child, and she does not help out at home. The mother is overwhelmed and does not know how to control the identified patient. The son is too attached to his mother and involved in supporting her, and he does not engage in age-appropriate social and play activities.

Life Context: The family is new to the United States, and the mother is disconnected from her host society (e.g., she has no English skills). The identified patient spends most of her time with acculturated peers who participate in drug use and risky sex.

Identified Patient: The identified patient is extremely rigid. The identified patient centralizes herself with her negative behavior. The relationships between the identified patient and other family members are characterized by intense negativity. This family has not identified other problems or persons as a concern.

Conflict Resolution: The typical pattern of interacting in the family is continuous conflict emergence without resolution.

General Discussion of the Diagnosis: In the Hernandez family, the mother is overwhelmed and is unable to manage her drug-abusing daughter's behavior. The daughter, in turn, has distanced herself from the family and spends the majority of her time with sexually active and drug-using friends. When the daughter is home, she and her mother fight constantly, with the brother intervening to take the mother's side against his sister. The brother's triangulating maneuvers serve only to further isolate the identified patient from her family. Cultural issues also need to be taken into account in diagnosing the Hernandez family. Upon their arrival in the United States from Colombia three years earlier, the members of this family began to drift apart from one another. Isabelita began learning English and associating with Americanized peers, whereas her mother remained socially and culturally isolated. Ms. Hernandez had become increasingly uncomfortable with Isabelita's acculturating behavior and choices of friends, but the widening chasm between mother and daughter discouraged Ms. Hernandez from addressing these issues with Isabelita. By the time Isabelita was referred to treatment, the family system had become completely dysfunctional, and Ms. Hernandez had ceded nearly all of her power and authority to her daughter.

Planning Treatment Based on Diagnosis: A powerful identified patient is typically joined first in order to engage the family into treatment. In this case, however, Isabelita did not present an engagement problem. Although angry and rebellious in her behavior, she was present in therapy and willing to voice her complaints and feelings. The counselor thus starts by joining both the mother and the identified patient. It is important very early in the therapy to work to restructure the dysfunctional family hierarchy. By supporting the mother, the counselor needs to help her break the cycle of conflict between herself and her daughter so that the mother can begin to recapture some control. Essentially, the counselor needs to help move the mother into an appropriate parental role. The brother's attempts at triangulation need to be blocked, allowing the mother and daughter to resolve their issues directly, between the two of them. This also would permit the brother to engage in more age-appropriate activities. Isabelita's disobedient behavior needs to be reframed as a cry for help in order to change the affective tone of her relationship with her mother, and, thus, to permit them to interact more positively.

The treatment plan that the counselor formulated for the Hernandez family addressed the following:

- ***Organization:*** A dysfunctional hierarchy exists in which the daughter holds the power and the mother is powerless and overwhelmed. Power must be transferred back to the mother.
- ***Organization:*** The son is triangulated into the relationship between the mother and the daughter. The son's attempts to triangulate must be blocked.
- ***Resonance:*** The mother and the daughter are enmeshed in a conflictive and explosive relationship; the daughter's behavior must be reframed as a call for help to reduce the negativity.
- ***Developmental Stage:*** The daughter's behavior at home is immature and demanding, the son is playing a "mother's partner" role, and the mother does not assume appropriate parenting leadership. The daughter must be shown how to express her feelings, the mother must be encouraged to elicit and validate the daughter's feelings, and the son must be prompted to participate in age appropriate social activities.
- ***Identified Patient:*** The daughter is designated as the source of the family's problems. The problem must be framed in terms of the whole family and addressed by changing the family's patterns of interaction.
- ***Life Context:*** Acculturation differences compound normative parent– adolescent disagreements and exacerbate the distance between the mother and the daughter. The counselor must help the two of them "get on the same page" in their interactions.
- ***Life Context:*** The daughter is associating with high-risk peers. As power is transferred back to the mother, peer selection must be brought up, and the mother needs to encourage the daughter to select different peers.
- ***Life Context:*** The mother and the son are socially isolated. The mother needs to familiarize herself with the English language and with American culture, and the son needs to associate with friends his own age.
- ***Conflict Resolution:*** The mother and the daughter tend to shout at and insult one another with no resolution. The

(*continued*)

family must be taught to stay on topic and resolve issues without leaving the room or resorting to personal attacks.

Producing Change: One week later, the counselor came for the second session, and the same exact incident reoccurred, with Isabelita coming home late, clearly on drugs. The counselor had already established a therapeutic relationship with the whole family. While the counselor sat with Ms. Hernandez waiting for Isabelita to show up, he used the time to explain how Ms. Hernandez could respond differently to Isabelita when she arrived home late (i.e., a reversal). The counselor coached Ms. Hernandez to remain calm, not let Isabelita engage her in a screaming match, and not provide or help her with food. When Isabelita arrived, her portion of the family dinner had been placed in the freezer. Upon her arrival, Isabelita as usual bolted to the kitchen and demanded food. Encouraged by the counselor, Ms. Hernandez continued to sit in the living room, which, in their small home, was just next to the kitchen. Isabelita came into the living room and began shouting at her mother about the food. The mother yelled back to Isabelita, "You are a drug addict," and this began anew the cycle of blaming and recrimination. The counselor stood up, walked up to Ms. Hernandez, and said, "You need to stay calm and not let her control you with her fighting."

After several such interventions, Ms. Hernandez finally looked at the counselor and said, "I am trying to do it, but it is very hard." This statement represented Ms. Hernandez's initial step in using the counselor to help her detach from the conflict with her daughter. Furthermore, when the son stepped in, the counselor encouraged the mother to hold him back as well. Isabelita continued to scream at her mother without getting a response for another 15 minutes before storming to her bedroom in a fury. Having been unsuccessful in engaging either her mother or brother in a fight, she was frustrated and gave up. After the counselor gave the mother ample support and praise for having controlled the situation and avoided a fight, the counselor moved the conversation to the next step. He discussed other ways in which Isabelita would "push her mother's buttons," and he gave Ms. Hernandez the task of using the newly learned skills on these other occasions.

This was a great gain for a single session, and it was clear that the gains from this session needed to be followed up and extended as soon as possible. The counselor told Ms. Hernandez that "we can keep making things better if we meet again in a few days." To Isabelita, the counselor said, "You see, these fights between you and your mom don't have to happen. If you'll agree to have me here again next week, we can keep working toward having peace in your life." As a result, both Ms. Hernandez and Isabelita agreed to hold another session the following week.

At the beginning of the next session, the counselor followed up on the previous week's gains by reviewing how Ms. Hernandez and Isabelita had made progress around the issue of fighting. The counselor intervened to block the brother's attempts to triangulate himself into interactions between Ms. Hernandez and Isabelita. Throughout the session, the counselor praised Ms. Hernandez whenever she avoided a fight, and empathized with her when she did not. ("I understand how hard it is, but I know you tried.") The counselor also praised Isabelita amply for her ability to follow her mother's lead in avoiding fights that are "so upsetting to you." Hence, both the mother and Isabelita received credit and praise for accomplishing changes in their relationship.

Having experienced a major accomplishment in placing the mother in control of the interactions, the counselor was now ready to move to the next level: negotiation of rules and consequences.

The counselor also began to reinforce changes in Isabelita's behavior, no matter how small, by showing empathy for "how difficult all of this must be for you." The counselor also took an active role in helping Ms. Hernandez move into a more appropriate parental role by gradually praising each of the mother's attempts to guide or set limits for her daughter. The counselor also consistently reframed Isabelita's disrespectful behavior as a cry for help and as her way of expressing pain.

Gradually, over time, Isabelita's externalizing behavior and drug abuse decreased. Ms. Hernandez learned to befriend her daughter and to remain calm and not engage in conflict (i.e., a reversal) whenever Isabelita would throw a tantrum. Isabelita began to phrase her complaints in the form of respectful disagreements rather than hostile attacks. The brother, sensing that the tension between his sister and mother was decreasing, slowly backed away from the triangulated relationship with them and began to seek out his own social activities.

Source: This case vignette was adapted from the *government document written by José Szapocznik, Olga Hervis, and Seth Schwartz and published by the National Institute on Drug Abuse titled* ***Brief Strategic Family Therapy for Adolescent Drug Abuse*** *(2003).*

Bibliography

Bennett, L. A. (1978). *Counseling in correctional environments.* New York: Human Science Press.

Bowen, M. (1978). *Family therapy in clinical practice.* New York: Jason Aronson.

Boyd-Franklin, N. (1989). *Black families in therapy: A multisystems approach.* New York: Guilford Press.

Brown, D., & Srebalus, J. (2003). *Introduction to the counseling profession* (3rd ed.). Pearson Education, Inc: New York.

Brucker, P. S., & Perry, B. J. (1998). American Indians: Presenting concerns and considerations for family therapists. *American Journal of Family Therapy, 26*(4), 307–320.

Cameron, S., & Turtle-Song, I. (2002). Learning to write case notes using the SOAP format. *Journal of Counseling & Development, 80*, 286–292.

Chang, P. (2000). Treating Asian/Pacific American addicts and their families. In J.-A. Krestan (Ed.). *Bridges to recovery: Addiction, family therapy, and multicultural treatment* (pp. 192–218). New York: Free Press.

Corey, G. (1996). *Theory and practice of counseling and psychotherapy* (5th ed.). Pacific Grove, CA: Brooks/Cole Publishing Company.

Duran, E., & Duran, B. (1996). *Native American postcolonial psychology.* Albany, NY: State University of New York Press.

Egan, G. (2007). *The skilled helper: A problem management and opportunity development approach to helping* (8th ed.). Thompson Brooks/Cole: Belmont, CA.

Falicov, C. J. (1998). *Latino families in therapy: A guide to multicultural Practice.* New York: Guilford Press.

Garcia-Preto, N. (1996). Latino families: An overview. In M. McGoldrick, J. Giordano, & J. K. Pearce (Eds.), *Ethnicity and family therapy* (pp. 141–154). New York: Guilford Press.

Gladding, S. T. (1996). *Counseling: A comprehensive profession* (3rd ed.). Englewood Cliffs, NJ: Prentice Hall.

Goldenberg, I., & Goldenberg, H. (1996). *Family therapy: An overview* (4th ed.). New York: Brooks/Cole.

Haley, J. (1984). *Ordeal therapy.* San Francisco: Jossey Bass.

Harper, F. D., & McFadden, J. (2003). *Culture and counseling: New approaches.* New York: Allyn & Bacon.

Holtzworth-Munroe, A., & Jacobson, N. S. (1991). Behavioral marital therapy. In A. S. Gunman & D. P. Kniskern (Eds.), *Handbook of family therapy* (Vol. II, pp. 96–132). New York: Brunner/Mazel.

Kaufman, E., & Borders, L. (1988). Ethnic family differences in adolescent substance use. In R. H. Coombs (Ed.), *The family context of adolescent drug use* (pp. 99–121). New York: Haworth Press.

Kazdin, A. E. (2001). *Behavior modification in applied settings* (6th ed.). Belmont, CA: Wadsworth/ Thomson Learning.

Kratcoski, P. C. (1981). *Correctional counseling and treatment.* Monterey, CA: Duxbury Press.

Lester, D. (1992). *Correctional counseling* (2nd ed.). Cincinnati, OH: Anderson Publishing.

Marín, G., & Marín, B. V. (1991). *Research with Hispanic populations.* Newbury Park, CA: Sage Publications.

May Lai, T. F. (2001). Ethnocultural background and substance abuse treatment of Chinese Americans. In S. L. A. Straussner (Ed.), *Ethnocultural factors in substance abuse treatment* (pp. 345–367). New York: Guilford Press.

McGoldrick, M., Gerson, R., & Shellenberger, S. (1999). *Genograms: Assessment and intervention.* New York: W. W. Norton and Co., Inc.

McGoldrick, M., Giordano, J., & Pearce, J. K. (1996). *Ethnicity and family therapy* (2nd ed.). New York: Guilford Press.

Paniagua, F. A. (1998). *Assessing and treating culturally diverse clients: A practical guide* (2nd ed.). Thousand Oaks, CA: Sage Publications.

Papero, D. (1990). *Bowen family systems theory.* Upper Saddle River, NJ: Allyn & Bacon.

Reid, D. J. (2000). Addiction, African Americans, and a Christian recovery. In J. A. Krestan (Ed.), *Bridges to recovery: Addiction, family therapy, and multicultural treatment* (pp. 145–172). New York: The Free Press.

Santisteban, D. A., Coatsworth, J. D., Perez-Vidal, A., Mitrani, V., Jean-Gilles, M., & Szapocznik, J. (1997). Brief structural/strategic family therapy with African American and Hispanic high-risk youth. *Journal of Community Psychology, 25*(5), 453–471.

Santisteban, D. A., Muir-Malcolm, J. A., Mitrani, V. B., & Szapocznik, J. (2002). Integrating the study of ethnic culture and family psychology intervention science. In H. A. Liddle, D. A. Santisteban, R. F. Levant, & J. H. Bray (Eds.), *Family psychology: Science-based interventions* (pp. 331–351). Washington, DC: American Psychological Association.

Skinner, B. F. (1953). *Science and human behavior.* New York: Macmillan.

Sutton, C. T., & Broken Nose, M. A. (1996). American Indian families: An overview. In M. McGoldrick, J. Giordano, & J. K. Pearce (Eds.), *Ethnicity and family therapy* (2nd ed., pp. 31–44). New York: Guilford Press.

Substance Abuse and Mental Health Services Administration. (2005). *Substance abuse treatment and family therapy.* Rockville, MD: Center for Substance Abuse Treatment.

Wright, E. M. (2001). Substance abuse in African American communities. In S. L. A. Straussner (Ed.), *Ethnocultural factors in substance abuse treatment* (pp. 31–51). New York: Guilford Press.

7

Group Therapy

CHAPTER OBJECTIVES

After reading this chapter, you will be able to:

1. Understand group facilitator skills.
2. Identify advantages of group counseling.
3. Identify disadvantages of group counseling.
4. Selection of group members.
5. Educating offenders about the group process.
6. Understand the four stages of the group process.
7. Intervening in the group process.
8. Counseling techniques in group settings.
9. Identify multicultural issues relevant to the group process.

INTRODUCTION

Group counseling is a very popular approach to working with offenders. It has been shown to be effective with a myriad of dysfunctional behaviors including domestic violence, substance abuse, anger, trauma, and sex offenders. Gladding (1996) provides an interesting point regarding the effectiveness of groups. A basic human need is interaction with others. It is through these interactions that we come to understand who we are and also realize that we are unique and worthy of love and acceptance. Especially for those who have had limited contact with others, group counseling can be extremely beneficial as acceptable behavior is taught and modeled. Groups also provide a great setting for many offenders to realize that they are not alone in their suffering as they interact with other offenders experiencing the same difficulties.

Generally, a group consists of two or more people who come together to work toward a common goal. For offenders, the goal is usually to better understand their psychological and emotional difficulties illuminated through their contact with the criminal justice system. Some groups are designed to assist offenders reenter society and others are designed to help offenders cope with life inside of jail or prison, both of which are very controlling institutions. As will be discussed throughout this chapter there are advantages and disadvantages to groups. In addition, we will provide specific guidelines that should be considered when forming groups as a counselor as well as the various processes within groups. The one factor that remains paramount is whether counseling individuals or groups is the leader's ability to be open, honest, and genuine. As noted in Chapter 5, offenders have a keen sense for identifying phoniness. Counselors or group members who are not genuine will be quickly identified and if not dealt with can cause great harm to the overall effectiveness of the group.

PART ONE: THE BASICS OF GROUP THERAPY

Group Facilitator Skills

ACTIVE LISTENING First, the qualities of effective group leaders are not different from the qualities of effective individual counselors. For example, effective group leaders will be active listeners. Active listening describes the process of being fully engaged with what an offender is saying both verbally and nonverbally. The active listener is often able to identify underlying feelings and emotion even when not directly communicated. Active listeners are also able to identify incongruencies in what an offender is verbalizing and what he or she is saying behaviorally. Active listening is a critical skill that counselors develop over time that allows them to efficiently and effectively guide offenders to real emotion attached to a circumstance or stimuli.

Active listening also helps build and maintain a positive alliance with the group. As noted, a positive therapeutic alliance vital to individual counseling is also vital to group counseling. By engaging in consistent active listening the leader is nonverbally stating to the group: "I am here for you; I am committed to you; I will not abandon you; I will give you my all and work to help you better your life. **I will not judge you.**" Exhibit 7.1 provides a good summation of active listening:

REFLECTION AND CLARIFICATION Active listeners are also well positioned to accurately reflect and clarify an offender's message. This is a critical task and serves to ensure that the message being heard by the counselor and the group is that which is intended by the offender. Oftentimes when group members have something important to share they will begin with only part of the real message they mean to impart. Some disclosures may be extremely risky and anxiety provoking. The counselor's ability to recognize the anxiety and gently guide the offender into the depth of the real message is very important.

EXHIBIT 7.1

Active Listening

Excellent listening skills are the keystone of any effective therapy. Therapeutic interventions require the clinician to perceive and to understand both verbal and nonverbal cues to meaning and metaphorical levels of meaning. In addition, leaders need to pay attention to the context from which meanings come. Does it pertain to the here and now of what is occurring in the group or the then and there history of the specific client?

Source: CSAT (2005).

QUESTIONING AND SUMMARIZING Questioning and summarizing, also closely related to active listening, is the ability to identify latent messages within an offender's verbalizations that uncover salient issues related to distress. The alert counselor will identify key words and phrases at which gentle but direct questions will be aimed. Direct questions are often very useful in cases where an offender is using generalizing statements. For example, an offender may state, "Most people have fears related to being in social situations with people they do not know." The counselor may follow up with, "What frightens YOU in social situations?"

Summarizing describes the process of articulating back to the offender what one believes has been said. Summarizing provides the vehicle through which counselors and group members clarify the essence of the offender's message and it also demonstrates to the offender that he or she has been heard. For many offenders, the simple act of being heard can be very therapeutic. Enhancing the therapeutic experience is likely when the counselor is able to accurately summarize the offender's message followed by direction and suggestions as to the underlying mechanisms supporting the distress.

ENCOURAGEMENT AND SUPPORT The group setting has the potential to provide great healing through members' show of encouragement and support. Much of the work done in groups takes place via the recapitulation of families of origin. For most offenders it is very likely that they rarely, if ever, received positive regard in the form encouragement or support. Self-esteem and egos can be destroyed by habitual neglect and harsh judgmentalism. The group often provides a wonderful opportunity for offenders to experience positive regard and encouragement. Counselors also must be very aware of how they respond to offenders. In addition, counselors must be able to govern the interactions between group members in such a way that everyone is able to express themselves, but in a way that does not cause damage. Similar to experiences in our families of origin, group members can sometimes be overly critical and judgmental. As depicted in Exhibit 7.2, counselors must work to maintain a healthy balance of freedom and disclosure while ensuring the overall tone is supportive and encouraging.

MODELING Modeling, within a group therapy setting, describes the process of demonstrating behavior and specific methods of articulation that are more likely to result in members getting their needs met. The concept of effective modeling cannot be overstated. Many offenders have never had the opportunity to witness healthy, functional behavior. In many cases, especially for persistent offenders, their primary caregivers may have been involved with criminality and substance abuse. As noted in differential association theory close, intimate relationships are powerful mechanisms in shaping one's behavior. Therefore, for those offenders who have had no previous exposure to appropriate behavior or cognition, a counselor's effective modeling will be their first exposure. For example, a domestic batterer may be taught that it is never appropriate to use violence within the relationship. For some offenders who grew up observing their fathers batter their mothers this may be the first they hear of such information. In addition to observing the violence they may have been told by the batterers that violence is the only way to keep a woman in her place. And, the violence is only carried out because he loves his wife.

In addition to the effective modeling of the counselor, the experience can be even more profound when more effective behavior is supported and further modeled by other group members. Peer support is a very powerful motivator. All humans have a tendency to compare themselves with others they see as most like them. In fact, this very point provides solid support for why groups can be so effective. Much learning takes place in the presence of peers

EXHIBIT 7.2

Jody's Arm

A long-term outpatient interpersonal process group meets in 90-minute sessions to support sustained recovery. The group, which includes five women and four men, is relatively stable and successfully abstinent. Many of the clients, however, still struggle with profound psychological concerns that require ongoing attention.

In one group session, all members are present except Jody, a 43-year-old client who is opioid dependent and has co-occurring psychiatric difficulties. Jody walks in approximately 35 minutes late, apologizing for her lateness. The group facilitator makes a mental note that Jody is wearing several sweatshirts, despite weather too mild to justify the need for layered clothing.

Approximately 15 minutes before the close of group, blood seeps through the top layer of clothing covering Jody's left arm. The group leader asks Jody if her injured arm is making some statement to the group members. Is there something specific that she wants from the group at this particular moment? The leader is confident that Jody is saying something very important not only to, but for, the group as a whole.

Jody indicates that the previous week she felt diminished by comments from a number of members in the group. In an effort to deal with the anxiety and shame associated with returning to the group, she has cut herself before attending.

A number of group members quickly share their concern for her and hopes that their comments of the previous week could be revisited and revised to be more supportive. Jody shows the group the cut on her forearm, which has all but stopped bleeding. She explains how deep her pain is and her desire for the group not to judge her for that pain.

Because Jody appears to be in no imminent danger, the leader chooses to continue with the group process, ending it at the regularly scheduled time. The group meets at a major medical center, so the leader is able to walk with Jody to the emergency room. The leader assures the group that Jody will receive the medical attention she needs.

The next week, the entire group makes substantial gains. They carefully examine their judgment and willingness to allow Jody to be the primary spokeswoman for the profound emotional pain that each of them feels. The dramatic and unexpected situation the previous week has not interrupted the group process. It has instead been used adroitly to make the group even more productive.

Note: This example is taken from a specific group session. The group in this example consists of members working with substance abuse issues. Students should pay particular attention to the impact of judgmentalism and how some members may react.

Source: CSAT (2005).

and caregivers who collectively make up groups. Therefore, it could be argued that if people learn criminality in groups the best way to unlearn is also in groups.

A quick note of caution is necessary for counselors modeling behavior for offenders. When working with offenders it is critical that counselors model and demonstrate behavior and cognitions that are realistic and capable of truly being carried out. In other words, counselors must be authentic and real or the seasoned offender will quickly recognize the suggestions as being ingenuous. When modeling behavior counselors must also be open to feedback from offenders. For example, an offender may simply state in response to the counselor's modeling "If I do that where I come from, I could get killed." In such circumstances the authentic counselor will accept this response with empathy as opposed to defensiveness and may solicit the help of the group to come up with appropriate responses that can then be modeled.

Advantages of Group Therapy

COST There are several advantages to counseling criminal offender in groups. The most significant advantage is "cost." It costs less for each member of the group when the counselor's fee is divided up evenly among the offenders. Most offenders, whether incarcerated or on probation, do not have an abundance of wealth. And, when one considers that licensed professional counselors can charge from $50 and up per hour it becomes clear that cost is a critical factor. Another fundamental advantage to group counseling is that more offenders have access to counseling. The current reality is that there are too many offenders for the number of professionally trained correctional counselors. Interestingly, correctional counselors are among the most sought after professionals within most correctional institutions. Until more counselors are hired and properly trained, however, the group process allows more offenders exposure to get help for a reasonable price.

CONFRONTATION BY PEERS Another advantage to group counseling is the concept of being confronted by peers. Being confronted by peers can be a profound experience for many offenders and this experience leads to real and lasting change. Remember that much learning takes place in groups with various associations with peers. Often deep learning is fostered in positive experiences with others the offender feels is mostly like him as opposed to authoritative figures who have no real concept of the offender's real world. Peers are often able to bridge the gap between the theoretical concepts offered by counselors and the practical circumstances of the institution or the poverty-stricken conditions of the offender's intimate community. In essence, peers are often able to assist counselors apply therapeutic techniques from perspectives the counselor may not appreciate as a result of his or her having different developmental experiences.

LEARN FROM MULTIPLE PERSPECTIVES Another advantage to group therapy is that offenders are afforded the opportunity to learn from multiple perspectives. The concept of learning from multiple perspectives shares the same basic theoretical foundation of learning that takes place while being confronted by peers. In group sessions offenders are able to experience different ideas and views relative to a common source of distress. In individual counseling it is often the case where a counselor's theoretical orientation and technique does not serve the client well. In such circumstances clients will often stop counseling altogether or will seek out a new therapist. Offenders, however, do not usually have the luxury of simply switching to a new counselor. Therefore, the multiple perspectives provided by group members often help to overcome this problem as offenders are usually able to find views and techniques they are comfortable with. In addition, the entire group benefits from multiple perspectives as the individual members are able to select items of what is being offered by each offender. Similar to the idea of integrative theories within scientific investigation, offenders are able to integrate various concepts that are most salient to their own individualized method of learning and life circumstances.

SENSE OF BELONGING Finally, a well-constructed group made up of offenders who feel free to share their thoughts fosters a very powerful sense of belonging. For many offenders, the sense of belonging or fitting in has never been realized. Human beings are social creatures; we need positive forms of socialization in order to meet our full range of psychological and emotional needs. A group of offenders who come together to work on common problems have the ability to create a sense of belonging that is extremely therapeutic.

Disadvantages of Group Counseling

LESS ONE-ON-ONE ATTENTION Although there are more advantages to group counseling than disadvantages, there are a few concerns that must be addressed. First, in a group setting there is less one-on-one attention. And as noted by Yalom (2005), it is generally a mistake to attempt individual psychotherapy in a group setting. For some offenders, especially those who have a difficult time speaking in front of others, the group setting can be overwhelming and intimidating. For some offenders the lack of individual attention may leave some areas of distress unexplored. In such cases where more individual attention is required it may prove beneficial to supplement group sessions with individual sessions where the availability of counselors and time permits. It may be that individual attention will be able to create the foundation needed to participate and benefit from the group.

CONFIDENTIALITY In addition to less one-on-one attention the issue of confidentiality is often a concern with group settings. Naturally, it is much more difficult to ensure confidentiality when working with multiple offenders. This fact must be disclosed to all members early in the group process. Ultimately, all the counselor can do is clearly articulate the importance of all information remaining confident and ask that each member uphold this request. It cannot, however, be guaranteed. In all cases, offenders should be provided with the following information (see Exhibit 7.3).

EXHIBIT 7.3
Confidentiality

Confidentiality is both an ethical and a legal issue. Federal law (Title 42, Part 2 or 42 C.F.R., Part 2, Confidentiality of Alcohol and Drug Abuse Patient Records) guarantees strict confidentiality of information about all people receiving substance abuse prevention and/or treatment services. Clients should be fully informed regarding issues of confidentiality, and group leaders should do all they can to build respect for confidentiality and anonymity within groups. There are six conditions under which limited disclosure is permitted under the regulations. These exceptions are:

1. The group member has signed a Release of Information document that allows the group facilitator to communicate with another professional and/or agency.
2. A group member threatens imminent harm to himself or herself, and the group facilitator believes that the client may act on this threat.
3. A client threatens imminent harm to another named person, and the group facilitator believes that there is a reasonable likelihood that the client will act on the threat.
4. A medical emergency requires that a client's drug and alcohol status be revealed in order to ensure that the client gets appropriate medical attention.
5. A client is suspected of child neglect and/or abuse, as defined by the laws of the state in which the substance abuse treatment services are being provided.
6. A direct court order mandates the release of specific information related to a client's history and/or treatment. However, an authorizing court order alone does not compel disclosure—for example, if the person authorized to disclose confidential information does not elect to make the disclosure, he or she cannot be forced to do so unless there is a valid subpoena (i.e., the subpoena has not expired) or other compulsory process introduced that would then compel disclosure. An appropriate judge issues a court order. It specifies the exact information to be provided about a particular client and is properly signed and dated.

Source: CSAT (2005).

GROUPTHINK Another disadvantage to group settings is the possibility for the formation of groupthink. Groupthink is a dangerous phenomenon of members conforming to attitudes and views expressed in the group that may not be their own (Robins, 2005). When groupthink sets in individuality is lost. This is the real problem as offenders may conform to the views of others and engage in actions that are not authentic. Individuals prone to group think include those who have a dysfunctional level of desire to fit in or be accepted by others. These individuals may have a difficult time stating their own opinions in the face of adversity. These offenders are likely to have endured strict control within their families of origin where expression was stymied and conformance demanded. Counselors must remain vigilant to the development of groupthink and confront its presence when necessary.

DIFFICULTY IN TRACKING ISSUES Finally, salient issues needing to be explored are often more difficult for the counselor to track in group settings. In individual settings this task is easier because the focus is on one person. In a group, however, there may be multiple issues that need to be addressed all of which are expressed by different offenders and nearly simultaneously as the discussion freely flows. The ability of the counselor to track individual and group needs is complex and probably best accomplished through experience. In essence, the counselor must be aware of two sets of needs that are not mutually exclusive of each other: (1) the individual and (2) the group. These needs are intertwined and can become confusing. What is important is that counselors understand this difficulty and confront it honestly. It may be that counselors, especially beginning counselors, periodically stop to check with the group to ensure that needs are being heard and addressed.

Selection of Group Members

"Some groups fail simply because the members of the group are not carefully selected" (Brown & Srebalus, 2005, p. 86). Selecting appropriate group members may be the most important task related to group counseling. Generally, there are three broad areas associated with selecting participants that counselors should be aware. First, all participants should be similar in the types of distress they are suffering. In order for group participants to benefit most it is beneficial that each offender share the main issue being addressed such as anger, depression, substance abuse, and so on. A group of offenders who are homogenous in regards to their dysfunctionality allows for continuity in the group and helps assure that each individual's distress is under constant consideration.

Second, although it is desired that all participants share common presenting problems group work is most beneficial when members have developed differing strategies aimed at coping with the problem. This allows for altering viewpoints or perspectives for dealing with issues that have proved troublesome for each offender. This is a very important component of forming effective groups. Human beings are complex and the greater the variation in responding to distress the more likely each member is to find a style of response that works best for him or her. Therefore, groups function best when members' presenting issues are homogenous and their responses are heterogeneous (Brown & Srebalus, 2005).

Finally, in order for the group experience to be meaningful, participants should be able to appropriately articulate feelings and possess a basic cognitive ability to make connections and understand the various views offered by the counselor and members. An important note that should be considered when forming groups is that overly aggressive and overly shy offenders have the potential to significantly disrupt the group process. When available these offenders should receive individual counseling prior to joining a group (Brown & Srebalus, 2005).

Educating Offenders about the Group Process

One way to help ensure that the group functions best is to take some time to educate members on the process of group counseling. Naturally, many offenders will be anxious about what is expected to take place in group counseling. Explaining the group process will help allay some of this anxiety and further serves to ensure that each offender is willing and capable of effectively participating in the group process.

Gladding (1996, pp. 340–341) draws on the work of Corey (1995) and provides six critical components that should be clearly articulated to each participant. First, the purpose and objectives of the group should not be a mystery. The purpose of the group should be clearly articulated so that each offender fully understands the foundation from which the group will function. Second, the group format, rules, and procedures need to be clear and agreed upon. In some cases it may prove beneficial to obtain a contract from each offender regarding his or her ability and willingness to conform to the rules of the group. Some groups purposefully create no rules signifying the group is free to present and react to information in whatever method it chooses. These group, however, are generally composed of members experienced with the group process. And, although these groups may provide a vehicle for extensive psychological and emotional growth for seasoned participants, they are not recommended for offenders inexperienced in group work. Third, there should be a clear statement summarizing the group counselor's credentials. Fourth, counselors should spend some time with each offender to ensure the individual is not only fit for the group but also that the counselor and individual offender are suited for meeting one's needs. Fifth, all offenders must be advised of the rights and responsibilities that accompany their participation in the group. Finally, counselors must be open about the limitations of group counseling. Confidentiality cannot be guaranteed and mere presence within a group setting does not ensure a successful experience.

According to Gladding (1996), there is an abundance of research that supports educating clients about basic functions and expectations of the group process. Most human beings are not comfortable entering into circumstances without some type of guidance of expectations. At its most basic level this anxiety is likely connected to basic needs of survival and is therefore powerful. And, as people become anxious their responses often become unpredictable. In essence, the more educated the offender is about the group process, the sooner he or she is able to concentrate on the objectives and processes aimed at improving his or her responses to aversive stimuli. Exhibit 7.4 contains an actual handout used to establish ground rules for a beginning group.

The Four Stages of the Group Process and Duties of the Counselor

In most cases, group counseling progresses through various stages. In this section we concentrate on four stages that seem to be most common. Before we discuss each stage it is important to note, however, that there may be variation in these stages as well as in the number of stages depending on the make-up and purpose of the group.

ORIENTATION STAGE The orientation stage is very similar to what we discussed above concerning educating the group. Generally, the orientation stage is where participants begin the process of getting to know each other. Discussions are generally "light" as each member attempts to get comfortable and acclimate themselves to the process. In the orientation stage, counselors reiterate expectations and goals and also serve as role models in beginning the process of teaching new behaviors. Some of the most important initial skills counselors begin to model include active listening as participants begin to introduce themselves. Counselors

EXHIBIT 7.4

Appleton Outpatient Psychotherapy Group Ground Rules

The behavior and feelings of members of the therapy group mirror in important ways behavior and feelings in other important relationships. Consequently, the group provides a setting in which to examine patterns of behavior in relationships. The group also provides a context in which members learn to identify, understand, and express their feelings. The therapist's role is to facilitate this group process. To foster these goals, we believe that several group ground rules are important. These are as follows:

1. Members joining long-term groups remain as long as they find the group useful in working on important issues in their lives. We recommend at least a year. Members are required to make an initial 3-month commitment in order to determine the usefulness of this particular group for them.
2. Regular and timely attendance at all sessions is expected. As a member, it is your responsibility to notify the group in advance when you know that you will be away or late for group. In the event of an unexpected absence, you should notify the group at least 24 hours in advance to avoid being charged for the missed session.
3. Members of Appleton substance abuse groups are committed to maintaining abstinence. If a relapse does occur, it must be discussed promptly in the group—as must thoughts or concerns about resuming drug/alcohol use. Members of ACOA (Adult Children of Alcoholics) and family groups are asked to be reflective about their own substance use and to bring up changes in patterns of use or concerns that may be associated with use.
4. Members will notify the group if they are considering leaving the group. Because leaving the group is a process, just as joining is, members are expected to see this process through for at least 3 weeks following notification of termination.
5. Members will have a commitment to talk about important issues in their lives that cause difficulty in relating to others or in living life fully.
6. Members will also have a commitment to talk about what is going on in the group itself as a way of better understanding their own interpersonal dynamics.
7. Members will treat matters that occur in the group with utmost confidentiality. To that end, members are expected not to discuss what happens in the group with people who are not members of the group.
8. Outside-of-group contact often has considerable impact on the group's therapeutic effectiveness. Therefore, any relevant interactions between members which occur outside the group should be brought back into the next meeting and shared with the entire group.
9. What you share in the group will be shared with other members of the treatment team when we feel that it is important to your treatment to do so.
10. Payments for group are due at the last meeting of the month unless other arrangements are discussed and explicitly worked out in the group. If for any reason timely payment becomes problematic, members are expected to discuss this in the group.

Original Source: Vannicelli (1992, pp. 295–296). Adapted from CSAT (2005).

also demonstrate the importance of nonjudgmentalism as each offender speaks and expresses differences in opinions and ideology. Counselors also demonstrate the process of sharing information. Sharing is certainly one of the most important behaviors counselors initially demonstrate. They may select a certain point expressed by each offender and expound with their own related experiences (Brown & Srebalus, 2005). Gladding (1996) notes that one of the most important and useful techniques used to assist offenders in the orientation phase is to make sure each offender knows what to expect in the initial session. A little mystery may be useful in later stages but not initially. If members will be expected to share relevant information about themselves in the opening meeting they should be informed about this expectation and even provided with some direction on what to say.

CONFLICT STAGE As the group progresses the second stage most often encountered is the conflict stage. In this stage members begin to jockey for position as they attempt to establish themselves in the group. The conflict stage is also where they begin transition from general, introductory speech to beginning the process of really working on presenting problems and issues. As this process takes place, a new round of anxiety sets in. Members will begin weighing whether they can trust other members with their deep, personal problems. Participants will often resist prods to share deeper and more meaningful information. Counselors may be questioned and even challenged as to whether they know what they are doing. **The most salient point to understand about the conflict stage is that much of the resistance is due to fear.** Many offenders will have never learned to share meaningful emotion. In their past experiences they were likely taught that showing or discussing emotion was a sign of weakness. Counselors must understand this process and not be baited into unhealthy exchanges with the offenders. The most resistant offenders will be those who are most afraid of sharing deep emotion. Counselors should work to comfort offenders as much as possible and take every opportunity to demonstrate trust and empathy in order to effectively reach the cohesion stage.

COHESION STAGE If the group successfully reaches the cohesion stage the odds are strong that significant learning and growth will take place. It is important to remember that group work functions as a recapitulation of one's family of origin. In one's family of origin, however, much of the learning was dysfunctional. The power of the group experience lies in the offender's ability to learn functional responses to group issues which are similar to many of the issues experienced in one's family and community. For example, there will be times where members may feel disrespected by other group participants. Similar circumstances in the community may result in violence. With the help of the group, however, one can explore alternative responses such as checking with the source of the perceived disrespect. With help and guidance the offender may state his or her feelings and ask if this is what was intended? Often, it will be learned that feeling disrespected was the least of intentions. The result is the offender learns that many circumstances are perceived erroneously and learns how to check them out before responding inappropriately.

TERMINATION STAGE As noted by the time-tested adage, "All (good) things come to an end," and groups are no different. This is also the case with top athletes as they will often enter a specific training camp for a specific challenge. Once the competition has come and gone they move onto the next training camp most capable of attending to their needs regarding the next challenge. The salient component of terminating the group is that the act of termination represents a death—the death of the group.

There are several important tasks for counselors during the termination stage. First, counselors must once again work to allay the members' impending anxiety about whether they are ready to carry on without the support of the group. Anxiety is the one disorder that counselors will have to address at each stage in order for the natural progression to take place. It is no surprise that Fosha (2000) describes anxiety as the mother of all pathology. Second, counselors need to ensure that all unfinished business has been addressed, especially interpersonal conflicts among group members. Finally, counselors help participants realize their progress and new skill with addressing aversive stimuli. Offenders are reminded that they can function successfully either in the institution or their communities of origin.

SECTION SUMMARY

Group counseling can be very effective when working with offenders. It is critical, however, that the group facilitator be skilled in keeping the session flowing and remaining on topic. This can be a difficult task as some offenders will work diligently to cognitively and emotionally remain in areas that are least threatening.

Selecting the appropriate members for a group is a very important task. For example, violent offenders may not be best suited for a group concentrating on anxiety issues that underlie acting out in the form of theft. It is wrong to assume that any offender can be placed into any group regardless of the objectives. In fact, if caution is not taken to ensure proper placement the result could be more harm to some of the participants.

Finally, offenders need to be educated on the group process and the expected objectives. For many offenders the group sessions may be their first exposure to any kind of counseling or therapeutic services. They may also arrive with certain perceptions and beliefs about counseling that need to be explored in order to ensure they have a realistic understanding of what to expect. Like all human beings, offenders will progress and learn most when their anxieties regarding the process have been allayed. Much of the anxiety can be diminished if the counselor spends an appropriate amount of time explaining what to expect and how the group will proceed.

LEARNING CHECK

1. Direct questions are rarely useful in group counseling sessions.
   a. True
   b. False
2. It is better to focus on the "big picture" and not pay too much attention on key words and phrases.
   a. True
   b. False
3. For offenders just beginning the counseling process it is best to create groups with no rules to allow for full exploration.
   a. True
   b. False
4. Peer confrontation should be avoided because it is likely to foster shame within the offender that is damaging to the group process.
   a. True
   b. False
5. Group work should never try to recapitulate the offender's family of origin.
   a. True
   b. False

PART TWO: GROUP THERAPY IN PRACTICE

Intervening in the Group Process

In this section we rely heavily on the work of Yalom (2005) and CSAT's Tip 41 (2005) except where otherwise noted. One of the most important tasks a group therapist must understand and figure out is working with difficult patients. Remember that resistance is going to usually be about fear and anxiety. Rare will be the case, however, where offenders will simply state, "I am feeling anxious so don't mind the rage filled rant on which I am about to embark." Instead the resistance and disruption will be cleverly cloaked with seemingly rational reasons as to why the therapist is not qualified or the entire group process is flawed.

INVOLVING MARGINAL MEMBERS Some offenders will attend regularly and always appear eager to explore whatever direction the group moves. They are not disruptive except for the fact that they are never fully engaged. Marginal members will often be very comfortable participating around the issues of other members, but will carefully guard and constrict messages directly related to their own issues. They will often have good advice for how other members should handle their problems. They may also appear to be very knowledgeable and experienced. The problem, however, is that the group never gets a chance to explore or get to know the real feelings of marginal members. This can be problematic in a group setting because members may feel as if marginal members feel superior to the rest of the group. Under most circumstances, this air of superiority will not be tolerated indefinitely and will need to be addressed. One technique that may be utilized to try and get greater and more meaningful involvement from marginal members is to use percentage questions. For example, the counselor may ask the marginal member, "What percentage of your feelings have you shared with the group?" "What percentage would you like to share?" "Do you have any thoughts on what may be keeping you from sharing more?" "Is there anything that you would like from the group that may help?"

ADDRESSING THE MONOPOLIST Another very common problem among groups is that of a monopolist. The monopolist will be the offender who seems to have to be talking constantly. The monopolist will not leave anything to chance. At the first sign of a lull in the group they will immediately take the floor and begin talking. Early in the group process the monopolist is often looked upon favorably because as long as the monopolist is talking everyone else can remain protected as they sit and listen. Monopolists tend to have a never-ending repertoire of stories and adventures. And, they will usually go into great detail as they hang on to the "floor" as long as possible. When others do have the opportunity to speak the monopolist will usually be ready to immediately follow up with, "Oh yeah, I am like that too, one time I even. . . ." And, once again they are off on elaborate stories about their experiences.

The problem with the monopolist is that although they may have provided a valuable service initially, now, no one else has the opportunity to be heard. Similar to experiences within families of origin, the monopolist soon becomes problematic and an issue the counselor must address. What is the incessant need to constantly talk really about? Of course, the reasons are legion, however, the foundation will usually be in relation to a fear of silence. For some offenders, silence may remind them of past experiences where violent outbursts followed periods of silence—"The calm before the storm." They may have experienced caregivers who were passive aggressive stating on the one hand that everything was fine and on the other become enraged for seemingly no reason. The constant chatter is an attempt to allay anxiety. In the mind of the monopolist, the group can be unpredictable just as caregivers were unpredictable.

Counselors must tend to the monopolist because, if left unchecked, no one else will be able to share their thoughts. Counselors can also employ the group to help in this process. For example, a counselor may ask the monopolist, "Would you be interested in hearing from the group and how they feel about you?" Other members may state, "We enjoy hearing from you, but we would like to be able to talk as well." The counselor may also ask the monopolist if he or she would like to share what it was like to endure the many "storms" that seem to follow the calm. The goal is to reassure the monopolist that he or she is safe with the group. The counselor may guide each individual in the group to reassure the monopolist using his or her own words. With the feeling of safety and security with the group the monopolist is usually able to refrain from the constant chatter and allow others the opportunity to share.

INVOLVING THE SILENT MEMBER The opposite of the monopolist is the offender who maintains silence. They may profess they have nothing to share and are learning a great deal from what everyone says. Generally, however, offenders who choose to remain silent will not benefit from the group. In long-term counseling group members will often abandon silent members as they will simply become exhausted with attempting to get to know them.

Silence is no different from any other defense or disruption. It will likely be cleverly cloaked but its basic origin is protection. It appears that the concept of judgmentalism is closely connected with silent behavior. Remaining silent is often due to extreme fears of self-disclosure, a need to be perfect, as well as control. Within a group, especially newly formed groups some offenders will employ silence to protect themselves from unpredictable attacks. It may be that silent offenders experienced harsh criticism from caregivers when attempting to communicate. They may have been told that their feelings or thoughts were not important and that the best method of action for everyone's well-being was to simply be quiet. When one attempts to share thoughts and is repeatedly criticized or judged (you are not worthy) the pain is immense and over time it significantly dulls affect.

Another concept that drives silence is perfection. Closely related to the origins of fear of disclosure, perfection is often adopted when one has experienced prolonged feelings of inadequacy or judgmentalism. Some offenders may feel that the only time they would be worthy of speaking is if they were able to say something in a manner so perfect that they would "wow" not only the other members but even the counselor. In essence, silent members decide that it is safer to remain silent than face the inevitable judgmentalism if they dared open their mouth. Many silent members will have experienced extreme, authoritative control at the hands of caregivers followed by severe punishment in the event they did not comply.

Another common motivation lurking below the surface of silent members is control. Some offenders may want to remain mysterious to the group as this may bring attention. Group members may prod the silent member with, "You seem to be so stable, you never show much emotion and you are always calm." Silence, therefore, works to garner attention. The paradox, however, is that silence will not work forever as the group will tire and eventually move on from the silence.

ENCOURAGING LEADERSHIP IN THE GROUP Encouraging leadership from group members is vital. Groups that are strictly controlled by authoritative counselors will not be as effective as groups where members are encouraged to lead themselves. Of course the counselor is there to guide and direct but the most effective leaders are those counselors who lead without force. A quick cautionary note regarding types of groups: It is important to understand that there are different types of groups. In psychoeducational groups, where the purpose is strictly to educate offenders, counselors will certainly take active roles and rely less on leadership from the group. In process groups, however, the focus is different and leadership from the group is essential. In essence, the group learns from itself. The goal is to recapitulate peer learning in the form of support and understanding.

OPERATING AS DIRECTIVE COUNSELORS At times counselors need to be directive (Yalom, 2005). At first blush, this statement may appear contradictory to the idea of group leadership. In reality it is not contradictory but rather complementary. Directives provided by the counselor, especially early in the group's formation, are what allows groups to eventually lead themselves. Directive counselor helps in modeling behavior and speech that is meaningful. It is a method of feedback that assists offenders with the process of tapping emotion as opposed to thoughts. For example, an offender may be asked to express his or her feelings based on what has been said in a particular group session. The offender may respond by saying, "It was informative, I didn't know that before." The directive counselor may say, "I am interested in your feelings, how would you complete the following statement 'When John said I have a tendency to talk too much I felt . . .' " With this direction the offender now responds with, "I felt attacked, and I also felt angry." Based on the counselor's direction the group is now operating with the realm of affect where meaningful change and growth is possible.

STAYING WITH THE THEME OF THE GROUP Staying with the theme of the group is a vital task that must be occasionally addressed by counselors. At times the group may attempt to venture outside of the real purpose of the group. In some cases this may be a method of trying to avoid real, presenting issues. The problem with avoiding the themes of the groups is that offenders will not benefit or learn new methods of coping with their distress. Groups of offenders convened to work on problems with substance abuse will benefit little from an in-depth discussion of the latest happenings on *Wall Street*.

Similarly, it is important that group rules be maintained. One of the most important tasks for counselors in maintaining group rules is to be sure that rules are clear and agreed upon by all participants. This helps remove the counselor from being the authoritative punisher and puts the responsibility among peers. An example of maintaining rules may be, "John, I know you are angry but we have agreed that shaming statements directed at other offenders is not allowed." The importance of maintaining rules is directly related to safety. If rules are not followed some offenders will become scared of sharing their feelings due to possible attack. When members no longer feel safe in the group the experience becomes meaningless.

CHECKING SUBGROUP FORMATION In group settings the formation of subgroups is inevitable. And, although subgroup formation may have certain benefits at times, they usually need to be addressed by the counselor. The main problem with subgroups is that they have a tendency to isolate members. In some cases the group may turn into several subgroups where members begin to battle each other and protect those within the subgroup. The unity of the group becomes fractured and can result in dysfunction similar to that which most offenders experienced in their families of origin.

The role of the counselor in responding to the formation of subgroups is to make them overt. The counselor may specifically note that John and Joe have seemed to form an alliance. The counselor may probe the subgroup to identify the differences between members of the subgroup and to remain members of the entire group. Ultimately the counselor must work to avoid subgroups stymieing the entire process. In some cases, offenders may be separated and seated in different places. In other cases, the counselor may need to be more direct and explain that the formation of subgroups will not be allowed.

Finally, the task of intervening in the group process is a delicate one. Problem behaviors will often conjure up the counselor's own negative emotion. In some cases the counselor may feel disrespected and have strong desires to lash out with damaging retorts. In spite of these powerful feelings, counselors must remain cognizant of the fact that most resistance is due to fear. In some cases where offenders choose to be inappropriately disruptive and the actions persist they will need to be removed from the group. Otherwise, the most helpful attitude a counselor can possess is one of empathic curiosity and interest as he or she attempts to reassure offenders they are not alone and they will not be abandoned. The group is there to assist them in their quest to find a more meaningful life.

Counseling Techniques in Group Settings

Specific therapeutic techniques used in group counseling are not different from those used in individual counseling. Many of the techniques were covered in Chapter 5 and are applicable to the group setting. As is the case with most therapeutic modalities used in individual counseling the focus of group therapy is to transform experience into what is being felt by offenders in the here and now. "What are you feeling now?" is the staple of what is trying to be accomplished. The task is to identify feelings and emotion being felt in the present that accompany past experiences. Regardless of the specific modality, effective transformation involves identifying, owning, and accepting powerful emotion coupled with examining cognitive structures that lead to behavior.

Some of the various techniques used in group counseling include confrontation, making the rounds, empty-chair work, role–play, and rehearsal, as well as challenging beliefs and reframing faulty cognitions. Each of these therapeutic techniques was developed in specific modalities. Modern counseling, however, is less concerned with specific modalities of therapy and more concerned with the manner in which the techniques are applied. This is not to imply that counselors should go out and engage offenders with techniques they do not fully understand. In fact, the opposite is of paramount importance; counselors should employ techniques that are capable of helping offenders enhance their emotional landscape and these techniques should be applied with honest, care, respect, and empathy. The following illustration provides an example of a counselor working to help a substance abusing client who is dealing with shame begin to reframe cognitions:

CASE VIGNETTE

Reframing Cognition

Shame

Often failed attachments in childhood and failed relationships thereafter result in shame, an internalized sense of being inferior, not good enough, or worthless. Shame flares whenever clients encounter the discrepancy between their drug-affected behavior and personal or social values. In group therapy, feelings of shame may be intensified because feelings of self-consciousness are elevated and other group members are present. The presence of other group members "often stimulates regressive longings" (Gans & Weber, 2000, p. 385). Furthermore, group members have a marked tendency to compare themselves with one another (Gans & Weber, 2000). In the past, when group facilitators used highly confrontational efforts to break through denial and resistance, an undesirable side effect was intensified shame, which increased the likelihood that group members would relapse or leave treatment. Shame interferes dramatically with attempts to heighten a client's self-esteem, which in turn is important to recovery (Alonso & Rutan, 1988).

Clients with addictions are often exquisitely sensitive and prone to project their shame onto relationships within the group. Often, at an unconscious level, they anticipate disapproval or hostility when none was intended. In this way, clients may demote themselves to the role of secondary player in the group.

One way to neutralize unintentionally shame-provoking comments is to reframe member-to-member communications. For example, if a group member asks, "Sally, where were you last week? You didn't come to group." Sally may interpret the question as a criticism or even an implication that she has returned to active use. The group facilitator may choose to reframe this member-to-member communication by speaking to the concern that the questioner really has for Sally's well-being.

This reframing would begin with the group leader asking why the group member wanted to know where Sally had been, adding something like, "I suspect your question reflects the feeling that you missed Sally last week and find group more enjoyable when she is here."

By focusing on positive interactions that reveal competency, the group facilitator helps move clients from shame to an affirmative image of themselves. The group leader should pay attention to member-to-member interaction, looking for instances of relational competence and support. The leader's supportive interactions eventually develop into group norms that combat the shame attached to addictive illness.

Source: CSAT (2005).

Before we begin to discuss the concept of multiculturalism within group settings we are inserting several important reminders meant to assist counselors responsible for leading groups. There is much to learn and remember in regard to counseling offenders in groups. Exhibit 7.5 is certainly not meant to be an exhaustive list of what to do in group sessions but instead a basic guide that may be useful in helping counselors stay focused on salient issues.

Multicultural Issues Relevant to Group Counseling

Similar to the population of the United States, offender populations are going to be heterogeneous. And although each offender will be suffering from a particular type of distress, the offenders themselves are likely to be from different cultures. In other words, each offender within a group will share a common form of distress (e.g., substance abuse); however, not all will be white males. Therefore, it is critical that counselors understand the influences of cultural experiences and how these experiences serve to govern the lives of each offender.

The greater the variation in ethnicity and culture the more likely biases will emerge (Brook, Gordon, & Meadow, 1998). These differing views within the group should be discussed and each offender should be reassured that at no time will the counselor or other participants ask anyone to give up or reject his or her culture views. In some cases offenders may decide to renounce certain views previously held because of their hindering effect on current growth, but this should always be done voluntarily and free of coercion.

Generally, cultural differences should be freely explored in the counseling setting. The group's ability to do this, however, is directly related to the counselor properly screening offenders for placement into the group. This is a critical process. When screening offenders, counselors should very carefully explore the offender's views and beliefs and also get a feel for the offender's openness to altering views. Counselors may even strategically express a statement contrary to the offender's cultural beliefs in an attempt to observe the offender's reactions. These free-flowing reactions to aversive, culturally related stimuli will often provide reliable readings of how the

EXHIBIT 7.5

Reminders for Each Group Session

Open.

Announcements: Who will be late? Absent? Does the leader plan any absences?
If there are new members, welcome them. Then explain the goals of the group.
Encourage new members to express their goals.
Track process.
To refocus the direction of the group, ask:

- How are things going (or feeling) in the group?
- What is happening right now?
- Does it feel as if we are on track?

Don't fight what is hard—use it!

Capitalize on the energy of resistance (the client's defense against the pain of self-examination) by

- Noticing it
- Validating it by welcoming honesty
- Linking it to group goals

Connect before tackling. Ally before confronting or stopping behavior.

Note the speaker's positive intentions or efforts. Then ask the speaker to examine his or her behavior or change course.

Encourage mutual connections among members.

Underscore resonating responses, either verbal or nonverbal. Ask how others are reacting to what is being shared.

Share the work.

Use the group to help you when the going gets rough:

- Share your conflict and ask the group to help with it.
- When a problem occurs, ask the group members to share their thoughts about how to proceed.

For example, "Max clearly has a lot on his mind. Do we go with that issue or stick to where we were headed a few minutes ago?"

Close.

Note that the time is up, or soon will be.
As you state the end boundary, ask if it is a hard time to end.

Source: CSAT (2005).

offender will respond in the group. The counselor is not looking for perfection; he or she is, however, scanning for signs that might illuminate the offender as being inappropriate for a particular group.

Another issue that must be addressed by counselors as they screen offenders for placement in the group is the offender's ability to speak the language of the group. If the group process is going to be carried out in English, all offenders should be fluent enough to

EXHIBIT 7.6

Preparing the Group

To promote cohesion, a positive group quality stemming from a sense of solidarity within the group, the group leader should do the following:

- Inform the group members in advance that people from a variety of backgrounds and racial and ethnic groups will be in the group.
- Discuss the differences at appropriate times in a sensitive way to provide an atmosphere of openness and tolerance.
- Set the tone for an open discussion of differences in beliefs and feelings.
- Help clients adapt to and cope with prejudice in effective ways, while maintaining their self-esteem.
- Integrate new clients into the group slowly, letting them set their own pace.
- When new members start to make comments about others or to accept feedback, encourage more participation.

Source: CSAT (2005).

comprehend fast-moving discussions. Offenders who are not able to do so may become frustrated and drop out, or other members may suffer by having to repeatedly go back and clarify, thus wasting valuable time. Once again, it is incumbent on the counselor to ensure that selected members are appropriate and equipped for the major objectives of the group. Below we provide two inserts to help operationalize this information. Exhibit 7.6 provides some general guidelines on preparing groups for issues concerning racial and ethnic minorities. Exhibit 7.7 provides guidance on how to work with offenders who have been hurt by the group as a result of their cultural beliefs.

EXHIBIT 7.7

Addressing Culture-related Conflict within the Group

A 33-year-old single, second-generation Chinese–Canadian woman joined a group after proper preparation. She was one of two non-Caucasians in this long-term, interpersonally focused, slow-turnover group. Unfortunately, in her first session, the group forcefully confronted an elderly man, who was emotionally abusive to his spouse and shirked responsibility for it. The new member froze throughout the session and was clearly very anxious. The therapist acknowledged her discomfort and the stressfulness of the situation for her. Nevertheless, the following day this client wanted to discontinue group, feeling very threatened by the directness of the confrontation and its target, the elderly father figure. Her anxiety was accepted as genuine and not seen as resistance by the therapist, who provided several individual sessions parallel to the group to clarify that this was not an attack on all fathers (including her own) in the group, and that it was done to help the elderly group member. This Chinese–Canadian client also was reassured that the other group members would be informed about the sociocultural reasons for her being upset, and that they would be empathic to her feelings on this matter. This intervention facilitated her integration in the group and her perception of the therapist as culturally credible and competent.

Original Source: Salvendy (1999, p. 451). Adapted from CSAT (2005).

SECTION SUMMARY

Understanding how to intervene in the group process is a skill that counselors develop over time and through experience. It is a delicate task that involves compassion, empathy, and sternness as well as the ability to identify the real underlying issues that are rarely stated directly. In essence, the counselor is constantly striving to answer a basic question—*What does the group need?* What are the real issues that need to be addressed in order to help each individual experience a greater sense of self and wholeness?

Successful intervention can be challenging, especially when trying to encourage the silent member to share his or her thoughts and feelings. Many offenders will state they are listeners and learn most by just listening to what the others have to say. The reality is that they are likely to grow exponentially if they are able to develop the courage to articulate their feelings and express their thoughts. Opposite the silent offender is the monopolist or the one who seems to have a strong desire to dominate the session. This form of control is aimed at the same construct driving the silent offender: *Fear*. The monopolist like his or her silent colleague is attempting to limit his or her exposure to piercing and often frightening emotion.

Throughout intervention counselors must maintain their composure and be keen to their own negative emotion that may surface within the group. It is also critical that counselors be familiar with the different cultural views and beliefs of the group members. Multiculturalism has received a lot of attention over the last decade leading to solid evidence that cultural experiences greatly influence the behaviors and cognitions of offenders. The offender population is diverse and complex and certainly requires a rich understanding of how this diversity will affect the dynamics of the group process.

LEARNING CHECK

1. Marginal members should not be encouraged to participate in the group process as this may produce further damage and greatly disrupt the group.
   a. True
   b. False
2. Confrontation should never be used in group counseling because some offenders are better off not understanding the foundation of their feelings.
   a. True
   b. False
3. Encouraging leadership from group members is rarely a good idea because it is likely to take away from the counselor's authority.
   a. True
   b. False
4. The most basic question that counselors should always remain cognizant of is, what does the group need?
   a. True
   b. False
5. Cultural differences should not be explored within the group setting as some offenders may feel vulnerable.
   a. True
   b. False

CONCLUSION

Group counseling is a very effective method of helping offenders learn new skills better able to serve them in their communities. The primary advantages of group counseling include cost reduction and also the fact that much learning takes place in the form peer interaction. This is a very powerful component of group therapy and is congruous with a basic postulate of sociological theory which is that much learning is in the form of groups interacting in social situations. Although there are some disadvantages to group counseling these factors can usually be mitigated by proper training and careful screening.

The most salient issue contained in this chapter is that resistance within the group will take place and it will be a result of fear and anxiety. Counselors must understand this concept and work with the resistance and not against it. The best armor counselors can possess to fade their own adverse reactions to resistance is personal congruence. In other words, counselors must not take the resistance personal or allow it to create circumstances where the counselor uses authority to "squash" the resistant behavior. This would likely be the same response the offender received from caregivers and would do great damage to the offender's ability to be helped by a group.

Finally, the counseling techniques used in group counseling are in large part no different from the techniques used in individual sessions. The goal is usually helping offenders experience dysfunction in the present and begin to better understand how cognitive restructuring can free vital energy previously directed at anger, shame, violence, and self-destruction. Counselor and group characteristics most able to foster change include active listening, empathy, honesty, and authenticity.

Essay Questions

1. Discuss the concept of *active listening*. Why is active listening so important in the group process?
2. Discuss the importance of modeling.
3. Discuss the advantages and disadvantages of group counseling. In your opinion, what is the most significant disadvantage to group counseling? How would you work to overcome this disadvantage?
4. Explain why proper preparation of all group members is so important?
5. Explain why cultural differences should be explored within the group?

Treatment Planning Exercise

Based on the following information identify several issues that should be immediately addressed within the group and also discuss the reasoning behind each of your selections.

Joe's Argument with His Roommate

Before the first meeting of a new problem-focused group, Joe had been arguing with his roommate because the roommate had forgotten to pay the phone bill the previous month. Joe had told his roommate, Mike, that he might remember to pay the bills on time if he were not smoking pot every day, and they began an angry discussion about the roommate's drug use. Joe tells the group that he wants to talk about his distrust of his roommate. Joe is not currently using drugs, but he is still struggling with attempts to control his drinking. Group members are generally supportive of Joe in his argument with his roommate. They express concern that he is living with someone who is actively using marijuana and other drugs. One group member, Jane, voices strong objections, however, to Joe's lack of trust for his roommate. Jane is struggling with her own abuse of prescription tranquilizers, and she is typically rather quiet and anxious in group. Nonetheless, she attacks Joe verbally with uncharacteristic vehemence.

Original Source: Flores (1997). Adapted from CSAT (2005).

Bibliography

Alonso, A., & Rutan, J. S. (1988). The experience of shame and the restoration of self-respect in group therapy. *International Journal of Group Psychotherapy, 38*(1): 3–14.

Brook, D. W., Gordon, C., & Meadow, H. (1998). Ethnicity, culture, and group psychotherapy. *Group, 22*(2): 53–80.

Brown, D., & Srebalus, D. J. (2005). *Introduction to the counseling profession* (3rd ed.). Boston, MA: Pearson Education, Inc.

Center for Substance Abuse Treatment. (2005). *Substance Abuse Treatment: Group Therapy.* Treatment Improvement Protocol (TIP) Series 41. DHHS Publication No. (SMA) 05-3991. Rockville, MD: Substance Abuse and Mental Health Services Administration.

Corey, G. (1995). *Theory and practice of group counseling* (4th ed.). Pacific Grove, CA: Brooks/Cole.

Flores, P. J. (1997). *Group psychotherapy with addicted populations: An integration of twelve-step and psychodynamic theory* (2nd ed.). New York: The Haworth Press.

Fosha, D. (2000). *The transforming power of affect: A model for accelerated change.* New York, NY: Basic Books.

Gans, J. S., & Weber, R. L. (2000). The detection of shame in group psychotherapy: Uncovering the hidden emotion. *International Journal of Group Psychotherapy, 50*, 381–396.

Gladding, S. T. (1996). *Counseling: A comprehensive profession* (3rd ed.). Englewood Cliffs, NJ: Prentice Hall.

Robins, S. (2005). *Organizational behavior* (11th ed.). Upper Saddle River, NJ: Pearson/Prentice Hall.

Salvendy, J. T. (1999). Ethnocultural considerations in group psychotherapy. *International Journal of Group Psychotherapy, 49*(4):429–464.

Vannicelli, M. (1992). *Removing the roadblocks: Group psychotherapy with substance abusers and family members.* New York: Guilford Press.

Yalom, I. D. (2005). *The theory and practice of group psychotherapy* (5th ed.). Cambridge, MA: Basic Books.

8

Substance Abuse Counseling and Co-occurring Disorders

CHAPTER OBJECTIVES

After reading this chapter, you will be able to:

1. Recognize substance dependence and substance abuse.
2. Know key diagnoses and definitions from the *DSM-IV-TR*.
3. Be aware of the various co-occurring disorders that are common to substance abusers.
4. Understand the various screening and assessment tools that are used in the treatment of substance abuse disorders.
5. Know the 12 core functions associated with substance abuse treatment.
6. Be aware of the impact that denial has on the addicted population's prognosis.
7. Understand the dynamics of relapse prevention.

INTRODUCTION

The prevalence of offenders suffering from substance use and abuse problems currently in the American Criminal Justice System is staggering. The massive increase in the number of convicted offenders suffering from substance abuse began in the 1980s and continues through the present. As Hanser (2006) points out, any informed discussion of drug offenders in the United States must begin with the war declared on drugs by the U.S. Government. As crack cocaine began to sweep through the nation in the early to mid-1980s an outcry shivered through the fabric of our society. Not only was the drug trade burgeoning and access to illegal substances becoming easier than ever, the violent crime rate was also increasing. A connection was quickly made between the expanding drug culture and the often violent incidents that occurred within its realm. This connection, along with societal upheaval, forced the government to take action in an attempt to rid ourselves from the evils and perils commonly associated with substance abuse and criminal behavior.

The resulting action taken by federal and state lawmakers has been to draft laws aimed at corralling illegal substance–using offenders. And, law enforcement efforts have been somewhat successful—successful at least in its ability to arrest a sufficient amount of drug-related offenders so that nearly every correctional agency in America is at or beyond capacity.

Once drafted these laws are enforced. In order to be enforced assets must be well equipped and mobilized. What is the primary ingredient for equipping and mobilizing assets? Money. As a country we have spent enormous amounts of money in attempt to halt the flow and usage of illegal substances. The money has primarily gone to two components of the criminal justice system: enforcement and corrections. Enforcement efforts are usually aimed at stopping the flow of illegal substances from entering our country; arresting those transporting and distributing illegal substances after they have entered the country; as well as, arresting those found to be using illegal substances. Enforcement efforts are carried out by a multitude of law enforcement agencies ranging from federal to state and local jurisdictions. Once arrested these offenders then become the responsibility of correctional agencies, also operating at local, state, and federal levels. In essence, we have filled every space available within the correctional component of criminal justice with a human inmate.

Closely related to substance use and abuse problems are co-occurring disorders. Co-occurring disorder is a phenomenon whereby individuals are not only suffering from substance abuse issues but they are also afflicted with psychological or emotional impairments that affect their overall health and well-being. For example, co-occurring disorder would be the appropriate concept used to describe an offender suffering from substance use or abuse in conjunction with some other ailment such as anxiety or depression. In fact, it is very rare to observe an offender with substance abuse issues but not also suffering from other psychological or emotional disorders. This is because, in general, substance use and abuse is a method of relieving or adapting to life circumstances that are experienced as unpleasant and troublesome. Psychologically and emotionally healthy human beings are generally not involved with the abuse of illegal substances because of their limiting effects. Humans function best in natural states of existence free of foreign substances. The ingestion of illegal substances by mostly psychologically and emotionally healthy individuals has a tendency to "gum things up" keeping them from functioning at their highest levels.

What we do know is that our correctional system is at full capacity. We also know that our correctional system is filled mostly with offenders suffering from co-occurring disorders. It would be difficult at best to refute these facts. The question then becomes, What do we do? How do we deal with our inmate population that is largely made up of offenders suffering from a multitude of psychological and emotional disorders coupled with the use and abuse of illegal substances?

First, it is important to point out that there are no simple answers or solutions. Our democratic style of government ensures checks and balances that work to limit one ideology from completely dominating policy and procedure. Conservatives may argue that the answer lies in building more prisons. The problems with this approach, however, are robust. How many more prisons would we need to build? Who would assume responsibility for the massive costs? On the other hand, liberals may argue that we need to decriminalize all forms of substance use. In relation to this postulate, the reality is that our society is not yet ready to seriously consider this approach as viable. Therefore, we are left to function somewhere between these two extremes.

Our contention is that we need a strong presence on different fronts. We need law enforcement to work diligently because many offenses, often violent, occur in conjunction with substance use and abuse. In addition, we need to create innovative approaches to address both the substance abuse issue among offenders as well as mental health issues that confront them. Among the innovations that have been incorporated, it is the use of both drug courts and mental health courts that has received widespread support and popularity within the criminal justice system. Students may recall the mention of these types of interventions from Chapter 1, noting again that

drug courts synthesize therapeutic treatment and judicial processes to optimize outcomes with the drug-addicted offender population (Watson, Hanrahan, Luchins, & Lurigio, 2001), while **mental health courts** consist of specialized dockets for defendants with mental illnesses (Bureau of Justice Assistance, 2004). Over the past two decades, there has been fervent support for drug courts and, upon the common realization that substances induce and correlate with other disorders, mental health course as well.

As can be seen, the trend is, and should be, to bear public resources on treating offenders who suffer from co-occurring disorders while in custody. Recidivism rates speak loudly and aggressively to this last postulate. As Hanser (2006) points out, recidivism rates are closely related to substance abuse. When considering co-occurring disorders recidivism rates are even higher. However, the complexities in providing the actual intervention for offenders who present with these multiple challenges are great. Therefore, the remaining portions of this chapter are aimed at identifying, describing, and treating those offenders suffering from substance use and abuse as well as co-occurring disorders. To begin, it is useful to define some of the concepts commonly used within the parameters of treating offenders suffering from substance abuse and co-occurring disorders. Many of these terms are commonly used interchangeably but as will be pointed out there are subtle differences that need to be illuminated.

PART ONE: RECOGNIZING SUBSTANCE DEPENDENCE AND SUBSTANCE ABUSE

Important Concepts Defined

The document most relied on to provide official definitions for most psychological and emotional concepts is the *Diagnostic Statistical Manual* (*DSM-IV-TR*) published by the American Psychological Association (APA). The latest version being the fourth edition published in 2000.

First, substance-related disorders are divided into substance use disorders and substance-induced disorders (CSAT, 2006). Substance use disorders are further divided into substance abuse and substance dependence. Substance use disorders are characterized by 11 categories provided by the APA (2000, p. 191):

1. Alcohol
2. Amphetamine or similarly acting sympathomimetics
3. Caffeine
4. Cannabis
5. Cocaine
6. Hallucinogens
7. Inhalants
8. Nicotine
9. Opioids
10. Phencyclidine (PCP) or similarly acting arylcyclohexylamines
11. Sedatives, hypnotics, or anxiolytics.

These 11 categories are separated by criteria into abuse and dependence. Substance abuse is often used to refer to both abuse and dependence. Also, substance dependence and addiction are often used interchangeably although there is strong debate as to whether this is appropriate (CSAT, 2006). Finally, the system of care responsible for treating substance-related disorders is commonly referred to as the substance abuse treatment system.

Substance Abuse—the *DSM-IV-TR* defines substance abuse as a "maladaptive pattern of substance use manifested by recurrent and significant adverse consequences related to the repeated use of substances" (APA, 2000, p. 198). Individuals who abuse substances are likely to experience harmful consequences such as, but not limited to, the following:

1. Repeated failure to fulfill roles for which they are responsible
2. Use in situations that are physically hazardous
3. Legal difficulties
4. Social and interpersonal problems.

Substance Dependence—is defined by the APA (2000) as "a cluster of cognitive, behavioral, and physiological symptoms indicating that the individual continues use of the substance despite significant substance-related problems" (p. 192). This harmful pattern of behavior includes all of the features of substance abuse as well as such features as:

1. "Increased tolerance for the drug, resulting in the need for ever-greater amounts of the substance to achieve the intended effect
2. An obsession with securing the drug and with its use
3. Persistence in using the drug in the face of serious physical or psychological problems" (CSAT, 2006, p. 1).

Substance-Induced Disorders—are characterized by three main facets which include substance intoxication, substance withdrawal, and group of symptoms that are "in excess of those usually associated with the intoxication or withdrawal that is characteristic of the particular substance and are sufficiently severe to warrant independent clinical attention" (APA, 2000, p. 210). Further exacerbating the problem of substance-induced disorders is the fact that individuals suffering from this ailment often present with a wide variety of symptoms characteristic of various mental disorders including delirium, dementia, amnesia, psychosis, mood disturbance, anxiety, sleep disorders, and sexual dysfunction (CSAT, 2006).

Co-occurring Disorders—a condition where individuals suffer from substance-related and mental disorders. Offenders suffering from co-occurring disorders will likely have one or more substance-related disorders operating in conjunction with one or more mental disorders (CSAT, 2006). The Center for Substance Abuse Treatment (CSAT) further defines co-occurring disorders, at the individual level, as a phenomenon where "at least one disorder of each type can be established independent of the other and is not simply a cluster of symptoms resulting from a single disorder" (CSAT, 2006, p. 3).

An important distinction noted by CSAT (2006) is that some offenders at particular points in time may present with symptoms that do not neatly fit the criteria for diagnoses found in the *DSM-IV-TR* categories. From a practical standpoint, however, these offenders are suffering from symptoms that are best addressed from a framework which assumes the presence of a co-occurring disorder. To address this distinction CSAT (2006) created a "**service definition of co-occurring disorder.**" The definition consists of three postulates:

1. "Individuals who are 'prediagnosis' in that an established diagnosis in one domain is matched with signs or symptoms of an evolving disorder in the other
2. Individuals who are 'postdiagnosis' in that either one or both of their substance-related or mental disorders may have resolved for a substantial period of time
3. Individuals with a 'unitary disorder and acute signs and/or symptoms of a co-occurring condition' who present for services. Suicidal ideation in the context of a diagnosed substance

use disorder is an excellent example of a mental health symptom that creates a severity problem, but itself does not necessarily meet criteria for a formal *DSM-IV-TR* diagnosis. Substance-related suicidal ideation can produce catastrophic consequences. Consequently, some individuals may exhibit symptoms that suggest the existence of co-occurring disorder but could be transitory (e.g., substance-induced mood disorders). While the intoxicated person in the emergency room with a diagnosis of a serious mental illness will not necessarily meet abuse or dependence criteria, he or she will still require co-occurring disorder assessment and treatment services" (p. 3).

How Substance Abuse Starts

First, it is important to state clearly that it is impossible to articulate a clear path to substance abuse to capture the path taken by all people. The paths are as complex and varied as human beings themselves. In addition, there has been much debate that still continues to try and place substance abuse within a particular domain. For example, in past years it was believed that substance abuse was primarily a moral issue. Addicts were viewed as morally deficient and corrupt (Dimoff, 2001). More recently, debate has shifted to consider substance abuse as a disease. This ideology places the enigma into the medical profession.

Today, it is mostly accepted that the issue of substance abuse is primarily grounded on at least two main components: heredity and environment, and/or a combination of the two. There is strong evidence that heredity is a major factor with powerful influence on the likelihood of some individuals engaging in substance abuse. Some reports claim individuals reared by parents who are substance users and abusers are four times more likely to be involved with substance abuse (Dimoff, 2001). Environmentally, the United States comprises of approximately 5–6 % of the world's population. Americans consume, however, three-quarters of all illegal drugs produced in the world making us the leading consumers of alcohol and prescription drugs.

Important to this discussion is one environmental factor that highlights current emphasis on "feeling good." With medical advances we now have a variety of medications aimed at soothing almost any ailment. If we do not feel good we turn to substances as a solution. And, this ideology has become big business for drug makers and pharmaceutical companies. This fact is quickly observed by the constant flow of media outlets telling us there is medication for whatever adverse feelings we may experience. Closely related to this phenomenon is the media-advanced depiction of what we should physically look like in order to be accepted and successful. In essence, if you are not thin and attractive you are relegated to the outer fringes of society. This ideology creates enormous social and environmental pressures which are impossible to achieve. There is a constant drive toward perfection. The problem with perfection, however, is that it is a very elusive concept that is usually characterized by such statements as, "If I were only able to be a little more . . . then I would be perfect." We mentally create scenarios that are impossible to achieve. And when we are unable to measure up to the impossible circumstances we create the result which is usually a feeling of shame or defectiveness. In order to alleviate the painful feelings of these emotions some turn to substances to dull the effects. A vicious circular cycle is created and rigidly adhered too and unfortunately this cycle is one that is incapable of producing the feelings we truly desire.

An additional component that may be most salient in the origins of substance abuse is the role or influence of parents or guardians. A strong consensus now exists that indicates much of a child's personality is formed by the age of eight. This includes values, morals, work ethic, and attitude. In most cases, parents will have the greatest influence on their children's psychological and emotional well-being. Ideally, children need to be given sufficient freedom to explore and learn their ever-expanding world. This freedom needs to be balanced with guidance and support aimed at showing the child what is right and wrong and also what is safe and dangerous. If children are not given sufficient freedom to learn and grow it is likely that deep emotional problems will result such as stress, low self-worth, depression, anxiety, and nervousness. These psychological and emotional disorders often contain negative feelings that are powerful influences on behavior. As children grow to adolescence and early adulthood it becomes very difficult to function in a normal and healthy manner. Not surprisingly, many will turn to substances to relieve the powerful pangs of anxiety, depression, shame, anger, and fear.

External pressures also contribute to the origins of substance use and abuse. External difficulties are commonly characterized by such issues as school problems, work difficulties, family problems, peer pressure, and relationship issues. All of these circumstances or environments are strong causal factors for individuals to experience feelings such as shame and defectiveness, which are described as being at the heart of addiction. As will be covered later in the chapter, substance abuse is really a symptom of psychological and emotional dysfunction. The issue is not so much treating substance abuse as it is treating repressed emotion and the psychological dysfunction that accompanies it.

Progressive Stages of Substance Abuse

It is important to recognize the different stages that usually lead to substance abuse. Obviously, these stages may vary for some individuals depending on particular circumstances. However, there is usually observable behavior that would fit the following five categories:

1. Compulsion to acquire and use substances and a preoccupation with their acquisition and use
2. Loss of control over substance use or substance-induced behavior
3. Continued substance use despite adverse consequences
4. A tendency toward relapse following periods of abstinence
5. Tolerance and or withdrawal symptoms (LASACT, 2004).

Compulsive behaviors usually result from users learning that good feelings can be produced by using substances. The individual may start out using substances at parties or on weekends to "take the edge off." Initially, powerful feelings of euphoria are experienced because of a lack of tolerance. And, generally there are no adverse behavioral effects because the substance has not yet begun to interfere with the user's lifestyle or obligations. In essence, there is a powerful feeling of euphoria with few consequences (Dimoff, 2001).

Due to the euphoric effects and initial lack of consequences, compulsive behaviors become more pronounced as users begin to actively plan both attainment and use of the substance(s). At this point use may still be controlled. For example, the individual may use only at "appropriate" times and places such as, not at work, not before 5:00 P.M. and certainly not in the mornings. Nonetheless, a very important and powerful process is now underway; tolerance is beginning to be developed.

Loss of control over substance use or substance-induced behavior usually becomes evident as the individual becomes more preoccupied with euphoric mood swings. There is generally an increase in the frequency of substance use and some of the self-imposed rules begin to be broken. The individual may engage in solitary use as opposed to only at parties or on the weekends with friends. In addition, more of the substance may be used than originally planned. At this point, the user is quickly approaching the realm of chemical dependency. This is where the individual's lifestyle begins to change. In fact, individuals who have become chemically dependent on a substance will usually arrange their life so that the substance and its obtainment and use are paramount. Everything else becomes secondary to the substance.

Once the individual has become dependent on a substance(s) a variety of destructive behaviors will usually become evident to the informed observer. Keep in mind that the dependent individual will likely be very clever in disguising his or her substance use and abuse. In fact, cognitive processes of these individuals may now be arranged in such fashion that their very survival is dependent on the substance. The individual begins to shift from using a substance to obtain euphoria to one of coping with negative emotions such as anger, guilt, fear, or anxiety. The individual's actions may become sneaky and mysterious as more effort is allocated to keeping his or her use a secret. Appreciate, that at this point the concept of control has shifted. The individual is no longer in control; the substance is in control.

Due to the shame that will accompany the loss of control, individuals will usually be irritable or angered easily. The individual will attempt to rationalize his or her behavior to avoid responsibility and become very adept at projecting one's problems to others. Personal relationships will begin to deteriorate as the substance will command more importance than other people, and also, the individual begins to repeatedly violate his or her own value system. All of these factors contribute to emotional distress perpetuating the circular cycle of what is now chemical dependence/addiction.

The concept of denial, which will be explored in greater detail later in the chapter, begins to take hold within the individual's methods of coping. In fact, denial is a concept often described as a person's way of coping with painful situations whereby the denial of the existence of a problem allows the individual not to deal with or assume responsibility for it. At this point, the person's use of a substance or substances can be described as chronic chemical dependency. Chronic chemical dependency can be described by the following characteristics:

1. Individual uses substance to feel normal and avoid pain rather than for achieving euphoria.
2. Individual experiences blackouts which progressively become longer and more frequent.
3. The desire to use the substance is now the most important factor in the individual's life.
4. The individual experiences complete loss of control.
5. The individual experiences paranoid thinking and may fear insanity.
6. Individual feels alone and isolated.
7. Individual is likely to experience a loss of desire to live.
8. Individual begins to experience physical problems (Dimoff, 2001).

During this phase of the substance abuse process there is usually a strong tendency toward relapse following periods of abstinence. In fact, some users may begin experimenting with the idea of not using. This is an attempt to show themselves or others that they really are not dependent and that they could halt usage if desired. This period of abstinence, however, is usually short lived and usage quickly resumes, resulting in relapse. It is important to note that relapse is not an isolated event. Relapse is a condition of becoming unable to cope with life without the use of substances. Relapse prevention is a critical strategy that will be given specific attention later in the chapter.

Finally, tolerance levels and withdrawal symptoms are such that the offender needs more of the substance and experiences noticeable difficulties during periods of abstinence. **Tolerance** is the "need for markedly increased amounts of the substance to achieve intoxication," or a "markedly diminished effect when using the same amount" (*DSM-IV*). **Withdrawal syndrome** is the characteristic group of signs and symptoms that typically develop after a rapid, marked decrease or discontinuation of a substance upon which an individual is dependent. The severity and duration of the withdrawal syndrome depends on several factors including the nature of the substance used, the half-life and duration of action of the substance, the length of time the substance has been used, the amount used, the use of other substances, the presence of other medical and psychiatric conditions, and other individual biopsychosocial variables.

Recognizing Substance Abuse

As a counselor in a correctional setting it is important to be able to recognize certain signs indicative of substance abuse. The proper recognition allows for proper assessment which in turn enables the institution to better provide appropriate services. Many offenders will under- or overreport their substance use and abuse problems. Even if not an intentional attempt at deception, it is rare that offenders will accurately depict their current reality concerning substance use and abuse. The following characteristics, provided by Dimoff (2001), are meant to provide a guide or framework for some of the more common characteristics displayed by offenders suffering from substance abuse. They are certainly not meant to be all inclusive:

Outward Physical and Mental Signs:

- Rapid weight loss or gain
- Discolored fingers
- Injection marks along veins—due to increased scrutiny of arms and other common injection points many offenders are now injecting substances in more concealed areas of the body including thighs, and over tattoos
- Wears long sleeve shirts on warm days.
- Dilated pupils
- Bloodshot or glassy eyes
- Poor balance
- Perspires excessively
- Health complaints
- Smells of alcohol or marijuana.
- Displays droopy eyelids or sleepy appearance.
- Frequently wears sunglasses at odd times.
- Uses gum or mints to cover breath.

Source: SACS, 2006.

Mental Impairments:

- Denial
- Delusional
- Paranoia
- Preoccupation
- Blackouts
- Memory impairment
- Poor judgment
- Difficulty concentrating
- Difficulty thinking

Co-occurring Disorders

Currently, there is strong movement on behalf of the federal government to address offenders suffering from co-occurring disorders. As previously stated, co-occurring disorder refers to any psychological or emotional disorder that is operating in conjunction with substance abuse. One such program being funded through SAMHSA is jail diversion. Jail diversion programs are aimed at identifying offenders who are suffering from substance abuse and/or co-occurring disorders. Once identified, those offenders meeting necessary criteria are diverted from jails and placed into comprehensive community service programs aimed at treating the offender's disorders. The theoretical structure on which jail diversion rests is that if those offenders suffering from co-occurring disorders are not treated then the likelihood of them being released and further acting out in ways that bring them into contact with criminal justice system is enhanced. It is important to note that most offenders, once assessed, will meet necessary criteria for dual diagnosis. "Dual diagnosis" is a term used to describe a phenomenon whereby offenders are suffering from a substance abuse disorder in concert with a mood disorder, anxiety disorder, personality disorder, or a psychotic disorder.

MOOD DISORDER **Mood** is a concept that describes a pervasive and sustained emotional state that may affect all aspects of an individual's life and perceptions (LASACT, 2004). Mood disorder describes a pathologically elevated or depressed disturbance of mood and includes full or partial episodes of depression or mania (LASACT, 2004). It is important to note the term "pathological" because this denotes the presence of disease. Elevated or depressed mood states are normal adjustments to daily activities and circumstances. In some instances where we are engaged in pleasurable activities it is considered normal and healthy to experience elevated moods. The same is true for circumstances that are experienced as painful such as the loss of a loved one. Moods become pathological when there is a persistence and prolonged nature of being in either a depressed or elevated state. In essence, we are not free to traverse different states of mood based on current life circumstances. The disorder works to keep us trapped so that we experience either depressed or elevated states of being, independent of our surroundings. The term used to describe an elevated mood state is "manic episode." A manic episode is a period of at least one week where an individual experiences a persistently elevated, euphoric, irritable, or expansive mood (LASACT, 2004). A manic episode is usually characterized by such symptoms as hyperactivity, grandiosity, flight of ideas, talkativeness, a decreased need for sleep, and distractibility (LASACT, 2004). A depressive episode, or major depressive episode, is used to describe a mood characterized by a depressed state. Major depressive episodes involve feelings of depression that are accompanied by loss of pleasure or indifference to most activities, most of the time for at least two weeks (LASACT, 2004). Some common examples of major depressive episodes include feelings of worthlessness and inappropriate guilt. In addition, some individuals may experience recurrent thoughts of death or suicide.

According to the Louisiana Association of Substance Abuse Counselors and Training (LASACT) (2004), there are four major components that are able to capture a wide range of cognitive and behavioral patterns described by the broad term of "mood disorder." These components consist of bipolar disorder, cyclothymia, dysthymia, and hypomanic episode and are listed below:

- ***Bipolar disorder***—is a condition that entails cycling mood changes from severe highs (mania) to severe lows (depression). In many cases, periods of normal mood levels will be mixed in-between. While clients are in the depression cycle, they will present with any or all of the symptoms of depression. While in the manic cycle, the client will likely be overactive, overtalkative, and will typically have an overabundance of energy. Further, manic states tend to affect thinking and judgment leading to impulsive and disproportionately exuberant social behaviors that can cause serious problems and/or embarrassment. For example, clients experiencing a manic phase may feel elated, engaging in anything from unwise business decisions to romantic sprees that are later regretted (National Institute of Mental Health, 2009).

- ***Cyclothymia***—is likened to a low-key form of bipolar disorder but, with cyclothymia, mood variability occurs with greater frequency and tends to be more chronic in nature (LASACT, 2004). Exhibited episodes of mania and depression are not severe enough to be diagnosed in the major category of severity but they are serious enough to disrupt the client's ability to lead a balanced and adjusted life (APA, 2000; LASACT, 2004).
- ***Dysthymia***—is described as a chronic mood disturbance that usually entails a loss of interest or pleasure in most day-to-day activities. The mood disturbance, however, is not sufficient to meet the full criteria for a clinical diagnosis of major depressive episode. Dysthymia is a mood disturbance that, while not debilitating to the client's day-to-day functioning, tends to diminish the client's ability to enjoy life; these individuals often have pessimistic outlooks and attitudes, regardless of their circumstances. In other words, a person diagnosed with dysthymia is often able to carry out normal duties and functions but there is no "zest" to life.
- ***Hypomanic episode***—is a condition described as a period, usually weeks or months, "of pathologically elevated mood that is similar to but less severe than a manic episode" (LASACT, 2004, p. 41). Similar to dysthymia, hypomanic disorders are usually not severe enough to cause overt and clearly observable impairment in functioning within social or occupational settings (LASACT, 2004).

SUBSTANCE-INDUCED MOOD DISORDER As mentioned, it is important to remember that many offenders will be suffering from more than one disorder. Substance abuse and mood disorder often exist in conjunction with the other. Any variation of mood disorders is sufficient to greatly diminish the joys of life. When people are unable to experience natural joy or pleasure their response will often be to turn to substances in order to change their mood.

A **substance-induced mood disorder** is described in the *DSM-IV-TR* as meeting the following criteria:

A. A prominent and persistent disturbance in mood characterized by either, or both, of the following:
   1. Depressed mood or markedly diminished interest or pleasure in all, or almost all activities
   2. Elevated, expansive, or irritable mood.

B. There is evidence from the history, physical examination, or laboratory findings of substance intoxication or withdrawal, and the symptoms in Criterion A developed during, or within a month of, significant substance intoxication or withdrawal.

C. The disturbance is not better accounted for by a mood disorder that is not substance induced. Evidence that the symptoms are better accounted for by a mood disorder that is not substance induced might include the following: The symptoms precede the onset of the substance abuse or dependence; they persist for a substantial period of time after the cessation of acute withdrawal or severe intoxication; they are substantially in excess of what would be expected given the character, duration, or amount of the substance used; or there is other evidence suggesting the existence of an independent non-substance-induced mood disorder.

D. The symptoms cause clinically significant distress or impairment in social, occupational, or other important areas of functioning.

E. The disturbance does not occur exclusively during the course of delirium.

In essence, a substance-induced mood disorder can be described as having manic features, depressive features, or mixed features that manifest during intoxication or withdrawal (LASACT, 2004).

ANXIETY DISORDERS **Anxiety disorders** are commonly noted as being the most common group of psychiatric disorders (LASACT, 2004). Fosha (2000) describes anxiety as being the mother of all pathologies. Anxiety is a concept that describes the sensations of nervousness, tension, apprehension, and fear that are experienced in anticipation of some type of danger. The danger may manifest itself through internal or external mechanisms. It is important to note that anxiety is also described as a normal reaction to stress. Anxiety may function as a motivator to get things done such as studying for an exam, completing necessary assignments in the office, and preparing for a speech. Anxiety becomes a disabling disorder when it grows to an excessive and irrational dread of everyday life and circumstances. Anxiety disorder refers to different clusters of signs and symptoms that may manifest themselves in a variety of ways including anxiety, panic, and phobias (LASACT, 2004).

A **panic attack** is described as a period of intense fear or discomfort that usually develops abruptly and reaches a peak within a few minutes. There is usually a manifestation of both physical and psychological symptoms. Physical symptoms may include hyperventilation, heart palpitations, trembling of body limbs, sweating, dizziness, hot flashes or chills, sensations of numbness or tingling, as well as nausea or choking. Psychological symptoms are mainly rooted in the emotion of fear. Common symptoms include the fear of fainting, dying, losing control, or losing one's mind. Individuals who suffer from panic attacks often describe the episodes as being extremely frightening. The fear of losing complete control can be so overwhelming that once the attack subsides a persistent fear reemerges with the thought of the recurrence of more panic attacks. In essence, those who experience panic attacks live in a constant state of fear and arousal that reaches climax during the attack and then subsides until the next (LASACT, 2004).

A **phobia** is a type of anxiety disorder where the focus of the anxiety is on an activity, person, or situation that is dreaded, feared, and avoided if at all possible. Phobia can be so powerful that one's life becomes restricted. For example, someone with a fear driving may only feel comfortable in their own home or places within walking distance. Some of the more common phobias include agoraphobia, social phobia, and simple or specific phobia (LASACT, 2004).

Agoraphobia is the fear of being caught in a situation or environment from which an exit would be impossible, difficult, or embarrassing. Embarrassment in this sense is usually in relation to the idea of being seen losing control in public. Typical situations in which agoraphobia may present include driving, standing in line, being in an auditorium, or just simply being outside of one's home. Agoraphobia will usually result in a pattern of avoidant behaviors, particularly avoidance of places or situations where an attack was experienced (LASACT, 2004).

Social phobia refers to persistent and irrational fear of embarrassment and humiliation in social situations. Often the fear is recognized as being irrational; however, the feelings are so powerful that one's cognitions are completely consumed. Individuals suffering from social phobia often view others as being much more competent and greatly exaggerate the effects of small or common mistakes. The most common social phobia is public speaking. However, symptoms of social phobias may also present when being around anyone other than those closest to the individual (LASACT, 2004).

Specific phobias are sometimes called single or simple phobias. Specific phobia is an intense, excessive, or unreasonable fear triggered by the presence or anticipation of a specific object or situation. Naturally occurring specific phobias may consist of rain, lightening, or spiders, whereas situational specific phobias have been known to manifest when one is faced with heights or riding in elevators (LASACT, 2004).

Another form of anxiety disorder is **obsessive compulsive disorder** (OCD). Obsessions are described as repetitive and intrusive thoughts, impulses, or images that trigger feelings of anxiety. Compulsions are described as repetitive rituals and acts that people are driven to perform, often reluctantly, in order to prevent or reduce stress. Oftentimes the obsessions or compulsions or both consist of thoughts and actions that are contrary to social norms. Some examples of OCD include harming others, becoming contaminated, excessive hand-washing, and silently counting and repeating words. Manifestations of OCD are extremely time consuming and significantly interfere with daily functioning (LASACT, 2004).

Post-traumatic stress disorder (PTSD) is a disorder where an individual experiences a psychologically traumatic stressor. In most cases PTSD is thought of in relation to severely traumatic events such as war, witnessing a death, experiencing a near-death situation, as well as sexual abuse. And, though these instances are more than sufficient to provide the necessary framework for PTSD, it is important to note that PTSD may result from situations and circumstances that are much less severe. Whether a person experiences the effects of PTSD depends on how they process the effects of certain circumstances. For example, the witnessing of a deadly automobile accident may leave permanent psychological scars for one individual thus inhibiting this individual from ever driving again. The same accident, however, witnessed by another person operating from a different cognitive structure may experience the wreck as tragic but is able to effectively move on and experiences little residual effects (LASACT, 2004).

PTSD consists of a persistent reexperiencing of a traumatic event through recurrent and intrusive images and thoughts (LASACT, 2004). These recurrent images may also manifest themselves in the form of dreams where the trauma is relived. Some of the symptoms experienced by people suffering from PTSD include insomnia, irritability, hypervigilance, and exaggerated startle responses. In addition, sufferers from PTSD will often avoid stimuli associated with the trauma including certain activities, feelings, and thoughts (LASACT, 2004).

PERSONALITY DISORDERS **Personality** refers to deeply ingrained patterns of thought and behavior that affect the way individuals perceive, relate to, and think about themselves and their world (LASACT, 2004). A **personality disorder** is generally described as a cluster of behaviors that are considered rigid, inflexible, and maladaptive. These behaviors are usually of sufficient severity to cause significant impairment in functioning or significant internal stress (LASACT, 2004). Additionally, personality disorders are enduring and persistent styles of behavior and thought; they are not atypical episodes that are uncommon behavior in certain circumstances.

Four personality disorders that present some of the greatest challenges to treatment providers include:

- Antisocial personality disorder
- Borderline personality disorder
- Narcissistic personality disorder
- Passive-aggressive personality disorder.

For an individual to be diagnosed with **antisocial personality disorder** there is usually a history of chronic antisocial behavior that begins before the age of 15 and continues into adulthood. Certain behaviors common to antisocial disorder include academic failure, poor job performance, illegal activities, recklessness, and impulsive behavior. Some of the symptoms common to antisocial personality disorder include dysphoria or an inability to tolerate boredom, feeling victimized, and a diminished capacity for experiencing intimacy (LASACT, 2004). Oftentimes offenders will describe their feelings just prior to committing an offense for which they were caught as being bored. They will make such statements as "there was nothing else to do," or "I was looking for some excitement and wanted to see if I could get away with it."

Borderline personality disorder is usually characterized by unstable moods and self images. These individuals will sometimes display extreme mannerisms of overidealization and devaluation along with drastic shifts from baseline to extreme moods or anxiety states. In addition, they are usually very impulsive. Offenders suffering from borderline personality disorder will usually be involved in very intense and unstable interpersonal relationships (LASACT, 2004). These relationships are often volatile and include periods of euphoria followed by extreme disruption that will often culminate in violence.

Narcissistic personality disorder is a concept that describes a pattern of grandiosity, lack of empathy, and hypersensitivity to evaluation of others. The pattern is pervasive and rigid (LASACT, 2004). Offenders suffering from narcissistic personality disorder will usually blame everyone but themselves for their circumstances. They lack empathy and are usually unable to experience compassion for others. In essence, a narcissistic individual will usually conclude that they are more intelligent than others and that their problems are due to the faults of those around them. In addition, they become extremely rigid when receiving feedback that is not positive.

The concept of **passive-aggressive personality disorder** describes a behavior that reflects hostility and aggression in passive ways. Offenders suffering from passive-aggressive personality disorder usually lack adaptive or assertive social skills, especially in relation to authority figures. These individuals likely endured strict control during formative years and have adapted by learning to substitute passive resistance for active resistance. This is because active resistance in the presence of a controlling authority figure was perceived as dangerous. Some common symptoms of passive-aggressive behavior include purposefully being late with social or job tasks, failing to do one's share of the work, criticizing authority figures in subtle ways, and having a constant negative attitude.

PSYCHOTIC DISORDERS **Psychosis** refers to a disintegration of the thinking process, involving the inability to distinguish external reality from internal fantasy (LASACT, 2004). A **psychotic disorder** is described as a mental disorder in which a person's personality is seriously disorganized and contact with reality is impaired. Some of the characteristics commonly associated with psychotic disorders include, but are not limited too, delusions, hallucinations, bizarre behavior, incoherent or disorganized speech, and disorganized behavior (LASACT, 2004). One of the most salient characteristics in the identification of psychosis will be the offender's inability to differentiate between information that originates from the external world and information that originates from the inner world of the mind (LASACT, 2004). In the following, some of the more common psychotic disorders are discussed along with attendant characteristics.

Schizophrenia is a formidable psychotic disorder where symptoms usually persist for at least six months resulting in deterioration of occupational and social functioning. Schizophrenia is best understood as a group of disorders with similar clinical profiles. Common characteristic symptoms include hallucinations, delusions, bizarre behaviors, and deterioration in general levels of functioning. In addition, one may experience severe disturbances in relation to language and communication, content of the thought processes, as well as perceptions, affect, and relationship to the external world. Schizophrenia can also be divided into subtypes that generally consist of the following:

- Paranoid type—usually characterized by delusions or hallucinations
- Disorganized type—usually characterized by speech and behavior problems
- Catatonic type—usually characterized by catalepsy or stupor, meaning a trance-like state with loss of sensation or consciousness, as well as extreme agitation or extreme negativism.
- Undifferentiated type—here there is no single clinical presentation that predominates. Usually consists of a cluster of characteristics with no one characteristic that is diagnosable within a particular subgroup.
- Residual type—at this point there are no predominant characteristics or psychotic symptoms. The disorder may have been successfully treated or the symptoms dormant.

Additional psychotic disorders that offenders may present with include **brief reactive psychosis.** "Brief reactive psychosis" is a term used to describe psychotic symptoms that result from being confronted by overwhelming stress. **Delusional disorders** describe prominent and often well-organized delusions but generally absent of hallucinations. Additional symptoms may include disorganized thought and behavior as well as abnormal affect. **Induced psychotic disorder** is a disorder in which psychotic behaviors or thoughts result from the acceptance of one person of the delusional beliefs of another. In essence, a dominant partner suffers from delusional psychosis and these delusions are believed and accepted by a more passive partner. Finally, **alcohol and other drug-induced psychotic disorder** (AOD) is a condition where individuals suffer conditions characterized by delusions or hallucinations as a result of psychoactive drug use.

SECTION SUMMARY

It is important to recognize that a large portion of offenders will be suffering from substance abuse problems. In addition, the literature is clear regarding the fact that most offenders suffering from substance abuse will also be suffering from various other psychological and emotional disorders. Therefore correctional counselors should anticipate the likelihood of having to address multiple issues stemming from a variety of sources. In fact, it is important that counselors understand that oftentimes substance abuse is a symptom of repressed emotion. In essence, the real task is to help guide offenders through the process of reconnecting with their repressed emotion and fully identify and express what they are feeling.

LEARNING CHECK

1. What does Fosha describe as the "mother of all pathology"?
   a. Depression
   b. Bipolar disorder
   c. Fear
   d. Anxiety
2. Common characteristics of schizophrenia include which of the following.
   a. Delusions
   b. Bizarre behaviors
   c. Hallucinations
   d. All of the above

3. Psychosis describes the process of being unable to distinguish between external reality and internal fantasy.
   a. True
   b. False
4. Common signs of substance abuse include which of the following.
   a. Rapid weight loss or gain
   b. Poor hygiene
   c. Blood shot or glassy eyes
   d. All of the above
5. Personality disorders generally describe behaviors that are inflexible, rigid, and maladaptive.
   a. True
   b. False

PART TWO: SCREENING, DIAGNOSIS, AND ASSESSMENT

Screening, diagnosis, and assessment are critical components in the process of deciding the depth and nature of services appropriate for offenders suffering from substance abuse and co-occurring disorders. In criminal justice settings, substance use and mental health disorders are often underdiagnosed which ultimately leads to misdiagnosis (Peters, 1992). When offenders are misdiagnosed it becomes difficult at best to employ proper interventions aimed at treating substance abuse and mental health disorders. It is for this reason that the proper assessment of substance abusers is critical to the ultimate prognosis. However, as noted before, it can be difficult to accurately assess the substance-abusing correctional client. Several reasons for nondetection of substance abuse and mental health disorders are commonplace. First, there is often a negative consequence associated with disclosure of symptoms; second, there is usually a lack of training on behalf of the staff concerning the diagnosis and management of substance abuse and co-occurring disorders (Peters & Bartoi, 1997).

Further adding to the enigma is the fact that mental health, substance abuse, and criminal justice systems often operate independently and do not adequately share critical information. In essence, each entity has a different, or at least slightly different, mission. This inadequate sharing of information often results in the nondetection of substance abuse and mental health disorders thereby stymieing the offender's opportunity to access integrated services (Peters & Bartoi, 1997). Kofoed, Dania, Walsh, and Atkinson (1986) suggest that integrated screening and assessment approaches are commonly found to produce more favorable outcomes. This is because there are very few, if any, validated single instruments capable of assessing co-occurring disorders inside or outside the criminal justice system (Peters & Bartoi, 1997). Therefore, for the purposes of screening and assessment the combination of specialized substance abuse and mental health instruments used in conjunction is most desired.

Definitions of Screening, Diagnosis, and Assessment

Screening is a concept used to describe the process of detecting mental health and substance abuse disorders along with indicators that reflect the need for treatment (Peters & Bartoi, 1997). Drake and Mercer-McFadden (1995) point out that screening is usually conducted early in the process of gathering information and usually precedes diagnosis and assessment. Common goals of the screening usually include the following:

- Detect current mental health and substance use disorders
- Identify individuals with a history of violence and/or severe medical problems
- Identify individuals suffering from severe cognitive deficits
- Identify individuals who would not be suitable for treatment of co-occurring disorders (Peters & Bartoi, 1997).

Diagnosis describes the process of reviewing symptoms related to *DSM-IV-TR* mental health and substance use disorders. Diagnosis is usually a more detailed description of the types of disorders detected in an offender. Diagnosis usually involves an interview, psychological assessment, review of archival records, as well as other types of testing (Peters & Bartoi, 1997). Diagnosis usually helps determine the primary focus of treatment and whether the focus will be substance abuse disorders, mental health disorders, or both. Some of the common goals of diagnosis include the following:

- Identify the presence of specific *DSM-IV-TR* mental health and substance use disorders.
- Develop hypotheses for psychosocial assessment (Peters & Bartoi, 1997).

Assessment is a concept describing a comprehensive examination of psychosocial needs and problems including the severity of disorders, the conditions associated with the occurrence and maintenance of the disorders, problems related to the disorders that may affect treatment, the offender's motivation for treatment, and specific areas for treatment interventions (Peters & Bartoi, 1997). Assessments are commonly conducted through interviews and/or specialized instruments and consist of the following goals:

- Examine the scope of mental health and substance abuse problems
- Assess the full spectrum of psychosocial problems that need to be addressed in treatment
- Provide a comprehensive foundation for treatment planning (Peters & Bartoi, 1997).

Selection of Screening, Diagnosis, and Assessment Instruments

In the following sections detailed information is provided concerning different instruments used to screen, diagnose, and assess offenders. Appreciate that the concepts of screening, diagnosing, and assessing offenders represent different stages in the process of identifying disorders in need of treatment, and to some degree represent different goals. It should also be noted that the following instruments presented in this discussion are not meant to be all inclusive. A cursory glance at the literature will yield hundreds of psychometric instruments designed to measure a wide range of psychiatric, psychological, emotional, and substance abuse disorders. Therefore, when reviewing the different instruments and deciding which to include in this discussion three important concepts were considered:

1. **Reliability**—a concept used to describe the accuracy of a measure. In other words, is the instrument accurately measuring a variable regardless of what the variable may be?
2. **Validity**—a concept used to describe whether an instrument is actually measuring what it is intended to measure. In other words, if the intended variable to be measured is depression, is the instrument truly measuring depression and not anxiety?
3. Has the instrument been **used in a criminal justice setting** (Peters & Bartoi, 1997)?

In addition, we include positive features as well as concerns for each of the instruments listed in order to assist practitioners and students in the selection of instruments most suitable for a particular agency.

Screening Instruments

A possible combination of screening instruments suggested by Peters and Bartoi (1997) include the following:

1. The Brief Symptoms Inventory (BSI) (Derogatis & Melisaratos, 1983) or the Referral Decision Scale (RDS) (Teplin & Schwartz, 1989) to measure mental health symptoms; and
2. Either the TCU Drug Dependence Screen (DDS) (Simpson, 1993), Simple Screening Instrument (SSI) (CSAT, 1994), or the combination of the Alcohol Dependence Scale (ADS) (Skinner & Horn, 1984) and the Addiction Survey Index (ASI) (McLellan et al., 1992) to measure substance abuse symptoms. These instruments have been found to be the most effective in identifying inmates with substance dependence problems (Peters & Greenbaum, 1996).

The **BSI** is comprised of 53 items and consists of three global indices of psychopathology and nine primary psychiatric dimensions.

Positive Features

- Brief to administer and requires no significant training.
- Only a sixth-grade reading level is required.
- Has adequate internal consistency and test-retest reliability.
- Adequate convergent validity with the Minnesota Multiphasic Personality Inventory (MMPI) (Hathaway & McKinley, 1989).

Concerns

- The BSI has poor discriminant validity.
- Has low construct validity and may be most useful as a general indicator of psychopathology (Boulet & Boss, 1991).

The **RDS** is a 14-item measure of mental health symptoms that was designed to identify individuals entering jails with significant mental health problems requiring treatment while in jail.

Positive Features

- Developed and validated in a criminal justice setting.
- Requires no training to administer.
- Can be self-administered.

Concerns

- Its validity has not been examined among offenders with co-occurring disorders.
- Examines only a few mental health disorders (depression, bipolar disorder, schizophrenia), however, in criminal justice settings these disorders are commonly the most problematic.

The **DDS** is a 19-item screen that examines diagnostic symptoms of drug use developed at the Texas Christian University, Institute of Behavioral Research.

Positive Features

- One of three screening instruments found to be most effective in identifying substance dependant inmates (Peters & Greenbaum, 1996).
- One of two screening instruments found to be most effective in identifying substance using inmates who were nondependent (Peters & Greenbaum, 1996).
- DDS is brief to administer.
- Because the DDS is a public domain instrument it is available at no cost.

Concerns

- The validity of the DDS has not been examined among offenders suffering from co-occurring disorders.
- The DDS does not examine quantity or frequency of recent or past substance use.

The **SSI** is a 16-item screening instrument that examines symptoms of alcohol and drug dependence. The SSI examines five different domains related to substance dependence including: (1) alcohol and/or drug consumption, (2) preoccupation and loss of control, (3) adverse consequences, (4) problem recognition, and (5) tolerance and withdrawal.

Positive Features

- The SSI was one of three screening instruments found to be most effective in identifying inmates considered to be substance dependent.
- The SSI had the highest sensitivity of all screening instruments in a study conducted by Peters and Greenbaum (1996).
- The SSI is brief to administer.
- The SSI is a public domain instrument available at no cost.

Concerns

- Validity has not been examined among offenders with co-occurring disorders.
- The SSI does not examine quantity or frequency of recent or past substance use.

The **ADS** is a 25-item instrument developed to screen for alcohol dependence symptoms. The instrument was developed and published by the Addiction Research Foundation in Toronto, Canada.

Positive Features

- The ADS, when used in conjunction with the ASI, was found to be one of three instruments most effective in substance dependent inmates (Peters & Greenbaum, 1996).
- The ADS, when used in conjunction with the ASI, was found to be very effective in identifying nondependent inmates.
- The ADS is brief to administer and easy to score.

Concerns

- The ADS is limited to screening for alcohol abuse.
- Although the cost is modest, the ADS is a commercial product and would need to be purchased.

The **ASI** is described as the most widely used substance abuse instrument and is commonly used for screening, assessment, and treatment planning (Peters & Bartoi, 1997). In addition, the ASI is commonly used in criminal justice settings. Seven areas of functioning commonly related to substance abuse are measured. These areas include drug or alcohol use, family or social relationships, employment or support status, and mental health status (Peters & Bartoi, 1997).

Positive Features

- In combination with the ADS, the ASI was found to be very effective in identifying substance dependent inmates.
- In combination with the ADS, the ASI was found to be very effective in identifying nondependent inmates.
- The ASI measures different psychosocial components related to substance abuse.
- The ASI is capable of capturing the history of substance abuse as well as recent and current use.
- Normative data are available for criminal justice populations (McLellan et al., 1992).
- The ASI is a public domain instrument and available at no cost.

Concerns

- The ASI requires significant training to administer and score.
- Administration of the entire ASI requires up to 75 minutes.

Aside from the suggestions of Peters and Bartoi (1997), we strongly recommend the **Substance Abuse Subtle Screening Inventory** (SASSI) as an alternate instrument for drug abuse screening. This instrument utilizes several criteria to detect personality profiles and/or characteristics that have a strong likelihood for substance abuse problems. In fact, the SASSI is designed to detect likely substance abuse among persons who are either in denial or who deliberately attempt to deceive the clinician. Because of this and because of the SASSI's effectiveness (substance abuse detection at 93% accuracy), it is a premier assessment tool. The SASSI is a brief and easily administered screening measure that helps identify individuals who probably suffer from a substance use disorder.

The SASSI Institute notes that "interpretations of SASSI profiles also produce hypotheses that clinicians may find useful in understanding clients and their treatment planning" (SASSI Institute presentation). The SASSI has enjoyed widespread popularity and is used in both criminal justice and mental health settings. This means that the SASSI is ideal for correctional counseling objectives, and, as the student may recall from Chapter 1, the continual generation of hypotheses augments the scientific method of inquiry and also aids in the refinement of treatment plans (see Chapter 2).

The SASSI consists of face valid items and subtle items that do not directly address substance abuse in a detectable manner. The questions are oblique in nature and instead ask about other lifecourse issues that often are commonplace with the substance-abusing lifestyle. The profiles generated provide several clinical inferences, and among these are the following: (1) indication of defensive responding, (2) level of insight and awareness of the effects of substance misuse, (3) evidence of emotional pain, and (4) likely future risk of involvement with the criminal justice system. It is clear from these other inferences that the SASSI is ideal for correctional treatment programs and that it appeals to both treatment and custodial-related concerns.

In addition, the SASSI can be administered by traditional pencil and paper format, computer and compact disc, or even online. Further, clinicians are given extensive support and guidance by the SASSI Institute, making its use "counselor friendly" and all the more easier to competently implement within the facility setting. Addictions professionals who are trained in a one-day SASSI workshop can effectively implement this screening tool. The SASSI Institute produces newsletters semiannually and provides phone and online support. The reason that we note these positive aspects of SASSI products is not to necessarily solicit our readers (we have no actual profit motive in recommending the SASSI) but to instead demonstrate that clinicians will find this tool both effective and easy to administer. We speak from experience when we note the effectiveness of the SASSI and when we note that the SASSI Institute provides ongoing and effective support to its consumers. It is with this in mind that correctional counselors may find this instrument to be a prudent choice in there drug abuse screening and assessment.

Lastly, one additional component of a comprehensive screening process includes measuring offenders' motivation and readiness for treatment. **Motivational screening instruments** are primarily designed to identify those offenders not suitable for treatment (Peters & Bartoi, 1997) and are able to predict dropout, as well as treatment outcome. In addition, those offenders who are not found to be ready for treatment can be diverted to other programs aimed at educating the offender regarding the effects of substance abuse and co-occurring disorders. One motivational screening instrument commonly used in correctional settings is the **Stages of Change Readiness and Treatment Eagerness Scale** (SOCRATES). The SOCRATES consists of a personal drinking questionnaire and a personal drug use questionnaire. Both instruments consist of 19 items and capture data in relation to three scales: ambivalence, recognition, and taking action. These scales reflect stages of offenders' motivation and readiness for treatment (Peters & Bartoi, 1997).

Positive Features

- According to Peters and Greenbaum (1996), the SOCRATES has been found to be highly reliable among correctional settings.
- The instrument is brief to administer and easily scored.
- It is a public domain document and free of charge.

Concerns

- Validity has not been determined among populations suffering from co-occurring disorders.
- The SOCRATES has not been validated for use in treatment matching in criminal justice settings.

Diagnostic Instruments

Diagnostic instruments are useful in identifying key questions or issues that will need to be addressed in the assessment stage as well as in the development of individual treatment plans (Drake & Mercer-McFadden, 1995). Diagnostic instruments are primarily used to examine symptoms of substance abuse and mental health disorders within the framework of the *DSM-IV-TR*. In essence, diagnostic instruments build on the information obtained during the initial assessment and provide a more in-depth look into the offender's psychosocial characteristics.

The **Diagnostic Interview Schedule** (DIS) (Robins, Helzer, Croughan, & Ratcliff, 1981) is a fully structured diagnostic instrument. The DIS measures such constructs as mood, anxiety, schizophrenia, eating, somatization, psychoactive substance abuse, and antisocial personality disorder (Peters & Bartoi, 1997).

Positive Features

- The DIS is able to measure antisocial personality disorder which is often associated with substance abuse.
- The DIS requires little training and can be administered by nonclinicians.

Concerns

- Structured instruments sometimes fail to detect up to 25% of those individuals abusing alcohol and it is possible that even a larger percentage of substance abusers go undetected (Drake et al., 1990; Stone, Greenstein, Gamble, & McLellan, 1993).
- According to Hasin and Grant (1987) the DIS may not be best suited to detect depression among offenders suffering from co-occurring disorders.

A second diagnostic instrument that may be useful is the **Structured Clinical Interview for DSM-IV Axis I Disorders** (SCID) (First, Spitzer, Gibbon, & Williams, 1996). The SCID examines 32 different Axis I diagnoses and includes major mental health and substance use disorders.

Positive Features

- Interrater reliability of the SCID is mostly good (0.64–0.72) among individuals suffering from co-occurring disorders (Corty, Lehman, & Myers, 1993).
- Peters and Greenbaum (1996) note the SCID has good test-retest reliability (77–100%) among male, prison inmates.

Concerns

- Similar to the DIS, the SCID also suffers from an inability to detect up to 25% of alcohol abusers and possibly even a higher number of substance abusers (Drake et al., 1990; Stone et al., 1993).
- The SCID requires clinical expertise to determine if symptoms meet the criteria of a particular disorder (Corty et al., 1993).
- Significant training is required for administration and scoring.

Assessment Instruments

The assessment of an offender usually entails a detailed and personalized gathering of information that is relied upon to develop a specific treatment plan. The assessment usually takes place after screening and diagnosis and once the offender has been referred to treatment services. One note important to the concept of assessment is that sufficient time should be given prior to an assessment to ensure the offender has been detoxified, is sober, and that any mental health symptoms are not the result of withdrawal (Weiss & Mirin, 1989). Some of the key components of a thorough assessment include examining skill deficits, the need for psychotropic medication, as well as the types of treatment and support services that will be needed to properly attend to the various disorders of a particular offender (Peters & Bartoi, 1997). In addition, Peters and Bartoi (1997) suggest the following types of information should be included in the assessment of co-occurring disorders:

- Criminal justice history and status
- Mental health history, current symptoms, and level of functioning
- Substance abuse history, current symptoms, and level of functioning
- History of interaction between mental health and substance use disorders
- Family history of mental health and substance use disorders
- Medical and health status
- Social/family relationships
- Interpersonal coping strategies, problem-solving abilities, and communication skills
- Employment/vocational status
- Educational history and status

- Literacy, IQ, and developmental disabilities
- Treatment history and response to treatment
- Prior experience with peer support groups
- Cognitive appraisal of treatment and recovery
  - Motivation and readiness for treatment
  - Self-efficacy in adopting lifestyle changes
  - Expectancies related to substance use
- Participant conceptualization of treatment needs
- Resources and limitations affecting the ability to participate in treatment.

When deciding on which instruments are most appropriate for assessment it is important to understand that an integrated approach is critical to success. There should be a comprehensive assessment of mental health and substance use disorders as well as an in-depth examination of criminal justice history and current status. Based on information provided by Peters and Bartoi (1997) the following combination of instruments may be best suited for assessing offenders' suffering from substance abuse and/or co-occurring disorders:

1. Either the Minnesota Multiphasic Personality Inventory-2 (MMPI-2) (Hathaway & McKinley, 1989), the Millon Clinical Multiaxial Inventory-III (MCMI-III) (Millon, 1992), or the Personality Assessment Inventory (PAI) (Morey, 1991).
2. The Addiction Severity Index (ASI) to examine substance abuse–related areas.

All three personality inventories (MMPI-2, MCMI-III, and PAI) are self-report measures that have undergone intense research and proven to be mostly reliable and valid instruments. The MMPI is a very robust instrument that is now used in a multitude of correctional settings. Students may recall that the MMPI-2 was discussed extensively in Chapter 2. The MCMI-III is useful in assessing personality disorders that may affect involvement in treatment. The MCMI-III also includes a drug abuse scale aimed at measuring personality characteristics associated with drug abuse. In addition to personality constructs, the PAI also includes measures of alcohol and drug problems (Peters & Bartoi, 1997). When used in conjunction with the ASI, previously described, this combination should yield mostly accurate depictions of offenders' current state regarding substance abuse and co-occurring disorders.

Threats to Accurate Screening, Diagnosis, and Assessment

It can be very difficult to obtain reliable and valid information from offenders suffering from substance abuse and co-occurring disorders. Many offenders vested in a criminal lifestyle will be hesitant to provide accurate and truthful information. There is often a lack of trust on behalf of offenders for anyone working in the various components of the justice and mental health system. As a result, screening, diagnosing, and assessing should be conducted on an ongoing basis throughout the duration of the offender's involvement with the justice system. It is important to note that in addition to the various psychometric instruments it is also important to engage offenders in interpersonal conversation aimed at assessing their overall mental and physical status. Some of the more common threats include the following:

- Inadequate staff training and poor familiarity with mental health and/or substance use disorders
- Inadequate amounts of time for proper screening and assessment
- Previous clinicians who may have avoided, or neglected, to provide screening for co-occurring disorders

- Incomplete or misleading records
- Extreme variation in the expression of co-occurring disorders
- An offender may be in temporary remission at the time of screening
- Considerable symptom interaction between co-occurring disorders
- Individuals suffering from co-occurring disorders may have difficulty providing accurate histories due to cognitive impairment, mental health symptoms, and confusion
- Individuals in the criminal justice system may anticipate negative consequences related to disclosure
- Symptoms may be feigned or exaggerated if an individual believes that this will lead to more favorable placement or disposition.

SECTION SUMMARY

Screening, diagnosing, and properly assessing offenders is a critical component of being able to effectively render appropriate services. The essence of each of these steps is to ascertain what types of services an offender needs. There are a variety of instruments available to help counselors properly screen, diagnose, and assess offenders. It is important that the counselor carefully identify certain instruments based on their reliability and validity. Also, it is important that counselors identify instruments that are capable of assessing both psychological and emotional disorders as well as substance abuse. This process usually consists of using several instruments because of the lack of single instruments able to capture the necessary components salient to the criminal justice system. Finally, it is important that counselors thoroughly familiarize themselves with the types of information produced by the instruments they use in order to maximize their utility.

LEARNING CHECK

1. Diagnosing describes the process of detecting mental health and substance abuse disorders that need to be treated.
   a. True
   b. False
2. Assessments are commonly conducted through interviews and/or specialized instruments.
   a. True
   b. False
3. A common threat to accurate screening, diagnosis, and assessment is the fact that many offenders distrust the criminal justice system and are hesitant to provide truthful information.
   a. True
   b. False
4. Motivational screening instruments are primarily used to identify offenders who are
   a. most suitable for treatment
   b. highly motivated
   c. not sure if they need treatment
   d. not suited for treatment
5. When choosing a particular instrument, it is not important to consider whether the instrument has been used in a criminal justice setting
   a. True
   b. False

PART THREE: TREATING ALCOHOL/SUBSTANCE ABUSE AND CO-OCCURRING DISORDERS

Treating offenders suffering from alcohol and/or substance abuse requires an informed and comprehensive approach that targets each area of the offender's life circumstance that may be contributing to the continued use. An informed treatment approach must be able to identify psychological and emotional characteristics, dynamics of interpersonal relationships, as well as the offender's physical surroundings that may be contributing to or causing the use of alcohol and/or other drugs. It is important to note that there are many different treatment paradigms that can be effective in treating alcohol and substance abuse as well as co-occurring disorders. The specifics of a particular treatment modality usually depend on the emphasis of a particular service provider as well as the training undergone by a particular counselor or mental health professional. The **12 core functions** that are presented below have been widely adopted by service providers throughout the world in treating alcohol and substance abuse. Each function is critical to the success of treating offenders. For the purposes of this text, we suggest these functions as a guide to be implemented according to the specific protocols of individual mental health and substance abuse providers.

1. ***Screening***—as mentioned above, this is usually the point at which the offender is determined to be eligible for admission to a particular program. During the screening an initial evaluation is conducted aimed at gathering information regarding psychological, social, and physiological signs and symptoms of substance abuse and co-occurring disorders.
2. ***Intake***—consists of administrative and initial diagnosis procedures for admission to a program. Clients are usually expected to fill out and complete necessary forms and documents including informed consents.
3. ***Orientation***—generally consists of describing to the client the general nature and goals of the program as well as rules governing client conduct and infractions that could lead to disciplinary actions or discharge from the program.
4. ***Assessment***—procedures consisting of an in-depth evaluation of a client's strengths, weaknesses, problems, and needs in order to develop a particular treatment plan. The assessment should consist of gathering relevant history including, but not limited to, alcohol and drug use; identifying methods and procedures for corroborating the client's history from significant secondary sources; identifying appropriate assessment tools; explaining to the client the rationale for using the assessment techniques; and finally, developing a comprehensive diagnostic evaluation of the client's substance abuse and/or co-occurring disorders in order to provide an integrated approach to treatment based on the client's strengths, weaknesses, and identified problems and needs. The results of the assessment should suggest the focus of the treatment.
5. ***Treatment planning***—the process by which the counselor and client, through collaboration, identify and rank problems needing resolution. In addition, the counselor and client establish immediate and long-term goals and decide on the appropriate treatment process and the resources to be utilized.
6. ***Counseling***—the process of using special skills to assist individuals, families, or groups in achieving objectives through exploring problems and their ramifications; examining attitudes and feelings; and consideration of alternative solutions and decision-making skills. In essence, counseling is the relationship whereby the counselor helps mobilize the client's resources to resolve problems and/or modify attitudes and values. Counselors need to have a working knowledge of various counseling theories. These theories may include reality therapy, transactional analysis, strategic family therapy, client-centered therapy, existential therapy, and so on.

7. ***Case management***—the process of bringing services, agencies, resources, and/or people together within a planned and coordinated framework with the goal of achieving identified goals. Case managers may perform counseling, however, the bulk of their responsibilities usually entail the coordination of multiple services needed to address specific needs of the offender. In addition, it is very important that case managers assume an active role in the treatment process where they are able to closely monitor the offender's progress or lack thereof.
8. ***Crisis intervention***—describes the process of delivering services that respond to an offender's needs during acute emotional and/or physical distress. A crisis is a decisive event in the course of treatment that threatens to compromise or destroy the rehabilitation effort. A crisis may consist of overdose or relapse as well as indirect circumstances such as the death of a loved one or divorce. It is critical that the counselor identify the crisis as quickly as possible and take immediate action to begin mitigating or resolving the salient problems.
9. ***Client education***—educating offenders is an important part of the overall treatment process. Education can be provided in a variety of ways including relevant psychosocial concepts, dangers and risks associate with certain behaviors, as well as describing self-help groups and other resources that may be available.
10. ***Referral***—the process of identifying the needs of an offender that cannot be met by the counselor and then following up by assisting the client in obtaining support and resources from other professionals that are able to provide appropriate services. It is important that counselors be aware of the referral process as well as the different community resources and their deliverables.
11. ***Report and record keeping***—the process of accurately recording the results of the assessment and treatment plan usually through writing reports, progress notes, discharge summaries, and other offender-related data. If performed properly, the process of reporting and record keeping will enhance the offender's entire treatment experience. Accurate reporting facilitates communication, timely feedback from supervisors, assists other programs that may provide services, and enhances the accountability of the program that may be necessary for licensing and funding.
12. ***Consultation with other professionals***—usually consists of communicating with in-house staff or outside professionals to ensure the best care possible for the offender. Consultations provide a good opportunity for professionals to gather in order to generate and share ideas regarding the treatment process of an offender.

In addition to the 12 core functions in treating alcohol and substance abuse, the Center for Substance Abuse Treatment (2006) provides 12 principles to address the needs of persons with co-occurring disorders. These principles were generated from the accumulated experience of mental health professionals over many decades of practice. Some of the information provided in the following principles may overlap with information already provided. We go forward, however, based on the belief that these areas of overlap cannot be emphasized enough.

- ***Principle 1***—Co-occurring disorders are to be expected in all behavioral health settings. In other words, it should be assumed that many offenders will be suffering from a multitude of disorders. Based on this assumption, all policies, regulations, funding mechanisms, and programming should reflect the need to serve people with co-occurring disorders.
- ***Principle 2***—An integrated system of mental health and addiction services that emphasizes continuity and quality is in the best interest of consumers, providers, programs, funders, and systems. This principle cannot be emphasized enough. A variety of services must be available and need to be matched with the specific needs of offenders.

- ***Principle 3***—The integrated system of care must be accessible from multiple points of entry and be perceived by the offender as caring and accepting. Many offenders suffering from substance abuse and co-occurring disorders lack the capacity to traverse complicated service systems and their attendant bureaucracy. In addition, a variety of barriers such as financial limitations, inadequate transportation, and so on may prevent some offenders from accessing or even seeking treatment. These barriers need to be removed whenever possible to avoid discouraging offenders from seeking treatment and continuing down the path of the untreated waiting for the next crisis.
- ***Principle 4***—The system of care for co-occurring disorders should not be limited to a single "correct" model or approach. Every individual is different, and what works for one may not work for the other. Systems of care need to be diversified and able to adapt to the specific needs and learning styles of particular offenders.
- ***Principle 5***—The system of care must reflect the importance of the partnership between science and service, and support both the application of evidence- and consensus-based practices for persons with co-occurring disorders and evaluation of the efforts of existing programs and services. In essence, there needs to be a constant effort aimed at enhancing services based on scientifically grounded evidence.
- ***Principle 6***—Behavioral health systems must collaborate with professionals in primary care, human services, housing, criminal justice, and education and related fields in order to meet the complex needs of persons with co-occurring disorders. This breadth of need is based on the fact that offenders suffering from co-occurring disorders are often among the most disadvantaged and impoverished members of society.
- ***Principle 7***—Co-occurring disorders must be expected when evaluating any offender, and clinical services should incorporate this assumption into all screening, diagnostic, assessment, and treatment planning.
- ***Principle 8***—Within the treatment context, both co-occurring disorders are considered primary. For offenders with co-occurring disorders, symptoms of either disorder may vary over time. One set of symptoms may be managed at a particular time while the other set causes impairment. This interactive nature requires each disorder to be continually assessed. This principle is based on the assumption that there is always a relationship between the disorders.
- ***Principle 9***—Empathy, respect, and belief in the individual's capacity for recovery are fundamental provider attitudes. Many offenders suffering from co-occurring disorders have experienced significant let-downs and disappointment throughout the course of their life. They are often very keen to any form of judgmentalism on behalf of the counselor and will likely feel demoralized, rejected, or disappointed once again. When faced with judgmentalism, whether real or perceived, many offenders will instinctively employ the defense mechanism of shutting down, which is an attempt at reducing emotional pain. Once cognitively and emotionally shut down real therapeutic progress is all but impossible.
- ***Principle 10***—Treatment should be individualized to accommodate the specific needs, personal goals, and cultural perspectives of unique individuals in different states of change. The concept of cultural competency on behalf of the service provider must be adhered to. Cultural differences must be learned, respected, and incorporated into all aspects of the treatment plan.
- ***Principle 11***—The special needs of children and adolescents must be explicitly recognized and addressed in all phases of assessment, treatment planning, and service delivery.

- ***Principle 12***—The contribution of the community to the course of recovery for consumers with co-occurring disorders and the contribution of consumers with co-occurring disorders to the community must be explicitly recognized in program policy, treatment planning, and consumer advocacy.

Denial as Clinical Treatment Issue

Counseling criminal justice offenders with substance abuse and/or co-occurring disorders is challenging work for a myriad of reasons. Often offenders will be resistant due to a lack of trust in the system; their only motivation for attending counseling sessions will be because they have been ordered to do so by the court; and the thought of getting in touch with emotion may be considered a weakness to be taken advantage of by others. In essence, many offenders will be unable to express and feel emotion. Their emotional landscape is barren due to past experiences that have left them feeling hurt and rejected. As a result, the thought of trying to reconnect with emotion and feeling, a critical part of the recovery process, will often provoke powerful feelings of anxiety.

One defense mechanism often employed to reduce the unpleasant feelings of anxiety, and particularly salient to offenders suffering from substance abuse and/or co-occurring disorders, is the concept of **denial.** Often offenders will deny the fact that they have a problem with the use of substances. This denial serves as an internal mechanism aimed at staving off powerful pangs of anxiety induced by the thought of living one's life without alcohol and/or drugs. Offenders seriously addicted to substances may be unable or unwilling to imagine their existence sober. The paradox, however, is that denial as a defense is only effective in the short term. As long as an offender is using denial as a coping mechanism he or she will be unable to experience or truly participate in lasting therapeutic change. Therefore, the goal is to assist and accompany offenders through the frightening process of rejecting the concept of denial as a defense mechanism and replacing it with acceptance and a true desire to recover their natural self.

There are a variety of strategies that can be effective in helping the offender move from denial to acceptance. The following strategies are meant to serve as guide that may be useful in assisting some offenders dismantle the concept of denial as a viable defense mechanism.

- ***Confront***—At some point the offender's use of denial as a defense mechanism will have to be confronted. In other words, it will have to be clearly articulated, in a manner in which the offender is able to comprehend, that the continued use of denial is counterproductive to the healing process. Even though the client may not be ready to accept the alternative, the counselor may be well served by further articulating that what needs to replace denial is acceptance of self; accepting the fact that he or she is a flawed but worthy human being deserving of love and freedom.
- ***Empathy/Compassion***—When offenders are using denial as a coping mechanism, they will often be resistant to much of the information being provided by a counselor. This resistance can trigger the counselors own negative emotions. For example, when an offender resists or rejects what the counselor is saying many counselors will begin to feel confused, panic, hurt, and even rejected (Egan, 2007). Based on these negative feelings counselors may react in ways that are counterproductive such as: becoming impatient and hostile; blaming the client and entering into a power struggle; or simply giving up (Egan, 2007). It is critical that counselors be aware of their own issues related to denial, resistance, and reluctance. In other words, how would you, the counselor, feel if you were being coerced or encouraged to do something that involved significant change? Or, as Egan (2007) points out, how do you avoid personal growth and development? By exploring these issues,

counselors are better equipped to appreciate the fear and anxiety being experienced by the offender. The ability to understand the offender's plight allows the counselor to genuinely express empathy and compassion free of judgmentalism.

- ***Understand that some reluctance on the part of the offender is normal***—Appreciate that many offenders will be heavily vested in the use of substances as a coping mechanism. Denial may be the only construct available that is strong enough to keep them from having to immediately face the realities of their destructive behaviors.
- ***Educate the offender as to why the concept of denial is so powerful***—Help the offender understand the underlying structure that is supporting the continued use of denial as a coping mechanism. For example, a counselor may suggest that the offender talk to his or her denial. The counselor may prompt the offender to complete this statement, "Denial, I am so glad I have you in my life. If it were not for you, denial, I would have to . . . " The likely completion of the aforementioned sentence would probably be something like, "Denial, if it were not for you I would have to admit that I have a drug or alcohol problem and it is destroying my life."
- ***Be realistic, it is ultimately up to the offender***—Try to remember that there are limits to what a counselor can do (Egan, 2007). Unrealistic expectations can lead to a power struggle that is counterproductive. Some clients may choose to reject help and continue on with their current lifestyle. As unfortunate as this may sound it is a reality that must accepted by the counselor.
- ***Strategies to remember***:
  - Show deep respect.
  - Relate with empathy and compassion.
  - Be genuine.
  - Maintain a sense of humor.
  - Be honest—admit when you are confused or do not understand.
  - Always try to relate to an offender in a nonjudgmental fashion. Judgmentalism will quickly erode any connection between the counselor and offender (Egan, 2007).

Alcoholics Anonymous (AA) and 12 Step Groups

Alcoholics Anonymous (AA) is a process carried out by self-help groups whose members suffer from alcoholism. AA was founded in the 1930s by Dr. Robert Smith and William Wilson (Alexander, 2000) and has been very successful in helping scores of individuals recover from alcoholism. AA is predicated on 12 steps that are to be followed by members in chronological order. A complete breakdown of the 12 steps can be found at http://www.aa.org.

Because AA and its 12 steps have been so successful it has served as a prototype for the treatment of other problems including Narcotics Anonymous, Al-Anon Family Groups, Gamblers Anonymous, Alateen, Adult Children of Alcoholics, Co-Dependents Anonymous, and others (Alexander, 2000).

There are several components of self-help groups that make them extremely effective for many people. First, usually everyone in the group is suffering from similar circumstances ranging from addiction, co-dependency, or living with family members who are drug addicts or alcoholics. This is an extremely powerful component and lets the individual know that they are not alone. Oftentimes people suffering from addiction or emotional/psychological disorders come to believe that they are the only ones suffering from these ailments. In addition, because they feel alone in their suffering they begin to feel as though they are defective which usually results in powerful feelings of shame. The group works to alleviate these negative emotions by providing an atmosphere of caring individuals suffering the same afflictions. Second, by working the 12 steps individuals are able to share their stories and circumstances and be heard. For some addicts, they may not have ever had the experience of truly being heard by others. They may not have had the opportunity to receive empathy and compassion unconditionally. In addition, the group may provide their first experience at being able to share their feelings and not be judged. These are powerful therapeutic forces that greatly enhance recovery efforts. Third, because members are addicts themselves they are able to provide practical guidance and support that has worked for them. Members are able to provide advice to others in regard to how they have traversed each of the steps.

SECTION SUMMARY

When attempting to treat offenders suffering from co-occurring disorders, it is important to recognize that an integrated system of care is necessary. Treatment should be individualized based on a specific offender's needs. It is important to avoid a "one-size–fits-all" mentality when working with offenders due to the myriad of factors that will be contributing to their problems. These factors are likely to be very specific to the individual and though some may appear to be common to most offenders the underlying characteristics are likely to be different. The primary reason for the differences is the fact that individuals have different cognitive processes for interpreting and responding to their environments. Counselors should always provide services with empathy and respect. Finally, it is important to recognize different cultural values and how they impact the offender's methods of reasoning.

LEARNING CHECK

1. A counselor should never admit to being confused or not understanding. This would reduce the counselor's credibility and hinder the ability to provide services.
   a. True
   b. False
2. In most circumstances where an offender is suffering from co-occurring disorders, the substance abuse problem should be considered primary.
   a. True
   b. False
3. Denial is a powerful defense mechanism primarily because of which of the following.
   a. Its ability to stave off powerful feelings of shame.
   b. Its ability to allow the offender to justify his or her actions.
   c. Its ability to allow the offender to pretend as though he or she does not have a problem.
   d. All of the above.
4. The primary concept that needs to replace the offender's denial is the acceptance of
   a. the situation
   b. oneself
   c. the fact that they will never change
   d. none of the above
   e. all of the above
5. One of the most powerful components of self-help groups is the fact that all of the members are suffering from similar circumstances.
   a. True
   b. False

PART FOUR: RELAPSE PREVENTION

Unfortunately, many offenders who undergo treatment while in the criminal justice system will go back to old environments and return to using alcohol and/or drugs. The recidivism statistics clearly show this to be a fact. For some, there is nothing really that can be done. In order to stay sober the offender must be fully committed to maintaining a substance-free life and willing to work diligently at maintaining an environment that is conducive to this success. The final segment of this chapter is aimed at those offenders who have successfully gotten clean and are committed to maintaining a life free of drugs and/or alcohol. Much of the information presented is drawn from the *Counselor's Manual for Relapse Prevention with Chemically Dependent Criminal Offenders*. The manual is part of the *Technical Assistance Publication Series* funded by SAMHSA.

Relapse prevention is the process of helping recovering addicts recognize and manage internal and external life circumstances that may lead to relapse. Relapse, in this context, is the process of becoming dysfunctional in recovery, which leads to a chemical use, physical or emotional collapse, or suicide. There are typically observable warning signs that precede episodes of relapse. Relapse usually progresses from bio/psycho/social stability through a period of distress that culminates with physical and/or emotional collapse. The symptoms intensify and the offender turns to substances for relief. Understanding and identifying the warning signs is a critical component in helping offenders stay clean. In essence, relapse occurs when offenders reverse the basic components of the recovery process. Therefore, it is possible to articulate a relapse process by first identifying the recovery process.

Process of Recovery:

1. Abstaining from alcohol and other drugs
2. Separating from people, places, and things that promote the use of alcohol or drugs, and establishing a social network that supports recovery
3. Stopping self-defeating behaviors that prevent awareness of painful feelings and irrational thoughts
4. Learning how to manage feelings and emotions responsibly without resorting to compulsive behavior or the use of alcohol or drugs
5. Learning to change addictive thinking patterns that create painful feelings and self-defeating behaviors
6. Identifying and changing the mistaken core beliefs about oneself, others, and the world that promote dysfunctional thinking.

Relapse Process:

1. Have a mistaken belief that causes dysfunctional thoughts
2. Begin to return to addictive thinking patterns that cause painful feelings
3. Engage in compulsive, self-defeating behaviors as a way to avoid the feelings
4. Seek out situation involving people who use alcohol and drugs
5. Find themselves in more pain, thinking less rationally, and behaving less responsibly
6. Find themselves in a situation where drug or alcohol use seems like a logical escape from their pain and as a result they use alcohol or drugs.

Based on the idea of being able to identify the relapse process a number of principles have been constructed specifically geared toward relapse prevention therapy. These principles are geared toward helping relapse-prone offenders maintain abstinence.

Principle 1: Self-Regulation

The risk of relapse decreases as the offender's capacity to self-regulate thinking, feeling, memory, judgment, and behavior increases. In essence, when the offender experiences disruptive stress he or she needs to be stabilized. The stabilization process often involves:

- Solving the immediate crises that threaten continued abstinence
- Learning skills to identify and manage withdrawal
- Establishing a daily structure that includes proper diet, exercise, stress management, and regular contact with treatment personnel and self-help groups.

Principle 2: Integration

The risk of relapse will decrease as the level of conscious understanding and acceptance of situations and events that have led to past relapses increase. The offender needs to become aware of critical issues that are capable of triggering relapse through a critical self-assessment. Identifying these critical issues allows the counselor to develop intervention plans, in conjunction with the offender, that enable the offender to work through crises before relapse occurs.

Principle 3: Understanding

The risk of relapse will decrease as the offender's awareness of the general factors that cause relapse increases. Oftentimes this process is carried out in structured education sessions and reading assignments. In addition, it is important to test offenders to ensure adequate comprehension and retention of the material.

Principle 4: Self-Knowledge

The risk of relapse will decrease as the offender's ability to recognize personal relapse warning signs increases. The offender should create a personalized warning sign list which includes circumstances and feelings that have led to past relapses. It is important that the list be developed and constantly revised as new problems arise.

Principle 5: Coping Skills

The risk of relapse will decrease as the ability to manage relapse warning signs increases. Once warning signs have been identified coping skills must be in place to help offenders deal with the problems that arise in a manner that fosters their ability to stay in recovery. First, offenders are taught to modify their behavioral responses in situations or circumstances that trigger warning signs. Second, through a cognitive behavioral approach offenders are taught to challenge dysfunctional thoughts. Third, offenders are taught to identify the core addictive and psychological issues that initially create the warning signs.

Principle 6: Change

The risk of relapse will decrease as the relationship between relapse warning signs and recovery program recommendations increases. The primary task is to identify a recovery activity for each warning sign on the offender's personalized list.

Principle 7: Awareness

The risk of relapse will decrease as the use of daily inventory techniques designed to identify relapse warning signs increases. The offender is taught to identify primary goals for each day, create a to-do list, and then carry out the necessary tasks for achieving the goals. At the end of the day the offender should review his or her warning sign list and recovery plan and determine whether any warning signs were present while carrying out the tasks.

Principle 8: Significant Others

The risk of relapse will decrease as the responsible involvement of significant others in recovery and in relapse prevention planning increases. Relapse-prone individuals are not likely to recover alone. They need help. A counselor should encourage significant others to be involved in the recovery process whenever possible.

Principle 9: Maintenance

The risk of relapse decreases if the relapse prevention is regularly updated during the first three years of sobriety. It is important to note that nearly two-thirds of all relapses occur within the first six months of recovery. In addition, less than one quarter of the variables that actually cause relapse can be predicted during the initial treatment phase. In essence, ongoing outpatient treatment is necessary for effective relapse prevention.

CONCLUSION

A lot of information has been presented in this chapter. We began by discussing substance abuse issues and some of the common issues concerning this disorder. As a counselor working with offenders it is important to be able to identify the common signs and symptoms that will usually be present among substance abusers. This is particularly salient when considering that many offenders will not freely admit their substance abuse problems. Oftentimes, this is because they are untrusting of the criminal justice system and will not want to get into further trouble. A detailed discussion was provided concerning common occurring mood, anxiety, personality, and psychiatric disorders. Appreciate that many offenders, once assessed, will be determined to be suffering from co-occurring disorders. If an offender is suffering from substance abuse problems it is extremely likely that they will also have another co-occurring disorder. Both disorders must be treated and both should be considered primary when attempting to devise a treatment plan.

The process of screening, diagnosing, and assessing offenders is the process whereby counselors and other professionals determine what disorders are present as well as the severity of each. Each step in the process builds upon the previous. Several psychometric instruments were presented in order to assist counselors with accurately identifying the various disorders from which offenders may be suffering. It is through each of these three components that we ultimately create an individualized treatment plan for each offender. The treatment plan serves as a roadmap for providing offenders with necessary counseling and information aimed at treating their disorders.

Many offenders suffering from co-occurring disorders require substantial counseling to modify or completely change old patterns of thinking and behaving. Counseling offenders is sometimes difficult due to their lack of trust as well as being heavily vested in ways and patterns of living. In addition, those offenders suffering from substance abuse issues will often be in denial regarding the seriousness of the disorder. Denial is a very common concept among populations of substance abusers. It will be critical to work with these offenders in a manner in which they are able to be guided through and out of the process of denial and begin to take ownership of their circumstances. This takes skill and vigilance on the part of the counselor. It is also important for the counselor to be intimately aware of his or her own emotions and vulnerabilities so as to avoid getting into power struggles and psychological games with offenders.

The importance and value of self-help groups cannot be overstated. One combination that may be particular beneficial is the use of self-groups in conjunction with counseling. Self-help groups provide support for many offenders and consist of others who are suffering the same symptoms and problems. Through sharing and support, offenders are able to learn that they are not alone and are also able to receive valuable feedback and guidance from their peers. Finally, relapse prevention must be considered a critical component to any mental health service provider attempting to treat offenders suffering from substance abuse and co-occurring disorders. Through relapse prevention techniques offenders are taught skills aimed at identifying situations in which they may be vulnerable and the ability to exercise new and better behaviors rather than drug use.

Essay Questions

1. Is there a difference between substance dependence and substance abuse? Is one more difficult to treat than other? Why or why not?
2. Define the concept of co-occurring disorders. Among the offender population, identify two of the most common co-occurring disorders. Why is it so important that counselors be familiar with and able to treat co-occurring disorders?
3. Discuss some of the key factors usually associated with how substance abuse starts. If you had to choose one, which factor would you identify as most important? Why?
4. What is the difference between a psychotic disorder and a personality disorder? Provide at least one example of each.
5. What is the primary purpose of denial? How does this concept affect the counselor's ability to effectively work with an offender? Discuss two methods of reducing or eliminating an offender's use of denial in relation to co-occurring disorders.

Treatment Planning Exercise

The case vignette presented below addresses substance abuse issues but also adds a twist for students; the client has co-occurring disorders. This makes the clinical case much more complicated but this is precisely the issue that confronts correctional counselors on a daily basis. It is seldom that counselors have clients with a singular issue. Rather, in many cases, the problems are multivariate and one clinical issue tends to compound the other. It is with this in mind that we present this case for students to address. Providing challenging treatment cases ensures that students understand the complexities with the treatment process and also ensures that material is not presented in an elementary or topical fashion. Further, co-occurring disorders tend to require the implementation of information from various chapters, thereby integrating the information that students acquire throughout the text and providing interlocking learning process where information is applied rather than being memorized. With this in mind, the student must do the following:

1. Refer back to Chapter 4 and explain how you would go about developing an effective therapeutic alliance with Mike? What challenges are you likely to encounter? How would you work to overcome these challenges?
2. What defense mechanisms and/or behaviors does Mike exhibit that is common to

substance abusers? How can you determine if this is a dimension of Mike's addiction or more a dimension of his potential for Narcissistic personality disorder?

3. What would you treat first, the drug abuse or the potential personality disorder? Would you treat them simultaneously?
4. How likely do you think it is that Mike will refrain from further drug use? How likely do you think it is that Mike will refrain from engaging in further criminal activity?
5. How would you motivate Mike to address his substance abuse issues? Explain some of the first initial processes that you might use when implementing the treatment planning process with Mike (some suggestions might come from Chapters 2 and 4).

The Case of Mike

Mike is a 20-year-old male who has just recently been released from jail. Mike is technically on probation for car theft, though he has been involved in crime to a much greater extent. Mike has been identified as a cocaine user and has been suspected, though not convicted, for dealing cocaine. Mike has been tested for drugs by his probation department and was found positive for cocaine. The county has mandated that Mike receive drug counseling, but as you continue counseling with Mike, you notice that he is very resistant to treatment. In fact, he denies issues with the severity of his drug use and blames either environmental circumstances or the behaviors of other people. When looking through his case file, you notice that at one time Mike was diagnosed by a psychologist to have *Narcissistic personality disorder*. This would then mean that he has comorbid issues that would need to be addressed.

Mike seems to have little regard for the feelings of others. Coupled with this is his extreme sensitivity to the comments of others. In fact, his prior fiancée has broken off her relationship with him due to what she calls his "constant need for admiration and attention. He is completely self-centered." After talking with Mike, you quickly find that he has no close friends. As he talks about people who have been close to him, he discounts them for one imperfection or another. These imperfections are all considered severe enough to warrant dismissing the person entirely. Mike makes a point of noting how many have betrayed their loyalty to him or have otherwise failed to give him the credit that he deserves.

When asked about getting caught in the auto theft, he remarks that "well my dumb partner got me out of a hot situation by driving me out in a stolen get-a-way car, we got nabbed only because the cop recognized the vehicle." (Word on the street has it that Mike was involved in a sour drug deal and was unlikely to have made it out alive if not for his partner.) Mike adds, "You know, I plan everything out perfectly, but you just cannot rely on anybody . . . if you want it done right, do it yourself." During this crime, Mike was high on a variety of stimulant drugs, including methamphetamine. In one group counseling session, he noted that his clarity is better with stimulants even though other members pointed out that his use of stimulants may actually be the reason that he finds himself in continual "bad luck" situations.

Mike recently has been involved with another woman (unknown to his prior fiancée) who has become pregnant. When she told Mike he said "Tough, you can go get an abortion or something, it isn't like we were in love or something." Then he laughed at her and told her to

(*continued*)

go find some other guy who would shack up with her.

Incidentally, Mike is a very attractive man and he likes to point that out on occasion. "Yeah, I was going to be a male model in L.A., but my agent did not know what he was doing . . . could never get things settled out right . . . so I had to fire him." Mike is very popular with women and has had a constant string of failed relationships due to what he calls "their inability to keep things exciting."

As Mike puts it "hey, I am too smart for this stuff. These people around me, they don't deserve the good life cause they're a bunch of dummies. But me, well I know how to run things and get over on people. And I am not about to let these dummies get in my way. I got it all figured out . . . see?"

Bibliography

Alexander, R. (2000). *Counseling, treatment, and intervention methods with juveniles and adult offenders.* Belmont, CA: Wadsworth/Thompson Learning.

American Psychiatric Association. (2000). *Diagnostic and statistical manual of mental disorders* (4th ed.). Washington, DC: American Psychiatric Association.

Boulet, J., & Boss, M. W. (1991). Reliability and validity of the brief symptom inventory. *Psychological Assessment, 3*(3), 433–437.

Bureau of Justice Assistance. (2004). *Mental health courts program.* Washington, DC: Office of Justice Programs, U.S. Department of Justice.

Center for Substance Abuse Treatment (CSAT). (1994). Simple screening instruments for outreach for alcohol and other drug abuse and infectious diseases. Treatment improvement protocol (TIP) series, #11. Rockville, MD: U.S. Department of Health and Human Services.

Center for Substance Abuse Treatment (CSAT). (2006). Definitions and terms relating to co-occurring disorders. COCE overview paper 1. DHHS publication No. (SMA) 06-4163. Rockville, MD: Substance abuse and mental health services administration and center for mental health services.

Corty, E., Lehman, A., & Myers, C. (1993). Influence of psychoactive substance use on the reliability of psychiatric diagnosis. *Journal of Consulting and Clinical Psychology, 61*(1), 165–170.

Derogatis, L. R., & Melisaratos, N. (1983). The brief symptom inventory: An introductionary report. *Psychological Medicine, 13,* 595–605.

Dimoff, T. A. (2001). *How to recognize substance abuse at work, at home, in athletics, anywhere.* Naperville, IL: Inside Advantage Publications.

Drake, R. E., & Mercer-McFadden, C. (1995). Assessment of substance use among persons with chronic mental illness. In A. F. Lehman & L. B. Dixon (Eds.), *Double jeopardy: Chronic mental illness* (pp. 47–62). Australia: Harwood Academic Publishers.

Drake, R. E., Osher, F. C., Noordsy, D. L., Hurlbut, S. C., Teague, G. B., & Beaudette, M. S. (1990). Diagnosis of alcohol use disorders in schizophrenia. *Schizophrenia Bulletin, 16*(1), 57–67.

Egan, G. (2007). *The skilled helper* (8th ed.). Belmont, CA: Thompson Brooks/Cole.

First, M. B., Spitzer, R. L., Gibbon, M., & Williams, J. B. W. (1996). Structured clinical Interview for DSM-IV Axis I Disorder—Patient edition (SCID-I/P. Version 2.0). New York, NY: Biometrics Research Department.

Fosha, D. (2000). *The transforming power of affect: A model for accelerated change.* New York: Basic Books.

Gorski, T. T., & Kelley, J. M. (1996). Counselor's manual for relapse prevention with chemically dependent criminal offenders: Technical Assistance Publication Series (19). Rockville, MD: Substance Abuse and Mental Health Services Administration.

Hanser, R. (2006). *Special needs offenders in the community.* Upper Saddle River, NJ: Prentice Hall.

Hasin, D. S., & Grant, B. F. (1987). Diagnosing depressive disorders in patients with alcohol and drug problems: A comparison of the SADS-L and the DIS. *Psychiatric Research, 21*(3), 301–311.

Hathaway, S. R., & McKinley, J. C. (1989). *Minnesota multiphasic personality inventory-2*. Minneapolis: University of Minnesota Press.

Kofoed, L., Dania, J., Walsh, T., & Atkinson, R. M. (1986). Outpatient treatment of patients with substance abuse and coexisting disorders. *American Journal of Psychiatry, 143*, 867–872.

Louisiana Association of Substance Abuse Counselors and Training (LASACT). (2004). *Assessment and treatment of co-occurring disorders: Alcohol, other drug abuse and mental illness*. Baton Rouge, LA: Louisiana Association of Substance Abuse Counselors and Trainers.

McLellan, A. T., et al. (1992). The fifth addition of the addiction severity index. *Journal of Substance Abuse Treatment, 9*, 199–213.

Millon, T. (1992). Millon clinical multiaxial inventory: I and II. *Journal of Counseling and Development, 70*(3), 421–426.

Morey, L. C. (1991). *The personality assessment inventory: Professional manual*. Odessa, FL: Personality Assessment Resources.

National Institute of Mental Health. (2009). *Depression: A treatable illness (fact sheet)*. Washington, DC: U.S. Department of Health and Human Services.

Peters, R. H. (1992). Referral and screening for substance abuse treatment in jails. *Journal of Mental Health Administration, 19*(1), 53–75.

Peters, R. H., & Bartoi, M. G. (1997). Screening and assessment of co-occurring disorders in the justice system. The National Gains Center for people with co-occurring disorders in the justice system. Policy Research Inc.

Peters, R. H., & Greenbaum, P. E. (1996). *Texas Department of Criminal Justice/Center for Substance Abuse Treatment Prison Substance Abuse Screening Project*. Millford, MA: Civigenics, Inc.

Robins, L. N., Helzer, J. E., Croughan, J., & Ratcliff, K. S. (1981). National institute of mental health diagnostic interview schedule: Its history, characteristics, and validity. *Archives of General Psychiatry, 38*, 381–389.

Simpson, D. D. (1993). *TCU Forms Manual: Drug abuse treatment for AIDS-risk reduction (DATAR)*. Fort Worth, TX: Texas Christian University Institute of Behavioral Research.

Skinner, H. A., & Horn, J. L. (1984). *Alcohol dependence scale: User's guide*. Toronto: Addiction Research Foundation.

Stone, A., Greenstein, R., Gamble, G., & McLellan, A. T. (1993). Cocaine use in chronic schizophrenia outpatients receiving depot neuroleptic medications. *Hospital and Community Psychiatry, 44*, 176–177.

Teplin, L. A., & Schwartz, J. (1989). Screening for severe mental disorder in jails. *Law and Human Behavior, 13*(1), 1–18.

Watson, A., Hanrahan, P., Luchins, D., & Lurigio, A. (2001). Mental health courts and the complex issue of mentally ill offenders. *Psychiatric Services, 52*(4), 477–481.

Weiss, R. D., & Mirin, S. M. (1989). The dual diagnosis alcoholic: Evaluation and treatment. *Psychiatric Annals, 19*(5), 261–265.

9

Youth Counseling and Juvenile Offenders

CHAPTER OBJECTIVES

After reading this chapter, you will be able to:

1. Identify and discuss the various mental health issues that compound the difficulties in treating juvenile offenders.
2. Explain how family-of-origin issues may be an important consideration for juvenile offenders.
3. Explain why sex counseling is particularly important for juvenile offender population.
4. Describe some of the topics that should be covered when delivering culturally competent interventions to juvenile offenders.
5. Identify and discuss the various reasons for youth obtaining gang affiliation.

PART ONE: BACKGROUND ISSUES

Introduction

Treatment of youth who are found to be delinquent is one of the most common types of work that exists within the correctional counseling arena. Though most youth are not kept in detention centers there is still a high demand for therapists who work with youth. Even if juveniles are required to stay in a detention facility, their stay is likely to be short term when compared to jail and prison sentences for adults. Thus, correctional counselors working with youth are likely to do so in community-based settings as much as they are likely to do so in structured facility settings.

For chronic youthful offenders, there are a number of risk factors that will be discussed later in this chapter. Further, there are differences in the type of offending and the type of resources that each youth may have. Most youthful offenders engage in minor delinquent activities. While this may consist of the majority of delinquent youth, this chapter will focus primarily on those youth who have committed more serious crimes or ones that are violent in nature. Thus, students should understand that this chapter is not one that deals with the run-of-the-mill youngster who engages in low-key delinquent and/or status offenses but instead those youth who commit serious forms of burglary, gang-related activity, sexual assault, substance abuse, physical assaults, arson, and/or other more serious behaviors.

Family Issues

Within the families of origin of many serious juvenile offenders, there is some sort of family violence that may have occurred. While this is not to say that all households with a youth who is processed through the justice system is automatically an abusive home, it is to say that in many cases serious delinquency also correlates with a tumultuous home life that tends to have some level of conflict and domestic abuse. In this section, we will not yet address the issue of child abuse and neglect, but will simply make note of the fact that domestic abuse and family strife is common within the backgrounds of seriously delinquent youth. For male juveniles who are institutionalized due to some form of assault, it is not uncommon for them to have committed their crime against a male stepparent who was abusive to the youth's mother. This is a common observation among juvenile workers who work with male teens who are transferred to adult court for crimes against a family member. In such cases, the young male is acting in defense of his mother. In other cases, particularly with female delinquents, there may be a tendency to leave the home or to use substances as a means of escape. Though in both of these examples the youth have not been specifically abused, the effects of domestic abuse within the home generate their reactions and behaviors that become problematic within the juvenile justice system.

SUBSTANCE ABUSE IN THE FAMILY Another common observation among homes with seriously delinquent youth is the existence of substance abuse. Substance abuse problems in the home can exist among the parents and/or adult caretakers as well as among other siblings. When substance abuse habits exist among the parents, this can naturally have a negative impact on the youth. Even when substances are relatively soft drugs this can leave the youth with negative social messages.

However, even when substance abuse consists of the use of legal drugs, the youth is not likely spared of the negative influence. For example, the use of alcohol is legal for adults but, if the youth's home is domestically violent, alcohol tends to exacerbate the violence and the frequency of that violence. Further, alcoholic families have a wide range of issues that must be addressed, such as the ability of the alcoholic to maintain employment and even caring for the alcoholic. In many alcoholic homes, the child is "parentified" and actually serves in a capacity that is similar to the parent of the alcoholic. These youth will tend to be fairly responsible in taking care of the house but they may have problems with the school system due to their sense of extended autonomy. In other words, these youth may fail to follow up with their school work due to the roles that they fill at home.

Homes where substance abuse problems are a chronic and routine issue seldom have any true stability. Indeed, when one or both parents are in and out of treatment over a number of years, this often tends to impair the relationship that is maintained with the child. As we will see in Chapter 11, female offenders tend to be the primary caretakers of their children. Thus, from one point in time to another, these women are likely to be in jail, residential treatment, or prison and will not likely have much contact with their children. Likewise, fathers in the home may also be absent on a routine basis if they are addicts. Just like female offenders, these men will tend to have intermittent stints in jail, residential treatment, or prison, with returns back into the community that tend to be short-lived.

The main point is that youth who grow up in family systems that are afflicted by drug or alcohol abuse tend to be fairly chaotic and unstable. Unstable homes tend to breed delinquency and more serious forms of criminality among youth. Therefore, youth who come from homes with substance abuse problems should be given specific group interventions to address this issue. This is even true if the drug or alcohol abuse was at the hands of a sibling rather than a parent or adult. Indeed, siblings can have a strong impact on one another and younger siblings are likely to emulate the actions of their older siblings, especially if the parents are absent due to their own chaotic drug-using lifestyle.

Child Abuse and Neglect: Correlates with Delinquency

When delinquent behavior occurs, it may bring about further abuse, resulting in a vicious cycle that generates behavior that continues to get worse and worse. Children and adolescents who exhibit patterns of delinquency that emanate from the home often imitate the behaviors of parents or other family members. In some extremely dysfunctional homes, children may even be instructed on how to commit crimes. Though this may sound unusual, it is not unheard of, and there have been court cases where such occurrences have specifically been noted. Consider also that the crime of **contributing to the delinquency of a minor** is a form of neglect where an adult specifically facilitates the ability of youth to commit delinquent or criminal acts and encourages these youth to engage in such acts.

Aside from circumstances where adults deliberately teach youth to commit crimes, it would seem that the trauma experienced because of abuse and neglect also fosters delinquency in children. For instance, Ireland, Smith, and Thornberry (2002) examined official records and utilized longitudinal survey data and found a strong relationship between maltreatment and delinquent behaviors. This was especially true with drug use among youth. Interestingly, Ireland et al. (2002) found that early childhood maltreatment that did not extend into later years of childhood had little impact on negative behaviors in adolescence. Contrasting with this, they found that maltreatment in adolescence, as well as persistent maltreatment from childhood through adolescence, was consistently related to various types of delinquency. This same pattern was known when drug use among youth was separately examined, without the effects of other delinquent behaviors.

The research by Ireland et al. (2002) is important because this aids in demonstrating where much of the more serious offending among youth and young adults may come from. Though this does not explain all juvenile misbehavior, it does tend to be consistent in explaining etiology within a substantial portion of the more serious youthful offending as well as later adult offending. Consider the research by English, Widom, Spatz, and Brandford (2002) who note that there is strong relationship between child abuse, neglect, delinquency, adult criminality, and future violent criminal behavior. The research by English et al. (2002) clearly underscores our contention that, for the majority of hard-core youthful offenders, the prior homelife circumstances are interlaced with the youth's offending behavior. English et al. (2002) further note that abused and neglected children were 4.8 times more likely to be arrested as juveniles, 2 times more likely to be arrested as an adult, and they were 3.1 times more likely to be arrested for a violent crime than were subjects who were members of a matched control group.

From the research just presented, it should be clear that youth who come from abusive homes do indeed have an increased likelihood of engaging in serious delinquency, drug abuse, and later adult criminality. The authors of this text believe that this is an important point to emphasize because the focus of this text is on the offender population. While we recognize that a large number of youth engage in minor forms of delinquency, we contend that much of the minor delinquency (i.e., teen age sex, use of alcohol at an occasional outing, speeding and minor traffic violations, violating minor ordinances) is actually part and parcel to the development of many teens. Indeed, these activities are often simply considered the process by which youth experience their newly budding sense of adolescent autonomy. However, when delinquency goes beyond the minor types of activity, such as with full-fledged burglaries (as opposed to petty shoplifting), drug use that goes beyond alcohol and marijuana, assaultive behavior, and other actions such as teen rape, we contend that in many cases prior childhood socialization and exposure to noxious family and peer influences are a common thread in etiology.

Other researchers share similar views on minor delinquent behavior among adolescents, going so far as to say that it is statistically normal among young boys growing up in the United States (Moffitt, 1993). According to Terrie Moffitt (1993), youthful antisocial and risk-prone acts are personal statements of independence. For example, these youth may engage in underage drinking or cigarette smoking, particularly with their peers, as a means of displaying "adult-like" behaviors. Another common form of delinquency for this group might be minor vandalism that is often perceived more as a "gag" rather than an act of victimization (actions such as the defacing of road signs, the destruction of residential mailboxes, and other petty forms of destruction). Shoplifting in various stores may also be encouraged among some members of this group for the occasional "five finger discount" in chosen music and/or clothing stores that are frequented by the adolescent peer group—displaying bravado among one's peers and, incidentally, obtaining an item that is valued by the individual and the peer group in the process. Lastly, some of these individuals may engage in occasional truancy from school, particularly if they are able to hide their absence. These adolescents typically commit acts of defiance or nonconformity simply as a means of expressing their developing sense of autonomy. However, these adolescents are not likely to continue their activities into late adulthood. Moffitt (1993) referred to these youth as **adolescent-only offenders**.

While youth who might be classified as adolescent-only offenders may occasionally be in need of some sort of counseling for any number of life-course issues, they seldom will need to see a treatment provider who specializes in the offender population. In more instances than not, these youth will age out of their behavior and will have no need for a correctional counselor. Rather, general counseling that addresses teen development, social pressure, peer groups, and other common aspects of development are likely to be more effective for this group.

On the other hand, some adolescents continue their delinquent behavior into and throughout adulthood; these are what Moffitt (1993) referred to as the **life-course-persistent juvenile** delinquents. Unlike the adolescent-limited delinquent, these adolescents lack many of the necessary social skills and opportunities possessed by the adolescent-limited delinquent. The reason for this difference in development is quite startling but nonetheless a common phenomenon to this group. For these offenders, the clue to their difference in conformative ability lies less in their adolescent years as much as it does with their early childhood development; many of these youth will have suffered from some sort of trauma and/or child abuse.

Indeed, it has been found that many life-course-persistent delinquents are children with inherited or acquired physiological deficiencies that develop either prenatally or in early childhood. To compound this problem, many of these same children often come from abusive social environments as well, reflecting the parental deficiencies that are transmitted intergenerationally from parent to child (Moffitt, 1993). This combination of the difficult child with an adverse child-rearing context (i.e., an abusive home) serves to place the child at risk for future delinquent behavior, setting the initial groundwork for a life-course-persistent pattern of antisocial behavior during years when the child is usually most impressionable (Moffit, 1993). Moffitt also found that early aggressive behavior is an important predictor of later delinquency and could possibly be a marker for the life-course-persistent offender.

TYPES OF CHILD ABUSE AND DETECTION OF ABUSE In many cases, juvenile youth are victims of various forms of neglect or abuse. This is a very important aspect of juvenile offending, particularly in community corrections. In many cases, community supervision officers will find themselves networking with child protection agencies and will likewise tend to have offenders on their caseloads who are in need of parenting assistance, whether the offender realizes it or not. Further, one must consider that over 70% of female offenders on community supervision are also the primary caretakers of their children. This is an important observation, especially when one considers that the proportion of female offenders on community supervision is much higher than those that are incarcerated. This means that community supervision officers are likely to come across issues related to the welfare of children on a fairly frequent basis. Further still, among a high number of delinquent youth, disproportionate rates of abuse and neglect occur.

In discussing these issues, we first turn our focus to child neglect since such maltreatment is often a precursor to later forms of abuse and also occurs in conjunction with abusive treatment. **Child neglect** occurs when a parent or caretaker of the child does not provide the proper or necessary support, education, medical, or other remedial care that is required by a given state's law, including food, shelter, and clothing. Child neglect also occurs when adult caretakers abandon a child that they are legally obligated to support (Cox, Allen, Hanser, & Conrad, 2008). Neglect is typically divided into three types: physical, emotional, and educational (Cox et al., 2008). **Physical neglect** includes abandonment; the expulsion of the child from the home (being kicked out of the house); excessive delay in or not seeking medical care for the child; inadequate supervision; and inadequate food, clothing, and shelter (Cox et al., 2008). **Emotional neglect** includes inadequate nurturing or affection, allowing the child to engage in inappropriate or illegal behavior such as drug or alcohol use, as well as ignoring a child's basic emotional needs (Cox et al., 2008). Lastly, **educational neglect** occurs when a parent or even a teacher permits chronic truancy or simply ignores the educational and/or special needs of a child (Cox et al., 2008).

The impact of neglect is not as readily observable as is abuse. Over time, however, the long-term effects to the child can be just as damaging as they are when a child is overtly abused. Among the offender population, child neglect is not at all uncommon. In cases where either the male or female parent is a serious drug abuser, it may be common for the child to be neglected. In fact, there are some circumstances where the oldest child may be *parentified* and delegated responsibility of caring for younger siblings while also taking care of the parent as well. As noted in the previous section of this text, **child parentification** occurs when he or she is placed in a position within a family system whereby they must assume the primary caretaker role for that family, often taking care of both children and adults within that family system. This is common in single head-of-household families where the adult caretaker is an alcoholic or drug abuser, and even in some dual adult household families, particularly those that are criminogenic in nature.

Interestingly, children that are neglected, including those that are parentified, often do not realize that they are necessarily being mistreated. Even if they do, many have no recourse and when coupled with the emotional bonds that they may have with their siblings, they are unlikely to leave or report such maltreatment on their own. These inappropriate family circumstances lead to very poor socialization in many cases, with children observing negative behaviors and developing criminogenic mindsets. Thus, these toxic family systems help to breed a new generation of persons who are susceptible to further perpetuation of the criminal lifestyle. It is because of this that community supervision officers overseeing juvenile offenders must take into account the family situation, encouraging family involvement when the family is functional and recommending family interventions when the family is not functional.

Beyond child neglect, acts of abuse are even more serious forms of maltreatment and include both physical and psychological forms of harm. **Child abuse** occurs when a child (under the age of 18 in most states) is maltreated by a parent, an immediate family member, or any person responsible for the child's welfare (Cox et al., 2008). Child maltreatment can include physical, sexual, and emotional abuse as well as physical, emotional, and even educational neglect from the caretaker (Cox et al., 2008). There are varying degrees of abuse and, in many cases, multiple forms of abuse may have been inflicted against the child. Further, these youth may also come from homes where there is domestic abuse between spouses or significant others. Research has shown that among juvenile sex offenders, the existence of child abuse is a common characteristic among such offenders in the United States as well as other countries (Hanser & Mire, 2008). The existence of abuse in a youth's background is an important observation to attend to, since aberrant behaviors are likely to have been learned from other dysfunctional family members. In some cases, the youth's behavior may be a form of acting-out against the stress and frustration of their toxic family environment.

According to Cox et al. (2008), **physical abuse** "can be defined as any physical acts that cause or can cause physical injury to a child" (p. 266). These authors go on to describe child abuse as a vicious cycle that involves parents who have unrealistic expectations of their children, thereby getting easily frustrated with the shortcomings that they perceive their children to have. It is not uncommon for such parents to have themselves been abused as children, resulting in an intergenerational transmission of violence through their abusive behavior. The extent of the harsh discipline tends to depend on the level of frustration that the parent feels, their ability to regulate their own emotions, and their views on appropriate parenting and discipline practices. The level of parenting skills and the age of the child often affect the type of abuse and frequency of abuse that is inflicted, since younger children are less able to defend themselves and/or perhaps run away.

Further, this type of treatment can greatly exacerbate any potential diagnoses that the young person might have (such as those just discussed in prior subsections) and this further complicates potential treatment approaches for that child. In fact, it may well be that the adult family members themselves have a number of mental health issues and this adds further difficulty to the family situation. Within such family environments, it is unlikely that the youth will be able to ever achieve any sense of normalcy or positive support. The parent's own challenges will tend to aggravate those problems facing the youth, and the youth's behavior will in turn serve as a further aggravating factor for their own maladaptive parenting. The two then will tend to continually fuel the dysfunction within the family system, thereby ensuring that the maladaptive system continues. In such cases, it is not likely that the juvenile should remain within the family system and it should be considered that the youth's behavior is perhaps a symptom of what is an unhealthy family grouping.

Psychological abuse is the third most frequently reported form of child abuse, with physical abuse and child neglect being the first and second most common types of abuse. Psychological abuse is somewhat vague and hard to define. Definitions that are too narrow are not likely to capture the various aspects of psychological abuse that might exist within an adult–child relationship that is abusive. On the other hand, definitions that are too broad may be nearly impossible to clearly identify in quantitative terms for research and/or in a legally substantive manner that could aid law enforcement and prosecutors. Because of these difficulties, this is the most difficult form of abuse to prosecute, being somewhat elusive when put to rigorous examination. Further, the difficulty in proving this abuse makes it likely that much of it goes unreported since it is so difficult to detect, prove, and document.

Psychological abuse is also sometimes referred to as emotional abuse and includes actions or the omission of actions by parents and other caregivers that could cause the child to have serious behavioral, emotional, or mental impairments. In some instances of psychological abuse, there is no clear or evident behavior of the adult caregiver that provides indication of the abuse. Rather, the child displays behavior that is impaired and/or has emotional disturbances that result from profound forms of emotional abuse, trauma, distance, or neglect. This is an issue that should be seriously considered when children present with diagnosable disorders, particularly those that are obsessive/compulsive, dissociative, anxiety-based, and/or oppositional/defiant in nature.

When considering children with disorders such as those just previously indicated, it should be taken to mean that the caregiver is necessarily the cause of the disorder, though that likelihood can certainly exist as well. Rather, it may well be that the child presents with these disorders and, due to frustration, the parent resorts to punishments that are bizarre or unorthodox in nature. For example, parents of a strongly oppositional child may resort to locking the child in a dark closet as a means of containing the child and also depriving him or her of stimuli that may heighten the child's emotionality. While this may have a basis of logic to it, this type of punishment is not appropriate yet may occur for long periods of time. In the process, the child's short-term behavior may be adjusted, but his or her sense of long-term maladjustment is further aggravated; in short, the parents contribute to the emotional disturbances that the child exhibits. On the other hand, parents who are psychologically abusive may also actually be a causal factor in a child developing any variety of emotional or adjustment disorders. Children who are psychologically abused may present with depression, anxiety, dissociative, and so forth. In such cases, the treatment from the caregiver negatively impacts that child's ability to thrive, resulting in an emotionally impaired child.

When neglect or abuse is detected within the home of a juvenile on a community supervision officer's caseload and/or when an adult offender is thought to be neglecting or abusing his or her children, correctional counselors must remember that they are under a legal obligation to report these actions to child protection services within that state. In reality, most all citizens are required to report this activity anytime they observe it occurring, but correctional counselors are especially liable and are required to make these reports. Further, the correctional counselor must make these reports even if he or she believes that others have already filed a report about the abuse. In short, the correctional counselor cannot simply rely on the good word of others that a report was filed. Once the abuse is reported, child protection officials typically then generate a risk assessment and make a decision regarding the best type of action to be taken that meets the best interests of the child.

Sexual abuse of youth consists of any sexual contact or attempted sexual contact that occurs between an adult or designated caretaker and a child. It should be noted that it is rare that physical indicators of sexual abuse are found. This means that most sexual abuse is detected due to behavioral indicators and/or when the youth discloses such acts. Possible behavioral indicators might include observations such as an unwillingness to change clothes or to participate in physical education classes; withdrawal, fantasy, or infantile behavior not typical of a teen; bizarre sexual behavior; sexual sophistication that is beyond the child's age (a bit hard to gauge with teens); delinquent runaway behavior; and reports of being sexually assaulted.

The behavior of parents also may provide indicators of sexual abuse. Such behaviors may include jealousy and being overprotective of a child. A parent may hesitate to report a spouse who is sexually abusing their child for fear of destroying the marriage or fear of retaliation. In some cases, intrafamilial sex may be considered a better option than extramarital sex. Lastly, sexual abuse of children can have numerous side effects, including guilt, shame, anxiety, fear, depression, anger, low self-esteem, concerns about secrecy, feelings of helplessness, and a strong need for others. In addition, victims of sexual abuse have higher level of school absenteeism, less participation in extracurricular activities, and lower grades.

Emotional Storm and Stress

During adolescence, there are substantial changes that take place within the development of youth. While this is common knowledge among parents, school teachers, and child development experts, this does not necessarily seem to be sufficiently touched upon by most texts on correctional counseling. We believe that it is important that the emotional aspects of the youth's development are covered, along with other issues that seem to be specifically relevant to adolescent youth.

Erik Erikson developed a theory of psychosocial development in 1975 that has continued to shape how modern day mental health and counseling experts view human development throughout the life span. According to Erik Erikson's (1975) theory of psychosocial development, youth who are in adolescence must contend with a developmental period where identity versus identity confusion becomes a primary hurdle in the youth's psychological formation. For the teen who is experiencing rapid growth and making a transition to adulthood, the search of one's place in society can be unpredictable, stressful, and frustrating.

Indeed, the roles open to teens are influenced by ethnic and racial background, geographic location, values within the family of origin, and their own peer-group social values. Correctional counselors who work with youthful offenders much keep these variables in mind when working with youth. Because of these vast differences in background, youth will have varying perceptions on what they should strive for and/or what is important. According to Davis and Palladino (2002), teens in the United States who have explored the alternatives and adopted a well-chosen set of values, goals, and sense of self will have reached identity achievement. In such cases, these youth will have a good sense of psychological well-being. But in other instances, the frustrations involved with meeting the challenges of this stage of development may prove so unpleasant as to result in a rejection of typical pro-social expectations. In such cases, the teen may adopt behaviors that are opposite to those that would be expected. This results in a **negative identity** and can affect the youth's sense of self and their view of their own place in the world.

In addition, youth who are not given support and guidance may experience **identity diffusion** (Erikson, 1975). This occurs when the teen has few goals and little motivation. These youth will often be indifferent to their schoolwork, the desire for friends, and/or planning for the future. These youth often have a sick sense of genuine self-identity. Youth who develop a negative identity and/or experience identity diffusion are at risk of engaging in delinquent behaviors. This is particularly true if their peer group is involved in delinquent activity.

ANGER AND AGGRESSION Anger is a normal response to frustration and interference (Morris, 1991). In some cases, anger can be appropriate and can even lead to a constructive outcome. For example, a youngster upset about unfair treatment in school may channel his or her anger to work constructively within a student organization or through some civic group to voice his or her desire for change. Others may channel their frustrations into other pursuits resulting in what is referred to as sublimation. **Sublimation** occurs when a person has pent up frustration, stress, and/or aggressive feelings and they channel those feelings toward some activity or pursuit that allows them to act on those feelings in a manner that is considered socially acceptable. For example, some youth who have feelings of aggression may find themselves drawn to heavy-contact sports such as football, wrestling, or boxing. These types of activities relieve tension through physical exercise and they provide a sense of mastery in defeating persons in competition. Others may find gratification from competitive activities that, while not physically grueling, provide a sense of mastery over circumstance and/or over persons in competition, such as with debate teams and/or even art competitions. This is not to imply that all competitive activities are simply ruses under which masked anger is allowed to manifest. Rather, this is just to demonstrate that some people who experience anger, stress, and frustration may utilize various mechanisms to exert that energy in a manner that does not lead to delinquency.

However, it is more often that anger leads to destructive forms of aggression. Aggression is any hostile action that is intended to harm, humiliate, or scare another person and it can be caused through physical or psychological means. Naturally, the use of overt violence is an act of aggression and when youth behave in such a manner they are engaged in an act of delinquent conduct. However aggression also occurs when we say or do something in anger to intentionally hurt someone's feelings and/or cause them psychological discomfort. Thus, when youth make sarcastic comments about another person, particularly in the presence of a peer group, and the comment is intended to embarrass the person (especially in front of one's peers), this is an act of psychological aggression. On the other extreme, if a group of youth decide to collectively refuse to speak to a member of the group and refuse to allow that youth to associate with the group, this is also an act of aggression.

Relational aggression is any behavior that is intended to harm someone by damaging or manipulating relationships with someone. This type of aggression can include gossip or rumors that are spread to humiliate or embarrass another youth. Teasing, taunting, and exclusion from a peer group are all psychological means of victimizing a person. This type of aggression is more often used by females than males, but even though this aggression is not physical and even though it may seem to be associated with feminine social cunning, it should not be discounted or taken lightly. Indeed, such activities can be quite mean spirited and even extend into the world of cyberspace where forms of cyberbullying can produce lethal outcomes for some youth. Cyberbullying may be direct communications with the victim or the simple posting of derogatory information online for other youth in the peer group to view.

While the purpose of this subsection is not to discuss specific acts of aggression in detail, it is hoped that the reader will understand that aggression comes in many forms and that it can take a serious toll on the development of a young person's sense of self. Further, the youth that correctional counselors are likely to see will have problems with anger and aggression in many cases. Later, in Chapter 10, we present specific information on anger management programs. These types of programs and the use of anger management group interventions are frequently required among many adjudicated youth. An understanding of how these groups are implemented as well as the underlying dynamics related to anger problems among youth is important for correctional counselors. Thus, students are encouraged to read the anger management section in Chapter 10 and, while doing so, to consider its application to both adult and juvenile clients.

UNHEALTHY SELF-EFFICACY Self-efficacy is an individual's own belief about his or her ability to successfully accomplish certain desired goals and/or behaviors. The greater a person's sense of self-efficacy, the more able he or she is to meet the challenges that exist in life. Self-efficacy is an important characteristic for juveniles and for adults. In the case of teens, self-efficacy is forming and is impacted by the experiences that are first encountered within the family and later within broader society. When children are encouraged and provided support, their sense of self-efficacy is likely to be high, or at least suitable for life's challenges. However, when children are subject to emotional or psychological abuse, their sense of self-efficacy will likely be low. This often results in the child (and later the teen) reacting in some manner that is problematic.

Children who do not think well of themselves are likely to internalize negative emotions. This is even more likely if the household itself is host to numerous negative relationships among family members and/or caretakers. When youth are raised in negative surroundings and if these youth are not involved with pro-social activities and are within the vicinity of delinquent peers, the likelihood that negative behaviors will occur is increased. In fact, there is a large body of criminological research that demonstrates the influence of delinquent peers upon a youth's involvement in delinquent activity. However, when youth have a healthy sense of self-efficacy, the pull of delinquency will not tend to be as great. While this is not to say that youth with high self-efficacy will not engage in delinquent acts, it is to say that such youth will be unlikely to engage in serious acts of delinquency and criminal activity, particularly on a long-term basis.

GRIEF Grief is commonly associated with a sense of loss. The grief response may include a flat affect and a lack of interest in positive activities. With grief some form of depression is common and this is a common reaction to the death of someone valued by a given person. Among today's youth, death and bereavement are not entirely uncommon, particularly among juveniles who grow up in impoverished areas of the United States where crime rates are high. Indeed, among youth who are members of gangs or who have grown up in domestically violent homes, a sense of grief may be a common emotion. Later, in Chapter 13, we will discuss the stages of grief and the treatment of grief.

It should be pointed out that grief can be experienced from any type of loss. For instance, divorce within the family may lead to a sense of grief among children over the loss of having both parents in the home. Children and adolescents may need time to process their emotional response to such developments where anxiety and depression are likely to emerge. Also, youth who have a parent incarcerated may feel a sense of grief since that parent will essentially be lost to the child while in the criminal justice system. Thus, grief manifests itself through a variety of means that commonly impact juvenile offenders.

DEPRESSION Depression is the feeling of being dejected and uninterested in committing to any particular action. A deflated sense of self, listlessness, low initiative, and other signs of unhappiness and a lack of caring characterize depression. Depression is often referred to as a type of mood disorder that includes major depressive disorder, bipolar disorder, and dystymic disorder. For purposes of this section and this chapter, we will restrict our discussion to major depressive disorders since these are the most problematic and most common among teens. Major depressive disorder is characterized by one or more major depressive episodes (i.e., at least two weeks of depressed mood or loss of interest accompanied by at least four additional symptoms of depression). Major depressive disorder is the most common mood disorder associated with the offender population (both adult and juvenile).

According to the *DSM-IV-TR*, the degree of impairment associated with **major depressive disorder** varies, but even in mild cases, there must be either clinically significant distress or some interference in social, occupational, or other important areas of functioning (p. 351). The afflicted youth will likely have decreased energy, tiredness, and fatigue without physical exertion. Even the smallest tasks may seem to require substantial effort. Further, these individuals often have a sense of worthlessness or guilt that may include unrealistic negative evaluations of one's worth or guilty preoccupations or ruminations over minor past failings. Such individuals often misinterpret neutral or trivial day-to-day events as evidence of personal defects and have an exaggerated sense of responsibility for untoward events (*DSM-IV-TR*, p. 350). There are multiple designations for depression within the *DSM-IV* and these various subcategories of diagnosis can be confusion and somewhat overly complicated for the layperson. Much of the differences in these categories have to do with the factors that led to the onset of depression such as life-course events, the use of toxic substances, or even physiological factors. To provide a complete overview of each of these types of depression would go well beyond the scope of this chapter. However, the following symptoms are included since they are the most frequently encountered among the gamut of depression categories of diagnosis. Specifically, the National Institute of Mental Health (2002) notes that a person experiencing major depression is likely to present with:

- Persistent sad, anxious, or "empty" mood
- Feelings of hopelessness, pessimism
- Feelings of guilt, worthlessness, helplessness
- Loss of interest or pleasure in hobbies and activities that were once enjoyed, including sex
- Decreased energy, fatigue, being "slowed down"
- Difficulty concentrating, remembering, making decisions
- Insomnia, early-morning awakening, or oversleeping
- Appetite and/or weight loss or overeating and weight gain
- Thoughts of death or suicide; suicide attempts
- Restlessness, irritability
- Persistent physical symptoms that do not respond to treatment, such as headaches, digestive disorders, and chronic pain.

The symptoms cited by the National Institute of Mental Health (NIMH) are common symptoms cited by most anyone presenting with depression. These symptoms were provided due to their compatibility with clinical symptoms in the *DSM-IV-TR* and to provide a general clinical overview of depression symptoms. However, there are some specific symptoms that are related to teens and that are not typically noted among adults. These symptoms should be seen as indicators of depression and might include attempts to run away from the family and/or home, problems with school performance (truancy or not paying attention in class), a lack of concern with appearance, persistent physical ailments that are not common to that age group (i.e., constant headaches, fatigue, or stomachaches), a reduction in contact with one's peer group and/or a sudden change in peer groups, a tendency to gravitate toward dark or somber topics, and/or self mutilation (Family First Aid, 2009).

Research on teen depression shows that youth are most vulnerable between the ages of 12 and 17, with older age ranges having more frequency of depression. One study, the National Survey on Drug Use and Health, provided specific percentages for youth ages 12 through 17 (Figure 9.1). It is important to point out that these percentages only include youth who have had major forms of depression but not youth with other less severe categories. If all categories had been considered, the percentages would likely be higher. Students should also keep in mind that Figure 9.1 refers only to depression in the past year among youth and does not include depression throughout the lifetime; if it did, the percentages would most assuredly be higher. Thus, Figure 9.1 illustrates a conservative presentation of the percentages of youth who present with depression.

It is unfortunate that so many teens suffer from depression but it is even more unfortunate that only roughly one in four youth receive treatment for this disorder (National Institute

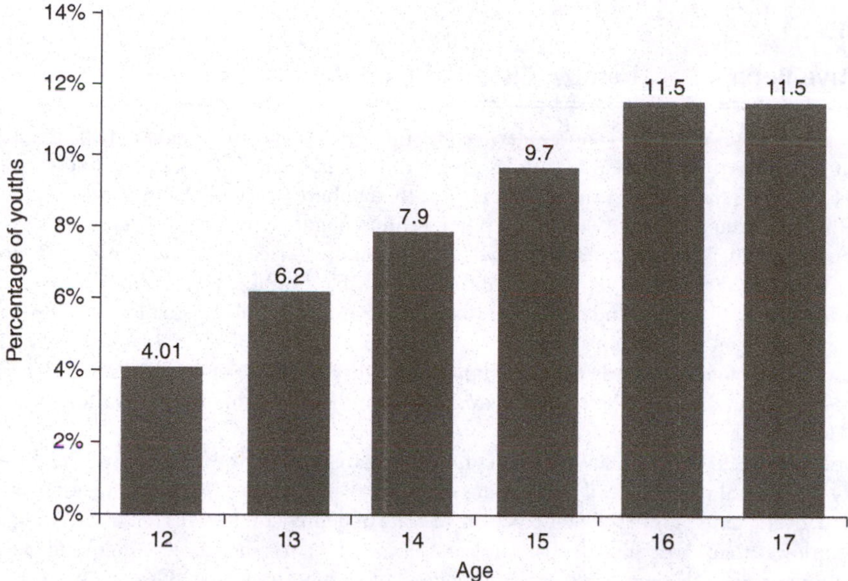

FIGURE 9.1 Percentage of Youths Aged 12–17 Who Experienced a Past-Year Major Depressive Episode (MDE), by Age (2004–2006) *Source:* Substance Abuse and Mental Health Services Administration, Office of Applied Studies. (2008). *The NSDUH report: Major depressive episode among youths aged 12 to 17 in the United States: 2004 to 2006*. Rockville, MD. Retrieved from: http://www.oas.samhsa.gov/2k8/youthDepress/youthDepress.pdf.

of Mental Health, 2009). Further, it has been found that depression in teens is quite treatable. Indeed, the Treatment for Adolescents with Depression (TADS) series of studies, sponsored and directed by the NIMH, found that combination treatment is a safe and very effective means of providing treatment for adolescents with depression (2004). By combination treatment, the NIMH is referring to treatments that use both medications as well as psychotherapy. The TADS study found that the combination of antidepressants (particularly SSRI inhibitors) and the use of cognitive behavioral therapy (CBT) were particularly effective. The use of CBT has been mentioned throughout this text as a premiere treatment modality. This type of therapy has consistently received empirical support throughout a variety of domains and with a diverse array of clients and client issues. Exhibit 9.1 provides additional insight on the effectiveness of this treatment modality.

FEAR, ANXIETY, AND POST-TRAUMATIC STRESS DISORDER It is important to first distinguish between fear and anxiety. Fear is typically used to describe a response to a specific and known threat. Anxiety, on the other hand, is more general in nature and is not always targeted at a specific source of concern or stress. Often, fear and anxiety may seem to be one and the same. But, fear is a response to the clearly perceived and understood aspects of a dangerous situation and anxiety is related to the less predictable aspects of a situation.

A primary reason that anxiety is presented is because it tends to occur among children who are in dysfunctional homes and it is also a common symptom among substance abusers and persons with depression. Further, the existence of post-traumatic stress disorder is common among

EXHIBIT 9.1

Cognitive Behavioral Therapy (CBT) and Teen Depression

While research from numerous sources have confirmed the efficacy of cognitive behavioral therapy (CBT), it is perhaps the Treatment for Adolescents with Depression (TADS) series of studies, sponsored and directed by the National Institute of Mental Health, that have proven to be the most comprehensive and multifaceted examination of depression among children and teens. The TADS research has consistently found that CBT is highly effective with depression among teens, just as it is with adults. In particular, one study in 2004 found that while medication and CBT combined was more effective than CBT alone, this same study did conclude that, over time, the effects of CBT alone tend to "catch up" with outcomes observed from the combination treatment (National Institute of Mental Health, 2004). Further, other research has found that, when stacked up against other modalities of treatment, CBT has consistently produced superior outcome effects with depression among adolescents (National Institute of Mental Health, 2009).

Specifically, the NIMH 2009 study sought to compare treatment outcomes between those using cognitive behavioral program and those using other types of affective-based therapeutic care. It was found that, over a nine-month follow-up period, the rate of depression in teens in the CBT program was 11 percent lower than those in the usual care condition—21.4% versus 32.7%. Adolescents in the prevention program also self-reported lower levels of depression symptoms than those in usual care. Among teens whose parents were not depressed at the beginning of the study, the program was more effective in preventing onset of depression than usual care—11.7% versus 40.5%. However, this advantage did not hold for youth in the CBT if they had a parent who was depressed at the start of the study. Such teens had significantly higher rates of depression than those without a currently depressed parent.

This study is just one of many that have consistently found that CBT interventions are superior to other types of interventions when sound and rigorous methodological research principles are utilized. Further, this government-funded research, as part of the TADS project, has utilized numerous clinics and facilities throughout the United States. Results are consistent with diverse populations and in different geographical locations throughout the nation. All of this lends to the generalizable nature of the research and demonstrates that CBT is perhaps the treatment of choice for youth with depression. This type of intervention has been shown to be more effective than those based on other orientations and, over time, it is even as effective as combined treatments. Though combined treatments may provide a quick positive outcome (useful in client circumstances that are crisis oriented) it is the CBT component, not the medication, that would appear to provide the long-term benefit for teens who face depression.

Sources: National Institute of Mental Health. (2004). *Combination treatment most effective in adolescents with depression.* Bethesda, MD: National Institute of Mental Health. Retrieved from: http://www.nimh.nih.gov/science-news/2004/combination-treatment-most-effective-in-adolescents-with-depression.shtml; National Institute of Mental Health (2009). *Re-shaping negative thoughts shields at-risk teens from depression.* Bethesda, MD: National Institute of Mental Health. Retrieved from: http://www.nimh.nih.gov/publicat/nimhdepression.pdf

victims of abuse and it is also included in this section since many juveniles (especially those suffering from serious physical and/or sexual abuse) may have symptoms of this disorder.

Post-traumatic stress disorder (PTSD) is a reaction that can occur when a person has been exposed to a traumatic event in which both of the following were present:

1. The person experienced, witnessed, or was confronted with an event or events that involved actual or threatened death or serious injury, or a threat to the physical integrity of self or others.
2. The person's response involved intense fear, helplessness, or horror.

Further, the individual must present with the following symptoms for a period that is longer than one month. The individual will have PTSD if the traumatic event is persistently reexperienced in one (or more) of the following ways:

1. Recurrent and intrusive distressing recollections of the event, including images, thoughts, or perceptions
2. Recurrent distressing dreams of the event
3. Acting or feeling as if the traumatic event were recurring
4. Intense psychological distress at exposure to internal or external cues that resemble the traumatic event
5. Physiological reactivity to the exposure to the internal or external cues that resemble the event.

Other factors that may indicate PTSD are persistent avoidance of stimuli that are associated with the trauma and numbing of general responsiveness, as indicated by three (or more) of the following:

1. Efforts to avoid thoughts, feelings, or conversations associated with the trauma
2. Efforts to avoid activities, places, or people that arouse recollections of the trauma
3. Inability to recall an important aspect of the trauma
4. Markedly diminished interest or participation in significant activities
5. Feeling of detachment or estrangement from others
6. Restricted range of affect
7. Sense of a foreshortened future.

Persistent symptoms of increased arousal (not present before the traumatic event), as indicated by two (or more) of the following:

1. Difficulty falling or staying asleep
2. Irritability or outbursts of anger
3. Difficulty concentrating
4. Hypervigilance
5. Exaggerated startle responses.

This disorder is commonly found among juvenile girls and among adult female offenders due to prior childhood sexual abuse. Quite often, the female offender (particularly those involved in the sex trade and/or having addiction problems) will have at least mild levels of this disorder. Likewise, as odd as it may seem, many juvenile sex offenders may present with this disorder due to similar childhood sexual abuse that has been inflicted against them. As it turns out, many juvenile sex offenders learn their means of acting out from having been victimized themselves. This is also consistent with the research that indicates that many sex offenders are themselves victims of prior childhood sexual abuse. The connection between the prior childhood sexual trauma and future sex offending by perpetrators is discussed in Chapter 12 on sex offender etiology and treatment.

SUICIDAL THOUGHTS Perhaps one of the most difficult and worrisome areas of dealing with juveniles would be the onset of suicidal ideation. Suicide is the third leading cause of death among teens in the United States. Aside from the fact that suicide happens to be a leading cause of death among teens, suicidal thoughts also intertwine with feelings of depression and, in some instances, a sense of grief. One researcher has found that in many cases, youth who feel incompetent in areas that are important to them (self-efficacy), as well as when they feel a lack of support from persons important in their lives such as parents or peers, feelings of hopelessness emerge

(Harter, 1990). Hopelessness then tends to lead to a depression composite, which includes low self-efficacy, general hopelessness, and a depressive affect.

Harter (1990) contends that there are powerful implications for both prevention and intervention. Harter (1990) notes that intervening at the front end, by influencing self-efficacy and social support, will have the greatest impact, since it is here that Harter has found that the chain of causal influences seem to begin. Thus, therapists should intervene to improve self-efficacy, by helping the individual to become more competent in areas in which he or she has aspirations or by aiding the individual to discount the importance of domains in which high levels of success are unlikely. Self-efficacy can also be improved by interventions that provide more opportunities for support and approval from significant others. Such interventions should not only enhance the youth's sense of self-efficacy, but it should also prevent further reinforcement of the insidious cycle that involves hopelessness, depression, and associated suicidal thoughts. Thus, the various points regarding juvenile development that have been discussed up until this point (i.e., self-efficacy, depression, grief, and anxiety) are ultimately relevant to ensuring the welfare of youth who may see no true purpose in continuing forward.

CONDUCT DISORDER It is the first five years of life that behavior related to child delinquency are established. This early years are closely dependent upon a child's individual characteristics and the family dynamics that exist. Risk factors at home include antisocial parents, mother suffering from depression, family poverty, marital strife, large family, history of family violence, and parents who abuse drugs or alcohol, discipline harshly and erratically, and rely on poor parenting practices.

In these cases, children that have persistent adjustment problems may present with a childhood disorder that is known as "conduct disorder." This term is the name of a diagnosis that is used by mental health practitioners and the criteria for this diagnosis is found in the *Diagnostic and Statistical Manual of Mental Disorders IV* (or the *DSM-IV-TR*). Certain characteristics of a child, such as a difficult temperament as an infant and depressed moods as a child, are risk factors for conduct disorder and/or future delinquency. If the child has been a victim of violence or if the child has been exposed to a steady dose of violence on television, in movies, and/or in video games, the child may be at increased risk of developing conduct disorder. Some factors stand out more than others but aggression seems to be the best predictor of conduct disorder. Thus, many factors can contribute to a child developing conduct disorder, including brain damage or trauma, child abuse, genetic vulnerability, school failure, or other traumatic life experiences.

Essentially, **conduct disorder** is a complex group of behavioral and emotional problems that are experienced by some children. The children and adolescents with this disorder have great difficulty following rules and behaving in a socially acceptable way. They are often viewed by other children, adults, and social agencies as "bad" or delinquent rather than disordered. According to the *DSM-IV-TR*, children with conduct disorder may exhibit a repetitive and persistent pattern of behavior in which the basic rights of others are violated. This is often manifested by the presence of three (or more) of the following criteria (all taken from the *DSM-IV-TR*) in the past 12 months, with at least one criterion present in the past six months:

Aggression to People and Animals

- bullies, threatens, or intimidates others
- often initiates physical fights
- has used a weapon that could cause serious physical harm to others (e.g., a bat, brick, broken bottle, knife, or gun)
- is physically cruel to people or animals

- steals from a victim while confronting them (e.g., assault)
- forces someone into sexual activity

Destruction of Property

- deliberately engaged in fire setting with the intention to cause damage
- deliberately destroys other's property

Deceitfulness, Lying, or Stealing

- has broken into someone else's building, house, or car
- lies to obtain goods or favors, or to avoid obligations
- steals items without confronting a victim (e.g., shoplifting, but without breaking and entering)

Serious Violations of Rules

- often stays out at night despite parental objections
- runs away from home
- often truant from school

Children that exhibit these behaviors should receive a comprehensive assessment. Many children with conduct disorder may have coexisting conditions as well, such as ADHD, learning disorders, or PSTD. Research shows that children with conduct disorder are more likely to have ongoing problems if they and their families do not receive early comprehensive treatment. Many children with conduct disorder are unable to adapt to the demands of adulthood and thus have repetitive problems with relationships, job performance, and legal issues. These children are at high risk of becoming a future adult offender.

SUBSTANCE ABUSE From the research, it is clear that youth are experimenting with drugs, alcohol, and tobacco at young ages. Typically, significant change in drug awareness and corresponding usage starts to take place around 12–13 years of ages. Indeed, youth around 13 years of age are three times more likely to know how to obtain marijuana or to know someone who uses illegal substances than are their 12-year-old counterparts (Ericson, 2001). Further, by the time youth enter eighth grade, roughly half will have tried alcohol, and about 1 in 5 will have smoked marijuana (Ericson, 2001). The use of drugs tends to increase mostly between eighth and ninth grade. Hess and Drowns make it clear, however, that although no single theory can explain the cause of juvenile delinquency, one fact is clear, "there is a direct connection between substance abuse and other forms of delinquency" (p. 86).

SECTION SUMMARY

In this section, it becomes clear that there is a multiplicity of issues to consider when providing interventions for juvenile offenders. When discussing interventions for juveniles, this chapter is largely focused on those offenders who are adjudicated for actions that are more seriously delinquent and/or criminal in nature. Many youth who present with serious offenses have a host of issues that negatively impact them. They may come from tumultuous family systems where abuse is common or their families may be plagued with substance abuse issues. These family-of-origin issues have a strong influence on the socialization of the youth and seem to exacerbate the likelihood that the youth will engage in serious forms of offending.

Likewise, adolescence is a period of storm and stress for most teens, and this is no different for youth who commit acts of delinquency. In fact, this is likely to be all the more true. Many youth who are adjudicated in the juvenile justice system tend to have a number of emotional and/or mental health challenges. For instance, anger problems and tendencies toward the use of aggression are common with these youth. Interventions that help youth identify their aggression and anger problems while teaching them to effectively utilize their assertiveness skills are important components of juvenile treatment. Further, many youth suffer from difficulties with their sense of self-efficacy. This impacts their overall self-identity, sense of confidence, and overall mental well-being. This is further exacerbated by the onset of substance abuse, depression, anxiety, and suicidal ideation, all of which are common and serious concerns with this population.

LEARNING CHECK

1. The use of aggression can be both physical and psychological.
   a. True
   b. False
2. The experience of child abuse is more common among the delinquent population than the non-delinquent juvenile population.
   a. True
   b. False
3. For the most part, fear and anxiety are the same concept.
   a. True
   b. False
4. Suicide is the number one cause of death among teens.
   a. True
   b. False
5. Many juveniles who have an adult substance abuser in the house are parentified and fulfill a family role of responsibility that exceeds what would normally be considered age appropriate.
   a. True
   b. False

PART TWO: SPECIAL ISSUES WITH YOUNG OFFENDERS

Counseling Offending Youth on Sex

When addressing youth on sex-related issues, it is important to keep in mind that many will already have a good idea about sex and sex-related topics. In fact, many will have been sexually active and even on a routine basis. However, many will not be conversant on specific anatomical issues associated with sexual activity and with the transmission of sexually transmitted diseases. In many cases, juvenile males will be much less informed than juvenile females. When conducting this type of counseling, it is recommended that correctional counselors use a youth-centered approach to counseling. This is similar to person-centered techniques discussed in Chapter 5; however, these techniques are geared toward reflection and listening to the youth's perspective. Importantly, youth-centered correctional counselors should provide pertinent and accurate information regarding sexuality, sexual health, and reproduction. Counselors in this role should work to demystify sexual myths, provide accurate and precise science-based information on sexuality, and provide practical strategies for the young person to act on the new information and skills learned. Among the typical counseling techniques and strategies, correctional counselors should use active listening to identify the youth's needs, and the counselor should express a sense of empathy. Keen observation of nonverbal behavior should be maintained with prompts from the counselor for relevant sexual health questions. Likewise, the correctional counselor using a youth-centered approach should provide reflection and summarization skills of the young client's personal situation and should develop a safe therapeutic relationship or alliance. The counselor is required to develop rapport and trust through appropriate self-disclosure while maintaining confidentiality. Lastly, it is very important that the counselor use age-appropriate language that the juvenile population will understand. The use of jargon and clinical terminology is to be avoided.

Confidentiality and consent issues are more complicated when working with adolescents. For adults, the choice to be tested is their own, and the process and results are confidential. For young people, guidelines vary on the age at which they can decide for themselves to be tested, as well as on when, or if, their parents or guardians must be notified of the test and the results. Naturally, this will be more relevant to youth who are on community supervision, but it may also be an important consideration when youth are in short-term detention. Correctional counselors should keep the following points in mind when working with juveniles:

- Youth often have different terminology for, and understanding of, sexual terms. In many cases there may be terms and slang that are used. It is recommended that the correctional counselor be well versed on this terminology. Though the counselor may know the terminology, it is not necessarily recommended that they incorporate the terminology in their own feedback and/or questions. If such use sounds artificial and/or if the youth seem uncomfortable with such informality from the counselor, then this technique should be avoided. On the other hand, if youth in therapy respond with additional dialogue and do not give indication that the use of common verbiage is not respected, then this can be a good means of joining and rapport building.
- Unlike many adults who seek counseling and testing for STDs and/or HIV, juveniles may actually be more interested in counseling and receiving information than in being tested. Youth who may not have initiated sex might be seeking support in making informed decisions about their sexual and reproductive health.
- Youth may not always be candid about their sexual experiences out of fear of stigma and labels. For instance, some youth may have engaged in sexual activity with the same sex, but due to number of reasons, these youth may not wish to divulge their experiences. Another example might be a youngster who had consensual sex with a sibling and/or another family member who due to self-consciousness of the taboo about incest may not wish to admit to the activity. Further, if the experience was with an adult, the youngster may avoid mentioning the encounter to protect the adult.
- Counseling adolescents often takes more time than working with adults, because young people often know less about their sexual health than adults do. Also, keep in mind that from some youth, particularly young males, some of the issues discussed may elicit humor and jokes, particularly jokes that are macho or male-dominated in nature. The correctional counselor should never join in such humor and should ensure that all topics are addressed in a serious and respectful manner.

Teenage Mothers and Unwanted Pregnancies

The United States has the highest rates of teen pregnancy and births in the Western industrialized world. Teen pregnancy costs the United States at least $7 billion annually. Indeed, 34% of young women become pregnant at least once before they reach the age of 20, which amounts to roughly 820,000 pregnancies a year by girls or young women. Roughly 80% of these teen pregnancies are unintended and 79% are to unmarried teens. Further, the younger an adolescent girl is when she first has sex, the more likely it is that her first sexual experience was actually unwanted or nonvoluntary in nature. Lastly, almost 40% of girls who first had intercourse at the age of 13 or 14 report that the sexual activity was not wanted. In addressing teen sex, young girls, and potential pregnancy, consider the following:

- Approximately one in five adolescents has had sexual intercourse before his or her 15th birthday.
- Approximately one in seven sexually experienced 14-year-old girls report having been pregnant. That translates into about 20,000 pregnancies each year and 8,000 births. (For those aged 15–19, the numbers are about 850,000 pregnancies and 450,000 births.)
- Teens who are 15 years and older who use drugs are more likely to be sexually experienced than are those teens who do not use drugs—72% of teens who use drugs have had sex, compared to 36% who have never used drugs.
- Teens who have used marijuana are four times more likely to have been pregnant or to have gotten someone pregnant than teens who have never used marijuana.

From the above information, it is clear that adolescents' early life-course sexual activity leads to pregnancy and it is also clear that much of the sexual activity occurs in tandem with drug use. Indeed, it would seem that some drug use further facilitates that likelihood of a future pregnancy. Given this, it is important to consider that in many families in which a daughter acts out sexually, the parents tend to be noncommunicative or they may be in constant conflict and turmoil with one another. In such cases, these teens do not feel comfortable talking with their parents due to the added strain and burden that the pregnancy is likely to add to the family household.

In trying to limit the amount of teen pregnancy, abstinence should be presented as one choice. Indeed, the primary reason that teenage girls who have never had intercourse give for abstaining from sex is that having sex would be against their religious or moral values. Other reasons cited include desire to avoid pregnancy, fear of contracting a sexually transmitted disease (STD), and not having met the appropriate partner. When educating juvenile girls on peer pressure and sexual activity, the correctional counselor should provide these youth with suggestions on how they can be assertive in resisting sexual advances from young men. Making facts clearer to girls, three-fourths of all girls at 14 who report having had sex state that they indulged mainly because their boyfriends wanted them to. Correctional counselors should ensure that young girls are aware of these facts and that they are aware of their own right to refuse such advances.

When attempting to prevent undesired pregnancies among juvenile girls, it may be useful to note that teens who have strong emotional attachments to their parents are much less likely to become sexually active at an early age and are therefore at a lower risk for teen pregnancy. In addition, contraceptive use among sexually active teens has consistently increased. This is a good trend since it has been found that sexually active teen who does not use contraception has a 90% chance of teen pregnancy within one year.

While it may be the view of the correctional counselor that these youth should simply abstain, the fact of the matter is that many will not. With this in mind, alternative safeguards against pregnancy should be discussed with juvenile girls, particularly if the young girl notes her intent to be sexually active. When correctional counselors work with juvenile girls, the discussions on use of contraceptives and decisions to engage in sexual activity can be very emotional for a young girl. Moreover, male counselors may also have some degree of discomfort discussing these issues. In cases where a female counselor is available, it may be useful to have same-gendered counselors discuss sex and pregnancy issues—but this should not at all be considered mandatory. If the juvenile girls are not uncomfortable with the male counselor's input and if the male correctional counselor is professionally adept with such topics, then there is an opportunity for the male counselor to provide some very effective and pro-social modeling. In fact, male counselors can demonstrate genuine care and consideration for the young girl's future and health.

On the other hand, male counselors working with juvenile girls should be careful to not seem "fatherly" or as if they are "lecturing" the youth. This is important because this is common among many father–daughter relationships and this can have an opposite effect than what is intended. Instead, the male counselor should ensure that he utilizes the youth-centered approach that was discussed earlier. This is important because the use of cross-gendered therapeutic interventions can have very positive effects if implemented correctly; and they can have very negative effects if they are not implemented correctly.

Lastly, when and where the opportunity exists, the use of both a male and a female cotherapist team might be most effective. The use of group interventions with young juvenile girls can allow the youth to discuss issues of sexual activity and pregnancy. The inclusion of peers can help to facilitate the intervention and also to create a stronger set of reinforcements for the young girl. The use of a cotherapist team can allow for effective modeling and even role-playing between the male and female therapist. These techniques can be very effective. As with most groupwork, the young girls can and should be encouraged to use techniques such as role-playing and assertiveness training within the group. Further, the feedback that juvenile girls gain from supportive peers can be very useful in providing the support and encouragement needed so that the girl can make her own independent choices regarding her own sexual behavior.

Parenting Classes and Parenting Issues

Though counseling regarding juvenile sex and teen pregnancy may be useful with many youth, some young girls will inevitably choose to engage in sexual activity that will conclude with a pregnancy. Further, the correctional counselor is likely to have juvenile girls in treatment who already have children when they are in the correctional system. In such cases, these youth may not be ready for parenthood and may need guidance and assistance on effective parenting techniques. Further, some of these juvenile girls will still be in contact with their male partners who are the biological fathers of the teen's child. In such cases, these juvenile fathers should also be encouraged to attend parenting classes. An example of a well-established curriculum for training on parenting would be the *Systematic Training for Effective Parenting,* which is published by STEP publishers. **Systematic Training for Effective Parenting** (STEP) is a comprehensive program to train parents on effective child-rearing techniques. The program emphasizes the use of "I" statements for personal responsibility, the use of reflective listening common to youth-centered counseling, and the use of appropriate consequences for desired and undesired behavior.

We advocate the use of the STEP program because it is based on extensive research that demonstrates the viability of this program. Indeed, the program has been tested on roughly 60 different occasions. From the evaluative research, it has been found that the program has also been used successfully with drug-addicted parents, abusive parents, foster parents, disadvantaged single mothers, and middle-class parents. In addition, STEP program research has looked at parents of antisocial children, low-GPA students, "problem" children, children with low self-concept, special needs children, and parents of adolescents who were hospitalized for emotional and behavioral problems. Lastly, this program has also been found effective within a multicultural context, having been studied with Chicana parents, Mexican-American parents, and parents from Appalachia, Canada, Puerto Rico, and Australia.

Lastly, an author of this text has had training in the use of this program and has even taught numerous families on effective parenting using this system. By all accounts, the author found this curriculum to be quite workable, both from a teaching standpoint and in regard to implementation. The curriculum is written in a clear and effective manner that is trainer friendly and parent friendly. For additional information regarding the STEP program, see Exhibit 9.2, which provides information on the STEP program for adolescents. The STEP/Teen curriculum is ideal for parents who are contending with a juvenile youth at home. The other STEP products can be used by teen mothers when raising their newborns.

In addition to providing parenting classes, it may be useful to include couple and/or family counseling as an intervention. In such cases, it may be that the juvenile girl and her partner are still in touch and/or involved with one another. In fact, it may even be the case that they intend to cohabitate or get married. This is especially true among the Latino-American culture where earlier pregnancies are not uncommon and where, due to culture (particularly based on religious orientation), young males will be expected to marry the young girl who is expecting to give birth. In such cases, family therapy can be even more productive if other family members (i.e., the parents of the juvenile female and/or the juvenile male) are also included in these interventions.

EXHIBIT 9.2

Systematic Training for Effective Parenting

The STEP/Teen's handbook is a useful tool for parents and for teenagers who are faced with accepting the responsibility of parenthood. This curriculum emphasizes positive approaches to parenting. The use of encouragement, teaching of consequences, and an understanding of the underlying goals of behavior are primary topics that parents will learn. However, recent additions to this classic parent training curriculum have included special and comprehensive suggestions for single parents and stepfamilies. In addition, this curriculum addresses specific and challenging topics such as drug use among youth, violence, and gang membership. Techniques for dealing with these issues are specifically provided. This makes the STEP process unique from other parenting guides. Further, the material designed for parents of teens is written in easy-to-understand language. This section also provides at-home activities to apply STEP/Teen techniques. The curriculum covers the following topics:

1. Understanding teens
2. Communication with teens
3. The use of encouragement
4. Healthy problem solving
5. Responsibility built through experiencing consequences.

This curriculum includes videos that are designed to be used with the curriculum. These videos are current and up-to-date, allowing parents and teens to view and discuss the scenarios. The primary key to this curriculum is the emphasis on effective communication and rapport building. Emphasizing accountability among youth and the need to consider consequences of one's behavior provides an effective approach to handling undesired behavior that provides parents with an alternative to punitive approaches. Lastly, this type of parenting curriculum is grounded in a balanced and realistic orientation toward parenting with today's youth. In other words, the realities and challenges of parenting youth in today's society are not side-stepped or ignored. Rather, the STEP process makes a point to address difficult and hard-to-answer problems that parents may face when raising teens.

Source: STEP Publishers. (2008). *Step into parenting: About STEP.* Retrieved from: http://www.steppublishers.com/does-it-work.

Indeed, in many cases, the parents of the juvenile female, and sometimes the juvenile male, will offer assistance in raising the newborn. Such family systems should be provided services to prepare them for the challenges that will undoubtedly emerge in the future.

Peer Groups, Subculture, Minority Issues, and Socialization

Peer groups are important for youth and, when seeing youth, the correctional counselor should keep this in mind. The peer group will likely be the primary source of socialization aside from the youth's family. Indeed, if the family was seriously dysfunctional, it is likely that the youth only identifies with his or her peer group. Among youth who are processed in the juvenile justice system and/or the criminal justice system, there exist a number of subcultural groupings that will be important reference points for youth seen by the counselor. In particular, it should be noted that the "gangsta" movement has had a particularly strong impact on youth culture, particularly among delinquent youth. The "thug" look and/or genre of music is fairly common among youth who are processed throughout the juvenile system. While other subcultural groups exist (i.e., Goths, alternative, etc.) they are not as well represented among the hard-core juvenile offender population. This is not to say that knowledge of such groups is not relevant to correctional counseling, but it is to say that these groups will not be as prevalent, largely due to the fact that they are simply not as widespread in popularity among today's youth and the public media.

Further, there are a disproportionate amount of minority youth who are processed through the justice system. Thus, in many juvenile systems, youth will tend to congregate along racial lines just as they might along subcultural lines. African-American and Latino-American youth are particularly represented, and these youth will likely affiliate with their own racial categories. In many cases, the youth from these minority groups will also come from families that are not affluent, with economic challenges being common to their background. These factors will tend to impact the socialization process that has been experienced by these youth and this is likely to be quite different from the backgrounds of many counselors. Because of this, the correctional counselor who works with the youth must also understand the cultural backgrounds common to the youth in their intervention programs. Knowledge of the locale from which the youth may have been raised can also be helpful for the correctional counselor.

Culturally Relevant Considerations

The cultural identity will be important for many youth that the correctional counselor may encounter within the juvenile and/or criminal justice system. This then requires that the correctional counselor be culturally competent in providing therapeutic services. With this in mind, there are several points that should be made about the content of culturally competent intervention services for juveniles. Certain key themes and issues should be included in these interventions when dealing with minority clients. Among these issues are those of acculturation, assimilation, migration history, race and institutional racism, and socioeconomic classism. These issues are likely to be directly relevant to most juvenile minorities who are processed within the formal system. Further, Caucasian youth in treatment should likewise be encouraged to explore their cultural roots, particularly with family-of-origin issues, for all the same reasons that minority youth would do so. In fact, there should be no distinction, as cultural beliefs are transmitted through all families and all youth can benefit from drawing on their cultural strengths and from learning about how issues such as racism and classism affect us all.

Correctional counselors should likewise discuss the importance of acculturation and assimilation—the former referring to the abilities and actions of the individual in adapting to the host culture and the latter referring to the permeability of the host culture (Smart & Smart, 1997). With respect to acculturation, minority youth should be encouraged to discuss how maintaining their own original culture and language can place them at cross purposes with the criminal justice system and American ideal of appropriate functioning. This should be compared with issues pertaining to assimilation, in which the minority juvenile is coerced to become more like the mainstream culture. The benefits and drawbacks to both options should be discussed openly in the group and youth should be given homework that causes them to reflect on these issues.

In addition, some juvenile youth may come from families that have only lived in the United States for a handful of years. Migration issues should be discussed as well, with difficulties in the adaptation process being discussed openly. Issues pertaining to first generation immigrants and the generations that follow should be discussed. Clients should be required through homework assignments to discuss immigration issues and cultural belief systems that were maintained or discarded by their families. In covering these topics, the self-efficacy of the youth is improved through the strengthening of their self-identity and understanding of the development of their family of origin in the broader society.

Also, issues of classism should be brought squarely into focus for the battering client. The effects of poverty on family relationships should not be overlooked. Economic levels affect the type and amount of service delivery that different populations receive in educational, medical, and political arenas. The effects of poverty can likewise affect feelings of power over one's environment, feelings of self-worth, and perceptions of victimization. Minority youth should be made aware of this and be provided with an environment where these issues can be openly discussed. Explorations into how social class can shape a youth's reactions to his or her sense of powerlessness should be made so that juveniles can readily identify with the social structures that put them at heightened "risk" of turning delinquent.

Gangs and Youth

When working with juveniles in the correctional setting, gang membership will be encountered on a fairly frequent basis. This is particularly true if the community supervision agency referring the youth is in a larger or mid-sized metropolitan area or if the correctional counselor works with youth who are in a state-operated facility. For correctional counselors who work with juveniles, it is advisable that they develop a working knowledge of the different gang groups in their area and among their juvenile population. An understanding of the tenets of a particular gang, how leadership structures operate, and gang alliances can be important in rapport building and can also provide the counselor with an understanding of the youth's world which will, undoubtedly, be influenced by the activities of their gang. This basic knowledge—and the correctional counselor should strive to learn more the basic information—will provide the counselor with the bare basics to competently provide services to these youth.

It is advisable that the correctional counselor have sufficient training with gangs and gang offenders if they plan to work with the offender population (both juvenile and adult) on a long-term basis. An excellent source of training and information for correctional counselors would be the **National Gang Crime Research Center** (NGCRC). The NGCRC is a nationally based non-profit organization of recognized gang experts from around the nation. This organization hosts an annual training conference where information regarding juvenile and adult gang issues are covered in a comprehensive manner. Organizations such as NGCRC should be consulted by correctional counselors if they have little or no experience with gang offending because a wealth of information may be available to enhance one's effectiveness when dealing with gang offenders.

There has been considerable debate as to why youth join gangs. It is our contention that many youth join gangs for a number of reasons, but, among all others, the primary reason is to have some sort of need met. There has been considerable research that has demonstrated that gangs provide many youth with basic human needs related to belonging. Some of these needs might include security, acceptance, friendship, food, shelter, discipline, belonging, status, respect, power, and money (Hess & Drowns, 2004; Valdez, 2000). Thus, gangs and gang membership likely results from any variety of personal, social, or economic factors.

In some cases, youth may be pressured into gangs. This is particularly true where rivalries are rampant and the need to recruit members exists. Peer pressure and intimidation may be the causal factor for some youth. Likewise, protection from victimization at the hands of other gang groups in the community might be another motivator. In addition, there may be expectations from older siblings and/or family members who have also joined a given gang. This is an important consideration because gangs in some areas of Chicago, Los Angeles, and New York have family memberships that may span three or more generations. Indeed, some neighborhoods in these metropolitan areas may have members throughout who are current members or, now well into adulthood, were once members before settling down. In such cases, it is not uncommon for that neighborhood to sympathize with the gang and to provide it with support.

These types of neighborhood dynamics can result in community-wide socialization that promotes gang membership. Hess and Drowns (2004) note that it is common among many underprivileged youth to experience frustration and feelings of deprivation from the predominantly middle-class values that pervade throughout broader society (Hess & Drowns, 2004). These youth are not afforded the same opportunities and privileges that more affluent families may have. Underprivileged youth eventually become aware of this and feel the stings of poverty that other middle-class youth avoid. To youth socialized in poor communities that are rampant with vice, crime, and violence, delinquency may not see to be anything abnormal or undesired (Hess & Drowns, 2004).

Amidst these neighborhood social conditions, the internal influences of the gang membership also work on the youth's development. The youngster may grow up knowing older gang members prior to himself becoming a member. He may learn to admire these members. Over time, an informal familiarization with the gang may develop. Eventually, the gang psyche is taught via the gang formal indoctrination process. This transformation of a youth into a gang member involves a slow process of assimilation (Hess & Drowns, 2004). Once the youth reaches an age at which he is able to prove his worth to the gang leadership, he is required to engage in some sort of ritual. In most cases this may consist of getting "jumped in," which is when the gang members beat the youth and the youth is expected to fight until they cannot continue to do so, or it may consist of getting "sexed in," in which some females may be required to have sex with male members to obtain affiliate status. Other cases may not require such ceremonies, particularly when the recruit is highly desired by the gang. Also, these forms of initiation are typical of male juvenile gangs but female gangs may not use the same types of initiation rites.

Among Latino and Asian juvenile gang members, the structure of their family of origin may consist of numerous immigrant members. In such cases, the parents may not speak English. Youth in these families learn the language and due to school influences become quickly comfortable with American society. In the process, some may lose respect for their parents and/or may seek to divest themselves of their cultural roots. In these cases, they quickly become experts at manipulating their parents and the parents lose the ability to regulate the behavior of their child. In such cases, it is very difficult to obtain any genuine reform of these youth unless they are separated out from any of their old influences prior to adjudication.

In these circumstances, the use of some type of family therapy is highly recommended. This is typically because the parents have little support and also because the structure of the family is being undermined. In such cases, the correctional counselor will find that the parents are more than willing to assist in regulating their youth, but they just are not able to because of linguistic and cultural limitations. It should be pointed out that these types of interventions require a correctional counselor who is either fluent in the client's primary language or an interpreter will be needed. One of the authors of this textbook has conducted therapy concerning similar issues through the use of an interpreter and found the process to be quite productive.

Consider further that many hard-core juvenile offenders come from abusive and/or neglectful homes. This is one key motivator for youth from these homes to join gangs. This motivation holds true for both male and female juvenile gang members. As was noted earlier in this chapter, the family of origin is the primary source for developing the youth's sense of belonging and self-worth. If these youth do not get this support at home, they are likely to seek this support from some other source; gangs provide that source (Hess & Drowns, 2004).

Certain commonalities exist with many families that have hard-core gang members. A family that has members who are also gang members is quite often a racial minority with underprivileged economic resources (Hess & Drowns, 2004). In many cases, the male role model may have a criminal history and/or may actually be incarcerated at the time that the youth obtains gang affiliation. Thus, the gang becomes a surrogate family, of a sort. Within the gang family, violence toward others is commonplace. Hess and Drowns (2004) note that "one reason for this is that gang members were often neglected or abused as children" (p. 194).

Naturally, the previous point dovetails with points made earlier in this chapter regarding the backgrounds of many juvenile offenders. Further, the issues related to economic deprivation and the desensitization toward gang affiliation and gang violence that may occur illustrates one reason why it is important to discuss issues related to classism and poverty with these youth. Thus, it is clear that many points made throughout the earlier segments of this chapter may serve as genuine causal factors for gang membership and for the maintenance of that affiliation over the span of years. As noted earlier, this may even become an intergenerational affiliation as entire families become enmeshed within the gang and neighborhood identity. Here again is an opportunity for family systems techniques, when and where some adult members do not wish to support a criminogenic lifestyle for their children. In some cases, even older members of a family who were gang members may not wish the same for their own offspring or kin. In such cases, it may be worthwhile to engage multiple family members into the intervention process, so long as these members do not seek to encourage delinquent or criminal activity among family members.

Gang Exit Strategies for Youth

As is clear, there are numerous incentives for youth to maintain membership with their gang affiliation. However, this affiliation stands at cross-purposes with the youth's ability to ultimately escape a life of crime. Thus, correctional counselors may find themselves in contact with programs that specialize in safely exiting juveniles from gang membership. In fact, some correctional counselors may work with gang offenders, leaving the door open for those youth who may decide to leave the gang life. Evans and Sawdon (2005) have provided a model process to facilitate the exit of youth from gang membership. This gang-exit program strategy has three components: (1) Assessment and intake, (2) intensive training and personal development, and (3) case management process.

Gang member assessment and intake is the phase that identifies interest and motivation of the gang member, the amount of gang involvement, and the member's family and social history (Evans &

Sawdon, 2005). During this phase, members are provided an orientation to the program. The next phase is the *gang member intensive training and personal development* phase. This phase implements two separate curricula, one for the male gang member and another for female gang members. Each curriculum involves up to 60 hours of intensive training. Topics during this training include anger management, aggression, sexism, racism, homophobia, and bullying. Communication skills training is also given during this phase. The last phase is the *gang member case management phase*, which involves individual support for the member but also requires ongoing group meetings for the ex-gang member. The intent is to reinforce what was learned at intake and to provide a proactive intervention when life takes some unforeseen turn for the prior gang member.

This program utilizes prior members who successfully complete the exit program as future facilitators with future members of the program. These prior gang members are tasked with being active in establishing community contacts and outreach. Participants visit local community centers and other youth services to provide information about the program. From this point, may prior members will engage in community presentations to help generate support (financial and otherwise) for the antigang program. This program trains these prior members who are "passing the word" with leadership skills training, empathy building, counseling, and the development of their own "personal stories," which are stories that explain how they became involved in gangs and why they have chosen cease involvement with the gang. This "story" is told in schools and other areas where the ex-gang member tries to warn against joining the gang life.

If it is possible to extract youth from the gang-oriented environment, then this option should be given priority. Indeed, the youth is much less likely to recidivate when away from the adverse peer group. In the absence of such an intervention, the next best strategy is to inoculate him or her from the effects of the gang world and to also replace the prior peer group with a new pro-social peer group. This is specifically what the gang-exit program attempts to do all the while working against the backdrop of the prior gang family's pressure to return. This is what makes the task so difficult for the offender and the community supervision officer and it is the strong tug of a subculture that eschews any attempt at reform made by the prior member.

SECTION SUMMARY

In this section, the issues associated with teen sex and sexuality are discussed. The need for counseling youth on safe-sex practices to avoid STDs and HIV as well as contraception strategies to avoid unwanted pregnancies were discussed. Correctional counselors who work with youth should be prepared to talk with male and female juveniles about these issues. Effective strategies for providing counseling on these topics were presented and specific mention of the STEP was presented as a premier approach to teaching young mothers and fathers skills for effective parenting.

Further, an understanding of peer-group subcultures is important for correctional counselors, as is the ability to provide culturally competent interventions. The various groupings and subgroupings by which juveniles gather are important since this will often be laced within their own sense of self-identity. In addition, the existence of juvenile gang offenders represents the most serious form of peer grouping. Juveniles join gangs for a number of reasons and the savvy correctional counselor will make a point to obtain knowledge and understanding of gang subculture.

LEARNING CHECK

1. Many youth who join gangs do so to gain acceptance and to have a sense of belonging.
   a. True
   b. False

2. The younger an adolescent girl is when she first has sex, the more likely it is that this first sexual experience was actually unwanted or nonvoluntary in nature.
   a. True
   b. False
3. Acculturation refers to the permeability of the host culture and assimilation refers to the abilities and actions of the individual in adapting to the host culture.
   a. True
   b. False
4. Youth whose parents are recent immigrants may fall into delinquency due to the ease with which they can manipulate their parents who, in many cases, may not know English or understand the broader American culture.
   a. True
   b. False
5. Teens who have used marijuana are four times more likely to have been pregnant or to have gotten someone pregnant than teens who have never used marijuana.
   a. True
   b. False

CONCLUSION

Juvenile offenders present with a variety of specialized needs and considerations that can prove challenging for even the most seasoned of correctional counselors. The issues that impact youth in their earliest of years can impact the likelihood of future delinquency occurring among a given youngster. The home life is the initial point of socialization and the early caretakers have a substantial (but not total) influence on the youth's future behavior. Many hard-core juvenile offenders come from homes that are substantially different from those where youth who commit minor acts of delinquency come from. Such homes more frequently have abusive or neglectful parental practices and substance abuse issues than do homes of less serious delinquents and non-delinquents.

Juveniles tend to have higher rates of clinical disorders than the general population. Indeed, depression, anxiety, and suicidal ideation are serious concerns among the adolescent population. Further, these problems are even worse among the delinquent population due to their increased likelihood of being victimized and their increased likelihood of abusing illicit substances. Both the abusive home life and the use of drugs and alcohol tend to simply make matters worse, though they serve as a coping mechanism for many youth (albeit a dysfunctional coping mechanism). Juvenile offenders tend to have difficulty with anger issues and the prevalence of conduct disorder among these youth is higher than is observed with other groups.

Teen sex and teen pregnancy is another important area that correctional counselors must attend to. Juvenile offenders are in particular need to have sex education that teaches them about safe-sex practices (in regard to STDs and HIV transmission) and they tend to be in need of information regarding fertility and birth control. Further, both male and female delinquents need this education and correctional counselors will need to be professional comfortable in addressing these issues with both male and female juvenile offenders. Similarly, some juvenile offenders have incurred parental responsibilities and are in need of parent training. The STEP is presented as a quality curriculum and training process of educating youth on this area of responsibility.

Correctional counselors should be informed on different subcultural groups and their prevalence within the juvenile justice system. In addition, multicultural competence is important and correctional counselors will need to be familiar with specific issues associated with different cultural and racial groups. The marginalization of many minority youth in the juvenile system truly provides few options for these youth. Further, community influences can point toward the support of gang membership. The lure of gang membership can be powerful, particularly when such membership is respected and idealized. Getting youth out of the gang life can be difficult but, with the aid of effective gang-exit strategies, this can be done. Ideally, such exit from gang affiliation will be indicative of future reform for the youth in question.

Essay Questions

1. Consider your readings from Chapter 5 regarding common theoretical counseling perspectives. In doing so, consider also the use of youth-centered counseling techniques that were mentioned within this chapter. Choose and discuss at least two theoretical approaches that you believe would be useful with juvenile clients. Be sure to explain your answer in some detail and provide specific examples.
2. Refer to your earlier readings in Chapter 7 on group therapy. Explain how and why group therapy might be an effective means of intervention with delinquent girls regarding safe-sex practices, birth control, and teen pregnancy. In which cases might this not be as effective an intervention? What are some variations in the group therapy process that you might employ?
3. Refer to your readings in Chapter 6 on family systems therapy. Explain how and why family systems therapy might be an effective means of intervention with delinquent youth. How might family systems be best in dealing with issues for immigrant families? What might be done in family systems therapy with homes that are abusive? Likewise, explain how family systems therapy might be beneficial for teen couples who will be contending with an unplanned pregnancy.
4. Consider a youth who is growing up in a gang-infested community. If you were counseling youth who were in such a location, what might you do to try to prevent youth from joining such an organization? How would you work with other youth who desired to leave the gang life? When might family systems therapy be effective and when might it not be?
5. Discuss some of the issues that impact many of the more serious juvenile offenders. Given these various issues that might emerge, explain what you might do if a youth disclosed that he or she were the victim of a prior childhood sexual assault. In addition, explain how you might intervene if the youth were presenting with signs of serious depression and if you suspected suicidal ideation.

Treatment Planning Exercise

For this treatment planning exercise, the student should consider their readings throughout this chapter as well as prior chapters. For this exercise, you should determine which, if any of the issues discussed in this chapter, apply to Danny's case. Be sure to identify those issues and explain how you would address them. Be sure to include a discussion of any corollary services that you might have the client utilize. In addition, explain whether a youth-centered approach would be appropriate with this client. Provide details on this aspect of your response.

The Case of Danny

Danny is a 17-year-old-male who has had a number of legal problems. Danny is currently on juvenile probation and has been referred to you by his juvenile probation officer. Danny's parents have also chosen to come to you for counseling because they feel that they have not done enough as parents.

Danny has constantly been in trouble at school and has just recently been placed on temporary suspension from the school grounds due

(*continued*)

to acts of vandalism. Danny is also fond of taking risks, such as jumping in the street to force cars to veer aside . . . all the while he throws eggs at the windshield to blind the driver.

When Danny was 10 years old he was diagnosed with oppositional defiance. He has continuously defied anything that is requested of him, unless there is a clear advantage for him when giving compliance.

Danny's parents are not naïve about his behavioral problems. In fact, they are very worried because he is now 17 and they feel as if they have completely failed as parents. They tell you that Danny will be made to attend treatment, and they will ensure it since they also plan to attend your clinic for couple's counseling. The counseling you are giving is in addition to his anger management and substance abuse counseling that he already receives as a mandatory condition of his probation. His parents tell you that they do not expect miracles; they just ask you to help if you can.

Bibliography

American Psychological Association (2004). *Mentally ill offender treatment and crime reduction act becomes law*. Washington, DC: American Psychological Association. Retrieved from: http://www.apa.org/releases/S1194_law.html.

Cox, S. M., Allen, J. M., Hanser, R. D., & Conrad, J. J. (2008). *Juvenile justice: A guide to theory, policy, and practice* (6th ed.). Thousand Oaks, CA: Sage Publications.

Davis, S. F., & Palladino, J. J. (2002). *Psychology* (3rd ed.). Upper Saddle River, NJ: Prentice Hall.

English, D. J., Widom, C. S., & Brandford, C. (2002). *Childhood victimization and delinquency, adult criminality, and violent criminal behavior: A replication and extension*. Washington, DC: National Institute of Justice.

Ericson, N. (2001). *Addressing the problem of juvenile bullying*. OJJDP Factsheet #27. Washington, DC: U.S. Government Printing Office.

Erikson, E. H. (1975). *Life history and the historical movement*. New York: Norton.

Evans, D. G., & Sawdon, J. (2005). The development of a gang exit strategy. *Corrections Today, 66*, 76–81.

Family First Aid: Help for Troubled Teens. (2009). *Teen depression, statistics, and warning signs*. Retrieved from: http://www.familyfirstaid.org/depression.html.

Hanser, R. D., & Mire, S. M. (2008). A comparison of juvenile sex offenders in the United States and Australia. *International Review of Law and Technology, 22*(1), 101–114.

Harter, S. (1990). *Visions of self beyond the me in the mirror*. Denver, CO: University of Denver.

Hess, K. M., & Drowns, R. W. (2004). *Juvenile justice* (4th ed.). Belmont, CA: Thompson/Wadsworth.

Ireland, T. O., Smith, C. A., & Thornberry, T. P. (2002). Developmental issues in the impact of child maltreatment on later delinquency and drug use. *Criminology, 40*(2), 358–380.

Moffitt, T. E. (1993). Adolescence-limited and life-course persistent antisocial behavior: A developmental taxonomy. *Psychological Review, 100*, 674–701.

Morris, C. G. (1991). *Contemporary psychology and effective behavior* (7th ed.). Glenview, IL: Scott, Foresman/Little, Brown Higher Education.

National Institute of Mental Health. (2002). *Depression*. Bethesda, MD: National Institute of Mental Health. Retrieved from: http://www.nimh.nih.gov/publicat/nimhdepression.pdf.

National Institute of Mental Health. (2004). *Combination treatment most effective in adolescents with depression*. Bethesda, MD: National Institute of Mental Health. Retrieved from: http://www.nimh.nih.gov/science-news/2004/combination-treatment-most-effective-in-adolescents-with-depression.shtml.

National Institute of Mental Health. (2009). *Re-shaping negative thoughts shields at-risk teens from depression*. Bethesda, MD: National Institute of Mental Health. Retrieved from: http://www.nimh.nih.gov/publicat/nimhdepression.pdf.

Smart, D. W., & Smart, J. F. (1997). DSM-IV and culturally sensitive diagnosis: Some observations for counselors. *Journal of Counseling and Development, 75*, 392–397.

Valdez, Al. 2000. *Gangs: A guide to understanding street gangs* (3rd ed.). San Clemente, CA: LawTech Publishing.

10

Anger Management and Domestic Abuse Counseling

CHAPTER OBJECTIVES

After reading this chapter, you will be able to:

1. Know the basic components and processes to anger management and domestic abuse group interventions.
2. Understand the underlying dynamics associated with domestic abuse.
3. Identify Groetsch's three categories of domestic batterers.
4. Match the appropriate treatment process with each category of batterer.
5. Be aware of corollary treatment issues relevant to domestic batterers.

PART ONE: PERSONS WITH ANGER PROBLEMS AND DOMESTIC BATTERERS

Though domestic violence issues have been given substantial public attention during the past two to three decades, there is still substantial confusion among the mainstream populace regarding distinctions between individuals with personal anger problems and those who are domestic batterers. Further, the term "anger management" has become one that is a source of humor, thereby almost normalizing the concept. Further, with the identification of phenomenon such as road rage and other commonly accepted terms for explosive behavior, it would seem as if the concept has been almost normalized within American culture. However, issues regarding domestic violence have not received as much lighthearted fanfare, generating social intolerance for this type of crime. Despite differing public perceptions regarding anger management and domestic battering, it is very common to see batterers mandated to anger management counseling, in some cases, without simultaneously attending a batterer's group. It is in this manner that one concept becomes equated with the other, but, among professionals, it is clear that anger management interventions are no substitute for a genuine domestic batterer treatment program.

While persons who have problems with anger control and emotional modulation may be in need of interventions to regulate their emotions, these dynamics are typically grounded in a sense of hurt or being aggrieved. Though this does not excuse extreme emotional outbursts or justify violent actions, it tends to be the case that most persons who have difficulties controlling their anger perceive some sort of slight, insult, or attack that has been aimed against them. In other cases, the anger may arise due to frustrations related to various stressors and/or persons who thwart the offender's ability to achieve some sort of goal or desired outcome.

While the factors just noted may help to explain the etiology to anger and even anger management problems, these factors do not, in and of themselves, explain the basis behind why domestic batterers commit such crimes. In the case of domestic batterers, the basis for much of the partner abuse that may occur is due to feelings of entitlement, particularly between male and female couples. In fact, many researchers (Pence & Paymar, 1993; Russell, 1996) note that belief systems grounded in patriarchy and male dominance tend to generate the abusive behaviors seen between batterers and their victims.

Further, domestic abuse is targeted at persons who reside with the offender and/or have some sort of relationship with the offender. This is in contrast with generalized anger control issues that may be sparked by any number of stimuli, including persons known to the offender as well as those who may be perfect strangers. This is an important point because many batterers may abuse their partners and/or children but they may not exhibit these behaviors when amongst others. Indeed, by all public appearances, they may seem to be very upright and even unassuming persons. But behind closed doors, they may be quite manipulative in how they psychologically and physically intimidate others. In this regard, domestic battering is often tied with the desire to control people and, in many cases, results in repetitive incidents between the perpetrator and the victim. On the other hand, simple anger control problems may manifest with much less calculation and may also have little or nothing to do with power and control within a family system.

Anger Management Groups

Anger management groups tend to use cognitive-behavioral techniques in intervention. In many groups, specific techniques are taught. For example, persons in anger management groups may be taught to take "time outs" when they feel twinges of anger are building. They may also be taught deep-breathing techniques as a means of maintaining their calm. Clients may be taught to use "I" statements as a means of taking responsibility for their emotions and behaviors and to avoid blaming others. In addition, clients may be given an exercise regimen to relieve stress and tension. It is also common for these groups to instruct clients to use anger logs or journals where clients are tasked with maintaining a record of what made them angry throughout the week. Naturally, clients are required to consider factors that trigger their anger. There are a number of other techniques that may be taught to clients who are in anger management groups.

Typically, anger management groups last only for a few weeks. In many cases, they may last for eight weeks or less. This short length of time tends to be true for clients who appear voluntarily as well as those who are court mandated. Throughout the course of these sessions, clients are required to consider those antecedent events that may trigger their anger and are also required to consider various means by which they can adjust and modify their reactions. Many intervention programs will use familiar techniques of thought stopping, cognitive restructuring, and an examination of one's self-talk.

Regardless of the agency, group, or professional expert who creates the curriculum, most all anger management interventions consist of the components that have been discussed in this subsection. Though some experts, such as Newton Hightower, Anderson and Anderson, and others, may have developed their own curricula that are well acclaimed throughout the nation (and perhaps the world), they all have similar themes in the manner by which anger is processed and by which it is treated. All of these interventions suggest some sort of approach that is cognitive-behavioral in nature. Further, these programs have not necessarily been tested for effectiveness through rigorous evaluative data. In addition, the training that counselors might seek from these programs can be quite expensive. Thus, casual students who would like to view a specific curriculum for anger management group process may find themselves unable to obtain this information without purchasing products by these vendors. Because of this, we recommend that students examine the manual and associated workbook published by the Substance Abuse and Mental Health Services (SAMHSA) manual titled *Anger Management for Substance Abuse and Mental Health Clients: A Cognitive Behavioral Therapy Manual*, written by Reilly and Shopshire (2002a). Though this manual has been constructed for group sessions with clients who have both anger management problems and substance abuse problems, we still recommend this manual to anyone interested in exploring how anger management groups are actually conducted. We particularly recommend this manual for persons who may later aspire to be correctional counselors.

The reasons for advocating for the work of Reilly and Shopshire (2002a) are many. First, this curriculum contains all of the more common ingredients that are found in other curricula. Second, as has been discussed in earlier chapters, the vast majority of the offender population has some sort of substance abuse issue, whether it be personal drug use or the association with other drug offenders. This means that most offenders who present to a correctional counselor will have both anger management problems coupled with substance abuse problems. Indeed, many of the explosive situations that lead to trouble with offenders also included the use of substances during the time of arrest. Third, this particular curriculum is designed to last 12 weeks in duration and is therefore a bit more extensive than some of the other types of anger management curricula that are used today. Fourth, because this manual is a publication of the federal government that falls within the realm of being public domain, it is absolutely free of charge to persons wishing to obtain copies. The associated workbook used by clients in the anger management group is likewise free. Both may be freely copied and utilized to as desired by treatment providers and they are available online. Lastly, it is the contention of this text's authors that the various products provided by SAMHSA are high quality and ideally targeted for the offender population. Thus, persons wishing to have a step-by-step guide on conducting an anger management group in addition to materials available to the participants of an anger management group only need to see the referenced entries for Reilly and Shopshire (2002a) included at the end of this text to directly obtain the materials for themselves.

An Overview of Domestic Battering Groups

The batterer's first contact with the program occurs when he arranges for an intake interview. At this time, the client signs release forms that give the program permission to contact his probation officer and his partner. The program then notifies the probation office that the client has chosen it for treatment. The first step of the intervention is the intake assessment, a process that can span one to eight weekly sessions. The initial session may be done as an individual interview or as part of a group orientation. Intake sessions serve several purposes:

- To get the client to agree with the terms and conditions of treatment and to sign the program contract;
- To begin to assess the nature and extent of the batterer's abusive behavior; and
- To screen for other problems such as substance abuse, mental illness, and illiteracy.

Beyond obtaining information solely related to domestic violence, the assessment typically includes questions about the batterer's family history, propensity for violence outside the family, and substance abuse. In many cases, this session will also be the start of a rapport that will be built between the therapist and the batterer, while also obtaining basic information necessary for further intervention. Approaches to assessment vary from program to program, but most all of them now provide at least a cursory exploration of potential mental health issues and substance abuse issues since these do tend to be common among this population. Throughout this process, some programs may screen for possible problems by using simple checklists and then referring the client for formal psychological evaluation if a substance abuse or mental health problem is suspected. Other programs may have the resources to run the entire gamut of assessments and evaluations, particularly if these programs have numerous mental health clinicians available to the agency.

After the initial intake session, most programs have an orientation process where the clients will meet for one or even several sessions during which the reeducation process begins. While conducting these initial sessions, counselors may use this time to further appraise the batterer since these will likely be the first few face-to-face observations that they may have with the client. In addition, this is a novel first meeting for the batterer who, while in the process of experiencing and adapting to the intervention process, may provide the therapist with clinical impressions and clues that further enhance the earlier assessment at intake. This is particularly true if the client has substance abuse or other mental health considerations.

The session then turns to the program goals and the rules for participating in the group. Some of the rules relate to attendance, punctuality, and payment of fees; others are related specifically to the group process, such as confidentiality, abstaining from alcohol and other drugs 24 hours before each group session, and participating constructively in group discussions (Healey, Smith, & O'Sullivan, 1999). Other rules may prohibit sexist or degrading language and insulting or intimidating counselors or other group members and require waiting in turn to speak. Finally, the program explicitly states the expectation that batterers will refrain from all violent, intimidating, or threatening behavior toward their partners. In addition to indoctrinating new members about program rules, orientation sessions are used to teach batterers the underlying assumptions of the program (Healey et al., 1999). When relaying these assumptions, therapists may do any of the following:

- Establish a broad definition of abuse that includes psychological and sexual abuse.
- Motivate batterers to change; counselors highlight the consequences of the batterer's abusive behavior on his children—often the best motivation to change.
- Counselors also begin to build empathy for their partners among batterers by discussing the consequences of abuse for the victim.
- Depending on the treatment approach, these sessions may also cover societal beliefs and norms that support.

The orientation sessions tend to be more like didactic classes than later sessions, which may take on a more therapeutic tone. One reason for the lecture-type format is to maintain order among new members who would sidetrack group discussions by turning attention away from their own behavior to complaints about their partner or the criminal justice system (Healey et al., 1999). Another, more subtle, reason for the structured format is to firmly establish norms for how to participate in group discussions before members graduate to more informal groups. The sessions also set a tone of active participation, making clear that clients will not be allowed to attend class without really participating in group discussions. Finally, the orientation phase—especially if it is extended over a number of weeks—can also serve as a screening device for the more therapeutic ongoing groups.

Once the orientation process has been completed, the group process will then shift toward the completion of some sort of scheduled curriculum. In many cases, this curriculum may span several months in duration, being much more in-depth than anger management curricula. In most cases, the batterer group intervention will last anywhere from 26 to 52 weeks in duration (Healey et al., 1999). It is the group intervention that has emerged as the intervention of choice for several reasons, which include the following:

- The group combats the implicit social approval of abusive behavior that many batterers perceive from family and friends. By sending consistent messages that do not condone any form of abuse and encourage nonviolent alternatives, the group serves as a healthy support system for batterers who wish to change.
- Successful group members can serve as role models to batterers who are just beginning to confront their own violent behavior, helping to break through a new member's minimization of his abuse.
- By providing a new source of support, the group reduces the batterer's excessive dependence on his partner to meet all his emotional needs.

However, group leaders must be alert and ready to intervene when batterers try to commiserate with one another, forming unhealthy bonds that excuse abusive behavior. As one set of group leaders advised, some programs are strictly structured, such as those using the Duluth curriculum (described below), prescribing the order in which topics are to be addressed. Other programs give discretion to group leaders to choose from a range of program content, while confronting batterers' behavior more directly. Program directors warned that some leaders may resort to a more flexible approach because they lack the skill to keep group discussions focused on the planned curriculum. It is important, therefore, to distinguish between a flexible curriculum and uncontrolled digressions from the set discussion schedule.

Whatever the structure or treatment approach, each group session typically begins with a round-robin style check-in, followed by the selected topic or educational piece for the meeting, ending with goal setting and check-outs. Check-ins are a way to introduce new members to the group and reinforce the program's focus on the batterer's behavior (Healey et al., 1999). They can be brief (each person states his name and one of the rules of the group) or more lengthy (each member describes his most recent or severe abusive behavior). In more therapeutically oriented programs, the check-ins can lead to discussions that take up the bulk of the session (Healey et al., 1999). For more educational programs, the check-ins are followed by a more structured presentation from the curriculum. Regardless of emphasis, at the end of the session programs typically assign homework that is designed to encourage each client to apply the session's topics directly to his life. Check-outs help participants summarize what they learned and clarify their behavioral goals for the coming week (Healey et al., 1999).

Most batterers deny or avoid accepting responsibility for their actions—that is, they refuse to view battering as a choice (Healey et al., 1999). As a result, one of the main goals of all reputable batterer intervention programs is to get the batterer to become accountable for his abusive behavior. Program staff have divided the most common tactics batterers use to avoid accountability into three categories:

- **Denying,** which is when the batterer denies that the abuse ever happened. For example, a batterer may claim "I didn't lay a hand on her; she made the whole thing up," despite the fact that a readily available police and/or hospital report clearly documents that the batterer is lying.

- **Minimizing** the abuse, which is done by downplaying the violent acts or underestimating effects of the assault. For instance, the batterer may claim "it was only a light slap" or that "She bruises easily," as a means of downplaying the seriousness of the assault.
- **Blaming**, which occurs when batterers attempt to find some cause external to themselves to which they attribute their battering behavior. The abuse of the victim, drugs or alcohol, or other life circumstances. In these types of situations, the batterer may blame the victim by stating "she drove me to it and should have known better," or he may claim that he was drunk and therefore the battering was beyond his control. It is also not uncommon for batterers to claim that life stressors (whether related to work or other circumstances) provided the causal explanation for their actions.

Because these tactics are so common, group leaders tend to be specially trained to look for these tactics. In most all programs, the group leader will be highly attuned to these tactics and will be very quick to confront those batterers who use them. In fact, the challenging of these tactics is one of the hallmark characteristics of batterer intervention programs. Thus, correctional counselors who intend to work with this population will find it useful to develop a keen ear for statements that resemble any of these three tactics.

As with anger management groups, domestic batterer groups also tend to be cognitive-behavioral in approach. The specific techniques that are used often aid the batterer in recognizing how he may fuel his own sense of rage through irrational "self-talk," the internal dialogue that the batterer uses to build himself up to an abusive incident. Examining the thoughts and feelings that precede the abuse helps the batterer to realize that he did not just lose his sense of control. In many cases, when the partner of the batterer does something unplanned or does not meet the expectations of the batterer, he will tend to repeat a series of negative thoughts about his partner which tend to build up the sense of anger and also to provide them with a justification for their violent actions. As this process occurs, the batterer repeats these negative thoughts to himself until his partner becomes an object that failed to perform as expected, and so violence becomes justified in his own mind. Essentially, cognitive-behavioral techniques used in batterer group-work tend to target three basic elements:

- What the batterer thinks about prior to an abusive incident;
- How the batterer feels, physically and emotionally, as a result of these thoughts;
- What the batterer does, such as yelling and throwing things, that builds up to acts of violence.

The group helps members to recognize and interrupt these thought patterns and the anger associated with them. In the process, the batterer learns to identify negative thoughts and feelings as precursors to his explosiveness and violence. As a result, he is taught to identify these cues at an early stage and to intervene with contrary thought that will prevent his typical reactions. Through the use of cognitive restructuring and other behavioral techniques such as time-outs, the batterer can practice the process so as to better interrupt the internal dialogues that occur prior to his overreactions. Further, he is taught to substitute his maladaptive thought patterns with reality checks and positive coping statements, while also reducing his state of physiological arousal through relaxation techniques (e.g., deep-breathing exercises, biofeedback) or noncompetitive forms of physical exercise that can reduce tension.

Lastly, most all states have a variety of guidelines that are required of batterer intervention programs, particularly those that receive funding (Hanser, 2007). One author of this text conducted a study of batterer intervention and prevention programs in the state of Texas and found that the various guidelines associated with that state's use of batterer interventions were consistent with the guidelines in other states. The *Battering Intervention and Prevention Project Guidelines* in the state of Texas were published by the Texas Council on Family Violence in tandem with the Texas Department of Criminal Justice and the Community Justice Assistance Division. The collaboration between these different organizations emphasizes the point that correctional counseling of batterers consists of a strong fusion between the criminal justice system and treatment providers. According to these guidelines, batterers are a special category of violent offenders who require specialized intervention. This is important because battering, in and of itself, is a behavior, not a clinical disorder, unto itself. There is no diagnosis for domestic batterers in the *DSM-IV-TR*, yet they are a very specialized type of offender who is obviously in need of change. The Texas guidelines go on to note that intervention programs should focus on both ending the violence committed by the offender *and* their capacity for change. Thus, the priority is to eliminate violent behavior through internal cognitive change.

The state of Texas guidelines, in outlining the benefits of group interventions, state that programs with groups with men who batter are more effective than individual counseling approaches because they

- Provide a greater opportunity for confrontation and accountability than do individual counseling approaches,
- Are more successful in decreasing the domestic batterer's fear of isolation and his overdependence on his partner, and
- Are more cost effective than individual approaches.

These benefits are of course similar to other benefits noted in the group therapy literature. It is apparent that these benefits are especially applicable to the battering population and it is for that reason that this chapter later provides two examples of group therapy programs for domestic batterers.

Among other guidelines, the state of Texas notes that during group sessions, correctional counselors will be specifically tasked with confronting any denying, blaming, minimizing, justifying, and/or rationalizing that is identified by the therapist. This again demonstrates the manipulative nature of the domestic batterer and highlights the three tactics of manipulation mentioned earlier in this population. In such cases, counselors are to provide such confrontation despite the existence of dysfunctional relationships, current stress factors, or previous trauma experienced by the offender; and counselors are guided to emphasize that the decision to engage in violent behavior is a choice made by the offender; it has not been imposed upon them and is not beyond their control. Other suggestions include the following:

- A "check-in" at the beginning of each session in which members report on recent behavior, homework assignments, and problem areas.
- Role-plays, group exercises, or written work promoting the participation of batterers and the application of program principles.
- A wrap-up concluding each session providing closure to deescalate heightened emotions and affirm the focal points and/or program principles.
- Assigned homework extending the application and practice of the session's focal points and program principles. Some form of community service may be required as part of the homework.

In addition, just as with most groups, it is recommended that domestic batterer groups should never exceed 15 clients and it is also recommended that coleaders be used, when and where possible. When using coleaders, the inclusion of counselors of both genders is the most effective strategy as this can allow the counselors to model equality in communications and in relationships. Lastly, group programs should also have some sort of follow-up system that also incorporates self-help and social support. These programs should be structured to reinforce the maintenance of nonviolence and address issues that go beyond their offending, such as parenting classes, stress management courses, and/or other forms of mental health intervention.

SECTION SUMMARY

The use of anger management groups has become a common intervention within the criminal justice system. Some correctional counselors may find themselves leading such groups. However, treatment for anger management is not identical to treatment for domestic abuse. While many of the techniques and methods of intervention are similar, there are substantial differences in the issues that lead to general anger-control problems and domestic abuse. Although, at times, these tend to overlap (i.e., most domestic batterers are angry at the time that they assault their partners), the two types of intervention should not be confused. Anger management programs typically last around eight weeks, with some lasting a few weeks longer and some being a couple of weeks less. Regardless, anger management groups are short-term groups.

Groups for domestic battering are much more long-term in nature. Further, these groups address deeply entrenched belief systems that relate to the many in which offenders view themselves and their partners within a relationship. Issues related to feelings of entitlement, control and manipulation of one's partner, the use of fear and intimidation, as well as societal influences are part of the treatment. Further, most programs last for nearly six months in duration. While anger control techniques are taught in batterer interventions, many more issues are addressed in these types of interventions, providing a more in-depth form of therapy designed to change the mindset of the batterer.

LEARNING CHECK

1. Most persons who have problems with anger control have a history of feeling of hurt or being aggrieved.
   a. True
   b. False
2. According to the authors, substance abuse problems are very common among batterers. This is so true that most programs should consider simultaneous treatment for substance abuse to be a common practice when operating batterer's groups.
   a. True
   b. False
3. Denying, minimizing, and blaming are common tactics used by batterers.
   a. True
   b. False
4. According to the authors, batterer group interventions typically last anywhere from 12 to 18 weeks in duration.
   a. True
   b. False
5. Generally speaking, group interventions are considered to be more effective than are individual sessions with domestic batterers.
   a. True
   b. False.

PART TWO: THE BATTERER

As was mentioned in the previous section, domestic batterers are offenders who are a unique class unto themselves. Though these offenders are violent, they are selective with who and how their violence will be utilized (Groetsch, 1996). This is also what separates them from offenders who have generalized problems with anger control. Offenders with anger control problems may manifest their anger in any number of circumstances that can be quite chaotic and unpredictable. However, the domestic batterer's violence is more focused and is rooted in numerous faulty belief patterns pertaining to their role and sense of entitlement within close relationships. Further, the reasons for their use of violence usually involve control and manipulation of an emotionally based relationship with the victim. While much attention has been given to the issue of domestic violence, it is the domestic batterer who is frequently misunderstood among both the general population and the body of criminal justice practitioners (Hanser, 2007).

One of these misunderstandings is the fact that not all batterers are the same, both in terms of the personal factors associated with their abusive behaviors and the lethality of their violence. In much of the early domestic violence literature, this distinction was minimized and a simple view of the domestic batterer was presented, one that simply purported that all batterers were in need of incarceration and punitive sanctions. It is our position that battering, like any other crime, is naturally an inappropriate behavior that warrants criminal justice consequence. However, this notion would be no different if the crime were some other form of assault, including simple or aggravated assault, as well as sexual assault. The simple point of the matter is that a crime of violence warrants a sanction. But yet, even with other types of offenders, there is recognition of distinctions between the types of offenders. Indeed, the justice system also considers a sundry array of mitigating and aggravating circumstances when trying cases. Thus, some variability between offenders should be recognized.

With this in mind, it is our position that batterers should be envisioned as falling along a continuum (Groetsch, 1996). Along this continuum, three specific categories of domestic batterers can be identified. This idea of creating specific categories within the battering population has become more accepted in recent years, particularly in regard to the development of psychological typologies. However, we will refer to the work of Groetsch (1996) for a couple of reasons. First, Groetsch is one of the first-known authors to suggest that there are clear and categorical distinctions between different types of batterers. Second, we believe that Groetsch's work is well suited for the correctional counselor, being readily easy to implement in actual treatment programs. Thus, throughout this chapter, we will refer to the three categories developed by Groetsch (1996), who based his categories on the potential dangerousness of the batterer himself.

The use of categories is helpful in determining which batterers are treatable from those who are simply beyond the scope of successful rehabilitation. In general, **category one batterers** are the least dangerous and most treatable, while category three batterers are very dangerous and not likely to complete treatment (Groetsch, 1996). **Category two batterers** fall between these two groups with prognoses that are the least predictable. The readers should note that these categories are in fact artificial for the most part but are simply a method by which classification and identification of likely prevention and treatment outcomes can be identified.

Category one batterers are often nonviolent in most circumstances, both in public and in private. These types of batterers are usually caught in abnormal circumstances that may be uniquely stressful to that person, such as child custody disputes, the loss of employment, or some other life-course difficulty. Their abuse tends to be situational and isolated with much of the cause for the incident being generated from what are referred to as "external" environmental factors rather than internal thoughts or belief system issues (Groetsch, 1996). These offenders will typically have no previous violent relationships with intimates and are the least likely to use weapons during their abuse. These offenders are also least likely to present with any mental health or life development issues.

What is perhaps most important is that these offenders do actually feel and express remorse over their actions. It is this last characteristic that makes this group treatable and truly separates them from the other two groups categorized in this chapter.

Category two batterers, on the other hand, often display several character defects, including substance abuse/addiction, non-domestic violent activity, and problems related to moral turpitude. Abuse by these batterers is not situational and it is not isolated (Groetsch, 1996). However, abuse by these batterers is likely to be unpredictable, sometimes with little or no apparent provocation. Interestingly, it is difficult to determine causal factors that weigh most in their abusiveness, with both external environmental and internal belief-system factors having near-equal effects and thus explaining, at least in part, their unpredictable use of violence (Groetsch, 1996). These batterers may have had previously violent relationships with other partners and may have inflicted premarital abuse upon their current partner (Groetsch, 1996). These abusers may use weapons, though they are not prone to lethal levels of weapon use. Instead, weapons are often used to threaten the victim rather than to inflict actual harm. Further, these offenders feel and express little remorse and are not necessarily amenable to treatment. This of course makes their treatment as unpredictable as the onset of their violence.

Category three batterers are high risk and often possess true personality disorders. These batterers often present ongoing and chronic patterns of abuse. Abuse among this population is largely based on internal belief-system issues regarding the rights of men in relationships with women (Groetsch, 1996). For this group, most all previous relationships with partners have been violent. Further, these batterers are likely to have exhibited some form of premarital violence toward their current partner. These abusers are likely to present and use dangerous weapons (Groetsch, 1996). In addition, these batterers demonstrate no remorse for their actions and seem to lack a conscience. These batterers are generally not considered to be amenable to treatment. In fact, it is most likely that a program of selective incapacitation would be the most pragmatic "intervention" when considering their extremely poor prognosis.

According to Groetsch (1996), these batterers frequently present with one or more personality disorders listed in the *DSM-IV-TR*, including Narcissistic, antisocial, borderline, histrionic, paranoid, and obsessive-compulsive personality disorders. Of course, these disorders may occur in conjunction with numerous other *DSM-IV-TR* disorders such as substance abuse or depression. Sadly, this group is that which is in the direst need for treatment yet the comorbid nature of disorders among this population make them the most difficult ones to treat. While it is true that many people who have one psychological disorder experience other disorders at the same time, this occurrence is particularly pronounced among the category three battering population. The simultaneous occurrence of disorders, or comorbidity (Davis & Palladino, 2002), increases the difficulty associated with making appropriate diagnoses and developing effective treatment plans for these batterers.

Treatment Approaches with Category One Batterers

Category one batterers very rarely appear in the criminal justice system. When they do, these types of batterers are likely to be receptive to both the punitive or deterrent effects of punishment and the treatment-related aspects of their criminal sanction (Groetsch, 1996). These batterers are often described as "family-only" abusers (Wexler, 2000). These abusers are often dependent on the affection from their significant other and they often express jealousy if it appears that this affection is not centered around them (i.e., if it is also given to the woman's children). As a manner of coping, they tend to suppress emotions and withdraw, later erupting into violence only after long periods of unexpressed negative emotions (Groetsch, 1996; Wexler, 2000). The acts of abuse are generally less severe than those of batterers and they do not tend to be aggressive in other circumstances (Groetsch, 1996). Importantly, these batterers also frequently express remorse for their abusive actions and they often voluntarily join groups in search of treatment. Many times, the mere threat that their partner will leave can influence them to seek genuine change.

Among court-mandated batterers, this group tends to be the least assaultive. Because these batterers are often genuinely remorseful, willingly seek change, and because they are not nearly as assaultive as other batterers, the notion of reconciliation between the batterer and the partner may be workable. Further, this group of batterers may not require group therapy but may be receptive to individual sessions, so long as the sessions are focused on accountability for the abuse and as long as the session is not focused on other issues corollary to the domestic abuse. Though other issues may be valid and may exist, those would be the topic of additional sessions which would not take the place of any intervention targeted at the offender's abusive behavior. Nevertheless, this group of batterers can still gain greatly from the traditional batterer's group intervention process, and correctional counselors are encouraged to use this approach with this group of batterers, when they feel it is appropriate. However, it may emerge that these offenders, due to their generally nonviolent history, may not fit well with a group of batterers whose abusiveness and offending history is much more serious and/or much more extensive in nature. In such cases, other group members may unduly challenge this type of batterer, thinking that this batterer may be minimizing his actions when, in fact, his actions are not near as severe as that found among other group members. This is not to say that category one batterers should be exonerated, but a failure to understand distinctions between these batterers can lead to serious clinical miscalculations throughout the treatment process. It can also create complications within the group dynamics where offenders are taught to challenge minimization and denial. According to Groetsch (1996), the following methods of intervention can be considered with category one batterers:

Individual Counseling. As noted previously, this type of counseling should make a point to directly address the client's abusive behavior, holding the client accountable for that behavior. However, in most cases, these batterers genuinely do come to terms with their responsibility for their actions and put forth the effort to change. With that in mind, other forms of one-on-one counseling may focus on the external issues that brought the offender's aggression to the surface. Naturally, other issues such as grief, substance abuse, stress, or other precursors to the aggression can and should be addressed in these corollary sessions.

Marriage Counseling. It should be noted that this type of intervention is typically NOT recommended for batterers. Such a recommendation is typically considered quite unorthodox, though it has been used in some instances in an effective manner that does not jeopardize the victim. However, it is important to remember that many category one batterers are voluntary participants who report for treatment to repair the damage that they have done in their relationship with their partner. Further, many victims of these abusers are likely to continue in the relationship with this type of batterer, particularly if the onset of physical assault is perceived by the victim to be generated by outside stressors. In addition, some partners may wish to engage in mutual therapy with the abuser, both to see if he is actually working on his issues in therapy and to also provide support in the relationship. Again, though this would not be an option with most battering offenders, category one batterers often self-report.

Support Groups. One-on-one counseling and marriage counseling are very limited in the time that a client spends in therapy. Support groups that focus on the specific issues or trauma that caused his violence are excellent means of reducing isolation, giving him exposure to others who understand his trauma, and providing him with an opportunity to establish peer relationship and fellowship. Support groups that address issues of stress, grief, substance abuse, and so on, and that employ a twelve-step program modality are excellent resources for such clients. If alcoholism is a concern, then victims should be simultaneously referred to Al-Anon.

Spiritual Needs. When applicable and when able, the correctional counselor should not refrain from incorporating the batterer's spiritual orientation, especially if the batterer alludes to his religious or spiritual beliefs. In fact, if possible, these beliefs and sources of pro-social support should be integrated into the treatment process. This is also an important consideration for those offenders who identify with a religious belief system or are members of a cultural group that holds a given set of spiritual tenets.

Treatment Approaches with Category Two Batterers

Category two batterers are more severe in the type of violence they employ and the frequency with which they employ that violence when compared to category one batterers. Unlike category one batterers, this group is likely to be deceitful and cunning when engaging in their abusive behavior. They are also likely to be much more devious and methodical than are category three batterers. While category two batterers are not as lethal as category three batterers, they are much more effective at hiding their abuse and evading law enforcement detection. Thus, extreme caution must be taken in the case of category two batterer. To illustrate this point, consider that many experienced intervention providers report very low success rates with these individuals.

According to Wexler (2000), this type of batterer is occasionally referred to as "emotionally volatile." This group tends to be violent mostly within their family, but they are often more socially isolated and socially incompetent than category one batterers. They exhibit higher levels of anger, depression, and jealousy (Wexler, 2000). Further, they find ways of misinterpreting their partners and blaming their partners for their own mood states. Depression and feelings of inadequacy are prominent among abusers of this category (Groetsch, 1996; Holtzworth-Munroe & Stuart, 1994; Wexler, 2000). Further, this category may have borderline or other personality disorders, though personality disorders are much more prevalent among the category three abuser. This group of batterers will typically have a poor treatment prognosis. Since this batterer's violence is based more on internal issues and defective character traits than external trauma, the treatment for a category two batterer should be of a different format than those of the category one batterer. Unless a holistic approach is taken with the category two abuser, there is little chance for a positive change. Groetsch (1996) discusses the basic approaches to counseling intervention, as presented below:

Individual Counseling. Generally, this type of therapy should not be used with this group. If used, it should be an adjunct form of treatment that focuses on the many defective character traits and internal issues of the category two batterer. Again, this type of therapy should not be allowed as a substitute for the use of standard group interventions.

Group Counseling. This type of counseling is the preferred modality because other batterers, who know and recognize manipulation from their cohorts, are able to assist in holding the batterer accountable for his behavior. This "group pressure" has been shown to be very effective with this population. However, it is not uncommon for members of such a group to get into behavioral collusion with one another whereby negative traits are actually reinforced.

A trained therapist should be aware of such a possibility and should counter peer collusion appropriately.

Educational Groups. Since much of the violence of the category two assailant is associated with learned behavior, an educational component to a group can be essential. This type of group will seek to modify elements of the batterer's socialization and will reeducate the batterer on matters involving gender roles, control, and sexism.

Support Groups. As with the category one batterer client, individual and group counseling time is very limited and expensive. While the therapist may spend one or two hours weekly with this client, the reality is that there are innumerable daily interactions throughout the week that can trigger relapse within this client. Support groups can serve as an excellent "back-up" to therapy and also can help to build rapport among other group members who are in the support group. These groups likewise can be more readily available at the time of crisis rather than during a rigidly scheduled point throughout the week.

Spiritual Needs. Just as with category one batterers, this area of batterer development can be of huge benefit in motivating the batterer toward change. As noted with category one batterers, this is an important consideration for those offenders who identify with a religious belief system or are members of a cultural group that holds a given set of spiritual tenets.

Treatment Approaches with Category Three Batterers

It is important to understand that this group of batterers are not only lethal but are very manipulative as well, being able to escape the detection of even the most seasoned therapists. This type of batterer is generally antisocial and more likely to engage in instrumental violence. By instrumental, it is meant that this violence is designed to gain a specific end or material outcome. In this case, violence "works" more successfully for this batterer in getting what they want (Holtzworth-Munroe & Stuart, 1994). They are limited in their capacity for empathy and attachment, and they hold the most rigid and conservative attitudes about women (Groetsch, 1996; Holtzworth-Munroe & Stuart, 1994; Wexler, 2000). They tend to be violent across situations and across different victims. They are generally more belligerent, more likely to abuse substances, and more likely to have a criminal history. This group is also unlikely to show remorse (Groetsch, 1996; Holtzworth-Munroe & Stuart, 1994; Wexler, 2000).

Within this category there is a certain population of battering men who could be best described as "**vagal reactors**" or "cobras" (Jacobson & Gottman, 1998) or, in a more general sense, psychopaths (Hare, 1993). Psycho-physiologically oriented studies have identified an unusual pattern among a subgroup of the most severe batterers (Gottman et al., 1998; Wexler, 2000). This group of batterers have actually shown reductions in measures of arousal during aggressive interactions with their partners—completely contrary to expectations and typical patterns during aggressive interactions (Gottman et al., 1998; Wexler, 2000). These batterers have been dubbed "vagal reactors" because their nervous system arousal is strangely disconnected from their behavior (Gottman et al., 1998; Wexler, 2000). These batterers deliberately and manipulatively control what goes on in the marital relationship (Wexler, 2000). Jacobson and Gottman (1998) call these men "cobras" because of their ability to become still and focused before striking their victim—this is in contrast to the more typical category two and three "**pit bulls**" who slowly burn in frustration and resentment before finally exploding (Wexler, 2000). Men who operate in this cold and calculating manner are not at all likely to be successfully treated (Groetsch, 1996; Wexler, 2000). In fact, the best intervention for this group is most likely simple incapacitation. They display many of the characteristics of classic psychopathic behavior—not necessarily typical of all category two and three abusers (Hare, 1993; Wexler, 2000). In short, these are the worst of the worst among the battering population.

Obviously, a healthy degree of skepticism must be utilized with this specific group of batterers and with category three batterers in general. Category three assailants who enter treatment generally do so in an effort to avoid criminal prosecution or in an attempt to lure their victims back into relationships. With category three batterers, Groetsch (1996) recommends that treatment specialists follow the recommended guidelines:

- Instead of promoting treatment for the category three batterer, promote boundaries such as court mandates, restraining orders, and restrictions that serve to protect the victim.
- Recognize that the criminal justice system refers batterers to treatment programs indiscriminately.
- Recognize that the chronic batterer has extensive levels of denial. This batterer will minimize, externalize, and rationalize all of his behaviors and violence.
- If you do provide treatment to the chronic batterer, never allow him to portray himself as a victim. While in some cases it may be true that he had a terrible childhood, he is now the perpetrator and should be confronted as such.
- Never consider the alcoholism or drug addiction of the category three batterer as the reason for his aggression. Substance abuse is not a direct causative factor for the violence. For chronic batterers, it is just one of the many symptoms of the personality disordered batterer.
- Remember, it is very common that this group of batterers will often present with separate personality disorders that aggravate the battering personality. These other disorders must be treated as well.

Additional Notes on Treatment Approaches

For all batterers, it is important to address all substance abuse issues first before other treatments have any chance of success. Without such primary interventions being established, the therapist will simply be reaching the "chemical" rather than the batterer's actual personality and belief system. This explains why it is common practice for batterers to continue drug counseling as an adjunct to their batterer's group counseling. This tactic naturally helps to prevent drug-induced relapse of domestic abuse. This is important to keep in mind because substance abuse correlates very strongly with aggressive behavior among batterers. This correlation has been found to be especially true with alcohol, which overwhelmingly emerges as a primary predictor of marital violence (Hanson, Venturelli, & Fleckenstein, 2002). In fact, one study found that rates of domestic violence were as much as 15 times higher in households where the husband was described as "often" being drunk rather than "never" being drunk (Collins & Messerschmidt, 1993; Hanson et al., 2002).

Research consistently shows that spouse abusers have numerous alcohol-related problems (Barnett, Miller-Perrin, & Perrin, 2004). Because drunkenness can precipitate domestic battering and can be used as an excuse, clinicians must address alcohol treatment and must not allow the batterer to evade responsibility by blaming the alcohol for the behavior. Further, treating alcohol or substance abuse problems alone is not thought to be sufficient, unto themselves, to rectify abusiveness among any category of batterer (Barnett et al., 2004; Healey et al., 1999). In fact, it could likely be the case that a batterer may be more prone to abusiveness when he stops drinking due to the stressful and unpleasant effects of withdrawal during their new-found sobriety (Barnett et al., 2004). On the other hand, treatments that combine behavioral marital therapy with treatment of alcoholism have been found to reduce abusiveness (Barnett et al., 2004; O'Farrell & Murphy, 1995). Findings such as these demonstrate the complexities involved in addressing the alcohol-violence correlation. Further, as discussed earlier in this chapter, substance abuse/addiction disorders tend to be comorbid with other disorders (i.e., depression and other mood disorders, emotional disorders, and the various personality disorders previously discussed in this chapter), providing a treatment picture that is convoluted at best.

Regardless of corollary issues in treatment, it is important to remember that in distinguishing between the three categories of batterers the main difference lies in the degree of the violence, how often it occurs, and the level at which the violence is sustained. This is crucial from a community supervision standpoint, as frequency and lethality of violence should be the primary concern in public safety risk-prediction decisions. Remember that while the category one abuser's violence is isolated, the category two batterer's abuse is sporadic and reoccurring. The abuse of the category three offender, on the other hand, is always ongoing and chronic. Making matters even more complicated is the fact that batterers will not always exhibit a perfect profile of category one, two, and three types of offenders. They frequently may fall somewhere between categories, making the diagnosis and corresponding risk-prediction of these offenders very difficult.

SECTION SUMMARY

Despite beliefs to the contrary, all batterers are not identical in the nature of their offending. This is a controversial view within some treatment circles since many early domestic abuse intervention programs would, in the process of working with corollary mental health issues, almost exonerate the batterer. In contemporary times, it is clear that some batterers may have a host of mental health considerations, substance abuse dependencies, and other factors that aggravate reform. However, they can and should still be held accountable for their abusive behavior. Still, one abuser may be quite different from another. Indeed, some abusers engage in violence in a routine pattern whereas others may do so as an isolated incident. To consider each to be one and the same would be a serious error in the assessment of lethality and in the treatment planning process.

This chapter provides the student with a process whereby batterers can be classified so that treatment programs can be better tailored for those in treatment. Category one, two, and three batterers are classified by level of dangerousness which then determines whether some treatment modalities are more appropriate than others. Further still, category three batterers are most likely to have corollary mental health issues and therefore have a more challenging prognosis. Lastly, research has consistently shown that drug and/or alcohol abuse is a common problem among the battering population. Thus, batterers should be in substance abuse treatment prior to beginning a domestic violence intervention. This is even true if no documented substance abuse problem is on record because it is likely that they have simply evaded detection. Substance abuse treatment should continue during the entire time the batterer participates in the batterer's group intervention.

LEARNING CHECK

1. Rather than emphasizing treatment for category three batterers, it is recommended that the setting of effective criminal justice boundaries be emphasized.
   a. True
   b. False

2. In many cases, category one batterers do express a sense of genuine remorse and are receptive to treatment.
   a. True
   b. False
3. "Vagal reactors" or "cobras" are likened to psychopaths.
   a. True
   b. False
4. Anger management can be an appropriate intervention for the various categories of batterers.
   a. True
   b. False
5. Given the prevalence of substance abuse problems among the battering population, it is recommended that all batterers be placed in some form of substance abuse treatment intervention, even if no documented substance abuse problem has been detected.
   a. True
   b. False

PART THREE: SPECIFIC DOMESTIC BATTERER GROUP INTERVENTION MODELS

The Duluth Model

Perhaps the most widely known curriculum is the Duluth model, which was initially constructed by Ellen Pence and Michael Paymar (1993). This was perhaps one of the earliest curricula to be designed as a full-range set of sessions for battering clients. This curriculum is so popular that many batterer intervention programs either adhere to or borrow from this psychoeducational and skills-building curriculum. This curriculum addresses a range of controlling behaviors, with the "power and control wheel" illustrating these behaviors in a unique but well-known diagram. This wheel depicts how physical violence is connected to male power and control through a number of "spokes" or control tactics: minimizing, denying, blaming; using intimidation, emotional abuse, isolation, children, male privilege, economic abuse, and threats. According to the Duluth model, the batterer maintains control over his partner through constant acts of coercion, intimidation, and isolation punctuated by periodic acts of violence.

The Duluth curriculum is taught in classes that emphasize the development of critical thinking skills centered around eight themes: (1) nonviolence, (2) nonthreatening behavior, (3) respect, (4) support and trust, (5) honesty and accountability, (6) sexual respect, (7) partnership, and (8) negotiation and fairness. Depending on the total length of the program, two or three sessions are devoted to each theme. Thus, the Duluth model of intervention is designed to last anywhere from 16 to 24 weeks in duration. The first session of each theme begins with a video vignette that demonstrates the controlling behavior from that portion of the wheel. Discussion revolves around the actions that the batterer in the story used to control his partner; the advantages he was trying to get out of the situation; the beliefs he expressed that supported his position; the feelings he was hiding through his behavior; and the means he used to minimize, deny, or blame the victim for his actions. At the close of each session, offenders are given homework: to identify these same elements in an incident when they exhibited similar controlling behaviors. During subsequent sessions devoted to the theme, each group member describes his own use of the controlling behavior, why he used it, and what its effects were. Alternative behaviors that can build a healthier, egalitarian relationship are then explored.

One of the drawbacks to this model of intervention is that it requires considerable skill on the part of group leaders. The curriculum is a bit open ended in approach meaning that the effectiveness of the intervention will tend to be related to the effectiveness of the correctional counselor(s) who facilitate the intervention. This is compounded by the fact that, with all group interventions for domestic batterers, group leaders have to be vigilant against both the active and passive ways batterers avoid taking responsibility for their abuse, both inside and outside of group. Because we believe that it is important to leave the student with a clear understanding of how interventions are implemented, a brief synopsis of each of the eight themes will be provided. Note that all information has been adapted from the work by Pence and Paymar (1993). Each session is presented in the discussion that follows.

Nonviolence. This is the primary theme during the first two or three group sessions. The first 15 minutes of the session consists of a check-in (discussed earlier in this chapter), where offenders report their progress on steps that they have agreed to take toward treatment. During the initial session (as well as others, if the counselor so desires) video vignettes may be used to illustrate the main theme for these sessions. The remainder of each of the three sessions will focus on addressing the offender's view on the use of violence and will consist of exercises where participants answer questions, examine past experiences, and role-play conflict resolution without the use of controlling or abusive behavior. Other group participants observe the role-play and provide their own observations and feedback.

Nonthreatening Behavior. During sessions four through six, nonthreatening behaviors are the primary theme or focus. As with all sessions, the first 15 minutes consists of a brief check-in. Afterwards, offenders are required to discuss and explore past acts of violence and intimidation that they have committed. Offenders are given specific exercises that identify the means by which violence, and the threat of violence, is used to control their relationship with their partner. Underlying payoffs for the use of intimidation are explored during these sessions.

Respect. During the next two or three sessions, issues of mutual respect are addressed, with specific focus being on the offender's use of emotional abuse as a weapon in the relationship. Indeed, Pence and Paymar (1993) contend that "emotional abuse is one of the most powerful weapons a batterer uses to control his partner. It provides the foundation for the use of almost all other abusive behaviors" against those he victimizes. Through the use of emotional abuse, the offender makes a psychological attack on his partner's self-esteem.

Trust and Support. This theme examines the tendency that batterers have to isolate their partners from external relationships and human contact. This sense of isolation may occur due to a lack of economic resources (with the batterer encouraging the partner to stay home and not work), a lack of transportation (there is only one car and the batterer uses it), or admonishment for associating with certain friends and/or family. The use of these isolation techniques makes their partner dependent upon them and this translates to power over their partner. It is important that correctional counselors are attuned to the various techniques that are used by batterers to control their victim. What might otherwise seem like a series of events that just "happened" then become part of a methodical process for the batterer to maintain power. These behaviors are identified and challenged by group members as well as the counselor.

Honesty and Accountability. During the sessions that address this theme, batterers are made to address their victim-blaming thoughts and words. During the sessions that address this theme, a variety of worksheets, role-plays, and other activities that require batterers to assume accountability for their actions are encouraged. The weeks that carry this theme tend to be met with more resistance than any other theme within the curriculum.

Sexual Respect. This theme addresses issues related to coerced sex in abusive relationships. In many instances, the partner may be manipulated, harassed, or made to feel guilty if she does not acquiesce to sexual demands. In many cases, offenders do not see these dynamics as problematic; rather this may be normalized by these offenders. This is largely due to beliefs that are egocentric where the offender views himself as having a right to sexual access. Further, many batterers may view their partner's unwillingness as a form of control by withholding something that is desired by the batterer.

Partnership. During the sessions that follow this theme, beliefs in strict gender roles are explored and challenged. Concepts such as male privilege and entitlement, economic abuse, and the balance of power in relationships are also specifically addressed. Inherent to this theme is that historic oppression and subjugation of women has occurred because men have defined most facets of society which has, in turn, led to a sexist belief system and the common acceptance of male privilege. Though this is naturally changing in the United States, many batterers still cling to the outdated notions that women should play subservient roles to men.

Negotiation and Fairness. This theme addresses the lack of negotiation skills that tend to be a common deficit among domestic batterers. According to Pence and Paymar, "the goal of negotiation is to balance the needs of two parties and to reach a resolution that is mutually satisfactory" (1993, p. 154). The sessions during which this theme occurs will consist of role-plays among the group participants as well as homework assignments designed to get the batterer to consider his own forms of controlling behavior that obstruct genuine negotiation.

Lastly, the most common approach in implementing the Duluth model is to have three weeks per theme. During the first week of each theme, there will usually be five activities that participants must complete. The group begins with a check-in, where the participants briefly discuss their progress toward their agreed-upon goals. This is followed by a brief discussion on the definition of the theme that is identified for that session. Then a three to five minute video or role-play is shown and the participants are required to take notes and incorporate the vignette into the session. The counselor may then provide lecture format information to participants followed by an assignment whereby participants record and analyze an abuse incident that is similar to the one discussed.

During weeks two and three, the process begins with a check-in. For week two there are usually only two activities. The majority of the session is then focused on the group analyzing their individual participant logs that identifies a personal example that fits with the overall theme of the session. Week three typically includes three activities, but these activities tend to consist of role-plays among group members where noncontrolling alternatives to abusive incidents are practiced. These incidents are typically chosen from a participant's control log, making the exercises even more relevant to the individuals in the group.

The Domestic Abuse Project Model

The origins of Domestic Abuse Project (DAP) date back to 1979 and it was developed during the same time period that the work by Pence and Paymar was developed. The DAP model begins with an orientation session that is followed by a cycle of at least 20 sessions. These sessions are arranged into two separate session tracks, with the first 10 sessions being educational in nature. After the educational sessions are completed, the client will attend an intake session, which ensures that the participant is fit for the process sessions that follow. The process sessions are the actual group therapy components, with the educational sessions providing baseline information to clients to ensure that they have the requisite understanding of power-and-control issues so as to be active participants during the group process sessions.

The orientation session occurs after initial contact with the intervention program. The meeting between treatment staff and the client allows the client to assess his own willingness to commit to treatment. At the same time, the correctional counselor is able to asses the offender's readiness to participate. The education sessions consist of the correctional counselor presenting information and materials in a lecture format to the entire group of offenders. During the course of the 10 education sessions, the group is assigned a new topic each week. Among these topics would be the costs and payoffs of abusive behavior, cultural violence, and the consequences of violence. A more detailed breakdown of the orientation session and the education sessions are provided as follows:

Orientation. The orientation session is divided into two parts. During part one, the correctional counselor should keep in mind that offenders typically experience a high level of anxiety and shame when they first begin a domestic abuse treatment program. The correctional counselor should attempt to provide information clearly and in a nonthreatening manner. Often, the use of a video during the orientation can help to facilitate conversation. During the orientation, offenders are informed of the philosophy and structure of the program. At the base of the DAP philosophy is the idea that power and control lie at the root of the violent behavior. During the second part of the orientation, offenders are introduced to the self-control plan (SCP), which is the cornerstone of the treatment regimen. The SCP is a cognitive-behavioral plan that helps to identify "cues" or antecedents to abusive behavior. The SCP is designed to assist the offender in early identification of these cues to enable him to make a healthier choice in his behavior before he feels that his actions are beyond his own control.

Education sessions. The education sessions are ongoing and open, meaning that as new participants join these groups, those who have completed the education series leave the group. Further, offenders must attend at least nine different sessions. If a participant misses more than one session, he must wait 10 weeks until the missed session comes up in the cycle again so that it can be attended.

Session 1—Costs and Payoffs of Abusive Behavior and Effects of Violence on Children: "The purpose of this session is to help group members realize that their abusive behavior may have short-term payoffs but will have long-term, detrimental consequences. Offenders learn how they can control and change their abusive behavior and implement more healthy alternatives for conflict resolution" (Domestic Abuse Project, 1993, p. 53).

Session 2—Responsibility versus Shame: "The purpose of this session is to define shame and understand how it prevents people from taking responsibility for and changing their abusive behavior. Offenders are taught to identify feelings associated with shame and the manner by which shame and guilt can generate defense mechanisms that prevent the offender from being accountable for their actions" (Domestic Abuse Project, 1993, p. 63).

Session 3—ABC Model and Stopping Negative Self-Talk: "The purpose of this session is to make the connection between emotional and behavioral responses and our core beliefs, attitudes, and self-talk. Choosing abusive behavior is based on negative self-talk about power, control, and expectations. Feelings of powerlessness, anger, and rage are based on these negative beliefs and serve as the basis for violent actions" (Domestic Abuse Project, 1993, p. 75). This session explains the ABC model with A being the activating event, B being a set of faulty beliefs, and C being the consequences of inappropriate actions.

Session 4—Responsible Assertive Communication Skills: "The purpose of this session is to define and recognize the four main styles of communication" (Domestic Abuse Project, 1993, p. 83). Special attention is given to assertive communications and active listening skills. Further, offenders are required to discuss how abuse impairs future communication skills.

Session 5—Responsible Assertiveness Role-Playing: "The purpose of this session is to identify the payoffs of developing assertive communication skill and an assertive belief system" (Domestic Abuse Project, 1993, p. 93).

Session 6—Culture of Origin I: "The purpose of this session is to examine how rigid stereotypes of gender roles perpetuate abuse, foster shame, encourage aggressive behavior, and keep men from experiencing intimacy in a relationship" (Domestic Abuse Project, 1993, p. 101).

Session 7—Culture of Origin II: The purpose of this session is to demonstrate that violence against a partner is not an isolated incident but occurs within a cultural and historical context that enforces a sense of power and control over one's partner (Domestic Abuse Project, 1993). This session explores violence used for oppression and issue related to ideas of male privilege and power derived from an unequal society.

Session 8—Ending Threats and Controlling Behavior: This session defines the use of threats and controlling behavior as abuse. It further explores how threatening and controlling behavior may have a profound impact on trust, honesty, and intimacy in a relationship. Lastly, possibilities of rebuilding trust and intimacy in relationships is explored (Domestic Abuse Project, 1993).

Session 9—Stress and Anger: This session is similar in theme and scope to the content included in many anger management programs. Offenders are taught to understand anger, hostility, and aggression. This session also explores various aspects of stress and the means of coping (Domestic Abuse Project, 1993).

Session 10—Therapist Exchange: This session typically has a visiting victim's advocate or therapist educate offenders on victim issues. Further, offenders are again taught that the domestic abuse is not the fault of their partner.

Once the offender completes the 10 education sessions, an individualized session is conducted with the offender and the correctional counselor. During this time, the correctional counselor will assess the client to determine if they are ready to engage in genuine therapy to change their abusive behavior. If the client is not ready, they may be sent back to repeat the education sessions or they may be sent out of the program, depending on the circumstances. Lastly, the process sessions allow group members to work through their feelings, discuss their abusive behavior, and engage in the feedback process with other members of the group. Lastly, while engaging in the process sessions, each offender is required to complete a set of three individual presentations to the group. The personal presentations cover topics related to each individual's own abusive behavior and the changes that have been or will be made.

SECTION SUMMARY

This section provides the reader with an overview of two different types of batterer group intervention programs. The Duluth model is probably the most widely recognized form of batterer group interventions throughout the United States. Many programs tend to either use the entire curriculum or borrow from that curriculum. The Duluth model has a psychoeducational and skills-building approach, with each session following a defined theme. This provides for a clear structure to the treatment process and allows the correctional counselor to address many specific and clearly defined issues that are related to domestic abuse.

However, there are other programs, such as the DAP model, that are likewise well disseminated and have a long history of use. This program also has themes throughout its sessions but divides the sessions between educational and process sessions. This means that batterers are given the requisite psychoeducation that is needed before they begin the second phase of sessions that is related to the treatment process. This again provides for a solid structure in intervention approach and also ensures that clients are ready for the group counseling experience before they start the actual treatment process. If an offender misses a session or is not deemed ready for further intervention by the correctional counselor, then further educational sessions are required. Further, the DAP model covers a broad array of issues and has a strong cognitive-behavioral approach, making it well suited for the criminal justice system.

LEARNING CHECK

1. The Duluth model of intervention is based around eight broad themes.
   a. True
   b. False
2. The Duluth model has two separate session tracks, one that is educational and one that is process oriented.
   a. True
   b. False
3. The DAP model has its basis in psychoanalytic forms of intervention and psychotherapy.
   a. True
   b. False
4. The DAP model addresses issues involving shame and guilt experienced by the offender.
   a. True
   b. False
5. One of the drawbacks to the Duluth model of intervention is that it requires considerable skill on the part of group leaders.
   a. True
   b. False

CONCLUSION

Issues related to anger management and domestic abuse are common to the offender population. In many cases, offenders have themselves come from abusive homes, and, when they are themselves perpetrators of family violence, they may be enacting a cycle that could extend across numerous generations throughout some family systems. While anger management and domestic abuse interventions may have many similar techniques, the two should not be confused as being one and the same. The factors that relate to each may be quite different, particularly since domestic abuse tends to be specific to others who are close to the batterer whereas episodes of anger from an offender may be generated by any number of persons, stressors, or sources of aggravation. There have been cases where courts have mandated domestic batterers to anger management rather than a domestic batterers group intervention; this should not occur. Domestic batterers require extensive intervention that goes beyond simply addressing anger control. Rather, issues of sexism, a sense of entitlement, views on relationships, and power and control must be addressed, among other things.

In addition, it is important to be able to discern between different types of batterers. Not all domestic abusers are equally dangerous nor do they all have the same prognosis for recovery. Some batterers may have a low likelihood of recidivism whereas others may be nearly beyond reform. Understanding the distinctions between the various types of batterers is important for victim safety concerns and for treatment planning purposes. Further still, domestic abusers may often have substance abuse issues that must be addressed. This is a very common occurrence and it is highly recommended that these offenders be required to attend treatment for any substance abuse problems that may exist. A failure to do so will most likely ensure that the batterer intervention is not successful. Lastly, mental health issues may also complicate the intervention process for many batterers. Correctional counselors must ensure that domestic batterers are screened for diagnosable disorders and that they receive assistance with those disorders.

Lastly, two model programs of group intervention were presented in this chapter, the Duluth model and the domestic abuse project model of group intervention. These two groups were chosen due to their longevity (they have both been in existence since the inception of the movement to recognize domestic violence) and due to their widespread use throughout the country. While many intervention programs may not use these models in their purest form, these models do tend to have many of the characteristics that are common to domestic group interventions around the nation. It is clear from the presentation of these models that domestic batterer groups emphasize the use of cognitive-behavioral approaches to intervention and the need for offender accountability for the crimes that they have committed. These two aspects of the intervention process are important since they tend to be the hallmark components of effective domestic batterer group interventions.

Essay Questions

1. Explain why the use of check-ins may be so common within domestic batterer group interventions. Further, explain some of the techniques used in interventions to make batterers track their behavior throughout the week between group sessions.
2. Provide at least one example of a cognitive-behavioral approach used in group interventions. In your opinion, why would cognitive-behavioral approaches be the perspective used in most batterer intervention programs? What are some techniques from your previous readings in Chapter 5 that would be effective with domestic abusers, given what you now know about domestic abuse group interventions?
3. From your previous readings, how do domestic abuser groups compare with the general group process presented in Chapter 7 of this text? What are some techniques from your previous readings in Chapter 7 that would be effective with domestic abusers, given what you now know about domestic abuse group interventions?
4. Discuss Groetsch's three categories of domestic batterers. Why is it important to classify batterers into different groups and how does this assist in the

treatment planning process? Also, explain which different types of interventions are likely to be effective with each category of domestic batterer.

5. Discuss some of the mental disorders that might be prevalent among the battering population. Explain how this might impact the likely success of treatment with batterers. Further, discuss why substance abuse treatment is important when considering the batterer population. From your previous readings in Chapter 8, what might be useful to consider when addressing substance abuse issues among batterers? Lastly, how would co-occurring disorders, in addition to the substance abuse issues, further complicate the treatment of a domestic batterer?

Treatment Planning Exercise

During this exercise, the student must consider the case of Jimmy and must determine whether Jimmy is being manipulative or whether the reasons that he gives are sincere. You must explain how you would confront Jimmy and how that may affect your rapport with Jimmy. Further, you must also consider how any confrontation might impair his relationship with his other treatment providers.

The Case of Jimmy

Jimmy is a domestic batterer who is in your group for his domestic abuse that meets on Monday evenings at 6:30 P.M. He is also in an additional group for anger management that meets at 7:00 on Wednesday evenings. Lastly, he is in another group for substance abuse issues at 7:00 on Thursday evenings. On Tuesday and Thursday mornings, he visits a local educational agency for GED preparation. In addition, Jimmy completes roughly eight hours of community service a week, attends AA meetings on Tuesday evening, and is also required to meet his probation officer five times per week since he is on intensive supervised probation. Jimmy has signed releases of confidentiality between all agencies and treatment providers enabling all persons involved with Jimmy's case to talk with one another without concern for confidentiality.

One day, Jimmy's addiction therapist calls you and explains that he is concerned. It seems that Jimmy is violating the bounds of confidentiality by leaking information regarding other members of his batterers' group. During the substance abuse group meeting on Thursday evenings, he routinely refers to clients in his Monday evening batterers' group by name and provides details regarding their relationships and their treatment progress. The therapist explains that he talked with Jimmy about this, and Jimmy got a bit angry. He was not volatile, but irritated and exclaimed, "Here I am trying to participate in the group session and you are downin' me, man! What gives with this, dude?"

When you ask Jimmy about this issue, he points out that he is so busy with therapy and meeting the conditions of his supervision that he cannot remember who is in what group and how to sort things out. He claims that he slips up by accident and that he just cannot keep up.

You screen his records and notice that the GED preparation and testing agency conducted a number of tests of cognitive functioning. They found that Jimmy has fairly significant cognitive deficits that affect his concentration. Whether this is induced by substance abuse is not clear, but it has been noted in his record (though Jimmy does not seem to be aware of this). On the other hand, you are keenly aware

(*continued*)

that batterers are very clever (though not necessarily smart academically), manipulative, and tend to be passive-aggressive by nature. In short, you suspect that Jimmy is manipulating his various treatment challenges to sabotage the therapy so that he can get reassigned. Lastly, you have been told by another offender in your batterer's group that Jimmy has stated many times that he does not like the therapist for his addiction group and has been wanting to leave that group for some time. It seems that Jimmy brings this up when the batterer's group members are outside smoking before the group work begins.

Bibliography

American Psychiatric Association. (2000). *Diagnostic and statistical manual of mental disorders: Text revision* (4th ed.). Washington, DC: American Psychiatric Association.

Barnett, O. W., Miller-Perrin, C., & Perrin, R. (2004) *Family violence across the lifespan* (2nd ed.). Thousand Oaks, CA: Sage Publications.

Collins, J. J., & Messerschmidt, M. A. (1993). Epidemiology of alcohol-related violence. U.S. DHHS NIAAA. *Alcohol, Health, and Research World, 17*, 93–100.

Davis, S. F., & Palladino, J. J. (2002). *Psychology* (3rd ed.). Upper Saddle River, NJ: Prentice Hall.

Domestic Abuse Project. (1993). *Men's group manual.* Minneapolis, MN: Domestic Abuse Project.

Gottman, J., Jacobson, N., Rushe, R., Shortt, J., Babcock, J., La Taillade, J., & Waltz, J. (1995). The relationship between heart rate activity, emotionally aggressive behavior, and general violence in batterers. *Journal of Family Psychology, 9*, 227–248.

Groetsch, M. (1996). *The battering syndrome: Why men beat women and the professional's guide to intervention*. Brookfield, WI: CPI Publishing.

Hanser, R. D. (2007). *Special needs offenders.* Upper Saddle River, NJ: Pearson Prentice Hall.

Hanson, G. R., Venturelli, P. J., & Fleckenstein, A. E. (2002). *Drugs and society* (7th ed.). Sudbury, MA: Jones and Bartlett Publishers.

Hare, R. (1993). *Without conscience.* New York: Pocket Books.

Healey, K., Smith, C., & O'Sullivan, C. (1999). *Batterer intervention: Program approaches and criminal justice strategies.* Washington, DC: National Institute of Justice.

Holtzworth-Munroe, A., & Stuart, G. L. (1994). Typology of male batterers: Three subtypes and the differences among them. *Psychological Bulletin, 116*(3), 476–497.

Jacobson, N., & Gottman, J. (1998). *When men batter women.* New York: Simon & Schuster.

O'Farrell, T. J., & Murphy, C. M. (1995). Marital violence before and after alcoholism treatment. *Journal of Consulting and Clinical Pscyhology, 63*, 256–262.

Pence, E., & Paymar, M. (1993). *Education groups for men who batter: The Duluth model.* New York: Springer Publishing.

Reilly, P. M., & Shopshire, M. S. (2002a). *Anger Management for Substance Abuse and Mental Health Clients: A Cognitive Behavioral Therapy Manual.* DHHS Pub. No. (SMA) 02-3661. Rockville, MD: Center for Substance Abuse Treatment, Substance Abuse and Mental Health Services Administration. Retrieved from: http://www.kap.samhsa.gov/products/manuals/pdfs/anger1.pdf.

Reilly, P. M., & Shopshire, M. S. (2002b). *Anger Management for Substance Abuse and Mental Health Clients: Participant Workbook*. DHHS Pub. No. (SMA) 02-3662. Rockville, MD: Center for Substance Abuse Treatment, Substance Abuse and Mental Health Services Administration. Retrieved from: http://kap.samhsa.gov/products/manuals/pdfs/anger2.pdf.

Russell, M. N. (1996). *Confronting abusive beliefs: Group treatment for abusive men.* Thousand Oaks, CA: Sage Publications.

Wexler, D. B. (2000). *Domestic violence 2000: An integrated skills program for men—Group leader's manual.* New York: W. W. Norton & Company.

11

Female Offenders and Correctional Counseling

CHAPTER OBJECTIVES

After reading this chapter, you will be able to:

1. Identify and discuss challenges that are more common for female offenders than for male offenders.
2. Explain how family-of-origin issues may be an important consideration for female offenders.
3. Explain why beliefs pertaining to sex and sexuality may be an important area of consideration for many female offenders.
4. Describe the underlying aspects of feminist therapy and how this may be applicable to female offenders.
5. Identify and discuss various issues related to females who come from minority groups that are more commonly represented in the criminal justice system of the United States.

INTRODUCTION

One specialized population that has gained quite a bit of attention since the mid-1990s is the female offender population. The rate of growth in the number of women in prison and on community supervision has continued to get higher, with the proportion of female offenders in treatment sharing a corresponding growth. It is not the focus of this chapter to determine the specific number of women nor the rate of growth of women in custody, but instead we simply wish to note that the female offender population has emerged as a substantive group within the correctional population. It is therefore important that correctional counselors be knowledgeable in providing interventions with this group of offenders. It is with this in mind that we now turn our attention to some of the common issues that are more specific to female offenders than male offenders.

PART ONE: WOMEN IN THERAPY

Parental Roles

Undoubtedly, the role as a mother has proven important within the identity of many female offenders (Hanser, 2007). In fact, the prognosis for successful correctional treatment is often linked with the woman's ability to maintain contact with her children (Hanser, 2007; Kassebaum, 1999). Further, it is important to consider that female offenders in the criminal justice system are mothers to approximately 1.3 million children. This then means that, at one point or another, issues related to parenting and childcare become important considerations for female offenders. This is particularly true since many women who are placed in treatment programs and/or put on community supervision may lose custody of their children. In some cases, the children may be kept by relatives of the female offender. In other cases, the children may be placed in foster care. When children are placed in foster care, caseworkers are expected to make concerted efforts to sustain family ties and to encourage family reunification (Bloom, Brown, & Chesney-Lind, 1996). Regardless of whether the offender is given incarceration or is kept on community supervision, the issue of child custody usually must be addressed for these offenders.

However, once released from custody to community corrections, mothers face numerous obstacles in reunifying with their children. They must navigate through a number of complex governmental and social service agencies in order to regain custody of their children. In the process, they often have to demonstrate that they are "fit" to have custody of their children. During this time, female offenders may need instruction on everything from pregnancy issues to parenting to child placement. Thus, it is important that correctional counselors see to it that female offenders gain parenting instruction, since many female offenders themselves have come from dysfunctional homes.

Substance Abuse

Substance abuse is a major contributor to female criminality. Substance abuse is correlated with a number of female crimes such as prostitution and shoplifting. Often these other crimes are committed to support the female offender's drug problem. Further, female offenders tend to use alcohol, cocaine, and heroin as drugs of choice. These are highly addictive drugs that require intensive treatment. Indeed, women are particularly in need of quality drug abuse interventions because female offenders are more likely than male offenders to use drugs, they use more serious drugs than male offenders, and they use them more frequently. Further, female offenders are more likely than male offenders to be under the influence of drugs at the time of their crimes (Kassebaum, 1999).

Not only are female offenders likely to be in more need of drug treatment but the intervention should be specifically tailored to the female population. Indeed, treating women in all-female rather than coeducational settings—where the environment can be more nurturing, supporting, and comfortable for speaking about such issues as domestic violence, sexual abuse and incest, shame, and self-esteem—is helpful (Kassebaum, 1999). Recently, women's treatment experts have been calling for new treatment models designed specifically for women. Adding special services to a male treatment model should not be considered sufficient. Rather, the female treatment program must be separate from the traditional male treatment models to ensure that it fits the psychological and social needs of women (Kassebaum, 1999).

Lastly, substance abuse issues for women are often tied to the relationships that they have with others, particularly their significant other. In most cases, a woman with a drug problem has been intimately involved with a man who also has a drug problem. In addition, many women report that a man introduced them to drugs, while men tend to more often begin using drugs with male peers. One study found that roughly 33% of female heroin addicts indicated that a male friend, spouse, or partner influenced their decision to use narcotics. On the other hand, only 2% of male addicts in the study indicated that a woman influenced their decision to use drugs (CASA, 1996). Kassebaum (1999) notes that it is probably accurate to say that some of these women are addicted both to the substance and to a man who is addicted. A man introduces them to drugs, and they depend on the man for their supply. In many cases, the woman's criminal behavior may simply result from dependent acquiescence in response to the desires of an addicted male partner.

Depression and Anxiety

Depression is perhaps the single most common *DSM-IV-TR* diagnosable disorder among female offenders. There are several reasons that contribute to this observation. First, within the general population of men and women, there is a slightly higher prevalence of depression and anxiety among women than men. In most cases, certain disorders in the *DSM-IV-TR* are represented more by one sex than the other: Women tend to present with depression more frequently than men. While this only accounts for cases that involve persons willing to report their symptoms, the general clinical landscape is one where depression and anxiety (anxiety tends to correlate with depression) are more commonly found among the female population.

Second, women tend to gravitate toward drug use, and this exacerbates their likelihood of reporting levels of depression and anxiety. It may be recalled from Chapter 8 that depression and anxiety are frequently found to be co-occurring disorders for substance abusers. Naturally then, this would be the case for female offenders just as it would be for male offenders. However, it is not clear if the female offending population tends to initially present with depression and anxiety which is then aggravated by the drug use, or if the drug use initiates and leads to long-term problems with depression and anxiety. The true answer is probably that both means of onset occur frequently among women processed in the criminal justice system, but it is probably more likely that women initially experience depression and anxiety prior to and aside from their drug use, given that the life-course profile of most female offenders tends to consist of a history or prior abuse, trauma, and deprivation.

This brings us to our last point regarding depression and anxiety among female offenders. Many women who are incarcerated and/or on community supervision often report some sort of abuse that has been experienced in their past. In childhood, it is not uncommon for sexual abuse and/or other forms of abuse to be reported. In adulthood, many female offenders report experiences with domestic abuse in their intimate relationships. These experiences often lead to some sort of trauma, including post-traumatic stress disorder (PTSD), which then also tends to correlate with anxiety (indeed, a traumatic event is anxiety producing) and depression. Thus, the life-course experiences of female offenders tend to add to the complications. Further still, experiences in the criminal justice system further aggravate the symptoms and severity of these disorders, particularly when long-term separation from their children tends to occur. Thus, issues related to these two disorders, depression and anxiety, are central to the effective treatment for female offenders.

Domestic Abuse

The research on the prevalence of domestic violence and its impact on women in the United States is so abundant and obvious that it goes beyond the scope of this chapter to discuss. However, when limiting the discussion to female offenders and their experiences with domestic violence, it appears that they are at greater risk for physical abuse than those in the general population. One survey of female offenders shows that incarcerated women are very likely to have histories of physical abuse (American Correctional Association, 1990). This study indicated that 53% of adult women and nearly 62% of juvenile girls had been victims of physical abuse. Nearly half of both these groups (49% of adults and 47% of juveniles) reported experiencing multiple episodes of physical abuse. Furthermore, this study found that this violence is most likely to have been perpetrated by a boyfriend or husband in the case of adult women offenders (50%) or by a parent in the case of juvenile girls (43%).

For juvenile girls, most of the cases of domestic violence occur between the ages of 10 and 14 years (Bloom, Owen, & Covington, 2003). Adult incarcerated women report being subjected to violence most at ages 15 to 24 (Bloom et al., 2003). This means that this abuse tends to follow the female offender throughout their life span, indicating that these offenders return to a lifestyle that is self-damaging. Because the women on probation and parole are likely to be somewhat socially isolated from common social circles, her peer network is likely to be limited (Bloom et al., 2003). At best it will include other women in a similar situation or perhaps persons from employment (keep in mind the educational level, unemployment rate, and vocational skills of these women). More likely, these women are likely to continue to associate within the subculture of origin, meaning that many of the friends and family that they return to are likely to be, or have been, criminal offenders themselves. This may be much more common since many women who offend often tend to do so as secondary accomplices with a male primary offender. Thus, these women are not likely to have many resources to rely on and may find themselves quite dependent on a man, including an abusive man.

Further, as was noted earlier in regard to the confluence of issues related to depression, anxiety, and past trauma issues (i.e., sexual assault and domestic violence), there has long been a noted relationship between substance abuse and domestic violence. For example, Miller et al. (1990) argue that female alcoholics are at significantly higher risk for becoming victims of domestic abuse. According to the same study, male parolees are at high risk for involvement as perpetrators of spousal abuse. Although Miller et al. (1990) do not address whether spouses or partners of male parolees are themselves former offenders, these findings clearly show that many women released on community supervision may be in abusive relationships. Further, since it is the case that many female offenders commit their crimes while acting in tandem with a primary male offender (i.e., transporting drugs for their drug smuggling boyfriends and husbands, having a pimp that they may associate with, or providing alibis and resources for the male offender during periods of crime commission), many of them simply return to these significant others (who are criminal offenders themselves) and therefore continue to be with men who are more likely to be abusive than otherwise noncriminal men. There is an added danger with this because these women already tend to be marginalized, and with the added stigma of being an offender on community supervision, along with worries of maintaining custody of any children that are likely to exist, the female offender may simply consign herself to such a dangerous and damaging lifestyle due to the lack of available options.

Physical and Sexual Abuse

A study on the self-reported prior abuse conducted by the Bureau of Justice Statistics in 1999 found that female offenders are abused more frequently than male offenders. State prison inmates reported both physical and sexual abuse experiences prior to their being sentenced. The results found that 57.2% of females had experienced abusive treatment compared to 16.1% of males. Of this same group, 36.7% of the female offenders and 14.4% of the male offenders reported that the abuse occurred during their childhood or teenage years. Other findings from this study are as follows:

1. Males tend to be mistreated as children, but females are mistreated as both children and adults.
2. Both genders reported much more abuse if they had lived in a foster home or other structured institution.
3. Higher levels of abuse were reported among offenders who had a family member who was incarcerated.
4. Offenders reporting prior abuse had higher levels of drug and alcohol abuse than those who did not report abuse. Further, female offenders abused drugs or alcohol more frequently than did male offenders.

PTSD Related to Sexual Assault and Prior Child Abuse

Post-traumatic stress disorder (PTSD) describes a series of symptoms where the victim's response to the experienced traumatic event involves intense fear, helplessness, or horror. The victim is likely to psychologically reexperience the traumatic event, while exhibiting persistent symptoms of anxiety or increased arousal that were not present before the traumatic incident (American Psychiatric Association, 2000). Further, the victim will likely have difficulty falling asleep and may have persistent nightmares related to the victimization. Displays of hypervigilance and exaggerated startle responses are also common (American Psychiatric Association, 2000; Daane, 2005). Lastly, it is very common for victims to avoid stimuli that are connected with the source of trauma or that remind the victim of the traumatic experience (American Psychiatric Association, 2000; Daane, 2005). The symptoms of PTSD have been observed as being fairly common among victims of rape and sexual assault, domestic abuse, and various types of child abuse.

When referring to the traumatic responses of victims to sexual assault and/or rape, the term **rape trauma syndrome** is sometimes used. Rape trauma syndrome consists of symptoms that include physical, emotional, and behavioral effects that result from an encounter with a life-threatening and psychologically damaging sexual victimization (Burgess & Holstrom, 1974; Daane, 2005). The trauma from rape tends to be comparable to any other life-threatening event regardless of the level of violence actually used during the attack (Daane, 2005). A great number of victims report fear of extreme bodily harm during their experience, such as mutilation or death. These victims also report the existence of symptoms such as nausea, startle responses, insomnia, and nightmares.

According to Burgess and Holstrom (1974), rape trauma syndrome is divided into two phases. The first phase, known as the acute phase, can last anywhere from several days to weeks. During this phase, the victim experiences reactions to the realization of her experience, which tends to occur within a matter of hours. There are two common forms of reaction among victims of rape trauma syndrome. One reaction results in visible signs of trauma such as crying, restlessness, or tenseness. Conversely, some victims present with a controlled reaction that results in the masking of feelings, with the victim appearing calm or having no emotion.

The reorganization phase is the second phase. This phase tends to last considerably longer, spanning anywhere from several months to several years (Burgess & Holstrom, 1974). During this phase, victims contend with the need to regain structure and order within their life and provide some of control (Burgess & Holstrom, 1974). Intermediate effects that often emerge during this phase may include a disruption and change in the victim's lifestyle, such as moving houses or changing jobs, increased dependence on family or friends, and fear of going out or being alone. During this phase, the victim may feel anger especially toward the offender, sometimes toward family or friends, or toward the legal system if the victim does not feel that some sense of justice was meted out against the offender (Daane, 2005).

It is important for correctional counselors to understand the symptoms to PTSD and rape trauma syndrome. Counselors may find that many of their clients suffer from residual elements of this syndrome, if not fully meeting the requirements of the syndrome. Thus, an understanding of the dynamics associated with rape victimization is important when working with female offenders because sexual abuse is very common in the history of female offenders. This may have occurred during childhood or during adulthood. Further still, many of these women may have been involved in the illicit sex industry, and, even though it may not be reported to police, these women are also likely to be the victims of rape. Indeed, the amount of rape that occurs among prostitutes and other sex workers tends to be vastly underreported due to apprehension of going to the police among this population.

In addition, as was noted in the prior section, the experience of domestic abuse, both during adulthood and in the female's prior childhood, can also lead to trauma that is PTSD inducing. In adulthood, this can even lead to a set of symptoms that have been dubbed the battered woman syndrome, and this will be discussed momentarily in the section that follows. The key point is that this, in addition to the increased sexual abuse among this population, tends to increase the likelihood of trauma among the female offending population. Lastly, the pain of domestic abuse may not necessarily be in the recent case history of the female offender. Rather, many offenders (both male and female) report prior child abuse and neglect.

Indeed, many female offenders come from violent and/or abusive families of origin; and, it may be speculated that, to some extent, female offenders learn to normalize abusive patterns of communicating. This means that they are likely to remain in later adult relationships that are abusive, simply because these dynamics will be familiar to them from their childhood experiences. Naturally, these prior experiences shape their views of their own childhood and this, in turn, is likely to affect how the female offender may parent her own young. In some cases, this may increase the likelihood that the female herself ends up committing acts of abuse or neglect against her own children (Barnett, Miller-Perrin, & Perrin, 2004). In addition, this is further compounded if the female offender, who has herself grown up in an abusive home, becomes involved with an adult partner who is abusive. In such cases, it is more common for these women to repeat the abuse and/or to fail to intervene when her children are abused (Barnett et al., 2004). Thus, the prior childhood experiences of the female offender can significantly shape many of the later aspects of her future adult relationships, family dynamics, and sources of trauma.

Just to further illustrate how these prior experiences can complicate an already muddled picture for female offenders, consider that one common experience among women who present with dissociative identity disorder (DID) is the experience of childhood abuse. The trauma from these experiences often lead to a "splitting off" of the personalities such that the "bad" personality will be the one associated with abusive treatment and the "good" personality is identified with positive treatment from parents and caretakers. While DID is a rare disorder, it is more common among the abused than nonabused population. Given that psychiatric "breaks" with reality (i.e., schizophrenia and other related disorders) have been noted to be higher among female inmates than male inmates in jails and prison throughout the United States, even this serious psychiatric disorder becomes an issue of specific concern when dealing with female offenders. In such cases, the placement of offenders in "lock down" or forms of isolation tends to exacerbate the vulnerability to the illness and magnify its symptoms. Thus, even serious psychiatric disorders can have their basis in the traumas of the female offender's past, and, depending on the criminal justice reaction, these problems can be either aggravated or alleviated.

From this and other sections in this chapter, it should become clear to the student that there are a number of co-occurring factors that impair women in treatment. Prior sexual abuse and domestic violence lead to experiences of trauma. This trauma induces fear, depression, anxiety, and other negative affective states. Further, substance abuse tends to be common among this population, quite possibly as a means of alleviating their negative affective states. The use of various stimulant and/or depressive drugs (including alcohol) may seemingly provide initial relief, but over time these drugs simply exacerbate their symptoms. This then means that ultimately the use of drugs as a coping mechanism ends up compounding the problem. This then leads to the further aggravation of disorders that are associated with drug use and, over time, the life-course experiences of these women and their involvement in-and-out of treatment becomes a vicious cycle. It is precisely this cycle that correctional counselors must interrupt if long-term recovery can be successful among these women.

Battered Woman Syndrome

Battered woman syndrome is, for our purposes, considered a form of PTSD. Essentially, this syndrome describes a set of psychological symptoms that are common to women who live in battering relationships, with the following four general characteristics of the syndrome:

1. The woman believes that the violence was her fault.
2. The woman has an inability to place the responsibility for the violence elsewhere.
3. The woman fears for her life and/or her children's lives.
4. The woman has an irrational belief that the abuser is omnipresent and omniscient.

As can be seen, these characteristics are grounded in a heightened and perhaps hyper state of fear of the batterer, to the point that the victim sees herself as powerless to prevent further abuse. The fear that grips such a person is based on psychological learning (reinforced over time) as well as real circumstances that are, in many instances, beyond her control to influence or mitigate. Regardless, the battered woman syndrome should not be equated to some form of mental disorder; rather it is the product of trauma. Lenore Walker, a preeminent pioneer within the domestic violence literature, has stated that "battered woman's syndrome is best understood as a subgroup of what the American Psychological Association defines as Post-traumatic Stress Disorder, rather than as a form of mental illness" (1989, p. 48).

When working with female offenders, it is important for the correctional counselor to understand that many of their clients will readily identify with this syndrome. While they may not have experienced the syndrome directly, they are highly likely to know someone (a friend or family member) who has suffered from this syndrome. Further, the female offender is, herself, at an increased likelihood of having experienced this syndrome. Even if not, many have experienced the ravages and trauma associated with domestic abuse and they will often still be able to readily sympathize and empathize with women who do experience this syndrome. Thus, the correctional counselor must be knowledgeable about the various dynamics associated with the domestic violence.

For example, knowledge of the well-known **cycle of violence**, which has three specific phases—the tension-building phase, the explosion or acute battering phase, and the calm respite or "honey moon" phase (Walker, 1979)—should be commonplace among correctional counselors who routinely see female offenders. Knowledge regarding the symptoms and signs of sexual abuse, child abuse, and other forms of domestic violence should be readily understood by the counselor to the point that they are fully conversant on these issues. In addition, as was noted in the prior subsection, the correctional counselor should be knowledgeable in regard to the symptoms of PTSD and in treating those symptoms.

STDs and HIV/AIDS

Because female offenders engage in risky behaviors such as unprotected sex and the use of alcohol and drugs, they tend to enter correctional facilities with high rates of sexually transmitted disease (STD). Rich et al. (2001) found that of all the women in the state of Rhode Island who had been incarcerated at some point between 1992 and 1998, roughly half of them had infectious syphilis. Other research has shown higher rates of gonorrhea, chlamydia, and trichomoniasis among incarcerated women than among women with no history of incarceration (Hammett, Harmon, & Rhodes, 2000; Shuter, 2002). Clearly, this demonstrates that female offenders are at an increased risk of having sexually transmitted diseases. Because correctional counselors may not necessarily be well versed on the specific symptoms and medical effects of various STDs and because medical care is often a critical issue among the female offender population, we have decided to include some brief information on the more common STDs that are encountered among the female offending population. The information provided has been derived from the Epigee Foundation (2004). These diseases are among those most commonly encountered within the offender population and are among those that are most problematic for correctional agencies. These diseases and their symptoms are listed below:

Human Papalloma Virus (HPV)—The most common STD with symptoms that include cauliflower-like warts developed on and inside the genitals, anus, and throat. It should be noted that condoms provide almost no protection against contracting the disease during sex and even more disturbing is the fact that there is no known cure. The warts can be suppressed by chemicals, freezing, laser therapy, and surgery.

Syphilis—The most common way of contracting the disease is through vaginal, anal, or oral sex. However, it can be spread by nonsexual contact if the sores (chancres), rashes, or mucous patches caused by syphilis come in contact with the broken skin of a noninfected individual. If untreated, syphilis may cause serious damage to the heart, brain, eyes, nervous system, bones, and joints and can lead to death. A person with active syphilis has an increased risk that exposure to HIV will lead to infection because the sores (chancres) provide an entry point for the AIDS virus. The disease can be cured with penicillin; however, damage done to body organs cannot be reversed. Latex condoms can reduce but not eliminate the risk of contracting the disease during sex. However, it is still possible to contract syphilis, even after using a condom, via sores in the genital area.

Chlamydia—This is a very dangerous STD as it usually has no symptoms; 75% of infected women and 25% of infected men have no symptoms at all. Infection can be cured with antibiotics. However, it cannot undo the damage done prior to treatment. Infected individuals are at greater risk of contracting HIV if exposed to the virus. Latex condoms can reduce but not eliminate the risk of contracting the disease during sex.

Gonorrhea—This is one of the most frequently reported STD. Infection can be cured with antibiotics. However, it cannot undo the damage done prior to treatment. Latex condoms can reduce but not eliminate the risk of contracting the disease during sex. Untreated gonorrhea can infect the joints, heart valves, and/or the brain and can cause sterility in men.

Herpes—This disease is painful and episodic; it can be treated but there's no cure. Herpes is spread by direct sexual skin-to-skin contact with the infected site during vaginal, anal, or oral sex. Abstaining from vaginal, anal, and oral sex with an infected person is the only 100% effective means of preventing the sexual transmission of genital herpes. Latex condoms can reduce but not eliminate the risk of contracting the disease during sex.

From the list above, it is clear that these diseases can easily be problematic to the correctional practitioner. Some of them (such as syphilis) do not even require sexual contact and can be transmitted by simply rubbing against the open sores. Thus, even though these diseases may not frequently be life-threatening, it is still prudent that interventions and educational efforts be provided to offenders for their own safety and for the safety of staff who must interact with them.

A large body of research shows that female criminals often have some sort of history of prostitution although the causal factor(s) and the order of causal factors are not very clear. This, in addition to risky drug use, contributes to the inflated likelihood that female offenders will present with STDs in correctional settings. This is an issue that cannot be ignored by correctional counselors, and it should be specifically noted that both male and female counselors must be conversant on the symptoms and treatments of STDs. Once these diseases are contracted, they often impact the overall prognosis of the offender.

Aside from the effects of sexually transmitted diseases, it is also important to note that the rate of HIV infection is higher for female offenders than for male offenders. According to the Bureau of Justice Statistics (Snell, 1994), among state prisoners tested for HIV, women were more likely to test positive. An estimated 3.3% of the women reported being HIV positive, compared to 2.1% of the men. Among prisoners who had shared needles to inject drugs, more women than men were likely to be HIV positive (10% vs. 6.7%). In the vast majority of cases, those who become infected with HIV will eventually develop AIDS and die of AIDS-related complications. As with STDs, the physical and psychological effects of having HIV can greatly impair treatment outcomes for female offenders.

Body Image, Sexuality, and Sexual Image

Body image is an often-cited issue of concern for women in the United States. Among female offenders the issue is just as relevant. Indeed, research has shown that substance abusers often suffer from a low sense of self-efficacy (Hanser, 2007). This is not necessarily surprising when one considers that depression is a common co-occurring disorder among substance abusers (a person who is depressed would likely have a poor sense of self-efficacy). This observation has been particularly noted among female drug offenders (Kassebaum, 1999).

In many cases, female offenders report feelings of low self-esteem, self-confidence, and ability. Many come from low socioeconomic backgrounds and this also seems to impact the feelings that these women may have about themselves and their own value in society. Further, many of these women have had their identities tied to sex and sexuality throughout much of their life. In many cases, the association with sex and/or sexuality has been abusive (sexual abuse as a child and/or an adult) or utilitarian in purpose (i.e., making money through prostitution). These types of sexual identification are not healthy and contribute to the negative self-image that female offenders may have if they have had these past experiences.

Given that many women in society often feel that they have to meet some sort of ideal standard in regard to beauty and given that women still grapple with equality in our society, two things should be made clear. First, just as with all other women in our society, female offenders experience the biases and the standards that are placed on women, with physical beauty being emphasized in our society in a manner that negatively impacts women. Second, the specific forms of victimization that female offenders are likely to have also increases the risk that these women will make negative and self-depreciating associations with their own physical image. Indeed, many women with eating disorders such as anorexia and bulimia nervosa have serious negative images of their own bodies. Thus, the factors related to body image are important for women in general, and, given the case histories of many female offenders, it is even more important for female offenders.

SECTION SUMMARY

In this section, it becomes clear that there are a multiplicity of issues that confront female offenders. These issues are often intertwined with one another, with one problem aggravating the other. For example, substance abuse has been noted as a particular problem for female offenders, as has the occurrence of depression and anxiety. However, it is not always clear if the onset of depression and anxiety is due to the use of substances or if these offenders tend to gravitate toward these substances as a means of coping with their depression and anxiety.

Female offenders tend to also suffer from the effects of abuse, both in childhood and in adulthood. Sexual abuse is experienced more often among the female offender population than among the remaining female population. Further, female offenders are frequently victims of domestic violence. Thus, rape trauma syndrome, battered woman syndrome, and other variants of PTSD are very common among this population. Correctional counselors must keep these background issues in mind when dealing with female offenders since these issues impact their prognosis for treatment.

Lastly, female offenders tend to be the primary caretakers for their children. In addition, contact with their children tends to aid in their overall treatment and reform from criminal activity. The loss of contact between the mother and the child has negative effects for the youngster and also negatively impacts the mother's likelihood of effective recovery. Thus, it is important that intervention programs provide mechanisms that foster and maintain the bond between the female offender and her children, for the welfare of the child and the mother.

LEARNING CHECK

1. Criminal activity by female offenders is often committed due to the desires of a significant other with whom the female offender has an intimate relationship.
   a. True
   b. False
2. Substance abuse issues with female offenders are often related to problems with self-efficacy.
   a. True
   b. False
3. Given that female offenders tend to have substantial activity in the sex industry, they are more susceptible to developing STDs than are male offenders.
   a. True
   b. False
4. Among female offenders with children, most are the primary caretakers of those children.
   a. True
   b. False
5. Issues related to mental health disorders, prior trauma, and substance abuse seem to be interlinked among many female offenders.
   a. True
   b. False

PART TWO: FEMINIST THERAPY, MARGINALIZATION, AND DIVERSITY

Perhaps one of the best-suited paradigms for counseling female offenders would be a feminist approach. While there are numerous scholars and therapeutic professionals who have written on this approach, it should be stated that there is no "typical" or "traditional" feminist therapeutic intervention process. However, there are some commonalities in this approach despite the differences that may be encountered from one therapist to the other. First, "there is a belief that patriarchy is *alive and sick* in sociopolitical life and the life of the family" (Corey, 1996, p. 414). This means that men are given privilege and this power imbalance leads to an unbalanced and sick family and society. Second, there is the consensus that the traditional nuclear family, the stereotypical family of the 1950s, was one that was not constructive for women but instead better met the needs of men. Third, feminist therapeutic approaches emphasize a supportive attitude toward women and toward female independence, explicit examination of gender disparities, and connecting how imbalanced and sexist personal relationships lead to an imbalanced and sexist society. Incidentally, this same concept works in reverse order as well; an imbalanced and sexist society fosters and maintains imbalanced and sexist personal relationships between women and men.

Emphasis on Gender Equality

The feminist perspective of counseling tends to operate from the perspective that dominant culture groups will maintain themselves and will advance views that benefit the powerful, while disenfranchising those who do not have power. Further, feminists tend to see patriarchy as the oldest and most universal dominant cultural position to have existed worldwide. Simply put, women have been subordinate to men throughout history and across most cultures. The feminist perspective seeks to obtain an egalitarian form of balance between men and women. Thus, feminist perspectives do not contend that women are better than men or that men should be subservient to women. Rather, this type of therapeutic approach calls for quality and mutuality among both men and women.

Empowerment of Women

This aspect of feminist intervention is important with female offenders due to the already-noted tendency to have a lowered sense of self-efficacy as well as having higher rates of anxiety and depression. When using empowerment groups, women are encouraged to explore the definitions and the limitations that have been put upon them, and, above that, they are to provide positive support for one another. The sense of mutual acceptance and mutual understanding of the dynamics that shape the female experience is integral to this approach, as is the understanding that the only long-lasting empowerment will be that which occurs at the social level.

In empowerment groups women are considered to be their own true experts on themselves and their own issues. In these groups, the correctional counselor will encourage the group to nurture clients, listen and respond empathetically, and identify those areas where the female client has made substantial or significant contributions to the community, their family, or some other cause. These groups also emphasize that communal qualities of interdependence, concern for others, emotional expression, and cooperation are valued and honored. Women are encouraged to identify their strengths, to value and nurture themselves, and to bond with other women. Language forms that devalue women are reframed from weakness to strengths (e.g., terms such as *enmeshed* and *fused* may be reframed as *caring, concerned,* and *nurturing*).

The primary issue involved is countering the devaluation of women and identifying the inherent strengths that women have. Further, the group process is considered superior to most individual types of therapy because other members will be able to frequently identify with the female member and to provide her with support. According to Worell (1993), feminist empowerment strategies should include the following emphases:

1. ***Self-evaluation:*** Improved self-esteem, self-affirmation
2. ***Comfort-distress ratio:*** Less distress and more comfort
3. ***Gender- and culture-role awareness:*** Behaviors informed by gender role and culture role and power analysis of continuing life situations
4. ***Personal control/self-efficacy:*** Improved perception of personal control and self-efficacy
5. ***Self-nurturance:*** Increase in self-nurturing behaviors and avoidance of self-abusing behaviors
6. ***Problem-solving skills:*** Improved problem-solving skills
7. ***Assertiveness increased:*** Use of respectful assertiveness skills
8. ***Resource access:*** Increased access to social, economic, and community support
9. ***Gender and cultural flexibility:*** Flexibility and choice in beliefs and behaviors informed by gender and cultural identity
10. ***Social activism:*** Involvement in social activism, institutional change.

Gender-Role Analysis, Power Analysis, and Intervention

This aspect of feminist interventions examines traditional roles such as being the caretaker of the family and/or one's significant other, particularly if that significant other is male. In many cases, women have been taught that it is their role to keep a family together and to keep the family functional. With belief system, family problems were thought to be the purview of the female member, and, if the family did not operate well, it was invariably considered due to the female's own inadequacies. On the other hand, women have been stereotyped as being dependent on men (emotionally and economically) and being enmeshed in their family issues. According to Worell and Remer (2007) the changing of gender roles to be more egalitarian would include, among other things, the following components:

1. ***Inclusiveness:*** Acknowledges that the social impact of gender is experienced unequally and unfairly for women with diverse personal and social identities, including ethnicity and culture, sexual orientation, socioeconomic status, nationality, age, and physical characteristics.
2. ***Equality:*** Recognition that the politics of gender are reflected in lower social status and unequal access to valued resources for a majority of women in most societies.
3. ***Knowledge:*** Striving for increased understanding about the diversity of women's experience as it is framed by multiple personal and social identities.
4. ***Attention to context:*** The realization that women's lives are embedded in the social, economic, and political contexts of their lives and should not be studied in isolation.
5. ***Making change efforts:*** A commitment to action to accomplish social, economic, and political change toward establishing equal justice for all persons.

By now, it should be clear to the reader that one of the primary issues regarding feminist therapy is the apparent power differential that has existed for women. This is fundamental to the social reality of female offenders, both in the micro and macro sense. In micro or personal terms, these offenders are likely to have suffered abuse at the hands of men, both in childhood and in adulthood. The high incidence of sexual abuse and other forms of abuse, most frequently at the hands of men, tends to create a landscape that is highly consistent with feminist thought. For female offenders, this is often a reality that they have lived with. On a macro level, these women are also likely to have suffered from various stereotypes and discrimination, as many women have. The loss of their children is, in itself, a taboo and source of shame for women in many parts of society, yet the same stigma is not as strong for male offenders. Further, as noted before, these women have a higher incidence of involvement in the sex industry. This industry is, in and of itself, driven by sex demands from men—men who are offenders. Yet, it is the female prostitute who bears the majority of the stigma, shame, and negative impact from this industry. Further, this industry simply confirms the notion that women are tools to meet the needs of men, adding further to the contextual framework from which female offenders are likely to identify.

The primary point is that for women in general, and female offenders in particular, there are factors that impact both their personal and community-level relationships. These issues are often associated with male privilege and social circumstances that have created a state of oppression. For female offenders, this may have existed throughout their entire life span, starting from early childhood and continuing through adolescence and adulthood. For these women, operating in a "one-down" position in regard to men may be the only reality that they have ever known. Correctional counselors must understand this and be empathetic to these challenges that have faced the female offender. A failure to do so will simply ensure that interventions are ineffective and, even worse, may serve to further reinforce the already imbalanced system that exists within our society and the criminal justice system.

Journal Writing

The use of this technique is fairly common in group treatment processes. In this case, the use of journaling allows the client to track various occurrences throughout the week. When doing this, the client is able to extend the value of the group session throughout the duration of the week. The correctional counselor can provide specific issues or topics that female offenders can provide in their journal, such as difficulties with assertiveness. Journal entries can then be used in group settings among clients or can even provide the basis for additional discussions in individual settings.

Another key use for journaling is to aid in the education process that is, to some extent, inherent in feminist therapy. Female offenders may not be attuned to the various means by which they themselves have been victimized. While this is not to necessarily create an excuse for their criminal offending, it is meant to point toward mitigating factors that exist for many female offenders. Further, this process can also allow these clients to identify those areas that have been sources of trauma. As the client makes observations in her journal, the idea is that they will see connections between the experiences in their own everyday life and those issues presented in a feminist-based treatment program. This then reinforces the client's ability to participate in the intervention since this, in essence, provides a degree of psychoeducation on feminist perspectives and their impact on women's needs in treatment.

Assertiveness Training

Ironically, this type of training is even recommended for clients who are at the other extreme of the spectrum from female offenders—domestic batterers. The reason for this is because many male domestic batterers do not exercise good impulse control and they are also unable to differentiate between aggression and assertiveness. For female offenders, this can also be the case where many may simply view conflicts as going from the point of little conflict or disagreement to dangerous form of conflict resolution that includes threats toward the person with whom they disagree. Thus, women in the criminal justice system often lack the skills necessary to effectively express their views and emotions in a manner that is clear, specific, and not subject to being dismissed or unheeded while also refraining from interaction patterns that aggravate the situation and/or lead to further conflict.

It is imperative that female offenders are able to express their view in a direct and accurate manner and without guilt or apology. All too often, these women have not been given appropriate consideration, and in many cases they may not have promoted their own interests. Female offenders must be able to do this without using methods that either make matters worse or place them in jeopardy with the criminal justice system. Since these clients may have never been taught these skills within their own family system, it is important that correctional counselors ensure that assertiveness training is provided for female offenders so that they will be able to better cope with stressors in a manner where they address the stressor rather than allowing others to override their feelings and thoughts that they may harbor.

Reframing and Cognitive Restructuring

The use of reframing consists of generating new or alternate interpretations of a problem or situation in an effort to provide alternative solutions to that problem. In other words, if the interpretation of a social situation is changed, the options involved when reacting to that situation should also change. Reframes are effective means of reinterpreting negative situations or circumstances into experiences that are more tenable. For example, a female offender may be told by her women's group that she is not a rape *victim* but that she is a rape *survivor*. The difference in the two terms is that one puts the client in a frail position while the other term is indicative of a person who has overcome and/or endured a serious injury. The use of the term "survivor" is meant to empower the client as she struggles to cope with the trauma associated with the experience of having been raped.

One point should be made about reframing: This technique is not intended to "make light" of serious situations. Rather, this technique is intended to empower the client and to open additional avenues of approaching a problem so as to aid her meeting her therapeutic goals. The use of reframes to dismiss the impact of a client's experience and/or to distract them from the key issue is a misuse of the technique. In some cases, clients and therapists may misuse this technique (accidentally) when this point is not kept in mind. The client should still face the problem that is before her, but effective reframes allow her to do so from a variety of angles.

Lastly, cognitive restructuring refers to the deliberate attempt to change ones' own dialogue that they have within themselves. In other words, we often consider a variety of options and circumstances and have an unspoken dialogue in which we make determinations about the world around us. This is the organizing aspect of thinking and our understanding of the world. A prerequisite to behavior change is that clients must notice how they think, feel, and behave and the impact that they have on others due to those thoughts, feelings, and behaviors. Accordingly, it is often the case that people have "scripts" within their thinking; these are predetermined means by which the world and our role in it are viewed. The use of cognitive restructuring helps to modify these scripts and the manner in which we interpret the world.

Further, the use of journaling (discussed earlier) is a technique that can enhance the outcome of cognitive restructuring. In fact, the clients may see trends in their own cognitive interpretations when they read their own journal entries at later points in the weeks or months that progress. This tool can provide them with a record of their perceptions and, at the same time, provide documentation of their progress. Further, writing and elaborating on the cognitive restructuring process will further reinforce the impact and effectiveness of this approach.

It should be pointed out that when using cognitive restructuring, the goal is not to create some sort of self-induced brainwashing to change our thoughts. Rather, we are challenged to interrupt the scripts that we use as a template to our thinking. For female offenders, this can be useful because they have often internalized scripts that include self-degrading views that are shaped by a system that has perpetuated this self-degrading means of interpreting one's place in the world. Thus, cognitive restructuring allows the female to supplant old scripts based in victimization and/or mistreatment, with new ways of empowered thinking. Naturally, it is expected that this will provide women with the ability to provide a more healthy and self-confident dialogue within themselves.

Role-Playing

Role-playing is an important component of many groups where practice at a given set of behaviors is required of clients. The use of role-plays also allows the correctional counselor and other group members to provide feedback to members who are observed during the role-play. The use of role-playing can also allow the correctional counselor to model effective behaviors and responses to difficult situations. For instance, some women may have difficulty in establishing boundaries with people in their lives and/or acting in an assertive manner. The use of role-playing allows the person to view how assertive means of communication may be conducted and it helps them to practice this type of behavior with the feedback of others. This can be a strong therapeutic tool if done correctly.

Autonomy Development

In many respects, this is simply an extension of assertiveness training and/or empowerment of the female offender. However, there is one specific area of functioning that should be considered in the development of autonomy among women—vocational and/or career autonomy. In many cases, female offenders are economically dependent and do not possess the requisite skills to be viable and competitive in the world of work. Employment is a key factor in the reintegration of offenders in society, and this is true regardless of whether the offender is male or female. In fact, employment has been cited as one of the strongest predictors of whether an offender will successfully reform from a life of crime. With the difficulties of women in the job market coupled with the difficulties that most offenders may have in obtaining employment due to the stigma of a criminal record, the link between employment and the development of autonomy among female offenders is perhaps easy to understand. Further, the emphasis on employment also comports well with many advocates of feminist counseling approaches.

For instance, Evans, Kincade, Marbley, and Seem (2005) note that one of the most significant messages of the feminist movement is that women should have the same opportunities for career choice as men. Throughout history, this has not been the case, particularly in homes where girls are taught to have roots and the boys are taught to have wings.

The challenge to the old adage "a woman's place is in the home" has changed social mores and has led to more women in the workforce. During the past two decades, there have been numerous advances in career counseling for women, and these benefits should be extended to female offenders as well. Naturally, this requires modification and/or differentiation from the traditional male-oriented theories.

As career counselors have moved from perceiving the "career woman" as an anomaly in the 1960s and 1970s to assuming that all women work—including a redefinition of homemaker as one who works in the home—this same concept should be advocated by the correctional counselor. This aids in empowering the clients and also provides a new "script" from which they may generate thoughts and beliefs regarding their own identities. In the current era, it is common for career counselors to address issues of discrimination, underemployment, traditional and nontraditional career choices, role conflicts, and sexual harassment (Evans et al., 2005). Thus, these issues should be addressed with female offenders, particularly those who are about to be released from prison and/or those who are in community supervision. The ability to find workable employment is a very serious challenge for many female offenders, particularly if they intend to also retain custody of their children.

Remember again that many female offenders are the primary caretakers of their children prior to their offending. Given that these women frequently face single parenthood, the need to maintain full-time employment, a treatment regimen for substance abuse and other mental health issues that warrant intervention, as well as the requirements of being on community supervision, these offenders have serious challenges that are not as common among the male offending population. When placed against the backdrop of heightened levels of prior abuse, the experience of domestically abusive relationships, and other noxious life experiences, it becomes clear that the female offenders have a unique set of challenges that the correctional counselor must be prepared to address. A failure to do so will result in an intervention that is inadequate and topical at best, sidestepping the important issues that confront the female offender.

Female Offenders and Domestic Abuse

As the women's movement continued to gain momentum during the 1960s and 1970s an increased awareness of domestic violence issues emerged within the United States. As women continued to demand equality within the professional arena, equality became an issue within the personal realm as well. Eventually, these demands within the personal realm extended to expectations within the marital relationship between men and women. By extension, feminist theory has provided a guiding framework for understanding and addressing domestic violence. Feminist theory ". . . has provided explanations of how it has come about that men and women's unequal status in society . . . and the differential socialization of male and female children perpetuated violence and abuse in the home" (Frances, 1995, p. 395). Feminist theory has been instrumental in raising the public consciousness about sex-role conditioning and how such conditioning can lead to belief systems that justify sexism, male privilege, and male socialization (Healey & Smith 1998). It is through the transmission of these belief systems that acts of domestic violence can reflect the patriarchal organization of society with the male partner exacting forced subservience from the female partner (Healey & Smith, 1998).

These views on domestic violence are consistent with many schools of feminist thought (particularly radical feminism) that contend that it is the use of violence that keeps women subjugated in the home and in society as a whole. Crimes such as sexual assault, stalking, marital rape, and domestic violence have two key underlying similarities: the perpetrator is most often male and the victim is most often female. In addition, all of these crimes serve to exploit and/or control the sexual and social freedom of women to have a lifestyle of equality both inside and outside the home. Since these crimes target women and since these crimes are most often committed by male perpetrators, it is easy to see the connection to feminist theory. This theoretical perspective has been used in therapeutic interventions for women (providing a framework and rationale for empowering victims) as well as programs designed for perpetrators (providing psychoeducation on the rights of women and enforcing accountability in the recognition of those rights). Thus it is that with the women's movement for equality in the broader society social changes simultaneously occurred that impacted the means and process of response to domestic violence issues during the decades that would follow.

Feminism, Diversity, and the Female Offender

Feminist scholars have bemoaned the fact that in addressing women's issues, the feminist movement has traditionally failed to provide adequate analysis of the unique issues presented to women of minority status (Hanser, 2002, 2007). Feminism has been likened to a theory based on the historical and social experiences of Caucasian middle-class women. But these experiences were often quite different from those of African-American, Latino-American, and Asian-American women. Indeed, during the early years of the feminist movement, there were documented cases of racism and discrimination between Caucasian-American and African-American feminists (Baird, 1992). Issues of race, racism, and institutional oppression will likely be relevant to African-American women but are not likely to be similarly relevant to the experiences of most Caucasian-American women (Baird, 1992; Hanser, 2002, 2007). Further, the socialization for Asian-American women and Latino-American women is likely to emphasize even further subservience and other dynamics that are laced with traditional values from their own respective cultures. Even further, there may be issues of religion as well as racial and cultural differences that should be taken into consideration (Shaheen, 1998). This is particularly true for women who are of the Muslim faith and/or community (Shaheen, 1998). Because of the vast array of differences that can be encountered between women and since many mainstream Caucasian-American women are not necessarily likely to be well versed on these cultural differences, an awareness has developed for the need to have feminist schools of thought that can address these differences in an effective and supportive manner.

As has been noted in previous sections of this chapter, feminism is personal and political. Nevertheless, the nuances of what this means for each individual woman will be different due to a variety of characteristics, such as race, culture, and class circumstances of individual women (Evans et al., 2005). Caucasian women have been benefactors of racial privilege. On the other hand, minority women have not experienced such privilege. Thus, there has been a movement to ensure that feminist therapists are sensitive to and knowledgeable about multiple issues important to women of color. Mental health practitioners have responded to criticism by feminists of color and have begun to be more inclusive of the issues of race, ethnicity, and social class (Evans et al., 2005). One current trend is the integration of race, gender, culture, and class in feminist writings and feminist-based therapy (Evans et al., 2005).

Counseling African-American Women

Though it may be appealing for correctional counselors to treat all clients the same, it would be a mistake to overlook the differences between cultural and racial groups that would likely result in a serious disservice to the client. Rather, it is important for the correctional counselor to be attuned to cultural differences that may be encountered since these aspects are part of the framework and perspective from which the client views and experiences the world. A correctional counselor who is not comfortable with making efforts to accommodate such difference will be ineffective with most minority clients, whether male or female. Further, the majority of professionals are Caucasian-American, and this makes it even more important that correctional counselors consider their values, beliefs, and expertise when working with minority groups.

For African-American women, it is frequently the case that family and religion are key aspects of their identity. Kanel (2003) speaks to the African-American family in a very concise and effective manner by stating that:

> When one considers the history of African-American, much of their family structure and value systems make sense. Raised in slavery, the African American family learned to

> exist in settings where roles were flexible and families were usually extended to several generations. These aspects can be readily seen in modern-day African American families. Elderly people as well as young adults tend to be supported by collective efforts of family members both within and outside the nuclear family. (p. 117)

The extended family plays a very important role in many African-American families. This is particularly true for female offenders who are African-American for two key reasons. First, there is a disproportionate rate of incarceration of African-American males throughout the United States. Specifically, the target age that would typically be most active in the workforce tends to be the age group among African-American males who are incarcerated. This means that the African-American community is affective economically and this affects African-American families as well. The ability to provide an income for children and other family members therefore tends to rest with the female and/or extended family when the male spouse or significant other is incarcerated, adding stress and strain to many women who are African-American. Second, when female offenders are incarcerated, issues with child custody tend to emerge, just as was noted in prior sections of this chapter. This naturally affects African-American female offenders and their children as well. In such cases, the extended family again becomes a vital resource since it is the extended family that is likely to raise children whose mother must serve a term of incarceration. Thus, correctional counselors must remember that extended kinship tends to be an important aspect of the African-American female offender.

Likewise, religion is an important aspect of family life in many African-American households. The church is often a forum where African-American women can be active and also obtain belonging. Correctional counselors should remember that, from the client's perspective, the church and figures associated with the church can be an important source of strength. Thus, correctional counselors should consider the role of prison clergy within facilities and/or the local church or affiliation if the offender is on community supervision. The integration of the church community can provide an effective therapeutic tool for many African-American women.

Afrocentrism and Feminism

According to Evans et al. (2005), the oppressive, brutal, and violent nature of slavery and racism over the span of four centuries has been considered a higher priority issue when compared to concerns about sexism among many African-Americans, both male and female. The prevailing sentiment has been that the survival of the African-American family and community is primary. Although African-American feminists were part of both the first and second wave of feminism, many found enough differences between their agenda and that of their white counterparts to found their own associations. African-American feminists have typically differentiated themselves from "mainstream" feminists because, for women of color, sexism was not the only demon that needed to be addressed in U.S. society. In fact, the feminist movement received very little support or participation from women of color or the African-American community (Evans et al., 2005). This lack of participation of women of color in the first, second, and third waves of feminism can be attributed to the multiple oppressions of race, gender, and class and the dynamic interplay of these oppressions with politics (Evans et al., 2005).

African-American feminism today is sometimes referred to as the "womanist" movement and perspective. This term tends to be more accepted among African-Americans and other women of color, perhaps because the term itself is different or perhaps because the term "womanist" includes man. The term "womanist," was first coined by Alice Walker (1983) in her essay *In Search of Our*

Mother's Gardens: Womanist Prose. According to Walker (1983), a womanist is an African-American feminist or other feminist who is from a minority group who celebrates the feminine qualities and strengths of women while promoting the survival and wholeness of all humans, male and female (Evans et al., 2005). The womanist participates in combating racial, gender, heterosexual, and class oppression simultaneously so that the multiple oppressions that have been experienced by women from various minority groups can be addressed (Evans et al., 2005). As has been noted in our prior discussion on feminism, the belief that the "personal is political" is critical to the womanist (Evans et al., 2005). However, the womanist does not limit her focus on uplifting females to the exclusion of men when combating oppression. Instead, the womanist is mainly concerned with uplifting an entire culture and, in the process, uplifting women as well (Evans et al., 2005).

Counseling Latino-American Women

Latino-American women are perhaps the second most likely encountered minority group of female offenders that the correctional counselor will encounter. For the most part, this group of female offenders will have a perspective that is substantively different from Caucasian and African-American women due to their distinct sources of cultural backgrounds and the fact that most will be bilingual, speaking Spanish as well as English. In fact, depending on the length of time that a specific female offender may have resided in the United States, this diversity in language may be an impediment for the correctional counselor, because these women may, on occasion, speak little English. Unless the correctional counselor is also fluent in Spanish, the ability to communicate (and establish a rapport) may be severely hampered.

Further, many Latino-Americans are Catholic in religious orientation and this tends to have a strong effect on the thought processes of female offenders. Religious affiliation will tend to be a strong source of support for most of these women, but some of the precepts that may be adhered to may also prevent the female offender's ability to develop a sense of autonomy and independence that is akin to what most feminist therapists would suggest. Indeed, traditional values regarding the family, the mother's role within the family, and the generally subservient nature afforded to women may work against attempts to develop autonomy. On the other hand, the various forms of fellowship and interconnectedness provided by the religious organization serve as a source of strength for many of these women.

Machismo, Marianismo, and Acculturation

Traditional and idealized Hispanic cultural expectations of appropriate male and female behavior are often referred to as machismo or marianismo. **Machismo** is described as being dominant, virile, and independent whereas **marianismo** emphasizes being submissive, chaste, and dependent (Raffaelli & Ontai, 2004). Although some research argues that these traditional gender roles are outdated and inapplicable, other studies show that they do influence behavior and interaction in Latino couples. The primary role emphasized for women in Latino-American families is that of mother instead of wife. This leads women to define themselves through their family and children instead of independently or as part of a couple. The role of martyr is also idealized, with women expected to be submissive and sacrifice themselves for their families. For marriage education providers, this stereotype provides both an opportunity and a challenge. It means that women will be extremely dedicated to their families and the good of their children, which can be a powerful motivator for participating in the counseling process.

In addition, the emphasis on the wife's quiet submission and the husband's dominance and independence may make it more difficult for Latino-American women to communicate directly and assertively with their husbands. Although Latinas immigrating to the United States may acculturate away from traditional behaviors, it is important to recognize that these cultural expectations can still remain. Furthermore, the definition of a "good" woman can vary dramatically across culture, country of origin, and level of acculturation. For example, some families that are less acculturated may not view egalitarianism as an important part of a healthy relationship. It is also necessary to remember that different members of a family may acculturate at different rates, particularly with regards to these traditional gender roles. For example, men often tend to acculturate more quickly than their wives because they often arrive in the United States before the rest of the family and have more exposure to mainstream culture through the workplace. Lastly, a stereotype does exist that more conservative gender roles, such as those just previously described, can lead to increased domestic violence in the Latino-American community. In fact, traditional Latino gender roles can be both oppressive and protective when it comes to domestic violence. The woman's role as sacrificing and subservient can lead to greater tolerance of domestic violence, as can the strong commitment to the family and the institution of marriage. The view of men as the dominant decision makers can also encourage controlling behaviors. Lastly, because of their role in the home, Latinas are often economically dependent on men, making it more difficult to leave the relationship.

Counseling Asian-American Women

Asian-Americans are not as frequently encountered within state and federal correctional systems throughout the United States. However, this group is perhaps the next more common group of minority offenders that correctional counselors may contend with. The exception may be in some areas of the United States (such as the Southwest) where Native Americans have a higher representation within the criminal justice system. However, female offenders are very infrequent among that population. Though Asian female offenders are not necessarily common, they are the more-often represented cultural racial group in the criminal justice system. It should be noted that there are a multitude of different ethnic Asian groups in the United States.

Acculturation and Assimilation

There has been a substantial amount of literature on the acculturation and assimilation of Asian-Americans in the United States. However, Shusta, Levine, Harris, and Wong (2005) provide one of the clearest yet pragmatic descriptions of this process by providing several categories or points of acculturation that Asian-Americans may fall within. These categories apply equally well to any Asian-American group, whether they be Chinese-American, Vietnamese-American, Asian Indian, or otherwise. These categories are adapted from Shusta et al. (2005) and are as follows:

1. Surviving—Includes individuals who have recently immigrated to the United States (within the last five years) and the majority of their socialization and experience will have been in their own nation of origin.
2. Preserving—This includes immigrants or refugees who have been in the United States for more than five years but who still had the majority of their socialization in their own nation of origin.
3. Adjusting—This includes the second-generation offspring of Asian-American immigrants.
4. Changing—This group includes immigrants, but these immigrants will have had the majority of their experiences within the United States.
5. Choosing—This category consists of third-generation (or later) Asian-Americans.

When considering each of these categories, it is important to understand the individual perspective from which these individuals view the world. For instance, those in the "surviving" category are typically in a survival mode and may have come from areas where police and other authority figures were oppressive and abusive. This then will tend to shape their frame of reference when dealing with police in the United States. Likewise, individuals in the "preserving" category seek to preserve their home culture and identity. Their own values and customs are preserved and this can be the source of intergenerational conflict within their family as youth become more "Americanized" and lose contact with their culture of origin. Among the remaining categories (adjusting, changing, and choosing), there is value for the homeland but there is also a realistic understanding that changes will need to be made (Shusta et al., 2005). This is particularly true for those in the changing and choosing categories, where decisions to include aspects of the old culture or to integrate aspects of the new culture are made. These individuals tend to be truly bicultural and it may be that many will use English as their primary language, allowing their proficiency with their native language to lapse. For these individuals, contact with law enforcement may be no different than that occurring between other citizens of the United States.

Proficiency with the English language is a particular hindrance that can cause serious misunderstandings between police officers and Asian-American citizens. This issue is somewhat tied to the generational status of the individual Asian-American since those groups that have immigrated most recently tend to be those with large percentages that do not speak English. This is particularly true among the Southeast Asian groups. Indeed, nearly 38% of all Vietnamese-Americans do not speak English (Shusta et al., 2005). In addition, it has been determined that an approximate 23% of Chinese-Americans also do not speak English (Shusta et al., 2005).

Family Honor

If norms are not followed in many Asian family systems, the family will experience a sense of shame, not only for their own actions but for the entire family (Kanel, 2003). This type of an honor system sometimes makes it necessary for a family to completely reject a certain member to avoid shaming or dishonoring the entire family. The differentiation between the family and the individual is not usually as distinct as is the case in European cultures. This is particularly true for Asian women in traditional family systems. In cases where a female continues to disobey the honor code of the family, it is likely that the other female members will ignore the violating family member and will, in many respects, use forms of social avoidance to either punish the female or to correct her for her prior act of disobedience.

This means that there may be quite a few family secrets that are simply not addressed. For example, a female member who has a drug problem will be expected to hide this from the public. Likewise, some Asian women may be in domestically abusive relationships but may continue to remain with their significant other due to family expectations. This then means that, in many cases, Asian-American women may be in precarious position. Correctional counselors must be aware of these dynamics as this will complicate treatment with Asian-American female offenders. This group tends to be distrusting of mental health interventions and it is then likely that the counselor will have difficulty contending with resistance from these clients since their belief system is one that emphasizes privacy within the family and the maintenance of harmony and the status quo.

Gender Roles

As can be seen, gender roles can be fairly well defined in Asian-American families. Traditional views are giving way to mainstream American beliefs on the role of men and women, but this has caused serious friction in many Asian families. This is particularly true when youth become acculturated into mainstream views while the older family members do not. Many young Asian-American women find themselves at odds with the expectations of their families and the reality that exists throughout broader society. For female offenders who are of Asian descent, these expectations will likely have a strong impact on their own self-identity and their sense of self-efficacy. Asian women are thought to be submissive to males in the household, particularly their spouses and their fathers. When Asian-American women attempt to break out of this role, conflict typically emerges and, in many cases, differences in gender-role expectations serve as the underlying basis for domestic abuse that occurs. It would seem that, at least in some families, those women who seek egalitarian standing are more at risk for victimization at the hands of abusive family members.

Lastly, among some Southeastern Asian-American girls and women, there may be a heightened risk for sexual victimization. As readers may be aware, Hmong and Vietnamese gangs exist in various areas of the United States and these gangs tend to victimize persons of their same cultural affiliation. In many cases, these gangs target young girls in their community who are also Hmong, Vietnamese, or some other Asian descent. This is important because for some Asian-American female offenders this type of victimization can be a source of trauma that lies at the base of other types of offending.

SECTION SUMMARY

This section addressed the use of feminist therapy as a paradigm for providing offender-specific intervention services. While women may have a number of individual needs for service, there are common experiences, due to being a woman, that tend to be constant among this group of offenders. The feminist perspective seeks to address these common issues since most other therapeutic orientations are not specifically tailored to meet the needs of women. Further, feminist perspectives target the victimization that has been common in the backgrounds of many female offenders and provides a paradigm that offers support, empathy, strength, and self-empowerment.

Lastly, while feminist perspectives hold substantial promise for female offenders, this approach does not have equal appeal for all women. Even further, women who are from minority groups may have different views on feminism and its applicability to their own personal and public lives. The marginalization experienced by many minority women tends to be even greater than that experienced by Caucasian-American women, meaning that interventions will need to be more culture specific to meet the needs of these offenders.

LEARNING CHECK

1. Feminist perspectives of counseling seek to give women identity and to empower them in society.
   a. True
   b. False
2. The experiences of African-American women may prevent traditional aspects of feminism from being optimally effective.
   a. True
   b. False
3. Assertiveness training is an important element of intervention with female offenders.
   a. True
   b. False

4. Feminist perspective of counseling teaches female offenders to blame men for the crimes that they commit.
   a. True
   b. False
5. Power differences between men and women add to the challenge of reform for many female offenders.
   a. True
   b. False

CONCLUSION

Female offenders have a host of therapeutic considerations that are distinct from those of their male counterparts. These differences go beyond simple physical differences between men and women in prison. Women throughout society experience a different socialization process than do men, and this must be included as a component within any treatment program for female offenders. Considerations for female offenders include social, psychological, and physiological aspects that must all be taken into account.

The variety of challenges that confront female offenders tend to be complicated and interwoven with one another. Seldom are the challenges for female offenders mutually exclusive from one another. This means that treatment interventions must address numerous concerns in a simultaneous fashion, including psychological, sociological, and medical concerns. Many of the issues confronting female offenders extend beyond the personal realm and include family-of-origin issues and the impact that their criminal activity has had on their children. As has been noted, a large proportion of the female offending population are also mothers of children. A failure to address the mother–child bond in an intervention program will limit the effectiveness of that program and will therefore not be as likely to reduce future recidivism.

Female offenders experience several co-occurring disorders that aggravate their challenges with substance abuse. The use of substances among the female offender population is common and has been found to be linked with a poor self-image and sense of self-efficacy. Female offenders tend to have poor self-image and this also correlates with the tendency to abuse substances. Sex, sexuality, and body image are all compounded issues where the media, society, and family expectations send contradictory messages that negatively affect the woman's sense of self-value.

Due to common problems of abuse in childhood and adulthood, female offenders tend to suffer from high levels of post-traumatic stress disorder. In addition, female offenders tend to be involved in high-risk relationships and to engage in risky behaviors. This is particularly true when it comes to sexual activity, and, due to their lifestyle choices, they tend to be at heightened risk of contracting STDs and/or HIV/AIDS. Drug use tends to aggravate their psychological coping and also impairs decision making when confronted with the opportunity to engage in high-risk behaviors.

The use of feminist therapy as a basis for intervention with female offenders was presented. Feminist perspectives address the victimization that has been a common experience among female offenders and provides a message of empowerment throughout the therapeutic process. Nevertheless, this approach should not be used in a one-size-fits-all manner because many of these women are from minority groups that have different views on feminism and its applicability to their own circumstances. Correctional counselors will need to keep this diversity in mind when providing interventions for female offenders.

Essay Questions

1. Consider your readings from Chapter 8 regarding substance abuse disorders and consider the discussion in this chapter regarding co-occurring disorders among the female offender population. What types of interventions will you recommend? Would you integrate this with a feminist perspective? If so, explain how you would do this. If not, explain why you would fail to do so.
2. Compare and contrast some of the differences that might exist when using feminist approaches with Caucasian-American women and those who come from minority groups such as African, Latino, or Asian-Americans. What are some of the issues you might consider to be similar? What issues might be different? Give reasons to your answers.
3. How is sex, sexuality, body image, and self-efficacy interrelated for many female offenders? Why would feminists say that these interrelations have occurred at the behest of men in society? How does such a claim comport with the observation that much of the crime committed by female offenders is in tandem with a male accomplice to whom the female is emotionally connected?
4. How might one make the point that female offenders are, in many cases, victims who have been turned into offenders? Provide at least three specific examples of how this might be true.
5. With reference to question number 4, explain some treatment approaches that you might use to aid a female offender who has herself suffered from a past of victimization. What techniques would you use? Would you use a feminist-based perspective or any one of the perspectives provided from Chapter 5 that provides an overview of the more common theoretical counseling perspectives?

Treatment Planning Exercise

In this exercise, students should consider their readings throughout this chapter as well as prior chapters when addressing this treatment planning exercise. For this exercise, you should determine which, if any, of the issues discussed in this chapter apply to Mary's case. Be sure to identify those issues and explain how you would address them. Be sure to include a discussion of any corollary services that you might have the client utilize. In addition, explain whether a feminist approach would be appropriate with this client. Provide details on this aspect of your response.

The Case of Mary

Mary appears in your office vibrant and full of energy. She is whirlwind of activity, straightening things in your office and talking at a vigorous and almost annoying pace. But as soon as you ask her to sit with you and focus on the reason she is here to see you, she begins to get irritated. "Look, I have a lot to do today and I really do not have time for this. I know I have to come here, but if I do not get started, then the whole day could be wasted."

When you ask her about the lethargic state that her boss had said she was in the week before, she tells you, "Well, we all have the dumps from time-to-time." Then she begins to tell, "But you know, my supervisor really does not know what he is doing. See, if I were boss, I could get that place running perfect in just two days."

Mary has been convicted and is on probation for check fraud and check forgery. It appears that Mary enjoys going on expensive spending sprees for brief periods of time. This is then followed by a cyclical period where she does not have the energy to even go to work.

During these times, Mary will often fail to pay her bills or even deposit her paycheck into her bank account. Thus, Mary has a long list of checks that have been returned for insufficient funds. Further, when she was on one of her spending sprees, she decided to use a few checks that belonged to her friend saying, "Well I am just like, well borrowing the money . . . I will tell her later."

As a result of financial difficulties and her prior husband's out-of-control temper, she divorced him about four years ago. He was into gambling and also drank heavily. He would complain about the lack of money, Mary's spending habits, and her radical mood swings. When aggravated and/or drunk, he would have screaming fits. Sometimes during the night when he was drunk he would also force Mary into sexual activity, even when she made it clear that she was not interested. Mary, on the other hand, tends to vacillate back and forth between the use of amphetamines and alcohol, often complicating her life and any chance for stability that she might have. Between her husband's problems and her own personal challenges, it was not surprising that the marriage did not last.

When Mary does have her periods of dark withdrawal, she completely neglects her medication. Further, she tends to neglect her two children, Tina (age 10) and Tony (age 8), letting them take care of themselves. Sometimes, Tina has to take care of mom as well. Both kids prepare themselves for school and walk to school on their own during these times. During these periods, Mary will simply mull over her thoughts and always seem tired and exhausted. She does not sleep well and claims that this impedes her ability to function throughout the day. Regardless, Mary does not exhibit the desire to accomplish her daily-life routines but instead simply allows things to fall apart.

Currently, Mary is upbeat and lively and wants to talk about her new boyfriend. From her prior case notes with other therapists, you can tell that "new boyfriends" tend to have a pattern that coincides with her manic episodes. What is interesting is Mary tends to neglect her children during these times as well while she is focusing on getting things right with her new "beau" or fixing her finances from the prior spending spree. This is of course then followed by self-loathing over neglecting her kids (who are neglected during this period as well) and the fact that her new "beau" has found her to be annoying or "moody," as many have put it.

Mary hates taking medication and does not really see why she needs to have therapy. All she really needs is for things to calm down and then she can get a grasp on her life. And according to Mary, "Time is running out as we speak, so can I go or what?"

Bibliography

American Correctional Association. (1990). *The female offender: What does the future hold?* Washington, DC: St. Mary's Press.

American Psychiatric Association (2000). *Diagnostic and statistical manual of mental disorders.* Arlington, VA: American Psychiatric Association.

Bloom, B., Brown, M., & Chesney-Lind, M. (1996). *Women on Probation and Parole.* In A. J. Lurigio (Ed.), *Community corrections in America: New directions and sounder investments for persons with mental illness and codisorders* (pp. 51–76). Washington, DC: National Institute of Corrections.

Bloom, B., Owen, B., & Covington, S. (2003). *Gender responsive strategies: Research, practice and guiding principles for women offenders.* Washington, DC: National Institute of Corrections. Retrieved from: http://www.nicic.org/Library/018017.

Baird, V. (1992). Simply: A history of feminism. *New Internationalist, 227.* Retrieved from: http://www.newint.org/issue227/simply.htm.

Barnett, O. W., Miller-Perrin, C., & Perrin, R. (2004). *Family violence across the lifespan* (2nd ed.). Thousand Oaks, CA: Sage.

Burgess, A. W., & Holstrom, L. L. (1974). Rape trauma syndrome. *American Journal of Psychiatry, 131*, 981–986.

Center on Addiction and Substance Abuse. (1996). *Encyclopedia on drugs, alcohol, and addictive behavior*. New York, NY: CASA.

Corey, G. (1996). *Theory and practice of counseling and psychotherapy* (5th ed.). Pacific Grove, CA: Brooks/Cole Publishing.

Daane, D. M. (2005). Victim response to sexual assault. In F. P. Reddingtion & B. W. Kreisel (Eds.), *Sexual assault: The victims, the perpetrators, and the criminal justice system* (pp. 77–106). Durham, NC: Carolina Academic Press.

Epigee Foundation. (2004). *Birth Control Guide on Sexually Transmitted Diseases*. Epigee Foundation. Retrieved from: http://www.epigee.org/guide/stds.html.

Evans, K., Kincade, E., Marbley, A. F., & Seem, S. R. (2005). Feminism and feminist therapy: Lessons from the past and hopes for the future. *Journal of Counseling and Development, 83*(3), 269–277.

Frances, R. (1995). An overview of community-based intervention programmes for men who are violent or abusive in the home. In R. E. Dobash, R. P. Dobash, & L. Noaks (Eds.). *Gender and crime* (pp. 390–409). Cardiff, UK: University of Wales Press.

Hammett, T. M., Harmon, M. P., & Rhodes, W. (2002). The burden of infectious disease among inmates of and releasees from correctional facilities. In The health status of soon-to-be-released inmates: A report to Congress: Vol. II. Chicago: National Commission on Correctional Health Care.

Hanser, R. D. (2002). *Multicultural aspects in batterer intervention programs*. Published Dissertation (UMI). Huntsville, TX: Sam Houston State University.

Hanser, R. D. (2007). Feminist theory. In N. A. Jackson (Ed.), *Encyclopedia of domestic violence*. New York: Routledge, Taylor, & Francis.

Healey, K., & Smith, C. (1998). *Batterer programs: What criminal justice agencies need to know* (BJS Publication No. NCJ 171683). Washington, DC: Bureau of Justice Statistics.

Jackson, N. A. (2007). *Encyclopedia of domestic violence*. New York: Routledge.

Kanel, K. (2003). *A guide to crisis intervention* (2nd ed.). Pacific Grove, CA: Brooks/Cole.

Kassebaum P. A. (1999). *Substance abuse treatment for women offenders*. Center for Substance Abuse Treatment, TAP 23; Rockville, MD.

Miller, B. A., Nochajski, T. H., Leonard, K. E., Blane, H. T., Gondoii, D. M., & Bowers, P. M. (1990). Spousal violence and alcohol/drug problems among parolees and their spouses. *Women and Criminal Justice, 2*, 55–72.

Raffaelli, M., & Ontai, L. L. (2004). Gender socialization in Latino/a families: Results from two retrospective studies. *Sex Roles: A Journal of Research, 50*, 287–299.

Rich, J. D., Hou, J. C., Charuvastra, A., Towe, C. W., Lally, M., Spaulding, A., Bandy, U., et al. (2001). Risk factors for syphilis among incarcerated women in Rhode Island. *AIDS Patient Care and STDS, 15*(11), 581–585.

Shaheen, A. (1998). American, Ambitious, and Muslim. *WIN: Women's International Net, 8b*. Retrieved from: http://www.geocities.com/Wellesley/3321/win8b.htm.

Shusta, M., Levine, D. R., Harris, P. R., & Wong, H. Z. (2005). *Multicultural law enforcement: Strategies for peacekeeping in a diverse society* (3rd ed.). Upper Saddle River, NJ: Prentice Hall.

Shuter, J. (2002). Public health opportunities for the correctional intervention on inmates with communicable disease. In The health status of soon-to-be-released inmates: A report to Congress: Vol. II. Chicago: National Commission on Correctional Health Care.

Snell, T. (1994). *Women in prison*. Washington, DC: Bureau of Justice Statistics.

Walker, A. (1983). *In search of our mother's gardens: Womanist prose*. Orlando, FL: Brace-Harcourt Publishers.

Walker, L. (1979). *The battered woman*. New York: Harper and Row.

Walker, L. (1989). *Terrifying love: Why battered women kill and how society responds*. New York: Harper and Row.

Worell, J. (1993, November). *What Do We Really Know about Feminist Therapies. Approaches to Research on Process and Outcome*. Invited presentation to the Texas Psychological Association, Austin, TX.

Worell, J., & Remer, P. (2007). *Feminist perspectives in therapy: Empowering diverse women* (2nd ed.). Hoboken, NJ: John Wiley & Sons, Inc.

12

Sex Offenders

CHAPTER OBJECTIVES

After reading this chapter, you will be able to:

1. Identify aspects of denial that are common to sex offenders.
2. Discuss the four domains of treatment used with sex offenders.
3. Identify the common cognitive-behavioral techniques used in sex offender interventions.
4. List and discuss the five Cs of treatment by William Prendergast.
5. Identify and discuss the two types of interrogation-based interventions used with sex offenders.
6. Explain how relapse prevention and consistency in treatment are necessary.
7. Explain why collaborative approaches between treatment providers and criminal justice personnel are so important.

PART ONE: ADDRESSING DENIAL AND THE FOUR DOMAINS OF TREATMENT

This section will provide the student with a detailed understanding of the common components associated with sex offender treatment programs. While each program may vary to some degree across the nation, the basic components noted in this section provide the more common aspects to such treatment interventions. Further, the information utilized in this section has been adapted from public domain information provided by the Center for Sex Offender Management (CSOM), which is a project of the Office of Justice Programs in affiliation with the U.S. Department of Justice.

Students may have noticed that many of the sources and resources in this text are derived from federal government publications and training materials. This is obviously no accident and reflects the fact that numerous high quality resources exist from various federal government programs. Most often, these resources are subjected to a great deal of rigor and are also the product of research conducted at the national level. Because of this, we believe that these resources tend to be superior to many other potential reference sources available. Further still, these resources are public domain and this allows us to direct readers to those specific sources if they would like to further study a topic and/or have access to the specific resources available. We consider this a very useful benefit for students and also a pragmatic approach to effectively integrate research material into this text.

Though the information released by the Center for Sex Offender Management (CSOM) is written primarily for nonclinical audiences, we believe that it is highly appropriate to be referred to in this text as this text is primarily geared toward criminal justice students who are interested in treatment programs common to most correctional agencies. Further, the information contained in this section is quite thorough when compared to many other correctional counseling texts, making this base source of information more than suitable for our purposes. Thus, we follow an organization of presentation similar to the curriculum advocated by CSOM, which is developed to assist probation and parole staff, treatment providers, victim advocates, law enforcement personnel, judges, prosecutors, and justice system educators to plan and develop their own live training events on a variety of specific issues related to sex offender management. Thus, this curriculum is ideal for purposes of familiarizing students to the means by which sex offender treatment programs operate.

Addressing Denial

First and foremost, it is important to note that just as is common with substance abusers, sex offenders tend to deny the commission of their offense and also tend to deny the seriousness of their offense. It is with this in mind that the correctional counselor must consider how he or she will treat an offender who is adamant and convincing with his or her denial. Though denial is a pervasive issue when working with sex offenders, the presence of denial does not, in and of itself, preclude effective treatment. Nevertheless, denial is a primary concern because most treatment programs hinge upon an offender's admission and willingness to agree that his or her behaviors are a problem.

Among those offenders who refuse to admit to their offense, issues discussed in treatment group meetings, such as cognitive distortions, deviant arousal, and offense cycles, will simply indicate that such problems are not applicable to their own situation. Naturally, this would make treatment nearly impossible and would undermine the therapeutic process for the other sex offenders in the group who admit their sex offense histories. Thus, before sex offender treatment can be effective, the offender must admit his offense history, at least in part. In this regard, the treatment of denial is an essential characteristic before genuine treatment can be pursued. Accordingly, there are two primary approaches for breaking through denial with sex offenders—the polygraph and the use of group treatment.

The use of polygraph examinations provides additional data that the correctional counselor can use, similar to information included in a police report. In these instances, counselors can refer to the results of the polygraph as a means of challenging the denial that some sex offenders will present. While it is not the intent of treatment to promote a sense of conflict within the therapeutic relationship, the level of manipulation that is common among these offenders warrants more concrete means of addressing offender denial. This is similar to earlier discussions in Chapter 10 regarding domestic batterers, who deny their actions as abuse, minimize damage from those actions, and blame other people or circumstances for their behavior. Sex offenders use these same tactics to avoid responsibility for these actions and the correctional counselor must be vigilant for these tactics.

Another technique of challenging denial is to invite offenders who are in an advanced treatment group to challenge offenders who deny their actions in the less experienced group. The idea is that more experienced offenders in treatment will be adept at challenging offenders in denial than others. In other circumstances, correctional counselors may find it more effective to simply create a group of offenders who all exhibit levels of denial. This technique is called the "deniers group," consisting of sex offenders who are all in denial. Essentially, this is a "pregroup" session that lasts from 12 to 16 weeks as a means of getting the offender in denial primed for the actual group therapy process. According to CSOM, treatment providers who employ this method report that the great majority of offenders are able to come out of their denial. This approach targets two major issues:

- Eliminating cognitive distortions—which, left intact, allow offenders to continue denying or minimizing; and
- Developing victimization awareness—which can allow offenders to understand the physical and psychological harm they inflict and, thus, render them more reluctant to commit future assaults.

This approach involves a number of techniques geared toward reaching these major issues. They may include:

> Forming a treatment group composed exclusively of individuals who have been convicted of a sex offense and who are in substantial denial (either of committing the offense at all or of having actually harmed the victim as a result of the offense).
>
> Articulating the assumption that denial is a normal reaction for those involved in sexual offending behavior and the reasons for that denial.
>
> Allowing the group itself to identify the cognitive distortions often employed by sex offenders in order to access and assault their victims through role-plays and discussions of what "other" offenders tell themselves in order to convince themselves that their behavior is okay.
>
> Utilizing videotaped or live statements of sexual assault victims to communicate to offenders the nature and extent of the trauma suffered by victims.
>
> Inviting sex offenders who were formerly deniers to visit the group and describe the reasons for their initial denial, the reasons they decided to admit, and a description of their sexual offenses.
>
> Allowing group members—as the culmination of this 12–16 week process—to describe their offense history.

One primary concern of group members is often related to confidentiality, particularly regarding information divulged by other group. One way to address this concern is to ask the group participants to come to an agreement about their own confidentiality, and in virtually every instance, the agreement they make among themselves is that what is discussed in the group does not get discussed outside of the group, as it pertains to anyone besides the person talking. Typically, it is best to have the group members come to this agreement among themselves rather than imposing such rules on them for two reasons. First, it is a simple way to begin their involvement in a discussion they are likely to understand and be interested in, without discussing any threatening content such as sex offending. This provides practice for what will be occurring in the group. Second, it requires that the group build cohesiveness and trust among its members, at least about this issue. Building trust among themselves can be a useful exercise because it leads to group members sensing that they can be helpful to each other.

Most of what occurs during group sessions is discussion among the participants. The facilitators' (or treatment providers') primary function is to introduce ideas, suggest discussion topics and activities, praise progress, and, most importantly, ensure that the therapeutic milieu remains pro-social. By this we mean that it is essential that as the group progresses, group members feel they will be rewarded—principally by other group members—for admitting their sexual assaults, which often is different from most others. Facilitators begin the "denier group" treatment by talking about definitions of and the continuum of denial, asking group members to define what is meant by denial, followed by a discussion of the degrees of denial that range from complete denial, such as "I wasn't even in the house at that time," to minimization. Next, the correctional counselor would initiate a more comprehensive discussion of denial by asking the group to consider and suggest examples of denial in three phases of sex offending: before the offense, during the offense, and after the offense.

A major component of many sex offenders' denial is not simply that they say they did not have sexual contact with their victims, but that their victims were in fact "partners" because they gave consent. This is a common facet of denial for many offenders, both those who commit acquaintance rape and those who sexually assault minors. Therefore, the concept of informed consent should be discussed at length both in sex offender denial treatment as well as in conventional sex offender treatment. Once this has been discussed, the correctional counselor will then conduct a role-play demonstration to illustrate this point. This role-play is illustrated in Exhibit 12.1.

EXHIBIT 12.1

An Example Role-Play for Denial Regarding Consent among Sex Offenders in Group Therapy

As the role-play begins, selva the facilitator stands next to an empty chair and asks the group to imagine that in the chair is an 11-year-old boy. The facilitator tells the group that he will be playing the role of a sex offender who believes what the group just concluded, namely that in order for children to give consent to sex, they must have a great deal of information. As a child molester who believes in children's right to consent, he will be telling the child what he needs to know about having sex with him, and then ask him if he wants to have sex.

Standing next to the empty chair, the facilitator speaks loudly enough for the group to hear as he looks at the imaginary child in the chair and says,

> *Johnny, I want to talk with you about something. I want to have sex with you.*
>
> *You look puzzled. Let me tell you what I mean, and what I hope we'll be doing. I know that you like to be with me, to come over to my house, and for us to do stuff together. You've been coming over here after school now since October, right? You like to play my video games, drink the Mountain Dew I always keep in the refrigerator for you, stuff like that, don't you?*
>
> *I know that you really like me, and I've acted like I really like you. I don't actually like you that much, but I've pretended that I do, and I think that's made you feel really good. It's not that I don't like you, but it's that if I get you thinking I like you really a lot, then you might be more willing to do what I want you to do.*
>
> *Anyway, let me tell you about what I'm hoping will be happening between us.*

The correctional counselor then proceeds to explain to the mythical child exactly what having sex with him means, graphically describing the physical act, describing the consequences he (the offender) will suffer if anyone finds out about it, and the great lengths he will go to in order to avoid being discovered and punished. This, of course, involves making the child out to be a liar if he ever were to disclose the behavior. He also goes into great detail about what the child will have to face should he have to go to court and from all the different people who will know about what has happened. He also describes in detail how the child will feel—including physical pain, feelings of guilt and isolation—immediately after the abuse and later, as an adult. He goes on to indicate that, when the child grows to the age of puberty, this experience may have longer-term consequences on his comfort with his adult sexuality. He concludes . . .

> *So, Johnny, now that you know about all this stuff, would you like to have sex with me?*

Source: Center for Sex Offender Management (2008). *An overview of sex offender treatment for a non-clinical audience.* Washington, DC: Office of Justice Programs, U.S. Department of Justice.

Once the role-play demonstration has been enacted, the therapist will invite group reactions. In most cases, clients discuss the fact that no child would voluntarily have sex with an adult if he or she knew all of the information pointed out in the role-play. The therapist will usually then point out that the information given to the child in the role-play is the information that most adults would be aware of. In other words, by the time people become adults, much of the information used in the role-play must have become common knowledge. Generally, by adulthood people would have learned about sex, about how people get other people to have sex with them, and so forth. However, children do not usually know this information, and, even if they did, they would not necessarily understand the information. Therefore, they are not able to give informed consent.

Despite this, sex offenders will often offer counter claims to justify inappropriate actions. Some common examples include the notion that the child wanted the sex, that the child should be considered old enough to have sex, that women like to be forced sexually, and/or that the sex is okay because the offender loves the child. Nevertheless, the seasoned group members tend to quickly challenge these various justifications, especially those of others, because they recognize these rationalizations as well or better because they themselves might have used similar tactics.

In most cases, sex offenders do not gain satisfaction from causing physical harm to their victims; rather they may pursue their behavior due to self-centered desires for gratification.

Regardless, these offenders cause trauma because they selfishly use their victims as objects and they disregard the harmful effects they cause. The exceptions to this are sexual sadists, who derive erotic arousal from causing victims to suffer, and psychopaths, who are indifferent to the pain that they cause others.

From this point, most treatment programs will seek to increase awareness of the victim and the impact that sexual abuse trauma has upon that person. It is generally believed that by increasing victimization awareness and empathy sex offenders will come to understand the harm they cause and, in the process, will be less likely to commit future sex offenses. Victimization awareness is a component of sex offender treatment for offenders in denial for the above reasons and because many sex offenders deny that their victims were truly victims, that is, they fail to see the harm done. Victimization awareness can be addressed in treatment groups in a variety of ways. First, by showing videotaped programs of sexual assault victims describing how they have been traumatized by sex offenders; second, by a live discussion whereby adult survivors of sexual assault visit the group to describe their experiences of trauma. The obvious advantage of using videotaped material is its accessibility and control—group facilitators choose the audiovisual materials carefully and they know exactly what the content will be. On the other hand, the advantage of live sexual assault survivors is that this approach is much more powerful than videotape, and there can be interaction in the form of questions and answers between the offenders and the sexual assault survivors.

It should be pointed out that the purpose of having group meetings with sexual assault survivors is not to instigate aggressive confrontation or anger. Rather, the point is to provide a forum for important education and thoughtful discussion that builds a sense of empathy on the part of the sex offender. This process takes considerable skill on the part of the correctional counselor who must regulate various dynamics of the group process. Among these dynamics would be the need for mutual respect and appropriate boundaries, clearly stating expectations, and ensuring that underlying agendas are not allowed to dominate the group process. Though this is a challenging process, it can be very rewarding since sex offenders and sexual assault survivors both tend to indicate that the experience was powerful, insightful, and instructive.

After this point in the denial group process, the next point in treatment includes a visit from sex offenders who were formerly in denial but now admit to their own offense histories and who are also vigilant in working on their treatment. It should be pointed out that the offenders who visit the group should be carefully selected by the correctional counselor from among his or her agency. These visiting offenders must have usually completed their own sex offender denial group session. Since the denial group sessions tend to last from 12 to 16 weeks in duration, they will have had three to four months of experience, at a minimum, with the group process.

The final point in the treatment for sex offenders who deny their crimes requires each participant to provide a sexual offense history. In this stage of treatment, each participant takes a turn at describing his or her offense history. Typically, correctional counselors conducting this type of group therapy find that 70 to 80% of the group members will admit to the offenses that they have committed. This allows the offender to then continue through further aspects of treatment. Treatment providers take different approaches to those offenders who persist in denial even after they have received significant therapy to assist them to break through denial. Some may proceed to use the polygraph, whereas others may provide the offender with another opportunity to participate in deniers treatment. Some therapists may decide that these offenders are simply no longer eligible for treatment. In such cases, the offender will most assuredly be incarcerated and will remain so until the expiration of their sentence.

The Four Domains of Treatment

For those offenders who either never express denial and/or those who successfully complete the deniers group, the genuine treatment process will begin. This will consist of additional group therapy that addresses a variety of issues related to sex offending and the manner by which offenders perceive their offending. Generally speaking, treatment programs address four broad domains, which are listed below:

- Deviant sexual interest, arousals, and preferences;
- Distorted attitudes;
- Interpersonal functioning; and
- Behavior management.

Although not all sex offenders have difficulties or deficits in each of the four domains listed above, the majority do. Therefore, it is important that treatment programs address all four of these domains. It is at this point that we discuss each of these domains of sex offender treatment. The student is again reminded that, up to this point, the sex offender treatment has simply been focused on the offender's denial. Challenging the offender's denial was a "pre-group" phase just to ensure that group members all had at least a common baseline of acceptance of their crime and how it impacted the victim/survivor of the sexual assault.

Deviant Sexual Interest, Arousal, and Preferences

The CSOM notes that offenders typically commit sex crimes for a wide variety of reasons. In fact, we contend (as does CSOM) that a large number of sex offenses are not committed due to a desire for power or control. In a large number of sex offenses, the offender genuinely seeks gratification rather than dominance over the victim. In other words, the exploitation by the offender is utilitarian to gaining access to sexual gratification. This does not comport with much of the traditional belief regarding sexual offending, which is that all sexual offending is grounded in the desire to exploit, dominate, and denigrate the victim. For instance, consider an offender who engages in sex with his 14- or 15-year-old step-daughter; this is likely to be more grounded in the desire for sexual gratification rather than an intent to humiliate the victim. As another example, consider an offender who uses rohypnol to subdue his victim, has sex with her, and then leaves the area. Being that the victim was unconscious there is little likelihood that denigration or exploitation was the primary intent. Also, considering that the offender left upon completion of the act, it is all the more likely that sexual gratification was the basis for the criminal offense.

This is not to say that many sex offenses are not grounded in the desire to have power and control over the victim—in fact, many are grounded in such a desire. Further, there are rapists who are misogynists in nature and others who are sadists. In both of these cases, the desire to humiliate and cause pain is certainly a strong motivation to their crimes. Still, it is our stance that this motivation does not account for the majority of the sex offender population. Going back to our example of the offender who encourages sex with his teenage stepdaughter, consider that, assuming he had no other criminal sexual history, if we were to measure his sexual arousal patterns in a laboratory, we likely would find that he is most erotically attracted to adult women, followed in intensity by adolescent girls, which is a normal sexual arousal pattern for a heterosexual adult male (CSOM, 2008). Thus, it might be concluded that his principal problem is likely to have more to do with his having used extremely poor judgment, having difficulties of impulse control, poor self-management, problems in his personal relationships, and other problems.

On the other hand, the person who is motivated to commit sexual assaults on children to satisfy his sexual arousal, or to force people to have sex with him, or to expose his genitals to strangers has problems in the area of sexual interests. Although it may seem surprising, some sex offender treatment programs do not directly and effectively address sexual interests in treatment. This is a serious oversight since the reinforcing sensation of gratification serves as a powerful motivator for many sex offenders. Thus, techniques designed to address the pairing between gratification and the action taken must be included in any type of comprehensive treatment regimen.

One technique that is often used is masturbatory satiation (Hanser, 2007). This technique is based on behavioral learning principles, with the treatment being based on the presumption that sexual arousal is, to some extent, a learned behavior that can likewise be unlearned and/or modified through a relearning process. This technique involves having the client masturbate to an appropriate fantasy, until he has an ejaculation (Hanser, 2007; Knopp, 1989). When the correctional counselor provides instruction on this technique, an explanation should be provided to the offender that he will be involved in a treatment approach that is intended to reduce his deviant sexual arousal while simultaneously increasing his arousal to nondeviant sexual stimuli. The offender will naturally complete this assigned technique in private. Prior to doing so, it is very important that the correctional counselor ensure that the offender understands the purpose to the assigned technique and that he conduct the exercise properly. Throughout the exercise, the offender is to record one's experience on an audiotape which the correctional counselor will later listen to.

Over time, this technique is intended to pair the intense pleasure associated with orgasm with healthy sexual fantasies. Likewise, it is expected that disinterest and/or even psychological discomfort will develop with deviant fantasies. Further, offenders may be requested to masturbate during their refractory period (the time right after they have achieved orgasm) because this typically induces boredom and some sense of physical discomfort. The purpose of this second aspect of the exercise is to have the offender experience negative reactions to deviant fantasies. Ideally, the attractiveness of the previously erotic (and deviant) stimuli is substantially diminished. By focusing on one aspect of his deviant arousal pattern, the offender will pair physical discomfort and extreme boredom with what typically would be arousing and pleasurable. Taken together, the pairing of healthy fantasies with the intense and positive experience of an orgasm is designed to strengthen healthy sexual interest and arousal patterns, while the pairing of discomfort, boredom with deviant fantasy can aid in reducing deviant fantasies and interests.

In most treatment programs, the sex offender is required to make three audiotapes a week. Each of these audiotaped sessions is intended to be approximately an hour in duration. The purpose for making the audiotapes is so that the correctional counselor can monitor compliance and ensure that the offender is conducting the exercise properly. This aspect of the treatment process typically lasts for approximately seven weeks with roughly 20 hours of homework being assigned throughout the entire period.

Distorted Attitudes

One of the key commonalities among sex offenders is the distorted attitudes that they tend to have (Prendergast, 2004). It is common for people to have various distortions in their perceptions. Often, such distortions serve as psychological defenses to justify what a person has done and/or to normalize his experiences. Sex offenders use distortions in perception as a means of rationalizing their offenses to make their offenses not seem as serious as they actually are. This protects the esteem of the offender and also distances them from any sense of guilt that they might otherwise experience.

COGNITIVE RESTRUCTURING Because sex offenders are aware that their behavior is illegal and/or harmful to the victim, they justify their behavior by creating rationalizations that minimize the negative impact of their actions. This is also intended to reduce dissonance that they might encounter, which leads to thinking errors or cognitive distortions. The purpose of cognitive restructuring with sex offenders is to have them identify and examine their cognitive distortions and to receive feedback that exposes the errors in their thinking. It is intended that the offender will develop an awareness of victim issues. The main goal is to circumvent the rationalizations that offenders use to justify their offending.

In most cases, this intervention begins with a discussion on how these distortions are used to justify aberrant behaviors. Through the use of group counseling processes, offenders eventually acknowledge that, regardless of the reasons, some behaviors are simply wrong and inappropriate. Group members are then asked to complete a sentence that essentially makes them confront the nature of their act. For example, an offender may be required to complete the following statement: "Even though I knew my sex offenses were wrong, or at least illegal, what I said to myself to make it seem okay was ____________." During these groups, offenders may be required to anonymously write down on paper a list of cognitive distortions that they have used. These lists of thinking distortions are later used as part of future group discussions, in which case the correctional counselor will read the various distortions one at a time and the group then discusses these distortions.

Another common technique used in these groups is the use of role-play exercises. One such role-play method involves group members playing the role of someone related to the victims, such as the father, with another offender playing a role that supports the offender to take responsibility for the offense, and yet another offender playing a pro-social role such as that of a community supervision officer. In this exercise, the correctional counselor would play the role of a sex offender who uses various cognitive distortions, defending these distortions to the three offenders playing their respective roles. It becomes the task of the offender role-players to explain to the correctional counselor (playing the role of offender) the faults and distortions that exist in his thinking. This is often a fairly easy task for offenders to do, because although they might have trouble challenging their own cognitive distortions, they tend to be adept at noting the distorted thinking that occurs among other offenders. This is especially true when different types of sex offenders, such as rapists and child molesters, are mixed in the same group.

VICTIM AWARENESS/EMPATHY TRAINING As was noted in the previous section on offenders in denial, another point in addressing distorted attitudes with sex offenders is the desire to increase their awareness of the victim's experience and to increase empathy, when this is possible. However, these techniques are not intended for offenders who are diagnosed as sexual sadists (see the *DSM-IV-TR*) and those persons who qualify as genuine psychopaths. Indeed, attempts to increase victimization awareness in offenders who have no capacity for empathy for others can actually make these offenders more likely, rather than less likely, to commit subsequent offenses. In regard to sexual sadists in particular, these individuals gain erotic gratification through the infliction of pain, suffering, and humiliation of their victims. Thus, teaching these offenders about the victim's pain and anguish is likely to excite and reinforce their crimes rather than extinguish them.

For those sex offenders who do not find gratification in the infliction of physical harm or psychological torment, the intent of victim awareness techniques is to simply increase the offender's understanding of the victim's trauma. The general logic is that, with such awareness acquired, the offender will be less likely to commit similar offenses in the future. Generally, sex offenders are capable of empathy but they tend to be less receptive to issues related to sex and sex offending. Because of this, the goals of this component of treatment require offenders to do the following:

- Understand the pervasive negative effects of sexual assault on victims and others;
- Know the likely consequences of their assaults on their victims and their families; and
- Learn empathy skills, especially the ability to empathize with their victims.

Other methods that are often utilized to enhance this component of treatment include requirements that offenders complete written assignments describing the offenses they have committed. However, with these exercises, the offender does not write this from their own perspective. Rather, these offenders are instructed to write the narrative from the perspectives of their victims. This is a direct attempt to build feelings of empathy. This kind of homework is read and critiqued by the correctional counselor. When needed, the correctional counselor will often require the offender to rewrite sections of their report, particularly when the use of minimization has been detected.

Interpersonal Functioning

In many cases, the criminal acts committed by sex offenders are manifestations of their poor interpersonal functioning. Examples include a man who is inadequate in meeting his responsibilities as an adult, and, a man who because of friction between himself and his wife sexually assaults his daughter to meet his sex needs. Another case might be a man who uses coercion, manipulation, or deceit to gain sex with women whom he dates. Yet another example might be a man who is unable to effectively develop adult peer relationships and therefore turns to children to meet his emotional and sexual intimacy needs. These are examples that commonly occur among sex offenders and these point to the need for interventions that train sex offenders to be more socially effective as adults.

These poor interpersonal skills, when combined with deviant sexual arousal, distorted attitudes, and poor impulse control, create an offender who is difficult to treat due to personality and cognitive challenges. Thus, the general idea among therapists is that if an offender can learn to live more functionally in the world of adults, they will find life more satisfying without the need to disregard the rights of others. However, it should be made clear that we do not mean to imply that a lack of social skills is the primary causal factor for sex offending; such is not the case. Rather, we simply mean to imply that it is much more difficult to treat a sex offender who has poor social skills and their risk of recidivism is greater since they are not as capable of developing appropriate adult sexual relationships as are persons who have effective social skills. Adding to this point, it is often the case among sex offenders that intimacy deficits and conflicts in intimate relationships have been found to correlate with sexual offending. The need for social skills training is less clearly specific than the rationale for reduction of deviant sexual arousal, but possession of effective social skills tend to improve the treatment prognosis. Put in another manner, if it is true that self-esteem and loneliness influence an offender's ability to function, then addressing social skills of the offender would seem to enhance the treatment process.

APPROPRIATE INTERACTIONS IN SOCIAL SITUATIONS The point to this aspect of treatment is to demonstrate that satisfying sexual interactions are extensions of social relationships. Because many sex offenders tend to see sexual activity as being an end unto itself within a relationship, this area of treatment emphasizes the role of friendship and intimate bonding with others. This treatment approach, like many others, utilizes participant role-playing exercises. In addition, offenders will likely be given homework assignments that require the offender to establish communication and relationship building. An example of such a homework assignment might be one in which the offender is required to talk with a given number of complete strangers and make a report about their experience when initiating such conversation.

The types of strangers that the sex offender will seek to communicate with will usually be identified by the correctional counselor. Obviously, some degree of discretion would need to be maintained. Thus, the offender may be asked to strike up conversation with a salesperson at a store or perhaps a person who attends a religious institution with the offender. Though the setting is not important, it is important that the offender be required to develop some sort of conversation and that they become adept at engaging in appropriate dialogue.

ASSERTIVENESS AS A TOOL TO AVOID FRUSTRATION AND POOR ANGER MANAGEMENT Another aspect of social skills that should be addressed with most sex offenders is the use of appropriate assertiveness. This area is relevant in the treatment of sex offenders for a variety of reasons. Sex offenders often mismanage anger, and assertiveness plays a significant role in anger reduction. In many cases, sex offenders suffer from insecurity in fearful attachment difficulties when establishing intimate relationships with adults. Some of this is due to fears of rejection and some due to a lack self-confidence and assertiveness skills. As a result, they may seek out contacts with people who are less likely to be rejecting, such as children.

Other problematic attachment styles have been found to be due to mistrustful and hostile approaches to interacting with others. Rather than dealing effectively and assertively with others, these offenders may harbor resentment and experience pervasive anger, which may lead them to act out aggressively. Assertiveness training promotes more effective means of managing anger and teaches individuals how to interact with others more effectively, and as a result, it can promote self-confidence, enhance self-esteem, and promote intimacy. This is considered important because deficits in intimacy conflicts in intimate relationships have been found to be correlated with sex offending (CSOM, 2008).

ADULT SEX EDUCATION On a cursory level, it may seem that the best message to give sex offenders is that they should not engage in any sexual thoughts, fantasies, or behaviors of any kind. Naturally, it is unrealistic to hope for this, thus the goal of treatment is to assist sex offenders in learning to be sexual beings without harming others. Thus, sex education is provided so that sex offenders develop a respect for the rights of others. This aspect of the treatment process is primarily psychoeducational in approach, with basic issues regarding safe sex, consensual sex, and other aspects of sexuality being covered. Throughout the educational component of sex offender treatment, considerable emphasis should be placed on the importance of verbal communication to promote clarity and ensure consent (because of their histories of having violated others). Correctional counselors should promote open, respectful, and clear communication related to sexual matters, teaching that sex is an important area for people to talk about (CSOM, 2008).

Behavior Management

Although deviant sexual arousal can motivate sex offending, distorted attitudes can promote it, and problems of interpersonal functioning can contribute to it, hence, ultimately sex offenders need to learn to manage their behavior. Deviant sexual arousal, distorted attitudes, and poor interpersonal functioning do not cause sexual offending, though they are correlated. Typically, the focus of this stage of treatment is on both the underlying issues and the behavioral acting out. One key component of sex offender treatment is teaching sex offenders very specifically how to manage their behavior. Behavior management is particularly important in situations where an offender easily could commit a sexual assault, such as being in the presence of someone who would be easy to victimize.

One of the key points to remember when monitoring behavior management of sex offenders is the ability of treatment and criminal justice agencies to work collaboratively to reinforce responsible behavior management among sex offenders. Community supervision agencies have the authority and ability to utilize a set of external controls, such as surveillance, the restriction of access to victims, and reducing opportunities to engage in high-risk behavior, which most treatment professionals lack. On the other hand, sex offender treatment providers have a set of therapeutic tools that are aimed at assisting the offender to develop his or her own internal controls over one's behavior. In some areas, these functions overlap and support one another. When taken together, both of these types of offender monitoring can contribute to successful offender management. Thus, it is important for correctional counselors to make routine contact with supervision personnel.

COVERT SENSITIZATION: VISUALIZING THE CONSEQUENCES OF SEXUAL ASSAULT One common behavior management technique is called covert sensitization. In many cases, sex offenders do not truly consider the long-range consequences of their behavior, but instead tend to focus on the immediate pleasure that they expect to achieve when committing their crime (Prendergast, 2004). This failure to consider the consequences of their actions is, in part, an outcome of the distortions and fallacies that exist within their thinking and perceptions. Therefore, if offenders learn to anticipate the consequences of their actions, it is then likely that this might prove to be some bit of a deterrent to their behavior. This is the underlying assumption to covert sensitization. With this in mind, the goal of covert sensitization is to teach offenders to have offenders substitute thinking about what is appealing about sex offending with considering instead possible negative consequences of committing sex offenses. This means that the correctional counselor will direct the sex offender toward taking a broader, more long-range view of their behaviors.

The specific process involved begins with the correctional counselor describing the reasons for the intervention. From that point, the group members are then required to identify and discuss their antecedent thoughts, their behaviors, and their cognitive distortions that occur prior to their offending. It has been found that sex offenders typically traverse a number of steps (that create circumstances where they can commit sexual assaults), both internally in their thinking and externally in their behavior (CSOM, 2008). Group members help one another to identify the thinking patterns prior to the offense as well as the patterns and strategies that they use to justify their actions.

Once the antecedent thoughts are identified, the offender is then asked to identify and describe imaginary neutral scenes where the offender is free to feel calm and relaxed, such as relaxing by the pool or engaging in a discussion with a good friend. After this, the offender is asked to identify some aversive scenarios. This must be reality based and serious enough so that, if they had actually occurred, the offender would have found them to be very unpleasant. The offender is then instructed to create several audiotapes as homework. When completing this homework, the offender starts by describing one of his neutral scenes which is then followed by a description of his antecedent behaviors that might likely lead to sexual offending.

Included in this homework would be the need for offenders to discuss the early stages of the commission of their crime, such as when they arrange to isolate their victim, to gain the victim's trust, and so on. Then, the offender is instructed to describe in detail an aversive scene, such as when he is arrested at his place of work by the police and is observed by those who are at his place of employment. The offender is required to spend at least two to five minutes focused on the aversive scene. The purpose of this exercise (particularly the aversive component) is to pair the experience of committing the sex offense with the aversive experiences. In addition, the correctional counselor might add an element to this technique by requiring the offender to imagine another scene where a consensual adult agrees to have sex with the offender. Though this aspect should only be interspersed between the precriminal scene and the aversive scene, it can help to pair the offender's interest with the appropriate behavior. This third scene is sometimes referred to as the escape scene (CSOM, 2008; Prendergast, 2004), because it provides an option beyond the aversive scene. The use of this escape scene is to highlight the fact that if sex offending is avoided, the offender can have a more pleasurable and satisfying life, including his sex life.

When conducting covert sensitization, offenders are typically required to complete about 10- to 15-minute covert sensitization audiotapes (CSOM, 2008). Correctional counselors are then required to review the covert sensitization audiotape homework and provide feedback to the offender, upon which time they erase the information and return the tapes to the offender. Naturally, if it does not seem that the offender is sincere in attempting this technique, the correctional counselor will need to challenge the offender's lack of effort and commitment.

RELAPSE PREVENTION Another treatment component related to sex offender behavior and self-management is relapse prevention (CSOM, 2008). The use of relapse prevention has its roots in the treatment of alcohol and other drug abuse, where it was found that getting people to stop drinking and using drugs was not nearly as difficult as was getting them to continue their abstinence (CSOM, 2008). Many of the notions and ideas regarding relapse prevention with drugs and alcohol have been borrowed and adapted to aid in sex offender treatment. When conducting relapse prevention with sex offenders, much of the focus is on the offender being required to asses his own offense patterns, his particular high-risk situations, and his coping strategies.

From this point, offenders learn how they can avoid lapses and relapses and how to monitor themselves for mood states and behaviors that might place them at increased risk of recidivism. The correctional counselor will assist offenders by providing feedback and homework assignments. Offenders are required to engage in this self-examination exercises, such as the task of writing an autobiography to gain a greater understanding of life patterns that result in offending, learning more effective problem-focused rather than emotion-focused coping strategies, avoiding high-risk situations, learning that urges that are not acted upon diminish with time, and practicing (such as with role-playing) how best to manage risky situations (CSOM, 2008). In completing these exercises, problem-focused coping strategies involve examining alternative methods to address the problem, deciding on the most effective strategies, and implementing the plan utilizing those strategies. On the other hand, emotion-focused coping strategies involve actions derived primarily from immediate emotions rather than considering various alternatives and the efficacy of each. Each of these approaches—problem based and emotion based—are important since they both address necessary aspects of relapse prevention. Thus, each should be given due attention among offenders to maximize the relapse prevention training.

SECTION SUMMARY

It is clear that sex offenders provide serious challenges for the correctional counselor. Chief among these challenges is the denial that will be encountered among most members of this population. In cases where mandated offenders refuse to assume accountability, placement in deniers pregroup may be necessary. During this time, the offender will engage in group interventions that address denial and the need for personal accountability for one's crime. If this phase of treatment is not successful in case of an offender, the offender will either be tested with interventions that are interrogation based or he will need to be incarcerated to ensure the public's safety.

Once issues regarding denial have been appropriately addressed, treatment will continue along four general domains of intervention. The first domain seeks to address deviant sexual interests and arousal that tend to be common among sex offenders. These deviant forms of arousal are typically learned (whether from prior sexual abuse or through other means), and the general consensus within the treatment literature is that aberrant forms of sexual arousal can also be unlearned. The next domain addresses distorted attitudes that sex offenders tend to have. In many cases, sex offenders have perceptions and beliefs that are not grounded in reality and they are subject to misread cues from their victims. Next, interpersonal functioning tends to be underdeveloped among many sex offenders, particularly among pedophiles. The inability to engage in relationships (both sexual and nonsexual) with adults and/or persons of equal stature and autonomy belies the insecurities that are common with many sex offenders. Lastly, behavior management is addressed in sex offender treatment. Regardless of the offender's psychological distortions, aberrant forms of arousal, and poor interpersonal functioning, the offender must be self-disciplined and capable of controlling his own actions. Behavior management techniques train sex offenders to effectively moderate their own behavior.

LEARNING CHECK

1. Before anything else in treatment can be accomplished, sex offenders must be willing to assume responsibility for their crimes.
   a. True
   b. False
2. Victim awareness technique is part of the domain of treatment that addresses deviant arousal.
   a. True
   b. False
3. Sex education is part of the interpersonal functioning domain of treatment.
   a. True
   b. False

4. Relapse prevention with sex offenders has its roots in relapse prevention programs used with drug offenders.
   a. True
   b. False
5. One aspect of social skills that should be addressed with most sex offenders is the use of appropriate assertiveness.
   a. True
   b. False

PART TWO: COMMON TREATMENT TECHNIQUES

While most students (particularly students of criminal justice) are aware that a variety of offenders may be given treatment, they are not typically aware of how these treatment techniques are utilized. In this section, we seek to clarify the various interventions by providing a brief overview of some of the techniques used in sex offender treatment. While some of these techniques may have been mentioned in the previous section, the presentation in this section should better organize their placement within the entire scheme of sex offender treatment. For purposes of this chapter, we consider the primary type of treatments to fall under one of two categories. These categories are cognitive-behavioral therapy and the interrogation-oriented approaches.

Neither of the approaches just mentioned emphasize affective-oriented styles of counseling and we think that this is noteworthy. Indeed, both perspectives are geared more toward the sex offender identifying with others, rather than being understood by others. We think that this is an important observation and refer to the work of Prendergast (2004) in clarifying this approach. Insight by Prendergast (2004) has provided several clear and easy-to-follow guidelines when providing therapeutic services to sex offenders. In short, the correctional counselor should not be duped by the manipulative nature of the sex offender but, at the same time, he or she must maintain a rapport with the offender.

Lastly, in this section we will provide much more extensive information regarding interrogation techniques. The use of criminal justice resources will be highlighted to demonstrate how collaboration between criminal justice personnel and the correctional counselor can optimize the prognosis for sex offenders. While this is true for all offenders who receive therapeutic services, this is particularly true for sex offenders due to their manipulative and convincing nature. The level of denial that is exhibited by sex offenders makes necessary the use of more invasive procedures when providing treatment interventions. Thus, we highlight the confrontational nature of sex offender treatment in this section of the chapter.

Cognitive-Behavioral Techniques Revisited

As noted earlier, cognitive-behavioral techniques are geared toward reducing and/or eliminating the deviant sexual arousal. There are many techniques commonly used by clinicians, each with a different rationale to their use. The first group of interventions teach impulse control, the second group of interventions teach arousal reduction, and the last group teach empathy to the offender. While each of these categories may overlap with information provided in the prior section, the current discussion seeks to simply clarify between the multiple techniques that are used with sex offenders. The impulse-control categories of cognitive-behavioral techniques include the following:

Thought stopping: This is used to disrupt a deviant thinking pattern. The offender is given pictures of arousing images and is forced to stop his thoughts when the image is seen.

The use of group confrontation, observation, and journaling assist in ensuring that this is accomplished (Knopp, 1989).

Thought shifting: This requires that the offender shift his thoughts to aversive imagery. The sex offender may be allowed to view or think about some arousing image but then is trained to think about something aversive, like an approaching police officer. Again, the use of group confrontation, observation, and journaling assist in ensuring that this is accomplished (Knopp, 1989).

Impulse charting: This is a method used to track points and times when certain thoughts and or desires seem more intense. The time of day, location, and number of times per week are to be noted. The offender will usually also be required to report the level of intensity of the impulse (i.e., 1–10 scale) and this will be tracked through a journaling process with the therapist (Knopp, 1989).

The arousal-reduction forms of cognitive-behavioral techniques include the following:

Scheduled overmasturbation: This intervention requires that the client routinely masturbate on a progressively more frequent schedule throughout the week. This is intended to reduce sexual drive and to make control easier for the offender. This exercise also teaches that the client does have some measure of control over his sexual arousal and use of sexual energy (Knopp, 1989).

Masturbatory reconditioning: This technique involves having the client masturbate to an appropriate fantasy, until he has an ejaculation (Knopp, 1989).

Aversion Therapy: This behavioral technique is often used in varying degrees within several sex offender programs. The aim of aversive techniques is to teach offenders to associate unpleasant stimuli with presently desirable yet unacceptable behaviors (Lester & Hurst, 2000). A wide range of physical or overt aversive stimuli have been used to treat sex offenders. Most notable ones are electric shock, foul odors and tastes, drugs that temporarily paralyze, and drugs that induce vomiting. Because of ethical and constitutional considerations, some of the more extreme forms of aversive stimuli are not used as frequently as they were some 20 to 30 years in the past.

Spouse monitoring: This involves supervision on the part of the spouse (if and when available, though other family members may be able to assist) or significant other to complete a daily checklist on the offender's compliance with the treatment and to ensure that any therapeutic homework given to the client is being completed at the prescribed times in the week. This increases the overall supervision that the offender has (Knopp, 1989).

Environmental manipulation: This helps to get the offender out of situations that are high risk for him and his potential victims. The offender should train himself to move out of the house, not to the victim (Knopp, 1989).

Cognitive-behavioral techniques that provide empathy training include the following:

Victim counselors: Victims are invited to attend the group meeting. In fact, the victim may colead the group. Offenders may be required to visit a victim advocate center, and, at their own expense, ask a victim counselor to explain his or her feelings on sex crimes.

Cognitive restructuring: The offender constructs scenes that cast him or significant others in the role of the victim. The client then focuses on typical rationalizations he uses to justify the assault (Knopp, 1989). Scenes are constructed where he utilizes and internalizes the rationalization. These scenes are then paired with aversive imagery. Lastly, alternate scenes are constructed where the offender catches himself in the distortion and counters with a reality-grounded message in which it is acknowledged that these actions do not end in the way that the offender hopes (Knopp, 1989).

Role-playing: The offender reenacts his own crime scene(s) with another offender and they take turns playing the role of victim. The remaining group offenders observe and later critique the role-play and allow for group processing of the effects on the victim.

The Five "Cs" in Sex Offender Treatment

This section introduces the work of Doctor William Prendergast (2004), an experienced therapist for sex offenders. We have chosen his work because he provides numerous points of no-nonsense insight into the treatment of sex offenders. He has extensive clinical experience and provides very clear and concrete guidance on the various dynamics that may occur between the correctional counselor and the sex offender client. While much of the previous information of this chapter has dealt with the process and techniques associated with sex offender treatment, Prendergast's (2004) work goes beyond this and highlights the interpersonal issues that are likely to impact therapy. In doing so, he points toward what he refers to as the "five Cs in sex offender treatment," which are confrontation, caution, confirmation, control, and consistency. We now provide an overview of each of these aspects of treatment.

CONFRONTATION Prendergast (2004) notes that due to the passivity, dependency, and seductiveness of many sex offenders, there can sometimes be a desire on the part of correctional counselors to be supportive, gentle, and parental in their approach. Prendergast (2004) notes that person-centered, Gestalt, and other affect-based approaches to therapy tend to be ineffective with this population. Rather, he contends that confrontation is the best method to reach the core of the sex offender's problems. Whatever the sex offender says, it should be heeded with a strong dose of skepticism, and, though this may be contrary to traditional counseling approaches, these offenders should be ready to validate statements or claims that they make in therapy.

One of the key observations regarding many sex offenders is that they are clever and tend to be adept at using vague generalities and/or utilizing psychological jargon as a means of mitigating or minimizing the impact of their offense (Prendergast, 2004). Thus, these offenders tend to become therapy-wise and begin to use the various technical terms to sanitize their actions and to place them within a clinical and sterile form of discussion. This tends to diminish the seriousness of their offense and, at the same time, creates the appearance of someone who is dedicated to the treatment regimen.

When using confrontation, Prendergast (2004) notes that long-winded statements and/or questions are ineffective because they interrupt the thought processes of the offender without steering them toward specific acceptance of responsibility. Prendergast recommends the use of "cue phrases" to prevent therapist interruptions and confrontation from turning to a means of avoidance or manipulation (2004, p. 148). The principle behind this is that the less said by the therapist, the better the challenge will be. Some suggested cue phrases are as follows:

- Because? I do not understand the motive or reasons for your actions/conclusions.
- Picture? You are being vague, and I don't get a clear understanding of the situation.

- Tilt! You're off the subject. Get back to what we were discussing.
- And? Not enough. Whatever you are telling me is incomplete. Something is missing.
- Pzzzzt! I don't believe you, or I don't buy that explanation/reason.

As can be seen, these forms of confrontation are direct and they do not operate on the presumption that the offender is being genuine or that the correctional counselor should be concerned about rapport building. Prendergast notes that most therapists have been trained in the use of "passive" treatment modalities and insist that these approaches, given time, will work (2004, p. 149). Invariably, these therapists find that traditional approaches seldom work with the sex offender.

Until a group is trained in the process and can function somewhat independently, the correctional counselor must direct, control, and keep the group on course (Prendergast, 2004). Since avoidance of any painful topic is to be expected, the correctional counselor must pay close attention not only to what is said but to what is *not* said in the session. Further, though offenders may challenge one another, there is a danger that the group may harm rather than help certain members. Indeed, Prendergast makes the insightful observation that sex offenders can become quite judgmental of one another, since this allows offenders to feel better about themselves in relation to other members. To mitigate this, the correctional counselor should always allow sufficient time at the end of each group meeting for (1) recovery from an emotional session; (2) a summary of what occurred in the session; and (3) each member to give feedback to other offenders who spoke of their problems. After each member gives his feedback, the correctional counselor should provide summary feedback. Lastly, it is critical that the correctional counselor show no favoritism or partiality when providing his or her feedback.

CAUTIONS Prendergast notes that in most cases, sex offenders both in the institution and in community treatment settings, tend to be well-mannered, polite, and behaved individuals. This is important because this can, in some cases, lead to a lax attitude toward the offender; this is to be avoided. This is particularly true since many sex offenders will attempt to make themselves likable to the correctional counselor and they will also then attempt to form some sort of personal connection with the therapist. Through this process, there is a tendency to normalize themselves into feeling equal to the correctional counselor. Once this is started, the offender will tend to distance himself from his peers in the group and begin to picture himself as being somehow superior and/or in a position that is similar to staff rather than the client population. Once this delusion starts, the denial mechanisms are entrenched and they fail to identify with their criminal behaviors, evading accountability. Naturally, the therapist should safeguard against this.

Prendergast also notes that female correctional counselors are at greater risk than are male treatment providers. Indeed, sex offenders often delude themselves into believing that the female treatment provider desires him for romantic purposes, and he will tend to misperceive even the most innocent of kind acts as indication of amorous feelings. In many cases, the correctional counselor is the last person to be aware of this. Once the offender's perception becomes known, it has usually worked itself deeply into his internal thoughts and will prove resistant to countering. According to Prendergast (2004), even if the correctional counselor makes it quite clear that she has no desires for the sex offender and even if she sets firm professional boundaries, the offender's delusional misperceptions will often result in the following forms of rationalization (p. 152):

- The authorities have made her act that way.
- She is worried about her job; but when I get out, we will be lovers.
- She really loves me but has to be fair to the rest of the group.
- She does not know that she loves me, but I will convince her.

The dangers to these rationalizations are apparent. It is also important to note that this in no way is the fault of the female correctional counselor. Rather, it is the intent of this section to note that female treatment providers are likely to encounter reactions that are fairly unique from most male treatment providers. Further, this is meant to simply educate students, both male and female, of the realities encountered when working with sex offenders.

CONFIRMATION Prendergast (2004) puts it simply by noting that treatment providers should simply "believe nothing" when working with sex offenders (p. 155). As was noted earlier in this chapter, truthfulness associated with sex offenders has less to do with what they do say and more to do with what they fail to mention. In essence, these offenders tell only part of the story. They are concerned with fear and rejection and have a difficult time coming to grips with their label as a sex offender. Further, most offenders will want to get the entire process of therapy over as quickly as possible, with minimal exposure or pain. Thus, these offenders will be very convincing and will seem sincere. It is in their best interest to not be honest in regard to their need for treatment. Thus, once the offender has passed through the denial phase of treatment, the correctional counselor will gain quick confirmation from the individual offender, who in many cases will seek to quickly claim that he sees the error of his ways. However, this should not be believed.

Rather, the correctional counselor should rely on the group therapy participants to provide an additional gauge on where the offender stands therapeutically. This is especially true in an institutional setting where the offenders will live, eat, and sleep within proximity of one another. Thus, it is likely that the group will be much better at evaluating the change or lack of change that has occurred among one of the members. While we are not suggesting that the therapist should make decisions based solely on the input from group members, we are noting that in cases where the counselor's assessment of the offender's progress is divergent from the feedback that other group members tend to provide, the correctional counselor should be doubly careful in making any determination.

Lastly, whenever possible, the correctional counselor is urged to seek input from family and/or other staff regarding an offender's progress. The confirmation process by group participants can be further improved by these other outside sources of information. Naturally, the counselor will need to ensure that family, friends, or other individuals are willing to provide such input and the counselor must remain receptive to the trauma of the victim, especially if they are a family member whom the counselor will ask for input. Prendergast (2004) notes that, when possible and if feasible, wives, parents, siblings, children (especially in cases of incest), neighbors, employers, and anyone else may be excellent sources of information regarding the offender's progress. The key is to go beyond the confines of the therapy session and to ask persons who might not be presented with impression management techniques. In this case, impression management is when the offender presents an impression that is most favorable, in the process failing to allow defects or genuine characteristics to be observed. Thus, it is likely that the offender's supervision officer will see a side of the offender that is also more positive than actually exists. While correctional counselors should work in tandem with community supervision officers, it is the input from others who are close to the sex offender during their day-to-day routine that will provide the most reliable information.

CONTROL Because therapy is typically built on a therapeutic alliance, there can be a tendency among novice correctional counselors to dwell more on relationship building in the group setting rather than boundary placement and maintenance of the group process. With sex offender group therapy, this is a mistake. This is particularly true given that sex offenders are most often skilled at manipulation and since many will try to ingratiate themselves to the counselor. Indeed, one of the major threats involved when a correctional counselor is too mild is that of a potential therapeutic conspiracy (Prendergast, 2004). In such cases, it is not uncommon for offenders to get together outside of the group sessions so that they can plan and stage reactions within the group setting. Indeed, some offenders may work together to rehearse reactions and/or feedback to present the impression that members are working together to make progress. This is an especially problematic issue when groups use peer review. *Peer review* is a constructive component of group therapy, but it should be used only by seasoned counselors who understand the challenges when dealing with sex offenders. As was noted earlier, the correctional counselor can augment the group input with other persons outside of therapy, such as family members, employers, and other persons who know the offender.

In addition, it is recommended that the counselor should maintain healthy psychological and professional distance from himself or herself and the group members. This prevents the impression that the counselor has favorites. Once the habit of distancing is established, none of the group participants will feel isolated or left out. Ultimately, this will have the effect of an increased and balanced sense of involvement among group members. Further, the correctional counselor must provide this distance while maintaining control of the group in a subtle manner. Prendergast (2004) recommends using noncondemning questions rather than pointed statements. For example, when the group begins to deviate off the topic, the correctional counselor might ask of the group, "Are we getting lost? I am losing the original thought of what was being said" or "Where are we going with this discussion? Does it apply to what was being said?" These types of questions aid in directing the group while providing some degree of subtlety when doing so.

CONSISTENCY In order for sex offenders to avoid recidivating, it is important that aftercare be provided once the treatment program has been completed. Access to follow-up assistance should be available on a 24-hour basis. In fact, private counselors and those working within agencies should have some sort of on-call system in place. It is important that therapeutic assistance be available to the offender even when the correctional counselor is gone on a vacation or for some other reason. Further, the additional therapeutic assistance should come from someone who is familiar with the offender's past history and treatment progress. When offenders are released from being incarcerated, it is often the case that community agencies will attempt to start therapy all over again, doing it according to their own preferences. While this is understandable, to some extent, every effort should be made between institutional treatment personnel to develop effective relationships with community-based treatment personnel who will provide services after incarceration. In doing so, it is hoped that treatment groups will devise means of treatment that enhance one another rather than working against each other.

Lastly, Prendergast (2004) notes that some sex offenders may never be completely cured, and they are then likely to experience recurrences. We completely concur with this point and would note that this means that sex offenders should have follow-up nearly indefinitely. Naturally, this can depend on the exact nature of the sex offense. In cases of statutory sex offenses without violence, particularly between persons close in age, this issue may not be relevant at all. But for pedophiles and rapists (particularly those who have used violence), it is important to have a long-term relapse prevention program in place. This notion is validated all the more by the criminal justice system where, in many states, certain categories of sex offenders are required to register with local law enforcement throughout the duration of their natural life. Such requirements are indication of the fact that sex offenders present a danger to society in the long run and are difficult to change.

Interrogation-Oriented Techniques

The next group of techniques used are designed to ensure that the offender is being honest in their feedback that they provide to program treatment staff. This is important and necessary since sex offenders are notorious for lying and manipulating. These tools assist the therapist and community supervision staff in determining whether progress is earnestly being made in the program. The two techniques presented require the use of mechanical instruments to ensure compliance with the program; the two instruments are the polygraph and the plethysmograph. The polygraph is a standard lie detector used to measure biological responses to deception. It is used in sex offender supervision to break through offender denial of the offense, assess the offender's honesty in reporting their sexual history, and to monitor the offender's compliance with probation conditions (Texas Council on Sex Offender Treatment, 2005). The penile plethysmograph uses a cup or band that is placed around the penis while the offender is in a private room. Once worn, the sex offender is presented with a variety of visual and auditory stimuli. While the offender is shown pictures and exposed to sounds, a computer program records the degree of sexual arousal that is experienced by the offender (Texas Council on Sex Offender Treatment, 2005).

THE POLYGRAPH AND SEX OFFENDERS According to the Texas Council on Sex Offender Treatment (TCSOT), polygraph testing, when combined with intensive treatment approaches, provides the most comprehensive means of accessing the offender's past deviant sexual history (2005). Further, it has been determined that the rate of "crossover" between adult and child victims among sex offenders is much higher when polygraph testing is used, as opposed to a reliance on standard interrogation techniques and/or disclosures to correctional counselors (Heil, Ahlmeyer, & Simons, 2003; TCSOT, 2005). This means that, without the use of the polygraph, it is very likely that criminal investigators and therapists alike are unable to gain an accurate picture of the criminal history of the offender. This is clear support for the use of polygraph testing and intensive sex offender treatment programming when seeking sexual offense history information (Heil et al., 2003).

Further, a research demonstrates that the use of polygraph interrogations of sex offenders is highly accurate—with 98%—in detecting falsifications (TCSOT, 2005). During the past 25 years, there has been an increased use of the polygraph to test the truthfulness of adult sex offenders, to break through denial, and to ensure compliance with their supervision conditions (TCSOT, 2005). Accordingly, it would seem that the polygraph is an effective tool for intervention and for eliciting admissions. This again demonstrates the therapeutic value of this instrument as well as the value to public safety and security. The admissions made by sex offenders are crucial to break down denial and to facilitate offender accountability (TCSOT, 2005). This then aids in the change process. It is expected that the appropriate mix of sanctions (for dishonesty) and privileges (for honest compliance with supervision and treatment requirements) will encourage sex offenders to disclose and address their criminal behaviors.

THE PENILE PLETHYSMOGRAPH AND SEX OFFENDERS In the past two decades, the plethysmograph has evolved into a sophisticated, computerized instrument that is capable of measuring slight changes in the circumference of the penis. The use of this instrument develops a diagnostic method used to assess sexual arousal by measuring the blood flow (tumescence) to the penis during the presentation of sexual stimuli (audio/visual) in a laboratory setting. It is interesting that the plethysmograph provides the identification of clients' arousal in response to sexual stimuli and, in the process, provides an indicator of the effectiveness of a given therapeutic intervention. Indeed, if the offender internalizes the methods taught to control his deviant arousal, there should be a corresponding decrease in deviant arousal. Further still, there should also be an increase to positive appropriate arousal. This means that the plethysmograph provides a nearly full-proof means of measuring the effectiveness of covert sensitization exercises. As the student may recall, these exercises are designed to elicit aversive reactions to inappropriate sexual arousal and, in other cases, reinforce appropriate sexual arousal. The effectiveness of these techniques (and the genuine effort of the offender) can be validated through the use of the penile plethysmograph.

Because sex offenders (especially highly compulsive offenders) have been found to ruminate over sexual fantasies involving the offense pattern, the phallometric assessments have been among the most successful at detecting the likelihood for relapse among these offenders. This is particularly true when, as noted in the prior section, one considers that these offenders will avoid disclosure of their fantasies at all costs. Thus, this process allows clinicians to identify those offenders who have deviant phallometry patterns; and the more deviant they are, the more likely that recidivism will occur (Lane Council, 2003; TCSOT, 2005).

One of the strengths of phallometric testing is that it provides an objective means of assessing offender progress in treatment. This can be much superior to the subjective impressions of the correctional counselor and/or community supervision personnel. This is an important point because sex offenders can be so convincing, even to people who are trained to detect their deceptions. The use of phallometric testing further refines the treatment process as it allows the correctional counselor to identify key aspects of the offender's challenges in treatment and provides guidance to the treatment professional when modifying and/or intensifying treatment approaches. Though phallometric assessments are considered valid and reliable, these test results are nonetheless interpreted in tandem with other relevant data to determine risk levels and revisions to the treatment regimen.

Because so many sex offenders either deny their culpability or minimize the extent of their interest in and involvement with sexual offending behavior, this instrument can augment the group process during the denial stage of treatment or it can provide a clear indicator of the progress that an offender has made. It is well established that the self-report of sex offenders cannot be assumed to be valid or to capable of indicating the scope of the offender's deviant fantasies, arousal patterns, or behaviors. Hence, psychophysiological assessment of sexual arousal patterns, which is one of the most effective means of breaking through the offender's denial, can be used. Many offenders reveal their deviant sexual interests when they are shown their positive physiologic responses to sexually inappropriate stimuli (Kercher, 1993). This instrument then serves to improve the treatment prognosis since the correctional counselor can then utilize probative techniques and assignments that target the thoughts and feelings of the offender that are otherwise undetected and therefore resistant to treatment.

SECTION SUMMARY

The use of cognitive-behavioral techniques has been widely accepted as the primary approach in sex offender treatment. There are many reasons for this, but most important among them is the fact that sex offender treatment must be designed in a manner that provides demonstrated evidence of the offender's progress. Given the public safety concerns involved with sex offenders, it is critical that interventions be grounded with clear indicators of progress. This then precludes many other modalities that are more affective based and/or person centered in orientation.

Indeed, given that sex offenders tend to be clever and manipulative, the typical approaches utilized by many treatment professionals may prove to be ineffective and may result in the therapist being misled.

Prendergast provides several excellent guidelines related to issues specific to sex offenders and their interpersonal dynamics with treatment providers. In this chapter, his five "Cs" of treatment are presented. The five "Cs" are confrontation, caution, confirmation, control, and consistency. All of these concepts provide a general approach to sex offender treatment that thwarts manipulation on the part of many sex offenders and also optimizes intervention techniques.

The use of interrogation techniques demonstrates the importance of ensuring compliance among sex offenders. This also provides further evidence that, in general, sex offender treatment is not built on the same type of trust-building relationship that might be used with other offenders. Indeed, the use of such invasive techniques does not exist with most all other types of offenders. Due to their manipulative nature, their resistance to treatment, and their danger to public safety, the sex offender tends to be set apart from most other offender typologies in the treatment and criminal justice literature.

LEARNING CHECK

1. In general, person-centered approaches should not be used within most sex offender group counseling interventions.
   a. True
   b. False
2. Masturbatory reconditioning involves having the client masturbate to an appropriate fantasy, until he has an ejaculation.
   a. True
   b. False
3. Aversion therapy is a cognitive-behavioral technique used to target impulse control deficits.
   a. True
   b. False
4. The phase known as "completion" is among Prendergast's five Cs of sex offender treatment.
   a. True
   b. False
5. The polygraph has been found to be roughly 98% accurate when used as an interrogation device with sex offenders.
   a. True
   b. False

CONCLUSION

The sex offending population is perhaps the most difficult and controversial group of offenders whom correctional counselors will treat. Indeed, it is sex offenders in general, and the pedophiles in particular, who bring to bear serious public concern and anger. Against that backdrop, the correctional counselor is tasked with providing treatment to this group of offenders, who on the surface often appear compliant but in most cases are resistant to treatment. Thus, the first order of business when providing therapeutic interventions for sex offenders is to address their denial.

If denial is particularly persistent, the use of a pregroup for deniers is warranted and/or the use of interrogation techniques that are administered by criminal justice personnel.

When sex offenders are willing to assume some level of accountability for their criminal offense, the treatment process tends to follow along four different domains. The first domain addresses deviant sexual interests, arousal, and preferences that the sex offender may possess. Because sexual behavior is largely learned, this approach presumes that aberrant forms of arousal can be unlearned. The next domain is focused on the distorted attitudes that sex offenders tend to possess. For many sex offenders, perceptions and beliefs regarding sexual behavior are not based on what would seem to be realistic or common expectations. The delusions by which these offenders operate must be challenged and the sex offender must articulate his beliefs so that exposure to group participants and the correctional counselor can allow for feedback to be given to the offender. The next step in treatment addresses the interpersonal functioning of the offender due to the fact that many sex offenders are socially challenged. Learning more effective social skills are intended to supplant those that are dysfunctional, over time. The last domain of treatment addresses behavior management. Though this is the most direct form of intervention, it provides clear and specific guidance to the offender on how to moderate his reactions to environmental stimuli that might help generate relapse.

From this chapter, it should be clear that cognitive-behavioral techniques are most often practiced in sex offender treatment programs. These techniques are a bit more direct than other techniques but they are also not as easily circumvented by sex offenders as are other techniques. This is a particular strength of the cognitive-behavioral approach to treatment. Likewise, Prendergast's five "Cs" of treatment help to reinforce the implementation of cognitive-behavioral approaches. Prendergast's directive style of therapy, replete with confrontational (but not aggressive) forms of implementation, help to maximize the likely effectiveness of cognitive-behavioral approaches.

Lastly, the use of interrogation techniques underscores the need to ensure compliance among sex offenders, both for therapeutic purposes and for public safety needs. Regardless of a correctional counselor's training, it is important to remember that the intervention with sex offenders is first and foremost an attempt to improve public safety. It is clear that sex offender treatment cannot be based on the same type of trusting relationship that exists with many other clients, including other types of offenders in the criminal justice system.

Essay Questions

1. Provide an explanation of why the initial stage of denial is so important in sex offender treatment. Further, discuss some specific aspects of treatment for sex offenders in denial. In addition, explain how interrogation techniques such as the polygraph and the penile plethysmograph can assist treatment providers in countering denial among sex offenders.
2. Provide at least one example of a cognitive-behavioral approach used in group interventions with sex offenders. Further, explain the reason that most programs utilize group interventions with sex offenders? What are some techniques from your previous readings in Chapter 5 that would be effective with sex offenders, given what you now know about sex offenders and group interventions?
3. Discuss the various cognitive-behavioral techniques outlined in the second section of this chapter. What is unique about these types of techniques compared to other techniques used with most other offenders. Further, explain why cognitive-behavioral techniques have proven to be the preferred approach to implementing sex offender treatment.
4. Discuss Prendergasts "five Cs in sex offender treatment." How does Prendergast's suggestions enhance the information provided by the Center for Sex Offender Management presented in the first

section of this chapter? In addition, explain how his suggestions enhance the various cognitive-behavioral interventions listed at the beginning of the second section of this chapter.

5. In your opinion, what might a new correctional counselor do to prepare himself or herself for working with the sex offender population? What are some particular challenges that might be encountered among some therapists? Lastly, how might professional collaboration be of use to correctional counselors who treat the sex offending population?

Treatment Planning Exercise

In this exercise, the student must consider the case of Nathan and determine whether Nathan is being manipulative or whether the reasons that he gives are sincere. You must explain how you would provide treatment for Nathan and you must consider how that may affect his final outcome. Further, you must identify specific techniques that you would use and discuss how you would determine those techniques did, in fact, work to reduce his likelihood of recidivism.

The Case of Nathan

Nathan is a 39-year-old Caucasian male. He lives alone in his rented home and is on intensive supervision probation. Nathan is a pedophile and the whole neighborhood knows it. Nathan is also divorced, and his previous wife left him after discovering that he had been molesting her seven-year-old son, Mark, for nearly two years. Prior to this, Nathan had been suspected of inappropriate relationships with other children when he was a substitute teacher at a local elementary school as well. Nathan's prior wife did not know of the dropped allegations that had been made against him. Nor did she know that he had lived with another woman, Sherry, who had two kids and suspected that Nathan was not to be trusted around her children.

Nathan is depressed because he really did care for Mark and really did not want to hurt Mark. Nathan really thought Mark was special, and Nathan was very attentive to Mark's needs. And, Nathan explains to you that "Deep down inside, I know Mark cared about me, too. I just do not know why he would tell his mom otherwise. I feel so betrayed!"

Nathan disclosed this during your last session with him. Instead of expressing remorse, he seems to be sorrowful over his loss of the "relationship" with Mark. Indeed, Nathan feigns commitment to treatment, but sometimes his comments indicate that he saw his molestation as consensual activity with Mark.

When Nathan was ultimately arrested, he was found with excessive amounts of pornography, but none of it included children as subjects. Further, his two prior adult female partners both noted that Nathan was capable of normal sexual activity but would go through periods of seeming "distracted" and uninterested in a normal sexual routine. This might last for weeks.

You can tell that Nathan genuinely does not desire to physically harm children, but his overpowering attraction to children is obvious. What is more, he acts as if he GENUINELY cared about these children as if they were some legitimate adult love interest. Further, he does not seem to have any deep-seated issues with adult women, and in fact he is capable of at least faking a relationship with women, though Sherry did note that Nathan always seemed a bit uninterested in their adult relationship and frequently found ways to involve the kids as a topic in their private discussions. Further, you can tell that Nathan is not really interested in treatment, but he goes along.

Nathan currently has a night job stocking freight at a local warehouse. He has numerous restrictions on his movement. His prognosis does not seem great and he seems to be keeping to himself. He has no real friends and you notice that he seems to spend an exorbitant amount of time at home alon.

Bibliography

Center for Sex Offender Management. (2008). *An overview of sex offender treatment for a non-clinical audience*. Washington, DC: Office of Justice Programs, U.S. Department of Justice.

Hanser, R. D. (2007). *Special needs offenders*. Upper Saddle River, NJ: Prentice Hall.

Heil, P., Ahlmeyer, S., & Simons, D. (2003). Crossover sexual offenses. *Sexual Abuse: A Journal of Research and Treatment, 15*(4), 221–236.

Kercher, G. (1993). *Use of the plethysmograph in the assessment and treatment of sex offenders*. Senate Interim Study Paper.

Knopp, F. H. (1989). Northwest treatment associates: A comprehensive community-based evaluation and treatment program for adult sex offenders. In P. C. Kratcoski (Ed.), *Correctional counseling and treatment* (2nd ed. , pp. 364–380). Prospect Heights, IL: Waveland Press, Inc.

Lane Council of Governments. (2003). *Managing sex offenders in the community: A national overview*. U.S. Department of Justice, Office of Justice Programs.

Lester, D., & Hurst, G. (2000). *Treating Sex Offenders*. In P. Van Voorhis, M. Braswell, & D. Lester (Eds.), *Correctional counseling & rehabilitation* (4th ed.). Cincinnati, OH: Anderson Publishing Company.

Prendergast, W. E. (2004). *Treating sex offenders: A guide to clinical practice with adults, clerics, children, and adolescents* (2nd ed.). New York, NY: Haworth Press, Inc.

Texas Council on Sex Offender Treatment. (2005). *Use of the polygraph in the assessment and treatment of sex offenders*. Retrieved from: http://www.dshs.state.tx.us/csot/csot_polygraphs.pdf.

13

HIV/AIDS, Older Offenders, Dying/Grief/Mourning, and Suicide Issues

CHAPTER OBJECTIVES

After reading this chapter, you will be able to:

1. Identify and discuss some of the stigmas and misconceptions associated with HIV/AIDS.
2. Discuss existential counseling and explain how and why it may be useful for offenders with HIV/AIDS and/or elderly offenders.
3. Identify the five stages of grief by Kübler-Ross and explain how they are used with persons experiencing trauma, particularly trauma due to the death of someone.
4. Identify and discuss the various typologies of elderly offenders. Be able to explain how they differ, one from the other.
5. Discuss the various approaches that correctional counselors might use to address the possibility of suicide among their offender clients.

PART ONE: HIV/AIDS

Introduction

This chapter will demonstrate how terminal illnesses, advanced age, and the bleak circumstances of many offenders put them in a world where death and loss are a commonplace experience. The student will be introduced to the basic aspects of HIV/AIDS among offenders with consideration given to how counselors can assist offenders with the dying process. Further, existential therapy and the use of a well-known grief-stage model are presented as a basic framework from which therapeutic interventions can be delivered. From this point, it becomes clear that many of the issues associated with awareness of one's mortality, the loss of loved ones, the sensation of medically deteriorating weaves a common theme in the grief and loss process. Further, the elderly are presented as being particularly at risk for contracting some type of virus or illness due to health challenges commonly encountered. Lastly, suicidal ideation is a threat that is frequently encountered within the offender population. The means by which suicide is assessed and treated is examined, with special attention given to several specialized populations that have been discussed within earlier chapters of this text. We now begin with our discussion of HIV/AIDS.

OVERVIEW OF HIV AND AIDS *Acquired Immune Deficiency Syndrome (AIDS)* is the official term given for the condition when a virus has invaded the body and disrupted the immune system to the point that it can no longer protect the body from a variety of deadly infections such as cancer or pneumonia (Kanel, 2003). This disease is most often terminal but there is a great degree of variability in how different person's bodies will react to the disease; some people will die within a few weeks while others might not die until several years have elapsed. AIDS came to the attention of medical authorities in the United States in 1981 when the Center for Disease Control first formally recognized its existence. Human immunodeficiency virus (HIV), the virus that actually leads to AIDS, was neither detected nor understood until 1983. Since 1981 roughly 750,000 cases of AIDS have been reported with approximately 83% being male and 17% being female in the outside population.

AIDS is caused by the HIV. A person infected with HIV may not present observable symptoms for several years. In fact, any indication will likely not be present until AIDS symptoms develop and this could take up to 10 or even 20 years until it becomes evident to the infected person or to others. Although they may not have symptoms, they are still very contagious.

However, as HIV progresses over time the infection becomes increasingly difficult to control and severe opportunistic infections such as tuberculosis, hepatitis, and pneumonia are much more likely to lead to death. Offenders who are intravenous drug users are at increased risk of contracting these illnesses due to sharing injection equipment that are contaminated with microorganisms that spread the infection. The proportion of AIDS cases among Intravenous Drug Users (IDUs) has remained consistent and accounts for approximately 25 to 29% of recently diagnosed cases (Hanson, Venturelli, & Fleckenstein, 2002). HIV is transmitted vaginally, orally, and especially through anal sex. HIV is of course also spread through infected blood or blood products and by sharing drug needles with an infected person. Likewise, HIV can be transmitted from infected mother to infant in utero, during birth, or while breastfeeding. When symptoms are experienced, they typically include flu-like symptoms including fever, loss of appetite, weight loss, fatigue, and enlarged lymph nodes. The symptoms usually disappear within a week to a month, and the virus can remain dormant for years. However, it continues to weaken the immune system, leaving the individual increasingly unable to fight opportunistic infections. It should be noted that virtually everyone who becomes infected with HIV will eventually develop AIDS and die of AIDS-related complications.

There are some common warning signs and symptoms for persons with AIDS, but it should be pointed out that these are not always certain because other diseases may actually be the primary source of the symptoms that are detected. Because AIDS itself is actually just a viral reduction in the operation of one's immune system, there may be few if any obvious symptoms. Perhaps the only real clue is that one might notice that their immune system is not as robust. A lowered constitution and inability to stave off illnesses may be a hint, depending on the circumstances. It is typically not until a person contracts another opportunistic infection (again, illnesses such as cancer and/or pneumonia) that it becomes truly apparent that one has AIDS. At this point, specific signs or symptoms may be noticed. Kanel (2003, p. 161) notes that any of the symptoms that follow warrant further investigation by a clinic or medical doctor:

1. Continuous fatigue
2. Fever and night sweats for more than a few weeks

3. Rapid, unexplained weight loss
4. Swollen glands in the neck, armpit, or groin
5. Pink or purplish blotches or bumps on or under the skin, or in the mouth, nose, eyelids, or rectum
6. Long-lasting, dry (unproductive) coughing
7. Fuzzy white patches on the tongue or in the mouth
8. Constant diarrhea
9. Loss of memory.

The best form of prevention is to abstain from sex with an infected person (especially anal sex), where body fluids, blood, semen, or vaginal secretions are likely to be exchanged. Latex condoms can reduce but not eliminate the risk of contracting the disease during sex. Naturally, individuals should avoid the use of intravenous drugs. It should be noted that there is no known cure for HIV. Antiviral drugs of various sorts are used to prolong the life and health of the infected individual. Other antiviral treatments are designed to simply buffer against the invasion of opportunistic infections to the person. Any holistic treatment program will also include a wide array of vitamin and lifestyle modifications.

Though AIDS/HIV has been publicly known for a number of years, misconceptions still persist regarding this disease. Indeed, publicity regarding HIV and AIDS has been generated for well over 20 years. Nevertheless, misunderstandings, myths, and misconceptions still continue. In fact, with the treatments for HIV/AIDS being improved and the media shock being subsided, there seems to be a more lax concern with this medical problem, leading to a less attentive understanding of the characteristics of HIV/AIDS. In some cases, this lax attitude and the misperceptions involved with HIV/AIDS have prompted the very behaviors that cause more people to become HIV positive. Although unanswered questions about HIV remain, researchers have learned a great deal. According to WebMD, there are a number of common myths associated with HIV. We present a selected set of these misconceptions below, along with the facts that dispute them.

Misconception 1: *I can get HIV by being around people who are HIV positive.*
The evidence shows that HIV is not spread through touch, tears, sweat, or saliva. You cannot be infected with HIV by:

Breathing the same air as someone who is HIV positive

Touching a toilet seat or doorknob handle after an HIV-positive person

Drinking from a water fountain

Hugging, kissing, or shaking hands with someone who is HIV positive

Sharing eating utensils with an HIV-positive person

Using exercise equipment at a fitness facility

You can get HIV from infected blood, semen, vaginal fluid, or mother's milk.

Misconception 2: *I don't need to worry about becoming HIV positive—new drugs will keep me well.*
Yes, antiretroviral medications are improving the lives of many people who are HIV positive. However, many of these drugs are expensive and produce serious side effects. None yet provides a cure. Also, drug-resistant strains of HIV make treatment an increasing challenge.

Misconception 3: *I can get HIV from mosquitoes.*
Because HIV is spread through blood, people are worried that biting or bloodsucking insects might spread HIV. Several studies, however, show no evidence to support this—even in areas

with lots of mosquitoes and cases of AIDS. When insects bite, they do not inject the blood of the person or animal they have last bitten. Also, HIV lives only for a short time inside an insect.

Misconception 4: *I'm HIV positive—my life is over.*
In the early years of the disease epidemic, the death rate from AIDS was extremely high. But today, antiretroviral drugs allow HIV-positive people—and even those with AIDS—to live much longer. In fact, from 2000 to 2004, the number of people living with AIDS increased by 30%.

Misconception 5: *You can't get HIV from oral sex.*
While it is true that oral sex is less risky than some other types of sex, you can get HIV by having oral sex with either a man or a woman who is HIV positive. Always use a latex barrier during oral sex.

From this list of misconceptions, it is clear that there is still need for preventative education. Further, the offender population tends to be particularly vulnerable since these individuals have a higher likelihood of engaging in risky behaviors. Likewise, misinformation is often provided as a means of encouraging persons into behaviors that would otherwise be unwise. Lastly, among the juvenile offending population, the inclusion of preventative education is particularly important. In Chapter 9 on Youth Counseling and Juvenile Offending, we discuss the need for safe-sex counseling. Given that these misconceptions are common among youth (especially the fifth misconception that was previously noted), we think that it is important that effective education be provided by correctional counselors and/or treatment programs, regardless of whether public school systems have or do cover similar material.

ADDRESSING THE STIGMA WITH THE AIDS VIRUS Public fear regarding HIV/AIDS has resulted in misunderstandings regarding the contraction of the virus as well as those who are infected by it. There are three types of stigma commonly associated with HIV: instrumental HIV-related stigma, symbolic HIV-related stigma, and courtesy HIV-related stigma. These types of stigma make the treatment process more difficult for the person afflicted with HIV and make the adjustment process all the more traumatic than it already would be. All of these types of stigma are discussed as follows.

Instrumental HIV-related stigma refers to the fear and apprehension that is experienced by the person with HIV/AIDS as well as those who discover that a person has the virus. This type of stigma is not surprising and, in actuality, is a common initial reaction. It is normal to have a degree of fear and apprehension when something threatening is introduced into our life. However, once protective precautions have been taken, knowledge is gained regarding the threat, and the immediacy of the threat is known, anxiety should be minimized, particularly among persons who are not afflicted with the virus. For those with the virus, the fear is quite natural and the process of working through that fear will undoubtedly require medical and (if the person is willing) mental health assistance. Whenever we examine our own mortality, anxiety is common.

Symbolic HIV-related stigma refers to the use of HIV/AIDS to express attitudes toward the social groups or "lifestyle" perceived to be associated with the disease. This is typically grounded in mistrust or dislike of specific groups that are vulnerable to the virus. Specifically, persons who dislike or are intolerant of the gay or lesbian population will manifest behavior that generates this type of stigma. Likewise, persons who show disdain and a lack of empathy for the drug-abusing population also fall into this category, since needle users are a group who are vulnerable to contracting and spreading the virus. As is now well known, HIV/AIDS can affect anyone and is not restricted to a given class or category of people.

Courtesy-related stigma is stigmatization of people connected to the issue of HIV/AIDS or HIV-positive people. This is often a reaction from others toward family members who are considerate and/or sympathetic to the person with HIV/AIDS. Not only is this type of stigma overly reactive, it may also be reflective of someone who has hate-based problems with persons who have HIV, especially if the person afflicted with HIV/AIDS is gay or lesbian in their sexual orientation.

All of these forms of stigma tend to result in a deterioration of interpersonal relations among others who the individual had been close to. Further, persons contending with HIV may feel varying degrees of guilt and anger, both in regard to their own actions (guilt) and in regard to the reactions of others (anger). It is not uncommon for persons to second-guess themselves or engage in wishful thinking of how they might have avoided the virus. Naturally, these persons will be under a great deal of stress, and depression is likely to be observed. Some persons may isolate themselves from others (especially if they have experienced rejection), while others may exhibit hostile behavior.

SELF-EFFICACY AND SOCIAL ISOLATION As was noted previously, it is common for anyone who is faced with his or her own mortality to have negative affect. For most persons, the notion of death is not considered pleasant, and, as a defense mechanism, many people simply avoid thinking about this reality. If they do ponder over their own demise, in many cases it is fleeting or topical, at most. Nevertheless, when we are confronted with our own terminal condition, even if there is some time until death will occur, there tends to be a sense of fear, loss, and anxiety. Further, many people with HIV/AIDS may experience a loss of self-efficacy and feel as if they are "second-rate" citizens, due to stigmas that abound regarding HIV/AIDS and their own negative affect regarding their plight. For some, there may be an emotional hollowing and sense of numbness to the entire ordeal.

Despite the fact that this sense of fear can lead to a depressive state, it should be noted that depression should be given separate and specific treatment that is in addition to any intervention for HIV/AIDS. This is because depression has to do with brain functioning and is not an inevitable clinical outcome for persons having HIV/AIDS. Many people contend with this virus and do not contract depression and this then means that, when persons do have depressive states, specific and targeted intervention should be provided. It is disturbing that in many cases depression is never specifically dealt with. It is important that persons with HIV/AIDS be screened for depression and that they have someone (a mental health professional or group worker) to talk with. The National Institutes of Health (2002) note that treatment for depression, when in conjunction with HIV or AIDS, should be managed by a mental health professional, who is in close professional communication with the medical physician who provides the HIV/AIDS treatment. This is true as a means of optimizing the treatment program and is also true if any type of antidepressant is recommended. Due to the potential for harmful drug–interaction effects, all parties should be aware of the various drugs taken by the client.

Some persons with HIV may choose to isolate themselves from others, becoming reclusive and knifing off relationships with the outside world. This is also a reaction that is likely to further the potential onset of depression. In addition, many persons going through HIV/AIDS may also know others with a similar affliction. In such cases, they may even know persons who have in fact died from the virus. In addition to their need for coping with their own mortality, they may also be coping with the potential loss of others. Because of these various issues that tend to co-occur with the onset of HIV/AIDS, it is strongly recommended that correctional counselors understand the grieving process and understand affect-based reactions to loss. Throughout this text, we have referred to the symptoms and treatment of depression and it is not necessary to again hash out the various aspects of depression. However, clinicians should be prepared to handle depression and grieving among their offender clients who present with HIV/AIDS while in correctional treatment.

EXISTENTIAL COUNSELING FOR THOSE WITH AIDS: MEANING TO LIFE AND DEATH This type of therapy is not based on specific techniques or a specific theoretical design. Rather, this type of therapy is more of a philosophical-based intervention, where the client is encouraged to explore the condition and purpose of his or her own existence. For persons who are facing their own mortality, this type of therapeutic approach can be quite constructive. With existential counseling, the basic conditions of human existence related to the freedom to make life choices, the freedom and responsibility to shape one's life, and the right to self-determination provide the primary content of the intervention.

Importantly, this type of therapy focuses on the awareness of death and our eventual demise. Corey (1996) provides one of the most clear and comprehensive explanations of existential counseling. His work on counseling theories is well known and it is from this work that we draw much of our own description of existential counseling. Existential counseling does not view death negatively but instead holds the awareness of death as a basic human condition that gives significance to living (Corey, 1996). According the existential view, a key human characteristic is the ability to grasp the reality of the future and the inevitability of death. In other words, it is important that we think about death if we are to also appreciate life (Corey, 1996). Thus, in this respect, death is simply another component to the continuum of existence. Indeed, according to Corey "if we realize that we are mortal, we know that we do not have an eternity to complete our projects and that each present moment is crucial. Our awareness of death is the source of zest for life and creativity" (1996, p. 180).

Thus, existential counseling is not necessarily somber but instead is empowering. This is particularly the case for persons who are undergoing serious and profound changes in life and/or who are experiencing serious loss that may make them question the meaning and purpose to their sense of loss, anguish, or pain. Corey (1996) describes the process of existential counseling as follows:

> During the initial phase, counselors assist clients in identifying and clarifying their assumptions about the world. Clients are invited to define and question the ways in which they perceive and make sense of their existence. They examine their values, beliefs, and assumptions to determine their validity. For many clients this is a difficult task, because they may initially present their problems as resulting almost entirely from external causes. They may focus on what other people "make them feel" or on how others are largely responsible for their actions or inaction. The counselor teaches them how to reflect on their own existence and to examine their role in creating their problems in living.
>
> During the middle phase of existential counseling, clients are encouraged to more fully examine the source and authority of their present value system. This process of self-exploration typically leads to new insights and some restructuring of their values and attitudes. Clients get a better idea of what kind of life they consider worthy to live. They develop a clearer sense of their internal valuing process.
>
> The final phase of existential counseling focuses on helping clients take what they are learning about themselves and put it into action. The aim of therapy is to

> enable clients to find ways of implementing their examined and internalized values in a concrete way. Clients typically discover their strengths and find ways to put them to the service of living a purposeful existence. (p. 185)

The above description of existential counseling demonstrates how this approach places meaning to our experiences in life, both positive and negative. This process puts meaning into one's life experiences and also, in the process, puts meaning into our own demise. Naturally, everything between these two points of existence is then given more significance. The key is to aid the client in developing an awareness and confronting his or her own sense of self once that awareness takes place. For many offenders, such deep introspection may initially seem silly; however, it is likely that they have wondered about their own place in society and in the cosmos. Many will have developed a hollow and jaded view of existence that will probably seem oversimplified to most clinicians. However, it is important that the correctional counselor not be deterred in encouraging the client to engage in personal discovery and exploration.

Throughout this process, clients may be given various readings by the correctional counselor, and this is typically referred to as bibliotherapy. When providing various forms of bibliotherapy, the classic works by Victor Frankl and/or Jean-Paul Sartre may be assigned. These two philosophers are known for their deep-searching probes into the meaning of life and the inherent sense of emptiness that many people have when faced with a trauma-inducing experience. Because the correctional counselor will be working with the offender population and because many of the offenders that he or she encounters will not necessarily have strong reading skills, it may be important that other works are utilized in the bibliotherapy process. However, it is not necessary that the work of great and admired scholars be utilized. Existential counseling homework can consist of videos, movies, or even self-made exercises. The key point is to have the client explore the depth of his or her own existence within the milieu of his or her own mortality, the sense of loss that comes with the understanding of a finite existence, and the grief that he or she may experience when losing persons or relationships that are meaningful in one's life.

GRIEF, LOSS, AND KÜBLER-ROSS'S FIVE STAGES The five stages of grief developed by Kübler-Ross are widely known by many therapists around the world. These five stages had their origin in the seminal book titled *On Death and Dying*, published in 1969 by Elisabeth Kübler-Ross. At the time, Kübler-Ross' book was considered revolutionary and served as a catalyst for examining how we view the grieving process and the notion of loss. The work of Kübler-Ross changed the way people handled bereavement from a process that people would not discuss to one where people in grief are given clear and specific attention that is focused on their loss and their ability to cope and adapt to that loss. Kübler-Ross' work was both outspoken and compassionate and it received acclaim from caretakers, the dying and the bereaved, and the medical community.

For this text, we present these stages as a means of dealing with death or the anticipated death of someone close to the client. Thus, this would likely be relevant for inmates on a cellblock who have lost a friend by any means, including death from HIV/AIDS. This would also be an effective means of working with families who have lost a loved one, providing a framework for the counselor to employ when doing so. However, it should be mentioned that these stages should not be necessarily restricted to grief over death. These stages of grief can be employed over any loss, such as divorce or becoming disabled. They can also be utilized with incidents that are trauma inducing.

We introduce these stages in this chapter, toward the end of the text, since their primary use has been with death and dying. Since AIDS, aging, death, and dying are the primary themes of this chapter, we felt that this content was most appropriate in this section of the text. However, these stages can be applied to any number of issues where a sense of loss or trauma has been encountered by the client. Students are encouraged to consider the application of these stages to other issues that may confront offender clients. In either event, we contend that death and bereavement are often trauma inducing, and the "grief cycle," as it is sometimes called, should be seen as a type of change model for helping clients understand and cope with personal reactions to trauma from death and dying.

Chapman (2008) explains that the five stages should not be observed as working in a lock-step fashion. Instead, there is some degree of fluidity with this model, depending on the specific circumstances of the client. We think that this is an important observation because many people tend to have a myopic understanding of stage models; we wish to avoid that. The counseling field utilizes a number stage-sequenced theories and interventions, but this is typically simply intended to be a means of presentation and organization of the information rather than an "etched–in-stone" process. It is due to this organization and the manner by which Kübler-Ross identifies the common human reactions to death and bereavement that make her theory ideal.

Further, we would like to point out that Kübler-Ross's model is one that is a *change* model, which implies that a continuation (of life) occurs and that some sort of transformation is made. We think that this is a particularly healthy means of addressing death and dying and we also believe that this approach comports well with existential counseling approaches that were presented earlier. In essence, we contend that correctional counselors should utilize both an existential approach as a background overlay while incorporating and integrating the five-stage grief cycle designed by Kübler-Ross. With this in mind, the five stages are presented below:

Denial: This is a conscious or unconscious refusal to accept facts, information, reality, and so on relating to the situation concerned. This is essentially a defense mechanism that is common and perfectly natural at the beginning points of the coping process. Eventually, almost everyone is forced to traverse this stage due to the simple fact that, try as one might, death is in fact permanent. Part of the denial process can include, in extreme cases, hallucinations or fabricated circumstances with the person who is lost, but these are extreme cases.

Anger: This stage can manifest in many different ways. Clients dealing with emotional turmoil can be angry with themselves, and/or with others, especially those close to them (Chapman, 2008). When processing these emotional reactions, correctional counselors should remain detached and nonjudgmental, reflecting affect and using person-centered techniques as much as possible.

Bargaining: In most cases, the bargaining stage can involve attempting to bargain with whatever higher power the client may believe in and/or luck or fate if the person is not given to religion. This approach is simply a process of negotiation with reality and does not usually work to assuage the person's sense of loss for very long.

Depression: At this point, the person is actually starting the genuine grieving process. Chapman (2008) notes that this is similar to a dress rehearsal or a practice run for the "aftermath" of what has been realized. This stage represents a form of acceptance, both of the loss that has been suffered and the emotions that are associated with that loss. The experience of sadness, sorrow, regret, and uncertainty is natural and clients should be allowed to conduct whatever emotional inventory that they feel is appropriate within the session. The worst thing that someone can do during this stage is use simple phrases such as "I know how you feel" and/or "it will get better." Instead, it is best to simply validate and reflect the emotional reactions of the client. It should be added that this form of depression is even specifically identified in the *DSM-IV-TR* and is considered both temporary and common among persons in similar circumstances.

Acceptance: At this point, the client is coming to terms with his or her loss, and, in a broad sense, he or she is beginning to achieve some degree of emotional detachment and objectivity. Chapman (2008) notes that people who are dying tend to enter this stage much earlier than people they leave behind, since others must pass through their own stages of grief.

These stages of grief, as outlined above, are effective in formulating an approach to the death and dying process. Further, when clients are facing their own terminality, such as with HIV/AIDS or perhaps due to chronic illness, these stages can assist in providing a buffer against the anxiety and fear that may develop. Placing that anxiety against an existential backdrop may help to make sense of the experience and provide meaning to that person's journey while an understanding of the five stages by Kübler-Ross can help to normalize the client's reactions, letting them know that they are not alone in their experience and that others experience similar reactions when coping with their own mortality or that of someone whom they love.

SECTION SUMMARY

In this section, students were presented with basic information regarding HIV and its progression to AIDS. The various emotional aspects involved with having HIV were discussed as were various sources of stigma associated with the virus. Misconceptions regarding HIV were also presented to demonstrate how a lack of knowledge or a misunderstanding of this affliction can put people at further risk of contracting the virus.

In addition, a brief introduction to existential counseling was provided. This type of counseling integrates a philosophical approach to counseling and relies less on technique than do other theoretical perspectives in counseling. However, the deep searching that is encouraged among clients and the emphasis on meaning and worth to our existence makes this form of counseling more fulfilling for many people who feel a void in their life, are going through some sort of grief or loss, and/or are experiencing some sort of serious change or transition in their life. Lastly, the five-stage model of grief cycle by Kübler-Ross was presented. This five-stage model is well known among mental health and bereavement experts due to its flexibility and utility with grief, loss, and trauma experiences. This section makes the point to demonstrate that the work of Kübler-Ross comports well with the existential approach to counseling, and the two, when taken together, provide an effective paradigms for persons experiencing any number of traumatizing experiences, especially those that may involve death or some other sort of serious loss

LEARNING CHECK

1. The work of Kübler-Ross contains four stages related to working through grief and loss.

a. True

b. False

2. Bibliotherapy is one type of technique used in existential counseling.

a. True

b. False

3. HIV itself is actually just a viral infection resulting in reduction in the operation of one's immune system. It is not until some other disease or illness is contracted and, due to the individual's lowered immune system, AIDS develops.
   a. True
   b. False
4. It is quite understandable that a person with HIV/AIDS might become withdrawn and depressed. However, depression is not inevitable and should be given specific and separate treatment alongside any HIV/AIDS intervention.
   a. True
   b. False
5. **Denial** is a conscious or unconscious refusal to accept facts, information, reality, and so on, relating to the situation concerned.
   a. True
   b. False

PART TWO: ELDERLY OFFENDERS

Categories of Elderly Offenders

When discussing elderly inmates, it becomes apparent that a "one-size-fits-all" approach will not adequately address the entire population. Indeed, the elderly offender population has different levels and types of criminal history that are important when making assessments related to public safety risks. From the offending patterns of elderly offenders, three basic typologies emerge: the **elderly first-time offender**, the **habitual elderly offender**, and the **offender turned elderly in prison.**

The rise in numbers of **habitual elderly offenders** and **offenders turned elderly in prison** has to do largely with the advent of "three strikes" felony sentencing in many states (Anno, Graham, Lawrence, & Shansky, 2004). These sentences require that third-time felony offenders serve mandatory sentences of at least 25 years up to life. It should be noted that the felony does not necessarily mean that the offender is violent in nature. Also adding to these statistics are the punitive sentencing measures associated with the War on Drugs of the 1980s and the 1990s where drug-using offenders were locked up at an all-time high, regardless of whether the crime involved violence or any form of drug trafficking (Anno et al., 2004). Lastly, 14 states and the federal Bureau of Prisons have eliminated parole, and state laws have increasingly required "truth in sentencing" so that inmates are sure to serve at least 85% of their prison term (Anno et al., 2004).

Thus, the habitual elderly offenders and the offenders turned elderly in prison are the result of a confluence of social factors and criminal justice policies. These offenders, for various reasons, have been given enhanced penalties that preclude their release in the community. This greatly distinguishes them from the elderly first-time offender who does not share a similar criminogenic background. Though they may look the same while in inmate clothes in the prison facility, they are usually quite different from one another and the public would be well served to keep this squarely in mind. States that have abolished parole and other community outlets may be well served to establish specialized court interventions for this type of offender. It is at this point that we turn our attention to the three typologies of elderly offenders, with each being briefly discussed in the paragraphs that follow.

ELDERLY FIRST-TIME OFFENDERS (EFTO) It is estimated that approximately 50% of elderly inmates are first-time offenders, incarcerated when they were 60 or older. New elderly offenders frequently commit crimes of passion. Conflicts in primary relationships appear to increase as social interactions diminish with age. Older first-time offenders often commit their offenses in a spontaneous manner that shows little planning but is instead an emotional reaction to perceived slights or disloyalties. These offenders do not typically view themselves as criminals, per se, but instead see their situation as unique and isolated from their primary identity. **Elderly first-time offenders** are those who commit their offense later in life. For those who commit violent crimes, these are usually crimes of passion rather than being premeditated crimes.

It should be noted that many of these offenses may unfortunately be the simple product of biological factors associated with the aging process. The higher rates of dementia among the elderly population is thought to have been a contributory causal explanation for acts that were otherwise nonexistent for the individual throughout the earlier life span. Rather, some forms of dementia are associated with a loss of inhibitory mechanisms (perhaps in the reticular activating system of the brain) in the brain. These losses of inhibitory ability mean that brain functions that regulated behavior cease to function correctly. The resulting behavior is often manifested in odd and illegal forms of sexual behavior, inflexibility, paranoia, and even aggression.

It should be noted that first-time offenders are more likely to be sentenced for violent offenses. These offenses will usually be directed at a family member due to proximity, if nothing else. Some experience crises of one sort or another due to disparity regarding the aging process. This is also thought to instill a sense of abandonment and resentfulness that may lead to aberrant forms of coping. Also, sexual offenses involving children are common among the first-time offending elderly. It should be noted that in the Tennessee prison system, nearly a third of their older inmates were incarcerated for sex crimes. For persons over the age of 65, aggravated assault is the violent offense most often committed, followed by murder (Aday, 1994).

The new elderly inmate probably was already maladjusted in society and was probably not good at changing with environmental demands. Other characteristics include a volatile personality and the propensity for suicide. These individuals were likely to have had mental health problems earlier in their life, and they are probably the type to withdraw when possible (Aday, 1994). These offenders are also the most likely to be victimized in prison as their irascible behavior and demeanor is likely to draw the attention of younger inmates rather than providing any form of deterrence from victimization within the institutional setting (Aday, 1994). These offenders are most likely to have strong community ties and are therefore usually the most amenable for community supervision because of this.

HABITUAL ELDERLY OFFENDERS (HEO) **Habitual elderly offenders** have a long history of crime and also have a prior record of imprisonment throughout their lifetime. These offenders are usually able to adjust well to prison life because they have been in and out of the environment throughout a substantial part of their life. Thus, they are well suited and adjusted to prison life. They are also a good source of support for first-time offenders and, if administrators are wise enough to implement this, are able to act as mentors for these first-time offenders. These offenders typically have substance abuse problems and other chronic problems that make coping with life on the outside difficult. Some of these inmates are not considered violent but instead serve several shorter sentences for lesser types of property crimes. This is the group that is most likely to end up as geriatric inmates who die in prison.

OFFENDER TURNED ELDERLY IN PRISON (OTEP) **Offenders turned elderly in prison** who have grown old in prison have long histories in the system and are the least likely to be discipline problems. Long-term offenders are very difficult to place upon release because they have few ties in the community and limited vocational background from which to earn a living. These offenders are often afraid to leave the prison and go back to the outside world because they have become so institutionalized within the predictable schedule of the prison. This also means that suicide may be considered among these individuals particularly prior to release, or even within a short time after release. This phenomenon is no difference from that noted in the classic movie *Shawshank Redemption* that portrays a released inmate who cannot cope with life on the outside, choosing instead to end his life prematurely by a self-hanging suicide.

Common Mental Health Issues

There are a number of common mental health issues that are observed among the elderly offender population. One study found that roughly 15 to 25% of the elderly suffer from mental illness (Morton, 1992). This has been found to be true in research both in the United States and in other countries like Canada and the United Kingdom. In fact, some of the international research contends that mental illness may be as high as 50% for those over 60 and in custody of the criminal justice system (BBC, 1999). This then demonstrates that dealing with the elderly offender is a complicated and multifaceted issue that will require correctional systems (both institutional and community-based) to provide some form of treatment since these offenders are not necessarily safe to be left on their own or place within society.

Among the forms of mental disorder or mental illness, depression has been found to be the most common mental disorder reported. Second most reported was dementia, which is associated with confusion, memory loss, and disorientation. The most serious form of dementia is Alzheimer's Disease. This disease is a serious concern for correctional systems because of the debilitating nature of the disease and the costs associated with treating it. Dementia of the Alzheimer's Type consists of memory impairment whereby the afflicted person has great difficulty learning new information and they are unable to recall information that had been learned in the past (American Psychiatric Association, 2000). In addition, persons with Alzheimer's will exhibit either aphasia (a disturbance in language construction and use), apraxia (impaired motor functioning), Anosia (failure to recognize persons or objects), or disturbances in planning or organizing as well as impaired abstract reasoning (American Psychiatric Association, 2000). While there are other details associated with Alzheimer's, the basic symptoms are as just outlined. It should be easy to see how such persons can prove problematic for correctional institutions that must safely house these offenders.

The third most problematic disorder is associated with substance abuse, particularly relating to alcohol abuse. Since many of these offenders have a history of substance abuse, correctional systems will need to be prepared to address mental health problems in this area with the elderly offender. Extensive use of substances will have depleted the offender's overall health, physically and mentally, and this effect aggravates trauma and insult associated with the vagaries of the criminal lifestyle and the noxious prison lifestyle.

As with offenders who confront their own mortality due to HIV/AIDS or some other illness, the elderly must also confront their own mortality as the years pass on, whether behind bars or while on community supervision. For these offenders, their fate is often largely sealed and out of their hands since many will have lost contact with their families, they will have a more difficult time obtaining regular full-time employment, and since their health will generally be in a state of decline. With these issues in mind, the correctional counselor should emphasize existential meaning to the offender's experience. In addition, among those offenders who do have contact with their family (whether in prison or on community supervision) it may be helpful to implement family counseling sessions. This may not always be feasible, but when and if it is, the sense of connection with loved ones can improve the prognosis considerably.

Ironically, for elderly offenders who are incarcerated, problems with anxiety may occur because they have adapted too well to their life in prison. Many older offenders who serve prolonged sentences behind bars begin to develop a form of "institutional dependency." This **institutional dependency** is defined as the process whereby the elderly inmate exchanges his or her prior life identity with a prison-based identity with reference groups changing from outside friends and family to those persons within the institution. More institutional dependency has been observed among unmarried older offenders, those incarcerated earlier in their lives, and chronic recidivists. This is not surprising since these groups spend the most total time in prison and therefore have the best opportunity to normalize the prison environment (Aday, 1994). Some researchers have examined elderly offenders and their adjustment to prison and have found some degree of satisfaction among older offenders who have become institutionally dependent. These offenders appear to develop strategies of coping that allow them to deal with the pains of imprisonment with little distress (Wooden & Parker, 1982). Correctional counselors should be aware of this phenomenon and should also note that the elderly offender is likely to be most anxious prior to his or her release. This is also when they tend to be at a high risk for suicide, particularly if they do not have extensive family connections outside of the institution.

It has been speculated that victimization and the fear of victimization has become a serious problem for elderly offenders. These offenders are more susceptible to being coerced into compliance than are more robust and younger offenders. While these offenders may cope with the pains of the imprisonment process itself, they may be unable to defend themselves effectively from the brutality of other inmates. This is one other aspect of anxiety that correctional counselors may find themselves addressing among elderly offenders who are incarcerated. In such cases, correctional counselors may find themselves noting these concerns to security administration on behalf of the elderly inmates. This can be a very challenging problem and correctional counselors will need to tread lightly with such issues so that conflicts of interest do not emerge as the therapist plays the role of treatment provider and liaison between inmates and staff regarding security.

The Susceptibility of Geriatric Offenders to HIV/AIDS

Changes that affect the immune system of the elderly make these offenders more susceptible to illness and require them to be immunized or reimmunized against certain illnesses (Morton, 1992). This means that older inmates are very vulnerable to tuberculosis and other contagious diseases and that they may need additional immunization. Communicable diseases are a serious problem in many correctional agencies. Further still, many agencies may not utilize widespread immunization due to cost factors. However, those agencies that have tight budgets should still consider using a form of "selective immunization" where the most at-risk offenders are identified and immunized. Failure to do this will simply ensure that the prison medical bill for inmates with communicable diseases continue to rise beyond the already exorbitant costs that now exist. And the elderly inmate will be more at risk of getting and spreading any viruses passed throughout the institution, making the failure to immunize ever more costly to the agency on a long-term basis. Thus, immunization of the elderly could save the agency substantial resources in the future.

Lastly, elderly offenders are at increased risk of HIV/AIDS due to their lengthy involvement in a high-risk lifestyle. The odds are more likely that such offenders have, at one time or another, engaged in risky sexual behavior and/or in drug usage that placed them at risk of contracting the virus. This is particularly true among elderly female offenders who are likely to have participated in some spectrum of the sex industry and, if nothing else, will often have been involved with male offenders who have led high-risk lives. Added to this, the fact that substance abuse issues are particularly pronounced for the female offender (remember Chapter 11) and the fact that elderly offenders will have a longer history of usage, it becomes clear that these offenders should be considered more susceptible to HIV/AIDS. None of this is to say that elderly male offenders are not also at an increased risk. These men have also been likely to engage in high-risk sexual activity, perhaps in many cases with the same women who are at an increased risk. Further, many of the long-term elderly males in treatment are more likely to have used needles if they have a history of hard-core drug use.

Since these offenders are not in good health and since they are likely to have physically deteriorated due to the vagaries of a rough-and-tumble lifestyle coupled with prison life, it is likely that they will also be more susceptible to some other disease or medical problem that the immune system would normally be able to stave off. Given that the elderly do not have the same hardy constitution of many younger inmates and given that many inmates will transmit infectious diseases within the facility, elderly are even more at risk of ultimately contracting AIDS. The fact that comobordity is also common among the elderly (consider just the effects of an alcoholic with Alzheimer's disease) helps to further demonstrate why this group of offenders is truly in danger of presenting with serious medical problems that may exacerbate the likelihood of contracting AIDS (Exhibit 13.1).

EXHIBIT 13.1

Treatment Recommendations for Elderly Offenders Considering Suicide

Given the comorbid nature of depression and suicide among the elderly, it is clear that the occurrence of each is often due to a multiplicity of issues that confront these offenders. This makes it difficult to know what should be done in response to this phenomenon. When considering various risk factors as well as the protective factors, elderly persons at risk of depression and/or suicide benefit from two key themes. First, there is an apparent need to have a sense of purpose. This seems to be lacking among many of the elderly that experience suicidal ideation. With this in mind, it is suggested that some sort of spiritual or religious intervention be made part and parcel to any response related to this phenomenon. Naturally, it would be up to the elderly person to determine the specific parameters involved with such an intervention, but such persons should be encouraged to fulfill any spiritual or religious interests that they might have.

In further elaborating on the need for purpose, the use of existentialist approaches to individual or group therapy might prove ideal. Such approaches to counseling would work well with the elderly person that is already spiritual and/or religious in orientation. This approach, being more philosophical in nature, is also highly suitable for those persons that are not spiritual or religious. In fact, persons that are agnostic or atheist can and do benefit from such approaches. Some notable existential philosophers (such as Sartre) were clearly atheist and did not hold much regard for those that clung to beliefs related to a higher power. Thus, regardless of one's sense of spirituality and regardless of a person's specific religion (i.e., Muslim, Christian, Hindu, Jewish, and so forth), existential approaches dovetail well with the given milieu. This is important because, as noted earlier, many elderly simply do not present to therapy. There is an apparent aversion to psychotherapeutic orientations, perhaps due to negative generational cohort perceptions of therapy or perhaps due to spurious occurrences. Either way, the elderly do not tend to prefer therapy but would be much more likely to find an approach that focuses on their point and purpose of existence to be rewarding and insightful. Since these issues are among those contemplated by many elderly persons, such an approach is ideal in developing a rapport and imparting therapeutic coping mechanisms (Rogers et al., 2007).

With respect to therapy, it is also recommended that family therapy be considered as a potential intervention whenever possible. Family belonging and connection is a strong protective factor and it is

(continued)

important to get the family involved in maintaining the elderly person's healthy state, whenever such involvement is possible (McGoldrick, Giordano, Pearce, & Giordano, 1996). Further, family therapy is also an excellent mechanism to help the caregivers who are responsible for the elderly person. Such forms of therapy provide a neutral ground where family interactions can be addressed and where family members can gain valuable guidance and support. Family therapists are typically more directive than are other types of therapists and the mechanisms that they use are often well suited to ensure that family members are given clear direction and support when coping with the caretaking role. Thus, this type of therapy can be very important for both the elderly person and the other family members. Further still, this type of intervention can further connect the elderly person to the family, both immediate and extended family members. Indeed, family therapy does not have to be restricted to those that are biologically related but can include persons that simply have a close relationship with the elderly person (McGoldrick et al., 1996). The point is that such therapy strengthens the bonds that the elderly person may have with others that are significant in their life. This type of therapy is also more likely to appeal to the elderly than is the typical one-on-one psychotherapy.

In addition, therapists may find it useful to learn alternative means of treating pain management, such as the use of hypnosis techniques or other modalities of intervention. The use of hypnosis, though still considered controversial in some circles, has actually been found effective in treating depression, gastrointestinal disorders, anxiety, addiction, and sleep disorders (Gafner, 2004). In many cases, the relaxation techniques associated with hypnotic induction can be effective in treating corollary issues associated with the older person's depressive affective state. For instance, the inability to obtain routine and adequate states of sleep and/or physiological symptoms that are stress/anxiety-related can be easily addressed by such techniques (Gafner, 2004). With sleep and anxiety issues being ameliorated for the client, it is likely that affective states will improve simply because the client is more likely to feel alert from better sleeping patterns and peaceful due to lowered states of anxiety. The lowering of anxiety is important because, as is commonly known by most all therapists, anxiety and depression are often intertwined. The connection between depression and anxiety is so profound that in many cases, anti-anxiety medications have positive effects for persons that are depressed and some antidepressants likewise have positive therapeutic benefits for clients suffering from anxiety and tension (American Psychiatric Association, 2000).

Source: Hanser, R. D., Hanser, P. A., Mire, S. M., & Henderson, H. (2008). The comorbidity of depressed affective states, medical factors, and mental health considerations in elderly suicide. *Contemporary Issues in Criminology and the Social Sciences, 2*(2), 109–130.

SECTION SUMMARY

The elderly offender in state correctional system and in community-based intervention programs is becoming more common as the graying of America occurs. While elderly offenders are likely to share many of the same health concerns, they are not all the same in regard to their level of criminality. Indeed, some such as the habitual elderly offender have persisted in a life of crime that has never ceased, others such as the offender turned elderly in prison may have committed a serious crime early in their life and have spent a lengthy period being incarcerated, and yet others may have lived crime free only to commit a crime in their later years that is serious enough to warrant their incarceration.

Each of these categories of offenders must be given different types of mental health treatment approaches because their perspectives are likely to be quite different from one another. On the other hand, these offenders are likely to have some common mental health issues, such as depression, anxiety, and Alzheimer's disease. Depending on their lifestyle outside of prison, they may also have serious substance abuse problems that will have aggravated their current mental health and the disorders that they possess.

Lastly, this section presented the fact that the elderly are more susceptible to illness, including AIDS. The reasons for this were provided, given their advanced age, physical deterioration behind bars, and any risky lifestyle behaviors that they may have pursued in the past. In addition, the elderly are more susceptible to suicidal ideation. As they become dependent on the institution, pondering over suicide may be observed if and when they face release from incarceration. Treatment recommendations for elderly offenders considering suicide were provided and this also helps to provide a transition to the section that follows where suicide prevention and treatment will be specific focus of discussion.

LEARNING CHECK

1. With respect to therapy with elderly offenders considering suicide, it is recommended that family therapy be considered as a potential intervention whenever possible. Family belonging and connection is a strong protective factor against suicide and can augment an existential approach that might be used.
   a. True
   b. False
2. Offenders turned elderly in prison who have grown old in prison have long histories in the system and are the least likely to be discipline problems.
   a. True
   b. False
3. Given the comorbid nature of depression and suicide among the elderly, it is clear that the occurrence of each is often due to a multiplicity of issues that confront these offenders.
   a. True
   b. False
4. Institutional dependency is defined as the process whereby the elderly inmate exchanges his or her prior life identity with a prison-based identity with reference groups changing from outside friends and family to those persons within the institution.
   a. True
   b. False
5. The connection between depression and anxiety is so profound that in many cases anti-anxiety medications have positive effects for persons who are depressed and some antidepressants likewise have positive therapeutic benefits for clients suffering from anxiety and tension.
   a. True
   b. False

PART THREE: SUICIDE

Prevention Management

Suicide ideation is a genuine threat among any high-risk population, and this is especially true among the offender population. When considering the issue of suicide within the offender population, there are points to consider both with the juvenile offender and the adult offender. Further, the issues related to suicide within the prison, jail, or detention center environment may be quite different from that experienced by offenders on community supervision. In addition, suicide among male and female offenders may be due to differing concerns and, if not incarcerated, may be through differing means of effecting the suicide or suicide attempt. For the ease of reading and also to stay within the intended scope and focus of this text, we will primarily focus on suicide within the correctional facility because this is where the greatest risk tends to occur. This is also where the greatest likelihood of liability will ensue for correctional counselors and for general criminal justice personnel. When appropriate, we will seek to distinguish between suicide among juveniles and adults and will integrate issues related to gender when they are deemed relevant.

When considering suicide, the first point of intervention actually should start with an effective form of prevention management. With such considerations, the first action taken by correctional officials should be to conduct a thorough and valid screening process at intake. In many cases, the detention facility, jail, or prison staff—referred to from henceforward as *custodial staff*—will conduct this screening since they will be the persons on hand during the booking and/or transfer of the inmate to the facility. Correctional counselors should ensure that they remain updated on suicide screens and that they are notified when an offender does warrant further intervention. However, even when custodial staff do not indicate such a need, correctional counselors should examine the intake screening paperwork of any clients on their caseload. In some cases, mental health practitioners may detect something that custodial staff will not detect.

The intake screening should take place immediately upon confinement and before any housing assignment is made. This process can be worked into other intake processes such as during medical screening, and it is advisable that facilities use a separate form for the suicide screen. Some sources may indicate that the screening questions can be included with other forms, but we recommend against this. The reason for this is simple: The intake process is hurried and full of distraction at many facilities. The use of a separate form sends a signal to the offender and the custodial personnel that the information about to be delivered is for a specific purpose. This prevents the information from being overlooked and from being underutilized. According to the National Institute of Corrections, NIC, (2001), all **screening** systems should, at a minimum, include the following:

1. Past suicidal ideation and/or attempts
2. Any current ideation, threats, or plans
3. Specificity of plans
4. Ability to carry out plans of suicide
5. Prior mental health treatment
6. Any recent and significant losses (such as a loved one, a divorce, or the loss of a job)
7. History of suicide within the family or close friends
8. Prior suicide risk level during other periods of confinement.

Lastly, this process must include procedures for referral to mental health and/or medical personnel. In addition, it should be noted that all of these factors are equally relevant to juvenile, female, and male offenders in the custodial setting and for those on community supervision.

The next component of an effective prevention program would revolve around **staff training.** The need for effective training should occur with custodial staff and with mental health staff. Ivanoff and Hayes (2001) note that very few suicides are actually prevented by mental health, medical, or other professional staff because suicides are usually attempted in inmate housing units and often during late evening hours or over the weekend when mental health staff are not readily on hand. The intake assessment and need for staff training are the baseline components for prevention.

Beyond this, there are 10 other specific components that the NIC (2001) recommends. Because this organization is the premiere organization in the United States on correctional standards and training, we also wish to incorporate their guidelines within this chapter when discussing the ingredients for an effective prevention program. However, it should be noted that, much of these issues have to do with the day-to-day operations of the facility itself. Though correctional counselors will not be directly involved in many of these details, they should still make a point to maintain an awareness of how the facility and its staff address suicide and they should provide follow-up with at-risk inmates to augment the efforts of security staff. Note that the list of components that will follow come directly from the 2001 training manual available from the NIC and this information is public domain, meaning that it has been directly taken from that manual verbatim since it is offered freely by that organization. With this in mind, the remaining components of an effective prevention program, according to the NIC, are as follows:

Assessment: This should be conducted by a qualified mental health professional, who designates the inmate's level of risk. Note, it is likely that you, the correctional counselor, may be the one who fulfills this function. In addition, please note that we will provide a discussion regarding the level of risk for suicide later in this section.

Monitoring: The plan should specify the facility's procedures for monitoring an inmate who has been identified as potentially suicidal. Regular, documented supervision should be maintained.

Housing: A suicidal inmate should not be housed or left alone. An appropriate level of observation must be maintained. If a sufficiently large staff is not available that constant supervision can be provided when needed, the inmate should not be isolated. Rather, s/he should be housed with another resident or in a dormitory and checked every 10–15 minutes. An inmate assess as being a high suicide risk always should be observed on a continuing, uninterrupted basis or transferred to an appropriate health care facility. The cell or room should be as nearly suicide proof as possible (i.e., without protrusions of any kind that would enable the inmate to hang him/herself).

Referral: The plan should specify the procedures for referring potentially suicidal inmates and attempted suicides to mental health care providers or facilities.

Communication: Procedures should exist for communication between health care (to include mental health) and correctional personnel regarding the status of the inmate.

Intervention: The plan should address how to handle a suicide in progress, including appropriate first-aid measures.

Notification: Procedures should be in place for notifying jail administrators, outside authorities, and family member of potential, attempted, or completed suicides.

Reporting: Procedures for documenting the identification and monitoring of potential or attempted suicides should be detailed, as should procedures for reporting a completed suicide.

Review: The plan should specify the procedures for medical, mental health, and administrative review if a suicide or a serious suicide attempt does occur.

Critical incident debriefing: Responding to and/or observing a suicide in progress can be extremely stressful for staff and inmates. The plan should specify the procedures for offering critical incident debriefing to all affected personnel and inmates.

Each of the previously listed features should be included in any type of suicide prevention program for a correctional agency. Given that part of the last few of these features eventually shifts to an intervention and a postintervention phase, it is important to note during the crisis response process aspects of treatment that are actually taking place to some extent. In fact, Ivanoff and Hayes (2001) note that when taken from a mental health perspective (as opposed to a custodial perspective), treatment begins at the point that crisis intervention or immediate response has occurred. Therefore, to some extent the division between prevention and intervention can become a bit blurred. Maintaining a distinction between these two forms of response is not really critical, and we contend it is even productive to allow both forms of response to be structured in such a manner that one enhances the other. For instance, after the intervention component there is a review process that occurs where staff examine the factors that lead to the suicide and/or the suicide attempt. This can be productive in helping to eliminate future potential suicides and this can also aid in staff training. This is also a productive exercise for the correctional counselor who can learn quite a bit about the at-risk offender population as well as the world of the correctional officer who deals with the offender population on a more routine basis.

When correctional counselors and custodial staff are both involved in the review process, this also creates a working rapport between both types of employees. Further, since the correctional counselor is a mental health practitioner, it is likely that they may find themselves aiding in the process of providing critical incident debriefing. While this may depend on the specific facility and/or agency, in cases where mental health professionals are not easily available, correctional counselors may "wear this additional hat," so to speak. This is actually good experience for the correctional counselor because it provides him or her with a perspective that is offered from the custodial staff in relation to potential trauma and responding to a suicidal attempt or actual death.

One of the authors of this textbook has provided such services to various correctional workers regarding traumatic incidents. This has even included sessions where custodial staff were debriefed after responding to a suicide death of an inmate in the facility. The same author has also responded to inmate suicide attempts on numerous occasions in a maximum security facility in a southwestern state and has also addressed suicide issues among teens and the addicted population at a community mental health center. The multiple contexts in responding to suicidal issue have provided a rich fabric of experience and it is for this reason that we believe that correctional counselors are well served by gaining familiarity with their own areas of intervention as well as those among custodial staff.

In many facilities, there is an apparent schism between custodial staff and correctional treatment staff. In many cases, each views the other as having opposing goals and functions. However, this should not at all be the case, and agencies should work to mitigate the friction and/or misunderstanding that can occur between these two groups of staff. Severson (2005) provides a very good discussion on the need for partnership between security and mental health professionals. Severson (2005) notes the following:

> To succeed in this endeavor requires us to do away with some of the myths of correctional treatment. Where or why these myths developed does not matter; what matters is that we recognize them as working against the institution's efforts to prevent suicides and emotionally disruptive behavior. The first two myths that must be discarded are those that suggest there must be total confidentiality of mental health services in jails and the notion that there are clear-cut boundary lines dividing the responsibilities of the security officer and mental health clinician. (p. 4)

Severson (2005) clearly supports collaboration between both groups of professionals and demonstrates that suicide prevention is an effort that includes everyone. Further, as he notes, confidentiality should not prevent the two groups from working together. Indeed, when a client is likely to harm himself or herself or another, most states allow clinicians to break confidentiality as a means of preventing future harm. Failing to do so in a custodial setting could be construed as negligence. Thus, therapists need to work with custodial staff and vice versa. Going further, Severson (2005) points toward other myths that should also be challenged:

1. The mental health clinician (perhaps by osmosis?) has some inherent and proprietary knowledge of suicide prevention;
2. The detention officer is the only person who may regard suicide as an inevitable occurrence;
3. The detention officer has too many other responsibilities to worry about and, therefore, should not be burdened with feedback about an inmate's mental state;
4. The mental health clinician is not concerned about the security of the facility; and finally
5. One professional is more capable, more intuitive, and more skilled than the other at preventing suicides and de-escalating volatile emotionally based reactions.

Clearly, there is no good rationale for maintaining territoriality when the saving of lives is at stake. For correctional counselors, input from custodial staff can help to augment the information that they gain during their sessions with the client. For the custodial staff, having the clinician's appraisals available may provide advanced warning so that an incident may be avoided. For custodial staff who must contend with the myriad details of day-to-day correctional work, the prevention of these types of crisis will usually be welcomed.

Assessing Risk Factors that Contribute to Suicide

Correctional counselors must be conversant on suicide risk and must also be trained on the use of assessment instruments and/or processes with suicide. This function will be a bit unusual when compared to the other work that many counselors conduct. In this case, the counselor will be expected to be conversant on the scale, any scoring that is involved, and any psychometric properties that may be included. Indeed, some scales that are too sophisticated may go beyond the expertise of the correctional counselor, depending on the clinician's training and experience. It is our belief that facilities, both juvenile and adult, should ensure that a formalized suicide risk assessment protocol is used and that it should be used by a qualified mental health professional (i.e., the correctional counselor). Further, the assessment should be performed within 24 hours of the time when suicide precautions are first considered.

This assessment by the correctional counselor should include (at a minimum) a description of the antecedent events and precipitating factors, any suicidal indicators that the correctional counselor discovers or knows about, a mental status examination, the previous psychiatric and suicide risk history, the level of lethality, the current medications that the offender is taking and any *DSM-IV-TR* diagnosis that has been given, and a treatment recommendation from the correctional counselor. In all cases, we believe that this should be double documented on both the suicide assessment form and in the health care record.

Further, the correctional counselor should talk with the client for a time period that is long enough to draw some conclusions about the client's sense of despondence and/or his or her source of angst. Specific questions regarding the offender's intent to commit suicide should be asked and the correctional counselor should not only listen to the client's comments but should note the nonverbal behaviors as well. The nonverbal behaviors should be noted in any paperwork that is kept to demonstrate that attention was provided in this area and to also show that the counselor did probe further than a simple check mark on the interview paperwork. In fact, nonverbal behaviors should be documented even if they indicate that the client is sincere and even if it turns out that the client is a very low risk for suicide. This level of observation can be very useful if the agency and/or the counselor later end up in court due to lawsuits alleging misconduct or negligence on the part of the facility.

Lastly, we recommend that the correctional counselor utilize some sort of standardized screening instrument, when and where possible. These instruments are beta tested and refined over time and will have a high degree of validity and reliability. Because of this, they are likely to be effective tools but they also will hold up in court much better than a "homemade" instrument. This is true unless the correctional counselor is in a state correctional facility, in which case the instrument is likely to be mandated and the counselor is best served staying within the compliance of the governmental regulations. But in the case of private facilities, small jails and local detention centers, and/or other such programs, the use of standardized instruments available on the market are recommended. They are not very expensive, and when used as an adjunct to good note-taking and effective counseling skills, they can provide an excellent means of demonstrating that quality care and attention were provided (Exhibit 13.2).

General Risk Factors and Emotional Causes

There are some common risk factors for suicide that have already been mentioned in earlier sections of this chapter. The primary risk factor is the existence of previous suicidal attempts in the offender's history. In addition, threats of suicide should not be taken lightly because, as it turns out, they are quite well correlated with later suicides that are completed (McDowell & Stewart, 2008). Though security personnel and even therapists may suspect some degree of manipulation in regard to these threats, the threats should still be taken seriously. In addition, personnel should pay attention to offenders who routinely talk about morbid topics. This is particularly true if this is not in line with their typical demeanor or character.

Quite naturally, the correctional counselor and security staff should take note if the offender makes preparations for death. Obviously, this would be very suspicious if the offender were a juvenile making such preparations, but suspicion is warranted even if the offender is elderly. Though this may seem logical when at an advanced age, it is still a warning sign, especially if heirlooms and such are being given away. In addition to giving items away and making arrangements for death, suicidal individuals will often socially withdraw. They typically have no reason for dialogue and may instead prefer to simply brood as they contemplate the various reasons that they have decided upon suicide. Lastly, if an offender leaves a note of any sort that suggests suicide, the correctional counselor should take this as a very serious indicator of suicide.

Emotional risk factors would include depression and anxiety. This has been referred to repetitively and these two disorders of affect and emotion are common co-occurring symptoms with a number of issues pertaining to the offender population. One key point to consider is that many offenders may suffer from profound feelings of shame or guilt over their crime. This is particularly true when they are first facing incarceration and/or when they are forced to confront their actions. The shame and guilt can also build up over time. In most cases, however, offenders will at least mention this before progressing to suicide. Unfortunately, many people may not listen to the offender's expression of shame and/or guilt, taking it for some sort of "con job" or some sort of manipulation.

EXHIBIT 13.2

Two Model Standardized Assessment Protocols for Correctional Counselors

Because of this uncertainty in classifying persons in regard to likely lethality, therapists may wish to consider a standardized scale for suicide detection, such as the *Adult Suicide Ideation Questionnaire* (ASIQ), available from Psychological Assessment Resources. The ASIQ is an objective screening tool that has been specifically designed with liability purposes in mind. In fact, this is a primary reason for its use: To reduce liability by identifying those persons who may need preventative action. This is a short 25-item self-report scale that is normed on 2,000 adults that includes psychiatric and normal adults (as well as college students) in its sample. The ASIQ has been found to be a valid measure of suicidal ideation with good internal consistency and test-retest reliability (Psychological Assessment Resources, 2007). Such objective scales give the clinician a more specific and solid form of protection against negligence suits.

While objective scales such as the ASIQ may aid in predicting suicide and may provide adequate documentation of screening to avoid negligence in the assessment of the offender client, the therapist must also consider assessment for treatment planning purposes. Indeed, failure to do so could be considered negligence in its own right. Thus, subjective methods can be useful when one wishes to engage the offender person in the suicide prevention process. One good example is the inclusive team-building method known as the *Collaborative Assessment and Management of Suicidality* (CAMS). The primary focus of this assessment process is that the client's own subjective suicidality is identified as the central clinical problem, regardless of any objective assessment or diagnosis that may be given (Jobes & Drozd, 2004; Toth, Schwartz, & Kurka, 2007). As Toth et al. (2007) explain, "by using the Suicide Status Form (SSF), both the clinician and the client develop a shared understanding of the client's suicidality by rating the client's current psychological pain, press (stress), perturbation (agitation), hopelessness, and poor self-regard" (p. 24). They go on to explain that "with the CAMS model, even the traditional face-to-face seating is changed once suicide is mentioned. The clinician asks for permission to sit side-by-side [with the] client while filling out the SSF in order to facilitate a more collaborative feeling" (Toth et al., 2007, p. 24). From this description, it is clear that such collaborative efforts engage the client and remove any judgmental element that might be associated with the assessment process.

Further, the CAMS model helps suicidal persons to identify reasons for living as well as for dying. From this process, the therapist can observe those protective factors that have kept the offender person from committing suicide up to the current point in time. Further, this process allows the therapist to engage the offender person in brainstorming exercises that can identify strengths for his or her treatment and also identify weaknesses that the client may possess, further refining the treatment process. When possible, the therapist should solicit such information from the offender client to generate a sense of rapport between the therapist and the offender client while also instilling a degree of self-ownership in the treatment process. This can thus accomplish two tasks at once: (1) create client motivation in the treatment planning process, and (2) generate alternative means of coping with the challenges facing the offender person.

Source: Hanser, R. D., Hanser, P. A., Mire, S. M., & Henderson, H. (2008). The comorbidity of depressed affective states, medical factors, and mental health considerations in elderly suicide. *Contemporary Issues in Criminology and the Social Sciences, 2*(2), 109–130.

Aside from the above common risk factors, there are other risk factors to consider with the incarcerated population. These are as follows:

1. First-time offenders who are extremely frightened and unsure of the jail and legal procedures are at high risk. The first 24 hours are particularly critical.
2. A young male who is a victim of sexual assault or the threat of sexual assault in the jail or prison. Particularly if this is their first incarceration experience.

3. Being placed in isolation increases the likelihood of suicide. This is true for males and females and it is particularly pronounced for females.
4. An inmate who faces a crisis situation, such as an eventual life sentence or the loss of a loved one by death or divorce. In such cases, existential counseling and/or the use of grief stage counseling can be effective.

Risk Factors for Teens in Confinement

Hayes (2004) notes that when dealing with juvenile offenders, those with documented mental disorders and those with substance abuse issues are perhaps among the most important set of risk factors for suicide among juveniles in the general population. Other risk factors included impulsive aggression, parental depression and substance abuse, family discord and abuse, and poor family support (Hayes, 2004). Life stressors, specifically interpersonal conflict and loss, as well as legal and disciplinary problems, were also associated with suicidal behavior in adolescents, particularly those who were substance abusers (Hayes, 2004). It has been argued that many of these risk factors are prevalent in youth confined in juvenile facilities. Researchers such as Sanislow, Grilo, Fehon, Axelrod, and McGlashan (2003) have found that high levels of depression, hopelessness, and acute situational stress due to confinement often lead to mental health profiles that mimic profiles of severely disturbed adolescents who are hospitalized in serious and acute psychiatric inpatient units. Thus, if all youth are at risk—to some degree or another—for suicide, then it may be the case that juveniles in confinement are at greater risk since they have life histories that predisposes them to suicide, such as with mental disorders, substance abuse, physical, sexual and emotional abuse, as well as prior ideations and/or attempts of suicide (Hayes, 2004).

We think that it is important that the point regarding life history experiences be given additional emphasis. Students should consider their readings in Chapter 9 on Youth Counseling and Juvenile Offenders. As one may recall, all of these points mentioned by Hayes (2004) were given specific, separate, and repetitive attention in that chapter. We cannot overemphasize how common these risk factors are among the more serious juvenile delinquent and criminal population. As one can see, these issues again become important when youth are in confinement, meaning that correctional counselors must be highly attentive to these risk factors with their juvenile clients, both when counseling in the institution and when counseling youth on community supervision.

For teens, chronic family fighting has been cited as one factor that can increase a youth to consider suicide. Kanel (2003) notes that the teen is often made to feel responsible for the arguments and tensions even though conflict is common among households with teens present. If the conflict is not dealt with in an effective manner, the family system may remain in crisis state for several years (Kanel, 2003). Further, youth who believe they are solely or primarily responsible for these conflicts can feel overwhelmed by this burden and constant turmoil and stress within the home. With these factors along with guilt regarding the discord that they perceive they have caused among their other family members, it may seem that suicide is an effective option for everyone (Kanel, 2003).

This is even more likely the case when youth are emotionally abused. When they are told that they are the primary reason for marital discord or when they are repetitively told that they are not smart, were a mistaken pregnancy, or that they are hated, this can increase the likelihood that the youth will consider suicide as an escape. Also, among delinquent youth who are caught committing some type of offense, they may find themselves unable to face their parents or other family members. This last point tends to depend on the type of offense and/or the type of parents who are involved. Obviously, suicide would be more likely if the youth committed some type of crime or an act of delinquency that was embarrassing and/or had extremely rigid and judgmental parents.

Risk Factors for Elderly Suicide

With being clear that suicide among the elderly entails a number of factors that correlate one with the other, it is reasonable to wonder what one can do to prevent such tragedies from occurring. One clear start would be to first know and recognize the warning signs of likely suicide. These warning signs can be seen as falling within four categories of occurrence, these being: verbal, behavioral, situational, and syndromatic. Among these, it is the verbal that is most basic and most direct. In such a case, the suicidal subject simply provides statements that give clear and overt warning that the person is contemplating suicide or it may be vague verbalized clues "such as the world might be better off without me" and other such indirect comments that allude to the possibility of suicide.

Just as with verbal clues, behavioral clues may be either direct or indirect. One of the most accurate predictors is whether the person has had a prior failed suicide attempt (U.S. Department of Health & Human Services, 2007). It is probably interesting to note that just as prior suicide attempts are strong predictors of likely future attempts, prior bouts of depression are strong indicators of likely future bouts of depression (as was discussed earlier in this draft). This is important because it may well be that there is a certain subset of the elderly population that are more at risk of suicide due to a set of personal characteristics and commonalities that have followed them through life rather than being at risk due to their elderly status. This could be very important since it might guide family members and caretakers in predicting tragic outcomes well in advance of the elderly years.

Regardless of the personality characteristics of the individual person being considered, it is clear that the elderly tend to make fewer attempts and are generally more effective at seeing a suicide to completion. In addition, any prior behavioral data that shows a prior attempt should instantly place that individual at high risk. In addition, there are numerous indirect behavioral indicators of possible suicide. The indicators that follow were obtained from the U.S. Department of Health and Human Services (2007):

- The stockpiling of medications
- Making or changing of a will
- Getting personal affairs in order as if they were about to leave
- Giving away property to others
- Self-neglect
- A marked decline in health, especially resembling the failure to thrive syndrome (Lantz, 2005).

These behaviors are not necessarily restricted to the elderly person that may be contemplating suicide. Indeed, these behaviors are reflective of almost any person considering such an act (American Psychiatric Association, 2000). But, these behaviors are important to keep in mind because among the elderly many may seem deceptively innocent. For instance, when the elderly make changes in their will or work to get their personal affairs in order, this may simply be seen as the person's attempt to simply be prepared for the inevitable and could even be perceived as the action of a social responsible person.

But, this then brings us to a variety of social indicators of suicide. The situational or contextual elements are important to understand because this will help to avoid potentially failed appraisals of the person's likely suicidal behavior. The social indicators are those that are perhaps most unique to the individual and are dependent on the relationship dynamics that the individual has in his or her life and as part of one's personality. For example, some people may be naturally introverted, having such characteristics throughout their entire life. In such a case, it would not be unusual for that person to act a bit withdrawn and perhaps self-absorbed, at least to some extent. For other persons in their elderly years, this could be a danger sign. The ability to accurately appraise such behavior is important and is probably most likely to occur among people who are familiar with the person on a long-term basis. Thus, family and friends are likely to be the best persons to make social appraisals of the elderly individual's status, simply because they will have known the individual for an adequate period of time and because they are closer to that individual. Included in the social indicators are any forms of psychosocial crisis, stressor, or debilitating experience that the individual may have encountered.

Thus, depressive symptoms are likely to have social causes and social manifestations (American Psychiatric Association, 2000). For instance, bereavement may be a common factor among elderly persons presenting with depression (American Foundation for Suicide Prevention, 2008; University of Toronto, 2003). As persons age, there is an increased likelihood that they will have to contend with the loss of a spouse, close friends, or family members. Depressive reactions to this loss are understandable and quite normal, but such forms of grief-based depression can eventually turn into more prolonged and globalized states of depression, if not attended to appropriately (American Psychiatric Association, 2000; University of Toronto, 2003). Likewise, there may be a slow shrinking of social networks for these individuals. This could be due to the loss of individuals, the lack of mobility that may accompany the aging process, or a lack of concern among other family members (University of Toronto, 2003). In a related sense, the person may experience bouts of social withdrawal that may exacerbate the shrinking social network. On the other hand, the shrinking of social networks (due to loss) may also encourage the elderly individual to isolate or withdraw from life, partly to avoid additional experiences of loss and also to avoid further obligations that are inherent to relationships with other persons. Lastly, those with a history of depression are likely to display this symptom later when they are older. It is likely that they will lapse back into depression if they have struggled with this in their earlier life.

To make matters worse, the elderly tend to leave behind fewer clues or indicators of their intent to commit suicide, yet at the same time these individuals possess characteristics and/or personal outlooks that would give them a high rank on most suicidal intent scores. In simpler terms, these individuals do not tend to talk about their intent to commit suicide, and, at the same time, they are more determined to do so than persons who are younger. Naturally, this makes detection and prevention efforts much more difficult among the elderly, as opposed to those utilized with younger at-risk populations.

Risk Factors for Women and Suicide

Among women, there are several distinct risk factors. However, it should be noted that females have a lower rate of actual suicides, but they do have a higher rate of attempted suicides than male offenders. As with other offenders, the onset of depression can increase the risk of suicidal behaviors among female offenders. However, it is the existence of impulse-control disorders, substance-use disorders, and anxiety disorders that are associated with a significantly higher risk of suicidal thoughts and attempts among women. As one may recall, each of these issues were covered in depth in Chapter 11 "Female Offenders and Correctional Counseling."

Depression is highly prevalent among women who die by suicide. The prevalence of depressive disorders in selected studies is between 59% and 91% for women (Chaudron & Claine, 2004).

In fact, it has been concluded that the prevalence of depression was greater among women who committed suicide than in the general population (Chaudron & Claine, 2004). Among women who die by suicide, alcohol abuse is also highly prevalent. In fact, many actually use alcohol while committing suicide. The use of alcohol at the time of suicide may reflect a substance use disorder, the need to be intoxicated to follow through, or the impulsivity associated with intoxication (Chaudron & Claine, 2004).

Lastly, it would appear that a lack of children also place female offenders at heightened risk of suicide. In fact, being pregnant and/or having young children in the home have each been found to be protective factors against female suicide (Chaudron & Claine, 2004). Further still, some studies suggest a higher rate of suicide among women who have undergone induced abortions. Given the risky lifestyles of many female offenders, a history of abortion is not necessarily uncommon. This sense of loss, especially if not dealt with appropriately, may leave painful emotional marks for years into the future.

Responses and Intervention

Kanel (2003) cites Lucy Steiner (1990) in noting the power in allowing clients to maintain their perspective that suicide is a right that is under their own complete control. In other words, the decision to live or die is ultimately determined by that person and this is a person's ultimate and most sacred sense of autonomy. This is a right that is reserved for the individual person and it is recommended that the correctional counselor avoid conflicts with potentially suicidal clients that can result from telling them that they have no right to kill themselves and/or that they should not do so for moral reasons (Kanel, 2003; Steiner, 1990). We also find that this approach is appropriate, particularly when dealing with the offender population that has so many oppositional personalities and where the environment is constantly laden with conflict or the threat of conflict. In many cases, these clients will feel as if the only control that they have over themselves and their life is the option of suicide (Kanel, 2003). In such a case, if the correctional counselor allows the client to simply have control over this option it can reduce the pressure that they may feel and this may alleviate a great deal of stress and tension for the client.

It is the therapist's task to diffuse the conflict, not to escalate it. Thus, the therapist will want to ensure that while they will not support a person into committing suicide, they understand fully well that choice is the individual's to make. Further, the correctional counselor will want to eliminate as much conflict as possible since this will also aid him or her in moderating his or her own stress during the encounter and will also ensure that the danger (and lethality) does not escalate. Thus, the correctional counselor should avoid adding conflict to any disagreements that may exist and avoid sounding judgmental or overly directive.

Rather, we contend that the therapist will need to listen and empathize with the client (McDowell & Stewart, 2008). This is important because in many cases, this is precisely what has been lacking for the individual. This is even more true with the offender population. The correctional counselor should utilize his or her active listening skills that have been discussed in earlier chapters of this text. The use of person-centered (or youth-centered if the suicidal person is a teen) techniques of reflection can be useful, particularly if the client detects the correctional counselor's genuine intent to understand the person's feelings and the reasons for having those feelings. This type of advanced empathy is the best approach to use with persons who are in pain, and, incidentally, it is the least likely of all responses to add conflict to the discussion.

Further, the counselor should affirm points made by the client (McDowell & Stewart, 2008). In this case, the counselor cannot affirm the right to commit flagrant violations of the institution and/or of his or her community supervision requirements, but the counselor can affirm feelings held by the client and can also provide a validity check for the client to ensure them that their feelings are normal and that their perspective holds value and a sense of logic. Likewise, the correctional counselor should be polite but direct in providing his or her input. Even then, the counselor's input should typically only occur if the client asks for such an input. The key is for the counselor to listen, not talk. Lastly, the correctional counselor should enlist the aid of the client when resolving the issue in a productive manner. If it should occur that the client is genuinely beyond the scope of common talk-therapy approaches then a referral may be in order. This is particularly true if medications will need to be prescribed as a means of addressing any latent depression or anxiety that is likely to be experienced by that client.

Lastly, we have noted earlier in this section the importance of discerning the level of lethality for suicidal offenders. In most cases, agencies will use a three- or four-tiered ranking system to rate the likely lethality of a person's suicidal tendencies. We adopt Kanel's use of low-, medium-, and high-risk suicidal clients for our purposes in this text (Kanel, 2003). According to Kanel (2003), **low-risk suicidal clients** are those who have pondered but never attempted suicide. These clients have adequate support systems and can usually be treated as outpatients. Therapy and educational interventions are encouraged. Next are **medium-risk suicidal clients** are individuals who contemplate suicide and feel depressed. These clients probably still have some hope, but they might also have a suicide plan. A no-suicide contract works as well for such persons as does a full suicide watch in most facilities. Thus, when these offenders are on community supervision, the correctional counselor can simply implement a suicide contract as a means of convincing the client to hold suicidal actions at bay. Nevertheless, crisis intervention with these offenders should be intense and frequent. **High-risk suicidal clients** are clients who have a plan, the means, and the intent for suicide, and they cannot be talked out of harming themselves. Hospitalization is often necessary for such clients.

The **no-suicide contract** is a formal written contract or a verbal agreement between the client and the correctional counselor in which the client makes a commitment to speak to the counselor before harming himself or herself. Follow-up phone calls (if the offender is on community supervision) or visits (if incarcerated) should occur after the creation of the contract; in most cases this is appreciated by the client. According to Kanel (2003), this is considered an effective intervention when used with low- and medium-risk clients. One of the authors of this text has used these contracts on several occasions and, from a practitioner's viewpoint, can validate Kanel's claim. The key is ensuring that the client is heard and that genuine empathy is conveyed. Further, the correctional counselor will want to avoid talking over the client or being baited into a conflict. Providing a sense of positive regard that is genuine (not technique sounding) and that encourages the client not to act in haste but to instead consider the possibilities that life may have to offer.

SECTION SUMMARY

This section provided a very extensive and detailed coverage of suicide issues in the custodial environment while also addressing suicide risk for offenders who are on community supervision. Suicide prevention programs are the first point of response to suicidal attempts within the institution, and many of the factors considered in prevention in the institution can and should be considered with offenders who are supervised in the community.

Further, the effective screening and assessment of suicidal potential is critical. Correctional counselors should familiarize themselves with these techniques and they should also become familiar with standardized instruments that are commonly used to assess suicide lethality. This will impact their later intervention during treatment planning and is also a very good safeguard against liability in the event that a suicide does occur. Correctional counselors should document closely their experience with the offender, conducting a structured interview that identifies nonverbal and verbal responses of the client when suicide is discussed.

Lastly, correctional counselors should utilize active listening skills when a person is considering suicide, being careful not to get embroiled in a conflict or to challenge the person's autonomy. This task is particularly challenging with youth who consider suicide. Rather, the correctional counselor, while not encouraging the act of suicide, should validate the client's right to self-direction. The use of approaches such as empathetic attending skills, active listening skills, and reflection of affect is recommended to the intervention process. Lastly, correctional counselors much consider the level of lethality of the client and will need to determine if hospitalization is necessary. If not, then the use of a suicide contract is recommended during the session and correctional counselors should provide empathetic follow-up during the week to demonstrate genuine care and concern for the client's welfare.

LEARNING CHECK

1. For teens, chronic family fighting has been cited as one factor that can increase a youth to consider suicide.
   a. True
   b. False
2. Assessment should be conducted by a qualified mental health professional, who designates the inmate's level of risk.
   a. True
   b. False
3. Typically, custodial staff and mental health staff have collaborated to optimize responses to suicidal inmates.
   a. True
   b. False
4. Among behavioral predictors of suicide, one of the most accurate is whether the person has had a prior failed suicide attempt.
   a. True
   b. False
5. Medium-risk suicidal clients are individuals who contemplate suicide and feel depressed.
   a. True
   b. False

CONCLUSION

This chapter has covered quite a bit of information—information that is crucial for correctional counselors. HIV/AIDS presents serious challenges for prisons and jails around the nation, and correctional counselors must be prepared to deal with the mental health aspects of this illness. The prevalence of HIV/AIDS is greater in the offender population than in the widespread community. This then makes it even more likely that correctional counselors will encounter this issue when conducting therapeutic interventions.

Importantly, the correctional counselor should be familiar with experiences of grief and loss, particularly when offenders are facing likely death. Understanding the various mental health issues associated with the death and dying process is important and must be given attention. Correctional counselors must be comfortable processing the emotional aspects of this process and will need to facilitate this for offenders who face such circumstances. In doing this, existential therapy was presented as an effective approach in providing the client with assistance and stability throughout this process. Integrating bibliotherapy and other forms of introspective media can aid the client in formulating their experiences and deriving meaning from those experiences. Correctional counselors who deal with terminal illness and/or offenders who are advanced in age must be prepared to assist offenders in developing a coping strategy that provides them with dignity and respect when facing death.

Despite the intent to add meaning and depth to living by understanding dying, offenders will still likely have some very predictable and understandable reactions. Many of these reactions will be similar to various stages identified by Kübler-Ross. It is important to understand that grieving and coping with trauma and loss is not identical for everyone. Thus, the use of the five-stage cycle of grief should not be used in a rigid application; some clients will experience these stages in a different order or they may not experience a stage to the same extreme as other offenders. Regardless, the correctional counselor must assist them in their emotional reactions to the grieving process and to the experience of trauma.

Next, elderly offenders will become increasingly common in many correctional facilties and community supervision programs around the country. While elderly offenders are likely to have many of the same health concerns, they should not be regarded as identical due to their different criminal histories. Some offenders, such as the habitual elderly offender, have persisted in a life of crime that has never ceased; others such as the offenders turned elderly in prison will have likely committed either a single serious crime or a set of crimes during the same relative time period, this occurring early in their life. Due to the seriousness of the crime, they may have spent a lengthy period being incarcerated. On the other hand, other elderly offenders may have lived crime free only to commit a crime in their later years that is serious enough to warrant their incarceration. Each of these categories of offender must be given different types of mental health treatment approaches because their perspectives are likely to be quite different from one another. Regardless, these offenders are likely to have some common mental health issues, such as depression, anxiety, Alzheimer's disease, and the potential for suicide.

Lastly, correctional counselors must be prepared to deal with suicide in the correctional setting. Clinicians should be familiar with screening and assessment techniques and also be familiar with standardized instruments that assess suicide lethality. This will be of use in their later intervention during treatment planning and is very important for correctional administrators as this is an effective safeguard against liability if a suicide does occur. As noted in our earlier section summary, correctional counselors should document closely their experience with the offender, conducting a structured interview that identifies nonverbal and verbal responses of the client when suicide is discussed. When providing interventions for suicide, correctional counselors should use active listening skills and they should ensure that they do not challenge the person's sense of autonomy. Instead, the counselor should provide understanding that uses reflection of affect and validates the client's right to self-determination. Though the likely lethality and risk of suicide will determine the specific course of action that should be taken in ensuring the client's safety, it is clear that attentiveness to the client, active listening skills, and reflection of affect are perhaps among the best forms of response when a person is in so much pain that they lose the will to go further with their life.

Essay Questions

1. Discuss the basic approach to existential counseling. Why might this approach be effective for HIV/AIDS victims, elderly offenders, and persons considering suicide. Also, explain why it is that existential counseling largely free of specific techniques. Explain how existential counseling is actually conducted with offenders who may need to engage in meaning self-reflection.
2. Identify, list, and discuss the five stages of grief and loss by Kübler-Ross and explain how these stages might be useful for an inmate who has HIV/AIDS. Also, explain how this stage process might aid persons facing other sources of trauma.
3. Explain how you might screen for suicidal intent and how you might implement a program for prevention. Further, explain how a correctional counselor might conduct an assessment of suicidal intent and lethality. Explain why the authors contend that some correctional counselors may want to use standardized suicide assessment tools.
4. Throughout this chapter, reference has been made to the notion that correctional counselors and custodial staff need to work together in collaboration. Provide some examples where this might be important and explain how this might be done in those examples.
5. How might the use of family systems therapy (see Chapter 6 "Family Systems Therapy and Counseling") be effective with an offender who has HIV/AIDS and is going through the process of coping with his or her own eventual demise? In addition, explain how family systems therapy might be useful for an elderly offender who is about to be released from prison. Lastly, explain how family interventions might be effective for youth who express suicidal intent.

Treatment Planning Exercise

In this exercise, the student must consider the case of Duane and determine how to address both his mental state and potential for suicide. You must explain how you would provide treatment for Duane, particularly in regard to his potential for suicide. You must also consider his dementia and determine how this is likely to affect his prognosis. Further, you must identify your specific theoretical approach and the techniques that you would use to provide an effective intervention for Duane.

The Case of Duane

Duane is currently on probation for voyeurism and indecent exposure. Yes, he has been arrested and convicted of both. The community supervision department has decided to send him to your office for mental health services. From the records given to you, it is obvious that Duane also suffers from dementia. Duane's records note a gradual onset and continuing cognitive decline over the past few years. He is also 64 years old and has numerous respiratory health problems related to heavy smoking. He has been diagnosed with **dementia of the Alzheimer's type, with early onset.**

Duane has been exhibiting bizarre behavior, including uncontrollable and unpredictable bursts of cursing and screaming, petty shoplifting in retail stores, and a concurring total loss of memory of the incidents.

He is beginning to demonstrate problems with spatial perception and has injured himself numerous times while in his own home. Duane has two daughters Jenny (age 28) and Tina (age 25), both of whom refuse to talk with him. He has exposed himself to one of his granddaughters (Jenny's five-year-old daughter), and he was caught spying on Tina when

(*continued*)

she was in bed with her husband. Both Jenny and Tina have had strained relationships with their father in the past and left home early. Incidentally, Duane is a widower and was retired early from the chemical plant that he had worked at.

Duane is often morose and sullen and has actually brought up doing something "crazy." One of his friends told a senior-care worker that Duane has thought about "going out with a bang" and described notions that he had been considering (i.e., committing bank robbery, a mass shooting, bombing some popular cite, etc.). Duane alludes to these possibilities as if they were a joke. You are not so sure.

You will be seeing Duane later this afternoon. It is not really clear-cut if anything can, in fact, be done to "fix" these problems. What do you do?

Bibliography

Aday, R. H. (1994). Aging in prison: A case study of new elderly offenders. *International Journal of Offender Therapy and Comparative Criminology, 38*(1), 121.

American Psychiatric Association. (2000). *Diagnostic and statistical manual of mental disorders*. Arlington, VA: American Psychiatric Association.

American Psychiatric Association. (2004). *Mentally ill offender treatment and crime reduction act becomes law*. Washington, DC: American Psychological Association. Retrieved from: http://www.apa.org/releases/S1194_law.html.

American Foundation for Suicide Prevention (2008). *Special populations: Facts and figures*. New York, NY: American Foundation for Suicide Prevention. Retrieved from: http://www.afsp.org/index.cfm?fuseaction=home.viewpage&page_id=050CDCA2-C158-FBAC-16ACCE9DC8B7026C.

Anno, B. J., Graham, C., Lawrence, J. E., & Shansky, R. (2004). *Correctional health care: Addressing the needs of elderly, chronically ill, and terminally ill inmates*. Washington, DC: National Institute of Corrections.

Ashford, J. B., Sales, B. D., & Reid, W. H. (2002). *Treating adult and juvenile offenders with special needs*. Washington, DC: American Psychological Association.BBC News. (1999). *Many elderly offenders "are mentally ill."* Retrieved from: http://news.bbc.co.uk/1/hi/health/294252.stm.

Brent, D. (1995). Risk factors for adolescent suicide and suicidal behavior: Mental and substance abuse disorders, family environmental factors, and life stress. *Suicide and Life Threatening Behavior, 25*(Suppl.), 52–63.

Chapman, A. (2008). *The Elisabeth Kubler-Ross grief cycle*. EKR Foundation. Retrieved from: www.businessballs.com.

Chaudron, L. H., & Claine, E. D. (2004). Suicide among women: A critical review. *Journal of the American Medical Women's Association, 59*(2), 125–134.

Corey, G. (1996). *Theory and practice of counseling and psychotherapy* (5th ed.). Pacific Grove, CA: Brooks/Cole Publishing.

Gafner, G. (2004). *More hypnotic inductions*. New York, NY: W. W. Norton & Company, Inc.

Hanser, R. D., Hanser, P. A., Mire, S. M., & Henderson, H. (2008). The comorbidity of depressed affective states, medical factors, and mental health considerations in elderly suicide. *Contemporary Issues in Criminology and the Social Sciences, 2*(2), 109–130.

Hanson, G. R., Venturelli, P. J., & Fleckenstein, A. E. (2002). *Drugs and society* (7th ed.). Sudbury, MA: Jones and Bartlett Publishers.

Hayes, L. M. (2004). *Juvenile suicide in confinement: A national survey*. Mansfield, MA: National Center on Institutions and Alternatives.

Ivanoff, A., & Hayes, L. (2001). Prevention of suicide and suicidal behavior in jail and prison. In J. B. Ashford & B. Sales (Eds.), *Treating offenders with mental disorders* (pp. 313–331). Washington, DC: American Psychological Association Press.

Jobes, D. A., & Drozd, J. F. (2004). The CAMS approach to working with suicidal patients. *Journal of Contemporary Psychotherapy, 34*, 73–85.

Kanel, K. (2003). *A guide to crisis intervention* (2nd ed.). Pacific Grove, CA: Brooks/Cole.

Lantz, M. S. (2005). Failure to thrive. *Clinical Geriatrics, 13*(3), 2–23.

McDowell, J., & Stewart, E. (2008). *My friend is struggling with thoughts of suicide.* Scotland, UK: Christian Focus Publications.

McGoldrick, M., Giordano, J., Pearce, J. K., & Giordano, J. (1996). *Ethnicity and family therapy* (2nd ed.). New York: Guilford Press.

Morton, J. B. (1992). *An administrative overview of the older inmate.* Washington, DC: National Institute of Corrections.

National Institute of Corrections. (2001). *Correctional healthcare: Suicide prevention.* Washington, DC: United States Department of Justice.

National Institutes of Health. (2002). *Depression and HIV/AIDS.* Washington, DC: U.S. Department of Health and Human Services.

Sanislow, C., Grilo, C., Fehon, D., Axelrod, S., & McGlashan, T. (2003). Correlates of suicide risk in juvenile detainees and adolescent in-patients. *Journal of the American Academy of Child and Adolescent Psychiatry, 42*(2), 234–240.

Steiner, L. (1990). *Suicide assessment and intervention.* Presentation at California State University Fullerton. As cited by Kristi Kanel (2003).

Toth, M., Schwartz, R. C., & Kurka, S. (2007). Strategies for understanding and assessing suicide risk in psychotherapy. *Annals of the American Psychotherapy Association, 10*(4), 18–27.

University of Toronto. (2003). The dwindles and failure to thrive. *Canadian Journal of CME, February,* 35–40.

U.S. Department of Health & Human Services. (2007). Evidence based protocol. Elderly suicide, secondary prevention. Retrieved from: http://www.guideline.gov/summary/summary.aspx?ss=15&doc_id=3308&nbr=2534#s21

WebMD (2008). The top 10 myths and misconceptions about HIV and AIDS. Retrieved from: http://www.webmd.com/hiv-aids/top-10-myths-misconceptions-about-hiv-aids?page=2.

Wooden, W. S., & Parker, J. (1982). *Men behind bars: Sexual Exploitation in prison.* New York: Plenum Press.

14

Evaluation, Effectiveness, and Offender Recidivism

LEARNING OBJECTIVES

After reading this chapter, you will be able to:

1. Discuss the importance of evaluative research and the role of the independent evaluator.
2. Explain the importance of quantitative processes in determining if treatment programs are evidence based in their practice.
3. Explain how validity and reliability are important to the evaluation process.
4. Identify some standardized instruments and explain why they are beneficial to the evaluation of treatment programs.
5. Explain how evaluations of drug treatment programs and sex offender treatment programs might be conducted.
6. Identify some of the ethical considerations when conducting evaluative research in mental health settings.
7. Discuss how evaluation results can be used to improve treatment program processes and outcomes.

PART ONE: INTRODUCTION TO THE EVALUATION PROCESS

When examining any program, whether therapeutic or otherwise, one of the first questions asked by politicians, policy makers, program administrators, and government officials is, "Does the treatment program work?" In such a case, the underlying desire is to know if money spent on a program is money that is well spent. In such cases, treatment providers will often be required to provide some sort of empirical "evidence" that the program is effective. This is often referred to as evidence-based program delivery. Treatment providers are increasingly being asked to demonstrate the effectiveness of their programs, particularly when such programs are grant funded. In turn, many correctional treatment programs seek money from grant-generating agencies, and, when they have some sort of documented program success, they increase their odds of securing such funds.

However, before going further, we would like to make one observation regarding correctional counseling and research. We believe that programs are best evaluated by researchers who themselves are treatment providers. This is particularly true if the researcher has had specific experience with the type of population that is the subject of the program evaluation. Both authors have conducted grant-funded evaluation research of treatment programs and have also studied and/or worked in a variety of treatment fields. One author in particular has worked with most typologies of offenders who have been presented in this text and has also conducted numerous evaluative studies of treatment programs that provide services to those offenders. We believe that this is important because such a practitioner is able to make sense of data that may seem confusing, uncertain, or contradictory, simply because they understand how the program and/or process of treatment intervention works within a given agency and/or with a specific offender population. With this said, it is at this point that we now turn our attention to the notion of evaluation research.

Evaluation Research

For the purposes of this text, we will refer to the Center for Program Evaluation and Performance Management which is a clearinghouse on evaluative research offered through the Bureau of Justice Assistance (BJA). This source, available online and referenced in this text, provides the reader with a very good overview of the evaluation process and also provides a number of examples pertaining to the evaluation of criminal justice and treatment programs. Because this is a federal government website, the information therein is public domain. In addition, we believe that this site provides a very clear, succinct, and effective overview of evaluation research from the eyes of the practitioner. It is for these reasons that this chapter is constructed from much of the organization and structure of the BJA website, providing the basics of evaluation research along with our own insights as to how that information is useful to correctional counselors.

Evaluation is a systematic and objective method for testing the success (or failure) of a given program. The primary purpose of conducting evaluative research is to determine if the intervention program is achieving its stated goals and objectives. In the field of correctional counseling, this is actually very important. It is the observation of the first author of this text that, in many cases, treatment programs provide their services but are not truly aware of whether they have actually "fixed" their clients; this is an important point to address. Treatment agencies must be able and willing to demonstrate the effectiveness of their program's intervention and this effectiveness should be expressed in quantitative terms. A failure to do so consists of negligence on the part of the agency and also leads to a potential public safety problem. Indeed, if the program does not truly work to reform offenders but the treatment staff continue to operate as if it does, offenders who are risks to public safety will just continue to enter society unchanged and just as dangerous or problematic as before.

Often, counselors and other personnel primarily geared toward offering therapeutic services do not necessarily understand the purpose of evaluative research. In addition, it is not uncommon for such practitioners to also discount the contributions of an evaluator, claiming that the evaluator cannot possibly know (better than themselves) whether clients are "getting better," so to speak. However, this is often based on intuition on the part of the therapist and is also not grounded in objective and detached observation. Evaluative research seeks to look at the process and outcome of correctional counseling in an objective and detached measure to determine the objective truth as to the efficacy of a given program.

All too often, treatment staff may provide anecdotal evidence and/or selected cases of success. This should be avoided as this is not sufficient to demonstrate effectiveness and as too much is left to interpretation. Rather, it is important that evaluations of therapeutic programs be conducted by persons who are neutral and detached from the delivery of therapeutic services and it is also important that quantitative as well as qualitative measures be included in that evaluation. Qualitative measures are those that are not numerical in nature and are based more on the context and circumstances of the observation. For instance, clinical case notes, open-ended interviews, and therapist observations would be examples of qualitative observations. On the other hand, quantitative measures are those that have a numerical quantity attached to them. Quantitative measures are those derived from standardized instruments that provide a numerical value to the information gathered from a client.

Working with an Outside Evaluator

One of the first issues that agencies will need to consider is whether to use an evaluation expert and whether that person can be from within the agency or whether they should instead come outside of the agency being evaluated. If the agency has funding available, it is recommended that they find a trained and experienced evaluator; such a person can be of great assistance to the treatment program throughout the evaluation process. However, it should be noted that agencies and agency staff must be receptive to the efforts of the evaluator. In many cases, agency staff may be defensive and/or guarded when providing information or records. In such cases, it is imperative that agency leadership ensure that hindrances to data collection and the communication of client outcomes be sufficiently addressed.

Regardless of whether the evaluator is from within or outside the agency, it is important that a trained and qualified evaluator be identified and secured. A failure to achieve this basic ingredient of the evaluation process will mean that counselors, clinicians, and perhaps clients, will "feel" as if the treatment regimen is working but they will not be able to provide any type of evidence-based support for their opinions. Obviously, this is not scientifically sound nor is it convincing to any potential skeptic who might examine the agency. Lastly, a qualified evaluator should have experience in evaluating treatment programs and, ideally, should have experience in evaluating treatment programs similar to the one operated by the agency in question. The evaluator should also attempt to balance the needs and concerns of various decision makers with the need for objectivity while conducting the evaluation.

Once it has been determined that the agency is ready for evaluation and who the evaluator will be, the process of developing an evaluation plan begins. Basically, an evaluation plan describes the process that will be used to conduct an evaluation of the treatment program (Bureau of Justice Assistance, 2008). According to the BJA (2008), key elements of an evaluation plan that should be addressed are (1) determining the target audience for the evaluation and the dissemination of its results; (2) identifying the evaluation questions that should be asked; (3) determining how the evaluation design will be developed; (4) deciding the type of data to be collected, how that data will be collected, and by whom; and (5) articulating the final products of the report that will be produced.

Lastly, the evaluation plan should detail the roles of various individuals who will contribute to the evaluation process; these individuals include the evaluator, the agency management, treatment staff, clients, family members of clients, and any other persons impacted by the research.

Likewise, an ideal evaluator will have had experience in delivery of therapeutic services that are the same or similar to those provided by the agency. This is important because it provides the evaluator with additional insight behind the data that is generated. Such insight can lead to a particularly useful blend of observations that dwell betwixt the world of the clinical practitioner and the academic researcher; this is the strongest and most useful type of evaluative research that can be produced.

Quantitative Evaluation of a Drug Treatment Program

An example of an evaluation plan that uses both quantitative and qualitative aspects of measurement is provided in the following evaluation description. This information consists of an evaluation model that the first author designed while working as an evaluator at a local drug treatment facility. This evaluation design demonstrates how the treatment staff and the evaluator may both provide observations, but it is the use of standardized instruments and collection methods that serve as the primary data used to determine client progress. (The use of standardized tools will be discussed later in this chapter.) Further, this example demonstrates that measures, to be effective, must be taken over a long period of time and among many different sources (i.e., agency staff, the evaluator, and/or family and friends of the client). It is in this manner that a composite profile of the client's overall progress is developed.

A. Evaluative Methods. This research design will follow a simple time-series design with repeated measures over the period of the grant-funded period. It is expected that the evaluative design will allow the agency to address all related program outcome questions as well as process questions, as required by this grant-funding opportunity. During the grant-funded period, weekly staff observations will be conducted to track client progress through the use of an evaluative rubric that is based on the basic tenets of operant conditioning strategies. When observing client progress, staff will ensure that their noted input is structured in such a manner as to optimize measurability while including contextual, subjective, and qualitative data that is deemed clinically useful or relevant. Further, staff will be required to provide a list of intervention techniques and behavior management tools that utilize each of the four categories.

B. Data Collection Instruments. In addition, several pretest and post-test measures will be taken to assess both the subject's recovery from alcohol or drug abuse and to assess their improvement in their other co-occurring mental health diagnoses. In addition to quantitative assessments of both of these areas of client outcome, semistructured qualitative client observations will be conducted by various staff at the pretest and post-test stages. One of these forms of interview is known as the **Addiction Severity Index** (ASI) and is commonly used in treatment facilities all over the United States. This will serve as an initial data collection process on clients and it is expected that this data will be more useful to treatment staff than to those having research objectives.

Four other measurement scales will be utilized at intake and at discharge (three months) of the first phase of treatment. These scales are as follows: The **Drug Abuse Screening Test** (Skinner, 1995), which is a widely recognized scale providing a quantitative index of the degree of problems related to drug and/or alcohol dependency. The **Substance Abuse Subtle Screening Instrument** (SASSI) is a screening measure that provides interpretations of client profiles and aids in developing hypotheses that clinicians or researchers may find useful in understanding persons in treatment. The **Behaviors, Attitudes, Drinking, & Driving Scale** (BADDS) will be administered at intake, program completion, and the three-month follow-up period. The BAADS is an evidence-based pre- and post-test psychological questionnaire that measures attitudes, behaviors, and intervention effectiveness related to impaired driving. Optionally, the **Maryland Addictions Questionnaire** (Western Psychological Services) may be given at intake. This scale determines severity of addiction; the motivation of the client; the risk of relapse; and treatment complications related to cognitive difficulties, anxiety, or depression. *When and where feasible, these scales will likewise be utilized with clients at the 6-month, 9-month, and 12-month periods for subjects in treatment.*

In addition, weekly observations will be conducted by staff and these observations will be provided in weekly case notes. Staff at the facility will specifically focus on observable and behavioral elements of the client's progress as this is considered a better method of judging the client's progress than are deductions that are made from the client's self-proclaimed introspective work. The staff at the facility are already accustomed to this approach of case review and will simply restrict their observations (particularly those placed in writing) to that which is observed through overt client behavior without any inference being drawn beyond what is clearly observable and thus measurable. This should not be a problem since the state of Louisiana already encourages this type of reference when compiling case notes and client progress evaluations.

Further, the **Substance Abuse Relapse Assessment** (Psychological Assessment Resources) will be administered to subjects at the 3-, 6-, 9-, and 12-month periods. This instrument is a structured interview developed for use by substance abuse treatment professionals to help recovering individuals recognize signs of relapse (Psychological Assessment Resources). Likewise, staff will conduct follow-up interviews during this period of time to provide an overall GAF scale rating for prior clients during the 3-, 6-, 9-, and 12-month period of the study. This will provide an additional metric (ratio data) measure during the aftercare stages of treatment. Staff will also be asked to rank the degree of success (on a scale from 1 to 100) that clients have made in reaching their original goals that were self-contracted in their plan of change. Staff will rank client success in goal achievement during the 4th, 7th, and 13th months of the study.

Upon completion of phase one, measures will also be taken at the close of the 4th, 7th, and 13th months through an informal survey of friends and family to determine if the subject is engaging in self-management strategies that were taught during phase one. These individuals will also be asked to rank the degree of success (on a scale from 1 to 100) that clients have made in reaching their original goals that were self-contracted in their plan of change. The information from these surveys will be triangulated with the information obtained from staff using the GAF checklist to provide a multidimensional view of the subject's progress. Further, subjects themselves will be asked to rank the degree of success (on a scale from 1 to 100) that they have made in reaching their original goals that were self-contracted in their plan of change during phase one. Subjects will rank their success in goal achievement during the 4th, 7th, and 13th months of the study.

In addition, agency cultural competence will be assessed using the **Agency Cultural Competence Checklist**, ACCC (Dana, Behn, & Gonwa, 1992). Specifically, the **ACCC** is an instrument that is designed to assess social service agency cultural competence with racial and ethnic minority groups. This checklist screens for both general cultural competence throughout the agency and culture-specific content within the assessment and intervention categories of that same agency. This instrument will be provided to staff members and to clients as a means of generating input on the adequacy of services in meeting minority needs and/or issues of faith or spirituality.

C. Human Subjects Research—Procedures and Protocols. All procedures as outlined by the Louisiana Office for Addictive Disorders and the Louisiana Association of Substance Abuse Counselors and Training (LASACT) will be followed when administering therapeutic services to clients. All procedures required by the Human Subjects Review Board of the University of Louisiana at Monroe will be followed as well. In addition, data collection/records keepers will ensure that all data is coded and completely unidentifiable by the researchers or by others viewing the records. The primary investigator will analyze the entered data coded by the data collection/records keepers but will not be familiar with either the physical hardcopy data sources nor will he or she have identifiable contact with or knowledge of the clients of each facility who will be the subjects for this study. It should be noted that Dr. Hanser is a Licensed Addictions (LAC) and a Licensed Professional Counselor (LPC) in the State of Louisiana and therefore has a very good understanding of legal and ethical issues related to addictions treatment and therapeutic interventions while also having a strong grasp of research ethics pertaining to human subject's safety and confidentiality.

Types of Data Collection

The evaluation plan just noted is a bit detailed but was designed to obtain a blend of different measures and to increase accountability among treatment staff to ensure that they focus on the outcomes of their efforts. This blend of different measures can come in several means but generally fall within four categories that include direct observation, the use of interviews, surveys and questionnaires, and official records. A description of each category was obtained from the BJA and is presented below:

1. ***Direct Observation:*** Obtaining data by on-site observation has the advantage of providing an opportunity to learn in detail how the project works, the context in which it exists, and what its various consequences are. However, this type of data collection can be expensive and time consuming. Observations conducted by program staff, as opposed to an outside evaluator, may also suffer from subjectivity.
2. ***Interviews:*** Interviews are an effective way of obtaining information about the perceptions of program staff and clients. An external evaluator will usually conduct interviews with program managers, staff members, and clients to obtain their perceptions of how well the program functions. Some of the disadvantages with conducting interviews are that they tend to be time consuming and costly. Further, interviews tend to produce subjective information.
3. ***Surveys and Questionnaires:*** Surveys of clients can provide information on attitudes, beliefs, and self-reported behaviors. An important benefit of surveys is that they provide anonymity to respondents, which can reduce the likelihood of biased reporting and increase data validity. There are many limitations that are associated with surveys and questionnaires, including the reading level of the client and cultural bias. However, the use of standardized instruments provides a number of benefits because they have been tested to ensure at least a modicum of validity and reliability. The use of standardized surveys, questionnaires, and instruments enhances the baseline data that is initially collected and this then adds to the strength of the evaluation. More information on standardized instruments will be provided later in this chapter.
4. ***Official Records:*** Official records and files are one of the most common sources of data for criminal justice evaluations. Arrest reports, court files, and prison records all contain much useful information for assessing program outcomes. Often these files are automated, making accessing these data easier and less expensive.

Regardless of the types of data-gathering process that is ultimately used, evaluators tend to conduct two general types of agency evaluation: program outcome evaluation and process evaluation. **Program outcome evaluation** entails an ongoing collection of data to determine if a program is successfully meeting its goals and objectives. In many cases, these measures address project activities and services delivered. Some examples of performance measures might include the following: the number of clients served, changes in attitude, and rates of recidivism. These types of evaluations tend to measure the overall outcome of the projects. Effective treatment programs produce positive outcomes among clients. As would be expected, these programs generate client change while they participate in the program, and, in the most successful programs, client progress continues even after the client is discharged from a particular treatment regimen. Areas of evaluation that might be used to demonstrate outcome effectiveness might include any of the following:

1. Cognitive ability (improvements in recall and/or overall testing scores or times)
2. Emotional/affective functioning (such as anxiety and depression)
3. Pro-social attitudes and/or values (such as improved empathy, honesty, etc.)
4. Education and vocational training progress (traditional achievement tests)
5. Behavior (evidenced by observable behaviors).

Process evaluations focus on the implementation of the program and its day-to-day operations. Typically, process evaluations address specific processes or procedures that are routinely done within the agency. In many cases, **process evaluation** refers to assessment of the effects of the program on clients while they are in the program, making it possible to assess the institution's intermediary goals. Process evaluation examines aspects of the program such as:

1. The type of services provided
2. The frequency of services provided
3. Client attendance in individual or group counseling sessions
4. The number of clients who are screened, admitted, reviewed, and discharged
5. The percentage of clients who successfully complete treatment.

Sex Offender Treatment Programs (SOTP): The Importance of Evaluation

One type of treatment program and treatment population who warrants routine assessment and evaluation would be sex offender treatment programs and the clients of these programs. The evaluation of these programs is quite naturally important because sex offenders have generated a high level of public concern. Determining whether treatment programs do indeed "work" or whether they do not do so is paramount to determining whether this population should be given treatment in lieu of simple incarceration. Further, effective evaluation allows programs to improve their implementation. Due to public safety concerns associated with sex offenders, effective evaluation has become a very important element in designing treatment programs for these programs.

Sex offender treatment programs entail a variety of approaches that are used to prevent convicted sex offenders from committing future sex offenses. Students should refer to Chapter 12 on sex offender treatment programs when considering the evaluation of such programs. As one may recall, these approaches include different types of therapy, community notification, and standardized assessments (Bureau of Justice Assistance, 2008). Given the high level of denial among sex offenders, it is important that assessment and evaluation components are able to measure both latent as well as manifest aspects of sex offender progress in treatment. In other words, the skilled evaluator will keep in mind that this population is inherently very manipulative and will need to ensure that their evaluation model is able to detect deceit and manipulation from data provided by these offenders.

Evaluations for sex offender treatment programs in prison are likely to have some differences from those in the community, particularly since public safety concerns are greater for those who are in the community. While some scales and processes will remain the same in both settings, evaluators in community-based settings will also need to consult with family and friends of the sex offender much more frequently than in a prison setting. The reasons for this are simply because such individuals are likely to have more direct observations of the offender, their behavior, and their apparent commitment to the treatment regimen.

Typically, there are three common therapeutic approaches to treating sex offenders. These approaches include (1) **cognitive-behavioral approach**, which focuses on changing thinking patterns related to sexual offending and changing deviant patterns of sexual behavior, (2) **psychoeducational approach**, which focuses on increasing offenders' empathy for the victim while also teaching them to take responsibility for their sexual offenses, and (3) **pharmacological approach**, which uses medication to reduce sexual response. As one may recall in Chapter 12, the primary types of treatment are cognitive-behavioral in approach but many may use psychoeducational aspects as well. The pharmacological approach has not been discussed in this text and will generally not be an area of intervention that will require substantial input from the correctional counselor. It is for this reason that, when discussing evaluation, we focus our attention on efforts to evaluate cognitive-behavioral and psychoeducational interventions.

Beyond the treatment staff, the supervision of sex offenders—and the evaluation of sex offender treatment programs—should include all parties who are involved with the case management of the sex offender, including law enforcement, corrections, victims (when appropriate), the court, and so on. All of these personnel can provide very useful information that may not be readily apparent to the evaluator. The key for the evaluator is to understand the one vantage point that each party provides from which he or she can view the sex offender treatment and/or supervision process. It is the composite picture, made up of the full range of individual observations, that should be used by the evaluator. Each party individually can provide valuable information in assessing the effectiveness and efficacy of the sex offender treatment program and supervision strategies (Bureau of Justice Assistance, 2008). Collectively, these parties provide a multifaceted view of the offender's progress.

Further, as was noted in Chapter 12, sex offenders are very manipulative, and even skilled therapists (and community supervision officers) may have difficulty discerning whether such an offender is making genuine and sincere progress. Because of this, it is important for the evaluator to get a comprehensive "snapshot" of the offender that is multidimensional in scope. The use of numerous observations and the comparison of those observations help to ferret out faulty data provided to the evaluator, whether the faulty data was provided deliberately (such as from the sex offender himself or herself) or accidentally/unknowingly from various personnel working with the offender. Naturally, the more comprehensive and the more accurate the evaluation, the more likely that agencies can refine their processes. Refined processes lead to more effective treatment and this then leads to increased public safety if the sex offender ceases recidivism due to effective treatment. Thus, the evaluator is a primary player in improving community safety through agency assistance in optimizing their service delivery.

As with our earlier example of an evaluative design for a substance abuse treatment organization, the use of standardized assessment instruments with sex offenders can greatly improve the validity and reliability of the evaluation. Standardized tools are more effective than "home grown" surveys and questionnaires because, as we noted in the previous subsection, they have been tested to ensure that they are valid and reliable in providing treatment planning information for counselors and security criteria for correctional administrators and supervision staff. Thus, standardized assessment tools tend to increase the likelihood of treatment efficacy and also better identify sex offenders who are at a heightened risk of recidivism (Bureau of Justice Assistance, 2008). A more in-depth discussion on the use of standardized instruments in the evaluation process will be provided in part two of this chapter. For now, we simply wish to note their constructive use when conducting evaluations.

Beyond the use of standardized data-gathering tools, evaluators tend to also address a number of specific areas of concern for publicly operated sex offender treatment programs. These areas of attention, as noted by the BJA (2008), include the following:

1. Attrition in sex offender programs with the hope of increasing the number of offenders who complete treatment
2. Identification of offense characteristics that predict treatment failure
3. Development of processes to better track high-risk sex offenders
4. Continual improvement of the validity and reliability of screening and assessment instruments that are used
5. Improving interventions for specific categories of sex offenders to improve one-size-fits-all treatment orientations.

When conducting evaluations of sex offender treatment programs, there are a number of program outcome measures that may be utilized. The program outcome measures noted below are among those that are more common and provide administrators with a general idea of what their program processes produce upon completion of the program:

1. Proportion of reconvictions for sexual offenses
2. Change in treatment motivation
3. Change in treatment engagement
4. Increase in offender emotional health or adjustment
5. Decrease in pro-offending attitudes
6. Decrease in inappropriate sexual drive
7. Decrease in aberrant sexual arousal and sexual fantasies.

In addition, process measures provide an understanding of the day-to-day operations of the treatment program. These types of measures aid clinical supervisors and agency administrators in determining specific areas of treatment that work well while identifying those areas that need some type of modification or improvement. Some of the common process measures examined include the following:

1. Number of face-to-face contacts between treatment provider and sex offender
2. Number of meetings between the sex offender, therapist, and probation officer
3. Number of visits by probation officers to the home of the sex offender
4. Number of urine screenings for drugs/alcohol
5. Number of medication-induced side effects
6. Level of community supervision received.

Lastly, the BJA (2008) has noted that there are numerous sex offender studies with different methodological problems such as small sample sizes, the lack of equivalence among control and experimental groups, and the use of low quality assessment scales. Despite this, some sex offender studies have provided evidence that suggests that treatment programs used today are more effective than those used in the 1980s and 1990s. Of interest is the fact that evaluations that have compared different therapeutic approaches have consistently demonstrated that cognitive-behavioral treatment approaches hold particular promise for reducing sex offender recidivism (Bureau of Justice Assistance, 2008).

As discussed in Chapter 12, cognitive-behavioral treatment with sex offenders is often provided in a group setting that focuses on cognitive distortions, denial of the offense while in treatment, deviant sexual thoughts and arousal, and a lack of empathy for victims. These programs lend themselves well to evaluation due to their clear processes of implementation and the ease by which those processes can be defined and quantified for research purposes. However, the ultimate litmus test of success is whether the sex offender recidivates, particularly through the commission of another sex offense. It is in this regard that cognitive-behavioral programs tend to demonstrate very good program outcome results because these programs tend to have more frequent and more significant reductions in recidivism than most other interventions that exist.

SECTION SUMMARY

Evaluative research is very important to treatment agencies since it is this process (and this process alone) that allows correctional counseling programs to operate as evidence-based programs. The use of internal evaluation is what ensures that counseling processes are in a state of continued refinement and improvement. This means that the evaluator, in many respects, must act in an independent fashion when conducting data collection and the research that will evaluate the agency. Likewise, the ideal evaluator is one who not only has sufficient credentials in research and statistical analysis but also has experience and expertise with the specific type of treatment program that is being evaluated. This will ensure that the evaluator will have a good contextual understanding of the dynamics within the agency and/or the challenges that tend to be encountered in a given area of treatment service. In addition, the evaluator should strive to have a cordial and warm rapport with agency staff, but it is their task to operate in a neutral and detached manner when determining quantitative outcomes for the agency.

When designing the evaluation plan, five key elements should be addressed. These five elements are as follows: (1) determining the target audience for the evaluation and the dissemination of its results; (2) identifying the evaluation questions that should be asked; (3) determining how the evaluation design will be developed; (4) deciding the type of data to be collected, how that data will be collected, and by whom; and (5) articulating the final products of the report that will be produced. This last element is what will be most important to the treatment program or facility since this will be the document that will determine whether the agency is viewed as a success or a failure (or neither).

Lastly, evaluators must provide measures for both processes and outcomes within the agency. Process measures are related to the day-to-day operations within the agency, such as techniques used in group therapy, number of sessions provided, or number of weeks that the client is in treatment. Outcome measures examine the final product once the program has been completed and might include the behavior of the client, emotional stability of the client, or a client's educational achievement while in the treatment program. In addition, an example of an evaluation project for a drug treatment program and for a sex offender treatment program were discussed. These examples demonstrated several key aspects of evaluation, such as the use of standardized instruments (discussed in more detail in part two of this chapter), the use of outcome and process measures in evaluation, and the need for treatment and evaluative personnel to work in a collaborative fashion. Lastly, drug treatment is one of the most often encountered forms of treatment provided within the correctional setting while sex offenders are one of the most manipulative offenders whom correctional counselors will encounter. It is for these reasons that examples were provided for the evaluation of programs addressing these types of clinical challenges.

LEARNING CHECK

1. Cognitive behavioral approaches have great deal of empirical research that supports their effectiveness with sex offenders.
   a. True
   b. False
2. Outcome measures examine the day-to-day operations of treatment programs.
   a. True
   b. False
3. Direct observation, interviews, surveys and questionnaires, and official records are the four primary means by which data are collected for evaluation projects.
   a. True
   b. False
4. The Addiction Severity Index (ASI) is commonly used in treatment facilities all over the United States.
   a. True
   b. False
5. Change in treatment motivation has been identified as a program outcome useful for many sex offender treatment programs.
   a. True
   b. False

PART TWO: CONSIDERATIONS IN FORMING THE EVALUATIVE DESIGN

The specific approach that a researcher may use to evaluate an agency may depend on a number of different factors. The needs of the agency, required reporting to grant funding agencies, ethical limitations, financial limitations with the research, process and outcome considerations, and feasibility of completing the research may all prove to be important factors in formulating the ultimate evaluative design. These initial considerations are very important and they will be instrumental in determining the appropriate approach in evaluation. Further, for many treatment programs (particularly those that are grant funded), the results of research projects can be very important in determining if programs continue to exist. Consider, as an example, that research related to the effectiveness of juvenile boot camp programs has tended to show that juvenile boot camp programs do not provide long-lasting changes in behavior of delinquent youth. These youth, once released, still tend to return to their criminal behaviors once they are returned to their old environments.

When such findings emerge, questions related to the accuracy of the results may also be generated. This is also just as true when we find that programs work exceptionally well. In such cases, we must be able to clearly demonstrate that our findings have been produced by the phenomenon that we believe have served as the causal factors. Consider again our example of the juvenile boot camp observation. How do we know if it is the structure of the juvenile boot camp intervention that is flawed? Could it be that juvenile boot camps are well designed and successful but some other spurious factors were causing recidivism among these youth? How do we determine and distinguish between these different potential explanations for juvenile recidivism after finishing a boot camp program? Answers to these questions can only be provided if we ensure that two primary constructs exist within our research. These constructs are known as validity and reliability.

Validity in Evaluative Research

Validity describes whether an instrument actually measures the construct or factor that we have intended to measure. For many students, it may seem strange that one could not know if they are measuring what they intend to measure; however, the mental health and counseling fields often are tasked with measuring concepts that cannot be readily and physically seen. For instance, the measurement of attitudes may be quite difficult, particularly if a client is deliberately being deceptive. In addition, some clinical disorders may consist of symptoms that also exist with other disorders, thereby making it difficult to distinguish the disorder that is actually being measured.

Further, some disorders may frequently coexist with other types of disorders, being so commonly connected that medications prescribed for one may be similar or identical to those prescribed for the other. An example of this would be the disorders of anxiety and depression. In many cases, psychiatrists may prescribe identical medications for both disorders. Further, it is frequent for persons with one of these disorders to also present with the other. Distinguishing whether a client engages in a behavior due to anxiety responses or depressive/affective responses may be important from a clinical perspective. Therefore, whatever measure the treatment program use it is important that it correctly and accurately discern between these two disorders if the desire is to optimize treatment outcomes. Though these two disorders may coexist, they are actually quite different from one another and individualized treatment plans must correctly distinguish between such clinical nuances if effective treatment outcomes are to be expected. Thus, the process used to distinguish between disorders must be valid; it must correctly measure the correct disorder that it is intended to measure without convoluted outcomes, thereby correctly providing for clinical diagnoses.

This type of clinical example can become even more important and even more complicated when other constructs, such as low self-esteem, are also added into the therapeutic equation. Indeed, many persons with low self-esteem suffer from either minor depression, anxiety, or both. The question then becomes "what is first, the low self-esteem followed by depression and/or anxiety or the existence of depression and/or anxiety with corresponding low self-esteem?" In order to correctly answer this question, one must be able to correctly identify between both clinical disorders as well as the general construct of low self-esteem. Only a valid measure will be able to do this. What is more, this measure must be very sensitive to underlying differences between disorders and constructs that have many latent interconnections; this further complicates the ability to achieve valid measurements but also demonstrates why this is all the more important. In theory, if you address the primary issue first, the other issues will tend to also subside on an exponential basis.

Though there are many more examples of clinical and nonclinical situations where invalid measures may be mistakenly used by researchers, we provide this example to demonstrate the complexity associated with distinguishing valid results in correctional treatment. We also provide this example to demonstrate why it is so important to correctly discern among various disorders and behavioral constructs. This is even more critical to public safety when behavioral symptoms include violent and/or medically risky behaviors. Therefore, it is important that evaluators of mental health programs ensure that their measures are valid and it is important for clinicians being evaluated to remain receptive to the requests of evaluators to provide exacting and detailed specificity as to observed symptoms, clinical impressions, and other aspects that the counselor may use to generate his or her own clinical judgments in treatment.

Reliability in Evaluative Research

Reliability is a concept that describes the accuracy of a measure which in turn describes the accuracy of a study. As an example, consider again an evaluation where measurements of client anxiety are taken. A reliable measure would provide a measure that accurately reflects the level of anxiety and this measure would consistently be provided over time and throughout multiple measures if interventions were not provided. This measure is reliable when it reflects the true level of anxiety that the client experiences accurately and on a consistent basis. The ability to gauge the level or intensity of a mental health symptom (such as anxiety) correctly and consistently over multiple measurement points makes a process reliable. It is important to clarify that the consistent reporting of results, in and of itself, is not the only consideration in determining reliability. Rather, it is also the ability to provide a measure that also correctly determines the modulation of that symptom. For example, a measure may consistently demonstrate that a client has low levels of anxiety when, in fact, they suffer from high levels of anxiety. Since the person does, in fact, suffer from anxiety this measure is valid; it is expected that anxiety is being measured and the instrument does indeed measure symptoms of anxiety. However, the instrument is not reliable because it consistently provides a measure that underrates the level of anxiety that the client consistently experiences. Consistently inaccurate measures cannot be considered reliable.

Validity and reliability are absolutely critical to conducting evaluative research; without them the research is essentially useless. Research in the field of correctional counseling is particularly important due to the implications that may emerge related to public safety and the continuation of programs. Therefore, the role of evaluators in treatment programs is one that is very important, both within the lone treatment facility and when making determinations for the funding of programs throughout a state or the nation. But the question then emerges, how do we ensure that the outcomes that are produced are, in fact, valid and reliable? One effective means of obtaining valid and reliable data would be to use standardized instruments that have been specifically designed to ensure that client information meets acceptable criteria with both constructs.

The Basics of Standardized Treatment Planning and Risk Assessment Instruments

As has been noted, the use of standardized instruments can add strength to any evaluation design. These instruments have been tested through a variety of processes and statistical analyses to ensure their validity and reliability, when properly used. It is the last part of the prior sentence—when properly used—that is important to note for correctional counselors. Many counselors who have the traditional graduate level education in counseling (this includes correctional counselors) will tend to have only one course that deals specifically with testing and assessment. Further, these programs often only require one class in research methods and, as is customary among counseling programs throughout the United States, there will be no specific course in statistics. This is because many counseling programs are designed to train therapists, not researchers.

On the other hand, the field of psychology tends to consistently require at least one research methods course, a separate statistics course, and will also have at least one (or more) courses in testing and assessment. Even with this increased emphasis on statistics and testing processes, persons with only a master's degree in psychology are not able to practice without obtaining some sort of supervision from a Ph.D. level psychologist. This is despite the fact that counselors with master's degree in counseling as well as advanced internships and practicum are licensed to conduct therapeutic services. These counselors are typically not qualified to conduct psychological testing on their own without additional training and, even then, there are limits to the types of tests that they may legally administer.

For laypersons and for paraprofessionals, the training in testing is even less than what is obtained by licensed counselors. In some treatment settings, paraprofessionals may conduct the majority of the day-to-day work, and they may even be required to read and utilize the results from standardized tests when performing their job. Naturally, these persons are not able to administer, score, or interpret such tests. They typically will simply use the results from an appraisal or evaluative specialist as a tool in treatment planning.

The reason for describing the credentials involved with the use of standardized tests is to demonstrate that few mental health professionals are able to administer, score, and interpret these tests without a doctoral level education. Further, many correctional treatment settings do not have full-time clinical psychologists and/or counselors who are qualified to conduct test administration. Thus, correctional counselors tend to not be well grounded in an understanding of the basic characteristics of a sound and empirically designed standardized instrument, particularly one with psychometric properties. This is an important point to note and this is precisely why we have included a brief overview of those characteristics of a valid and reliable testing mechanism.

Before proceeding further, students should understand that standardized tests tend to be used for two key purposes in correctional counseling: treatment planning and security classification. As has been noted in earlier chapters (specifically Chapters 1 through 3), correctional counselors must not only attend to therapeutic concerns of offenders who are clients, but they must also consider public safety when determining the prognosis of their clients. In other words, they must be concerned as to whether their clients will cause additional harm in society once they are released from a correctional facility and/or from community supervision. Because of this, correctional counselors will sometimes deal with standardized assessment tools that serve both a treatment planning and a security classification purpose.

Thus, it is useful for correctional counselors (and especially treatment evaluators) to understand some of the common principles associated with standardized treatment planning and classification instruments. A failure to understand these basic statistical and/or methodological considerations can lead to the misuse of these instruments among clinicians. James Austin (2006) provides six basic suggestions for correctional treatment professionals who may wish to know whether their instruments are effective. Many of Austin's comments have to do with the methodology that was used to construct the testing instrument, which then relates to the validity and reliability of that given instrument. Thus, knowing these basic concepts can help correctional counselors to ensure that instruments that they use and/or integrate into their treatment planning are appropriate and this also can ensure that correctional counselors use those instruments appropriately in their day-to-day operation. According to Austin (2006), the following points should be considered when utilizing standardized form for treatment planning, classification, and/or evaluative purposes:

1. *Selected Standardized Instruments Must Be Tested on Your Correctional Population and Separately Normed for Males and Females.* Austin (2006) notes that when assessment tools are tested on the offender populations in one area of the nation, they may not be as relevant to offenders in another area. For example, consider the state of California as compared to the state of Nebraska. It is likely that the offender populations in each state will differ, one from the other. Because of this, treatment programs and treatment program evaluators should use instruments that are essentially normed on—or tailored to—the characteristics of offender populations that are similar to those that they work with. Austin (2006) points out that "in research terms this issue has to do with the 'external validity' of the instrument and the ability to generalize the findings of a single study of the instrument to other jurisdictions" (p. 1). Therefore, if an instrument is normed on an offender population that is substantially different from the one that the evaluator is assessing, it is likely that the assessment and the evaluation outcomes will not be as accurate (Hanser, 2009).

Further, male and female offenders differ in both their treatment needs and security concerns. Characteristics associated with criminal behavior and prognoses for treatment tend to differ between male and female offenders (Hanser, 2009). Because of this, standardized instruments should be different for male and female offenders or instruments should have built-in mechanisms that are designed to differentiate between both populations; but in many cases separate instruments are not used and typically used instruments do not sufficiently differentiate between the needs of male and female offenders. To be reliable, assessment tools must give appropriate weight to gender differences among offenders, both in treatment planning and in the evaluative process (Hanser, 2009). Austin (2006) comments further that "recidivism and career criminal studies consistently show that females are less involved in criminal behavior, are less likely to commit violent crimes and are less likely to recidivate after being placed on probation or parole" (p. 1).

2. ***Interrater Reliability Tests Must Be Conducted with Instruments that Are Selected.*** Austin (2006) states that both an interraterreliability test and validity test must be completed by independent researchers prior to using a test for treatment planning, assessment, or evaluation. Further, these reliability and validity safeguards should be assured by researchers who accrue no monetary or political benefit when determining whether a standardized test is reliable and/or valid (Austin, 2006; Hanser, 2009). In simple terms, interrater reliability has to do with the consistency of the results that are obtained from an instrument. Interrater reliability should consistently yield the same outcomes regardless of the person who has conducted the test of the instrument (Hanser, 2009). This is very important for evaluative research and resounds the points made earlier in our previous subsection regarding reliability in the evaluation design.

3. ***A Validity Test Must Be Conducted.*** As with evaluative designs, the instruments used in those designs must also be valid. As has been explained earlier, validity ensures that the instrument is actually measuring what the evaluator and/or correctional counselor believe is being measured. As we noted in our example with valid measures of anxiety (see our earlier subsection), instruments can provide measures that correlate with a given issue but the cause of that correlation may be due to some unknown factor (Hanser, 2009).

4. ***The Instruments Must Allow for Dynamic and Static Risk Factors.*** Students should recall from Chapter 3 the distinctions between dynamic and static risk factors. Dynamic risk factors include characteristics such as age, marital status, and custody level (Hanser, 2006, 2009). The key commonality among dynamic risk factors is that they can and do change over time. Static risk factors include characteristics such as age at first arrest, crime seriousness, and prior convictions. Once established, these characteristics do not fluctuate over time (Hanser, 2006, 2009). Both of these factors are important for treatment planning while the offender is on supervision, risk prediction during release from incarceration, and in evaluating offender outcomes in treatment programs. For example, one author of this text who is also an independent evaluator for a drug treatment center for female offenders sought to determine if age had a significant correlation with various aspects of treatment success. In this case, a dynamic risk factor was utilized to analyze offender outcomes. In addition, this same evaluator sought to determine if the number of prior convictions was significantly correlated with treatment success; this is an example where a static risk factor was used to evaluate client treatment outcomes.

5. *Instruments Must Be Compatible with the Skill Level of Treatment Staff.* As was discussed earlier, different treatment staff will tend to have different levels of credentialing (i.e., laypersons, paraprofessionals, counselors and psychologists with master's degrees, counselors with doctorate degrees and specific training in psychometrics, and clinical psychologists with doctorate degrees). The level of credential can be important since this determines whether a person may be qualified to administer a specific test. Indeed, the accuracy of an assessment instrument can be just as dependent upon the skill of the person administering the tool as is its construction. It is not enough for a clinician and/or evaluator to use a well-developed instrument, but they must also have sufficient training in statistical analysis, research design, and testing processes and they must have adequate training before they can properly administer many standardized tests. Naturally, some tests are more complicated than others and it is because of this that different tests may require different levels of credentialed qualifications.

In addition, evaluators must have experience administering those instruments or instruments similar to those that they use. Training or education alone is not sufficient; there is simply no replacement for the skill and familiarity that is acquired through the process of repetitive administration of a given instrument.

The importance of these qualifications cannot be overstated. Further, many evaluative efforts may not always include standardized instruments as they can be costly to purchase, they may entail high costs in obtaining qualified personnel, and the process can be complicated and demanding. However, these costs and drawbacks do not offset the value that is added to an evaluative design for those agencies who truly wish to improve their service delivery and the treatment outcomes of clients in their programs. The importance of professional qualifications is often evidenced by the fact that companies such as Western Psychological Services (WPS) and Psychological Assessment Resources (PAR), two well-known companies that copyright and sell standardized instruments, require persons ordering such instruments to provide proof of their credentials, training, and/or experience with similar instruments.

6. *The Assessment Instrument Must Have Face Validity.* Lastly, the instrument and the process of assessment must be understood and recognized as credible by treatment staff and clients of the program that is being evaluated. Indeed, instruments that are only understood by academics will not be widely accepted by most treatment staff and such instruments can often confuse offenders who, in many cases, do not have well-developed reading skills. Further, if the instrument is perceived as being too "bookish" in nature and not applicable to the realities of the "street," so to speak, clients are likely to view the instrument as artificial and sterile, not really being able to probe the true reality of what an offender may (or may not) experience (Hanser, 2009). With this in mind, students should understand that a lack of "face validity" means that the instrument is not recognized as valid on its face, or at initial glance, by those who judge its ability to assess or appraise a set of characteristics (Hanser, 2009).

Ethics in Evaluation

Ethics refers to what is right and wrong in relation to human conduct. This is a vital component to any research endeavor and should be taken seriously. At no time should human subjects be placed in undue harm while attempting to carry out a research project. One of the best ways to ensure ethical standards is to be open and honest with participants. Each component of the research design should be clearly explained to all participants. And, participants should be given the opportunity to freely choose whether to consent or refuse to participate in the study. In addition, great care should be taken to ensure that the identity of each participant remain anonymous. Three ethical principles were established by the Department of Health, Education, and Welfare in 1979 aimed at protecting human subjects and eliminating human rights violations:

1. Respect for persons—treating persons as autonomous agents and protecting those with diminished autonomy;
2. Beneficence—minimizing possible harms and maximizing benefits;
3. Justice—distributing benefits and risks of research fairly (Schutt, 2006, p. 81).

All research proposals should be reviewed by the appropriate Institutional Review Board (IRB). The primary purpose of the IRB is to ensure that ethical standards clearly resonate in all facets of the proposal and risk to human subjects is minimal. Especially, when conducting human subject research, IRB approval is critical. In fact, some research projects may require IRB approval from multiple agencies. In addition, we strongly recommend that students visit the APA's website on "Ethical Principles of Psychologists and Code of Conduct." In particular, evaluators should take heed of Section 8 on "Research and Publication," which notes that participants (particularly agency clients in treatment) informed consent must be provided. The following is list of points paraphrased from requirements noted by the American Psychiatric Association (2009) that should be communicated to clients in treatment who are part of the evaluation process:

1. The purpose of the evaluation, the procedures involved, and the duration of the evaluative process
2. The voluntary nature of participation in the research and their right to cease participation at any time that they desire
3. Any potential consequences of declining or withdrawing
4. Possible risks, discomfort, or adverse effects involved (if any) with participation
5. Potential benefits to the client and/or the agency that the evaluative research might produce
6. The general limits of confidentiality (students should refer back to Chapter 2 for additional information on confidentiality)
7. Any incentives provided to get clients to participate
8. Information on their rights and notice of a contact person to who questions can be directed regarding the evaluation process.

Reviewing Evaluation Findings

Once the evaluator has designed and implemented the evaluation process within a treatment agency, it is not enough for that person to simply "crunch numbers" and provide statistical reports. Rather, they must communicate the outcome of the evaluation and provide feedback and/or suggestions to treatment personnel so that they can refine their techniques and approach. Creation of this feedback loop is critical; without it, the evaluation simply sits stale and useless within the treatment agency. Because evaluators must interpret and explain their findings, it is important for the evaluator to have worked as treatment provider, if at all possible. This allows the evaluator to understand the nuances and unspoken complications in providing therapeutic services. Without such insight, evaluators are limited to a one dimensional understanding of the treatment process, being restricted to the limitations of their data when interpreting results.

Beyond the process of collecting data and conducting analyses, evaluators are often trusted by treatment programs to provide interpretations and to produce conclusions resulting from their analysis. Along with this, evaluators may provide recommendations that are based on the findings. The evaluator, in providing such recommendations, will usually discuss the outcome with agency supervisors. In such cases, correctional counselors would be well served to heed the information provided by evaluators since their analysis is likely to be free of the subjective impressions that counselors tend to form of clients and their clinical situation. This is not to say that, in all cases, the evaluator's interpretation of treatment effectiveness is more accurate than the therapist's who work in a given treatment facility. Rather, it is to say that the evaluator's observations can serve as a good counterbalance to subjective observations of program staff. This is perhaps one of the best means by which clinicians can optimize their interventions and, in the process, establish their treatment program as being evidence-based in nature.

Incorporating the Evaluation Research Findings into Therapy

The primary goal of evaluation research is to enhance the services provided to offenders. We need to know what is working and what types of interventions are able to enact meaningful change and help keep offenders out of future contact with the criminal justice system. This is a critical component for creating and maintaining credibility of the counseling profession in working with offenders. Criminal justice is a discipline that frequently sees the theoretical pendulum swing from tougher incarceration policies to those more focused on rehabilitation and counseling. In order for counseling to remain viable we need to strive toward implementing practices that are theoretically sound and able to adapt to the peculiarities of individuals within the offender population and their particular needs.

Relapse and **recidivism** are concepts that generally represent different disciplines but are inextricably connected. In counseling we use relapse to signify an individual's reengagement in problem behavior. In criminal justice we use recidivism to describe the process of committing a criminal act that brings an individual back into the justice system. From the perspective of correctional counseling these concepts are best viewed as part of a singular process, meaning that, generally, offenders who recidivate are going to be offenders who have also relapsed into some type of problem behavior. Indeed, further proof of the interchangeable nature of these terms is seen in recent grant Requests for Proposals (RFPs) released by SAMHSA, where specific grant projects call for programs that simultaneously address substance abuse relapse and criminal recidivism.

Correctional counselors will eventually select a style of counseling that most suits their own personality and expertise. The selected style of counseling should be one that allows each counselor to operate from his or her authentic self. In addition to each counselor's individual knowledge of his or her particular therapeutic modality it is very important that counselors listen to offenders as they share their own reasons for relapse and recidivism. The offender's **self-reported reasons** for engaging in the behavior that led to his or her arrest is rich information for the counselor to explore. It may be that there are intricacies within a story that are unique to an offender and require specialized interventions that aim to reframe cognitions and alter behavior. Self-reported data also provide a good source of validating information that may have been captured in standardized instruments used by many facilities at intake. Common standardized assessment instruments measure an offender's levels of depression, anxiety, and trauma. These initial assessment instruments and self-report data usually provide a baseline from which subsequent counseling services can be gauged in regard to whether an offender's psychological and emotional outlook is improving (Figure 14.1).

Creating a Feedback Loop in Therapy

The process of refining one's method of counseling should be constant. Much of the refinement should be based on both quantitative and qualitative information gained from the process of

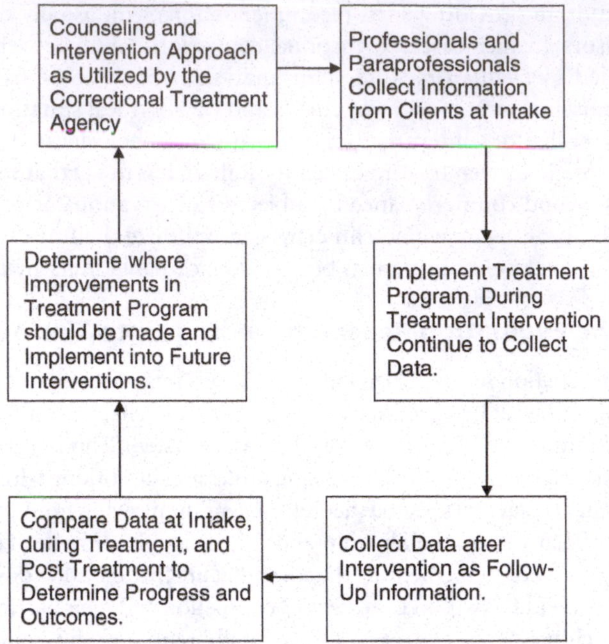

FIGURE 14.1 The Means by which Data Collection and Evaluation Create Feedback Loops that Impact Agency Interventions.

interacting with offenders and delivering treatment. When the data collection process adheres to acceptable standards of scientific investigation, the data produced should be relied upon heavily to "drive" future counseling sessions. In essence, the entire process of counseling offenders is best viewed as a circular phenomenon that mirrors the process of scientific inquiry. We begin with a distressed offender and begin the attempt to understand the particulars of the distress. We then proceed to the implementation of counseling techniques in an effort to reduce the distress. During this process we are constantly evaluating whether the treatment is effective. If the offender shows signs of improvement based on an intervention we will likely continue with subsequent application. If the offender does not seem to be responding well, or improving, it may be that we need to adjust our methods of intervention and then reassess after a reasonable period of time. This process continues until the offender is deemed suitable to proceed without further treatment.

Improving Therapy: A Final Note

The best counselors are personally congruent; they are authentic and provide realness in which discussions and disclosures are meaningful. Counselors who are not authentic will likely hide behind the delivery of scripted techniques and sanitized disclosure incapable of prompting genuine exchange able to heal old wounds. Counselors must be aware of their own psychological and emotional needs. Our own ability to attend to these needs in professional settings models our ability and willingness to make changes and can be very beneficial to offenders. Change is frightening for all human beings. But, imagine the level of trepidation for those offenders who have never had the opportunity to observe another person take the risk of disclosing personal information in hopes of a better life. Counselors have the opportunity to be meaningful change agents for many of the offenders they encounter. Whether the change will be meaningful and lasting, however, will in large part hinge on the counselor's own psychological and emotional depth. This is precisely why counselors should take every opportunity to engage in training aimed at enhancing their own self-understanding. A guiding question that should always be on the mind of counselors is: "Would I be willing to do what I am asking the offender to do?"

Indeed, the process of obtaining continued education is one that is mandated by most all ethical governing bodies within the counseling field. This is because the field of counseling (including correctional counseling) is always changing and improving. Therefore, when correctional counselors pursue further education throughout their careers, they are the benefactors of evaluative research that determines those approaches that "work" from those that do not. This is a continual improvement process where one utilizes an approach, tests that approach, gets results from the test of the approach, and based on the findings modifies future intervention approaches. Simply put, counselors must make a point to stay abreast of such research and to grow along with their discipline. To fail to do so produces a serious shortcoming in their competency to provide services and also shows professionally negligence. Further still, this failure would also be a failure to our client's welfare. Thus research is important since it guides us on how our field and our own individual careers should develop. In essence, we are all a work in progress and the best treatment professional is one who knows that they never stop growing, both personally and professionally. To fail to do so would essentially mean that we have decided to stop caring. Nothing could be more contradictory to the spirit, point, and purpose of the counseling profession.

SECTION SUMMARY

When conducting evaluative research, there are a number of issues to consider prior to starting the actual evaluation. First and foremost, the evaluator must consider issues related to the validity and reliability of the research that is conducted. Without addressing these two important concepts, the evaluation of the treatment program is likely to have no useful outcome. One way to facilitate valid and reliable data collection is to use standardized instruments. Gaining data from clients and staff through the use of standardized instruments can ensure that at least a minimal degree of validity and reliability is inherent to the data that is obtained. However, the simple use of these instruments does not, in and of itself, ensure that the evaluation will automatically be successful. The evaluator and relevant agency staff must be trained on the use of these instruments. If these instruments are not used properly, the evaluation will consist of essentially useless information.

Further, ethics in research should be given a priority, particularly in regard to the boundaries of confidentiality, ensuring that clients have informed consent prior to participating in the evaluation process. Once the evaluator has considered the validity and reliability of the evaluation design and once they have ensured that ethical safeguards are in place, they should proceed with the evaluative process. When completing the evaluation, they should provide feedback to treatment staff (particularly supervisory clinical staff) to disseminate the results of their findings. Further, evaluators should work with treatment staff and administrators to integrate findings within the processes of the agency's day-to-day operations. It is in this manner that feedback loops are built so that the evaluative process can further aid and support the continual refinement of treatment interventions.

LEARNING CHECK

1. Relapse and recidivism are two concepts that should not be considered related.
   a. True
   b. False
2. Validity is the ability to get consistent measurements.
   a. True
   b. False
3. Reliability describes the accuracy of a measure.
   a. True
   b. False
4. The primary goal of evaluation research is to refine treatment program efforts aimed at rehabilitating offenders.
   a. True
   b. False
5. It is not necessary for correctional counselors to understand evaluation research.
   a. True
   b. False

CONCLUSION

Research and assessment of correctional counseling programs is vital. It is through this process that we are able to identify program strengths and weaknesses that serve to inform the literature. It is also through the evaluative process that we are able to determine if our programs actually work to improve relapse and recidivism rates among offenders. Afterall, if these programs simply "feel good" but, in reality, provide little actual and observable benefit to society in general and the offender in particular, their usefulness is questionable. It is important that agencies engage in earnest and sincere evaluation and that the use of evidence-based approaches is emphasized. By being evidence based, agencies provide means of demonstrating their positive impact on society and, due to the evidence that they produce, provide the means by which other agencies can replicate their practices.

It is important for correctional counselors to understand the importance of evaluative research and to understand that the role of the evaluator is one that is helpful. Indeed, the best evaluator is one who has also worked in the treatment field, particularly in the same field that is being subjected to their evaluation. Such evaluators usually are more in tune with the processes that they evaluate and they are also better able to interpret and explain outcomes that are observed. Such evaluators also tend to be effective in explaining their results to agency staff and demonstrating how future interventions can be optimized.

Further, it is important that evaluation designs ensure for both validity and reliability. Where validity ensures that one is measuring what one intends to measure, reliability ensures that the measure is accurate in intensity and/or degree of measure and that the measurement consistently provides these accurate measures over time. In the field of correctional counseling, issues that are evaluated require that specific attention is given to the validity and reliability of the evaluation process. The use of standardized instruments helps to facilitate this process since they have been tested for their ability to provide valid and reliable data. Presuming the evaluator ensures that appropriate methodological principles are used, evaluations that use standardized instruments will typically be superior to those that do not.

Lastly, ethics in research should be maintained by the evaluator. Just as with correctional counselors, the issue of confidentiality is important. Clients should be provided full consent as to the nature of the study and their rights when participating in research. Though clients will have likely been apprised of their rights to confidentiality during their initial entry into the treatment program, research evaluators should also cover these parameters with clients to ensure that they understand their role, the nature of the research, and their own right to autonomy. This is an important issue, particularly in cases where clients are court mandated. Beyond the participation of clients, agency staff should be encouraged to participate. In such cases, evaluators can integrate information from staff to provide a more multifaceted appraisal of the processes involved within the treatment facility. Further, staff will ultimately be participants and recipients of the evaluative output since agencies will usually find it necessary to consider changes and modifications to their programs as evaluations of their effectiveness are provided. It is in this manner, through the incorporation of evaluative data, that agencies can continually refine and improve their services and become evidence-based treatment providers in the truest sense of the term.

Essay Questions

1. Why is evaluative research important to improving correctional counseling processes?
2. Discuss the purpose of evaluation research. What might be some consequences of not conducting evaluation research?
3. Why are standardized instruments considered particularly valuable in evaluative research? What are some necessary characteristics of standardized assessment tools?
4. Discuss the various ethical principles related to conducting research with offenders. What are some of the recommendations noted by the American Psychological Association?

Treatment Planning Exercise

For this exercise, you will need to consider your readings in this chapter as they apply to prior readings from **Chapter 8 on Substance Abuse Counseling and Co-occurring Disorders** and from **Chapter 9 on Youth Counseling and Juvenile Offenders.** Your assignment is as follows:

You are a researcher and a correctional counselor who has recently been hired by the community supervision system in your area. You have been asked to design and evaluate a treatment program for **adolescent substance abusers** that has been implemented within one of the larger cities in your state. Specifically, you are asked to examine how various aspects of social learning theory may lead to learned substance abuse within families of origin and within juvenile peer groups. With this in mind, you must then explain how various treatment options might best address domestic battering issues with this population. The program that you will evaluate uses all of the interventions listed in Chapter 8 and you are free to select any theoretical orientation that you desire from Chapters 5, 6, or 7 of this text. Lastly, you will need to provide a clear methodology for testing and evaluating your proposed program, including such factors as validity and reliability of your study as well as the validity and reliability of your assessment instruments (if any), the use of control and experimental groups, as well as ethical issues that might be involved with conducting such research.

Bibliography

American Psychiatric Association (2000). *Diagnostic and statistical manual of mental disorders*. Arlington, VA: American Psychiatric Association.

Austin, J. (2006). How much risk can we take? The misuse of risk assessment in corrections. *Federal Probation, 20*(2). Retrieved from: http://www.uscourts.gov/fedprob/September_2006/risk.html#basics.

Belenko, S. (2001). *Research on Drug Courts: A Critical Review. 2001 Update*. New York: National Center on Addiction and Substance Abuse. Retrieved from: www.drugpolicy.org/docUploads/2001drug-courts.pdf.

Bureau of Justice Assistance. (2008). Center for program evaluation and performance measurement. Washington, DC: Bureau of Justice Assistance. Retrieved from: http://www.ojp.usdoj.gov/BJA/evaluation/index.html.

Campbell, D. T., & Stanley, J. C. (1963). *Experimental and Quasi-Experimental Designs for Research*. Boston, MA: Houghton Mifflin Company.

Center for Substance Abuse Treatment. (2005). *Substance Abuse Treatment for Adults in the Criminal Justice System*. Treatment Improvement Protocol (TIP) Series 44. DHHS Publication No. (SMA) 05-4056. Rockville, MD: Substance Abuse and Mental Health Services Administration.

Dana, R. H., Behn, J. D., & Gonwa, T. (1992). A checklist for the examination of cultural competence in social service agencies. *Research of Social Work Practice, 2*, 220–233.

Hanser, R. D. (2006). *Special needs offenders in the community*. Upper Saddle River, NJ: Prentice Hall.

Hanser, R. D. (2009). *Community corrections*. Belmont, CA: Sage Publications.

Lempert, R. O., & Visher, C. A. (Eds.). (1987). *Randomized field experiments in criminal justice agencies: Workshop proceedings*. Washington, DC: National Research Council.

McCollister, K. E., & French, M. T. (2001). *The economic cost of substance abuse treatment in criminal justice settings*. Miami, FL: University of Miami. Retrieved from: www.amityfoundation.com/lib/libarch/CostPrisonTreatment.pdf.

Mire, S. M., Forsyth, C., & Hanser, R. D. (2007). Jail diversion: Addressing the needs of offenders with mental illness and co-occurring disorders. *Journal of Offender Rehabilitation, 45*(1/2), 19–31.

National Institute of Justice. (1992). *Evaluating Drug Control and System Improvement Projects: Guidelines for Projects Supported by the Bureau of Justice Assistance.*

Schutt, R. K. (2006). *Investigating the social world: The process and practice of research* (5th ed.). Thousand Oaks, CA: Pine Forge Press.

Skinner, H. (1995). *Drug Abuse Screening Test*. Toronto, Canada: Addiction Research Foundation.

ANSWERS TO LEARNING CHECK

Chapter 1

PART ONE

1. a. True
2. c. Counseling
3. a. True
4. a. True
5. d. All of the above

PART TWO

1. a. True
2. b. False
3. a. True
4. a. True
5. a. True

PART THREE

1. a. True
2. a. True
3. a. True
4. b. False
5. a. True

Chapter 2

PART ONE

1. b. Informed consent
2. b. False
3. b. Dual relationship
4. a. True
5. b. False

PART TWO

1. b. False
2. b. False
3. d. All of the above
4. a. True
5. b. False

PART THREE

1. b. False
2. b. False
3. b. False
4. a. True
5. b. False

Chapter 3

PART ONE

1. b. False
2. a. Dynamic risk factors
3. a. True
4. a. True
5. a. True

PART TWO

1. b. False
2. b. Axis II
3. b. False
4. a. Axis I
5. d. Axis IV

PART THREE

1. b. True Positive
2. d. False Negative
3. a. True
4. e. All of the above
5. c. True Negative

Chapter 4

PART ONE

1. a. True
2. a. True
3. b. False
4. b. False
5. b. False

PART TWO

1. b. False
2. a. True
3. b. False
4. b. False
5. b. False

PART THREE

1. b. False
2. a. True
3. b. False
4. a. True
5. a. True

Chapter 5

PART ONE

1. b. False
2. b. False
3. a. True
4. a. True
5. a. True

PART TWO

1. b. False
2. b. False
3. a. True
4. a. True
5. b. False

PART THREE

1. b. False
2. a. True
3. b. False
4. a. True
5. b. False

PART FOUR

1. b. False
2. b. False
3. a. True
4. b. False
5. b. False

Chapter 6

PART ONE

1. a. Differentiation of self
2. e. Homeostasis
3. a. True
4. a. True
5. a. True

PART TWO

1. a. True
2. e. Emotional cut-off
3. a. True
4. a. True
5. a. True

PART THREE

1. d. Negative punishment
2. b. Negative reinforcement
3. a. True
4. a. Positive reinforcement
5. c. Positive punishment

Chapter 7

PART ONE

1. b. False
2. b. False
3. b. False
4. b. False
5. b. False

PART TWO

1. b. False
2. b. False
3. b. False
4. a. True
5. b. False

Chapter 8

PART ONE

1. d. Anxiety
2. d. All of the above
3. a. True
4. d. All of the above
5. a. True

PART TWO

1. b. False
2. a. True
3. a. True
4. d. True
5. b. False

PART THREE

1. b. False
2. b. False
3. d. All of the above
4. b. oneself
5. a. True

Chapter 9

PART ONE

1. a. True
2. a. True
3. b. False
4. b. False
5. a. True

PART TWO

1. a. True
2. a. True
3. b. False
4. a. True
5. a. True

Chapter 10

PART ONE

1. a. True
2. a. True
3. a. True
4. b. False
5. a. True

PART TWO

1. a. True
2. a. True
3. a. True
4. b. False
5. a. True

PART THREE

1. a. True
2. b. False
3. b. False
4. a. True
5. a. True

Chapter 11

PART ONE

1. a. True
2. a. True
3. a. True
4. a. True
5. a. True

PART TWO

1. a. True
2. a. True
3. a. True
4. b. False
5. a. True

Chapter 12

PART ONE

1. a. True
2. b. False
3. a. True
4. a. True
5. a. True

PART TWO

1. a. True
2. a. True
3. b. False
4. b. False
5. a. True

Chapter 13

PART ONE

1. b. False
2. a. True
3. a. True
4. a. True
5. a. True

PART TWO

1. a. True
2. a. True
3. a. True
4. a. True
5. a. True

PART THREE

1. a. True
2. a. True
3. b. False
4. a. True
5. a. True

Chapter 14

PART ONE

1. a. True
2. b. False
3. a. True
4. a. True
5. a. True

PART TWO

1. b. False
2. b. False
3. a. True
4. a. True
5. b. False

INDEX